Introduction to the Social Sciences

Rick Booth, Editor

NELSON EDUCATION

NELSON EDUCATION

ISBN-13: 978-0-17-663807-8
ISBN-10: 0-17-663807-5

Consists of Selections from:

Natural Science in Western History, 1st Edition
Frederick Gregory
ISBN 0-618-22410-6, © 2007

First Steps: A Guide to Social Research, 4th Edition
Michael Del Balso, Alan D Lewis
ISBN 0-17-644266-9, © 2008

Essentials of Economics, 6th Edition
N. Gregory Mankiw
ISBN 0-538-45308-7, © 2012

Canadian Politics, Concise 5th Edition
Rand Dyck
ISBN 0-17-650343-9, © 2012

Sociology: Your Compass for A New World , 3rd Edition
Robert J. Brym, John Lie, Steven Rytina
ISBN 0-17-650062-6, © 2010

An Introduction To Government and Politics: A Conceptual Approach , 8th Edition
Mark O. Dickerson, Thomas Flanagan, Brenda O'Neill
ISBN 0-17-650042-1, © 2010

Studying Politics: An Introduction to Political Science , 3rd Edition
Rand Dyck
ISBN 0-17-610539-5, © 2009

Cover Credit:

Whitney Denman/Shutterstock

Table of Contents

Chapter 1: Introduction to the Social Sciences

The Ancient Western Heritage

In the world of the ancient Near East there was no such thing as natural science as we understand it today, in the twenty-first century. The early civilizations of Egypt and Mesopotamia did, however, attempt to make sense of nature. They achieved a coherence in their understanding of nature through the development of a tradition of myths, and sometimes with the help of mathematical calculation. Natural processes, as we shall see, were directly linked to the presence of gods.

In ancient Greece, prior to the time of Plato, depictions of the natural world also revolved around the activities of divine beings. Then, at the end of the sixth century B.C., a distinctly Greek approach that emphasized the world's *rational* structure made its appearance. Scholars have referred to the unique perspective on nature that began to emerge in the Ionian region at this time as the Greek miracle. This ancient Ionian view of nature contained aspects that contrasted with the more personal understandings of the natural world that had been dominant previously in the West.

Two thinkers from ancient Greece whose ideas proved to be crucial for the development of systematic depictions of the natural world were the philosophers Plato (ca. 427–ca. 347 B.C.) and Aristotle (384–322 B.C.). As we shall see, they were responsible for defining fundamental issues that would occupy thinkers for centuries to come.

◎ Nature in Ancient Civilizations ◎

The Near East

In what one scholar has identified as a mythopoeic view of nature, ancient peoples of Egypt and Mesopotamia viewed nature itself as an expression of deities, and natural processes as the direct actions of these gods. For example, ancient Egyptians invoked the sky goddess, Nut, to account for the appearance of the heavens. As she

1

CHAPTER 2

―――――――――――◎―――――――――――

Learning in the Middle Ages

At the beginning of the fourth century of the Christian era, a Germanic people known as Visigoths, from the delta of the Danube River, began to invade northern Italy. By A.D. 410 they were successful in their attempt to take Rome. And this was not the only time Rome was sacked in the fifth century—it occurred again at mid-century. The lack of political and social stability that resulted from these wars meant that the pursuit of intellectual matters, and even the cultivation of education, took a back seat to more pressing concerns.

At the same time, the growth and development of Christianity as a religion brought with it a new institution—monasticism. Monasteries were places where those who wished to devote themselves to Christian holiness could focus on that task. To the extent that monasteries were self-supporting, they functioned as separate communities. This meant that in addition to requiring practical knowledge about such mundane matters as carpentry, food production, or the growing of herbs for medicines and spices, monks were responsible for whatever formal education was provided in the monastery.

For the most part, education was directed toward spiritual edification. There were exceptions, but in general the heritage of Greek natural philosophy did not hold great appeal in monasteries, where the primary goal was spiritual betterment. Monks consulted classical thought and sought new knowledge about nature only when it served a higher purpose, namely, the understanding of spiritual truth. But that is not to say that monasteries made no contribution at all to the intellectual development of the Latin West. Although monasteries differed about which secular works might be relevant to spiritual development, those with the broadest vision made sure that Greek works were translated into Latin. Through this activity, through the study of scripture, and eventually through the development of theology, the monasteries kept literacy and scholarship alive.

23

It must be said, however, that in the period from A.D. 400 to 1000 there was no intellectual activity on a par with that of earlier Greek natural philosophy. We look in vain during this time for a Roman Ptolemy or Archimedes, figures distinguished by their grasp of earlier scholarly work and by their creative genius in developing new ideas about the natural world. Further, many Greek works on natural philosophy and mathematics were not translated and thus dropped from view.

◎ Transmission of Greek ◎ Learning to the Near East

The early development of Western Christianity drew its organization from the basic structure of the Roman Empire; that is, while local churches were self-governing, there emerged by the fourth century a structure that was modeled on the organization of the Empire itself. In this structure groups of churches were arranged into provinces, with preference given to churches of the large cities. By the fifth century there were five major patriarchies, the two most important being Rome, the oldest center of the Roman Empire, and Constantinople, to which the Emperor Constantine moved the seat of the Empire in 330.

In spite of their common religious origins, the development of the Eastern and Western churches reflected differences in language and outlook. For example, Latin became the universal language of liturgy in the West, while in the East the church

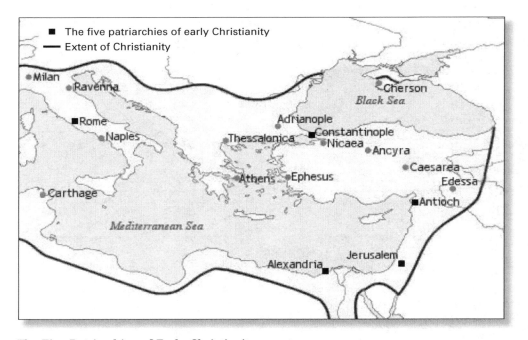

The Five Patriarchies of Early Christianity

CHAPTER 3

Early Modern Innovations

Dynamic changes began to emerge in the fourteenth and fifteenth centuries in the Latin West. On the intellectual level the recovery of ancient texts captured the attention of scholars, making them rethink the synthesis of Christianity and Aristotelian thought Thomas Aquinas had crafted. The invention of printing, which increased the dispersion of new ideas, contributed to the growing awareness of newness. And with explorers penetrating farther and farther into unknown waters, knowledge of the Earth itself expanded in unanticipated ways, opening up whole new worlds to the European imagination.

By this time the landscape of power was changing as well. The most obvious difference from earlier times was the erosion of the power of the papacy. In earlier years the pope, as the leader of a unified Western Christianity, exercised considerable political power. But with the growth of the power of kings, whose interests were regional and secular, respect for papal authority weakened.

The disruption of the Vatican's power became openly transparent during the 1300s and 1400s. Philip IV of France actually captured Pope Boniface VIII at the beginning of the fourteenth century in the course of a dispute over the king's right to imprison a bishop. As the result of Philip's action, the papacy moved from Rome to Avignon in France in 1309. From then until 1377 the popes, all French, were located in Avignon during what is known as the Babylonian Captivity. No sooner had the papacy been relocated to Rome near the end of the century when another crisis arose. In hostile reaction to decisions of the new pope, Urban VI, cardinals fled Rome and declared the papal election invalid. They then proceeded to elect a second pope, who simultaneously ruled from Avignon and produced a schism in church leadership that lasted until 1417. At one point during this so-called Great Schism there were three popes, none of whom recognized the legitimacy of the others!

45

◎

CHAPTER 4

The Renaissance of Natural Knowledge

The meaning of *renaissance,* when applied to the early modern period, is "rebirth," or "beginning again." Evidence of a renaissance of European society in the period from the fifteenth through the seventeenth centuries consists of a number of developments. For example, commerce, industry, and cultural life expanded as the number and role of middle class burghers—residents of the town—increased and altered older feudal relations. Among the educated elites, new intellectual institutions emerged to offer an alternative to those predominant in the medieval world. And on the level of religious culture, there appeared a new secular outlook that challenged the dominance of the clergy's conception of learning.

These changes occurred first in Italy as the republican city-states began to give way to powerful leaders who wished to consolidate their authority in central governments. Everywhere in Italy the values of rebirth were evident. But they did not remain confined to Italy alone. Especially as the sixteenth century dawned, the notion of new beginnings spread to the countries of central and northern Europe.

◎ Humanism ◎

One particular expression of this rebirth of European society was named *humanism* by scholars in the nineteenth century. It is of interest to us as far as the natural sciences of anatomy, natural history, and astronomy are concerned. Humanism concerns the life of the mind, in particular, the acquisition of knowledge and the interpretation of its meaning. The fundamental assumption of this aspect of the Renaissance was that humans in the past had crafted a wisdom that had been lost, should be restored, and could serve as the foundation on which to build a new outlook. This ancient wisdom had been compiled by thinkers of old whose writings had

CHAPTER 27

———————————⊚———————————

Ongoing Issues

There is a natural human tendency to make critical judgments about the outlook and specific views of people who, like those from the past, hold opinions that are very different from our own. This is certainly the case where knowledge of the natural world is concerned and in many instances such a judgment is well justified. But when it becomes clear, for example, that meteorites have indeed fallen to Earth from space, then it no longer is acceptable to assert, as did some natural philosophers of the eighteenth century, that peasant reports of rocks falling from the sky were preposterous claims of the uneducated.

As we evaluate the science of the past we do well to realize that our outlook in the present is not so privileged by the current state of knowledge that it represents final truth. Some textbooks of science (though by no means all), wishing to underscore the solidity of a modern theory, contrast it with a past theory that has been rejected. When such a text introduces the current view, students often read that, in contrast to the discarded idea of the past, "we now know" what the real explanation is. While there is no explicit claim that the modern theory will never change, it frequently does not occur to textbook authors to mention that prospect. Science is therefore presented merely as a body of knowledge acquired through the hard work of methodological research and analysis, not as a constantly changing articulation of our best attempts at understanding in light of factors that are dominant in a given time.

A broader perspective that is not completely focused on the present helps bring understanding to the issues of contemporary science because history is an important factor shaping current questions in the physical and biological sciences. Fundamental issues that have characterized the development of Western natural science over time continue to exert their influence in the present. For example, like the ancient Ionians, many modern physicists believe that scientific explanation of the physical world should not consist of patchwork accounts of individual aspects of nature; rather, separate facets should be brought together into a unified explanation. And in modern biological science the historical challenges about how to use scientific knowledge of living things without running roughshod over moral and ethical concerns are, if anything, more pointed today than they have ever been. These and other enduring themes from the past continue to persist in the ongoing issues of the natural sciences.

◎ The Physical Sciences ◎

Among the broad issues from the history of the physical sciences that continue today are those dealing with our theoretical understanding of matter and force, others concerned with our understanding of the universe in which we find ourselves, and still others that arise from our need to utilize our knowledge for the benefit of humankind. While these three topics do not represent the only ongoing questions of physical science of interest today, they do provide an opportunity to consider questions about science itself and about its interaction with contemporary culture.

Dreams of a Final Theory

Writing in 1986, the physicist and historian of science Gerald Holton described an age-old outlook that, he said, continues to characterize the deepest aim of modern fundamental research. A decade later Holton attached to this stance the label by which it has since become identified—"the Ionian enchantment." It is "to achieve one logically unified and parsimoniously constructed system of thought that provides the conceptual comprehension, as complete as humanly possible, of the scientifically accessible sense experiences in their full diversity." Such an ambition, he noted, "embodies a telos of scientific work itself, and it has done so since the rise of science in the Western world."

Early examples of the drive for unification.   One of the ways in which the Ionian enchantment has shown itself in the history of the physical sciences is the drive for unification evident in the theories of force that have emerged. We have observed the various stages of the drive to unify nature's forces in earlier chapters. When Isaac Newton declared that the same force that caused apples to fall affected the moon in its orbit, he introduced the idea of *universal* gravitation—that every body in the universe exerts a force on every other body. By uniting together the regions of the heavens and the Earth, Newton underscored the rejection of Aristotle's understanding, already suggested by Newton's predecessors, that they constituted totally separate realms, with different laws and even different kinds of matter.

As other forces—electrical, magnetic, chemical, thermal, and optical—caught the attention of natural philosophers in the eighteenth and nineteenth centuries, the wish to unite them showed itself quickly. We observed in Chapter 16 how German romantic nature philosophers, convinced of the unity of nature, were inspired to search for the relationship among forces. With the invention of the battery at the turn of the nineteenth century the relationship between electrical and chemical forces was uncovered. In 1820 Hans Christian Oersted succeeded in showing that electricity and magnetism occurred together. Later in the century

has not generated a great deal of opposition, embryo cloning has. Here, human embryos are produced in order to extract from them a certain kind of cell, called a stem cell, that can be used to generate specialized cells in the human body. While this capability holds great promise for the understanding of human development and the treatment of disease, it is controversial, because extracting the stem cells from the cloned human embryos destroys the embryos and with them, in the minds of some, potential human lives. Should scientists learn to produce stem cells from skin cells or other non-embryonic cells, much of the moral issue will removed.

We cannot assume that genetic testing always produces reliable results. This introduces an additional responsibility for the scientific community to evaluate the accuracy, reliability, and usefulness of the tests they develop and for health care workers to assess and communicate to patients the degrees of reliability of the information they impart. On occasion we acquire information about the existence of a link between genetic makeup and disease when no treatment exists for the disease. Should testing even be done in this instance?

Finally, we must consider the potential long-term impact of genetic information. Genetically altered foods may bring social benefits to the population at large and profits to commercial enterprises. Are they safe for individuals and for the environment? Are they marketed only among certain populations? And what of the possible evolutionary implications of human manipulation of genetic information? To what extent are our actions irreversible? All of these questions remain ongoing issues bequeathed to humankind by increasing scientific knowledge.

◎ Understanding the Nature of Science ◎

It is a common mistake to assume that understanding the nature of science can be achieved from but one avenue of approach. Historians of science sometimes portray themselves as the true spokespeople for science because they have examined its theories and the contexts in which science has been practiced over the long haul. This, they think, has resulted in an accurate and balanced view of all aspects of science, not just those that have emerged at one particular time.

Scientists understandably believe that *they* are the ones who truly understand what science is. After all, they are the ones who actually engage in scientific investigation. They know what it really means to do science. They are the ones whose passion for research sustains them through the drudgery of daily work and the frustration of experimental failure in order to be rewarded occasionally with the thrill of scientific discovery.

But philosophers, anthropologists, and sociologists of science, plus science writers and even the politicians who must decide what scientific projects are funded, are also convinced that they possess a perspective crucial to the larger understanding of science. To give a thorough representation of the nature of science, then, requires input from a variety of perspectives that would carry us well beyond the scope of this textbook.

Here we have made use of history to shed light on the nature of science. While the historical perspective is important and even vital, we do not claim that the contribution to the understanding of science that emerges from this textbook is in any sense sufficient by itself. On the contrary, along the way we have pointed out the limitations under which historical analysis operates.

The Changing Role of the History of Science

Just as scientific theories and the practice of science have not remained unaltered over the years, so too has the writing of the history of science changed over time. Especially near the end of the twentieth century, historians of science turned their attention to the various characteristics that have marked their discipline at different points in the past. This investigation has made it clear that historians have always brought assumptions to their work. From this realization has come a concern with historiography, which among other things refers to the methods of historical research. In recent years disagreements about how the history of science should be approached have even contributed to larger controversies about how we are to understand the nature of science.

Early histories of science.   Already in the eighteenth century natural philosophers began writing about the history of science. Joseph Priestley (see Chapter 10), for example, composed a history of electricity and another of vision, light, and color, both before 1775. In the nineteenth century some writers moved beyond the histories of individual sciences to more general vistas. The Cambridge professor William Whewell (1794–1866) wrote two volumes on *The History of the Inductive Sciences: From the Earliest to the Present Time* in 1837, and followed them with two more volumes on the philosophy of the inductive sciences "founded on their history" in 1840.

What characterized Whewell's and other early general histories of science was the presence of an overt agenda. Whewell wished to use history to convey what he saw as the essential component of natural science—its use of inductive reasoning from particular facts to general theories. Others trumpeted different agendas. John William Draper (1811–1882) and Andrew Dickson White (1832–1918) wrote separate histories of science in 1874 and 1896, respectively, whose purpose was to illustrate, as White's title eloquently declared, the *History of the Warfare of Science with Theology in Christendom.* A more philosophical examination of the meaning of natural science pervaded the four-volume *History of European Thought in the Nineteenth Century* by John Theodore Merz (1840–1922), which appeared between 1904 and 1912. The first two volumes were devoted specifically to scientific thought. Merz wanted to underscore what he saw as an erosion in science of a sense of contact with reality at its most basic level. He believed that this erosion had been brought about by the gradual shift to investigating the purely mechanical order of things.

After World War I, histories of science were more frequent, many written by scientists about their own fields. Perhaps the best-known general history was the multivolume *Introduction to the History of Science,* which began appearing in 1927 from the pen of the Belgian immigrant to America, George Sarton (1884–1956). Before leaving Europe during the occupation of his homeland by German troops, Sarton had begun editing a journal, *Isis,* devoted to the history of science. The war years interrupted its continuation, but he resumed publication in 1919 and remained editor until 1952. Sarton's goal in his publications was to use the historical investigation of science to illustrate the progress of humankind. He was also committed to creating a new discipline in the United States—the history of science. The success of this venture became evident in 1924, when the History of Science Society, which adopted *Isis* as its official journal, was established.

New directions in the history of science.   Study of the history of science, and with it claims regarding the nature of science itself, underwent substantial change in the 1930s as historians turned their attention to the forces they regarded as responsible for shaping science. For these scholars science did not develop in a vacuum; rather, more basic external factors directed how science unfolded. There were, however, disagreements about what these outside influences were.

A generation of Marxist scholars emphasized the material basis of human social experience, with its emphasis on economic factors, as the source of scientific ideas. For example, at the second International Congress of the History of Science in London in 1931, one delegate presented a paper on "The Socio-Economic Roots of Newton's Principia." The Marxist contributions to the congress later inspired a young British scientist, J. D. Bernal (1901–1971), to write a broader work in 1954, entitled *Science in History,* which attempted to examine the significance of science through its social and material context.

Others preferred to focus on human intellectual needs as the shaping force of science. In 1924, E. A. Burtt (1892–1989) published *The Metaphysical Foundations of Modern Science,* in which he claimed that the philosophical distinction between primary and secondary qualities made by the principal architects of the scientific revolution of the seventeenth century was ultimately responsible for the emergence of an understanding of nature as a vast system of mechanical motions. From this conception it followed that mathematical depictions of these mechanical motions constituted scientific explanation. The French thinker Alexandre Koyré (1892–1964) reinforced the priority of intellectual concerns. Because the intellect was the highest faculty in human beings, intellectual history was for Koyré the highest type of history. His *Galilean Studies* of 1939 examined not only Galileo's scientific writings, but also the philosophical implications of Galileo's conceptual innovations and the intellectual background against which they were introduced. For Burtt and Koyré the history of science was a special branch of philosophy.

Yet other directions began to appear as the 1950s neared and more appeared in the 1960s. In 1949 the British historian Herbert Butterfield (1900–1979), building on an earlier work in which he had objected to distorting the historical record by forcing it to reveal a story of progress, attempted to depict the history of science between 1300 and 1800 on its own terms. He opposed using history to narrate a story of success; hence he represented Copernicus as a conservative, the last representative of the Ptolemaic astronomers, not the revolutionary father of modern astronomy.

Early in the 1950s a young Princeton historian of science named Charles Gillispie (b. 1918), writing on the testy subject of *Genesis and Geology,* deliberately refused to worry about whether his subjects were making valid or invalid claims. He did not, he said, wish to "fret about epistemology;" rather, Gillispie wanted to understand why

15

the individuals in his study of science and religion thought as they did. He had become convinced that scientific beliefs were conditioned by social and religious opinion, that every scientist was a creature of his or her social milieu. Gillispie was by no means arguing that scientific ideas were *caused* by social factors, but he did maintain that they played a key role in how scientific theories were received.

The impact of Thomas Kuhn.   No single work has influenced the historiography of science as much as *The Structure of Scientific Revolutions,* by Thomas Kuhn (1922–1996). Published in 1962, it quickly became known as a work that purported to reveal something fundamental about the nature of scientific development from an examination of the history of science. The book exerted an influence well beyond Kuhn's own discipline; in fact, one of its central metaphors, the paradigm shift, made its way into American popular culture and was even borrowed by television advertisers in their quest to sell products.

Trained as a physicist, Kuhn changed disciplines from physics to the history of science after receiving his doctorate in 1948. The decision was made in part because of an experience he had had the previous summer. He had begun to immerse himself in the works of the past, but found himself frustrated as a modern scientist in his attempt to bring his critical skills to bear on Aristotle's physics. Then he suddenly realized that what seemed to be wrong and even absurd in Aristotle's ideas made complete sense if he adopted Aristotle's system and purposes. Aristotle was not writing bad physics; he was writing good Greek philosophy. From this epiphany came the conviction that the historian must be committed to the sympathetic reading of texts.

Using this new insight Kuhn completed a study in 1957 of the Copernican revolution in which he attempted to treat incongruities with present-day scientific

Thomas Kuhn

views not as errors, but as clues to understanding figures from the past. When he found a passage that made no sense to him, even on repeated readings, Kuhn assumed that it was *his* problem, not that of the author from the past. He had to so immerse himself in the outlook of his subject that the passage *would* make sense.

What all this suggested to Kuhn became clear in his famous book of 1962. There Kuhn introduced the idea of a paradigm, by which he meant an outlook or framework, which is constructed from both open and unspoken assumptions. What the historian must do is identify, as much as possible, the paradigms operating in historical periods and for historical figures and try to see things from within that paradigm. Critics later pointed out that Kuhn used the concept of a paradigm in many different ways, from the very general level of worldview to more specific theoretical viewpoints. But the notion that the historian must be sympathetic to the past remained clear.

Armed with his new tool, Kuhn set out to examine what happens when there is a scientific revolution—what Kuhn called extraordinary science. He asserted that what occurred in extraordinary science was a shift from one paradigm to another. Such a shift contrasted with the "normal science" that usually characterized the work of natural philosophers or scientists. Normal science was the solving of puzzles using the assumptions and outlook of the paradigm. It was a matter of drawing out all the possibilities entailed in a certain outlook, or what Kuhn called "articulating the paradigm."

Something different happens in extraordinary science, according to Kuhn. There, someone realizes that a piece of a puzzle that has proven problematic to everyone will never fit because it belongs to a *different* puzzle. By seeing things from the vantage point of a new puzzle—a new paradigm—the extraordinary scientist can make sense of it and of other pieces of the old puzzle. By seeing the Earth as a moving body, for example, Copernicus was able to construct a new paradigm that answered his need for internal harmony, something he did not find in the older Ptolemaic system.

Kuhn emphasized that scientific revolutions take time to develop because they require the appearance of anomalies and the development of a sense of crisis within the old paradigm. In addition to identifying the structural sequence they follow, Kuhn insisted that the shift from one paradigm to the next was not the result of a logical process. Paradigms, he said, were incommensurable with each other; that is, the assumptions characteristic of one are different enough from those of another that the move from one to the other is much more like a conversion experience or a gestalt switch than an inference or deduction.

Kuhn's conclusions about how science developed in the past, although no doubt influenced by his training as a scientist, came primarily from his immersion in the history of science. He maintained that his was not an idealized picture of how science ought to be viewed, but one based on a historian's best analysis of how it actually has unfolded. But the results of his analysis ran counter to the understanding of science present in many quarters, both at the time his book appeared and since.

Central to the objection to Kuhn's analysis, articulated frequently by scientists themselves, is the claim that science is not carrying humankind closer to nature's truth. In 1992 Kuhn noted in a lecture that if there is no external standard by which we can judge a paradigm shift (because in his view we are all in one paradigm or another and cannot simply shift back and forth between them), then it is hard to imagine what could be meant by the phrase that a scientific theory takes us "closer to the truth." In reply to Kuhn's position, physicist Steven Weinberg once asked: "If one scientific theory is only better than another in its ability to solve problems . . . then why not save ourselves a lot of trouble by putting those problems out of our minds?" What drives scientists, Weinberg continued, "is precisely the sense that there are truths out there to be discovered."

In fairness to Kuhn it must be noted that he never wished to abandon the idea of truth or to suggest that our focus should be solely on the context (paradigm) in which a scientific discovery is made to the neglect of the discovery itself. Kuhn did believe that the presence of paradigms prevents us from ever reaching final scientific truth. But, as the American intellectual historian David Hollinger has pointed out, Kuhn's work meant that historians and scientists have had to learn to bear the tension between not knowing truth and having to aim at it anyway.

Ongoing Debates in the Historiography of Science

In spite of Kuhn's own caution regarding the need to retain truth at least as the goal toward which we strive in both history and science, others have been less convinced. As a result of a number of developments in several disciplines, numerous scholars questioned the standards of traditional scholarship to a much more radical degree than did Kuhn. Some took the position that the social context of a scientific discovery was so important that all other considerations, including the content of the discovery itself, paled in light of it. As a result, the history of science expanded to include scholars who did not come to the field from the sciences themselves, but were drawn by an interest in scientific institutions or science in its relationships to politics, religion, literature, the arts, or public policy.

In the 1970s the growing number of historians of science engaged in a debate between so-called internal versus external history, as if it were a matter of choosing between the content of a scientific theory or the social context in which it emerged. Externalists pointed out that the noble dream of attaining objective reality in history or in science was so problematic that it should be discarded. Internalists insisted that the truth or falsity of a historical claim or scientific theory was not only germane but central to its historical significance.

This debate faded as even more radical positions emerged within the field of history in general, precipitating a rift among historians of science. In what has come to be known as the postmodern perspective, even the externalists came in for criticism on the grounds that their idea of a "social context" was just as problematic as that of "objective reality." The social structures externalists identified were, so the criticism went, arbitrary and subjective. History was not about finding causal explanations according to some structured grand narrative. In place of trying to tie together a particular scientific development with the social context in which it occurred, postmodern historians argued that history should depict the interests and the power relationships

The NATURE of SCIENCE

The Science Wars

Natural scientists themselves generally have expressed little sympathy for postmodern interpreters of science and its history. In 1994 a biting criticism of this trend by two authors, a scientist and a mathematician, appeared under the title *Higher Superstition*. It was followed three years later by a large collection of critiques by scientists, historians, and others opposed to the postmodern approach, entitled *The Flight from Science and Reason*. And in 1996 a professor of physics at New York University submitted a paper to a postmodern journal on what he called the "transformative hermeneutics of quantum gravity." When it was published in the journal, its author declared that it was a hoax, that he had filled it with nothing more than fawning references, grandiose quotations, and outright nonsense. All these developments, which were picked up by the press, became known as the "science wars" and brought to the attention of the public the fundamental disagreements over the nature of science that divided academics, including many historians of science.

The rift that divided scholars at the end of the twentieth century ran deep, so much so that each side regarded the other as dogmatic. Those who wished to defend the relevance of structure, to insist on a set of standards of scholarship, and to preserve a cognitive element in the historian's work were labeled by their postmodern opponents as "self-designated guardians of orthodoxy." Those who insisted that historical texts must be liberated of all constraints, including even those of the author's intent, were portrayed by the critics of postmodernism as intellectual anarchists.

The science wars exposed positions that were holy to each side. For one group it was crucial that a proper understanding of science, past and present, included ideas that truth existed and that it should be the goal of scientific research. The other side was equally convinced that there was no such thing as scientific truth because of the constantly changing subjective criteria employed by human beings in their acquisition and construction of knowledge. We are still struggling to incorporate the positive aspects from each perspective.

among peoples linked together in a culture. An obvious gain in this "cultural studies" approach was the desire to include in historical work individuals at the margins of society who have previously tended to be overlooked, especially as they illustrate the relationships of power present in the society. And yet, as Thomas Kuhn had said earlier about extreme interpretations of science, they seemed to leave historians with no "useful notions of how science works and of what scientific progress is."

◎   The Challenge Ahead   ◎

While no resolution to the disagreements among historians of science has emerged, the deep polarization and sharp divisions that marked the closing years of the previous century have dulled somewhat in the new millennium. Cultural critics of science, in their intense focus on how the historian or scientist shapes the very world we know, rightly continue to remind us that knowledge of the world or of the past is not something that simply comes to us directly from nature or the historical record unmediated by the scientist or the historian. At the same time, empirical scientists and historians who insist on the centrality of historical evidence correctly emphasize that we are not free to overlook or even deemphasize the realities that limit our interpretations.

Neither scientists nor historians have yet learned how to represent with precision the interaction between the constraints imposed by reality and the interventions of those who would know it. Until there is consensus on this knotty problem, all those who strive to understand how science has developed in the past and how it continues to operate in the present must retain open minds. In the situation where embracing one intellectual position automatically excludes the other, our only recourse is to make toleration an act of will. In so doing we display the modicum of humility that acknowledges that our position, while based firmly on our own convictions, is in the end not more than our own convictions.

Suggestions for Reading

David Cahan, ed., *From Natural Philosophy to the Sciences* (Chicago: University of Chicago Press, 2003).

John Horgan, *The End of Science: Facing the Limits of Knowledge in the Twilight of the Scientific Age* (Reading, Mass.: Addison-Wesley, 1996).

Thomas Kuhn, *The Structure of Scientific Revolutions* (Chicago: University of Chicago Press, 1996).

Spencer Weart, *The Discovery of Global Warming* (Cambridge, Mass.: Harvard University Press, 2003).

Why Know about Social Science Research?

What You Will Learn

- what is particular about social research
- why social research is important
- how the social science disciplines developed
- what the basic steps are in carrying out social research

INTRODUCTION

Controlling for personal and family characteristics, perceived weight status was signifi-cantly associated with suicidal thoughts and actions in middle school boys and girls.
Whetstone, Lauren M., Morrissey, Susan L., & Cummings, Doyle M. (2007). Children at risk: the association between perceived weight status and suicidal thoughts and attempts in middle school youth. *Journal of School Health, 77,* 59–67. InfoTrac record number: **A158907083**.*

Brand placements are appearing in greater numbers and in more diverse places including video games. . . . [V]ideo game players are processing the brand placements in video games and their implicit memory is influenced by these placements.
Yang, Moonhee, Roskos-Ewoldsen, David R., Dinu, Lucian, & Arpan, Laura M. (2006). The effectiveness of "in-game" advertising: comparing college students' explicit and implicit memory for brand names. *Journal of Advertising, 35,* 143–153. InfoTrac record number: **A156736058**.

[V]olleyball, wrestling, and hockey officials all possess the same degree of personality characteristics as the normal population. However, they are perceived by athletes and fans as being deficient in all of the domains of Extraversion, Openness, Agreeableness and Conscientiousness, while possessing an excess of Neuroticism.
Balch, Marcie J., & Scott, David (2007). Contrary to popular belief, refs are people too! Personality and perceptions of officials. *Journal of Sport Behavior, 30,* 3–21. InfoTrac record number: **A159644775**.

[C]oncerns about weight and shape emerge as early as the third grade. Hence, it may be argued that prevention programs for eating disorders should begin as early as the third grade rather than in adolescence when the behaviors may be more difficult to modify. . . .

---

*Throughout this book we have included references to articles available in full on the InfoTrac® College Edition database. A free temporary subscription to the database is included with this textbook. Please see the Preface for a quick and easy way to retrieve articles from InfoTrac using the record number.

[F]athers are an important factor in the development of their daughters' views about their weight and shape. Thus, the role of fathers cannot be neglected in prevention or treatment programs.

Agras, W. Stewart, Bryson, Susan, Hammer, Lawrence D., & Kraemer, Helena C. (2007). Childhood risk factors for thin body preoccupation and social pressure to be thin. *Journal of the American Academy of Child and Adolescent Psychiatry, 46,* 171–179. InfoTrac record number: **A159183349**.

The above statements are examples of results obtained from social science research studies using diverse methods. Practically every day we read or hear of results achieved through social science research carried out by researchers in academia, as well as in public and private organizations. The purpose of this book is to show you how social scientists undertake research, and to explain why these procedures are appropriate ways of discovering the facts of social life and explaining them.

We are all interested in questions about our lives and the world around us, which is one of the many important reasons why we should understand research methods. Questions about human beings and their social world have been raised since antiquity. However, for countless generations the answers were based on superstition, intuition, and speculation. This situation has changed over the last two centuries or so, as more systematic modes of inquiry have developed. Intuition and speculation have given way increasingly to a scientific way of collecting verifiable facts. The result has been a remarkable expansion of our knowledge about ourselves and about our social world. With the development of scientific modes of inquiry, social science disciplines gradually emerged that focused on studying human beings and their societies. The broad category of **social sciences** includes anthropology, economics, political science, psychology, sociology, history, geography, and related areas such as business studies and communications.

Social science research is unlike everyday social inquiry, which often relies on common sense. Common-sense explanations are not entirely useless, but if we rely only on common sense we have no way of knowing whether our assumptions are correct. For centuries people believed it was "common sense" that the earth was flat or that the earth was the centre of the universe. Only when individuals raised questions about these cherished beliefs and started looking for verifiable evidence were these views eventually dismissed.

Social science research—and scientific research in general—has become part of our daily life. The mass media are full of reports and debates about scientific research. Have crime rates increased in the past year? Is there a rise in the rate of high school dropouts? Has the income gap between males and females narrowed in the past decade? Is the family falling apart? The reported findings influence our lives in far more ways than we may realize.

Consider, for example, how social research helps to shape some of our opinions and behaviour. Suppose this morning's paper reports that the unemployment rate sharply increased last month. Another article cites a study showing that workers are generally pessimistic about their future employment. Worse still, those working in the very occupation you were hoping to enter in the future are the most concerned. These articles, all of which would likely be based on social research, will undoubtedly have an impact on what you think about the state of the economy and about whether you should pursue a particular career.

Peruse any major newspaper or magazine and you are bound to find articles that cite findings generated by social research. Some findings are even headline news; this is particularly true of the latest information on Canada's unemployment rate, the gross domestic product, and the consumer price index. Furthermore, politicians who design social policies that have a profound impact on our lives will often defend these policies by citing findings from social research studies. These studies, it would seem, give scientific justification for the policies. But are you able to critically assess the reported findings? Do you know what the purposes of the cited studies were? Are the conclusions and the weaknesses of these studies assessed in media reports?

Private organizations also use the findings of social research to assist them in various business and managerial decisions. As well, they use the findings of social research to determine ways to influence consumers to buy their products. Advertisements and commercials tell us that tests show one product is better than another, or that a survey shows consumers prefer one product to another. Are these tests and surveys valid?

Because of these widespread uses of social research, it is clearly in our best interest to understand the benefits and critically evaluate social research. In this book we will explore how certain types of high-quality information are possible as a result of social science research. By considering the research process used to collect that information, you will be able to critically evaluate the quality of the information. But why do we need this high-quality information? What is wrong with common sense or nonscientific information? To answer these questions, we need to look at information generally and to explore the contrasts between common sense and science.

FACTUAL INFORMATION AND CASUAL RESEARCH

In our everyday lives we accumulate a lot of information. In our social activities we need to make sense of or be informed about our surroundings in order to act effectively and reasonably. We need to know what is going on and why, and what people expect us to do. We often refer to this information or knowledge as our beliefs, opinions, and values. In certain areas we think we know the "facts" because we have read a magazine or newspaper article or have seen a documentary. Or we may have looked up information on the Internet or read one or two books on a subject. As we grow older this knowledge increases, we gain experience, and we may trust our insights and intuitions more. It may come as a great shock to learn that all this "knowledge" we base our lives on is questioned by science! For people engaged in scientific research, all of the socially acceptable ways of attaining knowledge in everyday life may be flawed.

Much of this potentially flawed information comes from parents, teachers, and other **moral authorities**. Such information is *traditional* or *customary*—it indicates the right way to proceed because it has always been right. Questioning or criticizing this type of information is considered blasphemous or deeply disrespectful. In earlier times this kind of information would have been almost all that was available. However, we are now exposed to the Internet, television, radio, newspapers, magazines, and books. When we go to school we find that teachers have different ideas from our parents and that our schoolmates have still other ideas. We soon discover that different people or information sources present different ideas of what is real, appropriate, or good.

How do we choose when there are conflicting or alternative ideas? Most of us become good at interpreting which rules apply to a particular situation, and we adjust our behaviour and attitudes accordingly. When we are with our friends and intimates we are relaxed and follow different codes of behaviour than we would, say, in a classroom or a work setting. In other words, we use social information *practically*, to cope with life. We do not think too deeply about the information itself—about whether it is logically consistent or is really "true."

What are the characteristics of this social information? Essentially, it consists of faith and folkways, or stereotyped rules of thumb. **Faith** means that something is unquestionably right and that it is simply wrong to disbelieve, criticize, or try to explore and evaluate a belief or an action. **Folkways** are working assumptions about ways of doing things and thinking about things, based on social routines and habits. These assumptions stabilize our experience and give it meaning and organization, whether or not reality actually works in accordance with the stereotypes. Prejudices are an extreme form of stereotyped rules; they identify a particular group or institution in a generalized way and define how an individual or a community should relate to that group. If someone does not fit the stereotype, that person becomes the "exception that proves the rule," rather than a reason for reexamining the stereotype. In ordinary, everyday life we use a lot of unquestioned information that *shapes our observations,* rather than being *shaped by observations.*

For example, assume you were brought up believing that members of a certain ethnic group with whom you have little contact are generally lazy and live on welfare. Would you question your view if you met one that was a successful professional? The tendency would be to see that person as an exception, rather than to question your view. Yet to truly know that group we would need to move beyond the stereotype and actually observe and study its members. Likewise we may dismiss criticisms of our cherished views by pointing to a case without recognizing that special factors may be involved. An example is someone who has always believed that smoking is not a health hazard and dismisses contrary views by pointing out that his healthy 95-year-old grandfather has been a heavy smoker since his teens.

Today, we also live in a world that values *factual information,* and we get much of this from media sources such as television and radio news documentaries, as well as from newspapers and magazines. You are aware, no doubt, that this information has its limitations. Newspapers and newsmagazines tend to have political biases that may colour the way news stories are written. Furthermore, the most successful media do not present much detail because that would reduce their ability to provide a variety of news items and might reduce audience interest. Instead of analyzing and going into the specific reasons for why things happen, television and radio newscasts in particular tend to briefly describe what happens, present the most dramatic aspects of an event, and focus on a particular personality connected with the event. There may be little follow-up on previous news stories, so we do not get the context that might help us to understand more about what is happening and why. Therefore, "news" often tends to become entertainment; only the highlights of the moment are presented, and these quickly disappear when another story emerges. It requires a lot of effort on our part to put together a coherent and meaningful story from this continuous stream of unrelated bits and pieces. Most of us do not have the time or the tools to do this. As well, we lack essential information that would allow us to do so.

The Internet is a recent addition to our sources of information. It is a communications technology that combines elements of the mass media, popular entertainment, the shopping mall, and the library in a form that is easily accessible from your home. Through the Internet you can download music, read newspaper and magazine articles, view films and TV programs, listen to radio broadcasts, shop online, check out what books are in your college library, and even take college courses and download class notes. You can also wander through innumerable chat rooms, newsgroups, and blogs. Perhaps the greatest problem with the Internet is the sheer volume of "stuff" that is accessible, and it suffers from the same problems and biases found in other media and entertainment sources. And of course the personal communication in discussion groups consists generally of opinions. Even much of the material found by means of search engines is often irrelevant, and thus searching for information may be time-consuming. The Internet is unlike the traditional library, which has professional "information specialists" (i.e., librarians) to help guide your search for information. However, when used properly the Internet is a valuable means of obtaining social science information, as we shall see throughout this book.

We have already identified some problems with various forms of everyday knowledge: faith cannot be questioned or analyzed; stereotyped routines shape our observations; and most news is fragmented and superficial. But what about factual knowledge drawn from the "serious" media or from encyclopedias and books? These sources do at least delve more deeply into particular subjects and are less superficial than ordinary news. Most of us treat newsmagazines, in-depth reporting, and nonfiction books with a special kind of respect. We assume that these sources are written by experts who know what they are talking about and who are telling us the truth. We do not normally ask ourselves exactly how the information was obtained, or whether the right people were interviewed. We assume that the reporters and writers have done their research properly and are presenting the facts correctly. But this means we are taking these reports on faith, unquestioningly.

This approach to factual information—taking the work of experts at face value—is the way most of us deal with experts in our lives. We believe our doctors, bank managers, and others without much questioning or cross-examining or looking around for second opinions. When we do research, for example, to buy a new car or MP3 player, we tend to do very quick checks using the most accessible sources of information. This way of proceeding might be called **casual** or **lay research**. How is it different from scientific research?

SCIENTIFIC RESEARCH

Science differs from other ways of knowing and doing research because of its aims and the procedures it uses to pursue those aims. Faith, folkways, and everyday factual information give us moral and social guidelines for solving immediate, practical problems in our lives. Science aims at objective knowledge—that is, knowledge that is not tied to immediate personal or practical problems, but is sought for its own sake.

To understand the procedures science uses, it is necessary to understand a little about its history. Scientific research is a recent development in human history. Ideas associated with science, such as experimentation, precise measurement, and the application of mathematics to description and explanation, developed mainly in the period between 1600 and 1800 in Western Europe (see Box 1.1).

During this period when people began to question long-cherished ideas that were at odds with their own observations, they were quickly challenged by the church and other authorities, who argued that the claims were fraudulent, or worse, blasphemous. Pioneer scientists had two strong ways to defend their claims. The first was to persuade critics to look at the evidence and at how it was obtained. If cardinals and bishops looked through the telescope, they too could see mountains on the moon; it was not just a subjective claim. Therefore, the more open scientists were about their findings and about the ways they had achieved these findings, the more likely they were to be believed. The second strong defence against their critics was to present the findings clearly and logically. Using closely reasoned logical arguments to justify their interpretations of their discoveries, scientists made it harder for traditional religious and moral objections to stand up. Logic could be used both to defend explanations of what they had found and to criticize those who argued against their reasoning. These two ways of challenging accepted ideas soon became a basic part of the **scientific method**. A major feature of the scientific method is the importance given to observation. As well, for research to be acceptable, it has to be logically reasoned, follow explicit procedures, and be open to inspection by others, even to the point of being repeatable by other researchers.

Above all, to be scientific means to carry out **systematic empirical research**. And to be systematic means to use specially developed procedures for gathering information and to use these procedures carefully and thoroughly. The aim of systematic empirical research is to observe, describe, explain, and predict in order to improve our understanding of reality. This is in contrast to casual research, which quickly gathers the most convenient and accessible information, often in a haphazard way, in order to solve a pressing problem. To be empirical means that you do not assume that you already know the answers; your research is not shaped by moral convictions or other traditional cultural assumptions that operate elsewhere in your life. On the contrary, you have to set these assumptions aside, be open-minded, and operate according to the special assumptions of scientific research.

THE EMERGENCE OF THE SOCIAL SCIENCES

The emergence of the social sciences was stimulated by the dramatic changes in European societies from the Renaissance onward: the discovery of sea routes to Asia and the Americas; the Protestant Reformation; and the scientific, commercial, and industrial revolutions. However, the social sciences first developed as a set of philosophical ideas and only later involved systematic empirical research. (See Box 1.2 for some early examples of pioneering empirical research. Note that most examples are from the 20th century.)

BOX 1.2   EXAMPLES OF PIONEERING EMPIRICAL SOCIAL RESEARCH

Principal Researcher	Research	Method
Charles Booth	Conducted several surveys on poverty and society in London. (1886–1903)	Survey (See Chapter 5.)
Wilhelm Wundt	Set up the first experimental laboratory. It was used to study human sensory experience such as vision and touch. (1879)	Laboratory experiment (See Chapter 6.)
Elton Mayo	With others, used different approaches to study the behaviour of industrial workers in their workplace, including the influence of illumination on productivity. (1927–1932)	Field experiment/ open-ended interviews (See Chapters 6 and 7.)
Bronislaw Malinowski	Studied the day-to-day life of the Trobriand Islanders of New Guinea by living with them. (1915–1918)	Fieldwork (See Chapter 7.)
Nels Anderson	Lived for some time as a homeless person during his studies of the urban homeless. (1921–1923)	Urban fieldwork (See Chapter 7.)
Harold Lasswell	Studied mass communication processes. One study focused on radio and print reports of enemy leaders' speeches. (1942)	Content analysis (See Chapter 8.)

The evolution of the social sciences into research-based, empirical disciplines involves several stages. One stage is the separation of a discipline from predecessors, such as philosophy, or from nonacademic fields such as art or journalism. A second stage is the development of the discipline in its own right, with a focus of study and an approach to its field that are distinct from those of other disciplines. Associated with these developments is the emergence of institutions that reinforce the practice of research as an open, shared process based on common interests and standards. Professional associations, journals in which research can be published, and universities where researchers can be trained and research can be sustained are the most important of these institutions.

Social Science Disciplines

Just as there is no single "science of nature" but rather several different natural sciences specializing in the study of various aspects of nature (physics, astronomy, chemistry, botany, etc.), so too are there different social science disciplines. Each discipline focuses on particular aspects of human life, develops its own theories in a language of its own making, and often uses certain **research methods** more than other social sciences do. Box 1.3 illustrates

BOX 1.3   SOCIAL SCIENCES PERSPECTIVES: EXAMPLES OF RESEARCH
APPROACHES TO THE PHENOMENON OF FAMILY PLANNING

Discipline	Emphasis	Family Planning Research
Anthropology	Systems of culture, including material artifacts	Differing patterns of population control in tribal and peasant societies
Economics	Rational choice in context of limited resources	Rise in family planning as a response to increasing costs of educating children as economy shifts from agriculture to industry
Geography	Spatial distribution	Patterns of spread of contraception and shifts in family size across rural versus urban areas
History	Time sequences	Rise in middle-class reform movements in industrial cities and key figures spearheading these movements
Political Science	Political, legal, and governmental organization	Variations in strengths of reform movements reflecting class, ideological, and political factors
Psychology	Personal and interpersonal feelings, ideas, and relationships	Patterns of trust, communication, and bonding between couples in relation to family planning
Sociology	Norms and pressures of group life	Class, ethnic, religious, and other community factors in relation to contraception

how different social science disciplines might undertake research on family planning as a result of the differences in their perspectives. Clearly, each discipline and different research approach makes important contributions to our better understanding of the phenomenon.

Anthropology studies the origin and varieties of human beings and their societies. Physical anthropology focuses on human evolution and variation and is closely tied to genetics and other life sciences. Cultural anthropology focuses on ways of life and varieties of beliefs, customs, language, and artifacts. Field research, whereby the social scientist lives with and participates in the life of the people studied, is a major research technique used in cultural anthropology.

The predecessors of anthropology in Canada were essentially the missionaries, explorers, and travellers of the past. But in 1910 a federal government department of anthropology was set up, headed by the famous American linguistic anthropologist Edward Sapir. He recruited various Canadians, including one who went on to establish the first centre for ethnography at Université Laval, which has specialized in the study of Quebec rural life. The first university department of anthropology was established in 1925 at the University of Toronto. The main anthropological association in Canada is the Canadian Anthropology Society, whose official publication *Anthropologica* is Canada's oldest journal of anthropology.

Economics studies how human beings allocate scarce resources to produce goods and services, and how these goods and services are distributed for consumption. It has two main branches: macroeconomics, which studies entire economies, and microeconomics, which focuses on individual firms, consumers, and other economic actors. Much of its research is based on economic and demographic information available from government sources such as Statistics Canada.

In Canada, economics was at first closely associated with amateur writing on policy issues by government officials and businesspeople and was known as *political economy*. But in 1918 the Dominion Bureau of Statistics (Statistics Canada's predecessor) was founded and provided standardized national and provincial statistics for economic analysis. University departments were created soon after, and in 1929 the Canadian Political Science Association, which included economists, was established. The association published the *Canadian Journal of Economics and Political Science* from 1935 until 1967, when economists set up the Canadian Economics Association. Since 1968 this association has published the *Canadian Journal of Economics*. For many years economic research among francophone academics was concentrated at École des hautes études commerciales de Montréal (HEC Montréal), founded in 1907, which began to publish *L'actualité économique* in 1925.

Geography is the study of physical environmental phenomena and their interrelations. Human geography focuses on the location and distribution of human populations and their activities, the environmental conditioning, and the environmental effects of location and distribution of human populations. In the late 20th century, geography became a synthesizing social science linking the physical and social sciences through a focus on spatial patterns and environmental factors shaping human history and culture.

Until World War II, to be a geographer in Canada generally meant being a cartographer trained in civil engineering, geology, or drafting. In 1922 the University of British Columbia established a department of geology and geography, and a first full department of geography was established at the University of Toronto in 1935. Over time, geographic expertise was increasingly demanded by governments concerned with strategic resources and economic development. The federal government first hired a full-time professional geographer in 1943, a practice followed by most provinces in the 1950s. While a nonprofessional Quebec Geographic Society had existed since 1877, the Canadian Association of Geographers was established by university-based and other professional geographers in 1951. Its publication is *The Canadian Geographer*.

History is the study of the human past. However, modern social scientific history is traced largely to the 18th and 19th centuries. At that time, the practice of using original records, documents, and letters and carefully cross-referencing these sources to establish the truth of facts or events and the accuracy of dates became the normal practice for historical research. Historians stress the importance of documentary evidence and its interpretation as their basic research technique.

In the 19th century much historical writing in Canada was mainly semifictional romantic or moralistic storytelling. The creation of the Public Archives of Canada in 1872, however, contributed to the compiling of objective records and common sources for historical analysis. By the 20th century some chairs of history had been established at various universities. In 1922 the Canadian Historical Association was founded. It publishes the *Journal of the Canadian Historical Association*. In francophone universities, departments of history were mainly set up after World War II. However, as early as 1915, the influential and controversial Father Lionel Groulx had set up a chair in Canadian history at the Montreal campus (present-day Université de Montréal) of Université Laval.

Political science studies the processes, institutions, and activities of governments and groups reacting to and involved in these processes. Political science mainly emerged as a discipline in the 18th and 19th centuries, when scholars attempted to classify the varieties of governments and explain why they existed. With the growth of democracy, the analysis of elections and voting patterns emerged. Consequently, much political science research involves the use of polls and other survey research techniques.

In Canadian anglophone universities, political science was dominated by economics, or "political economy," until after World War II. The Canadian Political Science Association and its journal, the *Canadian Journal of Economics and Political Science*, noted earlier, were primarily devoted to economics. When economists formed their own association and started publishing their own journal, the Canadian Political Science Association founded the *Canadian Journal of Political Science*. The development of political science in francophone universities largely coincided with the rapid social and political changes in Quebec in the 1950s and 1960s. Political science expanded along with the various francophone universities, and a francophone association of political scientists was set up in the early 1960s, now known as the Société québécoise de science politique, and began publishing the journal *Politique*.

Psychology is the study of behaviour and thought processes. Psychologists do research in such areas as perceptions, memory, problem solving, learning and using language, adjusting to the physical and social environment, and normal and abnormal development of these processes from infancy to old age. The two most widely used techniques for studying behaviour are observing the behaviour of humans and animals and conducting experimental studies on the effects of various stimuli on behaviour.

In Canada before the 20th century, psychology was seen as a subdivision of philosophy, and the first experimental laboratory was set up in 1889 by James Mark Baldwin of the University of Toronto philosophy department. University departments of psychology began to be created in Canada mainly during the 1920s. The Canadian Psychology

Association was established in 1939 and among its various publications are three journals: *Canadian Journal of Experimental Psychology; Canadian Journal of Behavioural Science;* and *Canadian Psychology.* Psychology departments in francophone universities were established in the early 1940s and were at first dominated by a Roman Catholic philosophical orientation until about the late 1950s, when the focus had turned to basic research.

Sociology emerged in the 19th century as the study of all aspects of social life in industrial or modern societies. It is now defined as the study of human social relationships, the rules and ideas that guide these relationships, and the development of institutions and movements that conserve and change society. Sociology is a broad discipline with many subdivisions and many overlaps with the other social sciences. Because of its breadth and variety, sociology does not lean toward any one research technique.

Sociology was a late developer in Canada despite the establishment of departments at McGill University and the University of Toronto in the 1920s and 1930s, respectively. In 1941 the prominent economist Harold Innis described it as "the Cinderella of the social sciences." But in Canadian universities, sociology began to emerge as an independent discipline in the 1940s. Until the 1960s sociologists mainly joined the Canadian Political Science Association, but in 1966 sociologists and anthropologists founded the Canadian Sociology and Anthropology Association. In 2006 the name of the association was changed to Canadian Sociological Association, and its journal, formerly called *Canadian Review of Sociology and Anthropology* was renamed *Canadian Review of Sociology.* In francophone universities sociology was at first under the influence of the Roman Catholic Church, but over the years the church's influence diminished. Sociology expanded and new journals were created, including *Sociologie et Société,* which began publishing in 1968.

SOCIAL SCIENCE RESEARCH

While the foundation of the social science disciplines rests on research, sharing the basic perspective and approach of the natural sciences, some features are unique to the social sciences. Whereas natural scientists study inanimate objects—chemicals, physical forces, stars, and so on—or animate but nonhuman beings, social scientists mainly study human beings with whom they can communicate. This focus gives social scientists special advantages and challenges in devising methods of research. Natural scientists may carefully and systematically observe and experiment but they cannot communicate with what they study. Social scientists can perform interviews and experiments, conduct surveys, read documents and letters written by long-dead individuals, and learn about cultures by participating or sharing in other people's lives and experiences. Social scientists, then, have a broader variety of research techniques available to them than do natural scientists.

However, since much of social science research involves the direct study of human beings with whom they can communicate, it brings up the possibility that the research may be coloured by emotions, political concerns, and other sources of bias. Social reality appears to be a much more difficult matter to investigate and about which to produce strong, firm conclusions and explanations. Experimentation in social life is much harder, so a researcher often cannot pin down exactly how one thing affects another. It is also much harder to identify clearly measurable qualities and characteristics in social life than it is in the natural world. Social phenomena often tend to be qualitative—describable in words but not as clearly and easily represented by numbers.

It is also difficult to pin down beginnings and endings of social phenomena. When did the Quiet Revolution in Quebec begin? When did it end? These points cannot be identified with any great precision. Social life is also continually and rapidly changing. The speed of social change makes it difficult for social scientists to keep up with and accurately describe the changes, let alone interpret and explain them. These complications mean that the social sciences are less able to produce small numbers of powerful explanations or general theories that apply to a large number of different phenomena. Instead, generalizations and explanations in social science apply to a small range of times and places, seem to have many exceptions, and are often intensely disputed. These characteristics continue to generate debates about the nature of the social sciences, their progress, usefulness, and comparisons with the natural sciences.

THE RESEARCH PROCESS

We have said that the scientific method involves following procedures that are acceptable to other scientific researchers. This book introduces you to these procedures so that you can understand how social science research takes place. With this understanding, you can become an informed and critical reader of social science literature, including what is reported in the media (e.g., see Reading 1.1), and you can begin to learn how to do your own research.

Reading 1.1

Every day the media report on social research of general public interest. Usually it is brief and highlights the main results. Likewise, we tend to retain what was said about the results and pay little or no attention to the aim and purpose of the research and how it was conducted. As a beginning step in understanding about social science research and becoming a more critical thinker of what is reported in the media, consider the following questions. In addition to the results, are we told about the objective of the study? How was the study carried out (i.e., the methodology)? Are we told about any weaknesses of the study? What was the researchers' general conclusion?

As you become more familiar with social science research, you will have more questions about the media reports. Read the newspaper article below and critically assess the information about the objective, methodology, results, and conclusion of the reported study. In addition, compare the newspaper article with the cited academic journal article whose reference is indicated below, and for now take note of the steps in the research process.

STUDY LINKS VIDEO GAMES TO RECKLESS DRIVING: Canadian Death Cited

Inspired by last year's death of Toronto taxi driver Tahir Khan, who was hit on a winding ravine road by a teenage street racer with a copy of the video game Need for Speed in his car, German psychologists have compiled the most extensive case yet that racing games cause reckless driving.

Playing such titles as Burnout, Midnight Racer and Need for Speed "increases risk-taking behaviour in critical road traffic situations," the team led by Peter Fischer reports today in the *Journal of Experimental Psychology: Applied*.

Writing about the Toronto case, in light of earlier examples of people reenacting video game scenarios to lethal effect, such as the Columbine school shootings, Prof. Fischer writes: "What if players of racing games similarly model their actual road traffic behaviour on their behaviour during these games?"

One of the team's experiments largely replicates a survey done last month by BSM, a British driving school.

Both showed that the more a person plays a racing game, the more likely he is to drive in an "obtrusive and competitive" manner. Both also come with the caveat that self-reporting is notoriously unreliable.

But the German team, from the elite Ludwig-Maximilians University in Munich, went further to look at whether playing a racing game can directly "prime" someone for risk-taking.

They had 68 university students play one of the three racing games mentioned above or one of three "neutral" games (Tak, Crash Bandicoot, or FIFA 2005). In keeping with previous research on video game psychology, subjects were allowed at least 20-minutes of playing to ensure they were sufficiently "in" the game.

The subjects then took a "Vienna Test," which measures risk-taking in actual road traffic situations, and is, in effect, another sort of video game. They watched reenactment videos of risky driving situations, such as passing on the highway and crossing train tracks, and were instructed to press a button at the moment they would abandon the manoeuvre.

"The time that had elapsed since participants gained their driver's licence, the number of accidents reported, sensation-seeking and enjoyment of the games had no significant effect on risk-taking behaviour," Prof. Fischer writes.

But simply playing the games seemed somehow to increase a subject's readiness to take "real-life" risks, a result that was "especially pronounced" for men.

"Practitioners in the field of road traffic safety should bear in mind the possibility that racing games indeed make road traffic less safe, not least because game players are mostly young adults, acknowledged as the highest accident rate group," Prof. Fischer writes.

Source: Brean, Joseph. *Study links video games to reckless driving: Canadian death cited.* (2007, March 19). National Post, p. A3.

A more elaborate and detailed analysis than what was reported in the newspaper article is available in the following academic article:

Fischer, Peter, Kubitzki, Jörg, Guter, Stephanie, & Frey, Dieter (2007). Virtual driving and risk taking: do racing games increase risk-taking cognitions, affect, and behaviors? Journal of Experimental Psychology: Applied, 13, *22–31.*

Social research that is acceptable to other social scientists follows certain steps, which are presented in Figure 1.1 and elaborated on in the following chapters. However, it should be noted that researchers develop their own styles of following this **research process**.

Figure 1.1 Research Process

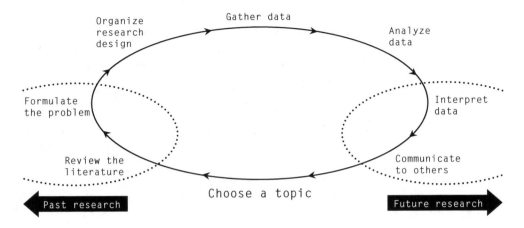

Here, we provide only an overview, and in Chapter 2 we elaborate on the process and introduce more terminology.

Social research requires careful preparation. The research process begins when we *choose a topic* from our knowledge base—that is, the general knowledge we have about an area. For example, you might decide to carry out a study to find out about the playing habits of college students who were avid players of violent video games in high school. Your interest in this subject may have been aroused from hearing parents and teachers claim that spending hours playing violent video games results in poor academic achievement and more aggressive behaviour. You wonder who actually purchases and plays violent video games, which are the more popular ones, whether some games have any educational purpose, and so on. You also know that some of your friends have had more exposure to such games than others, and that they do not all play the same games. These general ideas form the beginning of a research topic or issue.

Your next goal is to be more precise about the issue you want to examine. To help you in this effort, you concentrate on relevant background information, including scholarly studies on the topic. In other words, you *review the literature*. In the process, you become aware of what specific issues other researchers have examined, what techniques they used to collect facts, how they defined certain terms to distinguish different types of video games, information on the video games industry, and much more. The review of other studies and discussions on the topic will help you to carefully *formulate the problem* that you intend to research. The stated problem has to be a clear, focused statement that will guide your search for evidence. For example, after reading and reviewing works on violent video games and aggressiveness, you may decide that the literature ignores whether college students who were avid violent video game players in high school lose interest in such games in college. You develop an idea that students' interest in violent video games declines as they adjust to college life. This speculative statement can be put to the test, and that becomes the goal of your research.

But how do you test the idea? This will involve several steps. You will have to develop a clear set of definitions of the different types of video games. For instance, how do you define violent video games? Should you consider different ratings for violent video games? Does playing an online game qualify as playing a video game? Should you categorize the games according to price, sales, the Entertainment Software Rating Board content rating, or by subjects such as sports, war, science fiction, and so on? Should you take into account if the video game is single-player or multi-player? Will you only consider violent video games played on gaming consoles or only those played on computers, or both?

Other issues also have to be sorted out. Is it essential for you to determine whether in high school a student was a casual player or an avid player? What games did they play? Did they play alone or with friends? Moreover, which students will you study? What year? What program? How will they be selected to be part of your study? How will you carry out the study? It is *your* study and therefore you must decide how to answer these questions. In other words, you need to *develop the research design* and justify it in light of what you want to study.

The next step is to *gather the data*, as spelled out in your research design. After you have collected and recorded the information, you need to *analyze the data*. The data have to be sorted, organized, and analyzed in order for you to interpret them. Do the data show the patterns of change in playing video games? Do the patterns confirm or refute what you expected to find? What can you conclude from the data? How do the data fit with the academic literature you have read on video games?

Finally, you will want to *communicate to others* your data and conclusions. This is usually done in a research report that traces each step of the research process. In other words, you should explain how you chose and developed the topic, how you conducted the research, what you found, and your interpretations of the data, and then draw a conclusion. In addition, you need to point out the limitations of your study and suggest areas for future research.

As you can see, social research is a process. It begins with a general question, usually one in which we have a personal interest, that we then make more specific in order to be able to search for an answer. We develop a research design, including special tools and techniques to seek out the desired data. We gather and evaluate data to answer the specific question and thereby shed light on our general question. Research contributes to the accumulation of knowledge about the issue and suggests further avenues to research. Consequently, research never really ends. As one study comes to a close, another begins and continues the process of expanding our knowledge about ourselves and our social world.

In Table 1.1 we indicate which chapters of this book deal with the various steps of the research process. Throughout, we present the steps in a simplified way, but

Table 1.1   Steps in the Research Process

1. Overview of the research process.	Chapter 2	What Is Social Science Research?
2. Choose a topic and review the literature.	Chapter 3	Finding and Refining the Topic
3. Choose whom or what to study.	Chapter 4	Sampling: Choosing Who or What to Study
4. Gather the data.	Chapter 5	Social Survey
	Chapter 6	Experimental Research
	Chapter 7	Field Research
	Chapter 8	Indirect or Nonreactive Methods
5. Analyze and interpret the data.	Chapter 9	What Are the Results?
6. Communicate to others.	Chapter 10	The Research Report: The End and the Beginning

comprehensively enough for you to carry out your own research or to assess the research of others. The book provides a guided tour of the social research process, but only by doing your own social research can you capture the excitement of this process.

What You Have Learned

- There are some important differences between faith, folkways, and casual knowledge, on the one hand, and scientific knowledge on the other.
- Science is concerned with systematic empirical observation and logical analysis in order to understand and interpret observations.
- Several social science disciplines have developed, which apply a variety of empirical research techniques to different aspects of human life.
- We should be aware of the possibility that social science research may be affected by emotions, political concerns, and other sources of bias on the part of the researchers.
- Research generally proceeds in a patterned series of steps and stages.

Focus Questions

1. What are the characteristics of faith and folkways as sources of information?
2. What are the problems associated with media-based information?
3. How have the social sciences evolved as they became research-based disciplines?
4. What distinguishes casual from scientific research?
5. What are the main steps in the scientific research process?

Review Exercises

1. Follow a major news story for two weeks, through the reports on radio and television, and in one newspaper. Identify how you can tell that the story is a major one. How does its presentation shift over the course of the two weeks?

2. Identify a social issue about which you believe you have some knowledge or a strong opinion. For example, "Why do students drop out of high school?" or "What are the characteristics of people addicted to drugs?" With the help of your instructor, a librarian, or a search on the InfoTrac database, try to find some social scientific research on the topic. Compare the ideas and findings of the researchers with your own knowledge or opinion. What have you learned in this process?

3. Select one of the articles cited at the beginning of this chapter and retrieve the full text from the InfoTrac database (see the Preface for instructions on retrieving articles from InfoTrac). In your own words, state the issue that was examined and how the research was designed. Don't worry if you cannot fully understand the content of the article, particularly the jargon and statistical analysis. For now, simply identify the steps in the research process.

Weblinks

The Internet is an invaluable tool for social scientists; for many academic, research, government, and international institutes, it is the principal means of disseminating information. But because of the abundance of websites and the vast quantity of information, it is often difficult or time-consuming to find relevant material. The websites listed below and at the end of the other chapters in this book will make this process easier.

Virtual Training Suite (Intute)

http://www.vts.intute.ac.uk

A long list of "teach yourself" Internet tutorials categorized by subject headings. Each tutorial illustrates how to use the Web to gather information and research in the particular subject. The tutorials have been prepared by college and university specialists in the U.K. This site is a useful place to begin to find out about how to gain the most from searching sites on the Internet for your studies. As an example, see the tutorial on "Social Research Methods."

Research Resources for the Social Sciences

http://www.socsciresearch.com/index.html

One of the earlier Internet sites to have been designed for social science disciplines. It continues to provide an exhaustive list of relevant links organized according to various disciplines.

Virtual Library—Social Sciences

http://www.dialogical.net/socialsciences

The site is part of the World Wide Web Virtual Library. It has certain features of a library, with links to a range of links categorized by directories of data sources, electronic journals, and scholarly societies, or alphabetically according to subjects or different resources. A brief content description is provided of each link.

Social Science Subjects and Social Sciences Podcast (Intute)

http://www.intute.ac.uk/socialsciences

A great advantage of this site is that links have been evaluated and categorized by specialists at U.K. universities. Each link is briefly described, making browsing the Internet for sources less time-consuming. It is easy to use and offers links to a wide array of social science subjects that can be searched by subject headings and keyword.

The site also offers the Social Sciences Podcast, each program of which offers social science–related information news, information on the latest selections added to the site, and more.

Canadian Scholarly Societies

Below are the URLs of various academic associations in Canada. Most contain material regarding the association, including the main journal of the association, information on the discipline, and links to relevant sites.

Canadian Anthropology Society: **http://casca.anthropologica.ca**
Canadian Association of Geographers: **http://www.cag-acg.ca**
Canadian Economics Association: **http://www.economics.ca**

Canadian Historical Association: **http://www.cha-shc.ca**
Canadian Political Science Association: **http://www.cpsa-acsp.ca**
Canadian Psychology Association: **http://www.cpa.ca**
Canadian Sociological Association: **http://www.csaa.ca**

Scholarly Societies

http://www.scholarly-societies.org

The site contains links to nearly 3,800 websites with information on over 4,100 scholarly societies worldwide. You can search by subject, country, language and founding date. The site also contains links to hundreds of websites of societies of wider scope, special kinds of scholarly societies, as well as links to resources and essays of relevant interest.

Dictionary of the Social Sciences

http://bitbucket.athabascau.ca/dict.pl

This is an online dictionary that provides definitions of social science terms.

InfoTrac College Edition

http://infotrac.thomsonlearning.com

The InfoTrac College Edition is an "online university library" that offers access to nearly 20 million full-text articles from about six thousand academic journals and popular publications. Four months of unlimited access to the database is included with this textbook. Throughout the book we have referred to articles available on the database. See our Preface for more on how to access the cited articles. For a more detailed guide on the various ways to search and retrieve articles, go to the InfoTrac home page and click on "User Guide."

Chapter 2:
The Nature and
Scope of Economics

Ten Principles of
Economics

The word *economy* comes from the Greek word *oikonomos*, which means "one who manages a household." At first, this origin might seem peculiar. But in fact, households and economies have much in common.

A household faces many decisions. It must decide which members of the household do which tasks and what each member gets in return: Who cooks dinner? Who does the laundry? Who gets the extra dessert at dinner? Who gets to choose what TV show to watch? In short, the household must allocate its scarce resources among its various members, taking into account each member's abilities, efforts, and desires.

Like a household, a society faces many decisions. A society must find some way to decide what jobs will be done and who will do them. It needs some people to grow food, other people to make clothing, and still others to design computer software. Once society has allocated people (as well as land, buildings, and machines) to various jobs, it must also allocate the output of goods and services

3

they produce. It must decide who will eat caviar and who will eat potatoes. It must decide who will drive a Ferrari and who will take the bus.

The management of society's resources is important because resources are scarce. **Scarcity** means that society has limited resources and therefore cannot produce all the goods and services people wish to have. Just as each member of a household cannot get everything he or she wants, each individual in a society cannot attain the highest standard of living to which he or she might aspire.

Economics is the study of how society manages its scarce resources. In most societies, resources are allocated not by an all-powerful dictator but through the combined actions of millions of households and firms. Economists therefore study how people make decisions: how much they work, what they buy, how much they save, and how they invest their savings. Economists also study how people interact with one another. For instance, they examine how the multitude of buyers and sellers of a good together determine the price at which the good is sold and the quantity that is sold. Finally, economists analyze forces and trends that affect the economy as a whole, including the growth in average income, the fraction of the population that cannot find work, and the rate at which prices are rising.

The study of economics has many facets, but it is unified by several central ideas. In this chapter, we look at *Ten Principles of Economics*. Don't worry if you don't understand them all at first or if you aren't completely convinced. We will explore these ideas more fully in later chapters. The ten principles are introduced here to give you an overview of what economics is all about. Consider this chapter a "preview of coming attractions."

scarcity
the limited nature of society's resources

economics
the study of how society manages its scarce resources

How People Make Decisions

There is no mystery to what an economy is. Whether we are talking about the economy of Los Angeles, the United States, or the whole world, an economy is just a group of people dealing with one another as they go about their lives. Because the behavior of an economy reflects the behavior of the individuals who make up the economy, we begin our study of economics with four principles of individual decision making.

Principle 1: People Face Trade-offs

You may have heard the old saying, "There ain't no such thing as a free lunch." Grammar aside, there is much truth to this adage. To get one thing that we like, we usually have to give up another thing that we like. Making decisions requires trading off one goal against another.

Consider a student who must decide how to allocate her most valuable resource—her time. She can spend all her time studying economics, spend all of it studying psychology, or divide it between the two fields. For every hour she studies one subject, she gives up an hour she could have used studying the other. And for every hour she spends studying, she gives up an hour that she could have spent napping, bike riding, watching TV, or working at her part-time job for some extra spending money.

Or consider parents deciding how to spend their family income. They can buy food, clothing, or a family vacation. Or they can save some of the family income for retirement or the children's college education. When they choose to spend an extra dollar on one of these goods, they have one less dollar to spend on some other good.

When people are grouped into societies, they face different kinds of trade-offs. One classic trade-off is between "guns and butter." The more a society spends on national defense (guns) to protect its shores from foreign aggressors, the less it can spend on consumer goods (butter) to raise the standard of living at home. Also important in modern society is the trade-off between a clean environment and a high level of income. Laws that require firms to reduce pollution raise the cost of producing goods and services. Because of the higher costs, these firms end up earning smaller profits, paying lower wages, charging higher prices, or some combination of these three. Thus, while pollution regulations yield the benefit of a cleaner environment and the improved health that comes with it, the regulations come at the cost of reducing the incomes of the regulated firms' owners, workers, and customers.

Another trade-off society faces is between efficiency and equality. **Efficiency** means that society is getting the maximum benefits from its scarce resources. **Equality** means that those benefits are distributed uniformly among society's members. In other words, efficiency refers to the size of the economic pie, and equality refers to how the pie is divided into individual slices.

When government policies are designed, these two goals often conflict. Consider, for instance, policies aimed at equalizing the distribution of economic well-being. Some of these policies, such as the welfare system or unemployment insurance, try to help the members of society who are most in need. Others, such as the individual income tax, ask the financially successful to contribute more than others to support the government. While achieving greater equality, these policies reduce efficiency. When the government redistributes income from the rich to the poor, it reduces the reward for working hard; as a result, people work less and produce fewer goods and services. In other words, when the government tries to cut the economic pie into more equal slices, the pie gets smaller.

Recognizing that people face trade-offs does not by itself tell us what decisions they will or should make. A student should not abandon the study of psychology just because doing so would increase the time available for the study of economics. Society should not stop protecting the environment just because environmental regulations reduce our material standard of living. The poor should not be ignored just because helping them distorts work incentives. Nonetheless, people are likely to make good decisions only if they understand the options they have available. Our study of economics, therefore, starts by acknowledging life's trade-offs.

efficiency
the property of society getting the most it can from its scarce resources

equality
the property of distributing economic prosperity uniformly among the members of society

Principle 2: The Cost of Something Is What You Give Up to Get It

Because people face trade-offs, making decisions requires comparing the costs and benefits of alternative courses of action. In many cases, however, the cost of an action is not as obvious as it might first appear.

Consider the decision to go to college. The main benefits are intellectual enrichment and a lifetime of better job opportunities. But what are the costs? To answer this question, you might be tempted to add up the money you spend on tuition, books, room, and board. Yet this total does not truly represent what you give up to spend a year in college.

There are two problems with this calculation. First, it includes some things that are not really costs of going to college. Even if you quit school, you need a place to sleep and food to eat. Room and board are costs of going to college only to the extent that they are more expensive at college than elsewhere. Second, this calculation ignores the largest cost of going to college—your time. When you spend a year listening to lectures, reading textbooks, and writing papers, you cannot spend that time working at a job. For most students, the earnings given up to attend school are the largest single cost of their education.

opportunity cost
whatever must be given up to obtain some item

The **opportunity cost** of an item is what you give up to get that item. When making any decision, decision makers should be aware of the opportunity costs that accompany each possible action. In fact, they usually are. College athletes who can earn millions if they drop out of school and play professional sports are well aware that their opportunity cost of college is very high. It is not surprising that they often decide that the benefit of a college education is not worth the cost.

Principle 3: Rational People Think at the Margin

rational people
people who systematically and purposefully do the best they can to achieve their objectives

Economists normally assume that people are rational. **Rational people** systematically and purposefully do the best they can to achieve their objectives, given the available opportunities. As you study economics, you will encounter firms that decide how many workers to hire and how much of their product to manufacture and sell to maximize profits. You will also encounter individuals who decide how much time to spend working and what goods and services to buy with the resulting income to achieve the highest possible level of satisfaction.

marginal change
a small incremental adjustment to a plan of action

Rational people know that decisions in life are rarely black and white but usually involve shades of gray. At dinnertime, the decision you face is not between fasting or eating like a pig but whether to take that extra spoonful of mashed potatoes. When exams roll around, your decision is not between blowing them off or studying 24 hours a day but whether to spend an extra hour reviewing your notes instead of watching TV. Economists use the term **marginal change** to describe a small incremental adjustment to an existing plan of action. Keep in mind that *margin* means "edge," so marginal changes are adjustments around the edges of what you are doing. Rational people often make decisions by comparing *marginal benefits* and *marginal costs*.

For example, consider an airline deciding how much to charge passengers who fly standby. Suppose that flying a 200-seat plane across the United States costs the airline $100,000. In this case, the average cost of each seat is $100,000/200, which is $500. One might be tempted to conclude that the airline should never sell a ticket for less than $500. Actually, a rational airline can often find ways to raise its profits by thinking at the margin. Imagine that a plane is about to take off with ten empty seats, and a standby passenger waiting at the gate will pay $300 for a seat. Should the airline sell the ticket? Of course it should. If the plane has empty seats, the cost of adding one more passenger is tiny. Although the *average* cost of flying a passenger is $500, the *marginal* cost is merely the cost of the bag of peanuts and can of soda that the extra passenger will consume. As long as the standby passenger pays more than the marginal cost, selling the ticket is profitable.

Marginal decision making can help explain some otherwise puzzling economic phenomena. Here is a classic question: Why is water so cheap, while diamonds are so expensive? Humans need water to survive, while diamonds are unnecessary; but for some reason, people are willing to pay much more for a diamond than for a cup of water. The reason is that a person's willingness to pay for a good is based on the marginal benefit that an extra unit of the good would yield. The marginal benefit, in turn, depends on how many units a person already has. Water is essential, but the marginal benefit of an extra cup is small because water is plentiful. By contrast, no one needs diamonds to survive, but because diamonds are so rare, people consider the marginal benefit of an extra diamond to be large.

A rational decision maker takes an action if and only if the marginal benefit of the action exceeds the marginal cost. This principle can explain why airlines are willing to sell a ticket below average cost and why people are willing to pay more for diamonds than for water. It can take some time to get used to the logic of marginal thinking, but the study of economics will give you ample opportunity to practice.

Principle 4: People Respond to Incentives

An **incentive** is something that induces a person to act, such as the prospect of a punishment or a reward. Because rational people make decisions by comparing costs and benefits, they respond to incentives. You will see that incentives play a central role in the study of economics. One economist went so far as to suggest that the entire field could be summarized simply: "People respond to incentives. The rest is commentary."

incentive
something that induces a person to act

Incentives are crucial to analyzing how markets work. For example, when the price of an apple rises, people decide to eat fewer apples. At the same time, apple orchards decide to hire more workers and harvest more apples. In other words, a higher price in a market provides an incentive for buyers to consume less and an incentive for sellers to produce more. As we will see, the influence of prices on the behavior of consumers and producers is crucial for how a market economy allocates scarce resources.

Public policymakers should never forget about incentives: Many policies change the costs or benefits that people face and, therefore, alter their behavior. A tax on gasoline, for instance, encourages people to drive smaller, more fuel-efficient cars. That is one reason people drive smaller cars in Europe, where gasoline taxes are high, than in the United States, where gasoline taxes are low. A gasoline tax also encourages people to carpool, take public transportation, and live closer to where they work. If the tax were larger, more people would be driving hybrid cars, and if it were large enough, they would switch to electric cars.

When policymakers fail to consider how their policies affect incentives, they often end up with unintended consequences. For example, consider public policy regarding auto safety. Today, all cars have seat belts, but this was not true 50 years ago. In the 1960s, Ralph Nader's book *Unsafe at Any Speed* generated much public concern over auto safety. Congress responded with laws requiring seat belts as standard equipment on new cars.

How does a seat belt law affect auto safety? The direct effect is obvious: When a person wears a seat belt, the probability of surviving an auto accident rises. But that's not the end of the story because the law also affects behavior by altering incentives. The relevant behavior here is the speed and care with which drivers operate their cars. Driving slowly and carefully is costly because it uses the driver's time and energy. When deciding how safely to drive, rational people compare, perhaps unconsciously, the marginal benefit from safer driving to the marginal cost. As a result, they drive more slowly and carefully when the benefit of increased safety is high. For example, when road conditions are icy, people drive more attentively and at lower speeds than they do when road conditions are clear.

Consider how a seat belt law alters a driver's cost–benefit calculation. Seat belts make accidents less costly because they reduce the likelihood of injury or death. In other words, seat belts reduce the benefits of slow and careful driving. People respond to seat belts as they would to an improvement in road conditions—by driving faster and less carefully. The result of a seat belt law, therefore, is a larger number of accidents. The decline in safe driving has a clear, adverse impact on pedestrians, who are more likely to find themselves in an accident but (unlike the drivers) don't have the benefit of added protection.

At first, this discussion of incentives and seat belts might seem like idle speculation. Yet in a classic 1975 study, economist Sam Peltzman argued that auto-safety laws have had many of these effects. According to Peltzman's evidence, these laws produce both fewer deaths per accident and more accidents. He concluded that the net result is little change in the number of driver deaths and an increase in the number of pedestrian deaths.

Peltzman's analysis of auto safety is an offbeat and controversial example of the general principle that people respond to incentives. When analyzing any policy, we must consider not only the direct effects but also the less obvious indirect effects that work through incentives. If the policy changes incentives, it will cause people to alter their behavior.

The Incentive Effects of Gasoline Prices

From 2005 to 2008 the price of oil in world oil markets skyrocketed, the result of limited supplies together with surging demand from robust world growth, especially in China. The price of gasoline in the United States rose from about $2 to about $4 a gallon. At the time, the news was filled with stories about how people responded to the increased incentive to conserve, sometimes in obvious ways, sometimes in less obvious ways.

Here is a sampling of various stories:

- "As Gas Prices Soar, Buyers Are Flocking to Small Cars"
- "As Gas Prices Climb, So Do Scooter Sales"
- "Gas Prices Knock Bicycles Sales, Repairs into Higher Gear"
- "Gas Prices Send Surge of Riders to Mass Transit"
- "Camel Demand Up as Oil Price Soars": Farmers in the Indian state of Rajasthan are rediscovering the humble camel. As the cost of running gas-guzzling tractors soars, even-toed ungulates are making a comeback.
- "The Airlines Are Suffering, But the Order Books of Boeing and Airbus Are Bulging": Demand for new, more fuel-efficient aircraft has never been greater. The latest versions of the Airbus A320 and Boeing 737, the single-aisle workhorses for which demand is strongest, are up to 40% cheaper to run than the vintage planes some American airlines still use.
- "Home Buying Practices Adjust to High Gas Prices": In his hunt for a new home, Demetrius Stroud crunched the numbers to find out that, with gas prices climbing, moving near an Amtrak station is the best thing for his wallet.
- "Gas Prices Drive Students to Online Courses": For Christy LaBadie, a sophomore at Northampton Community College, the 30-minute drive from her home to the Bethlehem, Pa., campus has become a financial hardship now that gasoline prices have soared to more than $4 a gallon. So this semester she decided to take an online course to save herself the trip—and the money.
- "Diddy Halts Private Jet Flights Over Fuel Prices": Fuel prices have grounded an unexpected frequent-flyer: Sean "Diddy" Combs. . . . The hip-hop mogul said he is now flying on commercial airlines instead of in private jets, which Combs said had previously cost him $200,000 and up for a roundtrip between New York and Los Angeles. "I'm actually flying commercial," Diddy said before walking onto an airplane, sitting in a first-class seat and flashing his boarding pass to the camera. "That's how high gas prices are."

Hip-hop mogul Sean "Diddy" Combs responds to incentives.

Many of these developments proved transitory. The economic downturn that began in 2008 and continued into 2009 reduced the world demand for oil, and the price of gasoline declined substantially. No word yet on whether Mr. Combs has returned to his private jet. ■

QUICK QUIZ   *Describe an important trade-off you recently faced.* • *Give an example of some action that has both a monetary and nonmonetary opportunity cost.* • *Describe an incentive your parents offered to you in an effort to influence your behavior.*

· in the news

> *Incentive Pay*

As this article illustrates, how people are paid affects their incentives and the decisions they make. (The article's author, by the way, subsequently became one of the chief economic advisers to President Barack Obama.)

Where the Buses Run on Time

BY AUSTAN GOOLSBEE

On a summer afternoon, the drive home from the University of Chicago to the north side of the city must be one of the most beautiful commutes in the world. On the left on Lake Shore Drive you pass Grant Park, some of the world's first skyscrapers, and the Sears Tower. On the right is the intense blue of Lake Michigan. But for all the beauty, the traffic can be hell. So, if you drive the route every day, you learn the shortcuts. You know that if it backs up from the Buckingham Fountain all the way to McCormick Place, you're better off taking the surface streets and getting back onto Lake Shore Drive a few miles north.

A lot of buses, however, wait in the traffic jams. I have always wondered about that: Why don't the bus drivers use the shortcuts? Surely they know about them—they drive the same route every day, and they probably avoid the traffic when they drive their own

cars. Buses don't stop on Lake Shore Drive, so they wouldn't strand anyone by detouring around the congestion. And when buses get delayed in heavy traffic, it wreaks havoc on the scheduled service. Instead of arriving once every 10 minutes, three buses come in at the same time after half an hour. That sort of bunching is the least efficient way to run a public transportation system. So, why not take the surface streets if that would keep the schedule properly spaced and on time?

You might think at first that the problem is that the drivers aren't paid enough to strategize. But Chicago bus drivers are the seventh-highest paid in the nation; full-timers earned more than $23 an hour, according to a November 2004 survey. The problem may have to do not with how much they are paid, but how they are paid. At least, that's the implication of a new study of Chilean bus drivers by Ryan Johnson and David Reiley of the University of Arizona and Juan Carlos Muñoz of Pontificia Universidad Católica de Chile.

Companies in Chile pay bus drivers one of two ways: either by the hour or by the passenger. Paying by the passenger leads to significantly shorter delays. Give them

incentives, and drivers start acting like regular people do. They take shortcuts when the traffic is bad. They take shorter meal breaks and bathroom breaks. They want to get on the road and pick up more passengers as quickly as they can. In short, their productivity increases....

Not everything about incentive pay is perfect, of course. When bus drivers start moving from place to place more quickly, they get in more accidents (just like the rest of us). Some passengers also complain that the rides make them nauseated because the drivers stomp on the gas as soon as the last passenger gets on the bus. Yet when given the choice, people overwhelmingly choose the bus companies that get them where they're going on time. More than 95 percent of the routes in Santiago use incentive pay.

Perhaps we should have known that incentive pay could increase bus driver productivity. After all, the taxis in Chicago take the shortcuts on Lake Shore Drive to avoid the traffic that buses just sit in. Since taxi drivers earn money for every trip they make, they want to get you home as quickly as possible so they can pick up somebody else.

Source: Slate.com, March 16, 2006.

How People Interact

The first four principles discussed how individuals make decisions. As we go about our lives, many of our decisions affect not only ourselves but other people as well. The next three principles concern how people interact with one another.

Principle 5: Trade Can Make Everyone Better Off

You may have heard on the news that the Japanese are our competitors in the world economy. In some ways, this is true because American and Japanese firms produce many of the same goods. Ford and Toyota compete for the same customers in the market for automobiles. Apple and Sony compete for the same customers in the market for digital music players.

Yet it is easy to be misled when thinking about competition among countries. Trade between the United States and Japan is not like a sports contest in which one side wins and the other side loses. In fact, the opposite is true: Trade between two countries can make each country better off.

To see why, consider how trade affects your family. When a member of your family looks for a job, he or she competes against members of other families who are looking for jobs. Families also compete against one another when they go shopping because each family wants to buy the best goods at the lowest prices. In a sense, each family in the economy is competing with all other families.

Despite this competition, your family would not be better off isolating itself from all other families. If it did, your family would need to grow its own food, make its own clothes, and build its own home. Clearly, your family gains much from its ability to trade with others. Trade allows each person to specialize in the activities he or she does best, whether it is farming, sewing, or home building. By trading with others, people can buy a greater variety of goods and services at lower cost.

Countries as well as families benefit from the ability to trade with one another. Trade allows countries to specialize in what they do best and to enjoy a greater variety of goods and services. The Japanese, as well as the French and the Egyptians and the Brazilians, are as much our partners in the world economy as they are our competitors.

Principle 6: Markets Are Usually a Good Way to Organize Economic Activity

The collapse of communism in the Soviet Union and Eastern Europe in the 1980s may be the most important change in the world during the past half century. Communist countries worked on the premise that government officials were in the best position to allocate the economy's scarce resources. These central planners decided what goods and services were produced, how much was produced, and who produced and consumed these goods and services. The theory behind central planning was that only the government could organize economic activity in a way that promoted economic well-being for the country as a whole.

Most countries that once had centrally planned economies have abandoned the system and are instead developing market economies. In a **market economy**, the decisions of a central planner are replaced by the decisions of millions of firms and households. Firms decide whom to hire and what to make. Households decide which firms to work for and what to buy with their incomes. These firms

"For $5 a week you can watch baseball without being nagged to cut the grass!"

market economy

an economy that allocates resources through the decentralized decisions of many firms and households as they interact in markets for goods and services

and households interact in the marketplace, where prices and self-interest guide their decisions.

At first glance, the success of market economies is puzzling. In a market economy, no one is looking out for the economic well-being of society as a whole. Free markets contain many buyers and sellers of numerous goods and services, and all of them are interested primarily in their own well-being. Yet despite decentralized decision making and self-interested decision makers, market economies have proven remarkably successful in organizing economic activity to promote overall economic well-being.

In his 1776 book *An Inquiry into the Nature and Causes of the Wealth of Nations*, economist Adam Smith made the most famous observation in all of economics: Households and firms interacting in markets act as if they are guided by an "invisible hand" that leads them to desirable market outcomes. One of our goals in this book is to understand how this invisible hand works its magic.

As you study economics, you will learn that prices are the instrument with which the invisible hand directs economic activity. In any market, buyers look at the price when determining how much to demand, and sellers look at the price when deciding how much to supply. As a result of the decisions that buyers and sellers make, market prices reflect both the value of a good to society and the cost to society of making the good. Smith's great insight was that prices adjust to guide these individual buyers and sellers to reach outcomes that, in many cases, maximize the well-being of society as a whole.

Smith's insight has an important corollary: When the government prevents prices from adjusting naturally to supply and demand, it impedes the invisible hand's ability to coordinate the decisions of the households and firms that make up the economy. This corollary explains why taxes adversely affect the allocation of resources, for they distort prices and thus the decisions of households and firms. It also explains the great harm caused by policies that directly control prices, such as rent control. And it explains the failure of communism. In communist countries, prices were not determined in the marketplace but were dictated by central planners. These planners lacked the necessary information about consumers' tastes and producers' costs, which in a market economy is reflected in prices. Central planners failed because they tried to run the economy with one hand tied behind their backs—the invisible hand of the marketplace.

Principle 7: Governments Can Sometimes Improve Market Outcomes

If the invisible hand of the market is so great, why do we need government? One purpose of studying economics is to refine your view about the proper role and scope of government policy.

One reason we need government is that the invisible hand can work its magic only if the government enforces the rules and maintains the institutions that are key to a market economy. Most important, market economies need institutions to enforce **property rights** so individuals can own and control scarce resources. A farmer won't grow food if he expects his crop to be stolen; a restaurant won't serve meals unless it is assured that customers will pay before they leave; and an entertainment company won't produce DVDs if too many potential customers avoid paying by making illegal copies. We all rely on government-provided police and courts to enforce our rights over the things we produce—and the invisible hand counts on our ability to enforce our rights.

property rights
the ability of an individual to own and exercise control over scarce resources

FYI

> ## Adam Smith and the Invisible Hand

It may be only a coincidence that Adam Smith's great book *The Wealth of Nations* was published in 1776, the exact year American revolutionaries signed the Declaration of Independence. But the two documents share a point of view that was prevalent at the time: Individuals are usually best left to their own devices, without the heavy hand of government guiding their actions. This political philosophy provides the intellectual basis for the market economy and for free society more generally.

Why do decentralized market economies work so well? Is it because people can be counted on to treat one another with love and kindness? Not at all. Here is Adam Smith's description of how people interact in a market economy:

Man has almost constant occasion for the help of his brethren, and it is in vain for him to expect it from their benevolence only. He will be more likely to prevail if he can interest their self-love in his favour, and show them that it is for their own advantage to do for him what he requires of them. . . . Give me that which I want, and you shall have this which you want, is the meaning of every such offer; and it is in this manner that we obtain from one another the far greater part of those good offices which we stand in need of.

Adam Smith

It is not from the benevolence of the butcher, the brewer, or the baker that we expect our dinner, but from their regard to their own interest. We address ourselves, not to their humanity but to their self-love, and never talk to them of our own necessities but of their advantages. Nobody but a beggar chooses to depend chiefly upon the benevolence of his fellow-citizens. . . .

Every individual . . . neither intends to promote the public interest, nor knows how much he is promoting it. . . . He intends only his own gain, and he is in this, as in many other cases, led by an invisible hand to promote an end which was no part of his intention. Nor is it always the worse for the society that it was no part of it. By pursuing his own interest he frequently promotes that of the society more effectually than when he really intends to promote it.

Smith is saying that participants in the economy are motivated by self-interest and that the "invisible hand" of the marketplace guides this self-interest into promoting general economic well-being.

Many of Smith's insights remain at the center of modern economics. Our analysis in the coming chapters will allow us to express Smith's conclusions more precisely and to analyze more fully the strengths and weaknesses of the market's invisible hand.

© BETTMANN/CORBIS

market failure
a situation in which a market left on its own fails to allocate resources efficiently

externality
the impact of one person's actions on the well-being of a bystander

Yet there is another reason we need government: The invisible hand is powerful, but it is not omnipotent. There are two broad reasons for a government to intervene in the economy and change the allocation of resources that people would choose on their own: to promote efficiency or to promote equality. That is, most policies aim either to enlarge the economic pie or to change how the pie is divided.

Consider first the goal of efficiency. Although the invisible hand usually leads markets to allocate resources to maximize the size of the economic pie, this is not always the case. Economists use the term **market failure** to refer to a situation in which the market on its own fails to produce an efficient allocation of resources. As we will see, one possible cause of market failure is an **externality,** which is the impact of one person's actions on the well-being of a bystander. The classic example of an externality is pollution. Another possible cause of market failure is **market power,** which refers to the ability of a single person (or small group) to unduly influence market prices. For example, if everyone in town needs water but there is only one well, the owner of the well is not subject to the rigorous competition with which the invisible hand normally keeps self-interest in check. In the presence of externalities or market power, well-designed public policy can enhance economic efficiency.

market power
the ability of a single economic actor (or small group of actors) to have a substantial influence on market prices

Now consider the goal of equality. Even when the invisible hand is yielding efficient outcomes, it can nonetheless leave sizable disparities in economic well-being. A market economy rewards people according to their ability to produce things that other people are willing to pay for. The world's best basketball player earns more than the world's best chess player simply because people are willing to pay more to watch basketball than chess. The invisible hand does not ensure that everyone has sufficient food, decent clothing, and adequate healthcare. This inequality may, depending on one's political philosophy, call for government intervention. In practice, many public policies, such as the income tax and the welfare system, aim to achieve a more equal distribution of economic well-being.

To say that the government *can* improve on market outcomes at times does not mean that it always *will*. Public policy is made not by angels but by a political process that is far from perfect. Sometimes policies are designed simply to reward the politically powerful. Sometimes they are made by well-intentioned leaders who are not fully informed. As you study economics, you will become a better judge of when a government policy is justifiable because it promotes efficiency or equality and when it is not.

QUICK QUIZ   *Why is a country better off not isolating itself from all other countries? • Why do we have markets, and, according to economists, what roles should government play in them?*

How the Economy as a Whole Works

We started by discussing how individuals make decisions and then looked at how people interact with one another. All these decisions and interactions together make up "the economy." The last three principles concern the workings of the economy as a whole.

Principle 8: A Country's Standard of Living Depends on Its Ability to Produce Goods and Services

The differences in living standards around the world are staggering. In 2008, the average American had an income of about $47,000. In the same year, the average Mexican earned about $10,000, and the average Nigerian earned only $1,400. Not surprisingly, this large variation in average income is reflected in various measures of the quality of life. Citizens of high-income countries have more TV sets, more cars, better nutrition, better healthcare, and a longer life expectancy than citizens of low-income countries.

Changes in living standards over time are also large. In the United States, incomes have historically grown about 2 percent per year (after adjusting for changes in the cost of living). At this rate, average income doubles every 35 years. Over the past century, average U.S. income has risen about eightfold.

What explains these large differences in living standards among countries and over time? The answer is surprisingly simple. Almost all variation in living standards is attributable to differences in countries' **productivity**—that is, the amount of goods and services produced from each unit of labor input. In nations where workers can produce a large quantity of goods and services per unit of time, most people enjoy a high standard of living; in nations where workers are less productive, most people endure a more meager existence. Similarly, the growth rate of a nation's productivity determines the growth rate of its average income.

The fundamental relationship between productivity and living standards is simple, but its implications are far-reaching. If productivity is the primary determinant of living standards, other explanations must be of secondary importance. For example, it might be tempting to credit labor unions or minimum-wage laws for the rise in living standards of American workers over the past century. Yet the real hero of American workers is their rising productivity. As another example, some commentators have claimed that increased competition from Japan and other countries explained the slow growth in U.S. incomes during the 1970s and 1980s. Yet the real villain was not competition from abroad but flagging productivity growth in the United States.

The relationship between productivity and living standards also has profound implications for public policy. When thinking about how any policy will affect living standards, the key question is how it will affect our ability to produce goods and services. To boost living standards, policymakers need to raise productivity by ensuring that workers are well educated, have the tools needed to produce goods and services, and have access to the best available technology.

productivity

the quantity of goods and services produced from each unit of labor input

in the news

> ### Why You Should Study Economics

In this excerpt from a commencement address, the former president of the Federal Reserve Bank of Dallas makes the case for studying economics

The Dismal Science? Hardly!

BY ROBERT D. MCTEER, JR.

My take on training in economics is that it becomes increasingly valuable as you move up the career ladder. I can't imagine a better major for corporate CEOs, congressmen, or American presidents. You've learned a systematic, disciplined way of thinking that will serve you well. By contrast, the economically challenged must be perplexed about how it is that economies work better the fewer people they have in charge. Who does the planning? Who makes decisions? Who decides what to produce?

For my money, Adam Smith's invisible hand is the most important thing you've learned by studying economics. You understand how we can each work for our own self-interest and still produce a desirable social outcome. You know how uncoordinated activity gets coordinated by the market to enhance the wealth of nations. You understand the magic of markets and the dangers of tampering with them too much. You know better what you first learned in kindergarten: that you shouldn't kill or cripple the goose that lays the golden eggs. . . .

Economics training will help you understand fallacies and unintended consequences.

Principle 9: Prices Rise When the Government Prints Too Much Money

In January 1921, a daily newspaper in Germany cost 0.30 marks. Less than two years later, in November 1922, the same newspaper cost 70,000,000 marks. All other prices in the economy rose by similar amounts. This episode is one of history's most spectacular examples of **inflation,** an increase in the overall level of prices in the economy.

Although the United States has never experienced inflation even close to that of Germany in the 1920s, inflation has at times been an economic problem. During the 1970s, for instance, when the overall level of prices more than doubled, President Gerald Ford called inflation "public enemy number one." By contrast, inflation in the first decade of the 21st century has run about 2½ percent per year; at this rate, it would take almost 30 years for prices to double. Because high inflation imposes various costs on society, keeping inflation at a low level is a goal of economic policymakers around the world.

What causes inflation? In almost all cases of large or persistent inflation, the culprit is growth in the quantity of money. When a government creates large quantities of the nation's money, the value of the money falls. In Germany in the early 1920s, when prices were on average tripling every month, the quantity of money was also tripling every month. Although less dramatic, the economic history of the United States points to a similar conclusion: The high inflation of the 1970s was associated with rapid growth in the quantity of money, and the low inflation of more recent experience was associated with slow growth in the quantity of money.

inflation
an increase in the overall level of prices in the economy

"Well it may have been 68 cents when you got in line, but it's 74 cents now!"

In fact, I am inclined to define economics as the study of how to anticipate unintended consequences. . . .

Little in the literature seems more relevant to contemporary economic debates than what usually is called the broken window fallacy. Whenever a government program is justified not on its merits but by the jobs it will create, remember the broken window: Some teenagers, being the little beasts that they are, toss a brick through a bakery window. A crowd gathers and laments, "What a shame." But before you know it, someone suggests a silver lining to the situation: Now the baker will have to spend money to have the window repaired. This will add to the income of the repairman, who will spend his additional income, which will add to another seller's income, and so on. You know the drill. The chain of spending will multiply and generate higher income and employment. If the broken window is large enough, it might produce an economic boom! . . .

Most voters fall for the broken window fallacy, but not economics majors. They will say, "Hey, wait a minute!" If the baker hadn't spent his money on window repair, he would have spent it on the new suit he was saving to buy. Then the tailor would have the new income to spend, and so on. The broken window didn't create net new spending; it just diverted spending from somewhere else. The broken window does not create new activity, just different activity. People see the activity that takes place. They don't see the activity that *would* have taken place.

The broken window fallacy is perpetuated in many forms. Whenever job creation or retention is the primary objective I call it the job-counting fallacy. Economics majors understand the non-intuitive reality that real progress comes from job destruction. It once took 90 percent of our population to grow our food. Now it takes 3 percent. Pardon me, Willie, but are we worse off because of the job losses in agriculture? The would-have-been farmers are now college professors and computer gurus. . . .

So instead of counting jobs, we should make every job count. We will occasionally hit a soft spot when we have a mismatch of supply and demand in the labor market. But that is temporary. Don't become a Luddite and destroy the machinery, or become a protectionist and try to grow bananas in New York City.

Source: *The Wall Street Journal,* June 4, 2003.

Principle 10: Society Faces a Short-Run Trade-off between Inflation and Unemployment

Although a higher level of prices is, in the long run, the primary effect of increasing the quantity of money, the short-run story is more complex and controversial. Most economists describe the short-run effects of monetary injections as follows:

- Increasing the amount of money in the economy stimulates the overall level of spending and thus the demand for goods and services.
- Higher demand may over time cause firms to raise their prices, but in the meantime, it also encourages them to hire more workers and produce a larger quantity of goods and services.
- More hiring means lower unemployment.

This line of reasoning leads to one final economy-wide trade-off: a short-run trade-off between inflation and unemployment.

Although some economists still question these ideas, most accept that society faces a short-run trade-off between inflation and unemployment. This simply means that, over a period of a year or two, many economic policies push inflation and unemployment in opposite directions. Policymakers face this trade-off regardless of whether inflation and unemployment both start out at high levels (as they did in the early 1980s), at low levels (as they did in the late 1990s), or someplace in between. This short-run trade-off plays a key role in the analysis of the **business cycle**—the irregular and largely unpredictable fluctuations in economic activity, as measured by the production of goods and services or the number of people employed.

business cycle

fluctuations in economic activity, such as employment and production

Policymakers can exploit the short-run trade-off between inflation and unemployment using various policy instruments. By changing the amount that the government spends, the amount it taxes, and the amount of money it prints, policymakers can influence the overall demand for goods and services. Changes in demand in turn influence the combination of inflation and unemployment that the economy experiences in the short run. Because these instruments of economic policy are potentially so powerful, how policymakers should use these instruments to control the economy, if at all, is a subject of continuing debate.

This debate heated up in the early years of Barack Obama's presidency. In 2008 and 2009, the U.S. economy, as well as many other economies around the world, experienced a deep economic downturn. Problems in the financial system, caused by bad bets on the housing market, spilled over into the rest of the economy, causing incomes to fall and unemployment to soar. Policymakers responded in various ways to increase the overall demand for goods and services. President Obama's first major initiative was a stimulus package of reduced taxes and increased government spending. At the same time, the nation's central bank, the Federal Reserve, increased the supply of money. The goal of these policies was to reduce unemployment. Some feared, however, that these policies might over time lead to an excessive level of inflation.

QUICK QUIZ   *List and briefly explain the three principles that describe how the economy as a whole works.*

FYI

How to Read This Book

Economics is fun, but it can also be hard to learn. My aim in writing this text is to make it as enjoyable and easy as possible. But you, the student, also have a role to play. Experience shows that if you are actively involved as you study this book, you will enjoy a better outcome both on your exams and in the years that follow. Here are a few tips about how best to read this book.

1. *Read before class.* Students do better when they read the relevant textbook chapter before attending a lecture. You will understand the lecture better, and your questions will be better focused on where you need extra help.

2. *Summarize, don't highlight.* Running a yellow marker over the text is too passive an activity to keep your mind engaged. Instead, when you come to the end of a section, take a minute and summarize what you just learned in your own words, writing your summary in the wide margins we've provided. When you've finished the chapter, compare your summaries with the one at the end of the chapter. Did you pick up the main points?

3. *Test yourself.* Throughout the book, Quick Quizzes offer instant feedback to find out if you've learned what you are supposed to. Take the opportunity to write down your answer, and then check it against the answers provided at this book's website. The quizzes are meant to test your basic comprehension. If your answer is incorrect, you probably need to review the section.

4. *Practice, practice, practice.* At the end of each chapter, Questions for Review test your understanding, and Problems and Applications ask you to apply and extend the material. Perhaps your instructor will assign some of these exercises as homework.

If so, do them. If not, do them anyway. The more you use your new knowledge, the more solid it becomes.

5. *Go online.* The publisher of this book maintains an extensive website to help you in your study of economics. It includes additional examples, applications, and problems, as well as quizzes so you can test yourself. Check it out. The website is www .cengage.com/economics/mankiw.

6. *Study in groups.* After you've read the book and worked problems on your own, get together with classmates to discuss the material. You will learn from each other—an example of the gains from trade.

7. *Teach someone.* As all teachers know, there is no better way to learn something than to teach it to someone else. Take the opportunity to teach new economic concepts to a study partner, a friend, a parent, or even a pet.

8. *Don't skip the real-world examples.* In the midst of all the numbers, graphs, and strange new words, it is easy to lose sight of what economics is all about. The Case Studies and In the News boxes sprinkled throughout this book should help remind you. They show how the theory is tied to events happening in all our lives.

9. *Apply economic thinking to your daily life.* Once you've read about how others apply economics to the real world, try it yourself! You can use economic analysis to better understand your own decisions, the economy around you, and the events you read about in the newspaper. The world may never look the same again.

Conclusion

You now have a taste of what economics is all about. In the coming chapters, we develop many specific insights about people, markets, and economies. Mastering these insights will take some effort, but it is not an overwhelming task. The field of economics is based on a few big ideas that can be applied in many different situations.

Throughout this book, we will refer back to the *Ten Principles of Economics* highlighted in this chapter and summarized in Table 1. Keep these building blocks in mind: Even the most sophisticated economic analysis is founded on the ten principles introduced here.

Table 1

Ten Principles of Economics

How People Make Decisions
1: People Face Trade-offs
2: The Cost of Something Is What You Give Up to Get It
3: Rational People Think at the Margin
4: People Respond to Incentives

How People Interact
5: Trade Can Make Everyone Better Off
6: Markets Are Usually a Good Way to Organize Economic Activity
7: Governments Can Sometimes Improve Market Outcomes

How the Economy as a Whole Works
8: A Country's Standard of Living Depends on Its Ability to Produce Goods and Services
9: Prices Rise When the Government Prints Too Much Money
10: Society Faces a Short-Run Trade-off between Inflation and Unemployment

SUMMARY

- The fundamental lessons about individual decision making are that people face trade-offs among alternative goals, that the cost of any action is measured in terms of forgone opportunities, that rational people make decisions by comparing marginal costs and marginal benefits, and that people change their behavior in response to the incentives they face.

- The fundamental lessons about interactions among people are that trade and interdependence can be mutually beneficial, that markets are usually a good way of coordinating economic activity among people, and that the government can potentially improve market outcomes by remedying a market failure or by promoting greater economic equality.

- The fundamental lessons about the economy as a whole are that productivity is the ultimate source of living standards, that growth in the quantity of money is the ultimate source of inflation, and that society faces a short-run trade-off between inflation and unemployment.

KEY CONCEPTS

scarcity, *p. 4*
economics, *p. 4*
efficiency, *p. 5*
equality, *p. 5*
opportunity cost, *p. 6*
rational people, *p. 6*

marginal change, *p. 6*
incentive, *p. 7*
market economy, *p. 10*
property rights, *p. 11*
market failure, *p. 12*
externality, *p. 12*

market power, *p. 13*
productivity, *p. 14*
inflation, *p. 15*
business cycle, *p. 16*

QUESTIONS FOR REVIEW

1. Give three examples of important trade-offs that you face in your life.
2. What is the opportunity cost of seeing a movie?
3. Water is necessary for life. Is the marginal benefit of a glass of water large or small?
4. Why should policymakers think about incentives?

5. Why isn't trade among countries like a game with some winners and some losers?
6. What does the "invisible hand" of the marketplace do?
7. Explain the two main causes of market failure and give an example of each.

8. Why is productivity important?
9. What is inflation and what causes it?
10. How are inflation and unemployment related in the short run?

PROBLEMS AND APPLICATIONS

1. Describe some of the trade-offs faced by each of the following:
   a. a family deciding whether to buy a new car
   b. a member of Congress deciding how much to spend on national parks
   c. a company president deciding whether to open a new factory
   d. a professor deciding how much to prepare for class
   e. a recent college graduate deciding whether to go to graduate school
2. You are trying to decide whether to take a vacation. Most of the costs of the vacation (airfare, hotel, and forgone wages) are measured in dollars, but the benefits of the vacation are psychological. How can you compare the benefits to the costs?
3. You were planning to spend Saturday working at your part-time job, but a friend asks you to go skiing. What is the true cost of going skiing? Now suppose you had been planning to spend the day studying at the library. What is the cost of going skiing in this case? Explain.
4. You win $100 in a basketball pool. You have a choice between spending the money now or putting it away for a year in a bank account that pays 5 percent interest. What is the opportunity cost of spending the $100 now?
5. The company that you manage has invested $5 million in developing a new product, but the development is not quite finished. At a recent meeting, your salespeople report that the introduction of competing products has reduced the expected sales of your new product to $3 million. If it would cost $1 million to finish development and make the product, should you go ahead and do so? What is the most that you should pay to complete development?
6. The Social Security system provides income for people over age 65. If a recipient of Social

Security decides to work and earn some income, the amount he or she receives in Social Security benefits is typically reduced.
   a. How does the provision of Social Security affect people's incentive to save while working?
   b. How does the reduction in benefits associated with higher earnings affect people's incentive to work past age 65?
7. A 1996 bill reforming the federal government's antipoverty programs limited many welfare recipients to only two years of benefits.
   a. How does this change affect the incentives for working?
   b. How might this change represent a trade-off between equality and efficiency?
8. Your roommate is a better cook than you are, but you can clean more quickly than your roommate can. If your roommate did all the cooking and you did all the cleaning, would your chores take you more or less time than if you divided each task evenly? Give a similar example of how specialization and trade can make two countries both better off.
9. Explain whether each of the following government activities is motivated by a concern about equality or a concern about efficiency. In the case of efficiency, discuss the type of market failure involved.
   a. regulating cable TV prices
   b. providing some poor people with vouchers that can be used to buy food
   c. prohibiting smoking in public places
   d. breaking up Standard Oil (which once owned 90 percent of all oil refineries) into several smaller companies
   e. imposing higher personal income tax rates on people with higher incomes
   f. instituting laws against driving while intoxicated

10. Discuss each of the following statements from the standpoints of equality and efficiency.
    a. "Everyone in society should be guaranteed the best healthcare possible."
    b. "When workers are laid off, they should be able to collect unemployment benefits until they find a new job."

11. In what ways is your standard of living different from that of your parents or grandparents when they were your age? Why have these changes occurred?

12. Suppose Americans decide to save more of their incomes. If banks lend this extra saving to businesses, which use the funds to build new factories, how might this lead to faster growth in productivity? Who do you suppose benefits from the higher productivity? Is society getting a free lunch?

13. In 2010, President Barack Obama and Congress enacted a healthcare reform bill in the United States. Two goals of the bill were to provide more Americans with health insurance (via subsidies for lower-income households financed by taxes on higher-income households) and to reduce the cost of healthcare (via various reforms in how healthcare is provided).
    a. How do these goals relate to equality and efficiency?
    b. How might healthcare reform increase productivity in the United States?
    c. How might healthcare reform decrease productivity in the United States?

14. During the Revolutionary War, the American colonies could not raise enough tax revenue to fully fund the war effort; to make up this difference, the colonies decided to print more money. Printing money to cover expenditures is sometimes referred to as an "inflation tax." Who do you think is being "taxed" when more money is printed? Why?

15. Imagine that you are a policymaker trying to decide whether to reduce the rate of inflation. To make an intelligent decision, what would you need to know about inflation, unemployment, and the trade-off between them?

16. A policymaker is deciding how to finance the construction of a new airport. He can either pay for it by increasing citizens' taxes or by printing more money. What are some of the short-run and long-run consequences of each option?

For further information on topics in this chapter, additional problems, applications, examples, online quizzes, and more, please visit our website at www.cengage.com/economics/mankiw.

Chapter 3:
Macroeconomics

Thinking Like an
Economist

Every field of study has its own language and its own way of thinking. Mathematicians talk about axioms, integrals, and vector spaces. Psychologists talk about ego, id, and cognitive dissonance. Lawyers talk about venue, torts, and promissory estoppel.

Economics is no different. Supply, demand, elasticity, comparative advantage, consumer surplus, deadweight loss—these terms are part of the economist's language. In the coming chapters, you will encounter many new terms and some familiar words that economists use in specialized ways. At first, this new language may seem needlessly arcane. But as you will see, its value lies in its ability to provide you with a new and useful way of thinking about the world in which you live.

The purpose of this book is to help you learn the economist's way of thinking. Just as you cannot become a mathematician, psychologist, or lawyer overnight, learning to think like an economist will take some time. Yet with a combination of

21

theory, case studies, and examples of economics in the news, this book will give you ample opportunity to develop and practice this skill.

Before delving into the substance and details of economics, it is helpful to have an overview of how economists approach the world. This chapter discusses the field's methodology. What is distinctive about how economists confront a question? What does it mean to think like an economist?

The Economist as Scientist

"I'm a social scientist, Michael. That means I can't explain electricity or anything like that, but if you ever want to know about people, I'm your man."

Economists try to address their subject with a scientist's objectivity. They approach the study of the economy in much the same way a physicist approaches the study of matter and a biologist approaches the study of life: They devise theories, collect data, and then analyze these data in an attempt to verify or refute their theories.

To beginners, it can seem odd to claim that economics is a science. After all, economists do not work with test tubes or telescopes. The essence of science, however, is the *scientific method*—the dispassionate development and testing of theories about how the world works. This method of inquiry is as applicable to studying a nation's economy as it is to studying the earth's gravity or a species' evolution. As Albert Einstein once put it, "The whole of science is nothing more than the refinement of everyday thinking."

Although Einstein's comment is as true for social sciences such as economics as it is for natural sciences such as physics, most people are not accustomed to looking at society through the eyes of a scientist. Let's discuss some of the ways in which economists apply the logic of science to examine how an economy works.

The Scientific Method: Observation, Theory, and More Observation

Isaac Newton, the famous 17th-century scientist and mathematician, allegedly became intrigued one day when he saw an apple fall from a tree. This observation motivated Newton to develop a theory of gravity that applies not only to an apple falling to the earth but to any two objects in the universe. Subsequent testing of Newton's theory has shown that it works well in many circumstances (although, as Einstein would later emphasize, not in all circumstances). Because Newton's theory has been so successful at explaining observation, it is still taught in undergraduate physics courses around the world.

This interplay between theory and observation also occurs in the field of economics. An economist might live in a country experiencing rapidly increasing prices and be moved by this observation to develop a theory of inflation. The theory might assert that high inflation arises when the government prints too much money. To test this theory, the economist could collect and analyze data on prices and money from many different countries. If growth in the quantity of money were not at all related to the rate at which prices are rising, the economist would start to doubt the validity of this theory of inflation. If money growth and inflation were strongly correlated in international data, as in fact they are, the economist would become more confident in the theory.

Although economists use theory and observation like other scientists, they face an obstacle that makes their task especially challenging: In economics, conducting experiments is often difficult and sometimes impossible. Physicists studying gravity can drop many objects in their laboratories to generate data to test their theories. By contrast, economists studying inflation are not allowed to manipulate a nation's monetary policy simply to generate useful data. Economists, like astronomers and evolutionary biologists, usually have to make do with whatever data the world happens to give them.

To find a substitute for laboratory experiments, economists pay close attention to the natural experiments offered by history. When a war in the Middle East interrupts the flow of crude oil, for instance, oil prices skyrocket around the world. For consumers of oil and oil products, such an event depresses living standards. For economic policymakers, it poses a difficult choice about how best to respond. But for economic scientists, the event provides an opportunity to study the effects of a key natural resource on the world's economies. Throughout this book, therefore, we consider many historical episodes. These episodes are valuable to study because they give us insight into the economy of the past and, more important, because they allow us to illustrate and evaluate economic theories of the present.

The Role of Assumptions

If you ask a physicist how long it would take a marble to fall from the top of a ten-story building, she will likely answer the question by assuming that the marble falls in a vacuum. Of course, this assumption is false. In fact, the building is surrounded by air, which exerts friction on the falling marble and slows it down. Yet the physicist will point out that the friction on the marble is so small that its effect is negligible. Assuming the marble falls in a vacuum simplifies the problem without substantially affecting the answer.

Economists make assumptions for the same reason: Assumptions can simplify the complex world and make it easier to understand. To study the effects of international trade, for example, we might assume that the world consists of only two countries and that each country produces only two goods. In reality, there are numerous countries, each of which produces thousands of different types of goods. But by assuming two countries and two goods, we can focus our thinking on the essence of the problem. Once we understand international trade in this simplified imaginary world, we are in a better position to understand international trade in the more complex world in which we live.

The art in scientific thinking—whether in physics, biology, or economics—is deciding which assumptions to make. Suppose, for instance, that instead of dropping a marble from the top of the building, we were dropping a beachball of the same weight. Our physicist would realize that the assumption of no friction is less accurate in this case: Friction exerts a greater force on a beachball than on a marble because a beachball is much larger. The assumption that gravity works in a vacuum is reasonable for studying a falling marble but not for studying a falling beachball.

Similarly, economists use different assumptions to answer different questions. Suppose that we want to study what happens to the economy when the government changes the number of dollars in circulation. An important piece of this analysis, it turns out, is how prices respond. Many prices in the economy change infrequently; the newsstand prices of magazines, for instance, change only every few years. Knowing this fact may lead us to make different assumptions when studying the effects of the policy change over different time horizons. For studying the short-run effects of the policy, we may assume that prices do not change much. We may even make the extreme and artificial assumption that all prices are completely fixed. For studying the long-run effects of the policy, however, we may assume that all prices are completely flexible. Just as a physicist uses different assumptions when studying falling marbles and falling beachballs, economists use different assumptions when studying the short-run and long-run effects of a change in the quantity of money.

Economic Models

High school biology teachers teach basic anatomy with plastic replicas of the human body. These models have all the major organs: the heart, the liver, the kidneys, and so on. The models allow teachers to show their students very simply how the important parts of the body fit together. Because these plastic models are stylized and omit many details, no one would mistake one of them for a real person. Despite this lack of realism—indeed, because of this lack of realism—studying these models is useful for learning how the human body works.

Economists also use models to learn about the world, but instead of being made of plastic, they are most often composed of diagrams and equations. Like a biology teacher's plastic model, economic models omit many details to allow us to see what is truly important. Just as the biology teacher's model does not include all the body's muscles and capillaries, an economist's model does not include every feature of the economy.

As we use models to examine various economic issues throughout this book, you will see that all the models are built with assumptions. Just as a physicist begins the analysis of a falling marble by assuming away the existence of friction, economists assume away many of the details of the economy that are irrelevant for studying the question at hand. All models—in physics, biology, and economics—simplify reality to improve our understanding of it.

Our First Model: The Circular-Flow Diagram

The economy consists of millions of people engaged in many activities—buying, selling, working, hiring, manufacturing, and so on. To understand how the economy works, we must find some way to simplify our thinking about all these activities. In other words, we need a model that explains, in general terms, how the economy is organized and how participants in the economy interact with one another.

circular-flow diagram

a visual model of the economy that shows how dollars flow through markets among households and firms

Figure 1 presents a visual model of the economy called a **circular-flow diagram.** In this model, the economy is simplified to include only two types of decision makers—firms and households. Firms produce goods and services using inputs, such as labor, land, and capital (buildings and machines). These inputs are called the *factors of production*. Households own the factors of production and consume all the goods and services that the firms produce.

Households and firms interact in two types of markets. In the *markets for goods and services*, households are buyers, and firms are sellers. In particular, households buy the output of goods and services that firms produce. In the *markets for the factors of production*, households are sellers, and firms are buyers. In these markets, households provide the inputs that firms use to produce goods and services. The circular-flow diagram offers a simple way of organizing the economic transactions that occur between households and firms in the economy.

The two loops of the circular-flow diagram are distinct but related. The inner loop represents the flows of inputs and outputs. The households sell the use of

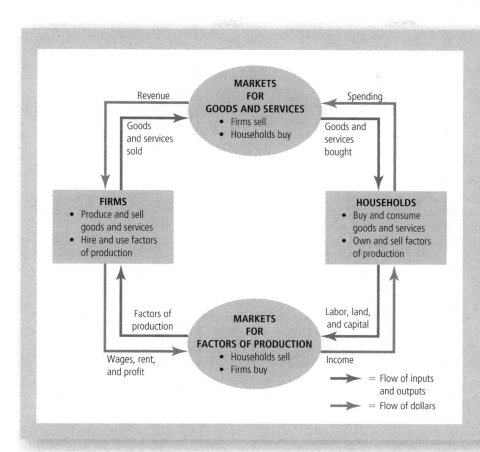

Figure 1

The Circular Flow
This diagram is a schematic representation of the organization of the economy. Decisions are made by households and firms. Households and firms interact in the markets for goods and services (where households are buyers and firms are sellers) and in the markets for the factors of production (where firms are buyers and households are sellers). The outer set of arrows shows the flow of dollars, and the inner set of arrows shows the corresponding flow of inputs and outputs.

their labor, land, and capital to the firms in the markets for the factors of production. The firms then use these factors to produce goods and services, which in turn are sold to households in the markets for goods and services. The outer loop of the diagram represents the corresponding flow of dollars. The households spend money to buy goods and services from the firms. The firms use some of the revenue from these sales to pay for the factors of production, such as the wages of their workers. What's left is the profit of the firm owners, who themselves are members of households.

Let's take a tour of the circular flow by following a dollar bill as it makes its way from person to person through the economy. Imagine that the dollar begins at a household, say, in your wallet. If you want to buy a cup of coffee, you take the dollar to one of the economy's markets for goods and services, such as your local Starbucks coffee shop. There, you spend it on your favorite drink. When the dollar moves into the Starbucks cash register, it becomes revenue for the firm. The dollar doesn't stay at Starbucks for long, however, because the firm uses it to buy inputs in the markets for the factors of production. Starbucks might use the dollar to pay rent to its landlord for the space it occupies or to pay the wages of its workers. In either case, the dollar enters the income of some household and, once again, is back in someone's wallet. At that point, the story of the economy's circular flow starts once again.

The circular-flow diagram in Figure 1 is a very simple model of the economy. It dispenses with details that, for some purposes, are significant. A more complex and realistic circular-flow model would include, for instance, the roles of government and international trade. (A portion of that dollar you gave to Starbucks might be used to pay taxes or to buy coffee beans from a farmer in Brazil.) Yet these details are not crucial for a basic understanding of how the economy is organized. Because of its simplicity, this circular-flow diagram is useful to keep in mind when thinking about how the pieces of the economy fit together.

Our Second Model: The Production Possibilities Frontier

Most economic models, unlike the circular-flow diagram, are built using the tools of mathematics. Here we use one of the simplest such models, called the production possibilities frontier, to illustrate some basic economic ideas.

Although real economies produce thousands of goods and services, let's assume an economy that produces only two goods—cars and computers. Together, the car industry and the computer industry use all of the economy's factors of production. The **production possibilities frontier** is a graph that shows the various combinations of output—in this case, cars and computers—that the economy can possibly produce given the available factors of production and the available production technology that firms use to turn these factors into output.

Figure 2 shows this economy's production possibilities frontier. If the economy uses all its resources in the car industry, it produces 1,000 cars and no computers. If it uses all its resources in the computer industry, it produces 3,000 computers and no cars. The two endpoints of the production possibilities frontier represent these extreme possibilities.

More likely, the economy divides its resources between the two industries, producing some cars and some computers. For example, it can produce 600 cars

production possibilities frontier
a graph that shows the combinations of output that the economy can possibly produce given the available factors of production and the available production technology

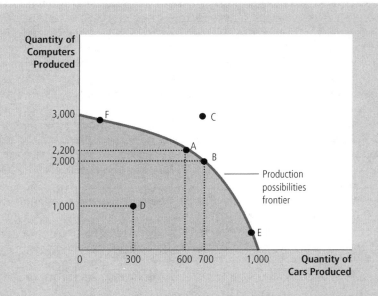

Figure 2

The Production Possibilities Frontier
The production possibilities frontier shows the combinations of output—in this case, cars and computers—that the economy can possibly produce. The economy can produce any combination on or inside the frontier. Points outside the frontier are not feasible given the economy's resources.

and 2,200 computers, shown in the figure by point A. Or, by moving some of the factors of production to the car industry from the computer industry, the economy can produce 700 cars and 2,000 computers, represented by point B.

Because resources are scarce, not every conceivable outcome is feasible. For example, no matter how resources are allocated between the two industries, the economy cannot produce the amount of cars and computers represented by point C. Given the technology available for manufacturing cars and computers, the economy does not have enough of the factors of production to support that level of output. With the resources it has, the economy can produce at any point on or inside the production possibilities frontier, but it cannot produce at points outside the frontier.

An outcome is said to be *efficient* if the economy is getting all it can from the scarce resources it has available. Points on (rather than inside) the production possibilities frontier represent efficient levels of production. When the economy is producing at such a point, say point A, there is no way to produce more of one good without producing less of the other. Point D represents an *inefficient* outcome. For some reason, perhaps widespread unemployment, the economy is producing less than it could from the resources it has available: It is producing only 300 cars and 1,000 computers. If the source of the inefficiency is eliminated, the economy can increase its production of both goods. For example, if the economy moves from point D to point A, its production of cars increases from 300 to 600, and its production of computers increases from 1,000 to 2,200.

One of the *Ten Principles of Economics* discussed in Chapter 1 is that people face trade-offs. The production possibilities frontier shows one trade-off that society faces. Once we have reached the efficient points on the frontier, the only way of producing more of one good is to produce less of the other. When the economy moves from point A to point B, for instance, society produces 100 more cars but at the expense of producing 200 fewer computers.

This trade-off helps us understand another of the *Ten Principles of Economics:* The cost of something is what you give up to get it. This is called the *opportunity cost*. The production possibilities frontier shows the opportunity cost of one good as measured in terms of the other good. When society moves from point A to point B, it gives up 200 computers to get 100 additional cars. That is, at point A, the opportunity cost of 100 cars is 200 computers. Put another way, the opportunity cost of each car is two computers. Notice that the opportunity cost of a car equals the slope of the production possibilities frontier. (If you don't recall what slope is, you can refresh your memory with the graphing appendix to this chapter.)

The opportunity cost of a car in terms of the number of computers is not constant in this economy but depends on how many cars and computers the economy is producing. This is reflected in the shape of the production possibilities frontier. Because the production possibilities frontier in Figure 2 is bowed outward, the opportunity cost of a car is highest when the economy is producing many cars and few computers, such as at point E, where the frontier is steep. When the economy is producing few cars and many computers, such as at point F, the frontier is flatter, and the opportunity cost of a car is lower.

Economists believe that production possibilities frontiers often have this bowed shape. When the economy is using most of its resources to make computers, such as at point F, the resources best suited to car production, such as skilled autoworkers, are being used in the computer industry. Because these workers probably aren't very good at making computers, the economy won't have to lose much computer production to increase car production by one unit. The opportunity cost of a car in terms of computers is small, and the frontier is relatively flat. By contrast, when the economy is using most of its resources to make cars, such as at point E, the resources best suited to making cars are already in the car industry. Producing an additional car means moving some of the best computer technicians out of the computer industry and making them autoworkers. As a result, producing an additional car will mean a substantial loss of computer output. The opportunity cost of a car is high, and the frontier is steep.

The production possibilities frontier shows the trade-off between the outputs of different goods at a given time, but the trade-off can change over time. For example, suppose a technological advance in the computer industry raises the number of computers that a worker can produce per week. This advance expands society's set of opportunities. For any given number of cars, the economy can make more computers. If the economy does not produce any computers, it can still produce 1,000 cars, so one endpoint of the frontier stays the same. But the rest of the production possibilities frontier shifts outward, as in Figure 3.

This figure illustrates economic growth. Society can move production from a point on the old frontier to a point on the new frontier. Which point it chooses depends on its preferences for the two goods. In this example, society moves from point A to point G, enjoying more computers (2,300 instead of 2,200) and more cars (650 instead of 600).

The production possibilities frontier simplifies a complex economy to highlight some basic but powerful ideas: scarcity, efficiency, trade-offs, opportunity cost,

A Shift in the Production Possibilities Frontier
A technological advance in the computer industry enables the economy to produce more computers for any given number of cars. As a result, the production possibilities frontier shifts outward. If the economy moves from point A to point G, then the production of both cars and computers increases.

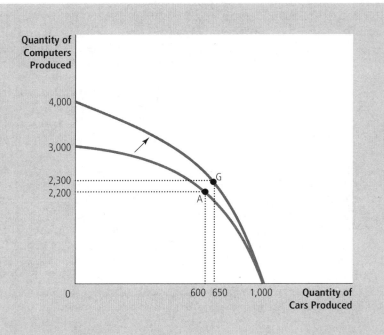

and economic growth. As you study economics, these ideas will recur in various forms. The production possibilities frontier offers one simple way of thinking about them.

Microeconomics and Macroeconomics

Many subjects are studied on various levels. Consider biology, for example. Molecular biologists study the chemical compounds that make up living things. Cellular biologists study cells, which are made up of many chemical compounds and, at the same time, are themselves the building blocks of living organisms. Evolutionary biologists study the many varieties of animals and plants and how species change gradually over the centuries.

Economics is also studied on various levels. We can study the decisions of individual households and firms. Or we can study the interaction of households and firms in markets for specific goods and services. Or we can study the operation of the economy as a whole, which is the sum of the activities of all these decision makers in all these markets.

The field of economics is traditionally divided into two broad subfields. **Microeconomics** is the study of how households and firms make decisions and how they interact in specific markets. **Macroeconomics** is the study of economywide phenomena. A microeconomist might study the effects of rent control on housing in New York City, the impact of foreign competition on the U.S. auto industry, or the effects of compulsory school attendance on workers' earnings. A macroeconomist might study the effects of borrowing by the federal government, the changes over time in the economy's rate of unemployment, or alternative policies to promote growth in national living standards.

Microeconomics and macroeconomics are closely intertwined. Because changes in the overall economy arise from the decisions of millions of individuals, it is impossible to understand macroeconomic developments without considering the associated microeconomic decisions. For example, a macroeconomist might study the effect of a federal income tax cut on the overall production of goods and services. But to analyze this issue, he or she must consider how the tax cut affects the decisions of households about how much to spend on goods and services.

Despite the inherent link between microeconomics and macroeconomics, the two fields are distinct. Because they address different questions, each field has its own set of models, which are often taught in separate courses.

microeconomics
the study of how households and firms make decisions and how they interact in markets

macroeconomics
the study of economywide phenomena, including inflation, unemployment, and economic growth

QUICK QUIZ   *In what sense is economics like a science?* • *Draw a production possibilities frontier for a society that produces food and clothing. Show an efficient point, an inefficient point, and an infeasible point. Show the effects of a drought.* • *Define* microeconomics *and* macroeconomics.

The Economist as Policy Adviser

Often, economists are asked to explain the causes of economic events. Why, for example, is unemployment higher for teenagers than for older workers? Sometimes, economists are asked to recommend policies to improve economic outcomes. What, for instance, should the government do to improve the economic

FYI

> ## Who Studies Economics?

As a college student, you might be asking yourself: How many economics classes should I take? How useful will this stuff be to me later in life? Economics can seem abstract at first, but the field is fundamentally very practical, and the study of economics is useful in many different career paths. Here is a small sampling of some well-known people who majored in economics when they were in college.

George H. W. Bush	Former President of the United States
Donald Trump	Business and TV Mogul
Meg Whitman	Former Chief Executive Officer of eBay
Danny Glover	Actor
Barbara Boxer	U.S. Senator
John Elway	Former NFL Quarterback
Kofi Annan	Former Secretary General, United Nations
Ted Turner	Founder of CNN
Lionel Richie	Singer

Diane von Furstenberg	Fashion Designer
Michael Kinsley	Journalist
Ben Stein	Political Speechwriter, Journalist, and Actor
Cate Blanchett	Actor
Anthony Zinni	General (ret.), U.S. Marine Corps
Steve Ballmer	Chief Executive Officer, Microsoft
Arnold Schwarzenegger	Governor of California

Sandra Day-O'Connor	Former Supreme Court Justice
Scott Adams	Cartoonist for *Dilbert*
Mick Jagger	Singer for the Rolling Stones

When asked in 2005 why The Rolling Stones were going on tour again, former economics major Mick Jagger replied, "Supply and demand." Keith Richards added, "If the demand's there, we'll supply."

Having studied at the London School of Economics may not help Mick Jagger hit the high notes, but it has probably given him some insight about how to invest the substantial sums he has earned during his rock 'n' roll career.

well-being of teenagers? When economists are trying to explain the world, they are scientists. When they are trying to help improve it, they are policy advisers.

Positive versus Normative Analysis

To help clarify the two roles that economists play, let's examine the use of language. Because scientists and policy advisers have different goals, they use language in different ways.

For example, suppose that two people are discussing minimum-wage laws. Here are two statements you might hear:

POLLY: Minimum-wage laws cause unemployment.
NORM: The government should raise the minimum wage.

Ignoring for now whether you agree with these statements, notice that Polly and Norm differ in what they are trying to do. Polly is speaking like a scientist: She is making a claim about how the world works. Norm is speaking like a policy adviser: He is making a claim about how he would like to change the world.

In general, statements about the world come in two types. One type, such as Polly's, is positive. **Positive statements** are descriptive. They make a claim about how the world *is*. A second type of statement, such as Norm's, is normative. **Normative statements** are prescriptive. They make a claim about how the world *ought to be*.

A key difference between positive and normative statements is how we judge their validity. We can, in principle, confirm or refute positive statements by examining evidence. An economist might evaluate Polly's statement by analyzing data on changes in minimum wages and changes in unemployment over time. By contrast, evaluating normative statements involves values as well as facts. Norm's statement cannot be judged using data alone. Deciding what is good or bad policy is not just a matter of science. It also involves our views on ethics, religion, and political philosophy.

Positive and normative statements are fundamentally different, but they are often intertwined in a person's set of beliefs. In particular, positive views about how the world works affect normative views about what policies are desirable. Polly's claim that the minimum wage causes unemployment, if true, might lead her to reject Norm's conclusion that the government should raise the minimum wage. Yet normative conclusions cannot come from positive analysis alone; they involve value judgments as well.

As you study economics, keep in mind the distinction between positive and normative statements because it will help you stay focused on the task at hand. Much of economics is positive: It just tries to explain how the economy works. Yet those who use economics often have normative goals: They want to learn how to improve the economy. When you hear economists making normative statements, you know they are speaking not as scientists but as policy advisers.

positive statements
claims that attempt to describe the world as it is

normative statements
claims that attempt to prescribe how the world should be

Economists in Washington

President Harry Truman once said that he wanted to find a one-armed economist. When he asked his economists for advice, they always answered, "On the one hand, . . . On the other hand, . . . "

Truman was right in realizing that economists' advice is not always straightforward. This tendency is rooted in one of the *Ten Principles of Economics*: People face trade-offs. Economists are aware that trade-offs are involved in most policy decisions. A policy might increase efficiency at the cost of equality. It might help future generations but hurt current generations. An economist who says that all policy decisions are easy is an economist not to be trusted.

Truman was not the only president who relied on the advice of economists. Since 1946, the president of the United States has received guidance from the Council of Economic Advisers, which consists of three members and a staff of a few dozen economists. The council, whose offices are just a few steps from the White House, has no duty other than to advise the president and to write the annual *Economic Report of the President*, which discusses recent developments in the economy and presents the council's analysis of current policy issues.

The president also receives input from economists in many administrative departments. Economists at the Office of Management and Budget help formulate spending plans and regulatory policies. Economists at the Department of the Treasury help design tax policy. Economists at the Department of Labor analyze data on workers and those looking for work to help formulate labor-market policies. Economists at the Department of Justice help enforce the nation's antitrust laws.

Economists are also found outside the administrative branch of government. To obtain independent evaluations of policy proposals, Congress relies on the advice of the Congressional Budget Office, which is staffed by economists. The

"Let's switch. I'll make the policy, you implement it, and he'll explain it."

in the news

> ## The Economics of President Obama

Here is how Larry Summers, a chief economic adviser to Barack Obama, describes the president's policies.

A Vision for Innovation, Growth, and Quality Jobs

BY LAWRENCE H. SUMMERS

President Obama laid out his vision for innovation, growth, and quality jobs earlier today at Hudson Valley Community College. This President's plan is grounded not only in the American tradition of entrepreneurship, but also in the traditions of robust economic thought.

During the past two years, the ideas propounded by John Maynard Keynes have assumed greater importance than most people would have thought in the previous generation. As Keynes famously observed, during those rare times of deep financial and economic crisis, when the "invisible hand" Adam Smith talked about has temporarily ceased to function, there is a more urgent need for government to play an active role in restoring markets to their healthy function.

The wisdom of Keynesian policies has been confirmed by the performance of the economy over the past year. After the collapse of Lehman Brothers last September, government policy moved in a strongly activist direction.

As a result of those policies, our outlook today has shifted from rescue to recovery, from worrying about the very real prospect of depression to thinking about what kind of an expansion we want to have.

An important aspect of any economic expansion is the role innovation plays as

Federal Reserve, the institution that sets the nation's monetary policy, employs hundreds of economists to analyze economic developments in the United States and throughout the world.

The influence of economists on policy goes beyond their role as advisers: Their research and writings often affect policy indirectly. Economist John Maynard Keynes offered this observation:

> The ideas of economists and political philosophers, both when they are right and when they are wrong, are more powerful than is commonly understood. Indeed, the world is ruled by little else. Practical men, who believe themselves to be quite exempt from intellectual influences, are usually the slaves of some defunct economist. Madmen in authority, who hear voices in the air, are distilling their frenzy from some academic scribbler of a few years back.

Although these words were written in 1935, they remain true. Indeed, the "academic scribbler" now influencing public policy is often Keynes himself.

Why Economists' Advice Is Not Always Followed

Any economist who advises presidents or other elected leaders knows that his or her recommendations are not always heeded. Frustrating as this can be, it is easy to understand. The process by which economic policy is actually made differs in many ways from the idealized policy process assumed in economics textbooks.

an engine of economic growth. In this regard, the most important economist of the twenty-first century might actually turn out to be not Smith or Keynes, but Joseph Schumpeter.

One of Schumpeter's most important contributions was the emphasis he placed on the tremendous power of innovation and entrepreneurial initiative to drive growth through a process he famously characterized as "creative destruction." His work captured not only an economic truth, but also the particular source of America's strength and dynamism.

One of the ways to view the trajectory of economic history is through the key technologies that have reverberated across the economy. In the nineteenth century, these included the transcontinental railroad, the telegraph, and the steam engine, among others. In the twentieth, the most powerful innovations included the automobile, the jet plane, and, over the last generation, information technology.

While we can't know exactly where the next great area of American innovation will be, we already see a number of prominent sectors where American entrepreneurs are unleashing explosive, innovative energy:

- In information technology, where tremendous potential remains for a range of applications to increase for years to come;
- In life-science technologies, where developments made at the National Institutes of Health and in research facilities around the country will have profound implications not just for human health, but also for the environment, agriculture, and a range of other areas that require technological creativity; and,
- In energy, where the combination of environmental and geopolitical imperatives have created the context for an enormously productive period in developing energy technologies as well.

Looking across the breadth of the U.S. economy, the prospects for transformational innovation to occur are enormous. But to ensure that the entrepreneurial spirit that Schumpeter recognized in the early twentieth century will continue to drive the American economy in the twenty-first century requires a role for government as well: to create an environment that is conducive to generating those developments.

© CHIP SOMODEVILLA/GETTY IMAGES

Source: The White House Blog, September 21, 2009. http://www.whitehouse.gov/blog/A-Vision-for-Innovation-Growth-and-Quality-Jobs/

Throughout this text, whenever we discuss economic policy, we often focus on one question: What is the best policy for the government to pursue? We act as if policy were set by a benevolent king. Once the king figures out the right policy, he has no trouble putting his ideas into action.

In the real world, figuring out the right policy is only part of a leader's job, sometimes the easiest part. After a president hears from his economic advisers about what policy is best from their perspective, he turns to other advisers for related input. His communications advisers will tell him how best to explain the proposed policy to the public, and they will try to anticipate any misunderstandings that might make the challenge more difficult. His press advisers will tell him how the news media will report on his proposal and what opinions will likely be expressed on the nation's editorial pages. His legislative affairs advisers will tell him how Congress will view the proposal, what amendments members of Congress will suggest, and the likelihood that Congress will pass some version of the president's proposal into law. His political advisers will tell him which groups will organize to support or oppose the proposed policy, how this proposal will affect his standing among different groups in the electorate, and whether it will affect support for any of the president's other policy initiatives. After hearing and weighing all this advice, the president then decides how to proceed.

Making economic policy in a representative democracy is a messy affair—and there are often good reasons presidents (and other politicians) do not advance the policies that economists advocate. Economists offer crucial input into the policy process, but their advice is only one ingredient of a complex recipe.

QUICK QUIZ   *Give an example of a positive statement and an example of a normative statement that somehow relates to your daily life. • Name three parts of government that regularly rely on advice from economists.*

Why Economists Disagree

"If all economists were laid end to end, they would not reach a conclusion." This quip from George Bernard Shaw is revealing. Economists as a group are often criticized for giving conflicting advice to policymakers. President Ronald Reagan once joked that if the game Trivial Pursuit were designed for economists, it would have 100 questions and 3,000 answers.

Why do economists so often appear to give conflicting advice to policymakers? There are two basic reasons:

- Economists may disagree about the validity of alternative positive theories about how the world works.
- Economists may have different values and therefore different normative views about what policy should try to accomplish.

Let's discuss each of these reasons.

Differences in Scientific Judgments

Several centuries ago, astronomers debated whether the earth or the sun was at the center of the solar system. More recently, meteorologists have debated whether the earth is experiencing global warming and, if so, why. Science is a search for understanding about the world around us. It is not surprising that as the search continues, scientists can disagree about the direction in which truth lies.

Economists often disagree for the same reason. Economics is a young science, and there is still much to be learned. Economists sometimes disagree because they have different hunches about the validity of alternative theories or about the size of important parameters that measure how economic variables are related.

For example, economists disagree about whether the government should tax a household's income or its consumption (spending). Advocates of a switch from the current income tax to a consumption tax believe that the change would encourage households to save more because income that is saved would not be taxed. Higher saving, in turn, would free resources for capital accumulation, leading to more rapid growth in productivity and living standards. Advocates of the current income tax system believe that household saving would not respond much to a change in the tax laws. These two groups of economists hold different normative views about the tax system because they have different positive views about the responsiveness of saving to tax incentives.

Differences in Values

Suppose that Peter and Paula both take the same amount of water from the town well. To pay for maintaining the well, the town taxes its residents. Peter has income of $100,000 and is taxed $10,000, or 10 percent of his income. Paula has income of $20,000 and is taxed $4,000, or 20 percent of her income.

Is this policy fair? If not, who pays too much and who pays too little? Does it matter whether Paula's low income is due to a medical disability or to her decision to pursue an acting career? Does it matter whether Peter's high income is due to a large inheritance or to his willingness to work long hours at a dreary job?

These are difficult questions on which people are likely to disagree. If the town hired two experts to study how the town should tax its residents to pay for the well, we would not be surprised if they offered conflicting advice.

This simple example shows why economists sometimes disagree about public policy. As we learned earlier in our discussion of normative and positive analysis, policies cannot be judged on scientific grounds alone. Economists give conflicting advice sometimes because they have different values. Perfecting the science of economics will not tell us whether Peter or Paula pays too much.

Perception versus Reality

Because of differences in scientific judgments and differences in values, some disagreement among economists is inevitable. Yet one should not overstate the amount of disagreement. Economists agree with one another far more than is sometimes understood.

Table 1 contains 20 propositions about economic policy. In surveys of professional economists, these propositions were endorsed by an overwhelming majority of respondents. Most of these propositions would fail to command a similar consensus among the public.

The first proposition in the table is about rent control, a policy that sets a legal maximum on the amount landlords can charge for their apartments. Almost all economists believe that rent control adversely affects the availability and quality of housing and is a costly way of helping the neediest members of society. Nonetheless, many city governments ignore the advice of economists and place ceilings on the rents that landlords may charge their tenants.

The second proposition in the table concerns tariffs and import quotas, two policies that restrict trade among nations. For reasons we discuss more fully later in this text, almost all economists oppose such barriers to free trade. Nonetheless, over the years, presidents and Congress have chosen to restrict the import of certain goods.

Why do policies such as rent control and trade barriers persist if the experts are united in their opposition? It may be that the realities of the political process stand as immovable obstacles. But it also may be that economists have not yet convinced enough of the public that these policies are undesirable. One purpose of this book is to help you understand the economist's view of these and other subjects and, perhaps, to persuade you that it is the right one.

QUICK QUIZ   *Why might economic advisers to the president disagree about a question of policy?*

Let's Get Going

The first two chapters of this book have introduced you to the ideas and methods of economics. We are now ready to get to work. In the next chapter, we start learning in more detail the principles of economic behavior and economic policy.

As you proceed through this book, you will be asked to draw on many of your intellectual skills. You might find it helpful to keep in mind some advice from the great economist John Maynard Keynes:

Table 1

Propositions about Which Most Economists Agree

Proposition (and percentage of economists who agree)

1. A ceiling on rents reduces the quantity and quality of housing available. (93%)
2. Tariffs and import quotas usually reduce general economic welfare. (93%)
3. Flexible and floating exchange rates offer an effective international monetary arrangement. (90%)
4. Fiscal policy (e.g., tax cut and/or government expenditure increase) has a significant stimulative impact on a less than fully employed economy. (90%)
5. The United States should not restrict employers from outsourcing work to foreign countries. (90%)
6. Economic growth in developed countries like the United States leads to greater levels of well-being. (88%)
7. The United States should eliminate agricultural subsidies. (85%)
8. An appropriately designed fiscal policy can increase the long-run rate of capital formation. (85%)
9. Local and state governments should eliminate subsidies to professional sports franchises. (85%)
10. If the federal budget is to be balanced, it should be done over the business cycle rather than yearly. (85%)
11. The gap between Social Security funds and expenditures will become unsustainably large within the next 50 years if current policies remain unchanged. (85%)
12. Cash payments increase the welfare of recipients to a greater degree than do transfers-in-kind of equal cash value. (84%)
13. A large federal budget deficit has an adverse effect on the economy. (83%)
14. The redistribution of income in the United State is a legitimate role for the government. (83%)
15. Inflation is caused primarily by too much growth in the money supply. (83%)
16. The United States should not ban genetically modified crops. (82%)
17. A minimum wage increases unemployment among young and unskilled workers. (79%)
18. The government should restructure the welfare system along the lines of a "negative income tax." (79%)
19. Effluent taxes and marketable pollution permits represent a better approach to pollution control than imposition of pollution ceilings. (78%)
20. Government subsidies on ethanol in the United States should be reduced or eliminated. (78%)

Source: Richard M. Alston, J. R. Kearl, and Michael B. Vaughn, "Is There Consensus among Economists in the 1990s?" *American Economic Review* (May 1992): 203–209; Dan Fuller and Doris Geide-Stevenson, "Consensus among Economists Revisited," *Journal of Economics Education* (Fall 2003): 369–387; Robert Whaples, "Do Economists Agree on Anything? Yes!" *Economists' Voice* (November 2006): 1–6; Robert Whaples, "The Policy Views of American Economic Association Members: The Results of a New Survey, *Econ Journal Watch* (September 2009): 337–348.

The study of economics does not seem to require any specialized gifts of an unusually high order. Is it not . . . a very easy subject compared with the higher branches of philosophy or pure science? An easy subject, at which very few excel! The paradox finds its explanation, perhaps, in that the master-economist must possess a rare *combination* of gifts. He must be mathematician, historian, statesman, philosopher—in some degree. He must understand symbols and speak in words. He must contemplate the particular in terms of the general, and touch abstract and concrete in the same flight of thought. He must study the present in the light of the past for the purposes of the future. No part of man's nature or his institutions must lie entirely outside his regard. He must be purposeful and disinterested in a simultaneous mood; as aloof and incorruptible as an artist, yet sometimes as near the earth as a politician.

It is a tall order. But with practice, you will become more and more accustomed to thinking like an economist.

in the news

> ### Environmental Economics
> *Some economists are helping to save the planet.*

Green Groups See Potent Tool in Economics

BY JESSICA E. VASCELLARO

Many economists dream of getting high-paying jobs on Wall Street, at prestigious think tanks and universities or at powerful government agencies like the Federal Reserve.

But a growing number are choosing to use their skills not to track inflation or interest rates but to rescue rivers and trees. These are the "green economists," more formally known as environmental economists, who use economic arguments and systems to persuade companies to clean up pollution and to help conserve natural areas.

Working at dozens of advocacy groups and a myriad of state and federal environmental agencies, they are helping to formulate the intellectual framework behind approaches to protecting endangered species, reducing pollution and preventing climate change. They also are becoming a link between left-leaning advocacy groups and the public and private sectors.

"In the past, many advocacy groups interpreted economics as how to make a profit or maximize income," says Lawrence Goulder, a professor of environmental and resource economics at Stanford University in Stanford, Calif. "More economists are realizing that it offers a framework for resource allocation where resources are not only labor and capital but natural resources as well."

Environmental economists are on the payroll of government agencies (the Environmental Protection Agency had about 164 on staff in 2004, up 36% from 1995) and groups like the Wilderness Society, a Washington-based conservation group, which has four of them to work on projects such as assessing the economic impact of building off-road driving trails. Environmental Defense, also based in Washington, was one of the first environmental-advocacy groups to hire economists and now has about eight, who do such things as develop market incentives to address environmental problems like climate change and water shortages. . . .

"There used to be this idea that we shouldn't have to monetize the environment because it is invaluable," says Caroline Alkire, who in 1991 joined the Wilderness Society, an advocacy group in Washington, D.C., as one of the group's first economists. "But if we are going to engage in debate on the Hill about drilling in the Arctic we need to be able to combat the financial arguments. We have to play that card or we are going to lose."

The field of environmental economics began to take form in the 1960s when academics started to apply the tools of economics to the nascent green movement. The discipline grew more popular throughout the 1980s when the Environmental Protection Agency adopted a system of tradable permits for phasing out leaded gasoline. It wasn't until the 1990 amendment to the Clean Air Act, however, that most environmentalists started to take economics seriously.

The amendment implemented a system of tradable allowances for acid rain, a program pushed by Environmental Defense. Under the law, plants that can reduce their emissions more cost-effectively may sell their allowances to more heavy polluters. Today, the program has exceeded its goal of reducing the amount of acid rain to half its 1980 level and is celebrated as evidence that markets can help achieve environmental goals.

Its success has convinced its former critics, who at the time contended that environmental regulation was a matter of ethics, not economics, and favored installing expensive acid rain removal technology in all power plants instead.

Greenpeace, the international environmental giant, was one of the leading opponents of the 1990 amendment. But Kert Davies, research director for Greenpeace USA, said its success and the lack of any significant action on climate policy throughout [the] early 1990s brought the organization around to the concept. "We now believe that [tradable permits] are the most straightforward system of reducing emissions and creating the incentives necessary for massive reductions."

Source: *The Wall Street Journal,* August 23, 2005.

SUMMARY

- Economists try to address their subject with a scientist's objectivity. Like all scientists, they make appropriate assumptions and build simplified models to understand the world around them. Two simple economic models are the circular-flow diagram and the production possibilities frontier.

- The field of economics is divided into two subfields: microeconomics and macroeconomics. Microeconomists study decision making by households and firms and the interaction among households and firms in the marketplace. Macroeconomists study the forces and trends that affect the economy as a whole.

- A positive statement is an assertion about how the world *is*. A normative statement is an assertion about how the world *ought to be*. When economists make normative statements, they are acting more as policy advisers than scientists.

- Economists who advise policymakers offer conflicting advice either because of differences in scientific judgments or because of differences in values. At other times, economists are united in the advice they offer, but policymakers may choose to ignore it.

KEY CONCEPTS

circular-flow diagram, *p. 24*
production possibilities
   frontier, *p. 26*

microeconomics, *p. 29*
macroeconomics, *p. 29*

positive statements, *p. 31*
normative statements, *p. 31*

QUESTIONS FOR REVIEW

1. How is economics a science?
2. Why do economists make assumptions?
3. Should an economic model describe reality exactly?
4. Name a way that your family interacts in the factor market and a way that it interacts in the product market.
5. Name one economic interaction that isn't covered by the simplified circular-flow diagram.
6. Draw and explain a production possibilities frontier for an economy that produces milk and

cookies. What happens to this frontier if disease kills half of the economy's cows?
7. Use a production possibilities frontier to describe the idea of "efficiency."
8. What are the two subfields into which economics is divided? Explain what each subfield studies.
9. What is the difference between a positive and a normative statement? Give an example of each.
10. Why do economists sometimes offer conflicting advice to policymakers?

PROBLEMS AND APPLICATIONS

1. Draw a circular-flow diagram. Identify the parts of the model that correspond to the flow of goods and services and the flow of dollars for each of the following activities.
   a. Selena pays a storekeeper $1 for a quart of milk.

   b. Stuart earns $4.50 per hour working at a fast-food restaurant.
   c. Shanna spends $30 to get a haircut.
   d. Sally earns $10,000 from her 10 percent ownership of Acme Industrial.

2. Imagine a society that produces military goods and consumer goods, which we'll call "guns" and "butter."
   a. Draw a production possibilities frontier for guns and butter. Using the concept of opportunity cost, explain why it most likely has a bowed-out shape.
   b. Show a point that is impossible for the economy to achieve. Show a point that is feasible but inefficient.
   c. Imagine that the society has two political parties, called the Hawks (who want a strong military) and the Doves (who want a smaller military). Show a point on your production possibilities frontier that the Hawks might choose and a point the Doves might choose.
   d. Imagine that an aggressive neighboring country reduces the size of its military. As a result, both the Hawks and the Doves reduce their desired production of guns by the same amount. Which party would get the bigger "peace dividend," measured by the increase in butter production? Explain.

3. The first principle of economics discussed in Chapter 1 is that people face trade-offs. Use a production possibilities frontier to illustrate society's trade-off between two "goods"—a clean environment and the quantity of industrial output. What do you suppose determines the shape and position of the frontier? Show what happens to the frontier if engineers develop a new way of producing electricity that emits fewer pollutants.

4. An economy consists of three workers: Larry, Moe, and Curly. Each works ten hours a day and can produce two services: mowing lawns and washing cars. In an hour, Larry can either mow one lawn or wash one car; Moe can either mow one lawn or wash two cars; and Curly can either mow two lawns or wash one car.
   a. Calculate how much of each service is produced under the following circumstances, which we label A, B, C, and D:
      • All three spend all their time mowing lawns. (A)
      • All three spend all their time washing cars. (B)
      • All three spend half their time on each activity. (C)
      • Larry spends half his time on each activity, while Moe only washes cars and Curly only mows lawns. (D)
   b. Graph the production possibilities frontier for this economy. Using your answers to part (a), identify points A, B, C, and D on your graph.
   c. Explain why the production possibilities frontier has the shape it does.
   d. Are any of the allocations calculated in part (a) inefficient? Explain.

5. Classify the following topics as relating to microeconomics or macroeconomics.
   a. a family's decision about how much income to save
   b. the effect of government regulations on auto emissions
   c. the impact of higher national saving on economic growth
   d. a firm's decision about how many workers to hire
   e. the relationship between the inflation rate and changes in the quantity of money

6. Classify each of the following statements as positive or normative. Explain.
   a. Society faces a short-run trade-off between inflation and unemployment.
   b. A reduction in the rate of money growth will reduce the rate of inflation.
   c. The Federal Reserve should reduce the rate of money growth.
   d. Society ought to require welfare recipients to look for jobs.
   e. Lower tax rates encourage more work and more saving.

7. If you were president, would you be more interested in your economic advisers' positive views or their normative views? Why?

For further information on topics in this chapter, additional problems, applications, examples, online quizzes, and more, please visit our website at www.cengage.com/economics/mankiw.

Appendix

Graphing: A Brief Review

Many of the concepts that economists study can be expressed with numbers—the price of bananas, the quantity of bananas sold, the cost of growing bananas, and so on. Often, these economic variables are related to one another: When the price of bananas rises, people buy fewer bananas. One way of expressing the relationships among variables is with graphs.

Graphs serve two purposes. First, when developing economic theories, graphs offer a way to visually express ideas that might be less clear if described with equations or words. Second, when analyzing economic data, graphs provide a powerful way of finding and interpreting patterns. Whether we are working with theory or with data, graphs provide a lens through which a recognizable forest emerges from a multitude of trees.

Numerical information can be expressed graphically in many ways, just as there are many ways to express a thought in words. A good writer chooses words that will make an argument clear, a description pleasing, or a scene dramatic. An effective economist chooses the type of graph that best suits the purpose at hand.

In this appendix, we discuss how economists use graphs to study the mathematical relationships among variables. We also discuss some of the pitfalls that can arise in the use of graphical methods.

Graphs of a Single Variable

Three common graphs are shown in Figure A-1. The *pie chart* in panel (a) shows how total income in the United States is divided among the sources of income, including compensation of employees, corporate profits, and so on. A slice of the

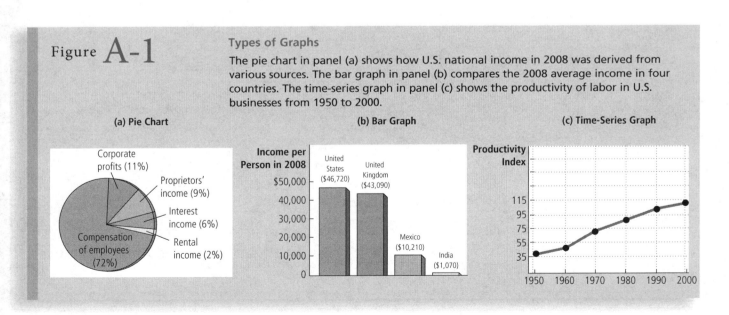

Figure A-1

Types of Graphs

The pie chart in panel (a) shows how U.S. national income in 2008 was derived from various sources. The bar graph in panel (b) compares the 2008 average income in four countries. The time-series graph in panel (c) shows the productivity of labor in U.S. businesses from 1950 to 2000.

(a) Pie Chart

Corporate profits (11%)
Proprietors' income (9%)
Interest income (6%)
Rental income (2%)
Compensation of employees (72%)

(b) Bar Graph

Income per Person in 2008

United States ($46,720)
United Kingdom ($43,090)
Mexico ($10,210)
India ($1,070)

$50,000
40,000
30,000
20,000
10,000
0

(c) Time-Series Graph

Productivity Index

115
95
75
55
35

1950 1960 1970 1980 1990 2000

pie represents each source's share of the total. The *bar graph* in panel (b) compares income for four countries. The height of each bar represents the average income in each country. The *time-series graph* in panel (c) traces the rising productivity in the U.S. business sector over time. The height of the line shows output per hour in each year. You have probably seen similar graphs in newspapers and magazines.

Graphs of Two Variables: The Coordinate System

The three graphs in Figure A-1 are useful in showing how a variable changes over time or across individuals, but they are limited in how much they can tell us. These graphs display information only on a single variable. Economists are often concerned with the relationships between variables. Thus, they need to display two variables on a single graph. The *coordinate system* makes this possible.

Suppose you want to examine the relationship between study time and grade point average. For each student in your class, you could record a pair of numbers: hours per week spent studying and grade point average. These numbers could then be placed in parentheses as an *ordered pair* and appear as a single point on the graph. Albert E., for instance, is represented by the ordered pair (25 hours/week, 3.5 GPA), while his "what-me-worry?" classmate Alfred E. is represented by the ordered pair (5 hours/week, 2.0 GPA).

We can graph these ordered pairs on a two-dimensional grid. The first number in each ordered pair, called the *x-coordinate*, tells us the horizontal location of the point. The second number, called the *y-coordinate*, tells us the vertical location of the point. The point with both an *x*-coordinate and a *y*-coordinate of zero is known as the *origin*. The two coordinates in the ordered pair tell us where the point is located in relation to the origin: *x* units to the right of the origin and *y* units above it.

Figure A-2 graphs grade point average against study time for Albert E., Alfred E., and their classmates. This type of graph is called a *scatterplot* because it plots scattered points. Looking at this graph, we immediately notice that points farther

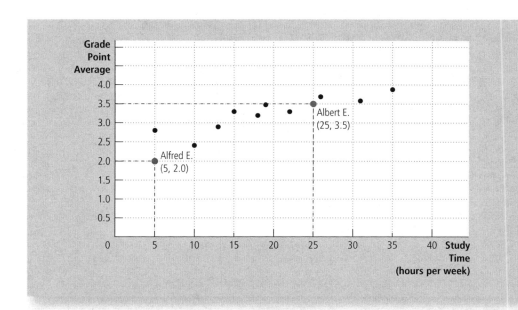

Figure **A-2**

Using the Coordinate System
Grade point average is measured on the vertical axis and study time on the horizontal axis. Albert E., Alfred E., and their classmates are represented by various points. We can see from the graph that students who study more tend to get higher grades.

to the right (indicating more study time) also tend to be higher (indicating a better grade point average). Because study time and grade point average typically move in the same direction, we say that these two variables have a *positive correlation*. By contrast, if we were to graph party time and grades, we would likely find that higher party time is associated with lower grades; because these variables typically move in opposite directions, we call this a *negative correlation*. In either case, the coordinate system makes the correlation between the two variables easy to see.

Curves in the Coordinate System

Students who study more do tend to get higher grades, but other factors also influence a student's grade. Previous preparation is an important factor, for instance, as are talent, attention from teachers, even eating a good breakfast. A scatterplot like Figure A-2 does not attempt to isolate the effect that studying has on grades from the effects of other variables. Often, however, economists prefer looking at how one variable affects another, holding everything else constant.

To see how this is done, let's consider one of the most important graphs in economics: the *demand curve*. The demand curve traces out the effect of a good's price on the quantity of the good consumers want to buy. Before showing a demand curve, however, consider Table A-1, which shows how the number of novels that Emma buys depends on her income and on the price of novels. When novels are cheap, Emma buys them in large quantities. As they become more expensive, she instead borrows books from the library or chooses to go to the movies rather than read. Similarly, at any given price, Emma buys more novels when she has a higher income. That is, when her income increases, she spends part of the additional income on novels and part on other goods.

We now have three variables—the price of novels, income, and the number of novels purchased—which are more than we can represent in two dimensions. To put the information from Table A-1 in graphical form, we need to hold one of the three variables constant and trace out the relationship between the other two. Because the demand curve represents the relationship between price and quantity demanded, we hold Emma's income constant and show how the number of novels she buys varies with the price of novels.

Suppose that Emma's income is $30,000 per year. If we place the number of novels Emma purchases on the *x*-axis and the price of novels on the *y*-axis, we

Table A-1

Novels Purchased by Emma
This table shows the number of novels Emma buys at various incomes and prices. For any given level of income, the data on price and quantity demanded can be graphed to produce Emma's demand curve for novels, as shown in Figures A-3 and A-4.

Price	For $20,000 Income:	For $30,000 Income:	For $40,000 Income:
$10	2 novels	5 novels	8 novels
9	6	9	12
8	10	13	16
7	14	17	20
6	18	21	24
5	22	25	28
	Demand curve, D_3	Demand curve, D_1	Demand curve, D_2

can graphically represent the middle column of Table A-1. When the points that represent these entries from the table—(5 novels, $10), (9 novels, $9), and so on—are connected, they form a line. This line, pictured in Figure A-3, is known as Emma's demand curve for novels; it tells us how many novels Emma purchases at any given price. The demand curve is downward sloping, indicating that a higher price reduces the quantity of novels demanded. Because the quantity of novels demanded and the price move in opposite directions, we say that the two variables are *negatively related*. (Conversely, when two variables move in the same direction, the curve relating them is upward sloping, and we say the variables are *positively related*.)

Now suppose that Emma's income rises to $40,000 per year. At any given price, Emma will purchase more novels than she did at her previous level of income. Just as earlier we drew Emma's demand curve for novels using the entries from the middle column of Table A-1, we now draw a new demand curve using the entries from the right column of the table. This new demand curve (curve D_2) is pictured alongside the old one (curve D_1) in Figure A-4; the new curve is a similar line drawn farther to the right. We therefore say that Emma's demand curve for novels *shifts* to the right when her income increases. Likewise, if Emma's income were to fall to $20,000 per year, she would buy fewer novels at any given price and her demand curve would shift to the left (to curve D_3).

In economics, it is important to distinguish between *movements along a curve* and *shifts of a curve*. As we can see from Figure A-3, if Emma earns $30,000 per year and novels cost $8 apiece, she will purchase 13 novels per year. If the price of novels falls to $7, Emma will increase her purchases of novels to 17 per year. The demand curve, however, stays fixed in the same place. Emma still buys the same

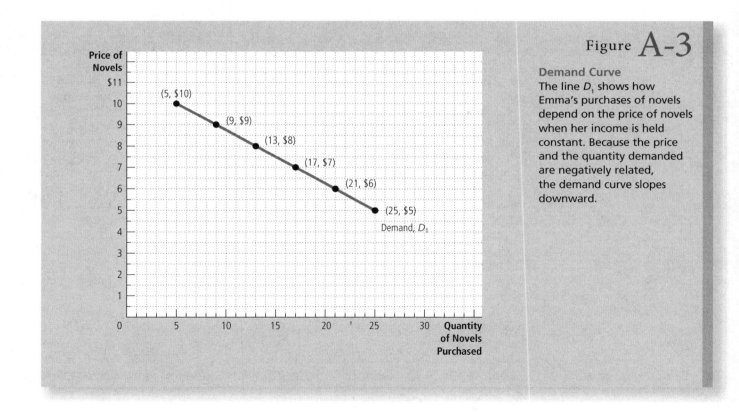

Figure A-3

Demand Curve
The line D_1 shows how Emma's purchases of novels depend on the price of novels when her income is held constant. Because the price and the quantity demanded are negatively related, the demand curve slopes downward.

Figure A-4

Shifting Demand Curves
The location of Emma's demand curve for novels depends on how much income she earns. The more she earns, the more novels she will purchase at any given price, and the farther to the right her demand curve will lie. Curve D_1 represents Emma's original demand curve when her income is $30,000 per year. If her income rises to $40,000 per year, her demand curve shifts to D_2. If her income falls to $20,000 per year, her demand curve shifts to D_3.

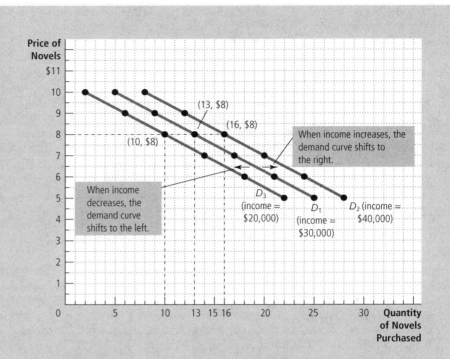

number of novels *at each price*, but as the price falls, she moves along her demand curve from left to right. By contrast, if the price of novels remains fixed at $8 but her income rises to $40,000, Emma increases her purchases of novels from 13 to 16 per year. Because Emma buys more novels *at each price*, her demand curve shifts out, as shown in Figure A-4.

There is a simple way to tell when it is necessary to shift a curve: *When a variable that is not named on either axis changes, the curve shifts.* Income is on neither the *x*-axis nor the *y*-axis of the graph, so when Emma's income changes, her demand curve must shift. The same is true for any change that affects Emma's purchasing habits besides a change in the price of novels. If, for instance, the public library closes and Emma must buy all the books she wants to read, she will demand more novels at each price, and her demand curve will shift to the right. Or if the price of movies falls and Emma spends more time at the movies and less time reading, she will demand fewer novels at each price, and her demand curve will shift to the left. By contrast, when a variable on an axis of the graph changes, the curve does not shift. We read the change as a movement along the curve.

Slope

One question we might want to ask about Emma is how much her purchasing habits respond to price. Look at the demand curve pictured in Figure A-5. If this curve is very steep, Emma purchases nearly the same number of novels regardless

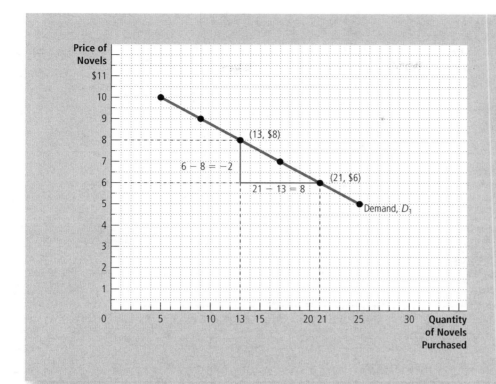

Figure A-5

Calculating the Slope of a Line
To calculate the slope of the demand curve, we can look at the changes in the *x*- and *y*-coordinates as we move from the point (21 novels, $6) to the point (13 novels, $8). The slope of the line is the ratio of the change in the *y*-coordinate (−2) to the change in the *x*-coordinate (+8), which equals −¼

of whether they are cheap or expensive. If this curve is much flatter, the number of novels Emma purchases is more sensitive to changes in the price. To answer questions about how much one variable responds to changes in another variable, we can use the concept of *slope*.

The slope of a line is the ratio of the vertical distance covered to the horizontal distance covered as we move along the line. This definition is usually written out in mathematical symbols as follows:

$$\text{slope} = \frac{\Delta y}{\Delta x},$$

where the Greek letter Δ (delta) stands for the change in a variable. In other words, the slope of a line is equal to the "rise" (change in *y*) divided by the "run" (change in *x*). The slope will be a small positive number for a fairly flat upward-sloping line, a large positive number for a steep upward-sloping line, and a negative number for a downward-sloping line. A horizontal line has a slope of zero because in this case the *y*-variable never changes; a vertical line is said to have an infinite slope because the *y*-variable can take any value without the *x*-variable changing at all.

What is the slope of Emma's demand curve for novels? First of all, because the curve slopes down, we know the slope will be negative. To calculate a numerical value for the slope, we must choose two points on the line. With Emma's income

85

at $30,000, she will purchase 21 novels at a price of $6 or 13 novels at a price of $8. When we apply the slope formula, we are concerned with the change between these two points; in other words, we are concerned with the difference between them, which lets us know that we will have to subtract one set of values from the other, as follows:

$$\text{slope} = \frac{\Delta y}{\Delta x} = \frac{\text{first } y\text{-coordinate} - \text{second } y\text{-coordinate}}{\text{first } x\text{-coordinate} - \text{second } x\text{-coordinate}} = \frac{6-8}{21-13} = \frac{-2}{8} = \frac{-1}{4}$$

Figure A-5 shows graphically how this calculation works. Try computing the slope of Emma's demand curve using two different points. You should get exactly the same result, −¼. One of the properties of a straight line is that it has the same slope everywhere. This is not true of other types of curves, which are steeper in some places than in others.

The slope of Emma's demand curve tells us something about how responsive her purchases are to changes in the price. A small slope (a number close to zero) means that Emma's demand curve is relatively flat; in this case, she adjusts the number of novels she buys substantially in response to a price change. A larger slope (a number farther from zero) means that Emma's demand curve is relatively steep; in this case, she adjusts the number of novels she buys only slightly in response to a price change.

Cause and Effect

Economists often use graphs to advance an argument about how the economy works. In other words, they use graphs to argue about how one set of events *causes* another set of events. With a graph like the demand curve, there is no doubt about cause and effect. Because we are varying price and holding all other variables constant, we know that changes in the price of novels cause changes in the quantity Emma demands. Remember, however, that our demand curve came from a hypothetical example. When graphing data from the real world, it is often more difficult to establish how one variable affects another.

The first problem is that it is difficult to hold everything else constant when studying the relationship between two variables. If we are not able to hold other variables constant, we might decide that one variable on our graph is causing changes in the other variable when actually those changes are caused by a third *omitted variable* not pictured on the graph. Even if we have identified the correct

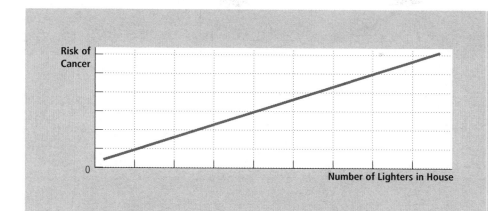

Figure A-6

Graph with an Omitted Variable
The upward-sloping curve shows that members of households with more cigarette lighters are more likely to develop cancer. Yet we should not conclude that ownership of lighters causes cancer because the graph does not take into account the number of cigarettes smoked.

two variables to look at, we might run into a second problem—*reverse causality.* In other words, we might decide that A causes B when in fact B causes A. The omitted-variable and reverse-causality traps require us to proceed with caution when using graphs to draw conclusions about causes and effects.

Omitted Variables   To see how omitting a variable can lead to a deceptive graph, let's consider an example. Imagine that the government, spurred by public concern about the large number of deaths from cancer, commissions an exhaustive study from Big Brother Statistical Services, Inc. Big Brother examines many of the items found in people's homes to see which of them are associated with the risk of cancer. Big Brother reports a strong relationship between two variables: the number of cigarette lighters that a household owns and the probability that someone in the household will develop cancer. Figure A-6 shows this relationship.

What should we make of this result? Big Brother advises a quick policy response. It recommends that the government discourage the ownership of cigarette lighters by taxing their sale. It also recommends that the government require warning labels: "Big Brother has determined that this lighter is dangerous to your health."

In judging the validity of Big Brother's analysis, one question is paramount: Has Big Brother held constant every relevant variable except the one under consideration? If the answer is no, the results are suspect. An easy explanation for Figure A-6 is that people who own more cigarette lighters are more likely to smoke cigarettes and that cigarettes, not lighters, cause cancer. If Figure A-6 does not hold constant the amount of smoking, it does not tell us the true effect of owning a cigarette lighter.

This story illustrates an important principle: When you see a graph used to support an argument about cause and effect, it is important to ask whether the movements of an omitted variable could explain the results you see.

Reverse Causality   Economists can also make mistakes about causality by misreading its direction. To see how this is possible, suppose the Association of American Anarchists commissions a study of crime in America and arrives at

87

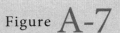

Figure A-7

Graph Suggesting Reverse Causality
The upward-sloping curve shows that cities with a higher concentration of police are more dangerous. Yet the graph does not tell us whether police cause crime or crime-plagued cities hire more police.

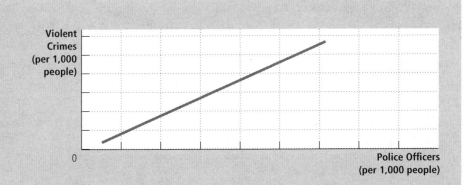

Figure A-7, which plots the number of violent crimes per thousand people in major cities against the number of police officers per thousand people. The anarchists note the curve's upward slope and argue that because police increase rather than decrease the amount of urban violence, law enforcement should be abolished.

If we could run a controlled experiment, we would avoid the danger of reverse causality. To run an experiment, we would set the number of police officers in different cities randomly and then examine the correlation between police and crime. Figure A-7, however, is not based on such an experiment. We simply observe that more dangerous cities have more police officers. The explanation for this may be that more dangerous cities hire more police. In other words, rather than police causing crime, crime may cause police. Nothing in the graph itself allows us to establish the direction of causality.

It might seem that an easy way to determine the direction of causality is to examine which variable moves first. If we see crime increase and then the police force expand, we reach one conclusion. If we see the police force expand and then crime increase, we reach the other. Yet there is also a flaw with this approach: Often, people change their behavior not in response to a change in their present conditions but in response to a change in their *expectations* of future conditions. A city that expects a major crime wave in the future, for instance, might hire more police now. This problem is even easier to see in the case of babies and minivans. Couples often buy a minivan in anticipation of the birth of a child. The minivan comes before the baby, but we wouldn't want to conclude that the sale of minivans causes the population to grow!

There is no complete set of rules that says when it is appropriate to draw causal conclusions from graphs. Yet just keeping in mind that cigarette lighters don't cause cancer (omitted variable) and minivans don't cause larger families (reverse causality) will keep you from falling for many faulty economic arguments.

Chapter 4:
The Canadian
Economy

Chapter 2

Geography, Economy, and Class

Canada's deep-seated geographic and economic divisions are some of its most obvious characteristics. Regional economic cleavages and regional identities are a daily fact of Canadian political life and many government decisions are direct responses to them. These cleavages and identities can be most usefully discussed in terms of distance and division, regional economic differences, regional economic conflicts, regional economic disparities, and regional identities. But economic divisions exist as well in non-geographic terms, usually referred to as class––that is, disparities and conflicts among people with different levels of income and wealth and varied degrees of economic power. Even though class-consciousness or class identities are not as prominent in Canada as might be expected, governments must also deal with such class conflicts on a regular basis.

Chapter Objectives

After you have completed this chapter, you should be able to:

Discuss how distance, division, and the distribution of population affect the operation of the Canadian political system

Identify the principal regions in Canada and the relationship between regions and provinces

Identify the key economic factors that distinguish one region from another

Enumerate the principal regional economic conflicts in Canada

Discuss different means of measuring regional economic disparities and programs that have been adopted to reduce them

Discuss regional identities in economic and non-economic terms

Define the concept of class

Identify the traditional demands made by the upper class, middle class, and working class

Discuss the causes, extent, and implications of poverty in Canada

Geography

Distance and Division

Canada's tremendous distances have always had a crucial influence on its political system. But such distances are immensely complicated by divisions caused by natural physical barriers running essentially in a north–south direction. Distance and division are constant factors in Canada in inducing regional identities and generating regional economic demands. Canada is usually divided into seven geographic regions, as shown in Figure 2.1.

Figure 2.1   Canada's Geographic Regions

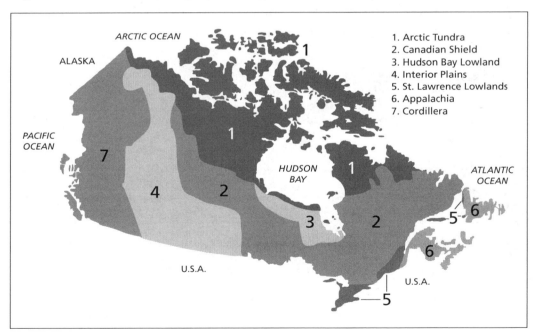

Source: Rand Dyck.

Demands to overcome distances and divisions have featured prominently in Canadian politics, and the establishment of great transportation and communications projects for this purpose dominated whole eras of Canadian history. Governments responded to these demands primarily by giving assistance to private corporations, establishing their own Crown corporations, and creating regulatory agencies in these fields.[1] The major transportation and communications links and agencies with which the federal government has been associated are as follows:

- Canadian Pacific Railway (CPR)
- Canadian National Railway (CNR)
- VIA Rail
- Trans-Canada Highway
- Trans-Canada Airlines/Air Canada
- Trans-Canada PipeLines
- Canadian Broadcasting Corporation (CBC)
- Canadian Radio-television and Telecommunications Commission (CRTC)

In short, in order to create and hold together a nation, Canadians built east–west institutions that ran counter to the natural north–south geographic features of the continent and the perpetual pull of the United States. The list ultimately included satellite services linking Canadians domestically and to the rest of the world. After 1985, however, successive federal governments deregulated, privatized, or reduced financial support for a number of these government operations.

Since people are not spread uniformly throughout Canada's gigantic territory, the distribution of population also complicates the distances involved. The overall density of the Canadian population is one of the lowest in the world, but what is really more significant is that there is no permanent settlement in nearly 90 percent of the country and that two-thirds of the population is huddled together within 100 kilometres of the U.S. border. The population of the various provinces in January 2010 can be seen in Table 2.1. Provincial population disparities affect the allocation of seats in the House of Commons—indeed, the whole power structure in Ottawa—and the calculation of federal transfer payments. Quebec is sensitive to the fact that in recent years its proportion of the total Canadian population has fallen below a symbolic 25 percent.

Ontario and Quebec combined contain about 62 percent of the population, and the Toronto–Ottawa–Montreal triangle obviously constitutes the "core" or "heartland" of Canada. While central Canada forms the political core of the country, it is also the economic heartland, with more large corporate head offices, especially in the Toronto area, than anywhere else. Moreover, it is the communications

TABLE 2.1 ESTIMATED POPULATION OF PROVINCES AND TERRITORIES, JANUARY 2010

	Number	Percentage
Ontario	13 134 455	38.7
Quebec	7 870 026	23.2
British Columbia	4 494 232	13.2
Alberta	3 711 845	10.9
Manitoba	1 228 984	3.6
Saskatchewan	1 038 018	3.1
Nova Scotia	940 744	2.8
New Brunswick	750 658	2.2
Newfoundland and Labrador	510 805	1.5
Prince Edward Island	141 232	0.4
Northwest Territories	43 281	0.1
Yukon	33 992	0.1
Nunavut	32 558	0.1
Canada	33 930 830	

Source: Adapted from Statistics Canada, *The Daily*, 11-001-XWE Thursday, March 25, 2010, http://www.statcan.gc.ca/daily-quotidien/100325/t100325a2-eng.htm (retrieved April 2, 2010).

and cultural core, containing the headquarters of CBC, CTV, Radio-Canada and private French-language television, the national newspapers, many Canadian cultural institutions, and much of the Canadian high-tech industry. Given such a concentration of population at the centre, the rest of the country, the "periphery" or "hinterland," regularly complains that it is overlooked by both public and private decision-makers.

Regions, Provinces, and Territories

In speaking of **regionalism** in Canada, then, we begin with great distances complicated by geographic barriers and concentrations of population that cause variations in political and economic power. In addition, it is partly because of such distances and divisions that the provinces and territories were created. The constitutional basis of such units is somewhat different from the natural, geographic basis of regions, however, and the fit between regionalism and provincialism is not perfect. Feelings of regionalism can exist within a province, such as in the northern parts of many provinces; regional sentiment can cut across provinces, as in the case of people in northwestern Ontario feeling psychologically closer to Manitoba than to southern Ontario; and provinces can be lumped into regions, such as the Maritimes or the Prairies. Nevertheless, as the 1979 Task Force on Canadian Unity pointed out, "the provinces ... are the basic building blocks of Canadian society and the logical units on which to focus a discussion of Canadian regionalism, even though they may not be the most 'natural' regions from an economic point of view."[2] It could be added that the creation of such provinces has served to enhance regional sentiment, as provincial politicians became exponents of regional problems and protectors of provincial interests.

In the 1990s, Quebec came closer than ever before to separating from the rest of Canada. If it were to leave with its existing borders intact (a somewhat debatable issue), Quebec would take with it almost one-quarter of the Canadian population, about 16 percent of the territory, and 20 percent of Canada's gross domestic product. From a strictly geographic point of view, the separation of Quebec would raise the question of continuing transportation links between Atlantic Canada and Ontario, border-crossing impediments, and jurisdiction over the St. Lawrence Seaway.

Regional Economic Cleavages

A discussion of the economies of the Canadian regions and provinces reveals striking regional economic differences that serve to reinforce their geographic distinctiveness and create another pattern of demands facing the Canadian political system.

Regional Economic Differences

Regional economic differences begin with primary industries or the natural resource base of the various provinces. The importance of natural resources to the national economy has been a central tenet of Canadian politics and economics for generations, usually termed the **staples theory** and identified with economic historian Harold Innis.[3] It postulates that Canadian economic development has relied on a succession of resource exports—furs, fish, timber, wheat, minerals, and energy—rather than manufacturing; Canadians are mere "hewers of wood and drawers of water."

Secondary industry consists of manufacturing, construction, and utilities, including electricity. Manufacturing includes the initial processing and refining of primary products as well as the making of finished goods. Generally speaking, the secondary sector produces more revenue and jobs than primary industry, is less seasonal, and commands higher wages. Primary and secondary industries are often combined as "goods-producing" industries.

Economists put transportation and communications, trade, finance, insurance and real estate, private services, and public administration into the "tertiary" or "services-producing" category. Manufacturing was never an important factor in the Canadian economy, and much political attention in this post-industrial era is focused on the services sector. The tertiary sector now furnishes about three-quarters of the employment in the country. With this background, let us highlight the economic differences among the various regions.

THE ATLANTIC PROVINCES

Historically, the Atlantic provinces had a distinctive and heavy reliance on fishing, especially in Newfoundland and Labrador. This industry fell into deep trouble in the 1990s, primarily due to a dramatic reduction in cod stocks; however, the abundance of shellfish has led to a partial recovery. The three Maritime provinces (New Brunswick, Nova Scotia, and Prince Edward Island) have a substantial agricultural base, while New Brunswick, Nova Scotia, and Newfoundland and Labrador also engage in forestry and mining, and there are great quantities of hydroelectric power in Labrador. Some processing and refining of natural resources takes place in the region, but the small local market and the distance from major population centres have left the region in a state of underdevelopment. Nevertheless, led by New Brunswick, a new emphasis on communications technology has revitalized the Atlantic provinces' economies to some extent, for in the modern technological world, physical distance is not the hindrance it was in the past. The Hibernia and other offshore oil projects have had a profound economic impact on Newfoundland and Labrador, as has the natural gas Sable Island Offshore Energy Project on Nova Scotia. The nickel mine at Voisey's Bay in Labrador should also provide badly needed income and employment.

QUEBEC

The Quebec economy is more diversified than that of the Atlantic region and it is somewhat more prosperous. Quebec's outstanding primary industries include farming in the St. Lawrence Lowlands and mining and forestry in the Canadian Shield.

The Shield is also traversed by numerous powerful rivers, making hydroelectricity Quebec's most valuable resource. Huge dams have been built on many of its rivers, including the controversial James Bay hydroelectric project. Electricity is the basis of Quebec's aluminum industry, as well as many other secondary industries. Quebec also stands out in the production of pulp and paper, especially newsprint, and is much stronger than the Atlantic region in the more sophisticated aspects of manufacturing, including aeronautics and pharmaceuticals. It also houses a large financial sector. The fact that economic power in Quebec used to rest largely in Anglo-Canadian and foreign hands fuelled the nationalist debate in that province. But since 1960 a major transformation has occurred, and both the public and francophone private sectors in Quebec have repatriated a great deal of economic power.

ONTARIO

Ontario historically had the most diversified and strongest economy of any region. The province has a great expanse of prime agricultural land in the south, as well as vast stretches of trees and almost every conceivable mineral in the Canadian Shield. Ontario's early development of hydroelectricity and of a steel industry gave it a head start over other regions. A skilled labour force, a large domestic market, proximity to the automobile industry in the United States, and the advantage of federal tariff and banking policies also helped to make it the manufacturing heartland of the country. This sector has weakened in recent years, however, and Ontario's dominance has also declined because it lacks the petroleum resources that are of increasing economic importance. But it continues to lead the country in the tertiary sector, especially finance.

THE PRAIRIE PROVINCES

The Prairie provinces are historically associated with agriculture, especially wheat, other grain, and livestock. Alberta doubles as Canada's petroleum province, now heavily dependent on the northern oil sands, and has become the richest part of the country by almost any measure. Petroleum is also of increasing significance in Saskatchewan, in concert with that province's other mineral resources, potash and uranium. Forestry is of some importance in Manitoba and Alberta, while Manitoba's hydroelectricity complements the petroleum of the other two Prairie provinces. The Prairies are also engaged in an increasing amount of manufacturing, as well as in finance, trade, and other service industries.

Supportive Alberta in abusive relationship with Ontario and Quebec
(Vance Rodewalt/Artizans.com)

BRITISH COLUMBIA

Mountainous British Columbia is the leading forestry province and also specializes in mining, especially of natural gas, copper, and coal. Several fertile river and lake valleys provide for farming, and B.C. also possesses a significant fishing industry. The mountains are the source of several large rivers that have been dammed for the production of hydroelectricity. Manufacturing is primarily related to the forestry, mining, and agricultural bases of the B.C. economy, and finance stands out among the services sector.

THE NORTH

The inhospitable climate, isolation, small and transient labour force, and poor transportation facilities conspire to retard economic development in the three northern territories. It is primarily mining that has inspired many southerners to venture north over the years. Northern Aboriginal peoples used to be self-sufficient in hunting, fishing, and trapping, activities that continue to occupy them to some extent, but their lives have been disrupted by the arrival of newcomers. Settlement of many Aboriginal land claims and increased autonomy from Ottawa should allow the Northern territories to better respond to local needs in the future. Tourism is on the increase, a Mackenzie Valley natural gas pipeline may be developed, and diamond mines are already making a difference.

Regional Economic Conflicts

As a result of such regional economic differences, the national government regularly faces demands to assist the economy of a single province, region, or industry. Such demands do not necessarily involve conflict between one region and another, and sometimes government responses to them are of general benefit. More often than not, however, demands from one region do conflict with those from another. Leaving aside Quebec, which will be examined in Chapter 3, the most common expression of such regional economic conflict has undoubtedly been between the Prairie and central regions. Since central Canada's regional interests have historically been persuasive with the federal government, the analysis is usually put in terms of the economic complaints of the West against the central core of the country.[4]

TRADITIONAL WESTERN ECONOMIC COMPLAINTS

The traditional complaints of Western Canada relate to natural resources, tariffs, and banking. For example, while the other provinces always had jurisdiction over their own natural resources, Ottawa decided to retain such control when Manitoba was created in 1870, as well as with Saskatchewan and Alberta in 1905. The logic of this discrimination was that the federal government (i.e., central Canada) should control such resources in the national interest, allowing Ottawa to guide the development of the West. The Prairie provinces fought vehemently against this discrimination and were finally successful in gaining control of their natural resources in 1930.

The West complained for generations that Canadian tariff policy was designed in the interests of Ontario at the expense of the Prairies. In the 1879 **National Policy**, John A. Macdonald saw the tariff as a means of promoting and protecting the industrial heartland of central Canada. Adding a tariff (an import tax) to the price of imported manufactured goods would raise their price above that of goods manufactured in Canada, allowing domestic goods to be sold more cheaply than imports. Ontario thus gained employment in producing tractors, for example, but Western Canadians felt that this was contrary to their interests. In the absence of such a tariff, they would have been able to buy cheaper tractors from the United States. The West demanded lower tariffs at every opportunity, and in the 1920s sent its own farmer representatives—the Progressive Party—to the House of Commons to fight on this front.

Canada deliberately developed a centralized branch banking system in an attempt to construct a sound, stable banking community that would avoid frequent local collapses. The result was a handful of large national banks with headquarters in Toronto or Montreal and local branches spread across the country. From a hinterland perspective, money deposited in the local branch of a national bank did not remain in the community to be lent out for local purposes but was sent to headquarters in central Canada to be used in the economic development of Ontario or Quebec. This was another reason for the farmers' revolt of the 1920s, and displeasure with the Canadian banking system had much to do with the rise of the Social Credit party in Alberta in the 1930s.

These policy areas can be put in a broader context called the metropolitan–hinterland thesis. It suggests that the West was created as a colony of central Canada and was intended to be held in a subordinate and dependent relationship.[5]

MODERN WESTERN ECONOMIC COMPLAINTS

Some of these traditional issues continue to rankle the West in different forms, and additional concerns have emerged in recent times. The conflict over natural resources re-emerged in the 1970s and 1980s, for example, especially with respect to petroleum pricing. After the OPEC (Organization of Petroleum Exporting Countries) cartel agreed on an artificial rise in the international price of oil in 1973, federal policy began to favour the consumer/manufacturing interest of central Canada at the expense of the producer interest of the West. The height of the regional economic conflict occurred in 1980 with the Trudeau government's **National Energy Program** (NEP), which imposed new federal taxes, kept the national price below the world level, encouraged frontier development, and promoted Canadianization of the industry, all objectives opposed by most Westerners. Eventually, a partial compromise between central and Western interests was reached in 1981, and the Mulroney government later scrapped the NEP entirely, but not before the program had had a profoundly isolating effect on the Western Canadian psyche.

Tariffs among all countries have gradually come down since 1945, but this issue took on a new life in the 1980s with the Western demand for a free trade agreement between Canada and the United States. By this time, business interests in central Canada also supported such a measure, and it was adopted to their mutual satisfaction.

Perhaps the most sensitive Western economic demand in the 21st century, at least from the Alberta perspective, is not to touch its petroleum industry, especially the development of the oil sands. This includes the threat of the imposition of federal environmental controls. Alberta was the leading opponent of the Kyoto Protocol and even though the oil sands are among the leading emitters of greenhouse gases, that province continues to resist restrictions that would hinder the incredible expansion of that industry.

OTHER ASPECTS OF REGIONAL ECONOMIC CONFLICTS

Many of the Western economic conflicts with central Canada have been echoed by the Atlantic provinces. Nova Scotia and New Brunswick entered Confederation in 1867 as proud and prosperous colonies, but their economies quickly declined. While changes in marine technology (from wooden sailing ships to steel steamships) were probably the principal factor responsible, Maritimers blamed federal economic policy for much of their difficulty. Post-Confederation tariff policy appeared to do the Maritimes more harm than good, and the Atlantic provinces fought for provincial ownership of offshore petroleum in the 1990s. They also complained that the federal government was not sufficiently aggressive when it came to protecting Atlantic fish stocks from foreign overfishing.

Smaller-scale regional economic disputes are also a routine occurrence in Canadian politics. Awarding the CF-18 maintenance contract to a company in Montreal infuriated supporters of a superior bid from a competitor in Winnipeg; extending drug patent protection for multinational pharmaceutical firms in Quebec offended Canadian generic drug producers in Ontario; and promoting frontier petroleum exploration (including federal assistance to Newfoundland's Hibernia project) upset conventional oil and gas producers in Alberta. Former Ontario premier Mike Harris complained that employment insurance premiums were too high, especially when Ontarians paid a large part of the premiums and residents of the five Eastern provinces collected a disproportionate amount of the payments.

Regional Economic Disparities

Conflicts between regions are exacerbated in Canada because of regional economic inequalities or disparities. Whatever the fault of federal policies, Canada's primary resources are not evenly distributed, the regions have different sizes and populations, they are located at variable distances from key export markets, and such markets affect them in particular ways.

Among the available ways to measure regional economic disparity is provincial gross domestic product (GDP), that is, the total value of all goods and services produced in a province. Because of great discrepancies in the size of provincial populations, it is more useful to divide each province's GDP by its population, giving the GDP per capita. A second measure of provincial disparities is per capita income, and a third is provincial unemployment rates. These measures are provided in Table 2.2, but have become quite divergent in recent years.

NEL

101

TABLE 2.2 PROVINCIAL GROSS DOMESTIC PRODUCT PER CAPITA (2008), PER CAPITA
INCOME (2008), AND UNEMPLOYMENT RATE (2009)

	GDP Per Capita ($)	Per Capita Income ($)	Unemployment Rate (Percent)
Newfoundland/Labrador	38 748	30 504	15.5
Prince Edward Island	29 950	28 963	12.0
Nova Scotia	31 312	31 938	9.2
New Brunswick	31 667	31 080	8.9
Quebec	34 657	33 406	8.5
Ontario	41 305	37 309	9.0
Manitoba	35 310	33 329	5.2
Saskatchewan	40 923	35 400	4.8
Alberta	52 168	48 110	6.6
British Columbia	37 466	36 457	7.6

Source: Adapted by author from Statistics Canada. Data, "Gross Domestic Product, Expenditure-Based, by Province and Territory," http://www40.statcan.ca/101/cst01/econ15-eng.htm, divided by 2008 provincial population; CANSIM, "Personal Income per Person," Table 384-0013; and "Labour Force, Employed and Unemployed, Numbers and Rates, by Province," http://www40.statcan.ca/101/cst01/labor07a-eng.htm, retrieved April 2, 2010.

In addition to developing national social programs and assisting various industries in a general way, successive federal governments have focused on two principal means to deal with the specific question of regional economic disparities. One is to give federal funding to have-not provincial governments, and the other is to provide grants to individual firms in designated have-not regions of the country.

EQUALIZATION PAYMENTS

In 1957, Ottawa finally responded to repeated demands to make **equalization payments** to have-not provinces. These payments are funded by various federal taxes levied in all provinces, but the revenue comes disproportionately from Ontario and Alberta. These annual cash grants to the have-not provinces are designed to allow them to raise their services to an acceptable national level but can be spent for any purpose. In other words, they are unconditional grants with no strings attached. The sums involved are quite impressive, as Table 2.3 reveals. For

TABLE 2.3 EQUALIZATION PAYMENTS, 2010–11

Quebec	$8 552 000 000
Manitoba	$1 826 000 000
New Brunswick	$1 581 000 000
Nova Scotia	$1 110 000 000
Ontario	$972 000 000
Prince Edward Island	$330 000 000
Total	$14 372 000 000

Source: Adapted from Department of Finance Canada, "Major transfers to provinces and territories, 2010–11" http://www.fin.gc.ca/fedprov/mtpt-ptfp10-eng.asp. Reproduced with the permission of the Minister of Public Works and Government Services, 2010.

several years, Newfoundland and Labrador and Nova Scotia complained, however, that when they took in additional natural resource revenues, they experienced a proportional decrease in their equalization payments. This issue caused a major conflict with the federal government, and the Martin and Harper governments responded with adjustments to the Equalization program. In fact, the 2007 budget was supposed to end the "fiscal imbalance" between the federal and provincial governments for all time. Two startling but contrary developments occurred as of 2009: Newfoundland and Labrador no longer qualified for equalization payments, while Ontario began to qualify. British Columbia and Saskatchewan joined Alberta as the other three have-provinces.

REGIONAL ECONOMIC DEVELOPMENT PROGRAMS

The second means of trying to reduce regional economic disparities is to establish federal regional economic development programs. The basic thrust of these programs is to designate those parts of the country that are in need of economic assistance, and then to provide grants to firms that would locate or expand existing operations in such areas. Some grants also go to provinces or municipalities in order to provide the basic infrastructure that might attract industry, such as highways, water and sewage systems, and industrial parks. Several separate regional economic development agencies now exist, principally the Atlantic Canada Opportunities Agency (ACOA), Federal Economic Development Initiative for Northern Ontario (FedNor), the new Southern Ontario Development Agency, Western Economic Diversification Canada (WD), and Canada Economic Development for Quebec Regions (CED).

What Do You Think?

To what extent should richer provinces share their wealth with poorer provinces, especially through the mechanism of federal equalization payments? To what extent do Quebec's superior social programs depend on contributions from other provinces?

Regional Identities

Many of the economic factors discussed above, reinforced by geography, have given rise to regional or provincial identities, a subject that was touched upon earlier. But there are also non-economic factors involved in such identities. In 1980, for example, **Western alienation** was defined as follows:

> A regionally distinct political culture through and within which are expressed economic discontent, the rejection of a semi-colonial status within the Canadian state, antipathy towards Quebec and French-Canadian influence within the national government, the irritation of the West's partisan weakness within a succession of Liberal national governments, and the demand from provincial political elites for greater jurisdictional autonomy.[6]

After it defeated the Liberals in 1984, the Mulroney Conservative government also gave priority to Quebec, leading to the formation of the Reform Party, whose initial slogan was "The West Wants In." The Reform Party won the majority of seats west of Ontario in the 1993 and 1997 elections, including almost all of the seats in British Columbia and Alberta. In 2000, the party changed its leader and name (to the Canadian Alliance) in an effort to become more appealing to the rest of the country. In 2003, it reabsorbed the Progressive Conservative Party and adopted another new name, but it retained its Alberta-based leader, Stephen Harper. Table 2.4 illustrates the regional support of the various political parties in the 2008 federal election and shows that the new Conservative Party of Canada continued to have a predominant Western base. On the other hand, the Harper government was at least as concerned as any party in power in the past 50 years to increase its representation in Quebec, risking the emergence of a new round of western alienation.

TABLE 2.4 REGIONAL DISTRIBUTION OF POPULAR VOTE BY PARTY, 2008 ELECTION (PERCENTAGES)

	Atlantic	Quebec	Ontario	West	North
Conservatives	29.6	21.7	39.2	52.4	35.1
Liberals	35.0	23.7	33.8	16.3	29.7
NDP	26.1	12.1	18.2	21.5	25.4
Bloc Québécois	—	38.1	—	—	—

Source: Elections Canada. Calculations by author.

What are other distinctive, non-economic elements of the Western regional identity? Given their relative prosperity, many Western Canadians tend to prefer individual self-reliance over collective, public solutions to demands being made. Since the principle of representation by population gives central Canada a majority of votes in the House of Commons, Westerners often propose to decentralize the federal system or to give the Senate more power to protect regional interests. Albertans generally take the most extreme positions on such issues as opposition to liberal interpretations of the Charter of Rights and Freedoms and to the requirement in the Canada Health Act that publicly funded health services be provided in the public sector. The Alberta government also wants a scaled-down gun registry and a role for provinces in international agreements that affect provincial jurisdiction. Other outlying regions in Canada feel isolated and discriminated against, too, sentiments that lead to regional identities in the Atlantic provinces and the North. Given the federal obsession with Quebec and a deteriorating economy, a distinctive Ontario identity may also be developing.

Class Cleavages

Let us turn from economic disparities based on geography to inequalities in individual incomes, wealth, and power, that is, to class cleavages. The concept of class is not as clear-cut as that of region, and Canadians are generally more aware of their regional and ethnic identities. In fact, because of such other divisions, class may not be as important a generator of political activity in Canada as it is in most countries. We do have significant class divisions but lack a strong consciousness of class and class conflict. This part of the chapter will begin by discussing various definitions and measurements of class, and will then examine the political role of the different classes.

Defining and Measuring Class

When dealing with the concept of class, it is customary to start with Karl Marx, who predicted that every capitalist economy would produce a class system consisting primarily of the bourgeoisie, the owners of the means of production, and the proletariat, the workers. Owners of the "means of production" are those who own mines, factories, banks, and other businesses. The proletariat would sell their labour for a price; the bourgeoisie would pay them as little as possible (and less than they were worth), thereby accumulating profit or surplus value. While religion and the prospect of a pleasant afterlife might keep them content for a while, the workers would come to resent their low wages and state of exploitation and eventually engage in a violent revolt.

Some social scientists continue to provide a neo-Marxist analysis of class cleavages in society, making provision for a new middle class as well. But others divide individuals and families into the upper, middle, and working classes primarily based on income. When such a measure is used, the divisions between the classes are less clear-cut than in Marxist analysis.

One means of measuring income inequality is to divide the population into five equal groups, or quintiles, from highest to lowest income, and to indicate the share of total income received by each group. Figure 2.2 presents such proportions for the year 2006. It also shows that the income shares before social program transfers (such as employment insurance and social assistance) were dramatically inequitable, and that the tax system takes only a little away from the rich to redistribute to the poor. Thus, even after taxes and transfers, the highest-earning 20 percent of the population still receive 44 percent of the total income, while the lowest 20 percent receive just five percent.

One of the problems in using the concept of class is the distinction between "objective" and "subjective" class. Objective class refers to the class into which analysts place a person, according to criteria such as type of work or level of income, while subjective class means the class to which people think or feel they belong, even if it contradicts objective standards. Many people who consider themselves to be middle-class would be categorized as working class by social scientists. Behaving as if they belonged to a different class than they really do, such people could be said to be lacking in **class-consciousness**, something that Marx also foresaw and called

Figure 2.2 **Income Shares of Quintiles: Market Income, Total Income (Income after Transfers and before Tax), and Income after Tax, 2006**

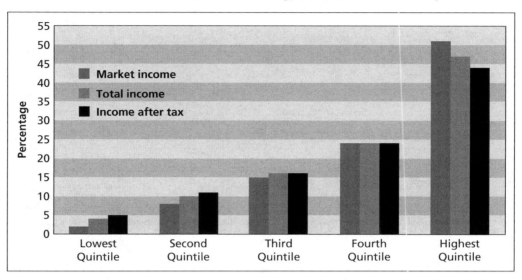

Source: Adapted from Statistics Canada, "Income in Canada, 2006," Catalogue 75-202-XTE 20060000 2006. Released May 5, 2008. http://www.statcan.gc.ca/pub/75-202-x200600-eng.htm

"false consciousness." This factor reduces the significance of class in motivating political activity.

The Upper Class and Corporate Elite

Canada is home to many fabulously rich entrepreneurs and some of the wealthiest families on earth. At the top of the 2009 edition of the *Canadian Business* "Rich 100" list, which included 55 Canadian billionaires, were the Thomson family, at $22 billion; the Irving family, at $7.3 billion; Galen Weston, at $6.5 billion; Jimmy Pattison, at $5 billion; the Rogers family, at $4.7 billion; and Paul Desmarais, at $4.3 billion.[7] The Thomson family now specializes in electronic databases and media companies; the Irving family owns most of New Brunswick, including large tracts of woodlands, pulp mills, oil refineries, gas stations, trucking firms, bus lines, railways, potato operations, and all the English-language daily newspapers in the province; and Galen Weston is the proprietor of Loblaws, Holt Renfrew, and Weston Bakeries. Jimmy Pattison owns a wide variety of companies centred in British Columbia; the Rogers family owns the vast Rogers Communications empire; and Paul Desmarais' holdings include Power Corp., Investors Group, and Great-West Life.

Another category of wealthy Canadians comprises the corporate chief executive officers who do not necessarily own their firms. According to the Canadian Centre for Policy Alternatives, the total average compensation of the top 100 CEOs in Canada in 2007—for one year alone—was over $10 million, which includes the value of salary, bonus, incentives, shares, stock options, and other benefits. This figure compared to $17 739 for the full year earnings of a person working at the average minimum wage, and $40 237 for the full year earnings at the average wage and salary in Canada.[8]

The general lines of the public policy demands of the upper class and corporate elite are easily drawn. Essentially, they want to be left alone; they prefer to minimize the role of government and have society rely more extensively on private market forces. They want to cut government spending on social programs so that their taxes can be minimized, balance the annual government budget, and reduce the accumulated national debt. If taxes are necessary, they want governments to avoid corporate and progressive individual taxes as much as possible and to provide generous loopholes, write-offs, and tax shelters. Their goal is to minimize government regulation, including labour standards and environmental protection.

Governments have normally been only too happy to respond to such demands. The Canadian state gives priority to big-business demands in the first place because it depends on the private sector to create jobs. Politicians are especially sensitive to a corporate threat to move to a country with more favourable policies. Second, corporate executives and politicians often come from the same ranks, including prime ministers and ministers of finance. Brian Mulroney and Paul Martin provide perfect examples. Third, companies have many avenues of influence available: making a direct, personal pitch for favourable decisions, using professional lobby firms to help them contact public decision-makers for a fee, and taking advantage of their membership in pressure groups. Among the hundreds of business groups in existence, the **Canadian Council of Chief Executives** is probably most powerful, representing the chief executive officers of the 150 largest firms in the country. Fourth, the corporate elite also control the mass media to a large extent and can use them to foster self-serving attitudes among authorities and the public. Finally, throughout their history, both the Conservative and Liberal parties were financed primarily by large corporate contributions. Such donations guaranteed access to decision-makers, if not specific favours, and it was not difficult to establish a link between corporate contributions and general public policy. As a result of actions taken by the Chrétien and Harper governments, however, corporations can no longer donate money to political parties and candidates.

The progressive nature of the personal income tax was reduced when the Mulroney government reduced ten tax brackets to three, and capital gains continue to be taxed at a lower rate than other forms of income. In her book *Behind Closed Doors*, Linda McQuaig shows how the rich use their political influence to obtain tax breaks that are paid for by those with lesser incomes.[9] Personal and corporate income taxes are riddled with loopholes, and Canada is one of the few countries in the world without a tax on wealth or inheritance, but the Harper government slashed corporate taxes. Beyond the recent moves toward deregulation, the various free trade agreements represent a commitment on the part of governments not to restrict the operations of corporations. Moreover, for a fee of $500 000, a corporation could send its CEO to address the national leaders at the Summit of the Americas in Quebec City in April 2001, while anti-globalization protesters were kept outside by a high fence and tear gas. And the reluctance of governments to enact effective measures to deal with climate change can be primarily explained by the opposition of large corporations, making the environment an issue related to class.

What Do You Think?

Do the economic elite—corporate owners and CEOs—owe their wealth and power to their own effort, creativity, and intelligence? Or have they largely inherited their wealth or gained it through exploiting their workers, deceiving consumers, and manipulating the political system—the tax laws, the labour laws, the environmental laws, etc.? Why don't more people see the political system in class terms?

Three principal exceptions to this corporate pressure to minimize the role of government must be noted. First, while the economic elite demands that government minimize spending on others, it often expects sizable chunks of public funds for itself, such as in government contracts and grants. Even after 25 years of primary reliance on free market forces, the Canadian government continues to give generous financial assistance to some of the largest companies in the country. A second exception is the rare occasion on which the economic elite actually favours new social programs. Such programs tend to increase the purchasing power of lower-income people, reduce the amounts that companies themselves have to pay in employee benefits, and ensure the basic stability of society so that upper classes do not have to worry about violent protests from the poor or unemployed. Third, business leaders expect government to provide such basics as roads, railways, and electricity that decrease their costs or increase their profits. Despite the overwhelming tendency of governments to respond to demands from the corporate elite, however, it should not be forgotten that politicians ultimately get elected by voters, the great majority of whom belong to other classes. Thus, other classes can influence events to some extent, but only if they act as a class.[10]

The Middle Class

On a subjective basis, a majority of Canadians probably think that they belong to the middle class. Academic analysts challenge this view, although they do agree that there is a large middle class in a modern society. They often divide the middle class between the upper middle class and the new middle class, the former being made up of small-business people, self-employed professionals (e.g., lawyers and doctors), and affluent farmers. The **new middle class** incorporates middle managers (who take orders from the corporate elite and give them to the working class), civil servants, teachers, nurses, and other salaried professionals. While the middle class is far from being a unified force, its members are normally well educated and receive above-average levels of income. Their main assets are their homes, their cars, and assorted other material possessions. While members enjoy such tax shelters as RRSPs, the middle class often claims that it pays a disproportionate amount of the taxes to finance government programs of all kinds. On the other hand, such groups as teachers and nurses increasingly feel that they are being treated by governments as if they belonged to the working class, and the proportion of the new middle class that belongs to public sector unions is constantly increasing.

The Working Class

The working class is generally identified as doing manual or routine work. Members of the working class are typically engaged in resource exploitation, assembly line production, secretarial and clerical work, sales, and a variety of crafts and trades.

Less affluent farmers might also be included. Some academic analysts put the bulk of the population into this category, even though many who are so labelled identify subjectively with the middle class. Normally lacking postsecondary education, members of the working class usually receive less income than those in the middle class.

Karl Marx's predictions of a violent proletarian revolt were dealt a blow when governments unexpectedly legalized trade unions and extended the franchise to the working class. Nevertheless, most governments and companies have been hostile toward the formation of labour unions, and Canada has experienced a large number of violent strikes, either over the formation of a union or over its subsequent demands. Among the key labour struggles in Canadian history were the 1919 Winnipeg General Strike, the 1937 General Motors Strike in Oshawa, the 1945 Ford Strike in Windsor, the 1949 Asbestos Strike in Quebec, and the woodworkers' strike in Newfoundland in 1959.[11] While legislation dealing with conciliation, mediation, arbitration, picketing, labour standards, occupational health and safety, and compensation for injury on the job is ostensibly passed to protect the working class, governments usually avoid offending their own corporate supporters in the design or implementation of labour laws.

Others things being equal, it is in the interests of members of the working class to belong to a trade union. Unionized employees usually have higher wages, more adequate benefits, better working conditions, and more protection against arbitrary dismissal than those who do not engage in collective bargaining. For example, unionized workers are much more likely to have private medical, dental, life, and disability insurance, as well as pension coverage. In spite of these advantages, the rate of unionization in Canada is very low (except in comparison to the United States) and is in decline. Total union membership in 2009 was 4.2 million, or about 30 percent of the paid workers in the country.[12]

Moreover, the number of blue-collar jobs is falling in such areas as resource industries, construction, and manufacturing, where unionization used to be most common. New jobs in the post-industrial society are found largely in sales and services, especially in the private sector, where workers are traditionally part-time, poorly paid, and hard to organize. Lacking a union, and given the nature of their job, those in sales and service occupations are not as likely to be class-conscious or to develop social democratic values as those who produce goods.

The composition of the unionized workforce is also changing in other ways. Once comprising primarily private sector, male, manual workers, it is increasingly composed of public sector unions, and over 50 percent of union members in Canada are now women. While only about 16 percent of private sector employees are unionized, the rate rises to 71 percent in the public sector. Indeed, public sector unions make up three of the seven largest unions in the country: the Canadian Union of Public Employees, the National Union of Public and General Employees, and the Public Service Alliance, along with the Canadian Auto Workers, the United Steelworkers of America, the United Food and Commercial Workers, and the Communications, Energy and Paperworkers Union.[13]

Given that most labour legislation is passed at the provincial level, the principal federal measure is the Employment Insurance (EI) Act. This program, originally called Unemployment Insurance, was introduced in 1941 to tide workers over between jobs. Given the high national unemployment rates in many years since, and the even higher rates in certain regions in every year, it is relied upon much more heavily than was originally anticipated. With such large numbers of workers drawing on the fund, it became a vital source of both individual and regional income, although governments repeatedly restricted its coverage in the 1980s and 1990s. The Chrétien and Martin governments siphoned off the significant surplus in the EI account to pay down the national debt and then loosened up the program, especially for Atlantic Canada, just prior to the 2000 and 2004 elections. Not surprisingly, the deficiencies in the EI program raised much controversy in the Great Recession of 2008–09.

Health care has become a serious problem on both federal and provincial political agendas. The rich can afford to take care of themselves, but public health care is a priority for many in the middle and working classes, to say nothing of the poor. The Canada Health Act requires that public institutions provide all basic medical care, so that public funds do not end up in profit-oriented firms. The Act also purports to prohibit two-tier health care in which those who can afford it can obtain faster care than those without such resources. The extent to which for-profit and two-tier health services are allowed has become a major class-based issue in modern times.

The **Canadian Labour Congress** (CLC) is the main lobbying body for over three million workers. The CLC is thus one of the largest pressure groups in the country and represents a significant number of voters. Its influence is diminished, however, by its outsider status in Ottawa, as well as by the fact that not all unions belong to it. The historic factionalism within the Canadian union movement has also hindered the cause of the working class.[14] Governments are often justified in assuming that a gap exists between labour leaders and rank-and-file members with respect to policy positions and party support. Union leaders often support the NDP, while large numbers of rank-and-file members vote for each of the other major parties.

NEL

Couple living in car hope to use home renovation tax credit
(Sue Dewar/Artizans.com)

The Poor

The poor can be defined as those living below the **poverty line**. The most widely accepted definition of poverty in Canada is the low-income cut-off provided annually by Statistics Canada. According to this measure, any individual or family that spends more than 64 percent of its income on food, clothing, and shelter is living in poverty (given that the average family spends 44 percent of its income on these three necessities). By this definition, Canada has over four million residents living in poverty, or about 15 percent of the population. Although these figures represent a decline since 1969, a large proportion of these people live far below the poverty line, and these figures do not include the large group of near-poor that exists just above it. Moreover, the gap between those with the lowest and highest incomes widened significantly between 1984 and 2005.[15]

Probably the most heartbreaking and most intractable aspect of poverty is that it includes about a million children. The high-school dropout rate among children from poor families is much higher than that of others, and the tie between low income and low education is self-perpetuating. *The Canadian Fact Book on Poverty* documents how children from low-income families stand out from their better-off peers:

> *They are less healthy, have less access to skill-building activities, have more destructive habits and behaviours, live more stressful lives, and are subject to more humiliation. In short, they have less stable and less secure existences and as a result they are likely to be less secure as adults.*[16]

Many poor people work full-time, and others part-time; in fact, the poor can be about equally divided between those who work and those who are unemployed or unemployable. The working poor try to scrape by on the minimum wage or on more than one low-paying job, but they are sometimes better off if they go on social assistance. Rather than raising the minimum wage, however, some provincial governments actually reduced welfare benefits in the last half of the 1990s, and only Quebec provided an adequate daycare program. From about 1995 to 2004, the most common government action was to cut taxes, even at the expense of social programs. The Centre for Social Justice points out that people living in poverty have no taxable income and so tax cuts are of no benefit to them; tax cuts merely create larger income disparities.[17]

As indicated earlier, improvement in the economy after 1995 resulted in a decline in the proportion of people living below the poverty line. Unfortunately, that decline came to an abrupt end with the worldwide economic meltdown at the end of 2008. Among the ideas for improving the lot of the poor are

- raising the federal minimum wage (partly as a model for the provinces and territories);
- restoring eligibility for Employment Insurance to earlier periods;
- creating an effective child benefit system that provides enough income support to keep parents out of poverty;
- building a universally accessible system of early child education and child care;
- expanding affordable housing to end homelessness; and
- renewing the national social safety net through the new Canada Social Transfer, with increased federal funding.[18]

One of the great weaknesses of the poor in the political system is that they are generally unorganized and collectively inarticulate. They lack the skills to organize effectively as advocacy groups, primarily because they are without the education, money, and time to develop such skills. Because of their low voter turnout rate, they tend to be ignored by both federal and provincial governments. Nevertheless, several groups and think tanks exist to research the poverty problem and to speak for the poor in the cacophony of the political process: the Canadian Council on Social Development, the National Council of Welfare, the National Anti-Poverty Organization, the Centre for Social Justice, the Caledon Institute of Social Policy, the Canadian Centre for Policy Alternatives, and Campaign 2000. Still, no one should expect any degree of equality in the struggle among interest groups representing different classes.

SUMMARY

The first part of the chapter deals with the political significance of geography and the economy. It begins by showing how distance, division, and the distribution of population have given rise to demands on the political system and influenced the nature of its responses, and notes the imperfect relationship between regions and provinces. The next section provides an overview of the economic differences among the various regions, especially between the West and the centre, both historically and in contemporary times. It presented statistics on measures of regional economic disparities, identified policies adopted to reduce them, and raised the question of regional identities such as Western alienation in economic and non-economic terms. The second part of the chapter discusses class cleavages, beginning with various definitions of class and the general lack of class-consciousness in Canada. It then lists the typical demands made by each of the main classes, along with the typical government responses. The chapter concludes with a discussion of poverty in Canada—who and how many are poor and what policies have been or could be adopted to improve the lot of poor Canadians.

DISCUSSION QUESTIONS

1. What should be the role of the federal government in overcoming Canada's great distances and divisions? To what extent can the private sector fulfill this function?
2. Are you conscious of living in a particular region, and if so, what regional and provincial complaints do you have about federal policies?
3. What, if anything, can be done to lessen the problem of regional economic disparities?
4. Why is union membership among the working class not higher? Why is class-consciousness in Canada relatively low?
5. Should Canada make a more concerted effort to reduce poverty? If so, how?

KEY TERMS

Canadian Council of Chief Executives The most powerful peak business pressure group in Canada, representing the 150 largest firms in the country.

Canadian Labour Congress The largest labour pressure group in Canada; the political voice of over three million members.

Class-consciousness An awareness of the social class to which one belongs.

Equalization payments Large annual cash payments made by the federal government to have-not provinces to help them provide a satisfactory level of public services.

National Energy Program The 1980 policy associated with Pierre Trudeau designed to skim off petroleum tax revenue for Ottawa, keep the price of petroleum below world levels, encourage conservation, and Canadianize the industry, which met with great opposition in Western Canada.

National Policy The broad nation-building 1879 policy of John A. Macdonald that included tariff protection for central Canadian manufacturing, massive immigration, and the construction of a national transportation system.

New middle class A term from class analysis describing salaried professionals such as teachers, public servants, and nurses.

Poverty line An amount of income such that anyone who received less would be living in poverty.

Regionalism Strong feelings of attachment to the region or province where one lives that often generate political activity.

Staples theory The notion that Canadian economic development has gone through a series of stages based on the exploitation of one natural resource or another and the export of such resources, without the development of a secondary or manufacturing sector.

Western alienation The feeling shared by many Western Canadians that their interests are not taken seriously in the national policymaking process.

FURTHER READING

Abella, Irving, ed. *On Strike*. Toronto: James Lewis & Samuel, 1974.

Braid, Don, and Sydney Sharpe. *Breakup: Why the West Feels Left Out of Canada*. Toronto: Key Porter Books, 1990.

Brownlee, Jamie. *Ruling Canada: Corporate Cohesion and Democracy*. Black Point, N.S.: Fernwood Publishing, 2005.

Gibbins, Roger, and Loleen Berdahl. *Western Visions, Western Futures*. Peterborough: Broadview Press, 2003.

Hale, Geoffrey. *The Uneasy Partnership: Politics of Business and Government in Canada*. Peterborough: Broadview Press, 2006.

Kerstetter, Steven. *Rags and Riches: Wealth Inequality in Canada*. Ottawa: Canadian Centre for Policy Alternatives, 2002.

McQuaig, Linda. *Shooting the Hippo: Death by Deficit and Other Canadian Myths.* Toronto: Viking, 1995.

Osberg, Lars. *A Quarter Century of Economic Inequality in Canada: 1981–2006.* Ottawa: Canadian Centre for Policy Alternatives, April 2008.

Savoie, Donald J. *Visiting Grandchildren: Economic Development in the Maritimes.* Toronto: University of Toronto Press, 2006.

Young, Lisa, and Keith Archer, eds. *Regionalism and Party Politics in Canada.* Toronto: Oxford University Press, 2002.

Chapter 5:
Sociology: Origins and Theory

CHAPTER

1

A Sociological Compass

In this chapter, you will learn that

- The causes of human behaviour lie mostly in the patterns of social relations that surround and permeate us.

- Sociology is the systematic study of human behaviour in the social context.

- Sociologists examine the connection between social relations and personal troubles.

- Sociologists are often motivated to do research by the desire to improve people's lives. At the same time, sociologists use scientific methods to test their ideas.

- Sociology originated during the Industrial Revolution. The founders of sociology diagnosed the massive social transformations of their day. They also suggested ways of overcoming the social problems created by the Industrial Revolution.

- Today's Postindustrial Revolution similarly challenges us. Sociology clarifies the scope, direction, and significance of social change. It also suggests ways of dealing with the social problems created by the Postindustrial Revolution.

- At the personal level, sociology can help to clarify the opportunities and constraints we all face. It suggests what each of us can become in today's social and historical context.

NEL

122

INTRODUCTION

Why You Need a Compass for a New World

"When I was a child, a cleaning lady came to our house twice a month," Robert Brym recalls. "Her name was Lena White, and she was what we then called an 'Indian.' I was fond of Lena because she possessed two apparently magical powers. First, she could let the ash at the end of her cigarette grow five centimetres before it fell off. I sometimes used to play where Lena was working just to see how long she could scrub, vacuum, climb the stepladder, and chatter before the ash made its inevitable descent to the floor. Second, Lena could tell stories. My mother would serve us lunch at the kitchen table. During dessert, as we sipped tea with milk, Lena would spin tales about Gluskap, the Creator of the world.

"I liked Gluskap because he was mischievous and enormously powerful. He fought giants, drove away monsters, taught people how to hunt and farm, and named the stars. But he also got into trouble and learned from his mistakes. For example, one day the wind was blowing so hard Gluskap couldn't paddle his canoe into the bay to hunt ducks. So he found the source of the wind: the flapping wings of the Wind Eagle. He then tricked the Wind Eagle into getting stuck in a crevice where he could flap no more. Now Gluskap could go hunting. However, the air soon grew so hot he found it difficult to breathe. The water became dirty and began to smell bad, and there was so much foam on it he found it hard to paddle. When he complained to his grandmother, she explained that the wind was needed to cool the air, wash the earth, and move the waters to keep them clean. And so Gluskap freed the Wind Eagle and the winds returned to the earth. Gluskap decided it was better to wait for good weather and then go duck hunting, rather than to conquer the winds.

"Like the tale of the Wind Eagle, many of the Gluskap stories Lena told me were about the need for harmony among humans and between humans and nature. You can imagine my surprise, therefore, when I got to school and learned about the European exploration of what was called the New World. My teachers taught me all about the glories of the *conquest* of nature—and of other people. I learned that in the New World, a Native population perhaps a hundredth as large as Europe's occupied a territory more than four times larger. I was taught that the New World was unimaginably rich in resources. European rulers saw that by controlling it they could increase their power and importance. Christians recognized new possibilities for spreading their religion. Explorers discerned fresh opportunities for rewarding adventures. A wave of excitement swelled as word spread of the New World's vast potential and challenges. I, too, became excited as I heard stories of conquest quite unlike the tales of Gluskap. Of course, I learned little about the violence required to conquer the New World."

In the 1950s I was caught between thrilling stories of conquest and reflective stories that questioned the wisdom of conquest. Today, I think many people are in a similar position. On the one hand, we feel like the European explorers because we, too, have reached the frontiers of a New World. Like them, we are full of anticipation. Our New World is one of instant long-distance communication, global economies and cultures, weakening nation-states, and technological advances that often make the daily news seem like reports from a distant planet. In a fundamental way, the world is not the same place it was just 50 years ago. Orbiting telescopes that peer to the fringes of the universe, human genetic code laid bare like a road map, fibre optic cable that carries a trillion bits of information per second, and spacecraft that transport robots to Mars help to make this a New World.

On the other hand, we understand that not all is hope and bright horizons. Our anticipation is mixed with dread. Gluskap stories make more sense than ever. Scientific breakthroughs are announced almost daily, but the global environment has never been in worse shape and AIDS is now the leading cause of death in Africa. Marriages and nations unexpectedly break up and then reconstitute themselves in new and unanticipated forms. We celebrate the advances made by women and minority groups only to find that some people oppose their progress, sometimes violently. Waves of people migrate between continents, establishing cooperation but also conflict between previously separated groups. New technologies make work more interesting and creative for some, offering unprecedented opportunities to become rich and famous. They also make jobs more onerous and routine for others. The standard of living goes up for many people but stagnates for many more.

Amid all this contradictory news, good and bad, uncertainty about the future prevails. That is why my colleagues and I wrote this book. We set out to show undergraduates that sociology can help them make sense of their lives, however uncertain they may appear to be. Five hundred years ago, the early European explorers of North and South America set themselves the task of mapping the contours of the New World. We set ourselves a similar task here. Their frontiers were physical; ours are social. Their maps were geographical; ours are sociological. But in terms of functionality, our maps are much like theirs. All maps allow us to find our place in the world and see ourselves in the context of larger forces. *Sociological* maps, as the famous American sociologist C. Wright Mills wrote, allow us to "grasp the interplay of [people] and society, of biography and history" (Mills, 1959: 4). This book, then, shows you how to draw sociological maps so you can see your place in the world, figure out how to navigate through it, and perhaps discover how to improve it. It is your sociological compass.

We emphasize that sociology can be a liberating practical activity, not just an abstract intellectual exercise. By revealing the opportunities and constraints you face, sociology can help teach you who you are and what you can become in today's social and historical context. We cannot know what the future will bring, but we can at least know the choices we confront and the likely consequences of our actions. From this point of view, sociology can help us create the best possible future. That has always been sociology's principal justification, and so it should be today.

The Goals of This Chapter

This chapter has three goals:

1. The first goal is to illustrate the power of sociology to dispel foggy assumptions and help us see the operation of the social world more clearly. To that end, we examine a phenomenon that at first glance appears to be solely the outcome of breakdowns in *individual* functioning: suicide. We show that, in fact, *social* relations powerfully influence suicide rates. This exercise introduces you to what is unique about the sociological perspective.
2. The chapter's second goal is to show that, from its origins, sociological research has been motivated by a desire to improve the social world. Thus, sociology is not just a dry, academic exercise but also a means of charting a better course for society. At the same time, however, sociologists use scientific methods to test their ideas, thus increasing the validity of the results. We illustrate these points by briefly analyzing the work of the founders of the discipline.
3. The chapter's third goal is to suggest that sociology can help you come to grips with your century, just as it helped the founders of sociology deal with theirs. Today we are witnessing massive and disorienting social changes. As was the case a hundred years ago, sociologists now try to understand social phenomena and suggest credible ways of improving society. By promising to make sociology relevant to you, this chapter is an open invitation to participate in sociology's challenge.

NEL

Before showing how sociology can help you understand and improve your world, we briefly examine the problem of suicide. That examination will help illustrate how the sociological perspective can clarify and sometimes overturn common-sense beliefs.

THE SOCIOLOGICAL PERSPECTIVE

Analyzing suicide sociologically tests the claim that sociology takes a unique, surprising, and enlightening perspective on social events. After all, suicide appears to be a supremely antisocial and non-social act. First, it is condemned by nearly everyone in society. Second, it is typically committed in private, far from the public's intrusive glare. Third, it is comparatively rare: In 2004, there were about 11 suicides for every 100 000 people in Canada (compared with the world average of about 16 suicides per 100 000 people; see Figure 1.1). And, finally, when you think about why people commit such acts, you are likely to focus on their individual states of mind rather than on the state of society. In other words, we are usually interested in the aspects of specific individuals' lives that caused them to become depressed or angry enough to do something as awful as killing themselves. We do not usually think about the patterns of social relations that might encourage or inhibit such actions in general. If sociology can reveal the hidden social causes of such an apparently non-social and antisocial phenomenon, there must be something to it!

The Sociological Explanation of Suicide

At the end of the nineteenth century, Émile Durkheim (1951 [1897]) demonstrated that suicide is more than just an individual act of desperation that results from a psychological disorder, as was commonly believed at the time. Suicide rates, Durkheim showed, are strongly influenced by social forces.

Durkheim made his case by examining the association between rates of suicide and rates of psychological disorder for different groups. The idea that psychological disorder causes suicide is supported, he reasoned, only if suicide rates tend to be high where rates of psychological disorder are high, and

Alex Colville's *Pacific* (1967)

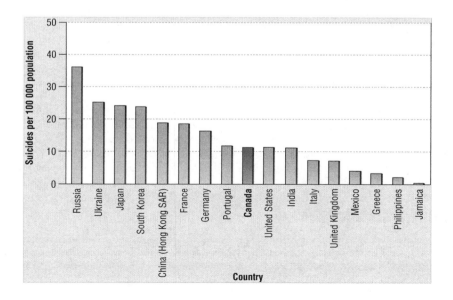

FIGURE 1.1

Suicide Rates, Selected Countries, circa 2004

Source: Rates were calculated based on data from World Health Organization, 2007, "Suicide Rates per 100,000 by Country, Year, and Sex (Table), Most Recent Year Available as of 2007." Retrieved January 3, 2008 (http://www.who.int/mental_health/prevention/suicide_rates/en/index.html).

FIGURE 1.2

Durkheim's Theory of Suicide

Durkheim argued that the suicide rate declines and then rises as social solidarity increases.

Durkheim called suicide in high-solidarity settings *altruistic*. Soldiers knowingly giving up their lives to protect comrades commit altruistic suicide. Suicide in low-solidarity settings is *egoistic* or *anomic*. *Egoistic suicide* results from the poor integration of people into society because of weak social ties to others. Someone who is unemployed is more likely to commit suicide than someone who is employed because the unemployed person has weaker social ties. *Anomic suicide* occurs when vague norms govern behaviour. The rate of anomic suicide is likely to be high among people living in a society lacking a widely shared code of morality.

Social solidarity refers to (1) the degree to which group members share beliefs and values, and (2) the intensity and frequency of their interaction.

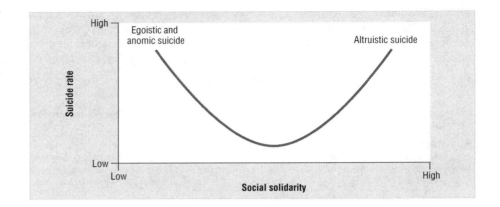

low where rates of psychological disorder are low. But his analysis of European government statistics, hospital records, and other sources revealed nothing of the kind. He discovered, for example, that there were slightly more women than men in insane asylums, but there were four male suicides for every female suicide. Jews had the highest rate of psychological disorder among the major religious groups in France, but they also had the lowest suicide rate. Psychological disorders occurred most frequently when a person reached maturity, but suicide rates increased steadily with age.

Clearly, suicide rates and rates of psychological disorder did not vary directly. In fact, they often appeared to vary inversely. Why? Durkheim argued that suicide rates varied as a result of differences in the degree of **social solidarity** in different categories of the population. According to Durkheim, the more beliefs and values a group's members share, and the more frequently and intensely they interact, the more social solidarity the group has. In turn, the more social solidarity a group has, the more firmly anchored individuals are to the social world and the less likely they are to take their own life if adversity strikes. In other words, Durkheim expected high-solidarity groups to have lower suicide rates than low-solidarity groups did—at least up to a certain point (see Figure 1.2).

To support his argument, Durkheim showed that married adults are half as likely as unmarried adults are to commit suicide. That is because marriage creates social ties and a kind of moral cement that bind the individual to society. Similarly, he argued that women are less likely to commit suicide than men are because women are more involved in the intimate social relations of family life. Jews, Durkheim wrote, are less likely to commit suicide than Christians are because centuries of persecution have turned them into a group that is more defensive and tightly knit. And the elderly are more prone than the young and the middle-aged are to take their own lives in the face of misfortune, because they are most likely to live alone, to have lost a spouse or partner, and to lack a job and a wide network of friends. In general, Durkheim wrote, "suicide varies with the degree of integration of the social groups of which the individual forms a part" (Durkheim, 1951 [1897]: 209). Of course, his generalization tells us nothing about why any particular individual may take his or her life. That explanation is the province of psychology. But it does tell us that a person's likelihood of committing suicide decreases with the degree to which he or she is anchored in society. And it says something surprising and uniquely sociological about how and why the suicide rate varies across groups.

Suicide in Canada Today

Durkheim's theory is not just a historical curiosity; it sheds light on the factors that account for variations in suicide rates today. Consider Figure 1.3, which shows suicide rates by age and sex in Canada. Comparing rates for men and women, we immediately see that, as in

Durkheim's France, men are about four times as likely as women are to commit suicide. In other respects, however, the Canadian data differ from the French data of more than a century ago. For example, when Durkheim wrote, suicide was extremely rare among youth. In Canada today, it is much more common, having increased substantially since the 1960s.

Although the rate of youth suicide was low in Durkheim's France, his theory of social solidarity helps us understand why it has risen in Canada. In brief, shared moral principles and strong social ties have eroded since the early 1960s, especially for Canada's youth. Consider the following facts:

Strong social bonds decrease the probability that a person will commit suicide if adversity strikes.

- Church, synagogue, mosque, and temple attendance is down, particularly among young people. Well over half of Canadians attended religious services weekly in the 1960s. Today the figure is below one-third and is only 15 percent for people born after 1960.
- Unemployment is up, again especially for youth. Thus, the unemployment rate was around 3 percent for most of the 1960s. It rose steadily to about 10 percent for most of the 1990s and reached 13.4 percent in 1994. Since then, the unemployment rate has declined, but it remains nearly twice as high for Canadians under the age of 25 as it is for Canadians above the age of 24 (in 2006, 11.6 percent compared with 6.3 percent).
- The rate of divorce has increased sixfold since the early 1960s. Births outside marriage are also much more common than they used to be. As a result, children are more often brought up in single-parent families now than in the past. This suggests that they enjoy less frequent and intimate social interaction with parents and less adult supervision.

In sum, the figures cited above suggest that the level of social solidarity is now lower than it was just a few decades ago, especially for young people. Less firmly rooted in society, and less likely to share moral standards, young people in Canada today are more likely than they were four decades ago to take their own lives if they happen to find themselves in a deep personal crisis (see also Box 1.1 on page 8).

FIGURE 1.3

Suicide Rates by Age and Sex, Canada, 2004

Sources: Statistics Canada, 2008, CANSIM, Table 102-0540. "Deaths by Cause, Chapter XX: External Causes of Morbidity and Mortality (V01 to Y89), Age, Group and Sex, Canada, Annual (Number) (44814 series)." Retrieved January 3, 2008 (http://www.statcan.ca/english/freepub/84F0209XIE/2003000/related.htm; Estimates of Population (2001 Census and Administrative Data), by Age Group and Sex, Canada, Provinces and Territories, Health Regions (June 2005 Boundaries) and Peer Groups, Annually (Number)." Retrieved January 3, 2008 (http://dc1.chass.utoronto.ca.myaccess.library.utoronto.ca/cgi-bin/cansimdim).

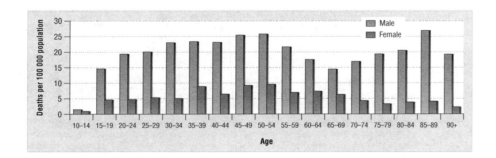

BOX 1.1
It's Your Choice

Suicide and the Innu of Labrador

The Canadians with the highest suicide rate are Aboriginal peoples. For example, the suicide rate of Aboriginal youth is five to six times as high as the national average and for Inuit youth it is 11 times as high. Suicide is the single greatest cause of injury-related deaths for Aboriginal people (Health Canada, 2004). Among Canada's Aboriginal peoples, the Innu of Labrador have the highest suicide rate. They are, in fact, the most suicide-prone people in the world. Among the Innu, the suicide rate is nearly 13 times as high as for all Canadians (Rogan, 2001; Samson, Wilson, and Mazower, 1999).

Durkheim's theory of suicide helps explain the Innu people's tragic propensity to commit suicide. Over the past half-century, the Innu's traditional norms and values have been destroyed. Moreover, the Innu have been prevented from participating in stable and meaningful patterns of social interaction. In other words, social solidarity among the Innu has been cut to an abysmally low level.

How did this happen? Historically, the Innu were a nomadic people who relied on hunting and trapping for their livelihood. In the mid-1950s, however, shortly after Newfoundland and Labrador became part of Canada, the provincial and federal governments were eager to gain more control of traditional Innu land so as to encourage economic development. Government officials felt that if new roads, mines, lumbering operations, hydroelectric projects, and low-level flight-training facilities for NATO air forces were to be built, the Innu would have to be concentrated in settlements. Furthermore, government officials believed that, to function in these new settlements, the Innu would have to learn practical and

cultural skills associated with a modern industrial society. As a result, governments put tremendous pressure on the Innu to give up their traditional way of life and settle in such places as Davis Inlet and Sheshatshui, the two communities where about 85 percent of the Innu now reside.[1]

In the new communities, Canadian laws, schools, and churches strongly discouraged the Innu from hunting, practising their religion, and raising their children in the traditional way. For example, Canadian hunting regulations limited Innu access to their age-old livelihood. Priests are known to have beaten children who missed church or school to go hunting, thus introducing interpersonal violence into a culture that formerly knew none. Teachers transmitted North American and European skills and culture, often denigrating Innu practices. In effect, Canadian authorities staged an assault on Innu culture as a whole. At the same time, few alternative jobs existed in the new communities. Most Innu wound up living in despair and on welfare. In the

absence of work, and lacking the stabilizing influence of their traditional culture, a people long known for nonviolence and their cooperative spirit became victims of widespread family breakdown, sexual abuse, drunkenness, and alcohol-related illness. Today in Sheshatshui, at least 20 percent of the children regularly get high by sniffing gasoline. In Davis Inlet, the figure is nearly 60 percent.

What is to be done about the tragedy of the Innu people? A study conducted in 1984 showed that a movement among the Innu to return to the land and their traditional hunting practices for up to seven months a year led to a dramatic improvement in their health. They lived a vigorous outdoor life. Alcohol abuse stopped. Diet improved. Their emotional and social environment stabilized and became meaningful. Suicide was unknown (Samson, Wilson, and Mazower, 1999: 25).

Unfortunately, a big political obstacle stands in the way of the Innu returning to their traditional lifestyle

NEL

on a wide scale. Simply put, the governments of Canada and New-foundland and Labrador will not allow it. A widespread Innu return to the land conflicts with government and private economic development plans. For instance, the Lower Churchill Falls hydroelectric project (the second-biggest hydroelectric project in the world) and the Voisey's Bay nickel mine (the world's biggest deposit of nickel) are located in the middle of traditional Innu hunting and burial grounds. The Innu are vigorously attempting to regain control of their land and what happens to it. They also want to be able to decide *on their own* when and how to use Canadian health services, training facilities, and the like. Whether some compromise can be worked out between government and private plans for economic development and the continuity of the Innu people is unclear. What is clear is that, as a Canadian citizen, the outcome is partly your choice.

From Personal Troubles to Social Structures

You have known for a long time that you live in a society. But until now, you may not have fully appreciated that society also lives in you. That is, patterns of social relations affect your innermost thoughts and feelings, influence your actions, and thus help shape who you are. As we have seen, one such pattern of social relations is the level of social solidarity characteristic of the various groups to which you belong.

Sociologists call relatively stable patterns of social relations **social structures.** One of the sociologist's main tasks is to identify and explain the connection between people's personal troubles and the social structures in which people are embedded. This is harder work than it may seem at first. In everyday life, we usually see things mainly from our own point of view. Our experiences seem unique to each of us. If we think about them at all, social structures may appear remote and impersonal. To see how social structures influence us, we require sociological training.

An important step in broadening our sociological awareness involves recognizing that three levels of social structure surround and permeate us. Think of these structures as concentric circles radiating out from you:

1. **Microstructures** are patterns of intimate social relations. They are formed during face-to-face interaction. Families, friendship circles, and work associations are all examples of microstructures.

    Understanding the operation of microstructures can be useful. Let's say you are looking for a job. You might think you would do best to ask as many close friends and relatives as possible for leads and contacts. However, sociological research shows that people you know well are likely to know many of the same people. After asking a couple of close connections for help landing a job, you would therefore do best to ask more remote acquaintances for leads and contacts. People to whom you are *weakly* connected (and who are weakly connected among themselves) are more likely to know *different* groups of people. Therefore, they will give you more information about job possibilities and ensure that word about your job search spreads farther. You are more likely to find a job faster if you understand "the strength of weak ties" in microstructural settings (Granovetter, 1973).
2. **Macrostructures** are patterns of social relations that lie outside and above your circle of intimates and acquaintances.[2] Macrostructures include class relations, bureaucracies, and **patriarchy,** the traditional system of economic and political inequality between women and men in most societies (see Chapter 11, Sexuality and Gender).

    Understanding the operation of macrostructures can also be useful. Consider, for example, one aspect of patriarchy. In our society, most married women who work full-time in the paid labour force are responsible for more housework, child care, and care for the elderly than their husbands are. Governments and businesses support this arrangement insofar as they provide little assistance to families in the form of nurseries, after-school programs for children, seniors' homes, and so forth. Yet an aspect of patriarchy—the unequal division of work in the household—is a major source of

Social structures are relatively stable patterns of social relations.

Microstructures are the patterns of relatively intimate social relations formed during face-to-face interaction. Families, friendship circles, and work associations are all examples of microstructures.

Macrostructures are overarching patterns of social relations that lie outside and above your circle of intimates and acquaintances. Macrostructures include classes, bureaucracies, and power systems, such as patriarchy.

Patriarchy is the traditional system of economic and political inequality between women and men.

dissatisfaction within marriages, especially in families that cannot afford to buy these services privately. Thus, sociological research shows that when spouses share domestic responsibilities equally, they are happier with their marriages and less likely to divorce (Hochschild with Machung, 1989). When a marriage is in danger of dissolving, it is common for partners to blame themselves and each other for their troubles. However, it should now be clear that forces other than incompatible personalities often put stress on families. Understanding how the macrostructure of patriarchy crops up in everyday life, and doing something to change that structure, can thus help people lead happier lives.

GLOBAL PERSPECTIVE

Global structures **are patterns of social relations that lie outside and above the national level. They include international organizations, patterns of worldwide travel and communication, and the economic relations between countries.**

3. The third level of society that surrounds and permeates us comprises **global structures.** International organizations, patterns of worldwide travel and communication, and economic relations between countries are examples of global structures. Global structures are increasingly important as inexpensive travel and communication allow all parts of the world to become interconnected culturally, economically, and politically.

   Understanding the operation of global structures can be useful, too. For instance, many people are concerned about the world's poor. They donate money to charities to help with famine and disaster relief. Some people also approve of the Canadian government giving aid to poor countries. However, many of these same people do not appreciate that charity and foreign aid alone do not seem able to end world poverty. That is because charity and foreign aid have been unable to overcome the structure of social relations among countries that have created and now sustain global inequality.

   Let us linger on this point for a moment. As we will see in Chapter 9 (Globalization, Inequality, and Development), Britain, France, and other imperial powers locked some countries into poverty when they colonized them between the seventeenth and nineteenth centuries. In the twentieth century, the poor (or "developing") countries borrowed money from these same rich countries and Western banks to pay for airports, roads, harbours, sanitation systems, basic health care, and so forth. Today, poor countries pay far more to rich countries and Western banks in interest on those loans than they receive in aid and charity. In recent years, foreign aid to the world's developing countries has been only one-seventh the amount that the developing countries pay to Western banks in loan interest (United Nations, 2004a: 201). Thus, it seems that relying exclusively on foreign aid and charity can do little to help solve the problem of world poverty. Understanding how the global structure of international relations created and helps maintain global inequality suggests new policy priorities for helping the world's poor. One such priority might involve campaigning for the cancellation of foreign debt in compensation for past injustices. Some Canadian and British government officials have been promoting this policy for the past few years.

As these examples illustrate, personal problems are connected to social structures at the micro-, macro-, and global levels. Whether the personal problem involves finding a job, keeping a marriage intact, or figuring out a way to act justly to end world poverty, social-structural considerations broaden our understanding of the problem and suggest appropriate courses of action.

The Sociological Imagination

The sociological imagination **is the quality of mind that enables a person to see the connection between personal troubles and social structures.**

Half a century ago, C. Wright Mills (1959) called the ability to see the connection between personal troubles and social structures the **sociological imagination**. He emphasized the difficulty of developing this quality of mind (see Box 1.2). His language is sexist by today's standards but his argument is as true and inspiring today as it was in the 1950s:

> When a society becomes industrialized, a peasant becomes a worker; a feudal lord is liquidated or becomes a businessman. When classes rise or fall, a man is employed or unemployed; when the rate of investment goes up or down, a man takes new heart or goes broke. When war happens, an insurance salesman becomes a rocket launcher; a store clerk, a radar man; a wife

lives alone; a child grows up without a father. Neither the life of an individual nor the history of a society can be understood without understanding both.

Yet men do not usually define the troubles they endure in terms of historical change. . . . The well-being they enjoy, they do not usually impute to the big ups and downs of the society in which they live. Seldom aware of the intricate connection between the patterns of their own lives and the course of world history, ordinary men do not usually know what this connection means for the kind of men they are becoming and for the kind of history-making in which they might take part. They do not possess the quality of mind essential to grasp the interplay of men and society, of biography and history, of self and world. They cannot cope with

BOX 1.2
Sociology at the Movies

NO.   ~~NE~~   **TAKE**   **ROLL**

Minority Report (2002)

The year is 2054 and the place is Washington, D.C. John Anderton (played by Tom Cruise) is a police officer who uses the latest technologies to apprehend murderers *before* they commit their crimes. This remarkable feat is possible because scientists have nearly perfected the use of "Pre-Cogs"—or, at least, so it seems. The Pre-Cog system consists of three psychics whose brains are wired together and who are sedated so they can develop a collective vision about impending murders. Together with powerful computers, the Pre-Cogs are apparently helping to create a crime-free society.

All is well until one of the psychics' visions shows Anderton himself murdering a stranger in less than 36 hours. Suddenly, Anderton is on the run from his own men. Desperate to figure out if the Pre-Cog system is somehow mistaken, he breaks into the system, unwires one of the psychics, and discovers that they do not always agree about what the future will bring. Sometimes there is a "minority report." Sometimes the minority report is correct. Sometimes people are arrested even though they never would have broken the law. The authorities have concealed this system flaw and allowed the arrest of potentially innocent people in their zeal to create a crime-free society.

In *Minority Report*, John Anderton (Tom Cruise) works with "Pre-Cogs" to track down criminals before they commit their crimes. When he discovers a flaw in the system, he realizes the future is not entirely fixed and that, within limits, he can change it. His insight holds an important sociological lesson for us.

And so Anderton comes to realize that not everything is predetermined—that, in his words, "It's not the future if you stop it." And stop it he does. Herein lies an important sociological lesson. Many people believe two contradictory ideas with equal conviction. First, they believe they are perfectly free to do whatever they want. Second, they believe the "system" (or "society") is so big and powerful they are unable to do anything to change it. Neither idea is accurate. As we emphasize throughout this book, social structures exert powerful influences on our behaviour; we are not perfectly free. Nonetheless, it is possible to change many aspects of society; we are not wholly predetermined either. As you will learn, changing social structures is possible under certain specifiable circumstances, with the aid of specialized knowledge and often through great individual and collective effort.

Understanding the social constraints and possibilities for freedom that envelop us requires an active sociological imagination. The sociological imagination urges us to connect our biography with history and social structure—to make sense of our lives against a larger historical and social background and to act in light of our understanding. Have you ever tried to put events in your own life in the context of history and social structure? Did the exercise help you make sense of your life? Did it in any way lead to a life more worth living? Is the sociological imagination a worthy goal?

Although movies are just entertainment to many people, they often achieve by different means what the sociological imagination aims for. Therefore, in each chapter of this book, we make the connection between a movie and a topic of sociological importance.

their personal troubles in such a way as to control the structural transformations that usually lie behind them.

What they need . . . is a quality of mind that will help them to [see] . . . what is going on in the world and . . . what may be happening within themselves. It is this quality . . . that . . . may be called the sociological imagination. (Mills, 1959: 3–4)

These words were penned in 1959, making "the sociological imagination" a recent addition to the human repertoire. True, in ancient and medieval times, some philosophers wrote about society. However, their thinking was not sociological. They believed God and nature controlled society. They spent much of their time sketching blueprints for the ideal society and urging people to follow those blueprints. They relied on speculation rather than on evidence to reach conclusions about how society works (see Figure 1.4).

Origins of the Sociological Imagination

The sociological imagination was born when three modern revolutions pushed people to think about society in an entirely new way:

1. The **Scientific Revolution** began about 1550. It encouraged the view that sound conclusions about the workings of society must be based on solid evidence, not just on speculation. People often link the Scientific Revolution to specific ideas, such as Newton's laws of motion and Copernicus's theory that the earth revolves around the sun. However, science is less a collection of ideas than a method of inquiry. For instance, in 1609 Galileo pointed his newly invented telescope at the heavens, made

The Scientific Revolution began about 1550. It encouraged the view that sound conclusions about the workings of society must be based on solid evidence, not just on speculation.

FIGURE 1.4

The European View of the World, about 1600

In Shakespeare's time, most educated Europeans pictured a universe in which God ultimately determines everything. Thus, in this early-seventeenth-century engraving, a chain extends from God's hand to the hand of a woman representing Nature; she in turn holds a chain extending to the "ape of Nature," representing humankind. This suggests that God and his intermediary, Nature, shape all human actions. Notice also that the engraving places humans at the centre of the universe, suggesting that God created the universe chiefly for human benefit. Finally, note that the engraving arranges all the elements of the universe—angels, heavenly objects, humans, animals, vegetables, minerals—in a hierarchy. It suggests that higher elements, such as the stars and the planets, influence lower elements, such as the fate of humans.

Source: Robert Fludd, *Ultriusque Cosmi Maioris Scilicet et Minoris Metaphysica, Physica Atqve Technica Historia.* 1617–19. (Oppenheim, Germany. Johan-Thedori de Bry.) By permission of Houghton Library, Harvard University.

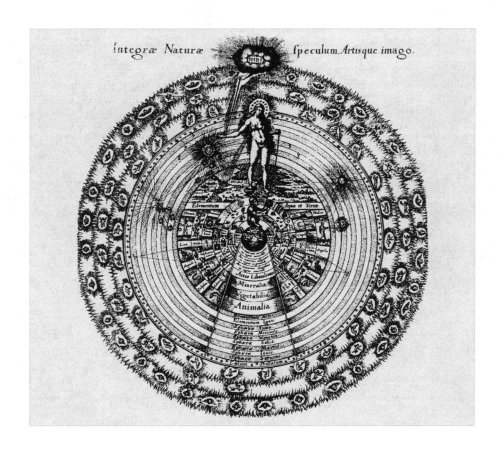

some careful observations, and showed that his observations fit Copernicus's theory. This is the core of the scientific method: using evidence to make a case for a particular point of view. By the mid-seventeenth century, some philosophers, such as Descartes in France and Hobbes in England, were calling for a science of society. When sociology emerged as a distinct discipline in the nineteenth century, commitment to the scientific method was one firm pillar of the sociological imagination.

2. The **Democratic Revolution** began about 1750. It suggested that people are responsible for organizing society and that human intervention can therefore solve social problems. Four hundred years ago, most Europeans thought otherwise. For them, God ordained the social order. The American Revolution (1775–83) and the French Revolution (1789–99) helped to undermine that idea. These democratic political upheavals showed that society could experience massive change in a short period. They proved that people could replace unsatisfactory rulers. They suggested that *people* control society. The implications for social thought were profound. For if it were possible to change society by human intervention, then a science of society could play a big role. The new science could help people find ways of overcoming social problems, improving the welfare of citizens and effectively reaching given goals. Much of the justification for sociology as a science arose out of the democratic revolutions that shook Europe and North America.

3. The **Industrial Revolution** began about 1780. It created a host of new and serious social problems that attracted the attention of social thinkers. As a result of the growth of industry, masses of people moved from countryside to city, worked agonizingly long hours in crowded and dangerous mines and factories, lost faith in their religions, confronted faceless bureaucracies, and reacted to the filth and poverty of their existence by means of strikes, crime, revolutions, and wars. Scholars had never seen a sociological laboratory like this. The Scientific Revolution suggested that a science of society was possible. The Democratic Revolution suggested that people could intervene to improve society. The Industrial Revolution presented social thinkers with a host of pressing social problems crying out for a solution. They responded by giving birth to the sociological imagination.

The Scientific Revolution began in Europe around 1550. Scientists proposed new theories about the structure of the universe and developed new methods to collect evidence so they could test those theories. Shown here is an astrolabe used by Copernicus to solve problems relating to the position of the sun, the planets, and the stars.

The **Democratic Revolution** began about 1750. It suggested that people are responsible for organizing society and that human intervention can therefore solve social problems.

The **Industrial Revolution**, often regarded as the most important event in world history since the development of agriculture and cities, refers to the rapid economic transformation that began in Britain in the 1780s. It involved the large-scale application of science and technology to industrial processes, the creation of factories, and the formation of a working class.

THEORY, RESEARCH, AND VALUES

French social thinker Auguste Comte (1798–1857) coined the term *sociology* in 1838 (Thompson, 1975). Comte tried to place the study of society on scientific foundations. He said he wanted to understand the social world as it was, not as he or anyone else imagined it should be. Yet there was a tension in his work: Although Comte was eager to adopt the scientific method in the study of society, he was a conservative thinker, motivated by strong opposition to rapid change in French society. This was evident in his writings. When he moved from his small, conservative hometown to Paris, Comte witnessed the democratic forces unleashed by the French Revolution, the early industrialization of society, and the rapid growth of cities. What he saw shocked and saddened him. Rapid social change was destroying much of what he valued, especially respect for traditional authority. He therefore urged slow change and the preservation of all that was traditional in social life. Thus, scientific methods of research *and* a vision of the ideal society were evident in sociology at its origins.

Although he praised the value of scientific methods, Comte never conducted any research. Neither did the second founder of sociology, British social theorist Herbert Spencer (1820–1903). However, Spencer believed that he had discovered scientific laws governing the operation of society. Strongly influenced by Charles Darwin's theory of evolution, he thought societies comprised interdependent parts, just as biological organisms did. These interdependent parts included families, governments, and the economy. According to Spencer, societies evolve in the same way as biological species do:

Eugene Delacroix's *Liberty Leading the People, July 28, 1830*. The democratic forces unleashed by the French Revolution suggested that people are responsible for organizing society and that human intervention can therefore solve social problems. As such, democracy was a foundation stone of sociology.

Individuals struggle to survive and the fittest succeed in this struggle; the least fit die before they can bear offspring. This allows societies to evolve from "barbaric" to "civilized." Deep social inequalities exist in society, but that is just as it should be if societies are to evolve, Spencer suggested (Spencer, 1975 [1897–1906]).

Spencer's ideas, which came to be known as "social Darwinism," were popular for a time in North America and Great Britain. Wealthy industrialists, like the oil baron John D. Rockefeller, found much to admire in a doctrine that justified social inequality and trumpeted the superiority of the wealthy and the powerful. Today, few sociologists think that societies are like biological systems. We have a better understanding of the complex economic, political, military, religious, and other forces that cause social change. We know that people can take things into their own hands and change their social environment in ways that no other species can. Spencer remains of interest because he was among the first social thinkers to assert that society operates according to scientific laws—and because his vision of the ideal society nonetheless showed through his writings.

To varying degrees, we see the same tension between belief in the importance of science and a vision of the ideal society in the work of the three giants in the early history of

Diego Rivera's *Detroit Industry, North Wall* (1932–33). Fresco (detail). Copyright 1997. The Detroit Institute of Arts. The first Industrial Revolution began in the late eighteenth century. The so-called Second Industrial Revolution began in the early twentieth century. Wealthy entrepreneurs formed large companies. Steel became a basic industrial material. Oil and electricity fuelled much industrial production. At the same time, Henry Ford's assembly lines and other mass-production technologies transformed the workplace.

sociology: Karl Marx (1818–83), Émile Durkheim (1858–1917), and Max Weber (pronounced VAY-ber; 1864–1920). The lives of these three men spanned just over a century. They witnessed various phases of Europe's wrenching transition to industrial capitalism. They wanted to explain the great transformation of Europe and suggest ways of improving people's lives. Like Comte and Spencer, they were committed to the scientific method of research. They actually adopted scientific research methods in their work. However, they also wanted to chart a better course for their societies. The ideas they developed are not just diagnostic tools from which we can still learn but, like many sociological ideas, are also prescriptions for combating social ills.

The tension between analysis and ideal, diagnosis and prescription, is evident throughout sociology. This becomes clear if we distinguish three important terms: theories, research, and values.

Theory

Sociological ideas are usually expressed in the form of theories. **Theories** are tentative explanations of some aspect of social life. They state how and why certain facts are related. For example, in his theory of suicide, Durkheim related facts about suicide rates to facts about social solidarity. This enabled him to explain suicide as a function of social solidarity. In our broad definition, even a hunch qualifies as a theory if it suggests how and why certain facts are related. As Albert Einstein wrote, "The whole of science is nothing more than a refinement of everyday thinking" (Einstein, 1954: 270).

Theories are tentative explanations of some aspect of social life that state how and why certain facts are related.

Research

After sociologists formulate theories, they can conduct research. **Research** is the process of carefully observing social reality, often to "test" a theory or assess its validity. For example, Durkheim collected suicide statistics from various government agencies to see whether the data supported or contradicted his theory. Because research can call the validity of a theory into question, theories are only *tentative* explanations. We discuss the research process in detail in Chapter 2, How Sociologists Do Research.

Research is the process of carefully observing reality to assess the validity of a theory.

Values

Before sociologists can formulate a theory, they must make certain judgments. For example, they must decide which problems are worth studying. They must make certain assumptions about how the parts of society fit together. If they are going to recommend ways of improving the operation of some aspect of society, they must even have an opinion about what the ideal society should look like. As we will soon see, these issues are shaped largely by sociologists' values. **Values** are ideas about what is right and wrong. Inevitably, values help sociologists formulate and favour certain theories over others (Edel, 1965; Kuhn, 1970 [1962]). As such, sociological theories may be modified and even rejected because of research, but they are often motivated by sociologists' values.

Values are ideas about what is right and wrong.

Durkheim, Marx, and Weber stood close to the origins of the major theoretical traditions in sociology: functionalism, conflict theory, and symbolic interactionism. A fourth theoretical tradition, feminism, has arisen in recent decades to correct some deficiencies in the three long-established traditions. It will become clear as you read this book that many more theories exist in addition to these four. However, because these four traditions have been especially influential in the development of sociology, we present a thumbnail sketch of each one.

SOCIOLOGICAL THEORY AND THEORISTS

Functionalism

Durkheim

Functionalism stresses that human behaviour is governed by relatively stable social structures. It underlines how social structures maintain or undermine social stability. It emphasizes that social structures are based mainly on shared values or preferences. And it suggests that re-establishing equilibrium can best solve most social problems.

Durkheim's theory of suicide is an early example of what sociologists now call **functionalism.** Functionalist theories incorporate these four features:

1. They stress that human behaviour is governed by relatively stable patterns of social relations or social structures. For example, Durkheim emphasized how suicide rates are influenced by patterns of social solidarity. Usually the social structures analyzed by functionalists are macrostructures.
2. Functionalist theories show how social structures maintain or undermine social stability. For example, Durkheim analyzed how the growth of industries and cities in nineteenth-century Europe lowered the level of social solidarity and contributed to social instability, one result of which was a higher suicide rate.
3. Functionalist theories emphasize that social structures are based mainly on shared values or preferences. Thus, when Durkheim wrote about social solidarity, he sometimes meant the frequency and intensity of social interaction, but more often he thought of social solidarity as a sort of moral cement that binds people together.
4. Functionalism suggests that re-establishing equilibrium can best solve most social problems. Thus, Durkheim said that social stability could be restored in late-nineteenth-century Europe by creating new associations of employers and workers that would lower workers' expectations about what they could get out of life. If, said Durkheim, more people could agree on wanting less, social solidarity would rise and there would be fewer strikes, fewer suicides, and so on. Functionalism, then, was a conservative response to widespread social unrest in late-nineteenth-century France. A more liberal or radical response would have been to argue that if people are expressing discontent because they are getting less out of life than they expect, discontent can be lowered by figuring out ways for them to get more out of life.

S. D. Clark (1910–2003) received his Ph.D. from the University of Toronto. He became the first chair of the Department of Sociology at that institution. Born in Lloydminster, Alberta, he is especially well known for his studies of Canadian social development as a process of dis-organization and reorganization on a series of economic frontiers (Clark, 1968). The influence of functionalism on his work is apparent in his emphasis on the way society re-establishes equilibrium after experiencing disruptions caused by economic change.

Functionalism in North America

Although functionalist thinking influenced North American sociology at the end of the nineteenth century, it was only during the continent's greatest economic crisis ever, the Great Depression of 1929–39, that functionalism took deep root here (Russett, 1966). With a quarter of the paid labour force unemployed and labour unrest rising, it is not entirely surprising that sociologists with a conservative frame of mind were attracted to a theory that focused on how social equilibrium could be restored. Functionalist theory remained popular for about 30 years. It experienced a minor revival in the early 1990s but never regained the dominance it had enjoyed from the 1930s to the early 1960s.

Harvard sociologist Talcott Parsons was the foremost North American proponent of functionalism. Parsons is best known for identifying how various institutions must work to ensure the smooth operation of society as a whole. He argued that society is well integrated and in equilibrium when the family successfully raises new generations, the military successfully defends society against external threats, schools are able to teach students the skills and values they need to function as productive adults, and religions create a shared moral code among the people (Parsons, 1951).

Parsons was criticized for exaggerating the degree to which members of society share common values and social institutions contribute to social harmony. This led North America's other leading functionalist, Robert Merton, to propose that social structures may have different consequences for different groups of people. Merton noted that some of those consequences

NEL

may be disruptive or **dysfunctional** (Merton, 1968 [1949]). Moreover, said Merton, although some functions are **manifest** (visible and intended), others are **latent** (unintended and less obvious). For instance, a manifest function of schools is to transmit skills from one generation to the next. A latent function of schools is to encourage the development of a separate youth culture that often conflicts with parents' values (Coleman, 1961; Hersch, 1998).

Similarly, to anticipate an argument we make below, the manifest function of clothing is to keep people warm in cool weather and cool in warm weather. Yet clothing may be fashionable or unfashionable. The particular style of clothing we adopt may indicate whom we want to associate with and whom we want to exclude from our social circle. What we wear may thus express the position we occupy in society, how we think of ourselves, and how we want to present ourselves to others. These are all latent functions of clothing.

> **Dysfunctional consequences** are effects of social structures that create social instability.
>
> **Manifest functions** are visible and intended effects of social structures.
>
> **Latent functions** are invisible and unintended effects of social structures.

Conflict Theory

The second major theoretical tradition in sociology emphasizes the centrality of conflict in social life. **Conflict theory** incorporates these features:

- It generally focuses on large macrolevel structures, such as "class relations" or patterns of domination, submission, and struggle between people of high and low standing.
- Conflict theory shows how major patterns of inequality in society produce social stability in some circumstances and social change in others.
- Conflict theory stresses how members of privileged groups try to maintain their advantages while subordinate groups struggle to increase theirs. From this point of view, social conditions at a given time are the expression of an ongoing power struggle between privileged and subordinate groups.
- Conflict theory typically leads to the suggestion that eliminating privilege will lower the level of conflict and increase total human welfare.

> **Conflict theory** generally focuses on large macrolevel structures and shows how major patterns of inequality in society produce social stability in some circumstances and social change in others.

Marx

Conflict theory originated in the work of German social thinker Karl Marx. A generation before Durkheim, Marx observed the destitution and discontent produced by the Industrial Revolution and proposed a sweeping argument about the way societies develop (Marx, 1904 [1859]; Marx and Engels, 1972 [1848]). Marx's theory was radically different from Durkheim's. **Class conflict**, the struggle between classes to resist and overcome the opposition of other classes, lies at the centre of his ideas.

> **Class conflict** is the struggle between classes to resist and overcome the opposition of other classes.

Marx argued that owners of industry are eager to improve the way work is organized and to adopt new tools, machines, and production methods. These innovations allow them to produce more efficiently, earn higher profits, and drive inefficient competitors out of business. However, the drive for profits also causes capitalists to concentrate workers in larger and larger establishments, keep wages as low as possible, and invest as little as possible in improving working conditions. Thus, said Marx, a large and growing class of poor workers opposes a small and shrinking class of wealthy owners.

Marx believed that workers would ultimately become aware of belonging to the same exploited class. He called this awareness "class consciousness." He believed working-class consciousness would encourage the growth of trade unions and labour parties. According to Marx, these organizations would eventually seek to end private ownership of property, replacing it with a "communist" society: a system in which there is no private property and everyone shares property and wealth.

Weber

Although some of Marx's ideas have been usefully adapted to the study of contemporary society, his predictions about the inevitable collapse of capitalism have been questioned. Max Weber, a German sociologist who wrote his major works a generation after Marx, was among the first to find flaws in Marx's argument (Weber, 1946). Weber noted the rapid

John Porter (1921–79) was Canada's premier sociologist in the 1960s and 1970s. Born in Vancouver, he received his Ph.D. from the London School of Economics. He spent his academic career at Carleton University in Ottawa, serving as chair of the Department of Sociology and Anthropology, dean of Arts and Science, and vice-president. His major work, *The Vertical Mosaic* (1965), is a study of class and power in Canada. Firmly rooted in conflict theory, it influenced a generation of Canadian sociologists in their studies on social inequality, elite groups, French–English relations, and Canadian–American relations.

The Protestant ethic is the belief that religious doubts can be reduced, and a state of grace ensured, if people work diligently and live ascetically. According to Weber, the Protestant work ethic had the unintended effect of increasing savings and investment and thus stimulating capitalist growth.

growth of the service sector of the economy, with its many non-manual workers and professionals. He argued that many members of these occupational groups stabilize society because they enjoy higher status and income than manual workers employed in manufacturing. In addition, Weber showed that class conflict is not the only driving force of history. In his view, politics and religion are also important sources of historical change (see below). Other writers pointed out that Marx did not understand how investing in technology would make it possible for workers to toil fewer hours under less oppressive conditions. Nor did he foresee that higher wages, better working conditions, and welfare state benefits would pacify manual workers. Thus, we see that Weber and other sociologists called into question many of the particulars of Marx's theory.

Conflict Theory in North America

Conflict theory had some advocates in North America before the 1960s. Most noteworthy is C. Wright Mills, who laid the foundations for modern conflict theory in the 1950s. Mills conducted pioneering research on American politics and class structure. One of his most important books is *The Power Elite*, a study of the several hundred men who occupied the "command posts" of the American economy, military, and government. He argued that power is highly concentrated in American society, which is therefore less of a democracy than we are often led to believe (Mills, 1956).

Exceptions like Mills notwithstanding, conflict theory did not really take hold in North America until the 1960s, a decade that was rocked by growing labour unrest, Quebec separatism, anti-Vietnam War protests, the rise of the black power movement, and the first stirrings of feminism. Strikes, demonstrations, and riots were almost daily occurrences in the 1960s and early 1970s, and therefore many sociologists of that era thought conflict among classes, nations, races, and generations was the very essence of society. Many of today's leading sociologists attended graduate school in the 1960s and 1970s and were strongly influenced by the spirit of the times. As you will see throughout this book, they have made important contributions to conflict theory during their professional careers.

Symbolic Interactionism

Weber, Mead, and Goffman

We noted above that Weber criticized Marx's interpretation of the development of capitalism. Among other things, Weber argued that early capitalist development was caused not just by favourable economic circumstances but that certain *religious* beliefs also facilitated robust capitalist growth (Weber 1958 [1904–05]). In particular, sixteenth- and seventeenth-century Protestants believed their religious doubts could be reduced and a state of grace ensured if they worked diligently and lived modestly. Weber called this belief the **Protestant ethic**. He believed it had an unintended effect: People who adhered to the Protestant ethic saved and invested more money than others did. Thus, capitalism developed most robustly where the Protestant ethic took hold. In much of his research, Weber emphasized the importance of empathetically understanding people's motives and the meanings they attach to things to gain a clear sense of the significance of their actions. He called this aspect of his approach to sociological research the method of *Verstehen* (which means "understanding" in German).

The idea that subjective meanings and motives must be analyzed in any complete sociological analysis was only one of Weber's contributions to early sociological theory. Weber was also an important conflict theorist, as you will learn in later chapters. It is enough to note here that his emphasis on subjective meanings found rich soil in the United States in the late nineteenth and early twentieth centuries because his ideas resonated deeply with the individualism of American culture. A century ago, people widely believed that individual talent and initiative could allow anyone to achieve just about anything in that land of opportunity. Small wonder then that much of early American sociology focused on the individual or, more precisely, on the connection between the individual and the larger society. This was certainly a focus of sociologists at the University of Chicago, the most influential Department of Sociology in the country before World War II. For example, the University of Chicago's George Herbert Mead (1863–1931) was the driving force behind the study of how the individual's sense of self is formed in the course of interaction with other people. We discuss his contribution in Chapter 4, Socialization. Here, we note only that the work of Mead and his colleagues gave birth to symbolic interactionism, a distinctively American theoretical tradition that continues to be a major force in sociology today.

Functionalist and conflict theories assume that people's group memberships—whether they are rich or poor, male or female, black or white—influence their behaviour. This can sometimes make people seem like balls on a pool table: They get knocked around and cannot choose their own destinies. We know from our everyday experience, however, that people are not like that. We often make choices, sometimes difficult ones. We sometimes change our minds. Moreover, two people with similar group memberships may react differently to similar social circumstances because they interpret those circumstances differently.

Recognizing these issues, some sociologists focus on the subjective side of social life. They work in the symbolic interactionist tradition, a school of thought that was given its name by sociologist Herbert Blumer (1900–86), Mead's student at the University of Chicago. **Symbolic interactionism** incorporates these features:

- Symbolic interactionism's focus on interpersonal communication in microlevel social settings distinguishes it from both functionalist and conflict theories.
- Symbolic interactionism emphasizes that social life is possible only because people attach meanings to things. It follows that an adequate explanation of social behaviour requires understanding the subjective meanings people associate with their social circumstances.
- Symbolic interactionism stresses that people help to create their social circumstances and do not merely react to them. For example, Canadian sociologist Erving Goffman (1922–82), one of the most influential symbolic interactionists, analyzed the many ways people present themselves to others in everyday life so as to appear in the best possible light. Goffman compared social interaction to a carefully staged play, complete with front stage, backstage, defined roles, and a wide range of props. In this play, a person's age, gender, race, and other characteristics may help to shape his or her actions, but there is much room for individual creativity as well (Goffman, 1959).
- By focusing on the subjective meanings people create in small social settings, symbolic interactionists sometimes validate unpopular and unofficial viewpoints. This increases our understanding and tolerance of people who may be different from us.

To understand symbolic interactionism better, let us briefly return to the problem of suicide. If a police officer discovers a dead person at the wheel of a car that has run into a tree, it may be difficult to establish whether the death was an accident or suicide. Interviewing friends and relatives to discover the driver's state of mind just before the crash may help rule out the possibility of suicide. As this example illustrates, understanding the intention or motive of the actor is critical to understanding the meaning of a social action and explaining it. A state of mind must be interpreted, usually by a coroner, before a dead body becomes a suicide statistic (Douglas, 1967).

For surviving family and friends, suicide is always painful and sometimes embarrassing. Insurance policies often deny payments to beneficiaries in the case of suicide. As a result, coroners are inclined to classify deaths as accidental whenever such an interpretation is plausible. Being human, they want to minimize a family's suffering after such a horrible event. Sociologists therefore believe that official suicide rates are about one-third lower than actual suicide rates.

Social Constructionism

One variant of symbolic interactionism that has become especially popular in recent years is **social constructionism**. Social constructionists argue that when people interact, they typically assume things are naturally or innately what they seem to be. However, apparently natural and innate features of life are often sustained by *social* processes that vary historically and

Erving Goffman (1922–82) was born in Mannville, Alberta. He studied sociology and anthropology at the University of Toronto. He completed his Ph.D. at the University of Chicago and pursued his academic career at the University of California, Berkeley, and the University of Pennsylvania. Goffman developed an international reputation for his "dramaturgical" approach to symbolic interactionism.

Symbolic interactionism **focuses on interaction in microlevel social settings and emphasizes that an adequate explanation of social behaviour requires understanding the subjective meanings people attach to their social circumstances.**

Social constructionism **argues that apparently natural or innate features of life are often sustained by social processes that vary historically and culturally.**

Margrit Eichler (1942–) was born in Berlin, Germany. She took her Ph.D. at Duke University in the United States before beginning her academic career in Canada. She served as chair of the Department of Sociology at the Ontario Institute for Studies in Education and became head of the Women's Studies Program at the University of Toronto. She is internationally known for her work on feminist methodology (Eichler, 1987). Her work on family policy in Canada has influenced students, professional sociologists, and policymakers for two decades (Eichler, 1988a).

Feminist theory claims that patriarchy is at least as important as class inequality in determining a person's opportunities in life. It holds that male domination and female subordination are determined not by biological necessity but by structures of power and social convention. It examines the operation of patriarchy in both micro and macro settings. And it contends that existing patterns of gender inequality can and should be changed for the benefit of all members of society.

culturally. For example, many people assume differences in the way women and men behave are the result of their different biological makeup. In contrast, social constructionists show that many of the presumably natural differences between women and men depend on the way power is distributed between them and the degree to which certain ideas about women and men are widely shared (see Chapter 11, Sexuality and Gender; Berger and Luckmann, 1966). People usually do such a good job of building natural-seeming social realities in their everyday interactions that they do not notice the materials used in the construction process. Social constructionists identify those materials and analyze how they are pieced together.

In sum, the study of the subjective side of social life helps us get beyond the official picture, deepening our understanding of how society works and supplementing the insights gained from macrolevel analysis. By stressing the importance and validity of subjective meanings, symbolic interactionists increase tolerance for minority and deviant viewpoints. By stressing how subjective meanings vary historically and culturally, social constructionists show that many seemingly natural features of social life actually require painstaking acts of social creation.

Feminist Theory

Few women figured prominently in the early history of sociology. The strict demands placed on them by the nineteenth-century family and the lack of opportunity in the larger society prevented most women from earning a higher education and making major contributions to the discipline. Women who made their mark on sociology in its early years tended to have unusual biographies. Some of these exceptional people introduced gender issues that were largely ignored by Marx, Durkheim, Weber, Mead, and other early sociologists. Appreciation for the sociological contribution of these pioneering women has grown in recent years because concern with gender issues has come to form a substantial part of the modern sociological enterprise.

Martineau and Addams

Harriet Martineau (1802–76) is often called the first female sociologist. Born in England to a prosperous family, she never married. She was able to support herself comfortably from her journalistic writings. Martineau translated Comte into English, and she wrote one of the first books on research methods. She undertook critical studies of slavery, factory laws, and gender inequality. She was a leading advocate of voting rights for women, higher education for women, and gender equality in the family. As such, Martineau was one of the first feminists (Yates, 1985).

In the United States in the early twentieth century, a few women from wealthy families attended university, received training as sociologists, and wanted to become professors of sociology, but they were denied faculty appointments. Typically, they turned to social activism and social work instead. A case in point is Jane Addams (1860–1935). Addams was co-founder of Hull House, a shelter for the destitute in Chicago's slums, and she spent a lifetime fighting for social reform. She also provided a research platform for sociologists from the University of Chicago, who often visited Hull House to interview its clients. In recognition of her efforts, Addams received the ultimate award in 1931—the Nobel Peace Prize.

Modern Feminism

Despite its early stirrings, feminist thinking had little impact on sociology until the mid-1960s, when the rise of the modern women's movement drew attention to the many remaining inequalities between women and men. Because of feminist theory's major influence on sociology, it may fairly be regarded as sociology's fourth major theoretical tradition. Modern feminism has several variants (see Chapter 11, Sexuality and Gender). However, the various strands of **feminist theory** share the following features:

•   Feminist theory focuses on various aspects of patriarchy, the system of male domination in society. Patriarchy, feminists contend, is as important as class inequality, if not more so, in determining a person's opportunities in life.

NEL

- Feminist theory holds that male domination and female subordination are determined not by biological necessity but by structures of power and social convention. From their point of view, women are subordinate to men only because men enjoy more legal, economic, political, and cultural rights.
- Feminist theory examines the operation of patriarchy in both microlevel and macrolevel settings.
- Feminist theory contends that existing patterns of gender inequality can and should be changed for the benefit of all members of society. The main sources of gender inequality include differences in the way boys and girls are reared; barriers to equal opportunity in education, paid work, and politics; and the unequal division of domestic responsibilities between women and men.

Summing Up

The theoretical traditions outlined above are summarized in Table 1.1 (see also Figure 1.5 on page 22). As you will see in the following pages, sociologists have applied them to all of the discipline's branches. They have elaborated and refined each of them. Some sociologists work exclusively within one tradition. Others conduct research that borrows from more than one tradition. But all sociologists are deeply indebted to the founders of the discipline.

To illustrate how much farther we are able to see using theory as our guide, we now consider how the four traditions outlined above improve our understanding of an aspect of social life familiar to everyone: the world of fashion.

Theoretical Tradition	Main Level of Analysis	Main Focus	Main Question	Image of Ideal Society
Functionalism	Macro	Values	How do the institutions of society contribute to social stability?	A state of equilibrium
Conflict theory	Macro	Class inequality	How do privileged groups seek to maintain their advantages and subordinate groups seek to increase theirs, often causing social change in the process?	The elimination of privilege, especially class privilege
Symbolic interactionism	Micro	Meaning	How do individuals communicate so as to make their social settings meaningful?	Respect for the validity of minority views
Feminist theory	Micro and macro	Patriarchy	Which social structures and interaction processes maintain male dominance and female subordination?	The elimination of gender inequality

TABLE 1.1
The Main Theoretical Traditions in Sociology

FIGURE 1.5

A Sociological Timeline of Some Major Figures in the Development of Sociological Theory, 1820–1960

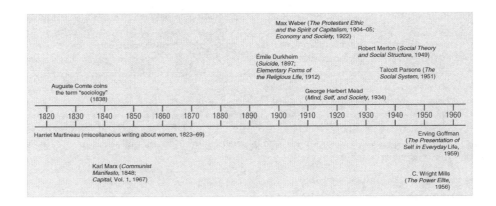

APPLYING THE FOUR THEORETICAL PERSPECTIVES: THE PROBLEM OF FASHION

"Oh. Two weeks ago I saw Cameron Diaz at Fred Segal and I talked her out of buying this truly heinous angora sweater. Whoever said orange is the new pink is seriously disturbed."
— Elle Woods (Reese Witherspoon) in *Legally Blonde* (2001)

In December 2002 the *Wall Street Journal* announced that Grunge might be back (Tkacik, 2002). Since 1998, one of the main fashion trends among white, middle-class, preteen and young teenage girls was the Britney Spears look: bare midriffs, highlighted hair, wide belts, glitter purses, big wedge shoes, and Skechers "energy" sneakers. But in 2002 a new pop star, Avril Lavigne, was rising in the pop charts. Nominated for a 2003 Grammy Award in the Best New Artist category, the 17-year-old skater-punk from Napanee in eastern Ontario (2001 population: 15 132; Statistics Canada, 2002d) affected a shaggy, unkempt look. She sported worn-out T-shirts, 1970s-style plaid Western shirts with snaps, low-rise blue jeans, baggy pants, undershirts, ties, backpacks, chain wallets, and, for shoes, Converse Chuck Taylors. The style was similar to the Grunge look of the early 1990s, when Nirvana and Pearl Jam were the big stars on MTV and Kurt Cobain was king of the music world.

Why in late 2002 were the glamorous trends of the pop era giving way in one market segment to "neo-Grunge"? Why, in general, do fashion shifts take place? Sociological theory has interesting things to say on this subject (Davis, 1992).

Until the 1960s, the standard sociological approach to explaining the ebb and flow of fashion trends was *functionalist.* In the functionalist view, fashion trends worked like this: Every season, exclusive fashion houses in Paris and, to a lesser extent, Milan, New York, and

Britney Spears versus Avril Lavigne

London, would show new styles. Some of the new styles would catch on among the exclusive clientele of Chanel, Dior, Givenchy, and other big-name designers. The main appeal of wearing expensive, new fashions was that wealthy clients could distinguish themselves from people who were less well off. Thus, fashion performed an important social function. By allowing people of different rank to distinguish themselves from one another, fashion helped to preserve the ordered layering of society into classes. ("It is an interesting question," wrote nineteenth-century American writer Henry David Thoreau in *Walden,* "how far [people] would retain their relative rank if they were divested of their clothes.") By the twentieth century, thanks to technological advances in clothes manufacturing, it didn't take long for inexpensive knockoffs to reach the market and trickle down to the lower classes. New styles then had to be introduced frequently so that fashion could continue to perform its function of helping to maintain an orderly class system. Hence the ebb and flow of fashion.

The functionalist theory was a fairly accurate account of the way fashion trends worked until the 1960s. Then, fashion became more democratic. Paris, Milan, New York, and London are still hugely important fashion centres today. However, new fashion trends are increasingly initiated by lower classes, minority groups, and people who spurn high fashion altogether. Napanee is, after all, pretty far from Paris, and today big-name designers are more likely to be influenced by the inner-city styles of hip-hop than vice versa. Avril Lavigne became the new face of Chanel in 2006, suggesting that new fashions no longer just trickle down from upper classes and a few high-fashion centres. Upper classes are nearly as likely to adopt lower-class fashion trends that emanate from just about anywhere. As a result, the functionalist theory no longer provides a satisfying explanation of fashion cycles.

Some sociologists have turned to conflict theory as an alternative view of the fashion world. Conflict theorists typically view fashion cycles as a means by which industry owners make big profits. Owners introduce new styles and render old styles unfashionable because they make more money when many people are encouraged to buy new clothes often. At the same time, conflict theorists think fashion keeps people distracted from the many social, economic, and political problems that might otherwise incite them to express dissatisfaction with the existing social order and even rebel against it. Conflict theorists, like functionalists, thus believe that fashion helps to maintain social stability. Unlike functionalists, however, they argue that social stability bestows advantages on industrial owners at the expense of non-owners.

Conflict theorists have a point. Fashion *is* a big and profitable business. Owners *do* introduce new styles to make more money. They have, for example, created the Color Marketing Group (known to insiders as the "Color Mafia"), a committee that meets regularly to help change the international palette of colour preferences for consumer products. According to one committee member, the Color Mafia makes sure that "the mass media, . . . fashion magazines and catalogs, home shopping shows, and big clothing chains all present the same options" (Mundell, 1993).

Yet the Color Mafia and other influential elements of the fashion industry are not all-powerful. Remember what Elle Woods said after she convinced Cameron Diaz not to buy that heinous angora sweater: "Whoever said orange is the new pink is seriously disturbed." Like many consumers, Elle Woods *rejected* the advice of the fashion industry. And, in fact, some of the fashion trends initiated by industry owners flop, one of the biggest being the introduction of the midi-dress (with a hemline midway between knee and ankle) in the mid-1970s. Despite a huge ad campaign, most women simply would not buy it.

This points to one of the main problems with the conflict interpretation: It incorrectly makes it seem as if fashion decisions are dictated from above. Reality is more complicated. Fashion decisions are made partly by consumers. This idea can best be understood by thinking of clothing as a form of *symbolic interaction,* a sort of wordless "language" that allows us to tell others who we are and to learn who they are.

If clothes speak, sociologist Fred Davis has perhaps done the most in recent years to help us see how we can decipher what they say (Davis, 1992). According to Davis, a person's identity is always a work in progress. True, we develop a sense of self as we mature. We come to think of ourselves as members of one or more families, occupations, communities, classes, ethnic and racial groups, and countries. We develop patterns of behaviour and belief associated with each of these social categories. Nonetheless, social categories change over time, and so do we as we move through them and as we age. As a result, our identities are always in flux. We often become anxious or insecure about who we are. Clothes help us express our shifting identities. For example, clothes can convey whether you are "straight," sexually available, athletic, conservative, and much else, thus telling others how you want them to see you and the kinds of people with whom you want to associate. At some point you may become less conservative, sexually available, and so on. Your clothing style is likely to change accordingly. (Of course, the messages you try to send are subject to interpretation and may be misunderstood.) For its part, the fashion industry feeds on the ambiguities within us, investing much effort in trying to discern which new styles might capture current needs for self-expression.

For example, capitalizing on the need for young girls' self-expression in the late 1990s, Britney Spears hit a chord. Feminist interpretations of the meaning and significance of Britney Spears are especially interesting in this respect because they focus on the gender aspects of fashion.

Traditionally, feminists have thought of fashion as a form of patriarchy, a means by which male dominance is maintained. They have argued that fashion is mainly a female preoccupation. It takes a lot of time and money to choose, buy, and clean clothes. Fashionable clothing is often impractical and uncomfortable, and some of it is even unhealthy. Modern fashion's focus on youth, slenderness, and eroticism diminishes women by turning them into sexual objects, say some feminists. Britney Spears is of interest to traditional feminists because she supposedly helps to lower the age at which girls fall under male domination.

In recent years, this traditional feminist view has given way to a feminist interpretation that is more compatible with symbolic interactionism ("Why Britney Spears Matters," 2001). Some feminists now applaud the "girl power" movement that crystallized in 1996 with the release of the Spice Girls' hit single "Wannabe." These feminists regard Britney Spears as part of that movement. In their judgment, Spears's music, dance routines, and dress style express a self-assuredness and assertiveness that resonate with the less submissive and more independent role that girls are now carving out for themselves. With her kicks, her shadow boxing, and her songs like the 2000 single "Stronger," Spears speaks for the *empowerment* of young women. Quite apart from her musical and dancing talent, then, some feminists think many young girls are wild about Britney Spears because she helps them express their own social and sexual power. Of course, not all young girls agree. Some, like Avril Lavigne, find Spears "phony" and too much of a "showgirl." They seek "more authentic" ways of asserting their identity through fashion (Pascual, 2002). Still, the symbolic interactionist and feminist interpretations of fashion help us see more clearly the ambiguities of identity that underlie the rise of new fashion trends.

Our analysis of fashion shows that each of the four theoretical perspectives—functionalism, conflict theory, symbolic interactionism, and feminist theory—can clarify different aspects of a sociological problem. This does not mean that each perspective always has equal validity. Often, the interpretations that derive from different theoretical perspectives are incompatible. They offer *competing* interpretations of the same social reality. It is then necessary to do research to determine which perspective works best for the case at hand. Nonetheless, all four theoretical perspectives usefully illuminate some aspects of the social world. We therefore refer to them often in this textbook.

A SOCIOLOGICAL COMPASS

Our summary of the major theoretical perspectives in sociology suggests that the founders of the discipline developed their ideas in an attempt to solve the great sociological puzzle of their time—the causes and consequences of the Industrial Revolution. This raises two interesting questions. What are the great sociological puzzles of *our* time? How are today's sociologists responding to the challenges presented by the social settings in which *we* live? We devote the

NEL

rest of this book to answering these questions in depth. In the remainder of this chapter, we outline what you can expect to learn from this book.

It would be wrong to suggest that the research of tens of thousands of sociologists around the world is animated by just a few key issues. Viewed up close, sociology today is a heterogeneous enterprise enlivened by hundreds of theoretical debates, some focused on small issues relevant to particular fields and geographical areas, others focused on big issues that seek to characterize the entire historical era for humanity as a whole.

Among the big issues, two stand out. Perhaps the greatest sociological puzzles of our time are the causes and consequences of the Postindustrial Revolution and globalization. The **Postindustrial Revolution** is the technology-driven shift from manufacturing to service industries—the shift from employment in factories to employment in offices—and the consequences of that shift for nearly all human activities (Bell, 1973; Toffler, 1990). For example, as a result of the Postindustrial Revolution, non-manual occupations now outnumber manual occupations, and women have been drawn into the system of higher education and the paid labour force in large numbers. The shift to service industries has transformed the way we work and study, our standard of living, the way we form families, and much else.

Globalization is the process by which formerly separate economies, states, and cultures become tied together and people become increasingly aware of their growing interdependence (Giddens, 1990: 64; Guillén, 2001). Especially in recent decades, rapid increases in the volume of international trade, travel, and communication have broken down the isolation and independence of most countries and people. Also contributing to globalization is the growth of many institutions that bind corporations, companies, and cultures together. These processes have caused people to depend more than ever on people in other countries for products, services, ideas, and even a sense of identity.

Sociologists agree that globalization and postindustrialism promise many exciting opportunities to enhance the quality of life and increase human freedom. However, they also see many social-structural barriers to the realization of that promise. We can summarize both the promise and the barriers by drawing a compass—a sociological compass (see Figure 1.6). Each axis of the compass contrasts a promise with the barriers to its realization. The vertical axis contrasts the promise of equality of opportunity with the barrier of inequality of opportunity. The horizontal axis contrasts the promise of individual freedom with the barrier of constraint on that freedom. Let us consider these axes in more detail because much of our discussion in the following chapters turns on them.

The Postindustrial Revolution **refers to the technology-driven shift from manufacturing to service industries and the consequences of that shift for virtually all human activities.**

Globalization **is the process by which formerly separate economies, states, and cultures become tied together and people becoming increasingly aware of their growing interdependence.**

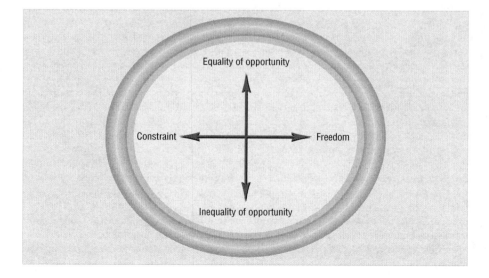

FIGURE 1.6
A Sociological Compass

Equality versus Inequality of Opportunity

Optimists forecast that postindustrialism will provide more opportunities for people to find creative, interesting, challenging, and rewarding work. In addition, the postindustrial era will generate more "equality of opportunity," that is, better chances for *all* people to get an education, influence government policy, and find good jobs.

You will find evidence to support these claims in this book. For example, we show that the average standard of living and the number of good jobs are increasing in postindustrial societies, such as Canada. Women are making rapid strides in the economy, the education system, and other institutions. Postindustrial societies like Canada are characterized by a decline in discrimination against members of minority groups, while democracy is spreading throughout the world. Desperately poor people form a declining percentage of the world's population.

Yet, as you read this book, it will also become clear that all these seemingly happy stories have a dark underside. For example, it turns out that the number of routine jobs with low pay and few benefits is growing faster than the number of creative, high-paying jobs. An enormous opportunity gulf still separates women from men. Racism and discrimination are still a part of our world. Our health care system is in crisis just as our population is aging rapidly and most in need of health care. Many of the world's new democracies are only superficially democratic, while Canadians and citizens of other postindustrial societies are increasingly cynical about the ability of their political systems to respond to their needs. Many people are looking for alternative forms of political expression. The *absolute* number of desperately poor people in the world continues to grow, as does the gap between rich and poor nations. Many people attribute the world's most serious problems to globalization. They have formed organizations and movements—some of them violent—to oppose it. In short, equality of opportunity is an undeniably attractive ideal, but it is unclear whether it is the inevitable outcome of a globalized, postindustrial society.

Freedom versus Constraint

Growing freedom is also evident—but within limits. In an earlier era, most people retained their religious, ethnic, racial, and sexual identities for a lifetime, even if they were not particularly comfortable with them. They often remained in social relationships that made them unhappy. One of the major themes of *Sociology: Your Compass for a New World* is that many people are now freer to construct their identities and form social relationships in ways that suit them. To a greater degree than ever before, it is possible to *choose* who you want to be, with whom you want to associate, and how you want to associate with them. The postindustrial and global era frees people from traditional constraints by encouraging virtually instant global communication, international migration, greater acceptance of sexual diversity and a variety of family forms, the growth of ethnically and racially diverse cities, and so forth. For instance, in the past people often stayed in marriages even if they were dissatisfied with them. Families often involved a father working in the paid labour force and a mother keeping house and raising children without pay. Today, people are freer to end unhappy marriages and create family structures that are more suited to their individual needs.

Again, however, we must face the less rosy aspects of postindustrialism and globalization. In many of the following chapters, we point out how increased freedom is experienced only within certain limits and how social diversity is limited by a strong push to conformity in some spheres of life. For example, we can choose a far wider variety of consumer products than ever before, but consumerism itself increasingly seems a compulsory way of life. Moreover, it is a way of life that threatens the natural environment. Meanwhile, some new technologies, such as surveillance cameras, cause us to modify our behaviour and act in more conformist ways. Large, impersonal bureaucracies and standardized products and services dehumanize both staff and customers. The tastes and the profit motive of vast media conglomerates, most of them American-owned, govern most of our cultural consumption and arguably threaten the survival of distinctive national cultures. Powerful interests are trying to shore up the traditional nuclear family even though it does not suit some people. As these examples show, the push to uniformity counters the trend toward growing social diversity. Postindustrialism and globalization may make us freer in some ways, but they also place new constraints on us.

WHY SOCIOLOGY?

Our overview of themes in *Sociology: Your Compass for a New World* drives home a point made by Anthony Giddens, renowned British sociologist and adviser to former British Prime Minister Tony Blair. According to Giddens, we live in an era "suspended between extraordinary opportunity . . . and global catastrophe" (Giddens, 1990: 166). A whole range of environmental issues; profound inequalities in the wealth of nations and of classes; religious, racial, and ethnic violence; and unsolved problems in the relations between women and men continue to profoundly affect the quality of our everyday lives.

Despair and apathy are possible responses to these complex issues, but they are not responses that humans favour. If it were our nature to give up hope, we would still be sitting around half-naked in the mud outside a cave.

People are more inclined to look for ways of improving their lives, and this period of human history is full of opportunities to do so. We have, for example, advanced to the point where, for the first time, we have the means to feed and educate everyone in the world. Similarly, it now seems possible to erode some of the inequalities that have always been the major source of human conflict.

Careers in Sociology

Sociology offers useful advice on how to achieve the goals of equality and freedom because it is more than just an intellectual exercise. Sociology is an applied science with practical, everyday uses in the realms of teaching and public policy, and the creation of laws and regulations by organizations and governments (see Box 1.3 on page 28). That is because sociologists are trained not just to see what is, but also to see what is possible.

WHERE DO
YOU FIT IN?

Students often ask: "Can I get a good job with a sociology degree?" "Exactly what kind of work could I do with a major in sociology?" "Aren't all the good jobs these days in technical areas and the natural sciences?" To answer these questions—and to help you decide whether it makes sense for you to major in sociology or another social science—consider the following data on the employment of Canadians with degrees in sociology and related fields.

A study based on 1988 data found that a higher percentage of Canadian sociology graduates were employed full-time than were graduates in the other social sciences (Guppy and Hedley, 1993). A study based mainly on 1996 data (Allen, 1999) showed that, in Canada,

- the unemployment rate among social science graduates was lower than among graduates in math, physics, engineering, agriculture, and biology.
- between 1991 and 1996, there were more new jobs for people with social science degrees than for people with degrees in other fields.
- although women earned less than men in all fields in 1996, the discrepancy between men's and women's income was smallest among social science graduates.

On the basis of these findings, it seems that sociology degrees promise more employment security for both men and women, and less income discrimination against women, than do other degrees. It also seems that the postindustrial economy requires more new employees with a social science background than new employees with a background in some technical and scientific fields.

Tens of thousands of Canadians have a B.A. in sociology. A sociology B.A. improves a person's understanding of the diverse social conditions affecting men and women; people with different sexual orientations; and people from different countries, regions, classes, races, and ethnic groups. Therefore, people with a B.A. in sociology tend to be attracted to

BOX 1.3
Social Policy: What Do You Think?

Are Corporate Scandals a Problem of Individual Ethics or Social Policy?

In 2002 the Sloan School of Management at the Massachusetts Institute of Technology conducted a survey of 600 graduates as part of its 50th anniversary observance. Sixty percent of survey respondents said that honesty, integrity, and ethics are the main characteristics of a good corporate leader. Most alumni felt that living a moral professional life is more important than pulling in large paycheques and generous perquisites.

Unfortunately, the behaviour of North American executives sometimes fails to reflect high ethical standards. In 2002, for example, investigators uncovered the biggest corporate scandals ever to rock the United States. Things got so bad that Andy Grove, a founder of Intel, said he was "embarrassed and ashamed" to be a corporate executive in America today (quoted in Hochberg, 2002), and the Wall Street investment firm of Charles Schwab ran a highly defensive television ad claiming to be "almost the opposite of a Wall Street firm." What brought about such astonishing statements was that several corporate giants, including Enron, WorldCom, Tyco, Global Crossings, and Adelphia Communications, were shown to have engaged in accounting fraud to make their earnings appear higher than they actually were. This practice kept their stock prices artificially high—until investigators made public what was going on, at which time their stock prices took a nosedive. Ordinary stockholders lost hundreds of billions of dollars. Many company employees lost their pensions (because they had been encouraged or compelled to place their retirement funds in company stock) and their jobs (because their companies soon filed for bankruptcy). In contrast, accounting fraud greatly benefited senior executives. They had received stock options as part of their compensation package. If you own stock options, you can buy company stock whenever you want at a fixed low price, even if the market price for the stock is much higher. Senior executives typically exercised their stock options *before* the stocks crashed, netting them billions of dollars in profit.

Canada has not been immune to unethical behaviour in the highest corporate ranks. For example, thousands of ordinary Canadians lost billions of dollars, including substantial pension savings, when senior executives of telecommunications giant Nortel grossly overstated the company's profitability and prospects, earned huge bonuses on the basis of false accounting, and then watched the stock slide from a high of $124.50 in July 2000 to 64 cents in October 2002. Several senior executives lost their jobs, but they were not prosecuted and they all kept their ill-gotten gains. In 2004, a group of Canadian investors launched a class-action lawsuit against newspaper baron Conrad Black and other executives of Hollinger International for $4 billion in damages. The suit claimed market losses may have been caused by controversies involving Black's management and allegations that he and associates quietly pocketed $400 million to which they were not entitled. (Black was eventually found guilty in an American court of fraud and obstruction of justice and was sentenced to a 6-1/2-year jail term.)

Can we rely on individual morality or ethics to show senior executives how to behave responsibly, that is, in the long-term interest of their companies and society as a whole? Ethics courses have been taught at all business schools for years but, as the dean of one business school noted, these courses can't "turn sinners into saints. . . . If a company does a lot of crazy stuff but its share price continues to rise, a lot of people will look the other way and not really care whether senior management is behaving ethically or not" (quoted in Goll, 2002).

Because individual ethics often seem weak in the face of greed, some observers have suggested that new public policies, that is, laws and regulations passed by organizations and governments, are required to regulate executive compensation. For example, some people think the practice of granting stock options to senior executives should be outlawed, stiff jail terms should be imposed on anyone who engages in accounting fraud, and strong legal protection should be offered to anyone who "blows the whistle" on executive wrongdoing.

Sociology helps us see what may appear to be personal issues in the larger context of public policy. Even our tendency to act ethically or unethically is shaped in part by public policy—or the lack of it. Therefore, we review a public policy debate in each chapter of this book. It is good exercise for the sociological imagination, and it will help you gain more control over the forces that shape your life.

jobs requiring good "people skills" and jobs involved in managing and promoting social change (see Table 1.2).

People with a B.A. in sociology often go on to take graduate and professional degrees in other fields, including law, urban planning, industrial relations, social work, and public

Government

Community affairs officer
Urban/regional planner
Legislative aide
Affirmative action/
  employment equity
  worker
Foreign service officer
Human rights officer
Personnel coordinator

Research

Social research specialist
Consumer researcher
Data analyst
Market researcher
Survey researcher
Census officer/analyst
Demographer/population
  analyst
Systems analyst

Community Affairs

Occupational/career
  counsellor
Homeless/housing worker

Public health/hospital
  administrator
Child development
  technician
Public administration
  assistant
Social assistance advocate
Resident planning aide
Group home worker
Rehabilitation program
  worker
Rural health outreach
  worker
Housing coordinator
Fundraising director/
  assistant
Caseworker/aide
Community organizer
Youth outreach worker

Corrections

Corrections officer
Criminology assistant
Police officer
Rehabilitation counsellor
Criminal investigator
Juvenile court worker
Parole officer

Teaching

College/university
  placement worker
Public health educator
Teacher
Admissions counsellor

Business

Market analyst
Project manager
Sales representative
Real estate agent
Journalist
Public relations officer
Actuary
Insurance agent
Human resources manager
Production manager
Labour relations officer
Administrative assistant
Quality control manager
Merchandiser/purchaser
Computer analyst
Data entry manager
Publishing officer
Advertising officer
Sales manager

TABLE 1.2

Jobs Commonly Held by
Canadians with Degrees
in Sociology

Source: Neil Guppy and R. Alan
Hedley. (1993). *Opportunities in
Sociology* (Montreal: Canadian
Sociology and Anthropology
Association). Reprinted with
permission of the Canadian
Sociology and Anthropology
Association.

policy. Most people with a graduate degree in sociology teach and conduct research in universities, with research being a more important component of the job in larger and more prestigious institutions. But many sociologists do not teach. Instead, they conduct research and give policy advice in a wide range of settings outside the system of higher education. In many federal government agencies, for example, sociologists are employed as researchers and policy consultants. Sociologists also conduct research and policy analysis in trade unions, non-governmental organizations, and professional and public interest associations. In the private sector, you can find sociologists practising their craft in firms specializing in public opinion polling, management consulting, market research, standardized testing, and evaluation research, which assesses the impact of particular policies and programs before or after they go into effect.

One way to see the benefits of a sociological education is to compile a list of some of the famous practical idealists who studied sociology in university. That list includes several former heads of state, among them President Fernando Cardoso of Brazil, President Tomas Masaryk of Czechoslovakia, Prime Minister Edward Seaga of Jamaica, and President Ronald Reagan of the United States. The former vice-president of the Liberal Party of Canada and president and vice-chancellor of York University in Toronto, Lorna Marsden, is a sociologist. Anthony Giddens, former director of the London School of Economics and adviser to former British Prime Minister Tony Blair, also holds a doctorate in sociology. So do Martin Goldfarb, chairman, president, and CEO of Goldfarb Consultants International, and Donna Dasko, senior vice-president of Environics; they head two of Canada's leading public opinion firms with offices and affiliates around the world. Alex Himelfarb, former clerk of the Privy Council and secretary to the Cabinet in Ottawa, and now the Canadian ambassador to Italy, holds a sociology Ph.D. too. British Columbia native Steve Nash of the Phoenix Suns is widely considered the best team player in professional basketball today, and his agent claims he is "the most color-blind person I've ever known" (Robbins, 2005). Arguably, Nash's sociology degree contributes to his team-building ability and his performance on the court by helping him to better understand the importance of groups and diverse social conditions in shaping human behaviour.

In sum, although sociology does not offer easy solutions to the question of how the goal of improving society may be accomplished, it does provide a useful way of understanding our current predicament and seeing possible ways of dealing with it, of leading us a little farther away from the mud outside the cave. You sampled sociology's ability to tie personal troubles to social-structural issues when we discussed suicide. You reviewed the major theoretical perspectives that enable sociologists to connect the personal with the social-structural. When we outlined the half-fulfilled promises of postindustrialism and globalization, you saw sociology's ability to provide an understanding of where we are and where we can go.

We frankly admit that the questions we raise in this book are tough to answer. Sharp controversy surrounds them all. However, we are sure that if you try to grapple with them, you will enhance your understanding of your society's, and your own, possibilities. In brief, sociology can help you figure out where you fit into society and how you can make society fit you.

NOTES

1. At the end of 2002, the Innu began to be relocated at government expense to new homes in Natuashish, a modern village carved out of the wilderness 15 kilometres west of Davis Inlet. By 2005, it was clear that modern dwellings alone were unable to solve the complex social problems of the Innu, which merely reproduced themselves in Natuashish.

2. Some sociologists also distinguish *mesostructures,* social relations that link microstructures and macrostructures. See Chapter 6, Networks, Groups, Bureaucracies, and Societies.

SUMMARY

1. What does the sociological study of suicide tell us about society and about sociology?
   Durkheim noted that suicide is an apparently non-social and antisocial action that people often, but unsuccessfully, try to explain psychologically. He showed that suicide rates are influenced by the level of social solidarity of the groups to which people belong. This theory suggests that a distinctively *social* realm influences all human behaviour.

2. What is the sociological perspective?
   The sociological perspective analyzes the connection between personal troubles and three levels of social structure: microstructures, macrostructures, and global structures.

3. How are values, theories, and research related?
   Values are ideas about what is right and wrong. Values often motivate sociologists to define which problems are worth studying and to make initial assumptions about how to explain sociological phenomena. A theory is a tentative explanation of some aspect of social life. It states how and why specific facts are connected. Research is the process of carefully observing social reality to test the validity of a theory. Sociological theories may be modified and even rejected through research, and those theories are often motivated by sociologists' values.

4. What are the major theoretical traditions in sociology?

Sociology has four major theoretical traditions. Functionalism analyzes how social order is supported by macrostructures. The conflict approach analyzes how social inequality is maintained and challenged. Symbolic interactionism analyzes how meaning is created when people communicate in microlevel settings. Feminist theories focus on the social sources of patriarchy in both macrolevel and microlevel settings.

5. What were the main influences on the rise of sociology?

The rise of sociology was stimulated by the Scientific, Industrial, and Democratic Revolutions. The Scientific Revolution encouraged the view that sound conclusions about the workings of society must be based on solid evidence, not just on speculation. The Democratic Revolution suggested that people are responsible for organizing society and that human intervention can therefore solve social problems. The Industrial Revolution created a host of new and serious social problems that attracted the attention of many social thinkers.

6. What are the main influences on sociology today and what are the main interests of sociology?

The Postindustrial Revolution is the technology-driven shift from manufacturing to service industries. Globalization is the process by which formerly separate economies, states, and cultures become tied together and people become increasingly aware of their growing interdependence. The causes and consequences of postindustrialism and globalization form the great sociological puzzles of our time. The tensions between equality and inequality of opportunity, and between freedom and constraint, are among the chief interests of sociology today.

KEY TERMS

class conflict (p. 17)	**patriarchy** (p. 9)
conflict theory (p. 17)	**Postindustrial Revolution** (p. 25)
Democratic Revolution (p. 13)	**Protestant ethic** (p. 18)
dysfunctional consequences (p. 17)	**research** (p. 15)
feminist theory (p. 20)	**Scientific Revolution** (p. 12)
functionalism (p. 16)	**social constructionism** (p. 19)
global structures (p. 10)	**social solidarity** (p. 6)
globalization (p. 25)	**social structures** (p. 9)
Industrial Revolution (p. 13)	**sociological imagination** (p. 10)
latent functions (p. 17)	**symbolic interactionism** (p. 19)
macrostructures (p. 9)	**theories** (p. 15)
manifest functions (p. 17)	**values** (p. 15)
microstructures (p. 9)	

QUESTIONS TO CONSIDER

1. What is the difference between objectivity and subjectivity? What roles do objectivity and subjectivity play in sociology?

2. What does Durkheim mean by "social solidarity"? How does he apply the term to the study of suicide? Comparing Canada 100 years ago with Canada today, how and why do you think the level of social solidarity has changed? What accounts for the change?

What are some consequences of the change? Has the level of social solidarity changed more for some groups than for others? If so, why and with what consequences?

3. Do you think Canadians have more or less freedom and equality of opportunity now than they did 100 years ago? Do you think we will have more or less freedom and equality of opportunity in 100 years than we do today? Justify your argument.

WEB RESOURCES

Companion Website for This Book

http://www.compass3e.nelson.com

Begin by clicking on the Student Resources section of the website. Next, select the chapter you are studying from the pull-down menu. From the Student Resources page you have easy access to InfoTrac® College Edition, additional Weblinks, and other resources. The website also has many useful tips to aid you in your study of sociology, including practice tests for each chapter.

InfoTrac® Search Terms

These search terms are provided to assist you in beginning to conduct research on this topic by visiting http://www.infotrac-college.com:

conflict theory
feminism
functionalism
social structure
suicide
symbolic interactionism

Recommended Websites

For an inspiring essay on the practice of the sociological craft by one of North America's leading sociologists, see Gary T. Marx, "Of Methods and Manners for Aspiring Sociologists: 37 Moral Imperatives," on the World Wide Web at http://web.mit.edu/gtmarx/www/37moral.html.

SocioWeb is a comprehensive guide to sociological resources on the World Wide Web at http://www.socioweb.com.

The Canadian Sociological Association (CSA) is the professional organization of Canadian sociologists. Visit the CSA website at http://www.csaa.ca.

CengageNOW™

http://hed.nelson.com

This online diagnostic tool identifies each student's unique needs with a Pretest that generates a personalized Study Plan for each chapter, helping students focus on concepts they're having the most difficulty mastering. Students then take a Posttest after reading the chapter to measure their understanding of the material. An Instructor Gradebook is available to track and monitor student progress.

Chapter 6:
Social Research Methods

CHAPTER

2

How Sociologists Do Research

In this chapter, you will learn that

- Scientific ideas differ from common sense and other forms of knowledge. Scientific ideas are assessed in the clear light of systematically collected evidence and public scrutiny.

- Sociological research depends not just on the rigorous testing of ideas but also on creative insight. Thus, the objective and subjective phases of inquiry are both important in good research.

- The main methods of collecting sociological data include experiments, surveys, systematic observations of natural social settings, and the analysis of existing documents and official statistics.

- Each data collection method has characteristic strengths and weaknesses. Each method is appropriate for different kinds of research problems.

SCIENCE AND EXPERIENCE

PERSONAL
ANECDOTE

OTTFFSSENT

"Okay, Mr. Smarty Pants, see if you can figure this one out." That's how Robert Brym's 11-year-old daughter, Talia, greeted him one day when she came home from school.

"I wrote some letters of the alphabet on this sheet of paper. They form a pattern. Take a look at the letters and tell me the pattern."

Robert took the sheet of paper from Talia and smiled confidently. "Like most North Americans, I'd had a lot of experience with this sort of puzzle," says Robert. "For example, most IQ and SAT tests ask you to find patterns in sequences of letters, and you learn certain ways of solving these problems. One of the most common methods is to see if the 'distance' between adjoining letters stays the same or varies predictably. For example, in the sequence ADGJ, there are two missing letters between each adjoining pair. Insert the missing letters and you get the first 10 letters of the alphabet: A(BC)D(EF)G(HI)J.

"This time, however, I was stumped. On the sheet of paper Talia had written the letters OTTFFSSENT. I tried to use the distance method to solve the problem. Nothing worked. After 10 minutes of head scratching, I gave up."

"The answer's easy," Talia said, clearly pleased at her father's failure. "Spell out the numbers 1 to 10. The first letter of each word—one, two, three, and so forth—spells OTTFFSSENT. Looks like you're not as smart as you thought. See ya." And with that she bounced off to her room.

"Later that day, it dawned on me that Talia had taught me more than just a puzzle. She had shown me that experience sometimes prevents people from seeing things. My experience with solving letter puzzles by using certain set methods kept me from solving the unusual problem of OTTFFSSENT." Said differently, reality (in this case, a pattern of letters) is not just a thing "out there" we can learn to perceive "objectively." As social scientists have appreciated for more than a century, *experience* helps determine how we perceive reality, including what patterns we see and whether we are able to see patterns at all (Hughes, 1967: 16).

The fact that experience filters perceptions is the single biggest problem for sociological research. In sociological research, the filtering occurs in four stages (see Figure 2.1). First, as noted in Chapter 1, A Sociological Compass, the real-life experiences and passions of sociologists motivate much research. That is, our *values* often help us decide which problems are worth investigating. These values may reflect the typical outlook of our class, race, gender, region, historical period, and so on. Second, our values lead us to formulate and adopt favoured *theories* for interpreting and explaining those problems. Third, sociologists' interpretations are influenced by *previous research,* which we consult to find out what we already know about a subject. And fourth, the *methods* we use to gather data mould our perceptions. The shape of our tools often helps determine which bits of reality we dig up.

FIGURE 2.1
How Research Filters
Perception

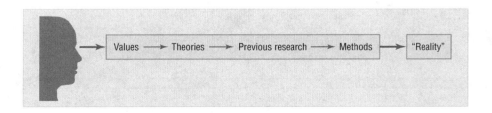

Given that values, theories, previous research, and research methods filter our perceptions, you are right to conclude that we can never perceive society in a pure or objective form.[1] What we can do is use techniques of data collection that minimize bias. We can also clearly and publicly describe the filters that influence our perceptions. Doing so enables us to eliminate obvious sources of bias. It also helps others see biases we miss and try to correct for them. The end result is a more accurate perception of reality than is possible by relying exclusively on blind prejudice or common sense.

It is thus clear that a healthy tension pervades all sociological scholarship. On the one hand, researchers generally try to be objective in order to perceive reality as clearly as possible. They follow the rules of the scientific method and design data collection techniques to minimize bias. On the other hand, the values and passions that grow out of personal experience are important sources of creativity. As Max Weber said, we choose to study "only those segments of reality which have become significant to us because of their value-relevance" (Weber, 1964 [1949]: 76). So objectivity and subjectivity each play an important role in science, including sociology. Oversimplifying a little, we can say that although objectivity is a reality check, subjectivity leads us to define which aspects of reality are worth checking on in the first place.

Most of this chapter is about the reality check. It explores how sociologists try to adhere to the rules of the scientific method. We first contrast scientific and unscientific thinking. We next discuss the steps involved in the sociological research process. We then describe the main methods of gathering sociological data and the decisions that have to be made during the research process. Finally, we return to the role of subjectivity in research.

Scientific versus Unscientific Thinking

In science, seeing is believing. In everyday life, believing is seeing. In other words, in everyday life our biases easily influence our observations. This often leads us to draw incorrect conclusions about what we see. In contrast, scientists, including sociologists, develop ways of collecting, observing, and thinking about evidence that minimize their chance of drawing biased conclusions.

On what basis do you decide statements are true in everyday life? Below we describe 10 types of unscientific thinking (Babbie, 2000). As you read about each one, ask yourself how frequently you think unscientifically. If you often think unscientifically, use this chapter to help you develop more objective ways of thinking.

WHERE DO
YOU FIT IN?

1. "Chicken soup helps get rid of a cold. *It worked for my grandparents, and it works for me.*" This statement represents knowledge based on *tradition*. Although some traditional knowledge is valid (sugar will rot your teeth), some is not (masturbation will not blind you). Science is required to separate valid from invalid knowledge.

2. "Weak magnets can be used to heal many illnesses. *I read all about it in the newspaper.*" This statement represents knowledge based on *authority*. We often think something is true because we read it in an authoritative source or hear it from an expert. But authoritative sources and experts can be wrong. For example, nineteenth-century Western physicians commonly bled their patients with leeches to draw "poisons" from their bodies. This often did more harm than good. As this example suggests, scientists should always question authority to arrive at more valid knowledge.

3. "The car that hit the cyclist was dark brown. I was going for a walk last night when *I saw the accident.*" This statement represents knowledge based on *casual observation*. Unfortunately, we are usually pretty careless observers. That is why good lawyers can often trip up eyewitnesses in courtrooms. Eyewitnesses are rarely certain about what they saw. In general, uncertainty can be reduced by observing in a conscious and deliberate manner and by recording observations. That is just what scientists do.

4. "If you work hard, you can get ahead. *I know because several of my parents' friends started off poor but are now comfortably middle class.*" This statement represents knowledge based on *overgeneralization*. For instance, if you know a few people who started off poor, worked

Perhaps the first major advance in modern medicine took place when doctors stopped using unproven interventions in their treatment of patients. One such intervention involved bleeding patients, shown here in a medieval drawing.

hard, and became rich you may think any poor person can become rich if he or she works hard enough. You may not know about the more numerous poor people who work hard and remain poor or about the rich people who never worked hard. Scientists, however, sample cases that are representative of entire populations. This enables them to avoid overgeneralization. They also avoid overgeneralization by repeating research, which ensures that they do not draw conclusions from an unusual set of research findings.

5. "I'm right because *I can't think of any contrary cases*." This statement represents knowledge based on *selective observation*. Sometimes we unconsciously ignore evidence that challenges our firmly held beliefs. Thus, you may actually know some people who work hard but remain poor. However, to maintain your belief that hard work results in wealth, you may keep them out of mind. The scientific requirement that evidence be drawn from representative samples of the population minimizes bias arising from selective observation.

6. "Mr. Smith is poor even though he works hard, but that's because he has a disability. People with disabilities are the only *exception to the rule* that if you work hard you can get ahead." This statement represents knowledge based on *qualification*. Qualifications or "exceptions to the rule" are often made in everyday life, and they are in science, too. The difference is that in everyday life, qualifications are easily accepted as valid, while in scientific inquiry they are treated as statements that must be carefully examined in the light of evidence.

7. "The Toronto Blue Jays won 50 percent of their baseball games over the last three months but 65 percent of the games they played on Thursdays. *Because it happened so often before*, I bet they'll win next Thursday." This statement represents knowledge based on *illogical reasoning*. In everyday life, we may expect the recurrence of events without reasonable cause, ignoring the fact that rare sequences of events occur just by chance. For example, it is possible for you to flip a coin 10 times and have it come up heads each time. On average, this will happen once every 1024 times you flip a coin 10 times. In the absence of any apparent reason for this happening, it is merely coincidental. It is illogical to believe otherwise. Scientists refrain from illogical reasoning. They also use statistical techniques to distinguish between events that are probably due to chance and those that are not.

8. "*I just can't be wrong*." This statement represents knowledge based on *ego-defence*. Even scientists may be passionately committed to the conclusions they reach in their research because they have invested much time, energy, and money in them. It is other scientists—more accurately, the whole institution of science, with its commitment to publishing research results and critically scrutinizing findings—that put strict limits on ego-defence in scientific understanding.

9. "*The matter is settled once and for all*." This statement represents knowledge based on the *premature closure of inquiry*. This way of thinking involves deciding that all the relevant evidence has been gathered on a particular subject. Science, however, is committed to the idea that all theories are only temporarily true. Matters are never settled.

10. "*There must be supernatural forces at work here*." This statement represents knowledge based on *mystification*. When we can find no rational explanation for a phenomenon, we may attribute it to forces that cannot be observed or fully understood. Although such forces may exist, scientists remain skeptical. They are committed to discovering observable causes of observable effects.

Even Albert Einstein, often hailed as the most intelligent person of the twentieth century, sometimes ignored evidence in favour of pet theories. However, the social institution of science, which makes ideas public and subjects them to careful scrutiny, often overcomes such bias.

CONDUCTING RESEARCH

The Research Cycle

Sociological research seeks to overcome the kind of unscientific thinking described above. It is a cyclical process that involves six steps (Figure 2.2).

First, the sociologist must *formulate a research question*. A research question must be stated so it can be answered by systematically collecting and analyzing sociological data.

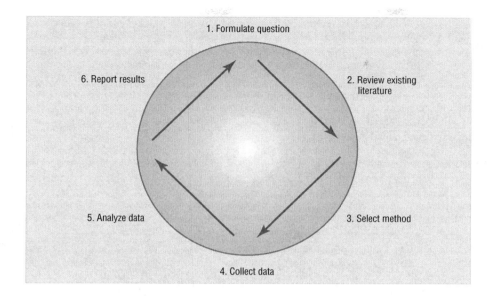

FIGURE 2.2
The Research Cycle

Sociological research cannot determine whether God exists or what the best political system is. Answers to such questions require faith more than evidence. Sociological research can determine why some people are more religious than others are and which political systems create more opportunities for higher education. Answers to such questions require evidence more than faith.

Second, the sociologist must *review the existing research literature.* Researchers must elaborate their research questions in light of what other sociologists have already debated and discovered. Why? Because reading the relevant sociological literature stimulates researchers' sociological imagination, allows them to refine their initial questions, and prevents duplication of effort.

Selecting a research method is the third step in the research cycle. As we will see in detail below, each data collection method has strengths and weaknesses. Each method is therefore best suited to studying a different kind of problem. When choosing a method, we must keep these strengths and weaknesses in mind. (In the ideal but, unfortunately, infrequent case, several methods are used simultaneously to study the same problem. This can overcome the drawbacks of any single method and increase confidence in the findings.)

Carol Wainio's *We Can Be Certain* (1982). Research involves taking the plunge from speculation to testing ideas against evidence.

NEL

The fourth stage of the research cycle involves *collecting data* by observing subjects, interviewing them, reading documents produced by or about them, and so forth. Many researchers think this is the most exciting stage of the research cycle because it brings them face to face with the puzzling sociological reality that so fascinates them.

Other researchers find the fifth step of the research cycle, *analyzing the data,* the most challenging. During data analysis you can learn things that nobody ever knew before. It is the time when data confirm some of your expectations and confound others, requiring you to think creatively about familiar issues, reconsider the relevant theoretical and research literature, and abandon pet ideas.

Of course, research is not much use to the sociological community, the subjects of the research, or the wider society if researchers do not *publish the results* in a report, a scientific journal, or a book. That is the research cycle's sixth step. Publication serves another important function, too. It allows other sociologists to scrutinize and criticize the research. On that basis, errors can be corrected and new and more sophisticated research questions can be formulated for the next round of research. In this sense, the practice of science is a social activity governed by rules defined and enforced by the scientific community.

It would be wrong to think that the research cycle always begins at the first stage and then proceeds to stage two, then to stage three, and so forth. The research cycle is a useful way of thinking about the stages of research—an ideal, if you will—but the exact starting point and progression of research varies from one project to the next. For example, sometimes research begins with a personal puzzle, sometimes with alternative interpretations of observations collected in a project, and sometimes with a skeptical perspective on the research literature.

Ethical Considerations

Throughout the research cycle, researchers must be mindful of the need to *respect their subjects' rights,* which means, in the first instance, that researchers must do their subjects no harm. This is the right to safety. People must have the right to decide whether they can be studied and, if so, in what way. Second, research subjects must have the right to decide whether their attitudes and behaviours may be revealed to the public and, if so, in what way. This is the right to privacy. Third, researchers cannot use data in a way that allows them to be traced to a particular subject. This is the subject's right to confidentiality. Fourth, subjects must be told how the information they supply will be used. They must also be allowed to judge the degree of personal risk involved in answering questions. This is the right to informed consent.

Ethical issues arise not only in the treatment of subjects but also in the treatment of research results. For example, plagiarism is a concern in academic life, especially among students, who write research papers and give them to professors for evaluation. A 2003 study found that 38 percent of college students admitted to committing "cut and paste" plagiarism when writing essays, up from just 10 percent in 2000 (Edmundson, 2003). Ready-made essays are also widely available for purchase.

Increased plagiarism is a consequence of the spread of the web and the growing view that everything on it is public and therefore does not have to be cited. That view is wrong. The Code of Ethics of the American Sociological Association states that we must "explicitly identify, credit, and reference the author" when we make any use of another person's written work, "whether it is published, unpublished, or electronically available" (American Sociological Association, 1999: 16).

Making such ethical standards better known can help remedy the problem of plagiarism. So can better policing. Powerful web-based applications are now available that help university and college instructors determine whether essays are plagiarized in whole or in part (visit http://www.turnitin.com). Perhaps the most effective remedy, however, is for instructors to ensure that what they teach really matters to their students. If they do, students won't be as inclined to plagiarize because they will regard essay writing as a process of personal discovery. You can't cut, paste, or buy enlightenment (Edmundson, 2003).

Bearing in mind our thumbnail sketch of the research cycle, we devote the rest of this chapter mainly to exploring its fourth and fifth stage, the gathering and analyzing of evidence. In this context we describe each of sociology's major research methods. These methods include participant observation, experiments, surveys, and the examination of existing documents and official statistics. We begin by describing participant observation research and related research methods.

THE MAIN METHODS OF SOCIOLOGY

Field Methods: From Detached Observation to "Going Native"

Eikoku News Digest published a column in the late 1990s by a supposed expert observer of English social life. It advised Japanese residents of England how to act English. One column informed readers that once they hear the words "You must come round for dinner!" they will have been accepted into English social life and must therefore know how to behave appropriately. The column advised readers to obey the following dinner party rules:

1. Arrive 20 minutes late because in England dinner always takes 20 minutes longer to prepare than expected.
2. Don't compliment the décor because in England everyone else's taste in décor is considered dreadful.
3. Bring a cheap wine because the English can't taste the difference.
4. Praise the food by saying "mmmm." The larger the number of "m"s, the greater the compliment.
5. After the meal, don't say it was good. "If someone asks how your dinner was, do not praise the food in detail. They will deduce that the conversation was boring. . . . And do not talk about the interesting conversation you had. They will assume that the food was particularly unpleasant." ("Going Native: Dinner Parties," 2003)

This advice was almost certainly meant as a joke. However, its absurdity serves to caution all students of social life about the dangers of drawing conclusions based on casual observation. By observing others casually, we can easily get things terribly wrong.

Some sociologists undertake **field research**, or research based on the observation of people in their natural settings. The field researcher goes wherever people meet. Settings investigated by field researchers include hospital intensive care units, the Yukon International Storytelling Festival, white teenage heavy-metal gangs, the studio audience of a daytime TV talk show, the gay community, the alternative hard rock scene, ethnic slums, and the rave subculture (Chambliss, 1996; Cruikshank, 1997; Gaines, 1990; Grindstaff, 1997; Humphreys, 1975; Schippers, 2002; Whyte, 1981 [1943]; Wilson, 2002). When they arrive in the field, however, researchers come prepared with strategies to avoid getting things terribly wrong.

One such strategy is *detached observation*. This approach involves classifying and counting the behaviour of interest according to a predetermined scheme. For example, a sociologist wanted to know more about how gender segregation originates. He observed children of different ages playing in summer camps and daycare centres in Canada and Poland. He recorded the gender composition of play groups, the ages at which children started playing in gender-segregated groups, and the kinds of play activities that became gender segregated (Richer, 1990). Similarly, two sociologists wanted to know more about why some American college students don't participate in class discussions. They sat in on classes and recorded the number of students who participated, the number of times they spoke, and the gender of the instructor and of the students who spoke (Karp and Yoels, 1976). In both research projects, the sociologists were interested in knowing how young people express gender in everyday behaviour, and they knew what to look for before they entered the field.

Field research is research based on the observation of people in their natural settings.

Two main problems confound direct observation. First, the presence of the researcher may itself affect the behaviour of the people being observed. Sociologists sometimes call this problem the *Hawthorne effect* because researchers at the Western Electric Company's Hawthorne factory in the 1930s claimed to find that workers' productivity increased no matter how they changed their work environment. Productivity increased, they said, just because the researchers were paying attention to the workers.[2] Similarly, some students may participate less in classroom discussion if researchers come in and start taking notes; the presence of the researchers may be intimidating. The second problem with direction observation is that the *meaning* of the observed behaviour may remain obscure to the researcher. The twitch of an eye may be an involuntary muscle contraction, an indication of a secret being kept, a sexual come-on, a parody of someone else twitching an eye, and so on. We cannot know what it means simply by observing the eye twitch.

To understand what an eye twitch (or any other behaviour) means we must be able to see it in its social context and from the point of view of the people we are observing. Anthropologists and a growing number of sociologists spend months or even years living with a people so they can learn their language, values, mannerisms—their entire culture— and develop an intimate understanding of their behaviour. This sort of research is called **ethnographic** when it describes the entire way of life of a people (*ethnos* means "nation" or "people" in Greek; Burawoy et al., 2000; Geertz, 1973; Gille and Riain, 2002).

In rare cases, ethnographic researchers have "gone native," actually giving up their research role and becoming members of the group they are studying. Going native is of no value to the sociological community because it does not result in the publication of new findings. However, going native is worth mentioning because it is the opposite of detached observation. Usually, field researchers employ techniques for collecting data between the two extremes of detached observation and going native. The field method they employ most often is participant observation.

Participant Observation

Sociologists engage in **participant observation** when they attempt to observe a social milieu objectively *and* take part in the activities of the people they are studying (Lofland and Lofland, 1995). By participating in the lives of their subjects, researchers are able to see the world from their subjects' point of view. This method allows them to achieve a deep and sympathetic understanding of people's beliefs, values, and motives. In addition, participant observation requires that sociologists step back and observe their subjects' milieu from an outsider's point of view. This helps them see their subjects more objectively. In participant-observation research, then, there is a tension between the goals of subjectivity and objectivity. As you will see, however, this is a healthy tension that enhances our understanding of many social settings.

The Professional Fence

A well-known example of participant-observation research is Carl B. Klockars's analysis of the professional "fence," a person who buys and sells stolen goods (Klockars, 1974). Among other things, Klockars wanted to understand how criminals can knowingly hurt people and live with the guilt. Are criminals capable of this because they are "sick" or unfeeling? Klockars came to a different conclusion by examining the case of Vincent Swaggi (a pseudonym).

Swaggi buys cheap stolen goods from thieves and then sells them in his store for a handsome profit. His buying is private and patently criminal. His selling is public and, to his customers, it appears to be legal. Consequently, Swaggi faces the moral dilemma shared by all criminals to varying degrees. He has to reconcile the very different moral codes of the two worlds he straddles, cancelling out any feelings of guilt he derives from conventional morality.

"The way I look at it, I'm a businessman," says Swaggi. "Sure I buy hot stuff, but I never stole nothing in my life. Some driver brings me a couple of cartons, though, I ain't gonna turn him away. If I don't buy it, somebody else will. So what's the difference? I might as

The **ethnographic** researcher spends months or even years living with a people to learn their language, values, mannerisms—their entire culture—and develop an intimate understanding of their behaviour.

Participant observation involves carefully observing people's face-to-face interactions and participating in their lives over a long period of time, thus achieving a deep and sympathetic understanding of what motivates them to act in the way they do.

well make money with him instead of somebody else." Swaggi thus denies responsibility for his actions. He also claims his actions never hurt anyone:

> Did you see the paper yesterday? You figure it out. Last year I musta had $25,000 wortha merchandise from Sears. In this city last year they could'a called it Sears, Roebuck, and Swaggi. Just yesterday I read where Sears just had the biggest year in history, made more money than ever before. Now if I had that much of Sears's stuff can you imagine how much they musta lost all told? Millions, must be millions. And they still had their biggest year ever. . . . You think they end up losing when they get clipped? Don't you believe it. They're no different from anybody else. If they don't get it back by takin' it off their taxes, they get it back from insurance. Who knows, maybe they do both.

And if he has done a few bad things in his life, then, says Swaggi, so has everyone else. Besides, he's also done a lot of good. In fact, he believes his virtuous acts more than compensate for the skeletons in his closet. Consider, for example, how he managed to protect one of his suppliers and get him a promotion at the same time:

> I had this guy bringin' me radios. Nice little clock radios, sold for $34.95. He worked in the warehouse. Two a day he'd bring me, an' I'd give him fifteen for the both of 'em. Well, after a while he told me his boss was gettin' suspicious 'cause inventory showed a big shortage. . . . So I ask him if anybody else is takin' much stuff. He says a couple of guys do. I tell him to lay off for a while an' the next time he sees one of the other guys take somethin' to tip off the boss. They'll fire the guy an' clear up the shortage. Well he did an' you know what happened? They made my man assistant shipper. Now once a month I get a carton delivered right to my store with my name on it. Clock radios, percolators, waffle irons, anything I want fifty off wholesale. (quoted in Klockars, 1974: 135–61)

Lessons in Method

Without Klockars's research, we might think that all criminals are able to live with their guilt only because they are pathological or lack empathy for their fellow human beings. But thanks partly to Klockars's research, we know better. We understand that criminals are able to avoid feeling guilty about their actions and get on with their work because they weave a blanket of rationalizations over their criminal activities. These justifications make their illegal activities appear morally acceptable and normal, at least to the criminals themselves. We understand this aspect of criminal activity better because Klockars spent 15 months befriending Swaggi and closely observing him on the job. He interviewed Swaggi for a total of about 400 hours, taking detailed "field notes" most of the time. He then wrote up his descriptions, quotations, and insights in a book that is now considered a minor classic in the sociology of crime and deviance.

Why is observation *and* participation necessary in participant-observation research? Because sociological insight is sharpest when researchers stand both inside and outside the lives of their subjects. Said differently, we see more clearly when we move back and forth between inside and outside.

By immersing themselves in their subjects' world, by learning their language and their culture in depth, insiders are able to experience the world just as their subjects do. Subjectivity can, however, go too far. After all, "natives" are rarely able to see their cultures with much objectivity and inmates of prisons and mental institutions do not have access to official information about themselves. It is only by regularly standing apart and observing their subjects from the point of view of outsiders that researchers can raise analytical issues and see things their subjects are blind to or are forbidden from seeing.

Objectivity can also go too far. Observers who try to attain complete objectivity will often not be able to make correct inferences about their subjects' behaviour. That is because they cannot fully understand the way their subjects experience the world and cannot ask them about their experiences. Instead, observers who seek complete objectivity must rely only on their own experiences to impute meaning to a social setting. Yet the meaning a situation holds for observers may differ from the meaning it holds for their subjects.

In short, opting for pure observation or pure participation compromises the researcher's ability to see the world sociologically. Instead, participant observation requires the researcher to keep walking a tightrope between the two extremes of objectivity and subjectivity.

It is often difficult for participant-observers to gain access to the groups they want to study. They must first win the confidence of their subjects, who must feel at ease in the presence of the researcher before they behave naturally. *Reactivity* occurs when the researcher's presence influences the subjects' behaviour (Webb, Campbell, Schwartz, and Sechrest, 1966). Reaching a state of non-reactivity requires patience and delicacy on the researcher's part. It took Klockars several months to meet and interview about 60 imprisoned thieves before one of them felt comfortable enough to recommend that he contact Swaggi. Klockars had to demonstrate genuine interest in the thieves' activities and convince them he was no threat to them before they opened up to him. Often, sociologists can minimize reactivity by gaining access to a group in stages. At first, researchers may simply attend a group meeting. After a time, they may start to attend more regularly. Then, when their faces are more familiar, they may strike up a conversation with some of the friendlier group members. Only later will they begin to explain their true motivation for attending.

Klockars and Swaggi are both white men. Their similarity made communication between them easier. In contrast, race, gender, class, and age differences sometimes make it difficult, and occasionally impossible, for some researchers to study some groups. We can scarcely imagine a sociologist nearing retirement conducting participant-observation research on youth gangs or a black sociologist using this research method to study skinheads. Nonetheless, in many participant-observation studies, the big social differences between sociologists and their subjects were overcome and resulted in excellent research (e.g., Liebow, 1967; Stack, 1974).

Exploratory research is an attempt to describe, understand, and develop a theory about a social phenomenon in the absence of, or with little, previous research on the subject.

Most participant-observation studies begin as **exploratory research**, which means researchers at first have only a vague sense of what they are looking for and perhaps no sense at all of what they will discover in the course of their study. They are equipped only with some hunches based on their own experience and their reading of the relevant research literature. They try, however, to treat these hunches as hypotheses. **Hypotheses** are unverified but testable statements about the phenomena that interest researchers. As they immerse themselves in the life of their subjects, their observations constitute sociological data that allow them to reject, accept, or modify their initial hypotheses. Indeed, researchers often purposely seek out observations that enable them to determine the validity and scope of their hypotheses. ("From previous research I know seniors are generally more religious than young people, and that seems to be true in this community, too. But does religiosity vary among people of the same age who are rich, middle class, working class, and poor? If so, why? If not, why not?") Purposively choosing observations results in the creation of a grounded theory. A **grounded theory** is an explanation of a phenomenon based not on mere speculation but on the controlled scrutiny of subjects (Glaser and Straus, 1967).

Hypotheses are unverified but testable statements about the relationship between two or more variables.

A grounded theory is an explanation of a phenomenon based not on mere speculation but on the controlled scrutiny of subjects.

Methodological Problems

Measurement

The great advantage of participant observation is that it lets researchers get "inside the minds" of their subjects and discover their view of the world in its full complexity. It is an especially valuable technique when little is known about the group or phenomenon under investigation and the sociologist is interested in constructing a theory about it. But participant observation has drawbacks too. To understand these problems, we must say a few words about measurement in sociology.

When researchers think about the social world, they use mental constructs or concepts, such as "race," "class," "gender," and so forth. Concepts that can have more than one value are called **variables**. Height and wealth are variables. Perhaps less obviously, affection and perceived beauty are, too. Just as a person can be 160 centimetres or 190 centimetres tall, rich or poor, someone can be passionately in love with, or indifferent to, the girl next

A variable is a concept that can take on more than one value.

door on the grounds that she is beautiful or plain. In each case, we know we are dealing with a variable because height, wealth, affection, and perceived beauty can take different values.

Once researchers identify the variables that interest them, they must decide which real-world observations correspond to each variable. Should "class," for example, be measured by determining people's annual income? Or should it be measured by determining their accumulated wealth, or years of formal education, or some combination of these or other indicators of rank? Deciding which observations to link to which variables is known as **operationalization**.

Sociological variables can sometimes be measured by casual observation. It is usually easy to tell whether someone is a man or a woman, and participant-observers can learn a great deal more about their subjects through extended discussion and careful observation. When researchers find out how much money their subjects earn, how satisfied they are with their marriages, whether they have ever been the victims of a criminal act, and so forth, they are measuring the values of the sociological variables embedded in their hypotheses.

Researchers must establish criteria for assigning values to variables. At exactly what level of annual income can someone be considered "upper class"? What are the precise characteristics of settlements that allow them to be characterized as "urban"? What features of a person permit us to say she is a "leader"? Answers to such questions all involve measurement decisions.

Reliability, Validity, Generalizability, and Causality

In a given research project, participant-observers usually work alone and usually investigate only one group or one type of group. Thus, when we read their research results, we must be convinced of three things if we are to accept their findings. We must be confident that another researcher would interpret things in the same way. We must be confident that their interpretations are accurate. And we must be confident that the findings extend beyond the single case examined. Let us examine each of these points in turn (see Figure 2.3 on page 44):

1. *Would another researcher interpret or measure things in the same way?* This is the problem of **reliability.** If a measurement procedure repeatedly yields consistent results, we consider it reliable. However, in the case of participant observation, there is usually only one person doing the measuring in only one setting. Therefore, we have no way of knowing whether repeating the procedures would yield consistent results.

2. *Are the researcher's interpretations accurate?* This is the problem of **validity**, the problem of whether confirmation of the measures can be found in the real world. If a measurement procedure measures what it is supposed to measure, then it is valid. All valid measures are reliable. However, not all reliable measures are valid. Measuring a person's shoe with a ruler may give us a reliable indicator of that person's shoe size. That is because the ruler repeatedly yields the same results. However, regardless of consistency, shoe size as measured by a ruler is a totally invalid measure of a person's annual income. Similarly, you may think you are measuring annual income by asking people how much they earn. Another interviewer at another time may get exactly the same result when posing the same question. But, despite such reliability, respondents may understate their true income. (A respondent is a person who answers the researcher's questions.) Our measure of annual income may therefore lack validity. Perfectly consistent measures may, in other words, have little truth-value.

   Participant-observers have every right to feel they are on solid ground when it comes to the question of validity. If anyone can tell whether respondents are understating their true income, surely it is someone who has spent months or even years getting to know everything about their lifestyle. Still, doubts may creep in if the criteria used by the participant-observers to assess the validity of their measures are all *internal* to the settings they are investigating. Our confidence in the validity of researchers' measures increases if we are able to use *external* validation criteria. Consider age.

Operationalization is the procedure by which researchers establish criteria for assigning values to variables.

Reliability is the degree to which a measurement procedure yields consistent results.

Validity is the degree to which a measure actually measures what it is intended to measure.

FIGURE 2.3

Measurement as Target
Practice: Validity, Reliability,
and Generalizability
Compared

Validity, reliability, and generalizability can be explained by drawing
an analogy between measuring a
variable and firing at a bull's-eye.
In case 1, above, shots (measures)
are far apart (not reliable) and far
from the bull's-eye (not valid). In
case 2, shots are close to each
other (reliable) but far from the
bull's-eye (not valid). In case 3,
shots are close to the bull's-eye
(valid) and close to each other
(reliable). In case 4, we use a
second target. Our shots are again
close to each other (reliable) and
close to the bull's-eye (valid).
Because our measures were valid
and reliable for both the targets in
cases 3 and 4, we conclude our
results are generalizable.

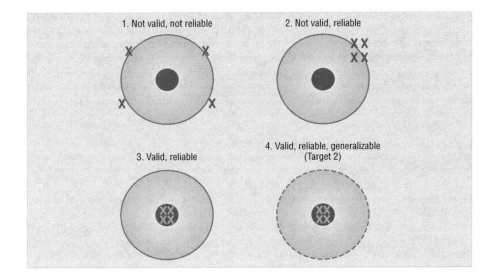

**Generalizability exists when
research findings apply
beyond the specific case
examined.**

**Causality involves the analysis
of causes and their effects.**

Asking people their age is one way to determine how old they are. The problem with
this measure is that people tend to exaggerate their age when they are young and understate it when they are old. A more valid way to determine people's age is to ask them
about their year of birth. Year of birth is generally reported more accurately than
responses to the question "How old are you?" It is therefore a more valid measure of
age. A still more valid measure of age can be found in the "year of birth" entry on
people's birth certificates. The point is that validity increases if we have some external
check on our measure of age.

3. *Do the research findings apply beyond the specific case examined?* This is the
problem of **generalizability**, and it is one of the most serious problems faced by
participant-observation studies. Klockars, for example, studied just one professional
fence in depth. Can we safely conclude his findings are relevant to all professional
fences? Do we dare apply his insights to all criminals? Are we foolhardy if we generalize his conclusions to nearly all of us on the grounds that most of us commit
deviant acts at one time or another and must deal with feelings of guilt? None of this
is clear from Klockars's research. Nor are questions of generalizability clearly
answered by many participant-observation studies, since they are usually studies of
single cases.

   Related to the issue of generalizability is that of **causality**, the analysis of causes
and their effects. Information on how widely or narrowly a research finding applies can
help us establish the causes of a social phenomenon. For instance, we might want to
know how gender, race, class, parental supervision, police surveillance, and other
factors shape the type and rate of juvenile delinquency. If so, we require information on
types and rates of criminal activity among teenagers who have a variety of social
characteristics and are in a variety of social settings. A participant-observation study of
crime is unlikely to provide that sort of information. It is more likely to clarify the
process by which a specific group of people in a single setting learns to become
criminal. Indeed, researchers who conduct participant-observation studies tend not to
think in somewhat mechanical, cause-and-effect terms at all. They prefer instead to
view their subjects as engaged in a fluid process of social interaction. As a result,
participant-observation is not the preferred method for discovering the general causes
of social phenomena.

In sum, participant observation has both strengths and weaknesses. It is especially useful in exploratory research, constructing grounded theory, creating internally valid measures, and developing a sympathetic understanding of the way people see the world. It is often deficient when it comes to establishing reliability, generalizability, and causality. As you will soon learn, these are precisely the strengths of surveys and experiments. Only a small percentage of sociologists conduct experiments. Nonetheless, experiments are important because they set certain standards that other more popular methods try to match. We can show this by discussing experiments concerning the effects of television on real-world violence.

Experiments

In the mid-1960s, about 15 years after the introduction of commercial TV in North America, rates of violent crime began to increase dramatically. Some people were not surprised. The first generation of North American children exposed to high levels of TV violence virtually from birth had reached their mid-teens. TV violence, some commentators said, legitimized violence in the real world, making it seem increasingly normal and acceptable. As a result, they concluded, North American teenagers in the 1960s and subsequent decades were more likely than pre-1960s teens to commit violent acts.

Social scientists soon started investigating the connection between TV and real-world violence by using experimental methods. An **experiment** is a carefully controlled artificial situation that allows researchers to isolate hypothesized causes and measure their effects precisely (Campbell and Stanley, 1963). It uses a special procedure called **randomization** to create two similar groups. Randomization involves assigning individuals to the two groups by chance processes. It then introduces the hypothesized cause to only one of the groups. By comparing the state of the two groups before and after only one of the groups has been exposed to the hypothesized cause, an experiment can determine whether the presumed cause has the predicted effect.

Here is how an experiment on the effects of TV violence on aggressive behaviour might work:

1. *Selection of subjects.* Researchers advertise in local newspapers for parents willing to allow their children to act as research subjects. Fifty children are selected for the experiment.
2. *Random assignment of subjects to experimental and control groups.* At random, each child draws a number from 1 to 50 from a box. The researchers assign children who draw odd numbers to the **experimental group**. This is the group that will be exposed to a violent TV program during the experiment. They assign children who draw even numbers to the **control group**. This is the group that will not be exposed to a violent TV program during the experiment.

   Note that randomization and repetition make the experimental and control groups similar. By assigning subjects to the two groups by using a chance process, and repeating the experiment many times, researchers ensure that the experimental and control groups are likely to have the same proportion of boys and girls, members of different races, children highly motivated to participate in the study, and so forth. Random assignment eliminates bias by allowing a chance process and only a chance process to decide which group each child is assigned to.
3. *Measurement of dependent variable in experimental and control groups.* The researchers put small groups of children in a room and give them toys to play with. They observe the children through a one-way mirror, rating each child in terms of the aggressiveness of his or her play. This is the child's pretest score on the dependent variable, aggressive behaviour. The **dependent variable** is the effect in any cause-and-effect relationship.
4. *Introduction of independent variable to experimental group.* The researchers show children in the experimental group an hour-long TV show in which many violent and aggressive acts take place. They do not show the film to children in the control

Aggressive behaviour among children is common, from siblings fighting to bullying in the school-yard. Since the inception of home TV in the 1950s, social scientists have sought to develop research designs capable of examining the causal effects, if any, of viewing violence on television.

An experiment is a carefully controlled artificial situation that allows researchers to isolate hypothesized causes and measure their effects precisely.

Random means "by chance"— for example, having an equal and nonzero probability of being sampled. Randomization involves assigning individuals to groups by chance processes.

An experimental group in an experiment is the group that is exposed to the independent variable.

A control group in an experiment is the group that is not exposed to the independent variable.

A dependent variable is the presumed effect in a cause-and-effect relationship.

group. In this experiment, the violent TV show is the independent variable. The **independent variable** is the presumed cause in any cause-and-effect relationship.

5. *Remeasurement of dependent variable in experimental and control groups.* Immediately after the children see the TV show, the researchers again observe the children in both groups at play. Each child's play is given a second aggressiveness rating—the posttest score.

6. *Assessment of experimental effect.* Posttest minus pretest scores are calculated for both the experimental and the control groups. If the posttest minus pretest score for the experimental group is significantly greater than the posttest minus pretest score for the control group, the researchers conclude the independent variable (watching violent TV) has a significant effect on the dependent variable (aggressive behaviour). This conclusion is warranted because the introduction of the independent variable is the only difference between the experimental and control groups.

Experiments on Television Violence

Experiments allow researchers to isolate the single cause of theoretical interest and measure its effect with high reliability, that is, consistently from one experiment to the next. Yet many sociologists argue that experiments are highly artificial situations. They believe that removing people from their natural social settings lowers the validity of experimental results, that is, the degree to which they measure what they are actually supposed to measure. Thus, many experiments show that exposure to media violence has a short-term effect on violent behaviour in young children, especially boys. However, the results of experiments are mixed when it comes to assessing longer-term effects, especially on older children and teenagers (Anderson and Bushman, 2002; Browne and Hamilton-Giachritsis, 2005; Freedman, 2002).

To understand why experiments on the effects of media violence may lack validity, consider that, in the real world, violent behaviour usually means attempting to harm another person physically. Shouting or kicking a toy is not the same thing. In fact, such acts may enable children to relieve frustrations in a fantasy world, lowering their chance of acting violently in the real world. Moreover, in a laboratory situation, aggressive behaviour may be encouraged because it is legitimized. Simply showing a violent TV program may suggest to subjects how the experimenter expects them to behave. Nor is aggressive behaviour punished or controlled in the laboratory setting as it is in the real world. If a boy watching a violent TV show stands up and delivers a karate kick to his brother, a parent or other caregiver is likely to take action to prevent a recurrence. This reaction usually teaches the boy not to engage in aggressive behaviour. In the lab, the lack of disciplinary control may facilitate unrealistically high levels of aggression (Felson, 1996).

Field and Natural Experiments

In an effort to overcome the validity problems noted above and still retain many of the benefits of experimental design, some sociologists have conducted experiments in natural settings. In such experiments, researchers forgo strict randomization of subjects. Instead, they compare groups that are already quite similar. They either introduce the independent variable themselves (this is called a *field experiment*) or observe what happens when the independent variable is introduced to one of the groups in the normal course of social life (this is called a *natural experiment*).

Some field experiments on media effects compare boys in institutionalized settings, such as boarding schools. The researchers expose half the boys to violent TV programming. Measures of aggressiveness taken before and after the introduction of violent programming allow researchers to calculate its effect on behaviour. One re-analysis of 28 such studies yielded mixed results. Although 16 of the field experiments (57 percent) suggested that subjects engage in more aggression following exposure to violent films, 12 (43 percent) did not (Wood, Wong, and Chachere, 1991).

Natural experiments have compared rates of aggressive behaviour in Canadian and other towns with and without TV service, but their results are inconclusive. They are also muddied by the fact that there are substantial differences among the towns apart from the presence or absence of TV service. It is therefore unclear whether differences in child aggressiveness are due to media effects.

Because of the validity problems noted above, it has not been convincingly demonstrated that TV violence generally encourages violent behaviour. The sociological consensus is that TV violence probably affects only a very small percentage of viewers. Some young people—those who are weakly connected to family, school, community, and peers—seem susceptible to translating media violence into violent behaviour. Lack of social support allows their personal problems to become greatly magnified—and if guns are readily available, these youth are prone to using violent media messages as models for their own behaviour. In contrast, for the overwhelming majority of young people, violence in the mass media is just a source of entertainment and a fantasy outlet for emotional issues, not a template for action (Anderson, 2003; Felson, 1996; Harding, Fox, and Mehta, 2002; Sullivan, 2002).

Surveys

Sampling

Surveys are part of the fabric of everyday life in North America. You see surveys in action when the CBC conducts a poll to discover the percentage of Canadians who approve of the prime minister's performance, when someone phones to ask about your taste in breakfast cereal, and when the late advice columnist Ann Landers asked her readers, "If you had to do it over again, would you have children?" In every **survey**, people are asked questions about their knowledge, attitudes, or behaviour, either in a face-to-face or telephone interview or in a paper-and-pencil format.

Remarkably, Ann Landers found that fully 70 percent of respondents would not have had children if they could make the choice again. She ran a shocking headline saying so. Should we have confidence in her finding? Hardly. As the letters from her readers indicated, many of the people who answered her question were angry with their children. All 10 000 respondents felt at least strongly enough about the issue to take the trouble to mail in their replies at their own expense. Like all survey researchers, Ann Landers wanted to study part of a group—a **sample**—in order to learn about the whole group—the **population** (in this case, all North American parents). The trouble is, she got replies from a *voluntary response sample,* a group of people who chose *themselves* in response to a general appeal. People who choose themselves are unlikely to be representative of the population of interest. In contrast, a *representative sample* is a group of people chosen so their characteristics closely match those of the population of interest. The difference in the quality of knowledge we can derive from the two types of samples cannot be overstated. Thus, a few months after Ann Landers

In a survey, **people are asked questions about their knowledge, attitudes, or behaviour, either in a face-to-face or telephone interview or in a paper-and-pencil format.**

A sample **is the part of the population of research interest that is selected for analysis.**

A population **is the entire group about which the researcher wants to generalize.**

Researchers collect information using surveys by asking people in a representative sample a set of identical questions. People interviewed on a downtown street corner do *not* constitute a representative sample of Canadian adults; the sample does not include people who live outside the urban core, it underestimates the number of seniors and people with disabilities, it does not take into account regional diversity, and so forth.

conducted her poll, a scientific survey based on a representative sample found that 91 percent of North American parents *would* have children again (Moore, 1995: 178).

How can survey researchers draw a representative sample? You might think that setting yourself up in a public place, such as a shopping mall, and asking willing passersby to answer some questions would work. However, this sort of *convenience sample,* which chooses the people who are easiest to reach, is also highly unlikely to be representative. People who go to malls are richer than average. Moreover, a larger proportion of homemakers, retired people, and teenagers visit malls than can be found in the Canadian population as a whole. Convenience samples are almost always unrepresentative.

To draw a representative sample, respondents cannot select themselves, as in the Ann Landers case. Nor can the researcher choose respondents, as in the mall example. Instead, respondents must be chosen at random, and an individual's chance of being chosen must be known and greater than zero. A sample with these characteristics is known as a **probability sample**.

In a probability sample, the units have a known and nonzero chance of being selected.

To draw a probability sample, you first need a *sampling frame.* This is a list of all the people in the population of interest. You also need a randomizing method. This is a way of ensuring every person in the sampling frame has a known and nonzero chance of being selected.

Up-to-date membership lists of organizations are useful sampling frames if you want to survey members of organizations. But if you want to investigate, say, the religious beliefs of Canadians, then the membership lists of places of worship are inadequate; many Canadians do not belong to such institutions. In such cases, you might turn to another frequently used sampling frame, the telephone directory. The telephone directory is now available for the entire country on CD-ROM. However, even the telephone directory lacks the names and addresses of some poor and homeless people (who do not have phones) and some rich people (who have unlisted phone numbers). Computer programs are available that dial residential phone numbers at random, including unlisted numbers. However, that still excludes about 1.3 percent of Canadian households from any survey that relies on the telephone directory as a sampling frame.

As the example of the telephone directory shows, few sampling frames are perfect. Even the largest and most expensive survey in Canada, the census, misses an estimated 2 percent of the population. Researchers believe that much of the undercounted population is composed of specific and identifiable groups, thus introducing sampling bias (see the section called "Analysis of Existing Documents and Official Statistics" later in this chapter). Nevertheless, researchers maximize the accuracy of their generalizations by using the least-biased sampling frames available and adjusting their analyses and conclusions to take account of known sampling bias.

Homelessness is increasingly a focus of public policy. But public support may not be adequate if the homeless are not counted properly in the census. Statistics Canada first included a count of the homeless in the 2001 census. However, because the count is based on information about the use of shelters and soup kitchens, combined with an attempt at street counts, these numbers are estimates.

Once a sampling frame has been chosen or created, individuals must be selected by a chance process. One way to do this is by picking, say, the 10th person on your list and then every 20th (or 30th or 100th) person after that, depending on how many people you need in your sample. A second method is to assign the number 1 to the first person in the sampling frame, the number 2 to the next person, and so on. Then you create a separate list of random numbers by using a computer or consulting a table of random numbers, which you can find at the back of almost any elementary statistics book or online. Your list of random numbers should have the same number of entries as the number of people you want in your sample. The individuals whose assigned numbers correspond to the list of random numbers are the people in your sample.

Sample Size and Statistical Significance

How many respondents do you need in a sample? That depends on how much inaccuracy you are willing to tolerate. Large samples give more precise results than small samples do. For most sociological purposes, however, a random sample of 1500 people will give acceptably accurate results, even if the population of interest is the entire adult population of Canada. More precisely, if you draw 20 random samples of 1500 individuals each, 19 of them will provide estimates that will be accurate within 2.5 percent of actual population values. Imagine, for example, that 50 percent of the people in a random sample of 1500 respondents say they support the Liberal Party. We can be reasonably confident that only 1 in 20 random samples of that size will not yield results between 47.5 percent and 52.5 percent. When we read that a finding is statistically significant, it usually means we can expect similar findings in 19 out of 20 samples of the same size. Said differently, researchers in the social sciences are generally prepared to tolerate a 5 percent chance that the characteristics of a population are different from the characteristics of their sample (1/20 = 5 percent). If the survey showed that 52 percent of the respondents support the Liberals and 48 percent support the Conservatives, the appropriate conclusion is *not* that the Liberals are in the lead. Instead, you should conclude that there is no detectable difference in support for the two parties given the 2.5 percent margin of error in the survey (see Figure 2.4).

In sum, probability sampling enables us to conduct surveys that permit us to generalize from a part (the sample) to the whole (the population) within known margins of error. Now let us consider the validity of survey data.

Survey Questions and Validity

We can conduct a survey in three main ways. Sometimes, a *self-administered questionnaire* is used. For example, a form containing questions and permitted responses can be mailed to the respondent and returned to the researcher through the mail system. The main advantage of this method is that it is relatively inexpensive. It also has drawbacks. For one thing, it sometimes results in unacceptably low *response rates*. The response rate is the number of people who answer the questionnaire divided by the number of people asked to do so, expressed as a percentage. Moreover, if you use mail questionnaires, an interviewer is not present to explain problematic questions and response options to the respondent. *Face-to-face interviews* are therefore generally preferred over mail questionnaires. In this type of survey, questions and allowable responses are presented to the respondent by the interviewer during a meeting. However, training interviewers and sending them around to conduct interviews is very expensive. That is why *telephone interviews* have become increasingly popular over the past two or three decades. They can elicit relatively high response rates and are relatively inexpensive to administer.

Questionnaires can contain two types of questions. A *closed-ended question* provides the respondent with a list of permitted answers. Each answer is given a numerical code so the data can later be easily input into a computer for statistical analysis. *Open-ended questions* allow respondents to answer questions in their own words. They are particularly useful in exploratory research, where the researcher does not have enough knowledge to create a meaningful and complete list of possible answers. Open-ended questions are more time-consuming to analyze than closed-ended questions are, although computer programs for analyzing text make the task easier.

Researchers want the answers elicited by surveys to be valid, to actually measure what they are supposed to. To maximize validity, researchers must guard against several dangers. We have already considered one threat to validity in survey research: *undercounting* some categories of the population because of an imperfect sampling frame.

FIGURE 2.4

The Margin of Error in a Sample

In a sample of 1500 people, 48 percent of the respondents support the Conservatives and 50 percent support the Liberals. However, because the 2.5 percent margins of error overlap, we cannot be sure whether support for the two parties differs in the population. To conclude that support for the two parties differs in the population, the margins of error must not overlap.

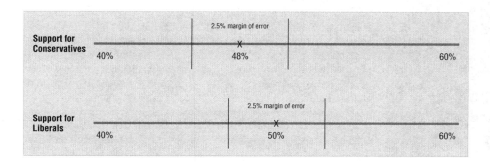

**TECHNOLOGY
BYTES**

Survey researchers who put their questionnaires on the World Wide Web confront a new variant of the problem of undercounting. Below each question they list allowable responses. Beside each allowable response they place a clickable box. They ask people who visit the website containing the questionnaire to read the questions and click the appropriate boxes to indicate their responses. Respondents' answers are automatically stored in a computerized database as soon as they click. For non-web surveys, data entry clerks must be hired to enter questionnaire responses into a computer. This expensive step is eliminated with web surveys. Web surveys also save the cost of postage and interviewers. However, the people who respond to web surveys select themselves in much the same fashion as the respondents to Ann Landers's parenthood question. Moreover, to answer a web survey, you have to have access to a computer connected to the Internet. A sample drawn from Internet users would not be representative of the Canadian population as a whole, let alone the population of a less-developed country where Internet access is rare. In 2000, 42 percent of Canadians had never used the Internet and another 10 percent used it rarely. The 52 percent of Canadians in this category tend to be seniors, have low incomes, and have no postsecondary education (Crompton, Ellison, and Stevenson, 2002). So although a web survey of Internet users might have validity, a web survey of the general population would likely give invalid results because of the unrepresentative nature of the sample on which it is based.

Other threats to validity in survey research aside from undercounting exist. Even if an individual is contacted about a survey, he or she may refuse to participate. This threat to validity is known as *non-response*. If non-respondents differ from respondents in ways that are relevant to the research topic, the conclusions drawn from the survey may be in jeopardy. For instance, some alcoholics may not want to participate in a survey on alcohol consumption because they regard the topic as sensitive. If so, a measure of the rate of alcohol consumption taken from the sample would not be an accurate reflection of the rate of alcohol consumption in the population. Actual alcohol consumption in the population would be higher than the rate in the sample.

Survey researchers pay careful attention to non-response. They try to discover whether non-respondents differ systematically from respondents so they can take this into account before drawing conclusions from their sample. They also take special measures to ensure that the response rate remains acceptably high—generally, around 70 percent or more of people contacted. Proven tactics ensure a high response rate. Researchers can notify potential respondents about the survey in advance. They can remind them to complete and mail in survey forms. They can have universities and other prestigious institutions sponsor the survey. They can stress the practical and scientific value of the research. And they can give people small rewards, such as a lottery ticket or a toonie, for participating.

If respondents do not answer questions accurately, a third threat to validity is present: *response bias*. The survey may focus on sensitive, unpopular, or illegal behaviour. As a result, some respondents may not be willing to answer questions frankly. The interviewer's attitude, gender, or race may suggest that some responses are preferred. This can elicit biased responses. Some of these problems can be overcome by carefully selecting and training interviewers and closely supervising their work. Response bias on questions about sensitive, unpopular, or illegal behaviour can be minimized by having such questions answered in private (Smith, 1992).

Fourth, validity may be compromised by *wording effects*. That is, the way questions are phrased or ordered can influence and invalidate responses. Experienced survey researchers have turned questionnaire construction into a respected craft. Increasingly, they refine the lessons learned from experience with evidence from field experiments. These experiments divide samples into two or more randomly chosen subsamples. Different question wording or ordering is then administered to the people in each subsample so that wording effects can be measured. Detected problems can then be resolved in future research.

Both experience and field experiments suggest that survey questions must be specific and simple. They should be expressed in plain, everyday language. They should be phrased neutrally, never leading the respondent to a particular answer and never using inflammatory terms. Because people's memories are often faulty, questions are more likely to elicit valid responses if they focus on important, singular, current events rather than on less salient, multiple, past events. Breaking these rules lowers the validity of survey findings (Converse and Presser, 1986; Ornstein, 1998).

Causality

In 1991, Erin Brockovich was down and out. She was a twice-divorced mother of three small children, and she had no university education. She had recently been seriously injured in a traffic accident, and she was unable to find work. She hired a law firm to argue her case but the $25 000 settlement covered only a fraction of her debts.[3]

Then came a turning point in Brockovich's life. She convinced the law firm that had settled her car accident case to hire her as a filing clerk at $1800 a month. Soon after she began working for the firm, Brockovich came across some medical records that piqued her curiosity. Her boss let her look into the matter. Brockovich's dogged investigation eventually established that a giant power utility had allowed a toxic chemical to leak into the groundwater of a nearby town, ruining the health of more than 600 residents. Although she was not a lawyer and had no formal education even as a law clerk or a paralegal, Brockovich spearheaded a court case that resulted in the largest legal settlement in North American history. In 1996, the power utility was ordered to pay $500 million to the victims. Brockovich herself received $3 million for her efforts. In 2000, these events were dramatized in the hit movie *Erin Brockovich,* starring Julia Roberts in the title role. The movie was nominated for five Academy Awards and Roberts won the best actress award for her portrayal of Brockovich (Ellis, 2002).

Erin Brockovich's story is unusual for two reasons. First, crimes committed by big corporations are rarely prosecuted successfully, and even successful prosecutions typically result in modest settlements (see Chapter 7, Deviance and Crime). Second, unemployed divorced women with small children and no university education rarely compete successfully against big-time lawyers, regardless of how bright and energetic they may be. Because of a lack of education and the demands of family, the cards are stacked too heavily against them (see Chapter 11, Sexuality and Gender). But what if we even out the playing field? What if we compare men and women who are more alike? What if we compare, say, male and female lawyers? Are male lawyers generally more successful? And if so, why? These are the questions sociologists Fiona Kay and John Hagan (1998) set out to answer in a survey of Ontario lawyers.[4]

Kay and Hagan analyzed self-administered questionnaires completed by a representative sample of 905 lawyers. The respondents had all been called to the Ontario

Erin Brockovich (2000) raises the question of why successful prosecutions of corporate crime are so rare. It also raises the question of why bright, energetic men often earn more than equally bright, energetic women.

bar between 1975 and 1990, remained in practice in 1990, and had begun practice on a partnership track.

Partnership is a measure of success in legal practice. Achieving the rank of partner means that a lawyer is one of the owners of his or her firm. Partnership enhances the lawyer's earnings and opens additional opportunities for career advancement. Kay and Hagan found that 46 percent of the men in their sample were partners, compared with just 25 percent of the women. That is, they found an **association** between gender and promotion. In general, an association exists between two variables if the value of one variable (in this case, partner versus non-partner) changes with the value of the other (in this case, male versus female).

An **association** exists between two variables if the value of one variable changes with the value of the other.

Why were men substantially more likely to become partners than women were? One explanation for why some people have more successful careers focuses on their "human capital," that is, the investments they make in their occupation. In this view, a person's success comes from improving his or her education, work experience, and work skills. If women devote more attention than men do to domestic labour and raising children, while men devote more attention to upgrading their education, work experience, and work skills, men will be more successful in their careers than women are (Becker, 1991).

We can test human capital theory by comparing male and female lawyers who have invested *equally* in human capital. Our confidence in human capital theory would *increase* if female lawyers who have invested as much in human capital as male lawyers have were as likely as male lawyers to become partners. Our confidence in human capital theory would *decrease* if male lawyers were more successful than female lawyers even when women and men made identical investments in their careers.

How can we measure investment in human capital? The number of years since graduation from law school is one measure, because it indicates years of job experience. A second measure is the number of years spent in law practice. If a person takes time off work to have children and raise them, that person will have less work experience. Significantly, when Kay and Hagan compared male and female lawyers with equal years of job experience and time since graduation, they found that men were still more likely to become partners than women were. Their findings thus decrease our confidence in human capital theory. That is because gender differences in success persist even when investment in human capital is the same for women and men.

Kay and Hagan (1998: 729) propose an alternative explanation for the greater career success of men: "[W]omen must display greater career commitment than men to receive the same, or even smaller, rewards." Their data support this argument. For example, Kay and Hagan's survey data show that women's career prospects improve if they are eager to engage in various "extracurricular" activities that enhance the reputation of their firms and attract clients. Such activities include being honoured by a professional organization, receiving public recognition for their work, and serving as a member of the bench in the Law Society of Upper Canada. Men's career prospects are unaffected by these activities. This illustrates that, to advance to the level of partner, women must display greater career commitment than men do.

In the course of developing an explanation for the association between gender and promotion, Kay and Hagan performed a causal analysis. They had to satisfy four conditions to establish causality. Since these four conditions must be satisfied in *any* causal analysis, they are worth considering at length.

First, Kay and Hagan had to be confident that the independent variable occurred before the dependent variable. This is the *time order* criterion. Time order is straightforward in the relationship between gender and promotion. Chronologically, gender precedes promotion.

Second, Kay and Hagan had to establish the existence of a correlation between the independent and dependent variables. This is the *association* criterion. We saw that 46 percent of men and 25 percent of women received promotions to partners. The association is not perfect. A perfect association would see 100 percent of men versus 0 percent of women receiving promotion. But clearly the partnership experiences of women and men differ substantially. If the difference between the percentages were 3 percent rather than 21 percent ($46 - 25 = 21$), we might be tempted to say that the difference is very small and probably due to chance fluctuation, that is, the individuals who happened to be included in the sample. However, a 21 percent difference establishes a sizable association between gender and partnership.

NEL

Men are usually more successful in the legal profession than women. By comparing male and female lawyers with similar levels of job experience, sociologists Fiona Kay and John Hagan (1998) found that female lawyers have to be more committed to their jobs than male lawyers are to be as successful.

Third, Kay and Hagan had to show that the effect resulted from the cause and not from some other factor. This is the *spuriousness* criterion. It may be that an association between independent and dependent variables is erroneous since the association may be due to the effect of a third variable. For instance, in Scandinavia there is an association between storks and babies. The more storks in a region, the higher the birth rate. Does this mean that storks bring babies? Of course not. Rural regions have more storks *and* more babies than urban regions do. If you look at rural regions only, there is no association at all between storks and the birth rate. The same holds true if you look at urban regions only. "Region" accounts for the association between storks and babies. It is a control variable. Statistical control removes the effect of a third variable (in this case, region) from an association (in this case, between storks and babies). Statistical **control** shows how the third variable influences the original association. Because in this case controlling for region makes the original association disappear, we say that the association between storks and babies is a **spurious association**. In general, spuriousness exists between an independent and a dependent variable when the introduction of a causally prior control variable makes the initial association disappear.

Similarly, Kay and Hagan wanted to see whether the association between gender and promotion was spurious. To find out, they examined the effect of human capital on the association. They found that human capital had no effect on the association. That is, men were still more likely to be promoted than women even when comparing women and men who had made equal investments in human capital. Unlike the association between storks and babies after controlling for region, the association between gender and promotion after controlling for human capital remained strong. This suggests that in Kay and Hagan's research, the control variable (human capital) is *not* responsible for the original association (between gender and promotion).

Fourth, Kay and Hagan had to demonstrate the existence of a mechanism or process linking the cause and the effect. This is the *rationale* criterion. Their rationale for the link between gender and promotion was the variable "work commitment." When Kay and Hagan controlled for work commitment, the association between gender and promotion disappeared. They found that if women displayed more work commitment than men did, they were as likely as men to be promoted. This is similar to the storks and babies example with region controlled. Just as region accounted for the association between storks and babies, work commitment accounted for the association between gender and promotion. Kay and Hagan's causal reasoning is illustrated in Figure 2.5 on page 54.

Control in statistics refers to removing the influence of one or more variables on the association between an independent and a dependent variable.

A **spurious association** exists between an independent variable and a dependent variable when the introduction of a causally prior control variable makes the initial association disappear.

NEL

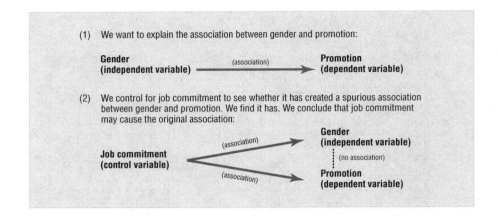

(1)　We want to explain the association between gender and promotion:

Gender
(independent variable) ——— (association) ———> Promotion
(dependent variable)

(2)　We control for job commitment to see whether it has created a spurious association
between gender and promotion. We find it has. We conclude that job commitment
may cause the original association:

Gender
(independent variable)

Job commitment
(control variable)　(association)　(no association)

Promotion
(dependent variable)　(association)

Analysis of survey data involves more than just testing for spurious associations. Many interesting and unexpected things can happen when a two-variable association is elaborated by controlling for a third variable (Hirschi and Selvin, 1972). The original association may remain unchanged. It may strengthen. It may weaken. It may disappear or weaken in only some categories of the control variable. It may even change direction entirely. Data analysis is therefore full of surprises, and accounting for the outcomes of statistical control requires a lot of creative theoretical thinking.

Reading Tables

A survey is not an ideal instrument for conducting exploratory research. It cannot provide the kind of deep and sympathetic understanding we gain from participant observation. However, surveys do produce results from which we can confidently generalize. If properly crafted, they provide valid measures of many sociologically important variables. Because they allow the same questions to be asked repeatedly, surveys enable researchers to establish the reliability of measures with relative ease. And, finally, as we have just seen, survey data are useful for discovering relationships among variables, including cause-and-effect relationships.

One of the most useful tools for analyzing survey data is the contingency table. A **contingency table** is a cross-classification of cases by at least two variables that allows you to see how, if at all, the variables are associated. To understand this definition better, consider Table 2.1, taken from a nationwide Canadian poll. One survey question was worded as follows: "As you may know, we have a number of genetically engineered or genetically modified foods in our food system. Do you strongly approve, somewhat approve, somewhat disapprove, or strongly disapprove of 'genetically engineered' or 'genetically modified' food?" Table 2.1 shows the results on this question for women and men. To simplify our analysis we combined the two categories of approval to form one category. We did the same for the two categories of disapproval. The table shows the number and percentage of Canadian women and men who approve and disapprove of genetically modified food. It allows us to see whether gender affects attitudes toward genetically modified food.

Note that gender, the independent variable (the presumed cause) is arrayed across the top of the table. Attitude toward genetically modified food (the presumed effect) is

A contingency table is a cross-classification of cases by at least two variables that allows you to see how, if at all, the variables are associated.

Sex of Respondent

Attitude to GM Food	Male	Female	Row Totals
Approve	468 (49.5%)	295 (32.5%)	763 (41.2%)
Disapprove	478 (50.5%)	612 (67.5%)	1090 (58.8%)
Column totals	946 (100.0%)	907 (100.0%)	1853 (100.0%)

NEL

arrayed along the side of the table. The table consists of four core cells, one defined by the cross-classification of approval and men, another by the cross-classification of approval and women, a third by the cross-classification of disapproval and men, and the fourth by the cross-classification of disapproval and women.

Although 2049 people were interviewed in the survey, 196 did not answer the question. All 1853 who responded can be assigned to cells of the table based on their characteristics. For example, men who approved of genetically modified food are assigned to the top left core cell. Women who disapproved are placed in the lower right core cell.

Do women and men differ in their attitude toward genetically modified food? Does the difference between the values of the independent variable produce a difference between the values of the dependent variable? Table 2.1 shows that 468 men and 295 women approved of genetically modified food. However, the absolute number of men and women in these cells tells us little because more men than women may have been interviewed. An easy way to take this into account is to convert the absolute numbers to percentages. Effectively, this asks: For every one hundred men, how many approved of genetically modified food? For every one hundred women, how many approved of genetically modified food?

The percentages are in parentheses in the table: 49.5 percent of men approved of genetically modified food ($468/946 \times 100 = 49.5$). The comparable figure for women is 32.5 percent. The independent variable (men versus women) produces a 17 percent difference in the approval of genetically modified food ($49.5 - 32.5 = 17$).

One reason for this difference might be that men are more politically conservative or right wing than women are (Everitt, 1998; Howell and Day, 2000). A simple way to measure political preferences is to ask people which federal political party they would vote for "if an election were held today." In our analysis we have combined the Conservative Party with the Alliance/Reform Party on the political right, kept the Liberal Party as a centrist party on its own, and combined the NDP and the Bloc Québécois on the political left.

The analysis becomes more complex with three variables in the analysis. In Table 2.2 you will quickly notice that we effectively have a sub-table for men (on the left) and another sub-table for women (on the right). As well, since some respondents did not state a party preference, we have only 1503 people in this table.

Are there differences in levels of approval of genetically modified food among people who have different political party preferences? Yes and no. For men, those who support parties on the right or in the centre tend to approve of genetically engineered food by a small margin (52.7 percent and 54.8 percent, respectively). However, men who favour parties on the left are not as approving (36.1 percent). So, yes, for men party preference does make a difference in approval levels. For women, there are virtually no differences by party preference. Only about a third of women approve of genetically modified foods, and approval does not differ by party preference.

So we see that contingency tables are effective tools for causal analysis. They enable us to see whether an association exists between two variables and to examine the effects of control variables on the original association.

Sex of Respondent	Male			Female		
Political Preference	Right	Centre	Left	Right	Centre	Left
Attitude to GM Food						
Approve	149 (52.7%)	207 (54.8%)	48 (36.1%)	57 (31.7%)	123 (34.1%)	55 (32.7%)
Disapprove	134 (47.3%)	171 (45.2%)	85 (63.9%)	123 (68.3%)	238 (65.9%)	113 (67.3%)
Column totals	283 (100.0%)	378 (100.0%)	133 (100.0%)	180 (100.0%)	361 (100.0%)	168 (100.0%)

TABLE 2.2
Attitude toward Genetically Modified Food by Sex, Controlling for Political Preference, Canada

Source: Environics Research Group, 1999.

NEL

Analysis of Existing Documents and Official Statistics

Apart from participant observation, experiments, and surveys, there is a fourth important sociological research method: the *analysis of existing documents and official statistics*. What do existing documents and official statistics have in common? They are created by people other than the researcher for purposes other than sociological research.

The three types of existing documents that sociologists have mined most widely and deeply are diaries, newspapers, and published historical works. For example, one of the early classics of American sociology, a study of Polish immigrants, is based on a close reading of immigrants' diaries and letters (Thomas and Znaniecki, 1958 [1918–20]). In recent decades, sociologists have made outstanding contributions to the study of political protest by systematically classifying nineteenth- and early-twentieth-century French, Italian, and British newspaper accounts of strikes and demonstrations (Tilly, Tilly, and Tilly, 1975).

In recent decades, sociologists have tried to discover the conditions that led some countries to dictatorship and others to democracy, some to economic development and others to underdevelopment, some to becoming thoroughly globalized and others to remaining less tied to global social processes. In trying to answer such broad questions, sociologists have had to rely on published histories as their main source of data. No other method would allow the breadth of coverage and depth of analysis required for such comparative and historical work. For example, Barrington Moore (1967) spent a decade reading the histories of Britain, France, Russia, Germany, China, India, and other countries to figure out the social origins of dictatorship and democracy in the modern world. Immanuel Wallerstein (1974–89) canvassed the history of virtually the entire world to make sense of why some countries became industrialized while others remain undeveloped. What distinguishes this type of research from purely historical work is the kind of questions posed by the researchers. Moore and Wallerstein asked the same kind of big, theoretical questions (and used the same kinds of research methods) as Marx and Weber did. They have inspired a generation of younger sociologists to adopt a similar approach. Comparative-historical research is therefore one of the growth areas of the discipline.

Census data, police crime reports, and records of key life events are perhaps the most frequently used sources of official statistics. Canadian censuses have been conducted regularly since 1871. The modern census tallies the number of Canadian residents and classifies them by place of residence, race, ethnic origin, occupation, age, and hundreds of other variables (see Box 2.1). Statistics Canada publishes an annual Uniform Crime Reporting (UCR) Survey that reports the number of crimes in Canada and classifies them by location and type of crime, age and sex of offenders and victims, and other variables. It also regularly publishes an *Annual Compendium of Vital Statistics* that reports births, deaths, marriages, and divorces by sex, age, and so forth.

BOX 2.1
It's Your Choice

Who Should Be Counted in the Canadian Census?

It may seem odd to say so, but the census is a political document. Often seen as little more than a dry, scientific compilation of numbers, of interest mainly to bureaucrats and bean-counters, the census is actually a record of the political interests and power struggles that have shaped Canadian history (Brym, 2009; Curtis, 2001). In particular, the census has always counted certain kinds of people and excluded others. By rendering some people and groups "invisible" it profoundly influences social policy.

The census excluded some people right from the beginning. Jean Talon completed New France's first census in 1666. The count: 3215 French settlers. Talon did not count the much larger population of Aboriginal peoples, did not even try to estimate their number and socioeconomic characteristics. That is because the first "Canadian" census was not a neutral tally of all residents of New France but a means of providing information that could be used to help wrest control of the territory from the Aboriginal peoples and establish a stable and prosperous French colony. Talon needed the numbers to rationalize the taxation of the French colonists, to further their economic development, to organize new colonization efforts, and, by implication, to interfere with, and even destroy, the livelihoods and lives of the Native population. The fact that Aboriginal peoples were not counted only added to the sense that they did not matter. In this respect, the first census added to the mythology that New France was empty, virgin territory, just waiting for European colonists to exploit its riches. Could there be a more political purpose?

That was the seventeenth century. You might think that the tendency of the census to exclude some kinds of people is ancient history. If so, you would be wrong. The census still undercounts Aboriginal peoples. Members of several reserves and settlements refuse to participate in the census as an act of political protest. They simply do not recognize the authority of the federal government. In addition, the census undercounts homeless people, who by definition have no fixed address. Still other Canadians refuse to participate in the census because they regard it as an invasion of their privacy.

Apart from undercounting certain types of individuals, the census renders certain *characteristics* of individuals invisible and denies the existence of certain *groups*. Consider the following:

- Until 1981, the census required every Canadian to specify one and only one ethnic or cultural origin.

The census has always counted certain kinds of people and excluded others. By rendering some people and groups "invisible" it profoundly influences social policy. Shown here is Tom Campbell's *Above the Street* (1995).

A person born to a Ukrainian-Canadian mother and an Italian-Canadian father may have felt attached to Ukrainian, Italian, *and* Canadian cultures. But such multiple ethnic attachments were not recognized by the census. People who felt they were of mixed heritage were counted as individuals in the census, but their multiple ethnic attachments were rendered invisible.

- Remarkably, it was only in 1996 that the census listed "Canadian" as a possible response to the ethnic question. Suddenly, "Canadian" became the most frequently chosen ethnic origin in the country. At midnight between May 13 and 14, 1996, Canada "lost" millions of

citizens who had formerly specified European, Asian, African, and other ancestries, and gained millions of "Canadians." Before the 1990s, the census made the Canadian ethnic group invisible.

- Until recently the census let people say they were from Jamaica or China but it did not allow them to identify themselves as members of a "visible minority." The recognition of the diverse *racial* origins of Canadians is something quite new.
- Some people lived common-law before 1981. However, the 1981 census was the first to ask people if they were living common-law.
- Women did most of the country's domestic labour before 1996 (as they do today), but only in 1996 did the census recognize unpaid domestic labour by asking questions about it.

People who perform domestic labour, people living common-law, members of visible minorities, members of the Canadian ethnic group, and people who identify with more than one ethnic group have been slighted by the Canadian census until recently. Homeless people and Aboriginal peoples still are. This matters because government programs and government funding are based on census counts. If some types of people are undercounted, what negative implications might this have for them? Can you think of types of people other than those listed above who are rendered invisible by the Canadian census? Should they be counted, too? As a Canadian citizen, it's your choice.

Existing documents and official statistics have four main advantages over other types of data. First, they can save the researcher time and money because they are usually available at no cost in libraries or on the World Wide Web. (See the Web Resources at the end of the chapter for useful websites containing official statistics.) Second, official statistics usually cover entire populations and are collected using rigorous and uniform methods, thus yielding high-quality data. Third, existing documents and official statistics are especially useful for historical analysis. The analysis of data from these sources is the only sociological method that does not require live subjects. Fourth, since the method does not require live subjects, reactivity is not a problem; the researcher's presence does not influence the subjects' behaviour.[5]

However, existing documents and official statistics share one big disadvantage. These data sources are not created with the researchers' needs in mind. They often contain biases that reflect the interests of the individuals and organizations that created them. Therefore, they may be less than ideal for research purposes and must always be treated cautiously.

To illustrate the potential bias of official statistics, consider how researchers compare the well-being of Canadians and people living in other countries. They sometimes use a measure called gross domestic product per capita (GDPpc). GDPpc is the total dollar value of goods and services produced in a country in a year divided by the number of people in the country. It is a convenient measure because all governments regularly publish GDPpc figures.

Most researchers are aware of a flaw in GDPpc, however. The cost of living varies from one country to the next. A dollar can buy you a cup of coffee in many Canadian restaurants but that same cup of coffee will cost you $6 in a Japanese restaurant. GDPpc looks at how many dollars you have, not at what the dollars can buy. Therefore, governments started publishing an official statistic called purchasing power parity (PPP). It takes the cost of goods and services in each country into account.

Significantly, however, both PPP and GDPpc ignore two serious problems. First, it is possible for GDPpc and PPP to go up while most people in a society become worse off. The richest people may earn all the newly created wealth while the incomes of most people fall. Any measure of well-being that ignores the *distribution* of well-being in society is biased toward measuring the well-being of the well-to-do. Second, in some countries the gap in well-being between women and men is greater than in others. A country like Kuwait ranks quite high on GDPpc and PPP. However, women benefit far less than men do from that country's prosperity. A measure of well-being that ignores the gender gap is biased toward measuring the well-being of men.

This story has a happy ending. Realizing the biases in official statistics, such as GDPpc and PPP, social scientists at the United Nations created two new measures of well-being in the mid-1990s. First, the human development index (HDI) combines PPP with a measure of average life expectancy and average level of education. The reasoning of the UN social scientists is that people living in countries that distribute well-being more equitably will live longer and be better educated. Second, the gender empowerment measure (GEM) combines the percentage of parliamentary seats, good jobs, and earned income controlled by women.

Table 2.3 lists the countries ranked first through fifth on all four measures of well-being we have mentioned. As you can see, the list of the top five countries differs for each measure. There is no "best" measure. Each measure has its own bias, and researchers have to be sensitive to these biases, as they must whenever they use official statistics.

GLOBAL
PERSPECTIVE

TABLE 2.3
Rank of Countries by Four Measures of Well-Being, 2007

Sources: United Nations, 2007, *Human Development Report 2007/2008,* New York. Retrieved January 3, 2008 (http://hdr.undp.org/en/media/hdr_20072008_en_complete.pdf), pp. 229, 330; International Monetary Fund, 2007, "Select Countries." Retrieved January 3, 2008 (http://www.imf.org/external/pubs/ft/weo/2007/02/weodata/weoselco.aspx?g=2001&sg=All+countries).

GDP Per Capita	Purchasing Power Parity	HDI	GEM
1. Luxembourg	1. Luxembourg	1. Iceland	1. Norway
2. Norway	2. United States	2. Norway	2. Sweden
3. Qatar	3. Norway	3. Australia	3. Finland
4. Iceland	4. Ireland	4. Canada	4. Denmark
5. Ireland	5. Iceland	5. Ireland	5. Iceland

NEL

THE IMPORTANCE OF BEING SUBJECTIVE

In the following chapters, we show how participant observation, experiments, surveys, and the analysis of existing documents and official statistics are used in sociological research. You are well equipped for the journey. By now you should have a pretty good idea of the basic methodological issues that confront any sociological research project. You should also understand the strengths and weaknesses of some of the most widely used data collection techniques (Table 2.4).

Our synopsis of sociology's "reality check" should not obscure the fact that sociological research questions often spring from real-life experiences and the pressing concerns of the day. But before sociological analysis, we rarely see things as they are. We see them as *we* are. Then, a sort of waltz begins. Subjectivity leads; objectivity follows. When the dance is finished, we see things more accurately (see Box 2.2).

Method	Strengths	Weaknesses
Participant observation	Allows researchers to get "inside" the minds of their subjects and discover their worldview; useful for exploratory research and the discovery of grounded theory; high internal validity	Low reliability; low external validity; low generalizability; not very useful for establishing cause-and-effect relationships
Experiments	High reliability; excellent for establishing cause-and-effect relationship	Low validity for many sociology problems (field and natural experiments somewhat better)
Surveys	Good reliability; useful for establishing cause-and-effect relationships; good generalizability	Some problems with validity (but techniques exist for boosting validity)
Analysis of existing documents and official statistics	Often inexpensive and easy to obtain, provides good coverage; useful for historical analysis; non-reactive	Often contains biases reflecting the interests of their creators and not the interests of the researcher

TABLE 2.4

Strengths and Weaknesses of Four Research Methods

BOX 2.2
Sociology at the Movies

NO. TAKE ROLL

Kinsey (2004)

In early-twentieth-century New Jersey, Alfred Kinsey's father sermonized that the telephone and the automobile were the devil's work. In his opinion, these conveniences increased interaction between young men and women, thereby promoting impure thoughts, petting, and all manner of sexual perversions.

Not surprisingly, the adolescent Alfred rejected his father's Puritanism and petty tyranny. He escaped to Harvard to study biology and zoology. He devoted 20 years to collecting and analyzing 100 000 specimens of the gall wasp, but underneath his mania for counting, classifying, and marvelling at natural diversity, his rebellion against sexual repression and imposed sexual uniformity never ended.

In the 1930s, now a full professor of zoology at Indiana University,

Kinsey began to investigate human sexual behaviour with the same fervour he had formerly invested in the gall wasp. Between 1938 and 1963, he and his associates conducted 18 216 in-depth interviews that formed the basis of two best-selling volumes on human sexual behaviour that astounded the North American public and put Kinsey on the cover of *Time* (Kinsey, Pomeroy, and Martin, 1948; Kinsey, Pomeroy, Martin, and Gebhard, 1953). In an era when masturbation, contraception, and premarital sex were widely considered sins, Kinsey's work sparked a revolution in attitudes toward sex by showing that even far more scandalous practices—extramarital affairs, homosexuality, and so forth—were commonplace. For many North Americans, his findings were liberating. For others, they were filthy lies that threatened to undermine the moral fibre of the nation. Both reactions, and the life of the man who caused them, are portrayed in *Kinsey* (2004), starring Liam Neeson in the title role.

Equipped with the information in this chapter, you can appreciate that Kinsey's methods were primitive and biased by modern sociological standards (Ericksen, 1998). We single out four main problems:

1. *Sampling.* Kinsey relied on what we today call a "convenience sample" of respondents. He and his colleagues interviewed accessible volunteers rather than a randomized and representative sample of the American population. About one-third of Kinsey's respondents had a known "sexual bias." They were prostitutes, members of secretive homosexual communities, patients in mental hospitals, residents of homes for unwed mothers, and the like. Two-thirds of these people were convicted felons. Five percent were male prostitutes. But even if we eliminate respondents with a

Liam Neeson as Alfred Kinsey

sexual bias, we do not have a representative sample. For example, 84 percent of the men without a sexual bias went to college. Most of them were from the Midwest, especially Indiana (Gebhard and Johnson, 1979). In Kinsey's defence, scientific sampling was in its infancy when he did his research. Still, we are obliged to conclude that it is difficult to generalize from Kinsey's work because his sample is unrepresentative.

2. *Questionnaire design.* Kinsey required that his interviewers memorize long questionnaires including 350 or more questions. He encouraged them to adapt the wording and ordering of the questions to suit the "level" of the respondent and the natural flow of conversation that emerged during the interview. Yet much research now shows that even subtle changes in question wording and ordering can produce sharply different results. A question about frequency of masturbation per month yields means between 4 and 15 depending on how the question is phrased (Bradburn and

Sudman, 1979). To avoid such problems, modern researchers prefer standardized questions. They also prefer questionnaires considerably briefer than Kinsey's because asking 350 questions can take hours and often results in "respondent fatigue," a desire on the part of respondents to offer quick and easy answers (as opposed to considered, truthful responses) so they can end the interview as quickly as possible.

3. *Interviewing.* People are generally reluctant to discuss sex with strangers, and Kinsey and his associates have often been praised for making their respondents feel at ease talking about the most intimate details of their personal life. Yet to establish rapport with respondents, Kinsey and his colleagues did not remain neutral. They expressed empathy with the pains and frustrations many respondents expressed, often reassuring them that their sexual histories were normal and decent. Today, researchers frown on any departure from neutrality in the interview situation because it may influence respondents to answer

questions in a less than truthful way. The reassurance and empathy expressed by Kinsey and his associates may have led some respondents to offer exaggerated reports of their behaviour.

4. *Data analysis.* It is unclear how Kinsey decided whether the effect of one variable on another was significant. He rarely used statistical tests for this purpose. He never introduced control variables to see if observed associations between variables were spurious. Moreover, he saw no problem in lumping together data collected over decades. Yet between 1938, when Kinsey started collecting data, and 1953, the year in which his second book was published, North America experienced unprecedented social change fuelled by economic depression and boom, war and peace. Sexual attitudes and behaviour undoubtedly changed, and we may wonder whether it is meaningful to analyze respondents from the late 1930s and the early 1950s together.

Since Kinsey, researchers have conducted more than 750 scientific surveys of the sexual behaviour of North Americans. Today, using modern research methods, we are able to describe and explain sexual behaviour more accurately and insightfully than did Kinsey and his pioneering colleagues. We know that many of the details of Kinsey's writings are suspect. But we also know that despite the serious methodological problems summarized above, his basic finding is accurate. The sexual behaviour of North Americans is highly diverse. As Kinsey says in the movie, "Variation is the only reality."

Herein, too, lies an important lesson about the relationship between subjectivity and objectivity in research. Clearly, Kinsey's biography and his passions helped to shape his innovative scientific agenda. There is nothing unusual in that; all good scientists are passionate about their work, and their research agendas are often rooted in their biographies. Like Kinsey, they try to be objective, but even if they fail, they can rely on the scientific community to uncover biases and discover the imaginative and valid core of every good theory. Without human emotions grounded in our subjectivity, there could never be a quest for truth; without research methods that improve our objectivity, there could never be a science.

Feminism provides a prime example of this process. Here is a *political* movement of people and ideas that, over the past 40 years, has helped shape the sociological *research* agenda. The division of labour in the household, violence against women, the effects of child-rearing responsibilities on women's careers, the social barriers to women's participation in politics and the armed forces, and many other related concerns were sociological "non-issues" before the rise of the modern feminist movement. Sociologists did not study these problems. Effectively, they did not exist for the sociological community (although they did, of course, exist for women). But subjectivity led. Feminism as a political movement brought these and many other concerns to the attention of the Canadian public. Objectivity followed. Large parts of the sociological community began doing rigorous research on feminist-inspired issues and greatly refined our knowledge of them.

The entire sociological perspective began to shift as a growing number of scholars abandoned gender-biased research (Eichler, 1988b; Tavris, 1992). Thus, approaching sociological problems from an exclusively male perspective is now less common than it used to be. For instance, it is less likely in 2009 than in 1969 that a sociologist would study work but ignore unpaid housework as one type of labour. Similarly, sociologists now frown on using data on one gender to draw conclusions about all people. As these advances in sociological thinking show, and as has often been the case in the history of the discipline, objective sociological knowledge has been enhanced as a result of subjective experiences. And so the waltz continues. As in *Alice in Wonderland,* the question now is, "Will you, won't you, will you, won't you, will you join the dance?"

APPENDIX

Four Statistics You Should Know

In this book we sometimes report the results of sociological research in statistical form. You need to know four basic statistics to understand this material:

1. The *mean* (or arithmetic average). Imagine we know the height and annual income of the first nine people who entered your sociology classroom today. The height and income data are arranged in Table 2.5. From Table 2.5 you can calculate the mean by summing the values for each student or *case* and dividing by the number of cases. For example, the nine students are a total of 1547 centimetres (609 in.) tall. Dividing 1547 by 9, we get the mean height—172 centimetres (67.7 in.).

2. The *median*. The mean can be deceiving when some cases have exceptionally high or low values. For example, in Table 2.5, the mean income is $37 667, but because one lucky fellow has an income of $200 000, the mean is higher than the income of seven of the nine students. It is therefore a poor measure of the centre of the income distribution. The median is a better measure. If you order the data from the lowest to the highest income, the median is the value of the case at the midpoint. The median income in our example is $15 000. Four students earn more than that; four earn less. (Note: If you have an even number of cases, the midpoint is the average of the middle two values.)

3. *Correlation.* We have seen how valuable contingency tables are for analyzing relationships among variables. However, for variables that can assume many values, such as height and income, contingency tables become impracticably large. In such cases, sociologists prefer to analyze relationships among variables by using *scatterplots*. Markers in the body of the graph indicate the score of each case on both the independent and the dependent variables. The pattern formed by the markers is inspected visually and through the use of statistics. The strength of the association between the two variables is measured by a statistic called the *correlation coefficient* (signified as r). The value of r can vary from -1.0 to 1.0. If the markers are scattered around a straight, upward-sloping trend line, r takes a positive value. A positive r suggests that, as the value of one variable increases, so does the value of the other (see Figure 2.6, scatterplot 1). If the markers are scattered around a straight, downward-sloping trend line, r takes a negative value. A negative r suggests that, as the value of one variable increases, the value of the other decreases (see Figure 2.6, scatterplot 2). Whether positive or negative, the magnitude (or absolute value) of r decreases the more widely scattered the markers are from the line. If the degree of scatter is very high, $r = 0$; that is, there is no association between the variables (see Figure 2.6,

TABLE 2.5

The Height and Annual Income of Nine Students

Student	Height (in cm and in.)	Income ($000)
1	170 (67)	5
2	165 (65)	8
3	152 (60)	9
4	163 (64)	12
5	183 (72)	40
6	173 (68)	15
7	178 (70)	20
8	175 (69)	30
9	188 (74)	200

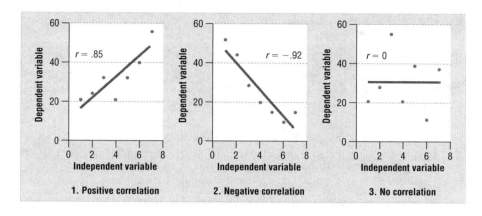

FIGURE 2.6
Correlation

1. Positive correlation   2. Negative correlation   3. No correlation

scatterplot 3). However, a low *r* or an *r* of zero may derive from a relationship between the two variables that does not look like a straight line. It may look like a curve. As a result, it is always necessary to inspect scatterplots visually and not just rely on statistics like *r* to interpret the data.

4. A *rate* lets you compare the values of a variable among groups of different size. For example, let's say 1000 women got married last year in a city of 100 000 people and 2000 women got married in a city of 300 000 people. If you want to compare the likelihood of women getting married in the two cities, you have to divide the number of women who got married in each city by the total number of women in each city. Since 1000/100 000 = 0.01, or 1 percent, and 2000/300 000 = 0.00666, or 0.67 percent, we can say that the *rate* of women marrying is higher in the first city even though fewer women got married there last year. Note that rates are often expressed in percentages. In general, dividing the number of times an event occurs (e.g., a woman getting married) by the total number of people to whom the event could occur in principle (e.g., the number of women in a city) will give you the rate at which an event occurs.

NOTES

1. Some scholars think it is possible to examine data without any preconceived notions and then formulate theories on the basis of this examination. However, they seem to form a small minority (Medawar, 1996: 12–32).

2. Subsequent analysis questioned the existence of a productivity effect in the Hawthorne study (Franke and Kaul, 1978). However, the general principle derived from the Hawthorne study—that social science researchers can influence their subjects—is now widely accepted (Webb et al., 1966).

3. Throughout, we convert U.S. dollars to Canadian dollars.

4. For clarity, we simplify Kay and Hagan's analysis.

5. When researchers finish analyzing survey data, they typically deposit computer-readable files of the data in an archive. This allows other researchers to conduct secondary analyses of survey data years later. Such data are widely used. They are not collected by government departments, but they have all the advantages of official statistics listed above, although they are based on samples rather than on populations. The largest social science data archive includes Canadian data and is housed at the University of Michigan's Inter-university Consortium for Political and Social Research (ICPSR). The ICPSR website, at http://www.icpsr.umich.edu, allows visitors to conduct elementary data analyses online.

SUMMARY

1. **What is the aim of science and how is it achieved?**
    The aim of science is to arrive at knowledge that is less subjective than other ways of knowing. A degree of objectivity is achieved by testing ideas against systematically collected data and leaving research open to public scrutiny.

2. **Does science have a subjective side?**
    It does. The subjective side of the research enterprise is no less important than the objective side. Creativity and the motivation to study new problems from new perspectives arise from individual passions and interests.

3. **What methodological issues must be addressed in any research project?**
    To maximize the scientific value of a research project, researchers must address issues of reliability (consistency in measurement), validity (precision in measurement), generalizability (the applicability of findings beyond the case studied), and causality (cause-and-effect relations among variables).

4. **What is participant observation?**
    Participant observation is one of the main sociological methods. It involves carefully observing people's face-to-face interactions and participating in their lives over a long period. Participant observation is particularly useful for doing exploratory research, constructing grounded theory, and validating measures on the basis of internal criteria. Issues of external validity, reliability, generalizability, and causality make participant observation less useful for other research purposes.

5. **What is an experiment?**
    An experiment is a carefully controlled artificial situation that allows researchers to isolate hypothesized causes and measure their effects by randomizing the allocation of subjects to experimental and control groups and exposing only the experimental group to an independent variable. Experiments get high marks for reliability and analysis of causality, but validity issues make them less than ideal for many research purposes.

6. **What is a survey?**
    In a survey, people are asked questions about their knowledge, attitudes, or behaviour, either in a face-to-face interview, telephone interview, or paper-and-pencil format. Surveys rank high on reliability and validity as long as researchers train interviewers well, phrase questions carefully, and take special measures to ensure high response rates. Generalizability is achieved through probability sampling, statistical control, and the analysis of causality by means of data manipulation.

7. **What are the advantages and disadvantages of using official documents and official statistics as sources of sociological data?**
    Existing documents and official statistics are inexpensive and convenient sources of high-quality data. However, they must be used cautiously because they often reflect the biases of the individuals or organizations that created them.

KEY TERMS

association (p. 52)	**ethnographic** (p. 40)
causality (p. 44)	**experiment** (p. 45)
contingency table (p. 54)	**experimental group** (p. 45)
control (p. 53)	**exploratory research** (p. 42)
control group (p. 45)	**field research** (p. 39)
dependent variable (p. 45)	**generalizability** (p. 44)

grounded theory (p. 42)

hypotheses (p. 42)

independent variable (p. 46)

operationalization (p. 43)

participant observation (p. 40)

population (p. 47)

probability sample (p. 48)

randomization (p. 45)

reliability (p. 43)

sample (p. 47)

spurious association (p. 53)

survey (p. 47)

validity (p. 43)

variable (p. 42)

QUESTIONS TO CONSIDER

1. What is the connection between objectivity and subjectivity in sociological research?

2. What criteria do sociologists apply to select one method of data collection over another?

3. What are the methodological strengths and weaknesses of various methods of data collection?

WEB RESOURCES

Companion Website for This Book

http://www.compass3e.nelson.com

Begin by clicking on the Student Resources section of the website. Next, select the chapter you are studying from the pull-down menu. From the Student Resources page you have easy access to InfoTrac® College Edition, additional Weblinks, and other resources. The website also has many useful tips to aid you in your study of sociology, including practice tests for each chapter.

InfoTrac® Search Terms

These search terms are provided to assist you in beginning to conduct research on this topic by visiting http://www.infotrac-college.com:

census

historical sociology

participant observation

sociological survey

sociology experiment

Recommended Websites

Bill Trochim at Cornell University has put together a comprehensive and impressive sociological research methods course at http://www.socialresearchmethods.net/kb.

For a comprehensive listing of websites devoted to qualitative research, go to http://www.nova.edu/ssss/QR/web.html.

"Statistics Every Writer Should Know" is an exceptionally clear presentation of basic statistics at http://www.robertniles.com/stats.

The World Wide Web contains many rich sources of official statistics. In preparing this book we relied heavily on data from the websites of Statistics Canada, http://www.statcan.ca, and the United Nations, http://www.un.org.

http://www.compass3e.nelson.com

CengageNOW™

http://hed.nelson.com

This online diagnostic tool identifies each student's unique needs with a Pretest that generates a personalized Study Plan for each chapter, helping students focus on concepts they're having the most difficulty mastering. Students then take a Posttest after reading the chapter to measure their understanding of the material. An Instructor Gradebook is available to track and monitor student progress.

What Is Social Science Research?

What You Will Learn

- how research begins
- the skeptical or critical values of research
- the scientific and the humanistic approaches to research
- basic steps in the research process and their pitfalls

INTRODUCTION

Imagine you met a student from a country with a different language and culture from your own. Before coming to Canada the student learned some English, read up on the history and politics of Canada, and became quite informed about the climate. Yet in his first week in Canada he feels disoriented, lost in the crowd, unsure of what to expect. He is particularly puzzled about a gesture that he has witnessed on a few occasions. At times when two people approach each other, they partly extend their right arms, open their hands, take each other's hand, and shake it. He is baffled by this gesture, especially since someone tried to do it with him and he did not know what to do.

Fortunately, the newcomer has become your friend and feels that he can turn to you for help. He asks, "What is that gesture?" Perhaps you are shocked that someone would have to ask, and so you answer, "It's a handshake." But your friend is still at a loss. He now asks, "How do you do it? When do you do it? Why do you do it?" You try your best to answer his questions, but it seems that every answer elicits more questions: "How far should I extend my arm? How strong should my grip be? Should I do the same thing with both males and females? Should I do it the same with different age groups? Should I . . . ?" You are stunned by the complications your friend sees in what to you, until now at least, was such a simple, common gesture. How would you answer these questions? What other questions do you think he might ask?

Now imagine yourself in a foreign country with different customs and language from your own. Suppose you too read up on the country and learned some of the language. But nothing prepared you for the first encounter with your host in the new country. Before you even have time to greet him with a handshake, he sticks out his tongue at you. Fortunately, he seems to mean well. You quickly offer him your hand, but he turns around. You are baffled by his behaviour, so you turn to him for help. His immediate response is to say, "It's an extended tongue." But you are still at a loss, and you ask: "What is that? How do you do it? Why do you do it?" Consider other questions you would want to ask your host. For example, how far should the tongue be extended?

None of us have taken Handshake 101, yet we know what it is, when to do it, and why we do it. But it can be quite bewildering for someone who is unfamiliar with the custom. Likewise, if we moved to another country, we would need to know more about the people and their customs. We would need to be able to communicate with them, so we would learn the language. However, we would also note many activities that they generally take for granted that would be strange to us. We would have many questions about these activities, and we would want to learn how, when, why, and so on.

At first, social scientific research may seem as baffling as trying to adapt to the ways of a new country. But with time, the logic and use of social research concepts will become routine, like greeting someone with a handshake.

As with the foreign student who already knew something about Canada but was unfamiliar with the handshake, you already know something about social research but you are not yet acquainted with many aspects of the process. You have heard of polls in the media, you have used the Internet and the library, and you probably have discussed theories in courses. You have even carried out casual research, such as informing yourself about various colleges and universities before deciding where to apply. But, as you may have realized after reading Chapter 1, these activities are not scientific research. As we noted, science is a way of knowing that is distinguishable from other socially acceptable ways of knowing. Therefore, social scientific research is different from casual research. But how is it different?

To answer this question, let us consider two basic questions about the research process. How do ideas for research begin or emerge? What are the aims and rules of scientific research? After answering these questions, we will elaborate on the steps in the research process.

Because we emphasize those aspects of scientific thinking that are different from common sense, you may find parts of this chapter challenging. Think of the ideas discussed here as a different language or as a new place to visit. Take time to become aware of the differences between what you know and the new language or place you do not know. As you become more familiar with a new language or place, you begin to feel more at home. As you read beyond this chapter, you should find that it makes even more sense. A simple "map" of some key differences between science and common sense is provided for your guidance in Table 2.1.

In this chapter we will look at three aspects of the research process:

1. How ideas for research begin or emerge
2. The norms and outlook of scientific research
3. The steps in the research process

HOW RESEARCH BEGINS

"How did they think of that?" "Where did they get the idea to do *that* research?" These are common reactions when people read about scientific research in the media. It is often hard to imagine how the researchers thought of doing the research in the first place. The popular image of scientists suggests that their research begins with a brilliant flash of insight—that they suddenly have an idea nobody else has thought of. This image of research is misleading; it suggests that all you need for research to begin is to come up with a brilliant, new idea. If this were the case, there would be far less research than there is, because brilliant ideas are always in extremely short supply.

It is true that research begins with an idea or a question that concerns the people willing to do research. But this idea is likely to have complicated origins in the way the researcher's background, current social circumstances, and ideas in the social sciences themselves come together.

Table 2.1 Science and Common Sense

	Common Sense	**Science**
Basic Foundation	Faith in unquestioned and unchanging truths	Working assumption of order in the universe
Examples	"Violent images in the media are always bad."	"Media images and audience responses are complex; so are the relations between them."
Community Rules	Folkways—commonly accepted ways of believing and behaving that are taken for granted	Objectivity, empirical verification, and open and clear communication, which are subject to critical examination
Examples	"We should ban violence in the media."	"We need to do research on: 1. The variety of media images: cartoons, horror, psychological thrillers, etc. 2. Circumstances in which people view these different images 3. The range of responses of different groups and individuals"
Searching for Knowledge	Casual research—what is needed to make a specific decision or to solve a particular problem	Systematic research—conscious attention to rules of description and explanation
Examples	"My children were so upset when they saw that movie. I'm never going to let them see another one like it."	Experiments—exposing groups of children in controlled ways to media images and then observing their behaviour

Personal experience can play an important role in shaping people's research interests. Refugees from Nazi Germany in the 1930s played a prominent part in conducting social scientific and historical research into totalitarianism and dictatorship in the 1940s and 1950s. Feminist ideas for social research emerged in the 1970s after an increasing number of women began to graduate from universities. The terrorist attacks of September 11, 2001 in the United States led many to research on related issues, such as community responses and the backlashes that followed.

Current social phenomena and social problems are likely to be of interest to many researchers, even if they themselves are not directly affected. For example, since the arrival of the personal computer, there has been a rapid growth of social science research into the impact of computer technology on work, leisure, education, and an emerging "new economy." The expansion of world trade has led to further interest in international relations, the future of nation-states, the influence of multinational firms, and the impacts of "globalization."

Perhaps most research is stimulated by the research of others. From the point of view of the individual researcher, this is intellectual stimulation—a game of ideas that may not connect directly to personal experience, a major social problem, or a contemporary event, but are nevertheless interesting and worth exploring further. Much historical research is like this. What was life like for the early settlers of Canada? Who supported Louis Riel and why? These are interesting questions in themselves, even though they may have no direct relation to contemporary issues and problems.

Other people's research can be a stimulus to further research in various ways. The research may have gaps or omissions. For example, there is a lot of research on the nursing profession as a "feminized" occupation—as one that has been primarily identified as a female occupation. Much of the research focuses on the way nurses are subordinated to the traditionally male role of doctors and surgeons. However, the numbers of male nurses and female doctors are growing. This growth suggests that doctor–nurse relations may well be changing as the gender compositions of the two occupations shift.

Research may be marked by controversy and disagreement. For example, there is much research into the relationship between media violence and aggressive behaviour, but a great deal of disagreement exists about what the data show or prove. Researchers often discover new information that is surprising but not easily explainable. The statisticians at Statistics Canada recently discovered that, with the exception of youth crimes, police reports indicate a decline in crime rates over the last several years. Apart from contradicting "common-sense" assumptions and impressions created by the media, these statistics were presented as bare facts without any explanation or interpretation. This lack of interpretation provides an opportunity for other researchers to develop satisfactory analyses and explanations.

What we are suggesting here is that the very beginnings of research are complicated. All of the factors we mention—personal experience, current social issues or problems, the stimulus of other people's research—often combine to pull people into undertaking social science research. What events or experiences in your own life could be beginning points of research? Can you think of current events that might even connect with your life or that interest you in some way? If you can say yes to any of these questions, you have taken the first step on the road of social research.

The next step is to narrow down your topic. For the research to get anywhere, it has to become focused, explicit, and developed enough to make it clear, communicable, and acceptable to a community of researchers, as well as to others who may be concerned with the practical results of your research. A clear and focused topic allows you to better communicate your research to others who may provide useful resources, inspiration, and aid.

THE AIMS AND RULES OF SCIENTIFIC RESEARCH

Having become interested in an issue or topic, your next problem is deciding how to follow it up. Becoming interested in an issue could lead you into different ways of expressing and exploring this interest. If your interest is in poverty, you could develop a political program to reform society; you could try your hand at a journalistic exposé of the issue; or you might try writing a novel or directing a documentary video about the experience of poverty. Each of these activities has its own aims and rules or procedures. Here, we shall look at the aims and procedures of a social scientific research approach.

If you have ever tried to read an article in a social science journal, you no doubt found it hard going. Even though the subject matter sounds interesting, the writing style and the terminology seem strange and abstract. This quality of writing results partly because each social science has developed special terms to express its ideas. As well, scientific researchers have developed rules and procedures to avoid the limitations and problems with intuition, experience, common sense, tradition, and authority. The terminology and the abstraction serve as reminders to the researchers themselves to be scientific in their outlook.

Since the articles are written for fellow professionals, the basic assumptions of scientific research are not spelled out. Hence, unless you already know the assumptions, the language of research will seem strange and difficult to comprehend. We are going to identify these assumptions and introduce some of the jargon associated with them.

Underlying the rules and procedures of social research are four basic values commonly held by researchers in all fields of science.

1. Researchers are committed to **objectivity** in their research work. That is, whatever their personal biases, researchers are committed to using the appropriate procedures for gathering and interpreting data and to presenting their discoveries honestly, even if these discoveries contradict cherished personal beliefs and values.

2. Scientific researchers aim for **empirical verification** of their ideas. That is, since scientific knowledge is based on observation in the world, scientific ideas must at some point be connected to observations to see if researchers' theories or speculations are in line with the facts. Researchers do not depend on personal experience, intuition, faith in authority, or tradition to provide answers to their questions.

3. Consequently, scientific research is designed to add to those discoveries by contributing to and building on other scientific knowledge. Research is viewed as a cooperative or *collective* endeavour; it builds on past research and lays the foundations for future research.

4. Finally, researchers can make a contribution only if they communicate their research clearly, honestly, and in enough detail that other researchers can fully understand how the research was carried out and how the data were interpreted. The logic and methods of research must be *transparent*, not hidden.

These basic values or aims can be summed up as **skepticism** (see Box 2.1). The value system of research leads researchers to disbelieve any statement that cannot be "proved" or supported by empirical evidence that has been discovered by following the accepted ways of doing research. Researchers, therefore, have developed procedures to ensure that their ideas are clearly and logically developed from previous research; that these ideas can become the basis of research plans that ensure empirical evidence is systematically gathered; and that the evidence is carefully analyzed and interpreted according to accepted rules and not according to the whims and personal beliefs of the researcher. These procedures will be outlined in the section on steps in the research process.

Skepticism could be called the negative or critical side of scientific inquiry. But research is also founded on some positive assumptions. The first assumption is that the universe is orderly or, as Einstein once put it, "God is not a madman." If there are regularities and patterns—events or processes that happen over and over again in nature and society—we should be able to discover them. This idea was advanced by ancient Greek thinkers. It

BOX 2.1   DOES SANTA CLAUS EXIST? ARE YOU SKEPTICAL?

Do you believe in Santa Claus? Recall the times you sat on Santa's lap and he asked you what presents you wanted, or you sent a letter or e-mail to the North Pole. There was no doubt that Santa existed and you had proof; he brought you gifts! So when did you stop believing? Why? Was it because you could prove that he did not exist? Or was it because you could not prove that he existed?

But while you now believe that Santa is just an imaginary construct, what about the claims of those who say they have supernatural powers? There are those who say they can solve crimes more easily than police investigators. One person has even become world-famous for supposedly bending spoons and keys with his mind.

Some psychics maintain that they can communicate with the dead. They have had their own TV shows and best-selling books, and have been featured on major television network programs. Indeed, one psychic had a TV show on which she claimed to have the power to tell to her guests the thoughts of their living or dead pets. And her guests were moved by what she told them.

Many faith healers claim to be able to jolt God into performing miracles. Thousands of people attend their services and many leave believing they *have* been healed, including from serious ailments such as cancer.

Today, as in the past, many continue to believe in astrology. Indeed, almost every major newspaper has a horoscope column. (When was the last time you read your horoscope?) There are also those who claim that by reading palms or tarot cards, looking into a crystal ball, or some other method, they can "read" your personality and foretell your future.

Can people really communicate with our dead relatives and pets? Can faith healers really heal us, and the astrologers and other psychics foretell our future or bend spoons with their minds? Rather than blindly accepting their claims we want proof. More specifically, we want to know if there is any reliable scientific evidence. In short, we are *skeptical.*

The word *skeptic* should not be confused with *cynic.* Whereas the cynic is simply distrustful, the skeptic demands to see the evidence. As noted in the magazine *Skeptic* (2007, Vol. 13, Iss. 2, page 5): "Ideally, skeptics do not go into an investigation closed to the possibility that a phenomenon might be real or that a claim might be true. When we say we are 'skeptical,' we mean that we must see compelling evidence before we believe."

Thus, by being skeptical we are prepared to change our minds, but only if there is reliable evidence that can be acquired using the scientific method. Being skeptical is therefore a common part of scientific research. Whatever the research, being scientific means there has to be an objective, rigorous, and reasoned search for verifiable evidence. We do not simply dismiss the claims, but rather seek appropriate, credible data.

distinguished them from their neighbours, who believed that nature was ruled by the whims and passions of gods, goddesses, spirits, and demons, and that the only way to cope with the resulting chaos was by following religious and magical rituals. These thinkers saw the universe as a disorderly place ruled by mysterious forces; it was impossible to understand how and why those forces worked the way they did, so magic was the key to survival.

The ancient Greeks also saw that if the universe is orderly, human thinking needs to reflect and express that order. They developed philosophical and mathematical ideas as the basis of rules for describing the orderliness of the universe, and emphasized the importance of **deductive reasoning**—that is, drawing particular conclusions from more general assumptions. For the Greeks, illogical thought and vague, unclear language were the main obstacles to scientific knowledge. Much later, during the scientific revolution in 17th-century Europe, other thinkers stressed the importance of empirical observations and **inductive reasoning**, which begins with particular observations and infers general patterns or principles from them. For these thinkers, purely logical ideas that had no reference to observation or that did not help to steer observation had no part in science. Scientific research is now understood to involve both types of reasoning.

Table 2.2 indicates how both types of logic fit with the research process. Deductive logic—thinking in terms of the relationships between ideas—is used when we move from a broad focus on the ideas of a theory to a narrow focus and then further refine the theory into a hypothesis. Inductive logic, by contrast, refers to thinking that organizes, summarizes, and interprets factual information and tries to draw implications or conclusions

Table 2.2 Logic, Theory, and Research

Emphasis on Deductive Logic	Emphasis on Inductive Logic
Theory building ←	← **Theory rebuilding**
The most general and abstract thought about research topics	Assessing and reformulating theories in light of data-based patterns, tests, and discoveries
↓	↑
Hypothesis development	**Data analysis and interpretation**
"Translating" general ideas into specific cause-and-effect statements	Coding, processing, and sorting data in relation to hypotheses
↓	↑
Operationalizing and measurement	**Data organization**
Developing empirical indicators of change or variation in the independent and dependent variables	Preliminary organization, coding, sorting, or processing of information prior to analysis

Data gathering

from observations. We use this kind of logic when we look for patterns in the data we have gathered. Both kinds of logic, then, are essential to the research process.

Another assumption, related to the idea of orderliness in nature and logic in thought, is the idea that order in nature can be explained. If you can clearly describe *how* things are the way they are, you should be able to develop ideas that explain *why* things are that way. The ultimate aim of research is to provide explanations, and the group of systematic, logically connected ideas that explain a factual discovery is called a **theory**. Research is never simply an accumulation of facts. Facts are important and meaningful only in relation to questions and ideas. Theories are the general ideas that give meaning to facts. They summarize and interrelate empirical data by explaining how and why things happen and by suggesting logical extensions and implications of these explanations. Stated differently, theories explain why things happen by linking **cause and effect**; they specify the circumstances or conditions under which things happen, and they permit us to **predict** events because we can look for those circumstances and conditions in advance of the outcome suggested by the theory.

Theories provide us with coherent, systematic syntheses of how we understand particular areas of reality. Yet scientific theories, unlike faith, are flexible. They are organized so that they are open to modification and development based on new empirical information arising from research. Such organization allows for the logical drawing of hypotheses from theories. **Hypotheses** are statements that express cause-and-effect relationships in a special language that indicates that they are not yet as supported by data, as are theories. Testing hypotheses through research extends the theory to new circumstances, conditions, and events. Without the process of hypothesis development and hypothesis testing, scientific theories would become closed, dogmatic, and unaffected by new research.

For example, theories of stratification or social class argue that economically based inequalities shape or determine political power and ideas, cultural patterns, family relationships, and so on. Such theories are very broad, general interpretations, which are not easy to test directly in relation to empirical evidence. For theory to be useful in guiding research, two things have to be done. First, we have to break the theory down into a more narrowly focused set of ideas; second, we need to reformulate these ideas into data-oriented, empirically testable hypotheses. For example:

Step 1

General theory: Economically based inequalities determine or shape the major features of social life.
Specific theory: Economically based inequalities shape the lifestyle (tastes, cultural expression, and consumption patterns) of individuals and groups.

Step 2

General hypothesis: Economic inequality determines consumption patterns.
Specific hypothesis: As income increases, the level of spending on entertainment increases.

Hypotheses are ideas put forward to be tested; they are designed to direct our attention to the "facts." Instead of speaking in terms of causes and effects, hypotheses refer to variables. **Variables** are parts or aspects of reality that can be seen to change or vary. Temperature, speed, and volume are variables in the physical world; social class, nationality, standard of living, and sexism are variables in the social world. Hypotheses usually take the form of "if . . . then" statements, such as "if the temperature of water decreases to the freezing point, its volume will increase," or "if income increases then the amount spent on entertainment will increase." In these hypotheses, temperature and income are called **independent variables**. They are identified as changing, but the causes of those changes are not specified; for the purpose of testing the hypothesis they are viewed as changing by themselves, *independently* of other factors. Volume and spending on entertainment are called **dependent variables** because their changes are linked to, or *depend on*, the changes in the independent variables. In other words, in our earlier hypothesis spending on entertainment "depends" on the level of income. Thus, the hypotheses assume that if there are no changes in the independent variables, there will be no changes in the dependent variables.

How can we tell whether there have been changes in any variable? We detect change by setting up ways of measuring or identifying changes. Setting up systems of **measurement** or identification of change is called **operationalizing**. Essentially, operationalizing means clearly laying out the rules for establishing changes in variables. In the physical sciences the rules have developed with instruments of measurement: temperature is measured by thermometers, speed by accelerometers, and so on. In the social sciences our instruments tend to be such things as sets of questions specially designed to establish how religious we are, how socially involved, or how satisfied with our work, or psychological tests designed to measure how intelligent, creative, depressed, addicted, and so forth, we are. Other measures are developed from available statistical data to measure unemployment, crime rates, and the cost of living, for example.

The process of operationalizing is one of moving from the *idea* of a phenomenon to a *definition* of the specific ways you intend to measure the existence and variation of a phenomenon in your research. For example, the idea of "intelligence" refers to a combination of skills and abilities, including linguistic, mathematical, and problem-solving or analytical reasoning. An **operational definition** of intelligence is "the skills and abilities measured by this (the researcher's) intelligence test." In other words, a researcher can show us what intelligence is by the operations of developing and applying questions that call for intelligent reasoning.

Take again our earlier hypothesis in step 2 above that states as income increases, the level of spending on entertainment increases. Our hypothesis is in the form of an "if . . . then" statement connecting variables, that is, if income increases then spending on entertainment increases. But we must now clarify what we mean by "increase in income" and "spending on entertainment." This has to be done by developing clear operational definitions. For example:

Step 3

Operational definition:
a. By "income" we mean . . . What do you mean by "income"? The definition must hold for the duration of your study and must resolve issues such as pre-tax or net income figures, earnings only or other income and wealth, individual or family incomes, the time period involved, etc.).
b. By "spending on entertainment" we mean . . . (What do you mean by "spending on entertainment"? The definition must hold for the duration of your study and must resolve such issues as: Do we include spending on tobacco and alcohol? How do we distinguish between "luxury clothing" worn at parties and regular or necessary clothing? Is eating out a necessity or a luxury/entertainment item?).

Let us take another example, that of "work satisfaction." The idea of work satisfaction might have been taken from general theories of social class and experience of social inequalities. Operationalizing the idea of work satisfaction requires that it be defined in such a way that the researcher can gather empirical evidence of work satisfaction levels through such measures as rates of absenteeism, rates of job turnover, measures of quality of job performance and productivity, and responses to questions about satisfaction with the job. Of course, these operational definitions and measures must be logically consistent with the underlying concepts and the broader general ideas or theories from which they are developed.

Moving from general, theoretical concepts to operationalized concepts of measurable variables is at times difficult and involves complications. Some of these are mentioned in later chapters in relation to specific research methods. A brief and simplified overview of these issues is presented in Box 2.2.

BOX 2.2 OPERATIONALIZATION AND MEASUREMENT ISSUES

ACCURACY

Does your measure produce accurate results or is there some built-in bias that leads to under- or overestimation?

For example, mainly asking questions on what people find unsatisfactory and negative about their jobs and work environment in a survey on work satisfaction might bias the results.

PRECISION

Is it possible to operationalize the variable so that it can be measured with a high level of refinement or precision?

For example, measuring "size of firm" by "number of employees" is more precise than distinguishing between "small," "medium," and "large" firms.

RELIABILITY

Will the method used to collect the data lead to consistent results? That is, does the measure produce similar results with repeated use?

For example, ambiguous or unclear questions in a standardized questionnaire may lead to inconsistent responses over several surveys using these same questions.

VALIDITY

Do the operationalized concepts of variables reflect the meaning of the broader theory?

For example, is work absenteeism a useful or realistic way of operationalizing the concept of work "alienation"?

Do the operationalized concepts cover the full range of the phenomena implied by the broader theory or research question?

continued

For example, do measures of "prejudice" apply to a researcher's concern with ethnic, racial, and religious prejudice, or do they really only measure ethnic prejudice?

Are the operationalized concepts plausible or reasonable reflections of the broader ideas in this field of research?

For example, does the operationalized concept of class include measures of economic wealth as well as measures of social status?

All of the measures identified so far have one thing in common: whether you are dealing with temperature, speed, IQ, work satisfaction, or the suicide rate, you can measure these variables in precise quantitative terms. For example, an IQ of 115, a temperature of 21 degrees Celsius, a work satisfaction rating of 7 out of 10, and a suicide rate of 3.5 per 100 000 are **quantitative variables**. But such quantitative precision may not be possible with many social characteristics that are treated as variables—religious differences, nationality, or sexual orientation, for example. These kinds of variations are classifiable as different and you can describe the differences, but you cannot numerically *measure* or rate such differences. Social scientists often deal with such **qualitative variables**, as well as with quantitatively measurable ones. Therefore, hypotheses in the social sciences are often less precise than those in the natural sciences. (This difference in the measurability of variables is discussed in Chapter 9.)

Statements linking independent and dependent variables translate abstract, theoretical ideas into specific, testable ideas. These statements focus on a small number of key factors (variables), and thus the researchers are forced to develop their ideas in terms of observation or data gathering (operationalizing). Thinking in terms of hypotheses requires researchers to identify how variables change, which can be done only by identifying what will be seen as variables change.

Such hypotheses are like pieces of a jigsaw puzzle. As hypotheses are tested, and assuming they survive the tests of observation and data gathering, they begin to accumulate and interconnect into a bigger picture covering more and more factors, events, and processes. This big picture is interpreted and described through theories that represent an overall understanding and explanation of the causes at work.

CAUSAL ANALYSIS

In everyday conversation we are quick to point to a cause. We may have an easy explanation for why there is a high dropout rate among high-school students, why there is air pollution, or why the price of gas may have increased, but to determine cause in research is complicated. The idea of cause is a difficult and controversial one that has long been debated by philosophers. Simply put, there are two basic positions in these debates. One side sees causality as a real, objective characteristic of the universe and considers that the researchers' task is to find evidence of this reality. The other side argues that cause is simply an idea—a logical principle that is a convenient way of organizing or interpreting our information or discoveries. Under this view, we do not find cause in reality; rather, we impose causes on our findings. Wherever their sympathies may lie in this debate, researchers tend to agree that four conditions need to be met in order to accept a causal interpretation of data:

1. *Temporal Order:* A cause must come before an effect.

   Students who work part-time will have lower grades.

   "A" (part-time work)　　**comes before**　　"B" (lower grades)

   Independent Variable　　　　　　　　　Dependent Variable

   This condition sounds obvious, and in many research situations it is. In the above situation, the student has to first work part-time to see if it affects grade performance. But social science research often involves chicken-and-egg puzzles, in which the sequence is not easily determined. For example, the "differential association" theory of juvenile delinquency argues that delinquency is a result of joining the wrong crowd. Yet it could just as easily be argued that the wrong crowd will attract a certain kind of individual. In which case being recruited into the wrong crowd is not a cause of delinquency, but rather is itself an **intervening** (in-between) **variable**. Furthermore, you could argue that wrong crowds and the problem personalities attracted to them are products of certain kinds of environments—they are both effects of a common cause. Sorting out sequences of causes and effects, then, is not always an easy task.

2. *Association or Correlation:* The researcher must show that the two variables change together in a consistent way.

   The more hours a student works, the lower the grades.

   "A" changes (increase in hours)　　**occur with**　　"B" changes (drop in grade performance)

   Independent Variable　　　　　　　　　Dependent Variable

   An increase in the number of hours worked will result in a drop in grade performance. That is, in most cases students who work more hours will have lower grades than students who work less. If there is no consistent pattern of association—that is, too many exceptions—it is unlikely there is a causal connection. How many exceptions still allow for a causal relationship to be inferred requires careful assessment, by statistical analysis if possible. Finding an association by itself does not mean that a causal relationship exists, and the other conditions outlined here must be satisfied.

3. *Elimination of Alternative Causal Influences*

   In our example there might be many other factors influencing grade performance that are unrelated to whether the student works part-time, such as course content. Causal or explanatory research requires controlling alternative causal factors so that clear conclusions can be drawn about the cause actually at work. Different research techniques use different means to establish such controls. The laboratory experiment is the most effective technique for eliminating alternative causal factors, but its use is often limited in social research. Consequently, other means, such as systematic comparison and statistical analysis, have been developed to perform this control function. These techniques, however, are much weaker than experimental controls. Hence, social science research is dogged by many disputes over causal explanations.

4. *Theoretical Consistency*

Finally, the discovery or interpretation of causal linkages must make sense or be acceptable in terms of the researchers' theoretical framework or assumptions. This is a difficult issue, because the researchers cannot be so attached to their theories that they "explain away" any results that do not fit. Such results or anomalies may be valuable in provoking the development of more adequate theories to replace the existing ones. However, much research consolidates and extends existing theoretical understanding rather than overthrowing it. Assessing the theoretical significance of research data—for example, whether it is an extension or an anomaly—can be very difficult.

Reading 2.1

Social science research can raise important issues about our well-being, and sometimes this research gets noted by the popular media. The newspaper article below reports on a study about teenagers reading magazine articles about dieting. What were the objective, the method, and conclusion of the study? What other questions do you have about the research that are not reported in the newspaper article? What practical advice does the study suggest? Given what you have read in the above section on causal analysis, can we say that reading magazine articles is the cause of unhealthy weight loss behaviour? Why or why not?

After reading the newspaper article you may want to read the original academic journal article on which it is based. The bibliographic information is listed below the newspaper article.

READ 'EM AND WEEP: Teenagers' Perusing of Diet Articles Linked to Eating Disorders Later

Magazine headlines entice teenage girls with promises: "Get the body you want" and "Hit your dream weight now!" But a new study suggests reading articles about diet and weight loss could have unhealthy consequences later.

Teenage girls who often read magazine articles about dieting were more likely five years later to practise extreme weight-loss measures such as vomiting than girls who never read such articles, the University of Minnesota study found.

It didn't seem to matter whether the girls were overweight when they started reading about weight loss, nor whether they considered their weight important. After taking those factors into account, researchers still found reading articles about dieting predicted later unhealthy weight loss behaviour.

Girls in middle school who read dieting articles were twice as likely five years later to try to lose weight by fasting or smoking cigarettes, compared with girls who never read such articles. They were three times more likely to use measures such as vomiting or taking laxatives, the study found.

"The articles may be offering advice such as cutting out trans fats and soda, and those are good ideas for everybody," said Alison Field of Harvard Medical School, who has done similar research but wasn't involved in the new study. "But the underlying messages these articles send are 'You should be concerned about your weight and you should be doing something.'"

The study appears in January's issue of the journal *Pediatrics*. Its findings were based on surveys and weight-height measurements of 2,516 middle school students in 1999 and again in 2004. About 45 per cent of the students were boys.

Only 14 per cent of boys reported reading diet articles often, compared with 44 per cent of girls. For those boys who did read about weight loss, there was no similar lasting effect.

In the new study, it was unclear whether it was the diet articles themselves or accompanying photographs of thin models that made a difference. The study didn't ask teenagers which magazines they read, only how often they read magazine articles "in which dieting or weight loss are discussed."

The study was based on students' self-reports about their behaviour and, like all surveys, could be skewed by teenagers telling researchers what they think they want to hear, said study co-author Patricia van den Berg.

She said parents should carefully consider whether they want their daughters reading about weight loss.

"It possibly would be helpful to teen girls if their mothers didn't have those types of magazines around," van den Berg said.

Parents also should discuss magazines' messages with their daughters, she said.

"Talk to your kids about where these messages are coming from," she said.

Doctors' waiting rooms are no place for magazines promoting diet and weight loss, she said, "in the same way you don't have materials promoting smoking in waiting rooms." . . .

Source: Carla K. Johnson, "Read 'em and weep: Teenagers' perusing of diet articles linked to eating disorders later," The Gazette, *January 2, 2007, p. A14.*

For the academic journal article on which the newspaper article is based, see:

van den Berg, Patricia, Neumark-Sztainer, Dianne, J. Hannan, Peter, & Haines, Jess (2007). Is dieting advice from magazines helpful or harmful? five-year associations with weight-control behaviors and psychological outcomes in adolescents. Pediatrics, 119, *e30–e37.* **InfoTrac record number: A157361009.**

ALTERNATIVE VIEWS OF SOCIAL SCIENCE RESEARCH

Some social scientists believe that social science research should not follow too closely the assumptions of natural science. They argue that social research is at least as **humanistic** as it is scientific. For these researchers, the task of social research is to bring out the uniquely human qualities of psychological and social reality. This task does not involve abandoning the assumption of an orderly universe or violating rules of logic, nor does it mean that social researchers should not care about empirical evidence. Rather, these researchers argue, social research should be devoted to careful description to bring out the richness and complexity of social and psychological life, and it should pay attention to the unique and the singular, not just to what can be generalized. Furthermore, social and psychological explanations have to be framed in terms of human motives and meanings, rather than focusing on the impersonal, mechanical causality favoured by natural science. (A brief introduction to these ideas is provided in Box 2.3.)

BOX 2.3 DIFFERENT VIEWS OF SOCIAL SCIENCE

Beginning in the 20th century, the natural sciences have made enormous progress and have contributed to the rise of increasingly powerful technologies. This progress has been extremely beneficial in areas such as medicine, agriculture, and energy production. Yet science and technology have also produced nuclear weaponry and manufacturing processes that pollute the environment. The growth of science has led, as well, to intensive research and debate about the nature of science itself. Such investigations have given us a greater sense of the complexity of science as a human activity and as a social institution.

Together, the effects of science and technology and the studies of the history and practices of science and scientists have contributed to critiques of the assumptions and the claims made on its behalf. In turn, these debates and critiques are found within the social sciences, as social researchers review the ways their disciplines follow or diverge from the natural sciences. To simplify, there are four differing views on the way social science is similar or dissimilar to natural science.

SOCIAL SCIENCE AS SCIENCE

The social sciences have developed and will continue to develop as all sciences have in the past. There are no logical differences between natural and social sciences—both are founded on the same principles of reasoning, ideas of causal explanation, and focus on observable experience. Although there are some differences in methods, both natural and social sciences use systematic methods of observation in order first to describe and then to develop explanations for phenomena. Historically, all sciences have similar phases of evolution: from speculation to increasingly accurate observation and description, and from qualitative description to increasingly explanatory and quantitative analysis, permitting increased prediction and control of the phenomena. This view, known as *positivism*, is still predominant among social science researchers, but it has been criticized by supporters of the following viewpoints.

HUMANISTIC/INTERPRETATIVE

The natural and social sciences share a fundamental framework of reasoning, but the observable experience or realities that each deals with are very different. Natural sciences deal with objects that can be observed only "externally" as objects, while the social sciences deal with human subjects with whom we share experiences. Thoughts, feelings, understandings, and intentions and their historical, cultural, social, and psychological variations are the focus of the social

continued

Box 2.3, *continued*

sciences. The methods of investigation and the modes of explanation, while logical and causal, are very different from those used in natural sciences.

CRITICAL/RADICAL

This approach is diverse and includes social scientists who combine a critical approach with the other perspectives mentioned here. Despite this diversity, these social scientists are united in viewing social science as a weapon or tool in political struggles and moral critique. Social science is not aimed at knowledge for its own sake. The purpose of social research is to expose oppression, exploitation, and injustice, and to make victims aware of these conditions so that they are moved to political action to overcome them.

POSTMODERNIST

This viewpoint is deeply skeptical of the entire framework of natural scientific thinking, which it sees as part of a culture that developed with European industrialization and aims for world dominance. Science is a cultural product emerging under specific historical, social, and political conditions, and so it cannot claim to be a universal, objective method of revealing truths for all times and places. Postmodernists argue that all human ideas are limited by their time and place of origin and cannot go beyond these limits. Because of these limitations, the objectivity of science, especially the social sciences, is an illusion.

Every social science is divided, to some extent, between the scientific and humanistic approaches, and there appears to be no end in sight to this division. Rather than take sides, we would like to point out that, as far as social research is concerned, both approaches are thoroughly empirical, and their work is generally *complementary* and not mutually exclusive. Valuable information and discoveries have been and continue to be contributed by both approaches.

STEPS IN THE RESEARCH PROCESS

Essentially, doing research involves, first, defining a topic in such a way that it is meaningful, significant, and researchable; second, developing an organized, systematic plan for researching the topic with reference to empirical data; third, following through on this plan; fourth, analyzing the data gathered; and fifth, communicating the results of the research in full—including the definition of the topic, the research plan, how the plan was implemented through gathering data, the results, and your interpretation of the results.

In this section we shall briefly look at this process step by step to give you a sense of how to proceed. Research is in fact more complicated than this, with lots of two-steps-forward–one-step-back movements. Lest we give you the wrong impression, scientific research is never problem-free. Researchers are human, after all; they make mistakes, they misinterpret their results, things fail to work out in the expected way, and all sorts of confusion may occur. Different kinds of things can go wrong at various stages of the research process, so along with identifying the steps themselves, we shall discuss some of the mistakes and problems that may occur at each step.

Step 1: Defining the Topic

As we have already stated, a researchable topic is not just a smart idea no one else has thought of. If you think you have an original idea, you first have to see whether it is really so original. As a basis for research, your idea also has to connect with empirical information. Consequently, the first step is to explore other people's research in order to find out what other people have thought and discovered and to see how your ideas relate or connect to these thoughts and discoveries. In the process, you will be able to clarify your initial idea, to rework it so that it takes advantage of and builds on other people's research. By fitting in with previous research, your ideas do not lose their originality or significance; rather, they become *more* important by becoming part of an ongoing set of discoveries and debates. The process of developing a research topic through examining other people's research is discussed in detail in Chapter 3.

Of course, things can go wrong even at this early stage. The area you are interested in may be controversial, such as the effects of violence in the media on children's behaviour. You may have strong ideas about the subject and want your research to support those ideas. Since the research on this topic is inconclusive, it is open to interpretation and selective reading. In most areas of social science, controversies are plentiful, so you will have to learn to be open-minded and fair in your reading. Any conclusions you draw should be made on the basis of the logical and empirical strengths and weaknesses of the research—they should not arise from your biases. Consequently, this initial step also involves identifying your own biases on the topic.

Misinterpretation of others' research also may occur through illogical reasoning, hasty reading, and omission of important or up-to-date information. These errors will undermine your research by introducing biases, one-sided interpretations, and mistaken interpretations, which will lessen the value of the entire research project. It is essential, then, that you launch the research properly, through a careful, critical examination of your initial ideas and the way they relate to the ideas and discoveries of other researchers in your chosen field.

Let us suppose that you have heard recent media reports about the squeegee kids who clean motorists' windshields when they are waiting at traffic lights. Perhaps you have heard about the Saturday night riot in Montreal, which was supposedly provoked by the police crackdown on these activities. Some radio interviews indicated that most squeegee kids are young high-school dropouts. You are aware that, over the past few years, the media have reported periodically on the phenomenon of dropping out of high school. Going beyond the media reports you have, with the help of your college librarian you read a number of government and academic reports on the issue. But now you have questions that these reports do not fully answer. How widespread is the problem? Has it grown worse in the past few years? Is it expected to worsen in the future? Who drops out? Why do they do so?

Step 2: Designing the Research Plan

Research begins with some questions that you want to find answers for, questions that may originate as personal curiosity but are refined and focused by reading previous research.

What kind of study you should plan on doing depends on the kinds of questions you wish to pursue. In turn, the nature of your study determines the kinds of research methods you will be using.

First, there is the issue of the general approach to be taken. Is your study to be exploratory, descriptive, or explanatory? You may conclude from your reading of others' research that there is so little information that what is needed is a probe into society to see what the reality is. Alternatively, you may find that there is some information on dropping out but that it is incomplete in certain ways. An **exploratory study** is designed to find out what things are like in situations where there is little firm information. "Is the rising dropout rate real, or is it a media myth?" is the kind of question asked in such a study. An exploratory study is designed to seek out as much information as possible from whatever sources that may be available about the subject.

Such a study might be qualitative or quantitative, or it might combine both types of information. An example of the former would be a **field study** (see Chapter 7) in which, to make contact with teenagers living on the streets, you do volunteer work at a drop-in centre or a community youth centre. You might also ask friends and teachers if they know individuals who have dropped out who would be willing to talk to you. As you make contacts and build up trust, you can find out about their lives and how they came to be in their current situation, and you might get leads to others in similar circumstances. In addition, you might be able to interview fellow volunteers and community-work professionals and find out what they know about the problem of dropouts. They too could pass you on to other experts or professionals, such as social workers or teachers. From these diverse sources you might put together a picture of dropping out combining both information on the experiences and lives of teenagers themselves, and various perspectives from people close to and informed about the problem.

The distinction between an exploratory and a **descriptive study** is not clear or rigid. However, it is logical to think of detailed description as something that follows from exploration. Once you have discovered some things about dropping out, the next step is to describe it clearly in all its variations. It is possible that the task of detailed and extensive description, then, is a project that follows from the initial exploratory research. Thus, you might go on to do detailed studies of male versus female dropouts, differences between runaways and dropouts living at home, differences in selected communities, and so on. Such studies would probably attempt to use different data-gathering techniques than those used in the initial, exploratory research. The exploratory researcher might use field research, case studies, expert testimony, documentary, and available data. In a descriptive study, the researcher would be more likely to use surveys by distributing questionnaires to community volunteers and professionals, which they would give to their clients, and to survey the volunteers and professionals themselves. Documentary research might be extended to cover a longer time period or to give greater range and detail and so on.

An **explanatory study** attempts to go beyond description by collecting data to show *why* things are the way they are. In our example, such a study would try to explain why dropping out has increased or decreased over a certain time period, or has increased more in some areas than in others; why youths with certain background characteristics seem to be more vulnerable to dropping out than others; or what specific conditions and circumstances seem common among dropouts. Explanatory studies tend to be more quantitative in their approach, to use specific techniques to select their informants, and to use systematic, questionnaire-based interviews or survey techniques and experimental procedures. These procedures allow researchers to draw conclusions more reliably than qualitative approaches do. However, explanatory research often includes exploratory, descriptive, and qualitative material to illustrate and support the arguments made on the basis of quantitative methods.

Consequently, deciding on whether your research approach is going to be exploratory–descriptive or explanatory will lead you to rely on different methods of observation or data gathering and will also tend to determine the relative balance between qualitative and quantitative analysis in your research.

Step 3: Following the Research Plan (Data Gathering)

Once you have developed your research plan and have decided on the aim of the research (exploratory–descriptive or explanatory) and the procedures you will be using to gather your data, you have to follow through on it. The bulk of this textbook (Chapters 5 to 8) discusses these procedures in detail. Here, we should just alert you to two important problems: sampling and errors in data gathering.

Most research involves sampling—that is, you will study only a small part of the reality you are interested in. You cannot track down and interview all dropouts; you will not have time to visit all drop-in centres or to talk to all experts; the government may have useful statistics since 1971 but not before; and so forth.

For various reasons, then, any factual study is restricted to a **sample**, or a part of what the researcher is concerned with. How that sample is made available or chosen for study is an important issue, as we shall see in Chapter 4. What is critical with respect to sampling is how confident you can be that the sample you have studied is representative of the whole. Without reasonable grounds for assuming your sample is representative, your study can be criticized as being potentially biased and as providing a distorted, selective view of reality.

The second problem is that all research procedures have the potential for creating **errors**. Questionnaires asking people to tick off an appropriate box provide opportunities for people to accidentally check off the wrong box, to skip the question, or to deliberately give the wrong reply. Experimenters cannot stop people from trying to guess the purpose of the experiment and altering their behaviour to help or hinder the experimenter from achieving the assumed purpose. Even the best participant observers may slightly alter the behaviour of the people they are observing. All these research procedures are necessary to gather data, but they also have the potential of producing erroneous information. Since these methods are the only ways we have of gathering data, the best we can do is try to be aware of their problems and limitations and attempt to minimize their sources of error.

Step 4: Analyzing and Interpreting the Data

Facts rarely, if ever, speak for themselves. The facts or data that are collected in the course of research always need organizing and analyzing before their patterns and implications can be seen or understood. Notes on fieldwork have to be read and reread before you can see what values, interests, and perceptions people share; the answers to dozens or even hundreds of questionnaires have to be coded and counted before you can identify patterns of opinions and connect these patterns with the characteristics of people with different opinions; statistics from government documents have to be sifted through and reorganized in order to discover trends or other patterns. These processes of analysis, interpretation, reorganization, and sifting and sorting make up the stage of **data analysis**, in which you find out what data you have gathered and what sense you can make of them. As we shall see in Chapter 9, data analysis takes different forms in quantitative and qualitative styles of social research.

Organizing the data badly can give unclear and misleading impressions. Two major problems encountered at this stage of research are drawing improper conclusions and "fudging" unexpected or surprising discoveries. We are often tempted to overgeneralize and to make strong claims on the basis of too few or too weak examples. Our tendency to want to fit observations into clear and distinct patterns may lead us to oversimplify and to force evidence into logical groupings in order to draw clear conclusions. With respect to the second problem, unexpected findings break through the logical groupings expressed in our hypotheses and research questions and leave us with the problem of how to account for these surprising facts. In our concern to explain all of our data, we may improvise new explanations to fit the facts without fully thinking through how these explanations fit with our initial ideas.

Step 5: Writing the Research Report

Research is meaningless if it remains known only by the original researcher. The entire point of research is to add to existing knowledge and, in the case of applied research, to improve our ability to do things effectively—to cure mental illness, reduce poverty, or improve job satisfaction. If no one else knows what you have found out, past mistakes go uncorrected, new conditions are not understood, and attempts to improve or cope with social problems are less effective than they might otherwise be.

Hence, the final step in the research process is writing and circulating a research report. This may take the form of an essay for your teacher, a paper written for publication in a journal, or a report submitted to a client or an organization. Regardless of the report's intended audience, it has to communicate clearly why you selected your problem, what your research design was and how you carried it out, and what the results were and how you interpreted them. Each of these points has to be presented with sufficient detail and clarity so that, in principle, other researchers could **replicate**, or repeat, your research if they so wished. In other words, other researchers may not be entirely convinced of your findings, and they should be able to try their hand at the same kind of research. If others come up with similar results, your research will be accepted as valid and as a foundation for others to build on. Of course, your research may be sufficiently convincing not to need repeating. In either case, at this point it is no longer *your* research. In a sense, it now belongs to all researchers; it has become "what everybody knows."

QUANTITATIVE AND QUALITATIVE RESEARCH

We have made a number of references to differences between quantitative and qualitative research in this chapter, since both approaches are present in each of the social science disciplines. Both are important to social research, and have developed as part of the increasing emphasis on the scientific nature of social science. In fact, many studies combine quantitative and qualitative research methods.

The two approaches are summarized in Table 2.3. Note that although the research strategies differ in some respects, the basic stages of quantitative and qualitative research

Table 2.3 Quantitative and Qualitative Research

Step 1: Defining the Topic

Selection of the topic and refining it into a hypothesis or research question

Step 2: Designing the Research Plan

	Quantitative Research	**Qualitative Research**
Aim	Descriptive or explanatory	Exploratory, descriptive, interpretative
Focus	Key variables	Broader interconnected factors
Operationalizing	Identifying or developing numerical empirical indicators for variables focused on	Identifying ranges of relevant qualitative data, open to modification as study continues
Sampling	Random sampling aimed for *(see Chapter 4)*	Nonrandom samples often used *(see Chapter 4)*
Instrument	Structured, and can involve experiment, survey, structured observation; the researcher uses inanimate instruments, such as questionnaires and tests *(see Chapters 5, 6, 8).*	Flexible, and can involve naturalistic observation, fieldwork, intensive interviews, interpretation of documents; the researcher is the main instrument who observes, interviews, and participates in social settings of interest *(see Chapter 7).*

Step 3: Data Gathering

	Proceeds according to the instrument(s) selected, and is kept separate from analysis and interpretation.	Data gathering is interconnected with data analysis (step 4) and they mutually inform each other.

Step 4: Data Analysis

	Deductive—involves descriptive and inferential statistics.	Inductive—involves largely qualitative interpretation by the researcher.

Step 5: Writing the Research Report

are similar. Both deliberately and systematically connect their research to previous research, and present the results in such a way that subsequent researchers could further develop the study. Which approach is used depends on the kinds of questions asked, the kind of study that is feasible, and the inclinations and skills of the researcher.

Quantitative research emphasizes precise measurement, the use of numerical data and, wherever possible, the use of sampling techniques that allow for more valid generalizations (see Chapter 4 for more on sampling). Quantitative research mainly involves using surveys, experimentation, or secondary data analysis in order to gather or produce data (discussed in Chapters 5, 6, and 8). This enables the researcher to describe relationships mathematically in the form of tables and graphs, to use descriptive statistics, and to test hypotheses through statistical analysis.

Qualitative research emphasizes detailed descriptions of people's actions, statements, and ways of life, often including their possessions, cultural objects, and environments (see Chapter 7). Qualitative research often uses case studies or unusual and "offbeat" situations to throw light on "normal" or general cases and circumstances. Qualitative research methods include naturalistic observation, fieldwork, open-ended interviews, and documentary interpretation. Qualitative research is characterized by a verbal or literary presentation of data, with much less concern for quantification.

In terms of the types of questions asked, quantitative researchers are concerned with establishing and measuring the strengths of the relationships between variables, and representing patterns and social trends in quantitative terms. An example of the first kind of research would be an investigation into the kinds of social and psychological variables that contribute to different patterns of health and illness. An example of the second kind of research would be an analysis of the increasing number of teleworkers. How many such workers are there? How rapid is the rate of growth of this kind of work? What kinds of firms do they work for? What types of work do they do?

Qualitative researchers tend to ask questions about the experiences and subjective meanings of social situations, such as what it is like to be a teleworker rather than a factory or office worker. Qualitative researchers also explore subcultures, such as the informal norms of peer groups in schools or friendships among workmates, and the ways these operate in the broader institutional culture promoted by teachers and managers. On a broader historical level, qualitative researchers are often interested in the social movements and conflicts surrounding changes in the identification and control of various substances such as drugs, or changes to the understanding and treatment of mental illnesses and similar large-scale cultural and institutional changes.

Certain kinds of research are more easily undertaken by one approach than by the other. It is often difficult to sample a large number of cult members or the homeless in order to undertake a quantitative study. Reliable census data are limited to the last century and a half in most industrialized societies, so historical studies have to use fragmentary statistics and combine these with qualitative data, even in studying demographic or economic topics. Studies comparing different time periods or different societies often involve data that have not been collected in similar ways, so that even when the data are quantitative, comparisons require careful qualitative interpretation.

Finally, all research depends on the skills, the creativity, and the interests of the researchers. Some researchers are more interested or excited by one research approach than the other, and develop better skills in their preferred approach.

CONSTRAINTS OF THE RESEARCH PROCESS

So far we have presented social science research as an almost entirely intellectual process. This is only part of the story. Research requires resources of all kinds, and part of the researcher's time, energy, and skills is spent in trying to obtain and manage the needed resources. In addition, research is a human activity—the researcher brings to it a variety of social and personal assumptions and perspectives. Those who are being researched are not always passive subjects opening up their lives for scientific inspection. A variety of social circumstances influence how research issues become important and how they are thought about and researched.

Resources

Doing research requires time, money, and other resources, all of which are in limited supply. Can you finish your report by the deadline? Can you afford to mail out questionnaires to a large enough sample? Will you be allowed to interview residents in an institution? People who undertake research for the first time are shocked to discover that so much of their time and energy is expended organizing these resources so that the research can actually be accomplished. You need to assess the amounts of time, money, and other resources you are going to need prior to starting the research. These considerations must be part of the development of the research plan, the second step in the research process. A *researchable* topic is one that is not only feasible in terms of its meaning and significance in relation to other research, but also practical in terms of the resources to which the researcher has access.

Ethics

Social researchers also face a variety of constraints arising from their subject matter—other human beings. The most important of these constraints involves **ethics**: What are researchers' responsibilities to the people with whom they interact in their research? Experiments involving human subjects are obviously limited by basic obligations to treat others with decency and dignity. But almost all social research methods raise ethical questions concerning how much stress the research should be permitted to impose, how much information should be extracted, and how much people's right to privacy should be protected. All professional social science associations have developed ethical guidelines for their researchers (see Box 2.4). Institutions that support research, such as universities and governments, routinely monitor studies by applying these guidelines. Ethical issues will be discussed as part of the presentation of each major research method in subsequent chapters.

BOX 2.4 ETHICAL CONSIDERATIONS

Is it right or wrong to observe people for a research study without them knowing? Is it right or wrong to ask for the racial origin of the respondent in a questionnaire? Is it right or wrong to force students in a university program to participate in a professor's research project? Is it right or wrong for a member of a research team to reveal the partial results of a study without the consent of the other members? For now, consider the following:

- A participant in a research project on attitudes is asked to be part of a half-hour group discussion on immigration. During the discussion, all of the other participants state their strong opposition to immigration and make racist

continued

remarks about various ethnic groups. At the end of the discussion, each is asked to complete a questionnaire on their attitudes toward the ethnic groups mentioned in the discussion. When the participant hands in the questionnaire, the researcher points out that the others in the group were actors. They had been told to state they were opposed to immigration and to make racist remarks about different ethnic groups. Are there ethical issues with this study? What should the researcher do or not do with the participant before, during, and after the group discussion? What else should the researcher do or not do?

- A researcher is carrying out a study of youth gangs. Part of the study involves the researcher spending time with the gangs, and the researcher becomes aware of some illegal activities. The police find out about the research and request the researcher to provide them with the names of the gang members. What should the researcher do or not do?
- Researchers carry out a study on the sexual behaviour of college students. In their introduction to their questionnaire they clearly state that the respondent's answers will be kept confidential. They do not ask for a name or any other information that they believe could possibly identify the student. However, in compiling the information from the questionnaires, they realize that because of a question related to age, they are able to identify some respondents. What should the researchers do or not do?
- A researcher wants to study the behaviour of children when they participate in certain arts and crafts activities. A friend who owns a summer camp agrees to allow the researcher to carry out the study at the camp. After preparing for the study, the researcher realizes that the parents have not been asked to give their consent, but the friend says it is too much trouble to ask the parents. It will take too much time, and the arts and crafts activities must be completed before the closure of the summer camp. The owner insists that the researcher simply carry out the study. What should the researcher do or not do?

Clearly, ethical concerns are primordial throughout the research process. Indeed, it is for this reason that we include a section on ethical considerations in each subsequent chapter on major research methods. Ethics should be taken into account from the very beginning of the research process and be part of your research design. In other words, before doing any other preparation, consider the possible ethical issues and how they will be handled. A suggestion for recognizing possible issues is to put yourself in the place of the participants in your study.

At times, no set rule exists to determine whether a situation calls for ethical considerations. A helpful source can be the ethical guidelines of a professional association, such as those listed in the Weblinks section at the end of Chapter 1, and the site indicated in the Weblinks section of this chapter. The various social science disciplines share ethical issues that are common to all of them, but each discipline may also encounter ethical issues unique to it. See the information on the home page of the interested professional association for documentation on their code of ethics.

Problems with Human Data

People can be troublesome to researchers for a variety of other reasons: they may be unwilling to be interviewed or to allow others to observe their activities; only a minority of people will return mail questionnaires; people in power—and deviants—tend to be secretive about their actions and resist studies of their lives; some people are inarticulate and unable to express their feelings and perceptions clearly; and historians often find it difficult to examine the lives of the humble majority who do not leave written documents and monuments behind as evidence of their actions. Social researchers, then, have to be extremely aware of the many ways human beings can hide and be hidden, deceive, and limit access to their lives and thoughts.

The Social Context and the Personal Equation

Another set of constraints or pressures arises from the social and personal circumstances surrounding research. Social research looks at quickly changing and controversial parts of reality: society, human relations, and human psychological characteristics. Not long ago spousal abuse was not a prominent topic for social research. In the 1970s Canadian social scientists debated and did research on the U.S. domination of the Canadian economy; in the 21st century many of these same social scientists are now doing research on the impact on Canada of the "global economy." Shifts like these arise from changing social conditions, which contribute to altering definitions of what are important issues, ideas, and phenomena in society. These shifts, in turn, encourage researchers to direct their attention to new areas and to lessen their interest in others.

In addition, social research can use a diverse range of designs and methods: laboratory experiments, surveys, fieldwork, analysis of documents, statistical analysis, and so on. There are many different *styles* of social research, ranging from the scientific style of experimentation and statistical analysis to the humanistic style of oral history and of many field studies. Each researcher develops an interest in specific issues and a taste for a certain style of research, because each of us brings our own concerns, outlook, and skills to research. Some may enjoy working with historical documents or personal letters and trying to recreate the lives and times of individuals and groups in a humanistic style. Others will enjoy the challenge of designing experiments or developing statistical interpretations of economic and demographic data.

As you learn the different approaches to research, you too will develop a leaning toward particular approaches, and you will become better at using these approaches than others in which you are less interested. This is not a problem as long as you are aware of the limitations of *all* research methods and realize that your way is not the only way of doing research. Each design and procedure has advantages and limitations; often the strengths of one method compensate for the weaknesses of others. The different research methods are each equally valuable and often can be used in a complementary way. Combining different methods in the same research design is often essential, as is remaining open-minded about all of the available methods for obtaining empirical evidence.

What You Have Learned

- Research may begin with questions or topics arising from personal issues or social issues or from the puzzles and questions posed by previous research.

- The initial issue or question needs to be developed and focused by relating it to what is already known and thought in a broader area of social science.
- All research follows basic guidelines requiring objectivity, empirical verification, and openness to inspection and analysis by others.
- These guidelines rest on certain assumptions that emphasize the orderliness of reality and the need for logical thinking.
- Much social science research is developed through testing hypotheses, which extend theories by focusing on a small number of variables that are assumed to be causally connected.
- Variables are defined in terms of the evidence required to show how they change—an approach called operationalization.
- Some social scientists deemphasize hypothesis testing and approach social research in a humanistic manner, stressing description over explanation.
- Research involves several steps: defining the topic appropriately; developing a research design and following it through; analyzing the data; and communicating the results.
- Research is affected by nonscientific factors, such as a scarcity of resources, ethical considerations, the social context, and the personal character of the researchers.

Focus Questions

1. Why might a researcher become interested in a specific research topic? Give several possible reasons.
2. What is scientific skepticism?
3. What are the basic assumptions of scientific inquiry?
4. What is explanatory research and when is it used?
5. What are the differences between the scientific and the humanistic approaches to social research?
6. What are variables? What kinds of variables are there?
7. What is the relationship between theory and hypothesis?
8. What problems may occur at different stages in the research process?
9. What factors hinder social research or make it difficult?
10. What are some of the ethical issues that deserve attention in research? When should researchers focus on the ethical issues in the research process?

Review Exercises

1. Do a subject or keyword search for a research-based article in a database on a topic in which you have a particular interest. Use a database to which your library subscribes or InfoTrac, for which a free limited subscription accompanies this textbook. Then answer the following questions.

    a. What is the issue or research question in the study discussed in the article?

    b. What is the source of the information in the article?

    c. Is a hypothesis being investigated or tested? If there is a hypothesis, what is the causal idea behind it? If there is no hypothesis, is there any causal idea? What are the variables in the hypothesis? Identify the dependent and the independent variables. How are these variables measured?

2. Discuss the various questions and issues raised on ethics in Box 2.4. Review and discuss the code of ethics of one of the professional associations listed in the Weblinks section of Chapter 1. Are some ethical issues unique to members of that profession?

Weblinks

The Research Process
http://www.ryerson.ca/%7Emjoppe/rp.htm

This website was designed by Professor Marion Joppe of Ryerson University to familiarize hospitality and tourism managers with the research process. It therefore briefly covers basic qualitative and quantitative approaches in the hospitality and tourism industries, and provides further explanations of research concepts.

The Web Center for Social Research Methods
http://www.socialresearchmethods.net

If you want a more advanced overview of issues examined in this chapter, visit this applied social research website created by Professor William M. K. Trochim of Cornell University. It covers an extensive array of topics. While it is intended mainly for upper undergraduate and graduate students, it could be very helpful.

The Research Room
http://www.uh.edu/%7Esrama/index.htm

This site contains an overview of the qualitative and quantitative research process. It was created by three professors at the University of Houston and the material can be used to supplement information in this and other chapters.

Qualitative and Quantitative Research (Guides)
http://writing.colostate.edu/collections/collection.cfm?id=24

This site contains guides to various research methods and related issues. The guides were prepared by graduate students at Colorado State University.

Methods for Social Researchers in Developing Countries (Book)
http://srmdc.net/index.htm

This site contains material from the book by the same title published by the Ahfad University for Women in the Sudan. It was specifically created for researchers in developing countries, but is also helpful for others.

Ethics on the World Wide Web
http://www.ethicsweb.ca

This site is a collection of mainly Canadian ethics-related websites. Of particular interest are those listed under "Applied Ethics Resources," which includes links to sites on research ethics and professional ethics. For more on the guidelines of scholarly associations see the sites of those listed in the Weblinks section of Chapter 1.

Chapter 7:
Social Inequality

Social Stratification: Canadian and Global Perspectives

In this chapter, you will learn that

- Income is unequally distributed in Canada and government plays a small, but important, role in redistributing money to children and families who are poor.

- Income inequality in Canada is lower than in the United States but consistent with most other postindustrial societies.

- As societies develop, inequality at first increases. Then, after passing the early stage of industrialization, inequality in society declines. In the postindustrial stage of development, inequality begins to increase again in some countries.

- Most theories of social inequality focus on its economic roots.

- Prestige and power are important non-economic sources of inequality.

- Although some sociologists used to think that talent and hard work alone determine a person's position in the socioeconomic hierarchy, it is now clear that being a member of certain groups limits opportunities for success. In this sense, social structure shapes the distribution of inequality.

PATTERNS OF SOCIAL INEQUALITY

Shipwrecks and Inequality

Writers and filmmakers sometimes tell stories about shipwrecks and their survivors to make a point about social inequality. They use the shipwreck as literary device. It allows them to sweep away all traces of privilege and social convention. What remains are human beings stripped to their essentials, guinea pigs in an imaginary laboratory for the study of wealth and poverty, power and powerlessness, esteem and disrespect.

Daniel Defoe's *Robinson Crusoe,* first published in 1719, is a classic novel in this tradition. Defoe writes of an Englishman marooned on a deserted island. The man's strong will, hard work, and inventiveness turn the island into a thriving colony. Defoe was one of the first writers to portray the work ethic of capitalism favourably. He believed that people get rich if they possess the virtues of good businesspeople—and stay poor if they don't.

The 1974 Italian movie *Swept Away* tells almost exactly the opposite story. In the movie a beautiful woman, one of the idle rich, cruises in the Mediterranean. She treats the hard-working deckhands in a condescending and abrupt way. The deckhands do their jobs but seethe with resentment. Then comes a storm. The beautiful woman and one handsome deckhand are swept onto a deserted island. The deckhand asserts his masculine prowess on an initially unwilling and reluctant woman. The two survivors soon have passionate sex and fall in love.

All is well until their rescue. On returning to the mainland, the woman resumes her haughty ways. She turns her back on the deckhand; he becomes a common labourer again. Thus, the movie sends the audience four harsh messages, each contrasting with themes in Defoe's *Robinson Crusoe.* First, you do not have to work hard to be rich, because you can inherit wealth. Second, hard work does not always make you rich. Third, something about the structure of society causes inequality, for it is only on the deserted island, without society as we know it, that class inequality disappears. *Swept Away* also focuses attention on unequal power between the sexes. The two survivors are not equals; male privilege exerts itself in a context in which class differences have been obliterated. Here, then, is a fourth harsh message. Inequality has many interrelated dimensions, including class, sex, and race, and different contexts highlight different conditions of power and exploitation.

And then there is *Titanic,* a characteristically American take on the shipwreck-and-inequality theme. At one level, the movie shows that class differences are important. For example, in first class, living conditions are luxurious, while in third class, they are cramped. Indeed, on the *Titanic,* class divisions spell the difference between life and death. After the *Titanic* strikes an iceberg off the coast of Newfoundland, the ship's crew prevents second- and third-class passengers from entering the few available lifeboats. Priority goes to first-class passengers.

As the tragedy of the *Titanic* unfolds, however, a different theme emerges. Under some circumstances, we learn, class differences can be erased. In the movie, the sinking of the *Titanic* is the backdrop to a fictional love story about a wealthy young woman in first class and a working-class youth from the decks below. The sinking of the *Titanic* and the collapse of its elaborate class structure give the young lovers an opportunity to cross class divisions and profess devotion to each other. At another level, then, *Titanic* is an optimistic tale that holds out hope for a society in which class differences no longer matter, a society much like that of the "American Dream."

Robinson Crusoe, Swept Away, and *Titanic* raise many of the issues we address in this chapter. What are the sources of social inequality? Do determination, industry, and ingenuity shape the distribution of advantages and disadvantages in society, as the tale of *Robinson Crusoe* portrays? Or is *Swept Away* more accurate? Do certain patterns of social relations underlie and shape that distribution? Is *Titanic*'s first message of social class differences still valid? Does social inequality still have big consequences for the way we live? What about *Titanic*'s second message? Can people overcome or reduce inequality in society? If so, how?

To answer these questions, we first sketch the pattern of social inequality in Canada and around the world. We pay special attention to change over time. We then critically review the major theories of social inequality. We assess explanations for differences in inequality in the light of logic and evidence. Periodically, we take a step back and identify issues needing resolution before we can achieve a fuller understanding of social inequality, one of the fundamentally important aspects of social life.

Economic Inequality in Canada

The musical *Cabaret,* set in the 1930s, contains a song based on the saying "Money makes the world go round." In the 1980s, Madonna repeated the theme in her hit song, "Material Girl": "They can beg and they can plead/But they can't see the light (that's right)/'Cause the boy with the cold hard cash/Is always Mister Right" (Brown and Rans, 1984).

TECHNOLOGY
BYTES

The idea that money is power is a perennial theme. Decade by decade, the saying "Everything has its price" becomes more and more accurate. Thus, the selling of blood, sperm, and ova is common in many countries. An international trade in the body parts of the living, and the dead, flourishes. These body parts are often used for education and research purposes. More controversial is the practice of purchasing human organs, in particular kidneys, for transplantation. In the typical supply and demand equation of modern commerce, as demand for available organs escalates, the supply of body parts expands. The global organ shortage "has encouraged the sale of organs, nowhere more conspicuously than in India. It has also stimulated the use of organs from executed prisoners, nowhere more systematically than in China. Thus, residents of Gulf States and other Asian countries frequently travel to India to obtain a kidney" (Rothman et al., 1997).

People selling body parts are almost invariably poor. People buying body parts are invariably rich. Though not a common practice, an increasing number of wealthy people travel to foreign countries with their own surgeons in tow in an attempt to prolong life through the purchase and use of body parts.

In North America, and especially in the United States, poor people are more likely than rich people are to suffer illnesses that could be alleviated by organ transplantation. However, they are less likely to be offered transplant opportunities (Wallich and Mukerjee, 1996). Especially in the United States, this is largely the result of the poor not having adequate private health insurance to cover transplantation expenses. However, it is also the case that the poor are more likely to be organ donors, even in Canada, because "the typical donor is still young and a victim of accidental or deliberate violence—which tends to strike the disadvantaged in disproportionate numbers" (Wallich and Mukerjee, 1996).

After weighing evidence and argument, an international report on organ trafficking "found no unarguable ethical principle that would justify a ban on the sale of organs" (Rothman et al., 1997). In particular, it notes that "a prohibition on sale might well cost would-be recipients their lives and infringe in important ways on the autonomy of would-be sellers" (Rothman et al., 1997). This latter point is particularly germane because it touches on a key debate about social inequality. From what perspective or standpoint can we make judgments about inequality and human misery? Who should make the choice between grinding poverty on the one hand and the sale of a kidney on the other? An easy response is to claim this is a false dichotomy. No one should have to make such a choice! Too easy. Such a response ignores all of human history, in which social inequality, the context of such a horrible choice, has existed always and every-where.

Materialism, the attempt to satisfy needs by buying products or experiences, is a defining characteristic of modern society. Never have so many people, at least in the Western industrial world, been able to share so widely in material comforts (such as central heating, ample food, appropriate clothing, and so forth). Economic prosperity has made Canada one of the best countries in the world in which to live.

The growth of prosperity in the post–World War II Canadian economy is easy to illustrate. Figure 8.1 shows the growth in the average earnings of Canadian households.

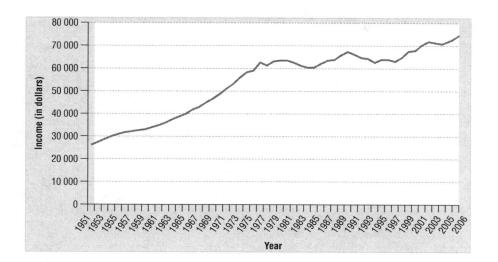

FIGURE 8.1

Average Income of Canadian Families, 1951 to 2006 (in 2003 dollars)

Source: Adapted from various documents from Statistics Canada and from the Canadian Council on Social Development.

In 2006, Canadian families earned an average income of more than $74 800. In the early 1950s, Canadian families earned less than $30 000 a year on average. Some of this increase may seem misleading since a soft drink that once cost a dime now costs a dollar. But the incomes in the graph are corrected for such inflation and still reveal a substantial increase.

The purchasing power of families rose because economic productivity was enhanced by improvements in workers' skills and by advances in the technologies used for production. Increases in family income, after adjusting for inflation, were most rapid from the end of World War II until the economic downturn that began around 1973.

Notice also from Figure 8.1 that the average earnings of Canadian families have increased at a slower rate recently. That is, the slope of the income line was flatter in the 1980s and 1990s than it was earlier. Recall, too, that the number of earners in a family increased over this recent interval as more women entered the paid labour force. Even so, the purchasing power of family earnings did not grow much. This difference has led to several recent public debates. Notably, the widespread demand for reduced taxes is, in part, a reaction to this relatively flat earnings trajectory. Despite working harder and longer, families' incomes have not grown proportionately. Coupled with this is the common awareness that the days of the single-breadwinner family of the 1950s and 1960s are past. Most families now have at least two earners, but the prospect of buying a house, and owning more of it than the bank does, is still a struggle.

Figure 8.1 simplifies reality because it is based on averages. Economic prosperity and the benefits of materialism are not equally shared. In your own experience you will have witnessed inequality when passing through skid row or the inner-city areas of many of our biggest communities. You may have seen the lineups for food banks or the poverty of some rural farmers. Here is a language and lifestyle of used clothes, of baloney and Spam, of fleas and roaches, of despair and depression. There is also a language of booze, illicit sex, welfare cheats, laziness, and cunning deceit. We will return to these contrasting descriptions later.

At the other end of the money spectrum is the luxury of our richest neighbourhoods, places you may have lived in or visited. This is the world of multimillion-dollar homes with indoor swimming pools and outdoor tennis courts, multi-car garages, and in-house security systems to deter those who might steal a piece of art. Here is a language and lifestyle of Gucci and Hugo Boss, of caviar and roast duckling, of coddled poodles and parakeets, of ambition and success. Here, too, is a different language, one of idle richness, of misbegotten inheritance, of greedy property owners, and of fraud and cunning deceit. This, too, is a contrast to which we will return (see Figure 8.2 on page 216).

The vast majority of us live between these two extremes. Many of us may have tasted both caviar and baloney, petted poodles and scratched fleas, but relatively few Canadians have

FIGURE 8.2

It's a Long Way to the Top:
Canadian Income Inequality,
2004

Note: Drawn to scale.

Source: Data from Brian Murphy, Paul
Roberts, and Michael Wolfson, 2007,
*A Profile of High-Income Canadians,
1982–2004,* Statistics Canada.
Retrieved May 1, 2008 (http://www.
statcan.ca/english/research/75F0002
MIE/75F0002MIE2007006.pdf).

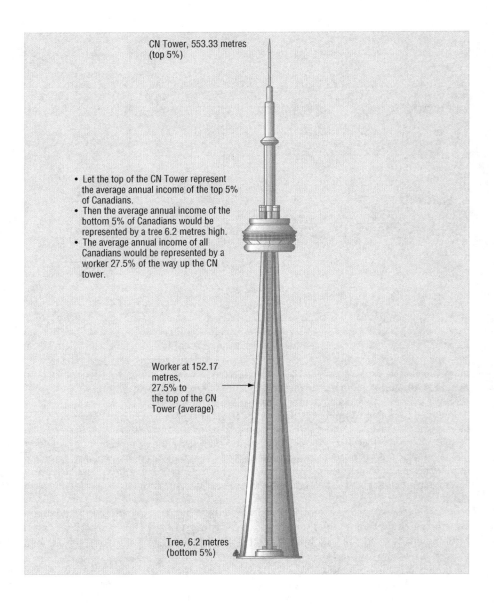

CN Tower, 553.33 metres
(top 5%)

- Let the top of the CN Tower represent the average annual income of the top 5% of Canadians.
- Then the average annual income of the bottom 5% of Canadians would be represented by a tree 6.2 metres high.
- The average annual income of all Canadians would be represented by a worker 27.5% of the way up the CN tower.

Worker at 152.17 metres, 27.5% to the top of the CN Tower (average)

Tree, 6.2 metres (bottom 5%)

continuing experience with either abject poverty or substantial wealth. How do we measure inequality that falls between these two extremes? Not all families earn $74 800 per year, even though that is close to the average. How do we understand fluctuations or variations around this average, and, most important, how they have changed? Is economic inequality growing or shrinking?

Social scientists have come up with a simple yet powerful way to display patterns of inequality. Here is the method, by way of analogy. Step one: Among your classmates, think of how much money each person might have earned in the past three months. A few people with full-time, well-paying, steady jobs may have earned more than $5000. Put those people at the front of a line, the highest earner first. Others will have struggled to find consistent work or may have opted not to work. Put them at the back of the line, with the lowest earner at the very end of the line.

Now, step two: Add up how much everyone in the line has earned. Imagine you have 100 students in your lineup and in sum they earned $300 000.

The Thomsons, Canada's wealthiest family, ranked 10th on the *Forbes Magazine* list of the world's richest people in 2007. Their assets totalled $25.35 billion. Sir Kenneth Thomson, who died in June 2006, handed over the reins of the Thomson electronic media, publishing, and information services empire to his son, David. The Thomsons are an example of success through both hard work and family connections.

Step three: Divide the line into five equal groups, with 20 percent of your classmates in each group—technically, these groups are known as quintiles.

Step four: Add up how much the members of each of the five groups or quintiles earned. The group at the head of the line will have earned the most given how we constructed the line. Imagine that together the members of this group earned $120 000. The group at the back of the line will have earned the least. Imagine that they collectively earned $12 000. Final step: Calculate the percentage of money each group earned. The top quintile has 40 percent of the earnings ($120 000/$300 000 × 100), while the bottom quintile has only 4 percent. The remainder (56 percent) is shared by the other three quintiles.

The most unequal distribution would be if the top quintile held 100 percent of the money. The opposite, an equal distribution, would result if each quintile held 20 percent of the money. This concept of the share of income held by each quintile is frequently used to investigate income inequality in Canada and elsewhere. It is an easy idea to visualize, and by looking at how the share of income changes over time, it allows researchers to determine whether inequality is growing or shrinking.

Figure 8.3 on page 218 shows that for 2005, the most recent year for which data are available, the lowest quintile of income earners received 6.1 percent of market income (that is, income before taxes and government transfers), while the top quintile received 42.5 percent. Almost half of all income was held by 20 percent of individuals and families.

This level of inequality can be put into perspective in two ways. First, how does income inequality in Canada compare with income inequality in other countries? Among rich countries, income inequality is lowest in Sweden and highest in the United States. Canada stands between these two extremes.

We can also ask how income inequality has changed within Canada over time. Figure 8.3 shows that the distribution has changed little between 1951 and 2005. In 2005 the bottom quintile received 6.1 percent of total income (before income tax), while in 1951 the figure was exactly the same. At the top end, the richest quintile increased its share of total income slightly, from 41.1 percent to 42.5 percent. In the past few decades, income inequality has widened in most rich countries, but not by much in Canada (Förster and Pellizzari, 2000).

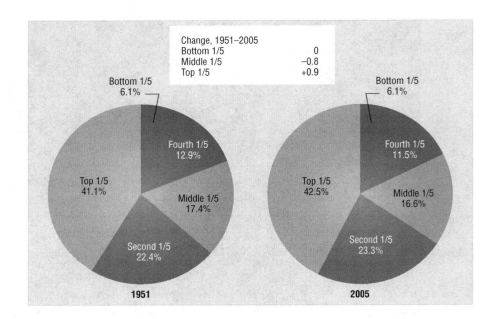

The incomes reported above and in Figure 8.3 are incomes Canadians receive before paying taxes. Given frequent reference to Canada as a "welfare state," you might imagine that after-tax income is distributed differently. The concept of a welfare state implies the image of Robin Hood, taking from the rich and giving to the poor. To what degree does the Canadian state act like Robin Hood?

As Table 8.1 illustrates, in 2005 the government redirected some income from the top quintile to the other quintiles. Compared with their pre-tax share of total income, the richest quintile of earners saw their income share decline by 2.9 percent. The after-tax income of all other quintiles rose modestly. Furthermore, since 1988 the redistributive effort of governments declined in Canada. Between 1988 and 2005, the share of after-tax income fell by 0.8 percent for the lowest quintile and rose by 2.8 percent for the richest quintile.

Explanations of Income Inequality

Why do some people fall into the highest quintile and others into the lowest quintile? What explains the distribution of income? The job a person holds plays a large role. Bank presidents are paid more than branch managers, who in turn make more than bank tellers do. Other jobs not only pay less well but also involve restricted hours of work or periods of unemployment. Thus, much about income inequality traces back to what kinds of work a person is able to obtain (see Table 8.2).

Some individuals earn unusually high salaries (and become famous) because they have natural talents at activities that are widely admired, in part because the activities are fulfilling recreations that many have attempted themselves. Jarome Iginla (hockey), Victoria Bertram

Quintile	Total Pre-tax Income Share	Total After-Tax Income Share	Gain/Loss
Lowest quintile	6.1	7.0	+0.9
Second quintile	11.5	12.6	+1.1
Third quintile	16.6	17.4	+0.8
Fourth quintile	23.3	23.4	+0.1
Highest quintile	42.5	39.6	−2.9

Occupation	Median Annual Income
Judges, lawyers and Quebec notaries	99 305
Specialist managers	80 027
Professional occupations in health	77 515
Professional occupations in natural and applied sciences	65 601
Mechanics	45 942
Construction trades	35 639
Clerical occupations	35 028
Secretaries	32 505
Labourers in processing, manufacturing, and utilities	31 538
Retail salespersons and sales clerks	27 225
Child care and home support workers	21 980
Cashiers	17 758
Occupations in food and beverage service	16 654

TABLE 8.2

Median Annual Income, Full-Time Workers, Selected Occupations, Canada, 2005

Sources: Statistics Canada, 2008, "Median Earnings and Employment for Full-Year, Full-Time Earners, All Occupations, Both Sexes, for Canada, Provinces and Territories—20% Sample Data." Retrieved May 1, 2008 (http://www12.statcan.ca/english/census06/data/highlights/earnings/Table801.cfm?Lang=E&T=801&GH=4&SC=1&SO=99&O=A); Statistics Canada, 2008, "Earnings and Incomes of Canadian over the Past Quarter Century, 2006 Census." Retrieved May 1, 2008 (http://www12.statcan.ca/english/census06/analysis/income/pdf/97-563-XIE2006001.pdf).

(ballet), Ben Heppner (opera), Lorie Kane (golf), Shania Twain (popular music), and Mike Weir (golf) are Canadians whose success on the world stage has provided them with substantial earnings. Although sheer talent or genetic gifts surely play a part, close examination of lives blessed by extraordinary success often reveals unusual determination and hard work.

Although talent and effort matter, rewards follow only when these are refined into particular skills. But who gets to develop which skills depends on access to learning environments. Many skills are relative: People can only develop to the level of those to whom they are exposed. Tennis is a good example: Full development of skills requires exposure to stiff competition. Many skills require recognition and encouragement for development.

The ability to lend guidance or assistance is often scarce and unequally accessible. Most people begin the journey toward adult employment within a family circle and are certain to be exposed to whatever is prevalent there. The more fortunate acquire a vocabulary and outlooks consistent with highly rewarded employment, while the less fortunate must unlearn and relearn if they are to catch up. It is somewhat easier to understand and learn what our parents know and somewhat harder to learn about things they did not experience. Thus, when individuals begin to participate in formal education, what they encounter varies in compatibility with earlier experience, mostly gained with family members.

Success at formal schooling is the key to acquiring economically valued skills. Since the Industrial Revolution, an ever-growing proportion of jobs have required formal schooling in ever-greater amounts. For the vast majority of income earners, it is their ability to communicate persuasively, think critically, reason logically, and work creatively that affects the occupations they hold and the incomes they receive. Natural talent and effort are important ingredients in this process, to be sure, but education matters a lot.

The importance of education as a determinant of occupation and income continues to increase (Baer, 1999). As the Canadian occupational structure moves further away from its traditional resource-based foundation to a more mature knowledge-driven economy, the importance of education will continue to grow.

Although educational opportunities have expanded enormously, in nearly all developed economies, including Canada, the chances of advancing in educational systems has consistently remained higher for people born into families that are relatively more educated (Breen and Goldthorpe, 1997). Individuals must supply talent and effort to accumulate **human capital** (useful knowledge and skills) but rates of success also depend on the human capital their families accumulated in previous generations.

Human capital is the sum of useful skills and knowledge that an individual possesses.

Human Capital Theory

Human capital theory stresses the increasing centrality of education as a factor affecting economic success. If physical capital is understood as investment in industrial plants and equipment, human capital is investment in education and training. In a manner analogous to the way productivity increases by upgrading manufacturing plants and introducing new technology, productivity gains can also result from investment in the skills and abilities of people. Knowledge-intensive jobs (that is, jobs requiring advanced skills) are increasingly numerous in Canada. Better-educated workers are more skilled and productive in these jobs because they have made investments in acquiring the research skills and knowledge base essential to the new economy (Betcherman and Lowe, 1997).

Much evidence supports a human capital interpretation of the link between schooling and incomes (Baer, 1999). However, this is not a complete explanation for why people earn what they earn. In Chapter 2 (How Sociologists Do Research), we discussed the work of Kay and Hagan (1998). We saw that in the legal profession almost everyone makes the same human capital investment. Everyone acquires a law degree, yet economic rewards vary even for people with the same experience and type of legal practice.

Part of the reason that people with the same amount of human capital may receive different economic rewards is that they possess different amounts of social capital. **Social capital** refers to people's networks or connections. Individuals are more likely to succeed if they have strong bonds of trust, cooperation, mutual respect, and obligation with well-positioned individuals or families. Knowing the right people, and having strong links to them, helps in attaining opportunities (Coleman, 1988).

A related version of this argument is captured in the notion of **cultural capital** as proposed by the French sociologist Pierre Bourdieu (Bourdieu and Passeron, 1990). Bourdieu focuses on taste and aesthetics—*savoir-faire*. Cultural capital emphasizes a set of social skills people have, their ability to impress others, to use language and images effectively, and to influence and persuade people. Although the notion of social capital stresses your networks and connections with others, the idea of cultural capital emphasizes your impression-management skills, your ability to influence others. In different ways, both concepts emphasize being part of the right "social club."

What both concepts also have in common is the idea that families higher in the social hierarchy enjoy more capital of all types. Connections and culture help you find a good job. Hiring new recruits, then, depends on the talent, effort, and skills that people bring to the interview, but it also depends on the connections and culture that people have. Indeed, culture and connections often influence who gets an interview.

In summary, natural talent and effort are important, and are especially significant in becoming a paid performer who excels at activities that many try (e.g., hockey player or popular singer). For most Canadians, level of education (or developed skill) is a critical factor in finding continuous, well-paying employment. In addition, social or cultural capital is consequential for many in finding economic success. Explaining an individual's position in the income hierarchy depends on several factors, but the four themes or perspectives outlined in Figure 8.4 are crucial.

Income versus Wealth

How long would it take you to spend a million dollars? If you spent $1000 a day, it would take you nearly three years. How long would it take you to spend a *billion* dollars? If you spent $2500 a day, you couldn't spend the entire sum in a lifetime—at that rate of spending, a billion dollars would last for more than 1000 years. (This scenario assumes you do not invest the money; if you invested it sensibly, you could not exhaust a billion dollars by spending $10 000 a day.) Thus, a billion dollars is an almost unimaginably large sum of

---

Social capital refers to the networks or connections that individuals possess.

Cultural capital is the stock of learning and skills that increases the chance of securing a superior job.

FIGURE 8.4

Explanations for Income Inequality

Natural talent ⟶ Rewards

Natural talent + Effort ⟶ Rewards

Natural talent + Effort + Skill-rich environments + Developed skills ⟶ Rewards

Natural talent + Effort + Skill-rich environments + Developed skills + Social and cultural capital ⟶ Rewards

money. Yet between 2004 and 2007, the estimated fortune of Canada's richest person, David Thomson, increased 17 percent, from $21.67 billion to $25.35 billion. In contrast, the annual income of a full-time worker earning the Ontario minimum wage in 2005 was $15 596. Just the *increase* in Thomson's wealth between 2004 and 2007 was equal to the total annual income of 196 717 minimum-wage earners! We list the 10 richest Canadians in Table 8.3.

What are the sources of the fortunes listed in Table 8.3? For some names on the list (Thomson, Irving, Weston), inheritance is a critical factor. These are family dynasties—families that John Porter (1965) and Wallace Clement (1975) called members of the "Canadian corporate elite" back in the 1960s and '70s. Other people on the top-10 list had merely well-to-do or solid middle-class parents. None rose from rags to riches. On the whole, Table 8.3 suggests a mix of family fortune, business acumen, and opportunism as key determinants of wealth.

Only a very few families acquire the great wealth of major business enterprises. But most families own assets and these add up to greater or lesser family wealth. For most adults, assets include a car (minus the car loan) and some appliances, furniture, and savings (minus the credit card balance). Somewhat wealthier families also have equity in a house (the market value minus the mortgage). More fortunate families are able to accumulate other assets, such as stocks and bonds, retirement savings, and vacation homes. Figure 8.5 on page 222 shows the distribution of wealth among Canadian families in 1984, 1999, and 2005. The families are divided into quintiles. Notice that the bottom 40 percent of families own almost no assets. In fact, the bottom 20 percent owe more than they own. Notice also that the assets owned by the bottom 40 percent of families shrank in the 21 years covered by the graph. The assets owned by the top 60 percent of families grew, and by far the biggest increase in wealth was experienced by the top quintile; its median net worth grew by almost two-thirds between 1984 and 2005.

Wealth inequality is thus increasing rapidly in Canada—but not as much as in the United States, where 62 percent of the increase in national wealth in the 1990s went to the richest 1 percent of Americans and fully 99 percent of the increase went to the richest 20 percent. The United States surpasses all other highly industrialized countries in wealth inequality. Between 50 percent and 80 percent of the net worth of American families derives from transfers and bequests, usually from parents (Hacker, 1997; Keister, 2000; Keister and Moller, 2000; Levy, 1998; Spilerman, 2000; Wolff, 1996).

Individual or Family	Estimated Wealth	Assets and Notes
Thomson family	$25.35 billion	Information distribution; Thomson-Reuters, Woodbridge Co. Ltd.
Ted Rogers	$7.6 billion	Communications; entertainment; Rogers Communications Inc.
Galen Weston	$7.27 billion	Food; groceries; retail; real estate; Holt Renfrew; George Weston Ltd.; Loblaw Cos. Ltd.; President's Choice; Zehrs; Connors Seafood
Paul Desmarais, Sr.	$5.64 billion	Financial services; media; broadcasting; oil; Power Corp. of Canada
Irving family	$5.3 billion	Oil; forestry products; building supply stores; media; frozen foods; transportation; Irving Oil; JD Irving Ltd
James Pattison	$4.52 billion	Auto sales; food; media; forest products; export services; financial services; Jim Pattison Group
Jeff Skoll	$4.48 billion	Internet; film production; eBay
Michael Lazaridis	$4.36 billion	Communications; Research in Motion
James Balsillie	$4.09 billion	Communications; Research in Motion
Bernard Sherman	$3.61 billion	Pharmaceuticals; Apotex Group

TABLE 8.3

Ten Wealthiest Canadians, 2007

Source: Reprinted with permission from *Canadian Business,* 2007 (http://www.canadianbusiness.com/after_hours/article.jsp?content=20071131_198701_198701).

NEL

FIGURE 8.5

Median Net Worth of
Canadian Families, 1984,
1999, and 2005

Note: To make the three surveys
comparable, the following items are
not included: employer-sponsored
pension plans, contents of the home,
collectibles and valuables, annuities,
and registered retirement income
funds. If it were possible to include
these items, wealth inequalities
would be greater than shown. Net
worth for the lowest quintile in
1984 was 0. Calculating the
percentage decline for this quintile
would require dividing by zero,
which of course is not possible.
Accordingly, for the lowest quintile,
we show the decline in net worth in
dollars rather than as a percentage.

Source: René Morisette and Xuelin
Zhang, 2006, "Revisiting Wealth
Inequality," *Pespectives* (Statistics
Canada). Retrieved May 1, 2008
(http://www.statcan.ca/english/free
pub/75-001-XIE/11206/art-1.pdf).

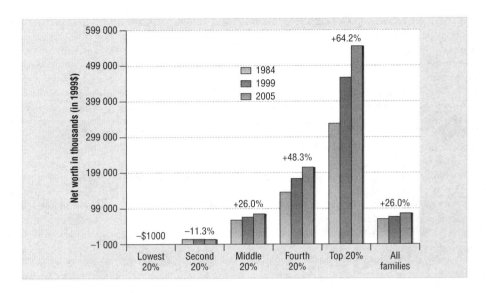

Note that only a modest correlation exists between income and wealth. Some wealthy people have low annual incomes and some people with high annual incomes have little accumulated wealth. As such, annual income may not be the best measure of a person's well-being. Policies that seek to redistribute income from the wealthy to the poor, such as income-tax laws, may not get at the root of economic inequality because income redistribution has little effect on the distribution of wealth (Conley, 1999; Oliver and Shapiro, 1995).

Income and Poverty

At the other extreme of the income distribution are the homeless. In recent decades the number of people with "no fixed address" has increased considerably. We do not know how many Canadians are homeless. Yet in cities across the country, people sleep under bridges, in back alleys, behind dumpsters, and in thickets in public parks. They do so night after night, month after month.

Homelessness is one manifestation of poverty. Exactly how many Canadians are poor is a matter of intense debate. Poverty lacks an agreed definition. A first disagreement occurs around whether poverty should be defined in absolute or relative terms. An absolute definition of poverty focuses on bare essentials, suggesting that poor families have resources inadequate to acquire the basic necessities of life (e.g., food, shelter, clothing). Agreement on "bare essentials" depends on values and judgments (Sarlo, 2001). What is essential varies from time to time, place to place, and group to group. Many of our ancestors lived without indoor plumbing, and some Canadians still do, but most people would define indoor plumbing as essential. A family could survive on a steady diet of cod and potatoes, but most would define such a family as poor.

What constitutes bare essentials depends on social context. Again, most Canadians would agree that the poverty experienced in Angola or Haiti or Ethiopia is not what should be used to define poverty in Canada. That is because most people think of poverty in relation to the social and economic context in which people live. Central heating is a necessity in Canada's cold climate but not in Ethiopia or Haiti.

A relative poverty line also has drawbacks. Two questions are central: Relative to what? How relative? Whether poverty ought to be defined narrowly, in terms of economic measures (e.g., income), or more broadly, with respect to community standards (e.g., safety of working conditions, environmental quality, housing stock), illustrates this second area of disagreement. Most definitions tend to be narrow, focusing primarily on income. But even if a relative poverty line is defined narrowly, how relative ought it to be? one-third of average income? one-half? some other fraction?

Yet another disagreement plagues any definition. Should poverty be defined on the basis of income or on the basis of consumption? Since "bare essentials" is a core idea in any definition of poverty, it makes good sense to ask about, and measure, poverty as the cost of purchasing bare essentials. Deprivation occurs when a family cannot acquire the essentials, not necessarily when income is too low. Income and consumption are correlated, of course, but people with high net wealth can live off their savings even with low income.

In one sense, the definition of poverty means little to a homeless man sleeping on top of a hot air vent. The immediate experience of poverty by families in remote coastal communities, by single parents in the urban core, and by farmers on the Prairies is unaffected by whether poverty is defined absolutely or relatively, narrowly or broadly, by income or by consumption. However, the definition of poverty is consequential for these people, because social policies are enacted, or not enacted, based on levels and trends in poverty. Definitions matter.

Social policy has a profound impact on the distribution of opportunities and rewards in Canada. Politics can reshape the distribution of income and the system of inequality by changing the laws governing people's right to own property. Witness First Nations land claims. Politicians can also alter patterns of inequality by entitling people to various welfare benefits and by redistributing income through tax policies. When politicians de-emphasize poverty, legislative efforts to maintain or expand welfare benefits and redistribute income are less likely. A definition of poverty showing fewer poor Canadians implies little need for government action. Conversely, for politicians and political parties supporting the poor, a definition of poverty showing a growing proportion of poor people is beneficial to their cause.

In addition to poverty definitions having political consequences, they are important research tools for the sociologist. A democratic society depends on the full participation of all citizens—everyone has the right to vote, anyone can run for political office, and the voice of everyone should influence political choices. As the National Council of Welfare (1999a: 4) argues, the proportion of Canadians who are poor is "one measure of how well our democracy is working." Can someone without a permanent home, someone in a family with bare cupboards, or someone with hand-me-down clothes participate fully in our national affairs?

Unlike some other countries, such as the United States, Canada does not have an official definition of poverty. Indeed, Statistics Canada argues that there is no internationally accepted definition of poverty and that any definition is arbitrary. Therefore, it does not attempt to estimate the number of Canadians who are poor. Instead, Statistics Canada reports what it calls a **low-income cutoff**. The low-income cutoff "represents an income threshold where a family is likely to spend 20% more of its income on food, shelter, and clothing than the average family" (Statistics Canada, 1999b). The threshold is reported for seven different family sizes and for five sizes of community since straitened circumstances depend on the number of people in your family and the place you live. Most advocates for the poor interpret these thresholds, shown for 2006 in Table 8.4 on page 224, as poverty lines. For example, in Canada's cities with a population of half a million or more, a family of four with an income of $33 221 or less after government transfer payments, such as GST credits and the Canada Child Tax Benefit, would be considered poor.

In recent decades, the prevalence of low income among Canadians peaked at 15.7 percent in 1996, declined to 11.6 percent in 2002, and rose to 15.3 percent in 2005. One difficulty in interpreting such overall rates, however, is that the risk of low income is different for different types of families. As Figure 8.6 on page 224 indicates, families without any earners are at especially high risk, especially if they are female lone-parent families; more than 81 percent of the latter are in the low-income category.

The rates reported in Table 8.4 are for the proportion of families living in low income at a given time. However, many families move in and out of poverty, most commonly because of unemployment, reduced work hours, and episodes of poor health. As Figure 8.7 indicates, larger proportions of families and individuals go through one or more spells of low income over

Low-income cutoff is Statistic Canada's term for the income threshold below which a family devotes a larger share of its income to the necessities of food, shelter, and clothing than an average family would, likely resulting in straitened circumstances.

NEL

TABLE 8.4

Low-Income Cutoffs after Taxes and Including Government Transfers, 2006

Source: Canadian Council on Social Development, 2007, "Stats and Facts." Retrieved May 1, 2008 (http://www.ccsd.ca/factsheets/economic_security/poverty/lico_06.htm).

* Includes cities with a population between 15 000 and 30 000 and small urban areas (fewer than 15 000)

	Population of Community of Residence				
Family Size	**500 000+**	**100 000–499 999**	**30 000–99 999**	**Fewer than 30 000***	**Rural**
1	$17 570	$14 859	$14 674	$13 154	$11 494
2	$21 384	$18 085	$17 860	$16 010	$13 989
3	$26 628	$22 519	$22 239	$19 934	$17 420
4	$33 221	$28 095	$27 745	$24 871	$21 731
5	$37 828	$31 992	$31 594	$28 321	$24 746
6	$41 953	$35 480	$35 039	$31 409	$27 444
7+	$46 077	$38 967	$38 483	$34 496	$30 142

several years. For example, more than 3 out of 10 Canadian children lived in a low-income family for at least part of the time during the five years summarized by Figure 8.7.

Myths about the Poor

We noted earlier the contrasting images that are sometimes constructed to portray the poor. Are people poor because they are lazy drunks, or are they poor despite working hard? Such imagery leads many people to differentiate between the "deserving" and the "undeserving" poor. Research conducted in the past few decades continues to show that many popular images about the poor are inaccurate.

Myth 1: People are poor because they don't want to work. In most poor families at least one family member works. In 2001, 64 percent of poor families with heads of household under age 65 had one family member working at least part of the year. The National Council of Welfare (2004: 101) estimates that 271 000 unattached people were poor in 2001 even though they worked between 49 and 52 weeks. They compose 26 percent of all poor, unattached people under age 65. Some 85 000 families were poor, even when husbands and wives together worked for 103 or more weeks during the year (National Council of Welfare, 2004: 100). They compose 10 percent of all poor families with heads under 65. Although a good job is one of the best forms of insurance against living in poverty, having a job is not a perfect insulator. In part, that is because individuals working at a minimum wage of $8 per

FIGURE 8.6

Low-Income Rates for Different Family Types, Canada, 2005

Source: Statistics Canada, 2008, "Earnings and Incomes of Canadians over the Past Quarter Century, 2006 Census." Retrieved May 1, 2008 (http://www12.statcan.ca/english/census06/analysis/income/pdf/97-563-XIE2006001.pdf).

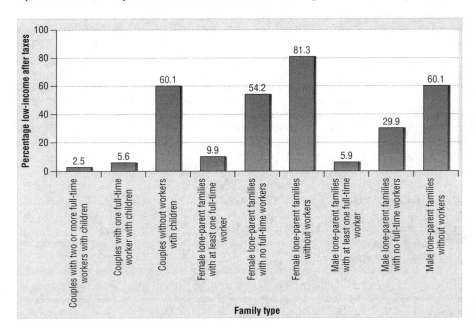

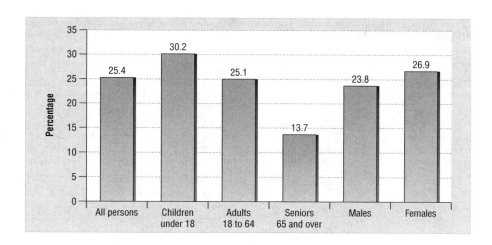

FIGURE 8.7

Persons Experiencing Low Income at Least One Year between 1996 and 2001

Source: Adapted from Statistics Canada, 2005, "Income in Canada, 2003," Catalogue 75-202, p. 123. Retreived at (http://www.statcan.ca/english/freepub/75-202-XIE/75-202-XIE2003000.pdf May 13, 2007)

hour have average annual incomes of $11 977, which is below the low-income cutoff for single individuals (National Council of Welfare, 2004: 105).

Myth 2: The overwhelming majority of poor people are immigrants. Individuals and family heads who are immigrants and who arrived in Canada before 1980 generally experience poverty at *lower* rates than native-born Canadians do (National Council of Welfare, 2004: 57). Higher poverty rates are evident among more recent immigrants who are less well established, but recent immigrants represent a fraction of all poor people.

Myth 3: The welfare rolls are crammed with young people who ought to be earning a living. In 1997 the National Council of Welfare (1998a) reported that only about 4 percent of welfare recipients were under the age of 20, and only 16 percent were under 25. Among single parents on welfare, only 3 percent were under the age of 20.

Myth 4: Most poor people are trapped in poverty. One in three people with a low income in 2002 had moved beyond it by 2003. Of the 25.4 percent of Canadians who experienced one or more years of low income (see Figure 8.7), only slightly more than one in eight of these (3.4 percent) lived in poverty for all six years. On average, those who experienced low income for at least one year spent 2.8 years or about one-half the total period in poverty (Statistics Canada, 2004d: 124). Thus, poverty for many is a result of family finances that are unstable; they slip into and out of difficult circumstances.

Explaining Poverty

Why are some Canadians poor? At one level, because poverty is a social construction—who is poor depends on the definition—the explanations focus on definitions. This explanation highlights the politics of poverty, in which levels and trends can be simply a consequence of definition. If we accept that some Canadians are poor, although granting that the number will vary depending on definition, then there is a second level of explanation. Here the question is, "Why are some people and families poor and others not?" Answers to this question vary from individual-level to structural explanations.

Individual-level explanations focus on the attributes of people who are poor, asking how these people differ from people who are not poor. This type of explanation focuses on causes that lie "within the person." Someone is poor, on this logic, because of a personal attribute, such as low intelligence or behaviour abnormality.

Some evidence suggests that individual attributes do explain a small amount of poverty. For example, we know that people who have physical disabilities or schizophrenia have a higher risk of living in poverty than others do. However, not all people with disabilities or with schizophrenia live in poverty, and the vast majority of people living in poverty have neither disabilities nor schizophrenia. On balance, this type of evidence teaches us that poverty is, for the most part, not a consequence of individual attributes, even though these are important in some cases.

NEL

A related form of explanation focuses more on the attitudes of individuals—not on attributes that are inherited, but on attributes or stigmas that are acquired. A social-psychological type of explanation emphasizes low self-esteem, lack of achievement motivation, and an inability to delay gratification. On this logic, poverty is perpetuated because poor families employ inadequate child-rearing practices that enhance bad attitudes. A related version of this argument stresses a "culture of poverty," a way of thinking and acting shared by poor families. This culture reinforces and perpetuates itself through poor upbringing and ill-formed personalities.

This type of reasoning is often dismissed by sociologists as "blaming the victim." You are poor, on this reasoning, because you have a poor work ethic, shoddy morals, no aspirations, no discipline, no fortitude, and so forth. Various objections undermine this type of explanation. First, there is a cause-and-effect, or chicken-and-egg, problem. People who are poor may develop "bad attitudes," but these may result from poverty and not be causes of poverty. The culture of poverty might provide an adequate description for some circumstances, but it is not an adequate explanation in general. Put differently, descriptions of poverty stressing a culture of depression, lack of hope, and fatalism may be accurate, but these effects of poverty ought not to be confused with the causes of poverty. Second, many people who are poor do work, are religious, don't smoke or drink, and so on. Therefore, evidence that supports explanations founded on personal deficits is often lacking.

Another form of explanation, one with greater currency in sociology, stresses the social organization of society, or subsystems in society, as explanations of poverty. The organization of our economy, for example, affects poverty. Capitalist economies feature cyclical booms and busts, periods of low unemployment and high profits followed by high unemployment and low profits. When unemployment rates rise, so do the numbers of families forced to live on reduced earnings, which for many means living in poverty. The right of employers to refuse to renew work contracts is an accepted part of our economic system. The reductions in income that result can hardly be attributed to changes in individual motivation. Low-wage jobs are also a part of the economy and some people in low-skill, nonunionized, part-year jobs will not earn enough to escape poverty. As Krahn and Lowe (1998: 405) summarize the situation, "a weak work ethic and a lack of effort" are seldom the explanation for individual poverty; "more often the problem is one of not enough good jobs."

Other analysts stress social policy as a factor affecting poverty levels. For example, as noted above, if you received the minimum hourly wage while working full time, full year, you would still be poor, especially if you had children to support. In this sense minimum-wage legislation is a social policy that creates a group of working poor. The social world is not quite so simple, of course, and if minimum wages were to rise, so too might the level of unemployment because some employers might not be able to afford to pay higher wages. Debate over these issues continues, but the point is that our social policies affect the well-being of people, and understanding the consequences of policies is critical.

The system of tax collection and tax allocation illustrates another way that social policies affect poverty. A progressive taxation system is one in which a greater proportion of income is paid in tax as incomes rise. For example, those who earn $100 000 pay a larger percentage of their income as tax than do those who earn $50 000. In Canada, although our income tax system is progressive, the overall tax system is relatively neutral. Most Canadian families pay about the same percentage of their total income in tax. This occurs because two interrelated factors undermine the "Robin Hood" effect of progressive income taxes. First, other taxes, such as GST and fuel taxes, are flat or neutral. They are not based on the income of the taxpayer. And since lower-income families typically spend higher proportions of their income on consumption, such taxes are somewhat regressive in impact. Second, those who earn more are able to shelter much of their income from taxation (e.g., in registered education saving plans, in registered retirement savings plans, through capital gains tax exemptions, and so forth). The net effect, as we saw above, is a system that does little to actually redistribute income and therefore relatively little to erode poverty.

Finally, other sociologists would stress ways of thinking, or ideological perspectives, as explanations for poverty. Negative images of various groups lead to an undervaluing of the ways of life of some people, such as First Nations and people with disabilities. Discrimination follows from this undervaluing, and discrimination seriously effects poverty. Undervaluing of talents and identities leads to less success in finding jobs. Even when employment is found, the work is often unsteady and low paying.

Is poverty an inevitable feature of society? It may be, at least to the extent that inequality is known to exist in all societies. However, the extent of poverty in Canada could be reduced if we chose to follow the examples of Western European nations. Many countries in Western Europe have poverty rates well below Canada's. That is because many European governments have established job-training and child-care programs that allow poor people to take jobs with livable wages and benefits. This is, however, a political choice. Many Canadians argue that providing welfare benefits dampens the work ethic and perpetuates poverty (see Box 8.1). Although the Western European evidence does not support that view, the political will does not currently exist in Canada to change our social policies to alleviate poverty.

BOX 8.1
It's Your Choice

Income Redistribution and Taxation

The idea of rugged individualism implies that our personal fortunes ought to rest on our own shoulders. "To each according to his or her abilities" is often held up as a supreme principle. Those who work hard, who persevere, who make wise decisions—those individuals supposedly deserve rewards, like Robinson Crusoe. By implication, those who are lazy and unwise deserve less.

A contrasting idea, the idea of collective responsibility, implies that as members of a community, we ought to look out for one another. In this view, "to each according to his or her need" ought to be a supreme principle. Those who have should share. The interests of the many should come before the riches of a few.

Few Canadians support either of these extreme ideas, but examples of each principle are easy to find. The unequal distribution of income in Canada and the high salaries of the presidents of large corporations are consistent with the theme of rugged individualism. Government support for postsecondary education and health

care illustrates the theme of collective responsibility. Both of these themes represent contrasting social policies, one focused on the supremacy of individual rights, the other emphasizing collective responsibility and the common good.

How much tax revenue should governments collect, and should they redistribute that revenue in ways that benefit lower income groups? Should governments act like Robin Hood and transfer some tax money to the poor? Should governments support hospitals and schools with tax dollars, or should individual families pay directly for medical care and education? These are questions of social policy.

Here are some of the arguments for and against income redistribution, arguments that are fundamental to some of the major political debates in many countries in recent years. What choices would you make if you and your colleagues could run the government for a few years?

Against Redistribution

1. Taking from the rich and giving to the poor decreases the motivation for people in both groups to work hard.

2. The cost of redistribution is high. Taking from one group and giving to another requires some agency first to collect money and then to allocate it.

3. Some individuals and families will cheat and deceive. Some will hide or misrepresent their earnings, either to pay less in tax or to receive more through welfare. Redistribution promotes both tax cheats and welfare frauds.

For Redistribution

1. A society with a reasonable degree of equality is a better place to live in than a society with heightened levels of inequality.

2. An extra dollar to a poor family is more helpful than an extra dollar to a rich family.

3. Improving the material well-being of a poor family through benevolence enhances the social well-being of a rich family.

4. Aid to poorer families reduces the risk of crime and political conflict since poorer families are thereby less likely to seek illegal means of earning income or to unite in protest over living conditions.

In sum, sociological explanations look not to the personal qualities of the poor but to the organization of society as a way of explaining why some people are poor and why poverty persists. Notice, too, that the solutions to poverty vary depending on the approach. One solution is to define the problem in a way that minimizes poverty. Another solution looks to change poor people's skills through job-training and job-search programs for adults and compensatory education programs for children so they are better able to find well-paying work. Still another set of solutions looks at the organization of society and asks whether we could change the way we do things so as to benefit the poor. This would involve altering the tax system, encouraging the creation of good jobs, reducing discrimination, and the like.

International Differences

Global Inequality

Despite growing income inequality in recent years and a large low-income population, Canada is one of the richest countries in the world. Angola is a world apart. Angola is an African country of 13.3 million people. More than 650 000 of its citizens were killed in a civil war that raged between 1975 and 2002. Angola is one of the poorest nations on earth.

Most Angolans live in houses made of cardboard, tin, and cement blocks. Few houses have running water. Average income is about $7800 a year. Life expectancy is 38 years. More than half the population is unemployed or underemployed, and the poverty rate is 70 percent (Central Intelligence Agency, 2008). Adding to the misery of Angola's citizens are the millions of landmines scattered throughout the countryside, regularly killing and maiming innocent passersby. About 85 percent of the population survives on subsistence agriculture.

However, multinational companies, such as Exxon and Chevron, drill for oil in Angola. Oil exports account for 85 percent of GDP. In the coastal capital of Luanda, an enclave of North Americans who work for Exxon and Chevron live in gated, heavily guarded communities that contain luxury homes, tennis courts, swimming pools, house cleaners, and SUVs. Here, side by side in the city of Luanda, is a microcosm of the chasm separating rich from poor in the world.

Some countries, such as Canada, are rich. Others, such as Angola, are poor. When sociologists study such differences between countries, they are studying **global inequality**. However, it is possible for country A and country B to be equally rich while inside country A, the gap between rich and poor is greater than inside country B. When sociologists compare such differences, they are studying **cross-national variations in internal stratification**.

The United States, Canada, Japan, Australia, and a dozen or so Western European countries, including Germany, France, and the United Kingdom, are the world's richest postindustrial societies. The world's poorest countries cover much of Africa, South America, and Asia. Inequality between rich and poor countries is staggering. Nearly a fifth of the world's

Global inequality refers to differences in the economic ranking of countries.

Cross-national variations in internal stratification are differences among countries in their stratification systems.

Inequality on a global scale. *Left*: An Angolan boy, a victim of a landmine, hops home in Luanda. *Right*: Children relax at home in Luanda's North American enclave, built by Exxon for its supervisors and executives and their families.

Country and Overall Rank	Life Expectancy (years)	Adult Literacy (percent)	School Enrolment Ratio	GDP per Capita ($US)
1. Norway	78.9	99.0	98	36 600
2. Sweden	80	99.0	100	26 050
3. Australia	79.1	99.0	100	28 260
4. Canada	79.3	99.0	95	29 480
5. Netherlands	78.3	99.0	99	29 100
173. Burundi	40.8	50.4	33	630
174. Mali	48.5	19	26	930
175. Burkina Faso	45.8	12.8	22	1 100
176. Niger	46	17.1	19	800
177. Sierra Leone	34.3	36	45	520
Least developed countries	64.6	76.7	60	4 054
High-income OECD (mature industrialized) countries	78.3	99	93	29 000

TABLE 8.5

United Nations Indicators of Human Development, 2004

Note: The United Nations publishes an annual index that combines four indicators of human development: life expectancy, adult literacy, school enrolment rates, and GDP per capita. The table lists the five highest-ranked countries, the five lowest-ranked, the value on each indicator for these countries, and some comparisons across the economic regions of the world.

Source: From United Nations, 2004, "Country Tables," *Human Development Report 2004*. Retrieved from http://hdr.undp.org/statistics/data/index_countries.cfm. Reprinted with permission. The United Nations is the author of the original material.

population lacks adequate shelter, and more than a fifth lacks safe water. About a third of the world's people are without electricity, and more than two-fifths lack adequate sanitation. In Canada, life expectancy is 79 years, annual income per person is more than $36 000, and inflation is about 3 percent (United Nations, 2004a; see Table 8.5). Canada has one of the highest enrolment rates in the world for postsecondary education but in many African countries, such as Angola, fewer than 50 percent of children are enrolled in primary schools. People living in poor countries are also more likely than people are in rich countries to experience extreme suffering on a mass scale. For example, because of political turmoil in many poor countries, tens of millions of people have been driven from their homes by force in recent years (Hampton, 1998). There are still about 27 million slaves in Mozambique, Sudan, and other African countries (Bales, 1999).

We devote much of Chapter 9 (Globalization, Inequality, and Development) to analyzing the causes, dimensions, and consequences of global inequality. You will learn that much of the wealth of the rich countries has been gained at the expense of the poor countries. We also discuss possible ways of dealing with this most vexing of social issues. For the moment, having merely noted the existence of the problem, we focus on the second type of international difference: cross-national variations in internal stratification.

Internal Stratification

Levels of global inequality aside, how does internal stratification differ from one country to the next? We can answer this question by first examining the **Gini index**, named after the Italian economist who invented it. The Gini index is a measure of income inequality. Its value ranges from zero to one. A Gini index of zero indicates that every household (or every income recipient) in the country earns exactly the same amount of money. At the opposite pole, a Gini index of one indicates that a single household earns the entire national income. These are theoretical extremes. In the real world, nearly all societies have Gini indices between 0.2 and 0.6.

Figure 8.8 on page 230 shows the Gini index for eight countries using the most recent international income data available. Of the eight countries, Sweden has the lowest Gini index (0.25) while Canada is around the middle at 0.331. The countries with the highest level of inequality include Russia (0.4), China (0.44), and the United States (0.45). Figure 8.8 suggests that among wealthy, postindustrial societies, income inequality in Canada is about average. Figure 8.8 also indicates that higher inequality and higher poverty rates tend to occur together.

The Gini index is a measure of income inequality. Its value ranges from zero (which means that every household earns exactly the same amount of money) to one (which means that all income is earned by a single household).

NEL

FIGURE 8.8

Household Income Inequality and Low Income, Selected Countries, 1995–2004

Note: Poverty data are not available for China.

Source: From Timothy M. Smeeding, 2004, "Public Policy and Economic Inequality: The United States in Comparative Perspective," Working Paper No. 367 (Maxwell School of Citizenship and Public Affairs, Syracuse University, NY). Retrieved June 24, 2006 (http://www. lisproject.org/publications/ LISwps367.pdf). Reprinted with permission.

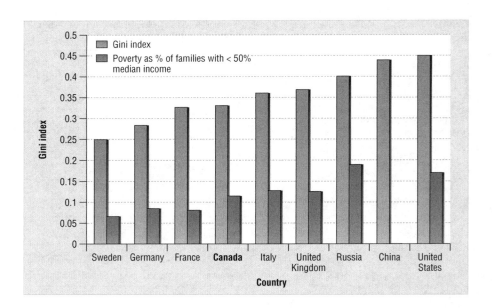

GLOBAL PERSPECTIVE

Development and Internal Stratification

What accounts for cross-national differences in internal stratification, such as those described in the previous section? Later in this chapter, you will learn that *political factors* explain some of the differences. For the moment, however, we focus on how *socioeconomic development* affects internal stratification.

You will recall from Chapter 6 (Networks, Groups, Bureaucracies, and Societies) that over the course of human history, as societies became richer and more complex, the level of social inequality first increased, then tapered off, and then began to decline (Lenski, 1966; Lenski, Nolan, and Lenski, 1995; see Figure 8.9). What follows is a recap.

Foraging Societies

For the first 90 000 years of human existence, people lived in nomadic bands of fewer than 100 people. To survive, they hunted wild animals and foraged for wild edible plants. Some foragers and hunters were undoubtedly more skilled than others were, but they did not hoard food. Instead, they shared food to ensure the survival of all band members. They produced little or nothing above what they required for subsistence. There were no rich and no poor.

FIGURE 8.9

Inequality and Development

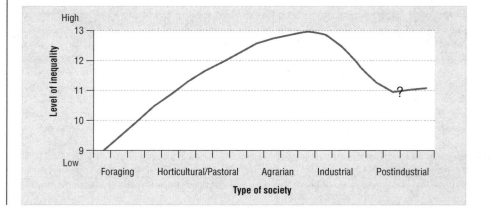

Horticultural and Pastoral Societies

About 10 000 years ago, people established the first agricultural settlements. These settlements were based on horticulture (the use of small hand tools to cultivate plants) and pastoralism (the domestication of animals). These technological innovations enabled people to produce wealth, a surplus above what they needed for subsistence. A small number of villagers controlled the surplus. Thus, significant **social stratification** emerged.

Agrarian Societies

About 5000 years ago, people developed plow agriculture. By attaching oxen and other large animals to plows, farmers could increase the amount they produced. Again thanks to technological innovation, surpluses grew. With more wealth came still sharper social stratification.

Agrarian societies developed religious beliefs justifying steeper inequality. People came to believe that kings and queens ruled by "divine right." They viewed large landowners as "lords." Moreover, if you were born a peasant, you and your children were likely to remain peasants. If you were born a lord, you and your children were likely to remain lords. In the vocabulary of modern sociology, we say that stratification in agrarian societies was based more on **ascription** than **achievement**. That is, a person's position in the stratification system was determined more by the features he or she was born with ("ascribed characteristics") than his or her accomplishments ("achieved characteristics"). Another way of saying this is that little **social mobility** took place.

A nearly purely ascriptive society existed in agrarian India. Society was divided into **castes**, four main groups and many subgroups arranged in a rigid hierarchy. Being born into a particular caste meant you had to work in the distinctive occupations reserved for that caste and marry someone from the same or an adjoining caste. The Hindu religion strictly reinforced the system (Srinivas, 1952). For example, Hinduism explained people's place in the caste system by their deeds in a previous life. If you were good, you were presumably rewarded by being born into a higher caste in your next life. If you were bad, you were presumably punished by being born into a lower caste. Belief in the sanctity of caste regulated even the most mundane aspects of life. Thus, someone from the lowest caste could dig a well for a member of the highest caste, but once the well was dug, the well digger could not so much as cast his shadow on the well. If he did, the well was considered polluted and upper-caste people were forbidden to drink from it.

Caste systems have existed in industrial times. For example, the system of **apartheid** existed in South Africa from 1948 until 1992. The white minority enjoyed the best jobs and other privileges, and they consigned the large black majority to menial jobs. Apartheid also prevented marriage between blacks and whites and erected separate public facilities for members of the two races. Asians and people of "mixed race" enjoyed privileges between these two extremes. However, apartheid was an exception. For the most part, industrialism causes a *decline* in inequality.

Industrial Societies

At first, the Industrial Revolution that began in the late eighteenth century did little to lower the level of social stratification. But improvements in the technology and social organization of manufacturing allowed people to produce more goods at a lower cost per unit, making a rise in living standards possible. Business leaders realized they could profit most by identifying, training, and hiring the most talented people, and they offered higher wages to recruit them. Workers used union power and growing political influence to win improvements in working conditions. As a result, social mobility became more widespread than ever before. Stratification declined as industrial societies developed.

Postindustrial Societies

Since the 1970s, social inequality has increased in nearly all postindustrial societies. Among rich countries, the United States exhibited the most social inequality in the 1970s, and since

Social stratification refers to the way in which society is organized in layers or strata.

An **ascription**-based stratification system is one in which the allocation of rank depends on characteristics a person is born with.

An **achievement**-based stratification system is one in which the allocation of rank depends on a person's accomplishments.

Social mobility refers to movement up or down the stratification system.

A **caste** system is an almost pure ascription-based stratification system in which occupations and marriage partners are assigned on the basis of caste membership.

Apartheid was a caste system based on race that existed in South Africa from 1948 to 1992. It consigned the large black majority to menial jobs, prevented marriage between blacks and whites, and erected separate public facilities for members of the two races. Asians and people of mixed race enjoyed privileges between these two extremes.

then inequality has grown faster in the United States than in any other rich country. The concentration of wealth in the hands of the wealthiest 1 percent of Americans is higher today than anytime in the past 100 years. The gap between rich and poor is bigger today than it has been for at least 50 years.

Technological factors are partly responsible for the trend toward growing inequality in most postindustrial countries. Many high-tech jobs have been created at the top of the stratification system over the past few decades. These jobs pay well. At the same time new technologies have made many jobs routine. Routine jobs require little training, and they pay poorly. Because the number of routine jobs is growing more quickly than the number of jobs at the top of the stratification system, the overall effect of technology today is to increase the level of inequality in most postindustrial societies. One reason for the especially high level of inequality in the United States is that it has proportionately more low-wage jobs than any other rich country does.

A second factor responsible for the growing trend toward social inequality is government policy. Through tax and social welfare policies, governments are able to prevent big income transfers to the rich. Among the rich postindustrial societies, however, only the French government has intervened to *lower* the level of inequality since the 1970s. The government that has done least to moderate the growth of inequality is that of the United States (Centre for Economic Policy Research, 2002; Smeeding, 2004).

These, then, are the basic patterns and trends in the history of social stratification. Bearing these descriptions in mind, we now examine how sociologists have explained social stratification. We begin with Karl Marx, who formulated the first major sociological theory of stratification 150 years ago (Marx and Engels, 1972 [1848]; Marx, 1904 [1859]).

THEORIES OF STRATIFICATION

Conflict Perspectives

Marx

In medieval Western Europe, peasants worked small plots of land owned by landlords. Peasants were legally obliged to give their landlords a set part of the harvest and to continue working for them under any circumstance. In turn, landlords were required to protect peasants from marauders. They were also obliged to open their storehouses and feed the peasants if crops failed. This arrangement was known as **feudalism**.

Feudalism was a legal arrangement in preindustrial Europe that bound peasants to the land and obliged them to give their landlords a set part of the harvest. In exchange, landlords were required to protect peasants from marauders and open their storehouses to feed the peasants if crops failed.

According to Marx, by the late fifteenth century, several forces were beginning to undermine feudalism. Most important was the growth of exploration and trade, which increased the demand for many goods and services in commerce, navigation, and industry. By the seventeenth and eighteenth centuries, some urban craftspeople and merchants had opened small manufacturing enterprises and saved enough capital to expand production. However, they faced a big problem: To increase profits they needed more workers. Yet the biggest potential source of workers—the peasantry—was legally bound to the land. Thus, feudalism had to wither if agricultural peasants were to become industrial workers. In Scotland, for example, enterprising landowners recognized they could make more money raising sheep and selling wool than by having their peasants till the soil. So they turned their cropland into pastures, forcing peasants off the land and into the cities. The former peasants had no choice but to take jobs as urban workers.

In Marx's view, relations between workers and industrialists first encouraged rapid technological change and economic growth. After all, industrial owners wanted to adopt new tools, machines, and production methods so they could produce more efficiently and earn higher profits. But this had unforeseen consequences. In the first place, some owners, driven out of business by more efficient competitors, were forced to become members of the working class. Together with former peasants pouring into the cities from the countryside, this caused the working class to grow. Second, the drive for profits motivated owners to concentrate workers in larger and larger factories, keep wages as low as possible, and invest as little as possible in improving working conditions. Thus, as the ownership class grew richer and smaller, the working class grew larger and more impoverished.

Marx felt that workers would ultimately become aware of their exploitation. Their sense of **class consciousness** would, he wrote, encourage the growth of unions and workers' political parties. These organizations would eventually try to create a communist system in which there would be no private wealth. Instead, under communism, everyone would share wealth, said Marx.

We must note several points about Marx's theory. First, according to Marx, a person's **class** is determined by the source of his or her income, or, to use Marx's term, by a person's "relationship to the means of production." For example, members of the capitalist class (or **bourgeoisie**) own the means of production, including factories, tools, and land. However, they do not do any physical labour. They are thus in a position to earn profits. In contrast, members of the working class (or **proletariat**) do physical labour. However, they do not own means of production. They are thus in a position to earn wages. It is the source of income, not the amount, that distinguishes classes in Marx's view.

A second noteworthy point about Marx's theory is that it recognizes more than two classes in any society. For example, Marx discussed the **petite bourgeoisie**. This is a class of small-scale capitalists who own means of production but employ only a few workers or none at all. This situation forces them to do physical work themselves. In Marx's view, however, members of the petty bourgeoisie are bound to disappear as capitalism develops because they are economically inefficient. Just two great classes characterize every economic era, said Marx: landlords and serfs during feudalism, bourgeoisie and proletariat during capitalism.

Finally, it is important to note that some of Marx's predictions about the development of capitalism turned out to be wrong. Nevertheless, Marx's ideas about social stratification have stimulated thinking and research on social stratification even today, as you will see below.

A Critique of Marx

Marx's ideas strongly influenced the development of sociological conflict theory (see Chapter 1, A Sociological Compass). Today, however, more than 125 years after Marx's death, it is generally agreed that Marx did not accurately foresee some aspects of capitalist development:

- Industrial societies did not polarize into two opposed classes engaged in bitter conflict. Instead, a large and heterogeneous middle class of "white-collar" workers emerged. Some of them are non-manual employees. Others are professionals. Many of them enjoy higher income and status than manual workers. With a bigger stake in capitalism than propertyless manual workers, non-manual employees and professionals have generally acted as a stabilizing force in society. To take account of these changes, some neo-Marxists recognize *two* main divisions in the social relations of work. Although owners control the assets of the business and determine its purpose, in today's large industrial organizations they cannot immediately supervise or direct the work of every employee. This is especially the case when a company is owned by a great many people, as it is in many major corporations today. Therefore, a class of supervisors has arisen. This class, sometimes called the "new middle class" to illustrate its recency and its intermediate position, is defined by relations of authority and supervision. New middle-class workers take direction from owners and are responsible for coordinating and directing the work of other employees. Sociologists Wallace Clement and John Myles (1994) provide an excellent application of this new way of thinking about class in their comparative analysis of the Canadian, American, and Scandinavian class structures.

Class consciousness **refers to being aware of membership in a class.**

Class, **in Marx's sense of the term, is determined by a person's relationship to the means of production. In Weber's usage, class is determined by a person's "market situation."**

The bourgeoisie **in Marx's usage are owners of the means of production, including factories, tools, and land. They do not do any physical labour. Their income derives from profits.**

The proletariat, **in Marx's usage, is the working class. Members of the proletariat do physical labour but do not own means of production. They are thus in a position to earn wages.**

The petite bourgeoisie, **in Marx's usage, is the class of small-scale capitalists who own means of production but employ only a few workers or none at all, forcing them to do physical work themselves.**

- Marx correctly argued that investment in technology makes it possible for capitalists to earn high profits. However, he did not expect investment in technology also to make it possible for workers to earn higher wages and toil fewer hours under less oppressive conditions. Yet that is just what happened. Their improved living standard tended to pacify workers, as did the availability of various welfare state benefits, such as employment insurance.
- Communism took root not where industry was most highly developed, as Marx predicted, but in semi-industrialized countries, such as Russia in 1917 and China in 1948. Moreover, instead of evolving into classless societies, new forms of privilege emerged under communism. For example, in communist Russia, income was more equal than in the West. However, membership in the Communist Party, and particularly membership in the so-called *nomenklatura,* a select group of professional state managers, brought special privileges. These included exclusive access to stores where they could purchase scarce Western goods at nominal prices, luxurious country homes, free trips abroad, and so forth. According to a Russian quip from the 1970s, "Under capitalism, one class exploits the other, but under communism it's the other way around."

Weber

Writing in the early twentieth century, Max Weber foretold most of these developments. For example, he did not think communism would create classlessness. He also understood the profound significance of the growth of the middle class. As a result, Weber developed an approach to social stratification much different from Marx's.

Weber, like Marx, saw classes as economic categories (Weber, 1946: 180–95). However, he did not think a single criterion—ownership versus non-ownership of property—determines class position. Class position, wrote Weber, is determined by a person's "market situation," including the possession of goods, opportunities for income, level of education, and degree of technical skill. From this point of view, there are four main classes according to Weber: large property owners, small property owners, propertyless but relatively highly educated and well-paid employees, and propertyless manual workers. Thus, white-collar employees and professionals emerge as a large class in Weber's scheme.

If Weber broadened Marx's idea of class, he also recognized that two types of groups other than class have a bearing on the way a society is stratified: status groups and parties.

Status groups differ from one another in the prestige or social honour they enjoy and in their style of life. Consider members of a particular minority ethnic community who have recently immigrated. They may earn relatively high income but endure relatively low prestige. The longer-established members of the majority ethnic community may look down on them as vulgar "new rich." If their cultural practices differ from those of the majority ethnic group, their style of life may also become a subject of scorn. Thus, the position of the minority ethnic group in the social hierarchy does not derive just from its economic position but also from the esteem in which it is held.

In Weber's usage, **parties** are not just political groups but, more generally, organizations that seek to impose their will on others. Control over parties, especially large bureaucratic organizations, does not depend just on wealth or another class criterion. One can head a military, scientific, or other bureaucracy without being rich, just as one can be rich and still have to endure low prestige.

So we see why Weber argued that to draw an accurate picture of a society's stratification system, we must analyze classes, status groups, and parties as somewhat independent bases of social inequality. But to what degree are they independent of one another? Weber said that the importance of status groups as a basis of stratification is greatest in pre-capitalist societies. Under capitalism, classes and parties (especially bureaucracies) become the main bases of stratification.

Although sociologists dissect inequalities into abstract schemes, the underlying differences exist quite apart from abstractions that theorists propose. For many people, the most tangible reality of class is how it sorts people into different neighbourhoods. There is no exact rule involved and various ranking criteria blend into a complex synthesis. Because the rule is inexact, people act on it without even agreeing on what, if anything, to call it.

Status groups differ from one another in terms of the prestige or social honour they enjoy and also in terms of their style of life.

Parties, in Weber's usage, are organizations that seek to impose their will on others.

PERSONAL
ANECDOTE

For example, Steven Rytina recalls: "When I was in elementary school, my family lived in a small coal-mining city. You could see the city's sharp stratification as your glance swept from the mine-owners' mansions on the hill to the shacks down by the river.

"One day when I was about 10, I was playing with some friends in what we knew as 'Perk's meadow.' One of my friends was over by the road when, for no apparent reason, a group of about a half-dozen boys came up and starting hitting him.

"We rushed over to help and they ran away. Who were they? We recognized only one of them. He lived about a half-block away but he never played in our ball games even though his house was closer to the field than were many of ours. We hardly knew him. Still, someone knew where he lived and so we ran over and barged into his house. But he wasn't there, so we retreated to the meadow and mobilized. We piled up a barrier of brush, collected apples and sticks for ammunition, and got the word out to the neighbourhoods up the hill.

"Over three days, larger and larger bodies of boys assembled from up-the-hill and from down-the-hill and met in the middle at Perk's meadow. There was lots of shouting, a little jostling, and bushels of apples thrown. On the final day, there were 30 or 40 on each side. By then, the fracas attracted the attention of some adults who put a quick end to it.

"It was only much later that I asked myself why people on both sides assumed that there were two sides and only two sides, and that boys would come, as they did, once they were told about the initial incident. (That no one invited girls was, in that time and place, not a puzzle.) Years later, the answer crystallized. The street that formed the boundary along Perk's meadow marked an abrupt transition. On the immediate up-hill side were the houses of the president of the local bank and the owner of the lumber mill. Almost without exception, families up the hill were business owners or professionals who belonged to the country club and enjoyed other privileges. Those on the down-hill side did not share in those privileges and the friendships they fostered. What both sides at Perk's meadow assumed, correctly even though nobody ever spoke of it directly, was that this class division existed and that their loyalty was to one and against the other. We were only kids, but the cleavages in the adult world were faithfully reflected in our little universe. We had no vocabulary to describe such differences and therefore no insight into why our loyalties (and living standards) turned so sharply on what our fathers did for a living. But everyone involved converged toward a common response as if this was somehow built into the very nature of things."

Functionalism

Marx and Weber were Germans who wrote their major works between the 1840s and the 1910s. Inevitably, their theories bear the stamp of the age in which they wrote. The next major developments in the field occurred in the United States in the mid-twentieth century. Just as inevitably, these innovations were coloured by the optimism, dynamism, and prejudices of that time and place.

Consider first in this connection the **functional theory of stratification**, proposed by Kingsley Davis and Wilbert Moore at the end of World War II (Davis and Moore, 1945). Davis and Moore observed that jobs differ in importance. A judge's work, for example, contributes more to society than the work of a janitor. This presents a problem: How can people be motivated to undergo the long training they need to serve as judges, physicians, engineers, and so forth? Higher education is expensive. You earn little money while training. Long and hard study rather than pleasure seeking is essential. Clearly, an incentive is needed to motivate the most talented people to train for the most important jobs. The incentives, said Davis and Moore, are money and prestige. More precisely, social stratification is necessary (or "functional") because the prospect of high rewards motivates people to undergo the sacrifices needed to get a higher education. Without substantial inequality, they conclude, the most talented people would have no incentive to become judges, physicians, and so forth.

Although the functional theory of stratification may at first seem plausible, we can conduct what Max Weber called a "thought experiment" to uncover one of its chief flaws. Imagine a society with just two classes of people—physicians and farmers. The farmers

The functional theory of stratification argues that (1) some jobs are more important than others are, (2) people must make sacrifices to train for important jobs, and (3) inequality is required to motivate people to undergo these sacrifices.

NEL

According to the functional theory of stratification, "important" jobs require more training than "less important" jobs. The promise of big salaries motivates people to undergo that training. Therefore, the functionalists conclude, social stratification is necessary. As the text makes clear, however, one of the problems with the functional theory of stratification is that it is difficult to establish which jobs are important, especially when we take a historical perspective.

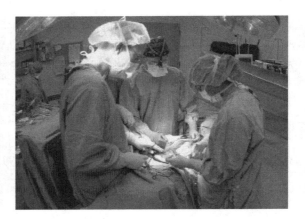

grow food. The physicians tend the ill. Then, one day, a rare and deadly virus strikes. The virus has the odd property of attacking only physicians. Within weeks, there are no more doctors in our imaginary society. As a result, the farmers are much worse off. Cures and treatments for their ailments are no long available. Soon the average farmer lives fewer years than his or her predecessors did. The society is less well off, though it survives.

Now imagine the reverse. Again we have a society comprising only physicians and farmers. Again a rare and lethal virus strikes. This time, however, the virus has the odd property of attacking only farmers. Within weeks, the physicians' stores of food are depleted. After a few more weeks, the physicians start dying of starvation. The physicians who try to become farmers catch the new virus and expire. Within months, there is no more society. Who, then, does the more important work, physicians or farmers? Our thought experiment suggests that farmers do, for without them society cannot exist.

From a historical point of view, we can say that *none* of the jobs regarded by Davis and Moore as "important" would exist without the physical labour done by people in "unimportant" jobs. To sustain the witch doctor in a tribal society, hunters and gatherers had to produce enough for their own subsistence plus a surplus to feed, clothe, and house the witch doctor. To sustain the royal court in an agrarian society, serfs had to produce enough for their own subsistence plus a surplus to support the royal family. By using taxes, tithes, and force, government and religious authorities have taken surpluses from ordinary working people for thousands of years. Among other things, these surpluses were used to establish the first institutions of higher learning in the thirteenth century. Out of these, modern universities developed.

The question of which occupations are most important is thus not clear-cut. To be sure, physicians earn a lot more money than farmers do today and they also enjoy a lot more prestige. But that is not because their work is more important in any objective sense of the word. (On the question of why physicians and other professionals earn more than non-professionals do, see Chapter 17, Education).

Other problems with the functional theory of stratification have been noted (Tumin, 1953). We mention two of the most important. First, the functional theory of stratification stresses how inequality helps society discover talent. However, it ignores the pool of talent lying undiscovered because of inequality. Bright and energetic adolescents may be forced to drop out of high school to help support themselves and their families. Capable and industrious high-school graduates may be forced to forgo a postsecondary education because they can't afford it. Inequality may encourage the discovery of talent but only among those who can afford to take advantage of the opportunities available to them. For the rest, inequality prevents talent from being discovered.

Second, the functional theory of stratification fails to examine how advantages are passed from generation to generation. Like Robinson Crusoe, the functional theory correctly emphasizes that talent and hard work often result in high material rewards. However, it is also the case that inheritance allows parents to transfer wealth to children regardless of their talent. For example, glancing back at Table 8.3, we see that many of the largest personal fortunes in Canada were inherited. Other examples strengthen the point. The McCain brothers are rich Canadians not because of their talent (although they surely have talent) but principally because their father gave them a food-processing empire.

Even rich people who do not inherit large fortunes often start near the top of the stratification system. Bill Gates, for example, is one of the richest people in the world. He did not inherit his fortune. However, his father was a partner in one of the most successful law firms in Seattle. Gates himself went to the most exclusive and expensive private schools in the city, followed by a stint at Harvard. In the late 1960s, his high school was one of the first in the world to boast a computer terminal connected to a nearby university mainframe. Gates's early fascination with computers dates from this period. Gates is without doubt a highly talented man, but surely the social advantages he was born with, and not just his talents, helped to elevate him to his present lofty status (Wallace and Erickson, 1992). An adequate theory of stratification must take inheritance into account, while recognizing how inequality prevents the discovery of talent.

Many of the ideas reviewed above emphasize the economic sources of inequality. However, as Weber correctly pointed out, inequality is not based on money alone. It is also based on prestige and power. We now turn to an examination of these non-economic sources of inequality.

NON-ECONOMIC DIMENSIONS OF INEQUALITY

Power

In November 1997, seven teenagers in Victoria, B.C.—six girls and a boy—attacked their schoolmate, 14-year-old Reena Virk, beating her unconscious and leaving her to drown. In March 2000, Hamed Nastoh, also 14, killed himself by jumping off the Pattullo Bridge between New Westminster and Surrey, B.C. Nine months later, 14-year-old Dawn-Marie Wesley of Mission, B.C., hanged herself in her bedroom with a dog leash. In April 2002, 14-year-old Emmet Fralick of Halifax shot and killed himself.

What do the cases of Virk, Nastoh, Wesley, and Fralick have in common? All four teenagers were bullied by their classmates. Three of them felt they had no recourse but to take their own lives. As Dawn-Marie Wesley wrote in her suicide note: "If I try to get help it will get worse. They are always looking for a new person to beat up and they are the toughest girls. If I ratted they would get suspended and there would be no stopping them. I love you all so much" (quoted in O'Malley and Ali, 2001).

Bullying was probably part of your upbringing, too. Recall your years in the schoolyard. Remember how some people had the power to "name," while others were forced to "wear" those names? "Four eyes," "fatty," and "spaz" were common names in many schools. If you had the misfortune of needing glasses, having a visible birthmark, or even having an unusual name, you might have been the victim of verbal abuse.

Why are so many children publicly shamed and humiliated? Because it makes those with the power to name feel superior and proud. The peer group is a place to "earn points" and win friends. To become one of the in-crowd, a child must commonly disparage outsiders. If a person is part of the out-crowd, he or she must commonly disparage members of the in-crowd as a defence aimed at maintaining self-esteem. Often it is cliques who do the mocking. Social class, ethnicity, grade level, and neighbourhood often define cliques.

Bullying is one form of power in action. Max Weber defined **power** as the ability of individuals or groups to get their own way, even in the face of resistance from others (Weber, 1947: 152). It would, however, be a mistake to think that power is an attribute that you either have or don't. That is because less powerful groups may organize and resist; and organization and resistance are themselves bases of power. Accordingly, less powerful groups may become more powerful when power holders seek to impose their will.

Power is ability to impose one's will on others.

Sometimes, less powerful groups may even prevent power holders from achieving their aims. Power is therefore not an all-or-nothing attribute but a *social relationship*, the exercise of which may cause less-powerful people to become more powerful.

Authority is legitimate, institutionalized power.

We must distinguish between power and authority. **Authority** rests on moral consent—I comply with your demands not because you force me to but because I believe they are legitimate. In this case, compliance occurs not because sanctions are or could be used, but because I agree your demands are valid. We agree that bringing a gun to school is inappropriate and that halting at stop signs is essential for safety. Most people obey these rules not out of fear of sanctions, but because they agree that they are sensible, legitimate practices.

It is also important to note that the use of power is often invisible. Powerful people often do not have to do anything to get their way because others understand that it would be futile to resist. Extremely powerful individuals or groups are even able to set agendas, frame issues, and shape ideas—to decide the topics that will be debated and how they will be debated. This enables them to exclude potentially contentious issues from debate. They may then win battles without having to fight them because others haven't even conceived of the need to raise certain issues or at least raise them in certain ways. This invisible use of power is less risky than allowing contentious issues to be put on an agenda, having less powerful individuals and groups organize and resist, and perhaps even having to use force to win an issue. The use of force is a sign of relative weakness.

Prestige and Taste

Let us now consider another non-economic dimension of social stratification: prestige or honour. Weber, you will recall, said status groups differ from one another in terms of their lifestyles and the honour in which they are held. Here we may add that members of status groups signal their rank by means of material and symbolic culture. That is, they seek to distinguish themselves from others by displays of "taste" in fashion, food, music, literature, manners, travel, and so forth.

The difference between *good taste, common taste,* and *bad taste* is not inherent in cultural objects themselves. Rather, cultural objects that are considered to be in the best taste are generally those that are least accessible.

To explain the connection between taste and accessibility, let us compare Bach's *The Well-Tempered Clavier* with Gershwin's *Rhapsody in Blue*. A survey by French sociologist Pierre Bourdieu showed different social groups prefer these two musical works (Bourdieu, 1984 [1979]: 17). Well-educated professionals, high-school teachers, professors, and artists prefer *The Well-Tempered Clavier*. Less well-educated clerks, secretaries,

The differences among *good taste, common taste,* and *bad taste* are not inherent in cultural objects themselves. Rather, cultural objects that are considered to be in the best taste are generally those that are least accessible. *Left*: Measha Brueggergosman. *Right*: Don Cherry.

and junior commercial and administrative executives favour *Rhapsody in Blue*. Why? The two works are certainly very different types of music. Gershwin evokes the jazzy dynamism of big-city America early in the twentieth century, Bach the almost mathematically ordered courtly life of early eighteenth-century Germany. But anyone would be hard-pressed to argue that *The Well-Tempered Clavier* is intrinsically superior music. Both are great art. Why then do more highly educated people prefer *The Well-Tempered Clavier* to *Rhapsody in Blue?* Because, according to Bourdieu, during their education they acquire specific cultural tastes associated with their social position. These tastes help to distinguish them from people in other social positions. Many of them come to regard lovers of Gershwin condescendingly, just as many lovers of Gershwin come to think of Bach enthusiasts as snobs. These distancing attitudes help the two status groups remain separate.

Bach is known for such musical innovations as counterpoint (playing two or more melodies simultaneously) and the fugue (in which instruments repeat the same melody with slight variations). His music is complex, and to really appreciate it a person may require some formal instruction. Many other elements of "high culture," such as opera and abstract art, are similarly inaccessible to most people because fully understanding them requires special education.

However, it is not just education that makes some cultural objects less accessible than others are. Purely financial considerations also enter the picture. A Mercedes costs four times more than a Ford, and a winter ski trip to Whistler can cost four times more than a week in a modest motel near the beach on Lake Erie or the Bay of Fundy. Of course, anyone can get from point A to point B quite comfortably in a Ford and have a perfectly enjoyable vacation in different places. Still, most people would prefer the Mercedes and Whistler, at least partly because they signal higher status. Access to tasteful cultural objects, then, is as much a matter of cost as of education.

Often, rich people engage in conspicuous displays of consumption, waste, and leisure not because they are necessary, useful, or pleasurable but simply to impress their peers and inferiors (Veblen, 1899). This display is evident if we consider how clothing acts as a sort of language that signals a person's status to others (Lurie, 1981).

For thousands of years, certain clothing styles have indicated rank. In ancient Egypt, only people in high positions were allowed to wear sandals. The ancient Greeks and Romans passed laws controlling the type, number, and colour of garments and the type of embroidery with which they could be trimmed. In medieval Europe, too, various aspects of dress were regulated to ensure that certain styles were specific to certain groups.

European laws governing the dress styles of different groups fell into disuse after about 1700, because a new method of control emerged as Europe became wealthier. From the eighteenth century on, the *cost* of clothing came to designate a person's rank. Expensive materials, styles that were difficult to care for, heavy jewellery, and superfluous trimmings became all the rage. It was not for comfort or utility that rich people wore elaborate powdered wigs, heavy damasked satins, the furs of rare animals, diamond tiaras, and patterned brocades and velvets. Such raiment was often hot, stiff, heavy, and itchy. They could scarcely move in many of these getups. And that was just their point—to prove not only that the wearer could afford enormous sums for handmade finery but also that he or she did not have to work to pay for them.

Today, we have different ways of using clothes to signal status. For instance, designer labels loudly proclaim the dollar value of garments. Another example: A great variety and quantity of clothing are required to maintain appearances. Thus, the well-to-do athletic type may have many different and expensive outfits that are "required" for jogging, hiking, cycling, aerobics, golf, tennis, and so forth. In fact, many people who really can't afford to obey the rules of conspicuous consumption, waste, and leisure feel compelled to do so anyway. As a result, they go into debt to maintain their wardrobes. Doing so helps them maintain prestige in the eyes of associates and strangers alike, even if their economic standing secretly falters.

NEL

SOCIAL MOBILITY

Mordecai Richler's *The Apprenticeship of Duddy Kravitz* (Richler, 1959) is one of the true classics of modern Canadian literature. Made into a 1974 film starring Richard Dreyfuss as Duddy, it is the story of a poor 18-year-old Jewish Montrealer in the mid-1940s desperately seeking to establish himself in the world. To that end, he waits on tables, smuggles drugs, drives a taxi, produces wedding and bar mitzvah films, and rents out pinball machines. He is an obnoxious charmer with relentless drive, a young man so fixed on making it that he is even willing to sacrifice his girlfriend and his only co-worker to achieve his goals. We cannot help but admire Duddy for his ambition and his artfulness even while being shocked by his guile and his single-mindedness.

Part of what makes *The Apprenticeship of Duddy Kravitz* universally appealing is that it could be a story about anyone on the make. It is not just some immigrants and their children who may start out as pushy little guys engaged in shady practices and unethical behaviour. As Richler reminds us in many places, some of the wealthiest establishment families in Canada and elsewhere started out in just this way. Duddy, then, is a universal symbol of "upward mobility"—and the compromises a person must sometimes make to achieve it (see Box 8.2).

Much of our discussion to this point has focused on how we describe inequality and how we explain its persistence. Now we take up a different, although related, set of questions. Is our position within the system of inequality fixed? To what extent, if at all, are we trapped in a disadvantaged social position or assured of maintaining an advantaged position? Canada is not a caste system. But at birth, do all people have the same freedom to gain wealth and fame? Are opportunities equally accessible to everyone?

Sociologists use the term *social mobility* to refer to the dynamics of the system of inequality and, in particular, to movement up and down the stratification system. If we think about inequality as either a hierarchy of more or less privileged positions or a set of higher and lower social classes, an important question is how much opportunity people have to change positions. Typically, change has been measured by using one of two benchmarks: your first position in the hierarchy (e.g., your first full-time job) or the position of your parents in the hierarchy. Comparing your first job to your current job is an examination of occupational or **intragenerational mobility**. Comparing the occupation(s) of parents to their children's current occupation is an examination of the inheritance of social position or **intergenerational mobility**.

Whichever benchmark is used, social mobility analysts are interested in the openness or fluidity of society. In open or fluid societies, there is greater equality of access to all positions in the hierarchy of inequality, both the low and the high. Regardless of your social origins, in more open societies you are more likely to rise or fall to a position that reflects your capabilities. In contrast, in closed or rigid societies, your social origins have major consequences for where you are located in the hierarchy of inequality. In such societies, poverty begets poverty, wealth begets wealth. In feudal Europe or in the Indian caste system, your birth determined your fate—you were a peasant or a lord based on the position of the family to which you were born.

More recently, societies have become more open in that your social origin does not completely determine your fate. Your chances in life are less dependent on the circumstances of your birth. Think about the changes in Canadian society over the last century. A mainly agrarian, resource-based economy has transformed into a modern, advanced postindustrial nation. We have experienced substantial growth in well-paying occupations in finance, marketing, management, and the professions. To what extent have people from all walks of life, from all economic backgrounds, been able to benefit from this transformation? This introduces a second, related theme to discussions of mobility—equality of opportunity.

As you can imagine from our earlier discussion, in the 1950s and 1960s proponents of the functional theory of stratification and human capital theory imagined that equality

Intragenerational mobility is social mobility that occurs within a single generation.

Intergenerational mobility is social mobility that occurs between generations.

BOX 8.2
Sociology at the Movies

TAKE ROLL

Sweet Home Alabama (2002)

Sweet Home Alabama is a Cinderella story with a twist: The successful heroine from humble beginnings gets the handsome prince but is not sure he is truly what she wants.

In the seven years since Melanie Carmichael (Reese Witherspoon) left her small-town Alabama home, she has achieved impressive upward social mobility. Beginning as a daughter of the working class, she has become a world-famous fashion designer in New York City. As the film begins, the mayor's son is courting Melanie. Andrew (Patrick Dempsey) proposes to her in Tiffany's, the upscale jewellery store that symbolizes upper-class consumption in the popular imagination. She says yes, but before she can marry him she has to clear up a not-so-minor detail: she needs a divorce from Jake (Josh Lucas), the childhood sweetheart she left behind.

Most of the story unfolds back in rural Alabama, in a town where friends climb the local water tower to drink beer and watch the folks pass by below, where major social events include Civil War re-enactments and catfish festivals, and where special hospitality is shown by offering guests hot pickles "right out of the grease." Melanie finds herself caught between two classes and two subcultures, and the film follows her struggle to reconcile her conflicting

Josh Lucas and Reese Witherspoon in *Sweet Home Alabama* (2002)

identities. Her dilemma will require her to acknowledge and reconnect with her mother (Mary Kay Place), who lives in a trailer park, while standing up to her future mother-in-law, the mayor of New York City (Candice Bergen).

In the end, Melanie returns to Jake, while Andrew, briefly heart-broken, pleases his mother by marrying a woman of his own class. Melanie's homecoming does not, however, require that she return to life in a trailer park. She discovers that while she was in New York, Jake had transformed himself. The working-class "loser" built a successful business as a glass blower. This change allows Melanie to imagine an upwardly mobile future by Jake's side.

Sweet Home Alabama sends the message that people are happiest when they marry within their own subculture. That message is comforting because it helps the audience reconcile itself to two realities. First, although many people may want to "marry up," most people do not in fact succeed in doing so. We tend to marry within our own class—and within our own religion and ethnic and racial group (Kalmijn, 1998: 406–08). Second, marrying outside your subculture is likely to be unsettling insofar as it involves abandoning old norms, roles, and values, and learning new ones. It is therefore a relief to learn from *Sweet Home Alabama* that you're better off marrying within your own subculture, especially since you will probably wind up doing just that.

The message has an ideological problem, however. Staying put in your own subculture denies the dream of upward mobility. *Sweet Home Alabama* resolves the problem by holding out the promise of upward mobility without having to leave home, as it were. Melanie and the transformed Jake can enjoy the best of both worlds, moving up the social hierarchy together without forsaking the community and the subculture they cherish. *Sweet Home Alabama* achieves a happy ending by denying the often difficult process of adapting to a new subculture while experiencing social mobility.

of opportunity would pervade society. They argued that as more and more skilled jobs are created in the new economy, the best and the brightest must rise to the top to take those jobs and perform them diligently. We would then move from a society based on ascription to one based on achievement. In a system of inequality based on ascription, your family's station in life determines your own fortunes. Conversely, in a system based on achievement, your own talents and your own merit determine your lot in life. If you achieve good grades in school, your chance of acquiring a professional or managerial job rises.

Other sociologists, however, have cautioned that this scenario of high individual social mobility might not follow from the transformation of the economy. These theorists, focusing more on the reproduction of inequality, emphasized how advantaged families have long attempted to ensure that their offspring inherit their advantages (Collins, 1979).

On the world stage, Blossfeld and Shavit (1993) demonstrated that in 11 of 13 advanced industrial countries, little evidence supports the view that there is greater equality of opportunity in societies with expanding education systems (Sweden and the Netherlands are the two exceptions). In short, the openness or fluidity of the system of inequality did not increase over the last half of the twentieth century.

Richard Wanner (1999) has tested these ideas at the postsecondary level by using Canadian data. He set himself the task of testing the idea that "Canada's investment in educational expansion reduced the amount of ascription in educational attainment" (Wanner, 1999: 409). What he was asking was this: Has the growth of education—more high schools, more colleges and universities—benefited people from all social backgrounds equally?

Socioeconomic status (SES) combines income, education, and occupational prestige data in a single index of a person's position in the socioeconomic hierarchy.

If ascription is weaker now than in previous decades, then parents' **socioeconomic status (SES)**—an index combining income, education, and occupational prestige data—should now have less effect on a child's education. In simple terms, if in earlier decades the chances of children from poorer families going to university were small, these chances should have increased in more recent decades if ascription was weakening. As measures of socioeconomic background, Wanner used mother's and father's education and father's occupation. He tested his central question by using detailed information from a sample of 31 500 Canadians.

Wanner found that class-based ascription still operates strongly. Despite the fact that more Canadians are acquiring more years of schooling and more degrees than ever before, the long arm of family socioeconomic background continues to exert a strong hold on educational attainment. The link between family advantage and children's educational achievement has not weakened.

Explanations for how and why this occurs remain a matter of controversy (Davies, 1999). The school system has become increasingly differentiated. Many routes through high-school vocational programs and college diploma programs are taken by students from lower socioeconomic backgrounds. Students from higher socioeconomic backgrounds typically continue on to university. Also, new high-school programs have proliferated. These include storefront schools for "at-risk" students in poorer neighbourhoods, language-immersion streams, private schools, and enriched learning tracks. These types of schools tend to enrol students from different socioeconomic backgrounds.

More recently, data from the National Longitudinal Survey of Children and Youth has demonstrated socioeconomic differences in children's preparedness or readiness for school (Ross, Roberts, and Scott, 2000). Children from households with incomes below $20 000 are 4.5 times as likely to have delayed vocabulary development as are children from families with incomes at or more than $50 000. Not only are they themselves less ready for school learning, but because family incomes are similar in the same neighbourhood, these students also often find themselves in schools with others who are less well prepared (Hertzman, 2000). A recent international study has replicated these findings, showing that a family's socioeconomic status affects a student's reading literacy, in this case among 15-year-olds. Importantly, however, the effect of socioeconomic status was less pronounced in Canada than in other countries (OECD, 2001).

Sociologists have also distinguished "equality of opportunity" from "equality of condition" to emphasize this point. Although everyone might have the legal opportunity to go to school, not everyone is socially able to take advantage of the opportunity. Coming to kindergarten hungry or not having been in high-quality child care before age five has an effect on how well a child will begin his or her formal schooling career. Equality of opportunity focuses on chances of participation, while equality of condition focuses on chances of succeeding. By way of analogy, we may all be able to enter the race, but if you come with track shoes and good coaching and I come with boots and no coaching, your chances of winning are higher, assuming that we have equal athletic skills.

POLITICS AND THE PERCEPTION OF CLASS INEQUALITY

WHERE DO
YOU FIT IN?

We expect you have had some strong reactions to our review of sociological theories and research on social stratification. You may therefore find it worthwhile to reflect more systematically on your own attitudes to social inequality. To start with, do you consider the family in which you grew up to have been lower class, working class, middle class, or upper class? Do you think the gaps between classes in Canadian society are big, moderate, or small? How strongly do you agree or disagree with the view that big gaps between classes are needed to motivate people to work hard and maintain national prosperity? How strongly do you agree or disagree with the view that inequality persists because it benefits the rich and the powerful? How strongly do you agree or disagree with the view that inequality persists because ordinary people don't join together to get rid of it? Answering these questions will help you clarify the way you perceive and evaluate the Canadian class structure and your place in it. If you take note of your answers, you can compare them with the responses of representative samples of Canadians, which we review below.

Surveys show that few Canadians have trouble placing themselves in the class structure when asked to do so. Most Canadians consider themselves to be middle class or working class. They also think that the gaps between classes are relatively large. But do Canadians think that these big gaps are needed to motivate people to work hard, thus increasing their own wealth and the wealth of the nation? Some Canadians think so, but most do not. A survey conducted in 18 countries, including Canada, asked more than 22 000 respondents if large differences in income are necessary for national prosperity. Canadians were among the most likely to disagree with that view (Pammett, 1997: 77).

So, Canadians know that they live in a class-divided society. They also tend to think that deep class divisions are not necessary for national prosperity. Why then do Canadians think inequality continues to exist? The 18-nation survey cited above sheds light on this issue. One of the survey questions asked respondents how strongly they agree or disagree with the view that "inequality continues because it benefits the rich and powerful." Most Canadians agreed with that statement. Only about a quarter of them disagreed with it in any way. Another question asked respondents how strongly they agree or disagree with the view that "inequality continues because ordinary people don't join together to get rid of it." Again, most Canadians agreed, with less than a third disagreeing in any way (Pammett, 1997: 77–78).

Despite widespread awareness of inequality and considerable dissatisfaction with it, most Canadians are opposed to the government playing an active role in reducing inequality. Most do not want government to provide citizens with a basic income. They tend to oppose government job-creation programs. They even resist the idea that government should reduce income differences through taxation (Pammett, 1997: 81). Most Canadians remain individualistic and self-reliant. On the whole, they persist in the belief that opportunities for mobility are abundant and that it is up to the individual to make something of those opportunities by means of talent and effort.

Significantly, however, all the attitudes summarized above vary by class position. For example, discontent with the level of inequality in Canadian society is stronger at the bottom of the stratification system than at the top. The belief that Canadian society is full of opportunities for upward mobility is stronger at the top of the class hierarchy than at the bottom. Considerably less opposition to the idea that government should reduce inequality exists as we move down the stratification system. This permits us to conclude that, if Canadians allow inequality to persist, it is because the balance of attitudes—and of power—favours continuity over change. We take up this important theme again in Chapter 14 (Politics), where we discuss the social roots of politics.

SUMMARY

1. **What is the difference between wealth and income? How are they distributed in Canada?**
    Wealth is assets minus liabilities. Income is the amount of money earned in a given period. Substantial inequality of both wealth and income exists in Canada but inequality of wealth is greater. Both types of inequality have increased over the past quarter of a century. Canada is less unequal than the United States in both regards, but Canada is more unequal in income than are several other wealthy societies.

2. **How does inequality change as societies develop?**
    Inequality increases as societies develop from the foraging to the early industrial stage. With increased industrialization, inequality declines. In the early stages of postindustrialism, inequality then increases in some countries (e.g., the United States) but not in others where governments take a more active role in redistributing income (e.g., France).

3. **What are the main differences between Marx's and Weber's theories of stratification?**
    Marx's theory of stratification distinguishes classes on the basis of their role in the productive process. It predicts inevitable conflict between bourgeoisie and proletariat and the birth of a communist system. Weber distinguished between classes on the basis of their "market relations." His model of stratification included four main classes. He argued that class consciousness may develop under some circumstances but is by no means inevitable. Weber also emphasized prestige and power as important non-economic sources of inequality.

4. **What is the functional theory of stratification?**
    Davis and Moore's functional theory of stratification argues that (1) some jobs are more important than others, (2) people have to make sacrifices to train for important jobs, and (3) inequality is required to motivate people to undergo these sacrifices. In this sense, stratification is "functional."

5. **Is stratification based only on economic criteria?**
    No. People often engage in conspicuous consumption, waste, and leisure to signal their position in the social hierarchy. Moreover, politics often influences the shape of stratification systems by changing the distribution of income, welfare entitlements, and property rights.

6. **How do Canadians view the class system?**
    Most Canadians are aware of the existence of the class system and their place in it. They believe that large inequalities are not necessary to achieve national prosperity. Most Canadians also believe that inequality persists because it serves the interests of the most advantaged members of society and because the disadvantaged do not join together to change things. However, most Canadians disapprove of government intervention to lower the level of inequality.

KEY TERMS

achievement (p. 231)

apartheid (p. 231)

ascription (p. 231)

authority (p. 238)

bourgeoisie (p. 233)

caste (p. 231)

class (p. 233)

class consciousness (p. 233)

cross-national variations in internal stratification (p. 228)

cultural capital (p. 220)

feudalism (p. 232)

functional theory of stratification (p. 235)

Gini index (p. 229)

global inequality (p. 228)

human capital (p. 219)

intergenerational mobility (p. 240)

intragenerational mobility (p. 240)

low-income cutoff (p. 223)

parties (p. 234)

petite bourgeoisie (p. 233)

power (p. 237)

proletariat (p. 233)

social capital (p. 220)

social mobility (p. 231)

social stratification (p. 231)

socioeconomic status (SES) (p. 242)

status groups (p. 234)

QUESTIONS TO CONSIDER

1. How do you think the Canadian and global stratification systems will change over the next 10 years? over the next 25 years? Why do you think these changes will occur?

2. Why do you think many Canadians oppose more government intervention to reduce the level of inequality in society? Before answering, think about the advantages that inequality brings to many people and the resources at their disposal for maintaining inequality.

3. Compare the number and quality of public facilities, such as playgrounds, public schools, and libraries, in various parts of your community. How is the distribution of public facilities related to the socioeconomic status of neighbourhoods? Why does this relationship exist?

4. Scientific advances in both microelectronics and biotechnology are significant features of this decade. How might these influence, and in turn be influenced by, inequality in contemporary Canada?

WEB RESOURCES

Companion Website for This Book

http://www.compass3e.nelson.com

Begin by clicking on the Student Resources section of the website. Next, select the chapter you are studying from the pull-down menu. From the Student Resources page you have easy access to InfoTrac® College Edition, additional Weblinks, and other resources. The website also has many useful tips to aid you in your study of sociology, including practice tests for each chapter.

InfoTrac® Search Terms

These search terms are provided to assist you in beginning to conduct research on this topic by visiting http://www.infotrac-college.com:

class

poverty

class consciousness

social mobility

global inequality

http://www.compass3e.nelson.com

NEL

Recommended Websites

For comprehensive income statistics about Canada, go to Statistics Canada at http://www.statcan.ca.

For financial information about Canada's publicly traded companies, go to the Toronto Stock Exchange at http://www.tsx.com.

For research on social and economic security, visit the Canadian Council on Social Development at http://www.ccsd.ca.

CengageNOW™

http://hed.nelson.com

This online diagnostic tool identifies each student's unique needs with a Pretest that generates a personalized Study Plan for each chapter, helping students focus on concepts they're having the most difficulty mastering. Students then take a Posttest after reading the chapter to measure their understanding of the material. An Instructor Gradebook is available to track and monitor student progress.

CHAPTER

11

Sexuality and Gender

In this chapter, you will learn that

- Whereas biology determines sex, social structure and culture largely determine gender or the expression of culturally appropriate masculine and feminine roles.

- The social construction of gender is evident in the way parents treat babies, teachers treat pupils, and the mass media portray ideal body images.

- The social forces pushing people to assume conventionally masculine or feminine roles are compelling.

- The social forces pushing people toward heterosexuality operate with even greater force.

- The social distinction between men and women serves as an important basis of inequality in the family and the workplace.

- Male aggression against women is rooted in gender inequality.

NEL

SEX VERSUS GENDER

Is It a Boy or a Girl?

TECHNOLOGY
BYTES

On April 27, 1966, eight-month-old identical twin boys were brought to a hospital in Winnipeg to be circumcised. An electrical cauterizing needle—a device that seals blood vessels as it cuts—was used for the procedure. However, because of equipment malfunction or doctor error, the needle entirely burned off one baby's penis. The parents desperately sought medical advice. No matter whom they consulted, they were given the same prognosis. As one psychiatrist summed up the baby's future, "He will be unable to consummate marriage or have normal heterosexual relations; he will have to recognize that he is incomplete, physically defective, and that he must live apart" (quoted in Colapinto, 1997: 58).

One evening, more than half a year after the accident, the parents, now deeply depressed, were watching TV. They heard Dr. John Money, a psychologist from Johns Hopkins Hospital in Baltimore, say that he could *assign* babies a male or female identity. Money had been the driving force behind the creation of the world's first "sex change" clinic at Johns Hopkins. He was well known for his research on **intersexed** infants, babies born with ambiguous genitals because of a hormone imbalance in the womb or some other cause. It was Money's opinion that infants with "unfinished genitals" should be assigned a sex by surgery and hormone treatments, and reared in accordance with their newly assigned sex. According to Money, these strategies would lead to the child developing a self-identity consistent with its assigned sex.

Intersexed infants are babies born with ambiguous genitals because of a hormone imbalance in the womb or some other cause.

The Winnipeg couple wrote to Dr. Money, who urged them to bring their child to Baltimore without delay. After consultation with various physicians and with Money, the parents agreed to have their son's sex reassigned. In anticipation of what would follow, the boy's parents stopped cutting his hair, dressed him in feminine clothes, and changed his name from Bruce to Brenda. Surgical castration was performed when the twin was 22 months old.

Early reports of the child's progress indicated success. In contrast to her biologically identical brother, Brenda was said to disdain cars, gas pumps, and tools. She was supposedly fascinated by dolls, a dollhouse, and a doll carriage. Brenda's mother reported that, at the age of four and a half, Brenda took pleasure in her feminine clothing: "[S]he is so feminine. I've never seen a little girl so neat and tidy . . . and yet my son is quite different. I can't wash his face for anything. . . . She is very proud of herself, when she puts on a new dress, or I set her hair" (quoted in Money and Ehrhardt, 1972: 11).

The "twins' case" generated worldwide attention. Textbooks in medicine and the social sciences were rewritten to incorporate Money's reports of the child's progress (Robertson, 1987: 316). But then, in March 1997, two researchers dropped a bombshell. A biologist from the University of Hawaii and a psychiatrist from the Canadian Ministry of Health unleashed a scientific scandal when they published an article showing that Bruce/Brenda had, in fact, struggled against his/her imposed girlhood from the start (Diamond and Sigmundson, 1999). Brenda insisted on urinating standing up, refused to undergo additional "feminizing" surgeries that had been planned, and, from age seven, daydreamed of her ideal future self "as a twenty-one-year-old male with a moustache, a sports car, and surrounded by admiring friends" (Colapinto, 2001: 93). She experienced academic failure and rejection and ridicule from her classmates, who dubbed her "Cavewoman." At age nine, Brenda had a nervous breakdown. At age 14, in a state of acute despair, she attempted suicide (Colapinto, 2001: 96, 262).

In 1980, Brenda learned the details of her sex reassignment from her father. At age 16, she decided to have her sex reassigned once more and to live as a man rather than as a woman. Advances in medical technology

David Reimer at about age 30.

NEL

made it possible for Brenda, who now adopted the name David, to have an artificial penis constructed. At age 25, David married a woman and adopted her three children, but that did not end his ordeal (Gorman, 1997). In May 2004, at the age of 38, David Reimer committed suicide.

Gender Identity and Gender Role

The story of Bruce/Brenda/David introduces the first big question of this chapter. What makes us male or female? Of course, part of the answer is biological. Your **sex** depends on whether you were born with distinct male or female genitals and a genetic program that released male or female hormones to stimulate the development of your reproductive system.

However, the case of Bruce/Brenda/David also shows that more is involved in becoming male or female than biological sex differences. Recalling his life as Brenda, David said, "[E]veryone is telling you that you're a girl. But you say to yourself, 'I don't *feel* like a girl.' You think girls are supposed to be delicate and *like* girl things—tea parties, things like that. But I like to *do* guy stuff. It doesn't match" (quoted in Colapinto, 1997: 66; our emphasis). As this quotation suggests, being male or female involves not just biology but also certain "masculine" and "feminine" feelings, attitudes, and behaviours. Accordingly, sociologists distinguish biological sex from sociological **gender**. A person's gender comprises the feelings, attitudes, and behaviours typically associated with being male or female. **Gender identity** is a person's identification with, or sense of belonging to, a particular sex—biologically, psychologically, and socially. When you behave according to widely shared expectations about how males or females are supposed to act, you adopt a **gender role**.

Contrary to first impressions, the case of Bruce/Brenda/David suggests that, unlike sex, gender is not determined just by biology. Research shows that babies first develop a vague sense of being a boy or a girl at about the age of one. They develop a full-blown sense of gender identity between the ages of two and three (Blum, 1997). We can therefore be confident that Bruce/Brenda/David already knew he was a boy when he was assigned a female gender identity at the age of 22 months. He had, after all, been raised as a boy by his parents and treated as a boy by his brother for almost two years. He had seen boys behaving differently from girls on TV and in storybooks. He had played with stereotypical boys' toys. After his gender reassignment, the constant presence of his twin brother reinforced those early lessons on how boys ought to behave. In short, baby Bruce's *social* learning of his gender identity was already far advanced by the time he had his sex-change operation. Many researchers believe that if gender reassignment occurs before the age of 18 months, it will usually be successful (Creighton and Mihto, 2001; Lightfoot-Klein, Chase, Hammond, and Goldman, 2000). However, once the social learning of gender takes hold, as with baby Bruce, it is apparently very difficult to undo, even by means of reconstructive surgery, hormones, and parental and professional pressure. The main lesson we draw from this story is not that biology is destiny but that the social learning of gender begins very early in life.

The first half of this chapter helps you to better understand what makes us male or female. We first outline two competing perspectives on gender differences. The first perspective argues that gender is inherent in our biological makeup and that society must reinforce those tendencies if it is to function smoothly. Functionalist theory is compatible with this argument. The second perspective argues that gender is constructed mainly by social influences and may be altered to benefit society's members. Conflict, feminist, and symbolic interactionist theories are compatible with the second perspective.

In our discussion we examine how people learn gender roles during socialization in the family and at school. We show how everyday social interactions and advertising reinforce gender roles. The imposition of relatively rigid gender roles consistent with patriarchy reduces options for both men and women, sometimes at substantial costs in personal fulfillment. We discuss how members of society enforce **heterosexuality**—the preference for members of the opposite sex as sexual partners. For reasons that are still poorly understood, some people

Your sex depends on whether you were born with distinct male or female genitals and a genetic program that released either male or female hormones to stimulate the development of your reproductive system.

Your gender is your sense of being male or female and your playing of masculine and feminine roles in ways defined as appropriate by your culture and society.

Gender identity is a person's identification with, or sense of belonging to, a particular sex—biologically, psychologically, and socially.

A gender role is the set of behaviours associated with widely shared expectations about how males and females are supposed to act.

Heterosexuality is the preference for members of the opposite sex as sexual partners.

resist and even reject the gender roles that are assigned to them based on their biological sex. When this occurs, negative sanctions are often applied to get them to conform or to punish them for their deviance. Members of society are often eager to use emotional and physical violence to enforce conventional gender roles.

The second half of the chapter examines one of the chief consequences of people learning conventional gender roles. Gender, as currently constructed, creates and maintains social inequality. We illustrate this in two ways. We investigate why gender is associated with an earnings gap between women and men in the paid labour force. We also show how gender inequality encourages sexual harassment and rape. In concluding our discussion of sexuality and gender, we discuss social policies that sociologists have recommended to decrease gender inequality and improve women's safety.

THEORIES OF GENDER

Most arguments about the origins of gender differences in human behaviour adopt one of two perspectives. Some analysts see gender differences as a reflection of naturally evolved dispositions. Sociologists call this perspective **essentialism** because it views gender as part of the nature or "essence" of a person's biological makeup (Weeks, 2000). Other analysts see gender differences as a reflection of the different social positions occupied by women and men. Sociologists call this perspective *social constructionism* because it views gender as "constructed" by social structure and culture. Conflict, feminist, and symbolic interactionist theories focus on various aspects of the social construction of gender. We now summarize and criticize essentialism. We then turn to social constructionism.

Essentialism **is a school of thought that views gender differences as a reflection of biological differences between women and men.**

Essentialism

Freud

Sigmund Freud (1977 [1905]) offered an early and influential essentialist explanation of male–female differences. He believed that differences in male and female anatomy account for the development of distinct masculine and feminine gender roles.

According to Freud, children around the age of three begin to pay attention to their genitals. As a young boy becomes preoccupied with his penis, he unconsciously develops a fantasy of sexually possessing the most conspicuous female in his life: his mother. Soon, he begins to resent his father because only his father is allowed to possess the mother sexually. Because he has seen his mother or another girl naked, the boy also develops anxiety that his father will castrate him for desiring his mother.[1] To resolve this fear, the boy represses his feelings for his mother. That is, he stores them in the unconscious part of his personality. In due course, repression allows him to begin identifying with his father. This leads to the development of a strong, independent masculine personality.

In contrast, the young girl begins to develop a feminine personality when she realizes she lacks a penis. According to Freud:

> [Girls] who notice the penis of a brother or playmate, strikingly visible and of large proportions, at once recognize it as the superior counterpart of their own small and inconspicuous organ, and from that time forward fall a victim to envy for the penis. . . . She has seen it and knows that she is without it and wants to have it. (quoted in Steinem, 1994: 50)

Because of her "penis envy," the young girl develops a sense of inferiority, according to Freud. She also grows angry with her mother, who, she naively thinks, is responsible for cutting off the penis she must have once had. She rejects her mother and develops an unconscious sexual desire for her father. Eventually, however, realizing she will never have a penis, the girl comes to identify with her mother. This is a way of vicariously acquiring her father's penis in Freud's view. In the "normal" development of a mature woman, the girl's wish to have a penis is transformed into a desire to have children. However, says Freud, since

NEL

women are never able to resolve their penis envy completely, they are "naturally" immature and dependent on men. This dependence is evident from the "fact" that women can be fully sexually satisfied only by vaginally induced orgasms.[2] Thus, a host of gender differences in personality and behaviour follow from the anatomical sex differences that children first observe around the age of three.

Sociobiology and Evolutionary Psychology

For the past three decades, sociobiologists and evolutionary psychologists have offered a second essentialist theory. We introduced this theory in Chapter 3, Culture. According to sociobiologists and evolutionary psychologists, all humans instinctively try to ensure that their genes are passed on to future generations. However, men and women develop different strategies to achieve this goal. A woman has a bigger investment than a man does in ensuring the survival of any offspring because she produces only a small number of eggs during her reproductive life and, at most, can give birth to about 20 children. It is therefore in a woman's best interest to maintain primary responsibility for her genetic children and to find the best mate with whom to intermix her eggs. He is the man who can best help support the children after birth. In contrast, most men can produce as many as a billion sperm in a single ejaculation and this number can be replicated often (Saxton, 1990: 94–5). Thus, a man increases the chance his and only his genes will be passed on to future generations if he is promiscuous yet jealously possessive of his partners. Moreover, since men compete with other men for sexual access to women, men evolve competitive and aggressive dispositions that include physical violence (DeSteno and Salovey, 2001). Women, says one evolutionary psychologist, are greedy for money, while men want casual sex with women, treat women's bodies as their property, and react violently to women who incite male sexual jealousy. These are "universal features of our evolved selves" that presumably contribute to the survival of the human species (Buss, 2000). From the point of view of sociobiology and evolutionary psychology, then, gender differences in behaviour are based in biological differences between women and men.

Functionalism and Essentialism

Functionalists reinforce the essentialist viewpoint when they claim that traditional gender roles help to integrate society (Parsons, 1942). In the family, wrote Talcott Parsons, women traditionally specialize in raising children and managing the household. Men traditionally work in the paid labour force. Each generation learns to perform these complementary roles by means of gender role socialization.

For boys, noted Parsons, the essence of masculinity is a series of "instrumental" traits, such as rationality, self-assuredness, and competitiveness. For girls, the essence of femininity is a series of "expressive" traits, such as nurturance and sensitivity to others. Boys and girls first learn their respective gender traits in the family as they see their parents going about their daily routines. The larger society also promotes gender role conformity. It instills in men the fear that they won't be attractive to women if the men are too feminine, and it instills in women the fear that they won't be attractive to men if the women are too masculine. In the functionalist view, then, learning the essential features of femininity and masculinity integrates society and allows it to function properly.

A Critique of Essentialism from the Conflict and Feminist Perspectives

Conflict and feminist theorists disagree sharply with the essentialist account. They have lodged four main criticisms against it.

First, *essentialists ignore the historical and cultural variability of gender and sexuality.* Wide variations exist in what constitutes masculinity and femininity. Moreover, the level of gender inequality, the rate of male violence against women, the criteria used for mate

Definitions of *male* and *female* traits vary across societies. For example, the ceremonial dress of male Wodaabe nomads in Niger may appear "feminine" by conventional North American standards.

selection, and other gender differences that appear universal to the essentialists vary widely too. This variation deflates the idea that there are essential and universal behavioural differences between women and men. Three examples help illustrate the point:

1. In societies with low levels of gender inequality, the tendency decreases for women to stress the good provider role in selecting male partners, as does the tendency for men to stress women's domestic skills (Eagley and Wood, 1999).
2. When women become corporate lawyers or police officers or take other jobs that involve competition or threat, their production of the hormone testosterone is stimulated, causing them to act more aggressively. Aggressiveness is partly role-related (Blum, 1997: 158–88).
3. Literally hundreds of studies conducted mainly in North America show that women are developing traits that were traditionally considered masculine. Women have become considerably more assertive, competitive, independent, and analytical in the past few decades (Biegler, 1999; Duffy, Gunther, and Walters, 1997; Nowell and Hedges, 1998; Twenge, 1997).

As these examples show, gender differences are not constants and they are not inherent in men and women. They vary with social conditions.

The second problem with essentialism is that *it tends to generalize from the average, ignoring variations within gender groups.* On average, women and men do differ in some respects. For example, one of the best-documented gender differences is that men are, on average, more verbally and physically aggressive than women are. However, when essentialists say men are inherently more aggressive than women are, they make it seem as if that is true of all men and all women. As Figure 11.1 shows, it is not. When trained researchers measure verbal or physical aggressiveness, scores vary widely within gender groups. There is considerable overlap in aggressiveness between women and men. Thus, many women are more aggressive than the average man and many men are less aggressive than the average woman.

Third, *little or no evidence directly supports the essentialists' major claims.* Sociobiologists and evolutionary psychologists have not identified any of the genes that, they claim, cause male jealousy, female nurturance, the unequal division of labour between men and women, and so forth. Freudians have not collected any experimental or survey data

NEL

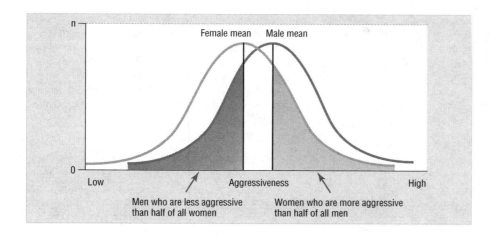

FIGURE 11.1
The Distribution of Aggressiveness among Men and Women

showing that boys are more independent than girls are because of their emotional reactions to the discovery of their sex organs.

Finally, *essentialists' explanations for gender differences ignore the role of power.* Essentialists assume that existing behaviour patterns help to ensure the survival of the species and the smooth functioning of society. However, as conflict and feminist theorists argue, essentialists generally ignore the fact that men are usually in a position of greater power and authority than women are.

Conflict theorists dating back to Marx's collaborator, Friedrich Engels, have located the root of male domination in class inequality (Engels, 1970 [1884]). According to Engels, men gained substantial power over women when preliterate societies were first able to produce more than the amount needed for their own subsistence. At that point, some men gained control over the economic surplus. They soon devised two means of ensuring that their offspring would inherit the surplus. First, they imposed the rule that only men could own property. Second, by means of socialization and force, they ensured that women remained sexually faithful to their husbands. As industrial capitalism developed, Engels wrote, male domination increased because industrial capitalism made men still wealthier and more powerful while it relegated women to subordinate, domestic roles.

Feminist theorists doubt that male domination is so closely linked to the development of industrial capitalism. For one thing, they note that gender inequality is greater in agrarian than in industrial capitalist societies. For another, male domination is evident in societies that call themselves socialist or communist. These observations lead many feminists to conclude that male domination is rooted less in industrial capitalism than in the patriarchal authority relations, family structures, and patterns of socialization and culture that exist in most societies (Lapidus, 1978: 7).

Despite this disagreement, conflict and feminist theorists concur that behavioural differences between women and men result less from any essential differences between them than from men being in a position to impose their interests over the interests of women. From the conflict and feminist viewpoints, functionalism, sociobiology, and evolutionary psychology can themselves be seen as examples of the exercise of male power, that is, as rationalizations for male domination and sexual aggression.

Social Constructionism and Symbolic Interactionism

Essentialism is the view that masculinity and femininity are inherent and universal traits of men and women, whether because of biological or social necessity or some combination of the two. In contrast, social constructionism is the view that *apparently* natural or innate features of life, such as gender, are actually sustained by *social* processes that vary historically

"Barbie was more than a doll to me. She was a way of living: the Ideal Woman."

and culturally. As such, conflict and feminist theories may be regarded as types of social constructionism. So may symbolic interactionism. Symbolic interactionists, you will recall, focus on the way people attach meaning to things in the course of their everyday communication. One of the things to which people attach meaning is what it means to be a man or a woman. We illustrate the symbolic interactionist approach by first considering how boys and girls learn masculine and feminine roles in the family and at school. We then show how gender roles are maintained in the course of everyday social interaction and through advertising in the mass media.

Gender Socialization

Barbie dolls have been around since 1959. Based on the creation of a German cartoonist, Barbie is the first modern doll modelled after an adult. (Lili, the German original, became a pornographic doll for men.) Some industry experts predicted mothers would never buy dolls with breasts for their little girls. Were *they* wrong! Mattel sells about 10 million Barbies and 20 million accompanying outfits annually. The Barbie trademark is worth US$1 billion.

What do girls learn when they play with Barbie? The author of a website devoted to Barbie undoubtedly speaks for millions when she writes, "Barbie was more than a doll to me. She was a way of living: the Ideal Woman. When I played with her, I could make her do and be ANYTHING I wanted. Never before or since have I found such an ideal method of living vicariously through anyone or anything. And I don't believe I am alone. I am certain that most people have, in fact, lived their dreams with Barbie as the role player" (Elliott, 1995; Nicolaiedis, 1998; Turkel, 1998).

One dream that Barbie stimulates among many girls concerns body image. After all, Barbie is a scale model of a woman with a 40-18-32 figure (Hamilton, 1996: 197). Researchers who compared Barbie's gravity-defying proportions with the actual proportions of several representative groups of adult women concluded that the probability of this body shape was less than 1 in 100 000 (Norton, Olds, Olive, and Dank, 1996). (Ken's body shape is far more realistic at 1 in 50.)

Nevertheless, for nearly half a century, Barbie has served as an identifiable symbol of stereotypical female beauty (Magro, 1997). Her pre-set Barbie Workout Scale registers a lithe 110 pounds (50 kilograms). The closets of her pink house are jammed with outfits. Bathrooms, gyms, and beauty parlours feature prominently among the Barbie sets available. Her quest for physical perfection seems largely geared to the benefit of Ken, her boyfriend (Nelson and Robinson, 2002: 131). When girls play with Barbie, they learn to want to be slim, blonde, shapely, and, implicitly, pleasing to men.

A comparable story, with competition and aggression as its theme, could be told about how boys' toys, such as GI Joe, teach stereotypical male roles. True, a movement to market more gender-neutral toys arose in the 1960s and 1970s. However, it has now been overtaken by the resumption of a strong tendency to market toys based on gender. As *The Wall Street Journal* pointed out, "gender-neutral is out, as more kids' marketers push single-sex products" (Bannon, 2000: B1). For example, in 2000, Toys "R" Us unveiled a new store design that included a store directory featuring Boy's World and Girl's World. The Boy's World section has action figures, sports collectibles, remote-controlled cars, Tonka trucks, boys' role-playing games, and walkie-talkies. The Girl's World section has Barbie dolls, baby dolls, collectible horses, play kitchens, housekeeping toys, girls' dress-up, jewellery, cosmetics, and bath and body products.

A movement to market more gender-neutral toys emerged in the 1960s and 1970s. However, it has now been overtaken by the resumption of a strong tendency to market toys based on gender.

Yet toys and the mass popular culture they represent are only part of the story of gender socialization and hardly its first or final chapter. Research shows that, from birth, infant boys and girls who are matched in length, weight, and general health are treated differently by parents—and by fathers in particular. Girls tend to be identified as delicate, weak, beautiful, and cute, boys as strong, alert, and well coordinated (Rubin, Provenzano,

NEL

and Lurra, 1974). Recent attempts to update and extend this investigation found that although parents' gender-stereotyped perceptions of newborns have declined, especially among fathers, they have not disappeared entirely (Fagot, Rodgers, and Leinbach, 2000; Gauvain, Fagot, Leve, and Kavanagh, 2002; Karraker, Vogel, and Lake, 1995). When viewing videotape of a nine-month-old infant, adult experimental subjects tend to label its startled reaction to a stimulus as "anger" if the child has earlier been identified by the experimenters as a boy and as "fear" if it has earlier been identified as a girl, *whatever the infant's actual sex* (Condry and Condry, 1976; see also Martin, 1999).

Parents, and especially fathers, are more likely to encourage their sons to engage in boisterous and competitive play and discourage their daughters from doing likewise. In general, parents tend to encourage girls to engage in cooperative, role-playing games (Fagot, Rodgers, and Leinbach, 2000; Gauvain et al., 2002; Parke, 2001, 2002). These different play patterns lead to the heightened development of verbal and emotional skills among girls, and to more concern with winning and the establishment of hierarchy among boys (Tannen, 1990). Boys are more likely than girls are to be praised for assertiveness, and girls are more likely than boys are to be rewarded for compliance (Kerig, Cowan, and Cowan, 1993). Given this early socialization, it seems perfectly "natural" that boys' toys stress aggression, competition, spatial manipulation, and outdoor activities, while girls' toys stress nurturing, physical attractiveness, and indoor activities (Hughes, 1995). Still, what seems natural must be continuously socially reinforced. Presented with a choice between playing with a tool set and a dish set, preschool boys are about as likely to choose one as the other—unless the dish set is presented as a girl's toy and they think their fathers would view playing with it as "bad." Then, they tend to pick the tool set (Raag and Rackliff, 1998).

It would take someone who has spent very little time in the company of children to think they are passive objects of socialization. They are not. Parents, teachers, and other authority figures typically try to impose their ideas of appropriate gender behaviour on children, but children creatively interpret, negotiate, resist, and self-impose these ideas all the time. Gender, we might say, is something that is done, not just given (Messner, 2000; West and Zimmerman, 1987). This fact is nowhere more evident than in the way children play.

Gender Segregation and Interaction

Consider the grade 4 and 5 classroom that sociologist Barrie Thorne (1993) observed. The teacher periodically asked the children to choose their own desks. With the exception of one girl, they always segregated *themselves* by gender. The teacher then drew on this self-segregation in pitting the boys against the girls in spelling and math contests. These contests were marked by cross-gender antagonism and expression of within-gender solidarity. Similarly, when children played chasing games in the schoolyard, groups often *spontaneously* crystallized along gender lines. These games had special names, some of which, such as "chase and kiss," had clear sexual meanings. Provocation, physical contact, and avoidance were all sexually charged parts of the game.

Although Thorne found that contests, chasing games, and other activities often involved self-segregation of boys and girls, she observed many cases of boys and girls playing together. She also noticed quite a lot of "boundary crossing." Boundary crossing involves boys playing stereotypically girls' games and girls playing stereotypically boys' games. The most common form of boundary crossing involved girls who were skilled at specific sports that were central to the boys' world—such sports as soccer, baseball, and basketball. If girls demonstrated skill at these activities, boys often accepted them as participants. Finally, Thorne noticed occasions in which boys and girls interacted without strain and without strong gender identities coming to the fore. For instance, activities requiring cooperation, such as a group radio show or art project, lessened attention to gender. Another situation that lessened strain between boys and girls, causing gender to recede in importance, occurred when adults organized mixed-gender encounters in the classroom and in physical education periods. On such occasions, adults legitimized cross-gender contact. Mixed-gender interaction was also more common in less public and crowded settings. Thus, boys

In her research on school-children, sociologist Barrie Thorne noticed quite a lot of "boundary crossing" between boys and girls. Most commonly, boys accepted girls as participants in soccer, baseball, and basketball games if the girls demonstrated skill at these sports.

A gender ideology is a set of interrelated ideas about what constitutes appropriate masculine and feminine roles and behaviour.

and girls were more likely to play together in a relaxed way in the relative privacy of their neighbourhoods. In contrast, in the schoolyard, where they were under the close scrutiny of their peers, gender segregation and antagonism were more evident.

In sum, Thorne's research makes two important contributions to our understanding of gender socialization. First, children are actively engaged in the process of constructing gender roles. They are not merely passive recipients of adult demands. Second, although schoolchildren tend to segregate themselves by gender, boundaries between boys and girls are sometimes fluid and sometimes rigid, depending on social circumstances. In other words, the content of children's gendered activities is by no means fixed.

This is not to suggest that adults have no gender demands and expectations. They do, and their demands and expectations contribute importantly to gender socialization. For instance, many school-teachers and guidance counsellors still expect boys to do better in the sciences and math and girls to achieve higher marks in English (Lips, 1999). Parents often reinforce these stereotypes in their evaluation of different activities (Eccles, Jacobs, and Harold, 1990). Although not all studies comparing mixed- and single-sex schools suggest that girls do much better in the latter, most do (Bornholt, 2001; Jackson and Smith, 2000). In single-sex schools, girls typically experience faster cognitive development; higher occupational aspirations and attainment; greater self-esteem and self-confidence; and more teacher attention, respect, and encouragement in the classroom. They also develop more egalitarian attitudes toward the role of women in society. Why? Because such schools place more emphasis on academic excellence and less on physical attractiveness and hetero-sexual popularity. They provide more successful same-sex role models. And they eliminate sex bias in teacher–student and student–student interaction since there are no boys around (Hesse-Biber and Carter, 2000: 99–100).

Adolescents must usually start choosing courses in school by the age of 14 or 15. By then, their **gender ideologies** are well formed. Gender ideologies are sets of interrelated ideas about what constitutes appropriate masculine and feminine roles and behaviour. One aspect of gender ideology becomes especially important around grades 9 and 10: adolescents' ideas about whether, as adults, they will focus mainly on the home, paid work, or a combination of the two. Adolescents usually make course choices with gender ideologies in mind. Boys are strongly inclined to consider only their careers in making course choices. Most girls are inclined to consider both home responsibilities and careers, although a minority considers only home responsibilities and another minority considers only careers. Consequently, boys tend to choose career-oriented courses, particularly in math and science, more often than girls do. In college and university, the pattern is accentuated. In 2006 women accounted for just 17 percent of Canadian university students in architecture and engineering (see Chapter 17, Education).

Young women tend to choose courses that lead to lower-paying jobs because they expect to devote a large part of their lives to child rearing and housework (Eccles, Roeser, Wigfield, and Freedman-Doen, 1999). When a sample of Canadian undergraduates were asked to identify their preference, 53 percent of the women but only 6 percent of the men selected "graduation, full-time work, marriage, children, stop working at least until youngest child is in school, then pursue a full-time job" as their preferred lifestyle sequence (Schroeder, Blood, and Maluso, 1993).

These choices sharply restrict women's career opportunities and earnings in science and business. In 2000, 76.5 percent of people working full-year, full-time in the 10 lowest-paid occupations in Canada were women. The average earnings of women in these occupations was $19 459 (Department of Justice Canada, 2004). We examine the wage gap between women and men in depth in the second half of this chapter.

The Mass Media and Body Image

The social construction of gender does not stop at the school steps. Outside school, children, adolescents, and adults continue to negotiate gender roles as they interact with the mass media. If you systematically observe the roles played by women and men in television, movies, magazines, music videos, TV commercials, and print media advertisements, you will probably discover a pattern noted by sociologists since the 1970s. Women will more frequently be seen cleaning house, taking care of children, modelling clothes, and acting as objects of male desire (Signorielli, 1998). Men will more frequently be seen in aggressive, action-oriented, and authoritative roles. The effect of these messages on viewers is much the same as that of the Disney movies and Harlequin romances we discussed in Chapter 4, Socialization: They reinforce the normality of traditional gender roles.

Steven Rytina learned just how powerful the mass media's lessons about traditional gender roles are when he was in his 20s. For several years, he worked in a daycare facility for children between the age of four and six. "It was the 1970s," Steven recalls, "and a big concern was to not pass on traditional gender stereotypes. Since most of the kids were from families where mothers and fathers had earned or were earning professional degrees, this project was popular and seemed straightforward. We were conscientious about using gender-neutral language, our storybooks were carefully screened to make sure they didn't portray women and men in stereotypical feminine and masculine roles, and so forth. Many of the kids' parents told me that they were trying to instill the same gender-neutral messages at home as we were at daycare.

PERSONAL ANECDOTE

"But to our surprise and dismay, it didn't work. When the kids played, their fantasies were the opposite of what we hoped for. For example, without exception, it was the little boys who turned towels into capes and the little girls who acted out peril, helplessness, and gratitude to their brave protectors. Strongly traditional gender themes were not merely apparent but overwhelmingly dominant.

"Finding out why was as simple as asking. We learned that the kids watched a lot of TV. The fantasies of Disney and Warner Brothers were far more compelling to them than any book or any teacher telling stories. I expect that most of the kids I worked with eventually adopted gender attitudes nearer what we hoped for. However, every one of them was at first fully immersed in stereotypes that their teachers and parents professed to disdain. My daycare experience taught me that it is very difficult to prevent children from absorbing the gender messages that dominate the mass media."

People even try to shape their bodies after the images portrayed in the mass media. The human body has always served as a sort of personal billboard that advertises gender. However, the importance of body image to our self-definition has grown over the past century. Just listen to the difference in emphasis on the body in the diary resolutions of two typical white, middle-class North American girls, separated by a mere 90 years. From 1892: "Resolved, not to talk about myself or feelings. To think before speaking. To work seriously. To be self restrained in conversation and actions. Not to let my thoughts wander. To be dignified. Interest myself more in others." From 1982: "I will try to make myself better in any way I possibly can with the help of my budget and baby-sitting money. I will lose weight, get new lenses, already got new haircut, good makeup, new clothes and accessories" (quoted in Brumberg, 1997: xxi).

As body image became more important for self-definition during the twentieth century, the ideal body image became thinner, especially for women. For example, although Miss America beauty pageant winners became only a little taller between 1922 and 1999, they became much thinner (Curran, 2000). As one eating disorders expert observed, "Beauty pageants, like the rest of our media-driven culture, give young women in particular a message, over and over again, that it's exceedingly important to be thin to be considered successful and attractive" (quoted in Curran, 2000).[3]

Why did body image become more important to people's self-definition during the twentieth century? Why was slimness stressed? Part of the answer to both questions is that more North Americans grew overweight as their lifestyles became more sedentary. As they became

The "White Rock Girl," featured on the logo of the White Rock beverage company, dropped 15 pounds between 1894 (left) and 1947 (right).

better educated, they also grew increasingly aware of the health problems associated with being overweight. The desire to slim down was, then, partly a reaction to bulking up. But that is not the whole story. The rake-thin models who populate modern ads are not promoting good health. They are promoting an extreme body shape that is virtually unattainable for most people (Tovee, Mason, Emery, McClusky, and Cohen-Tovee, 1997). They do so because it is good business. The fitness, diet, low-calorie food, and cosmetic surgery industries do billions of dollars of business a year in North America (Hesse-Biber, 1996). Bankrolled by these industries, advertising in the mass media blankets us with images of slim bodies and makes these body types appealing. Once people become convinced that they need to develop bodies like the ones they see in ads, many of them are really in trouble because these body images are impossible for most people to attain.

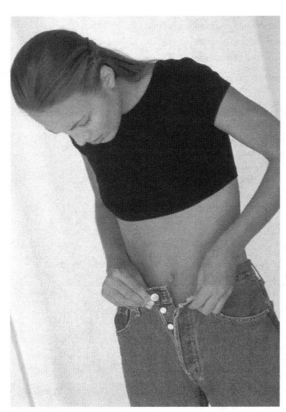

The low-calorie and diet food industry promotes an ideal of slimness that is often impossible to attain and that generates widespread body dissatisfaction.

Survey data show just how widespread dissatisfaction with our bodies is and how important a role the mass media play in generating our discomfort. One survey of North American university graduates showed that 56 percent of women and 43 percent of men were dissatisfied with their overall appearance (Garner, 1997). Only 3 percent of the dissatisfied women, but 22 percent of the dissatisfied men, wanted to gain weight. This difference reflects the greater desire of men for muscular, stereotypically male physiques. Most of the dissatisfied men, and even more of the dissatisfied women (89 percent), wanted to lose weight. This finding reflects the general societal push toward slimness and its greater effect on women. According to the National Population Health Survey, even though Canadian women are almost five times more likely than Canadian men to be *underweight* (14 percent and 3 percent, respectively), they are more likely to report recent attempts to lose weight: "This desire to lose weight extended to many women who were already within the healthy weight range" (Health Canada, 1999a: 118).

Figure 11.2 reveals gender differences in body ideals in a different way. It compares North American women's and men's attitudes toward their stomachs. It also compares women's attitudes toward their breasts with men's attitudes toward their chests. It shows, first, that women are more concerned about their stomachs than men are about their own. Second, it shows that men are more concerned about their chests than women are about their breasts. Clearly, then, people's body ideals are influenced by their gender. Note also that Figure 11.2 shows trends over time. North Americans' anxiety about their bodies increased substantially between 1972 and 1997.

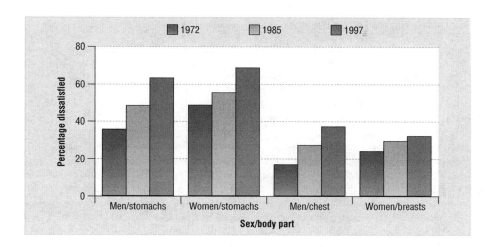

FIGURE 11.2

Body Dissatisfaction,
North America, 1972–1997
(in percent, *n* = 4000)

Note: The *n* of 4000 refers to the
1997 survey only. The number of
respondents in the earlier surveys
was not given.

Source: From "The 1997 Body Image
Results" by David M. Garner,
Psychology Today, Vol. 30, No. 1,
pp. 30–44. Reprinted from *Psychology
Today Magazine*, copyright © (1997)
Sussex Publishers, Inc.

Table 11.1 suggests that advertising is highly influential in creating anxiety and insecurity about appearance, and particularly about body weight. We see that nearly 30 percent of North American women compared themselves with the fashion models they saw in advertisements, felt insecure about their own appearance, and wanted to lose weight as a result. Among women who were dissatisfied with their appearance, the percentages were much larger, with about 45 percent making comparisons with fashion models and two-thirds feeling insecure and wanting to lose weight. It seems safe to conclude that fashion models stimulate body dissatisfaction among many North American women.

Body dissatisfaction, in turn, motivates many women to diet. Because of anxiety about their weight, 84 percent of North American women in the 1997 survey said they had dieted. The comparable figure for men was 54 percent. Just how important is it for people to achieve their weight goals? According to the survey, it's a life or death issue: 24 percent of women and 17 percent of men said they would willingly trade more than three years of their lives to achieve their weight goals.

Body dissatisfaction prompts some people to take dangerous and even life-threatening measures to reduce their size. In the 1997 survey, 50 percent of female smokers and 30 percent of male smokers said they smoked to control their weight. Other surveys suggest that between 1 percent and 5 percent of North American women suffer from anorexia nervosa (characterized by weight loss, excessive exercise, food aversion, distorted body image, and an intense and irrational fear of body fat and weight gain). About the same percentage of North American female university students suffer from bulimia, characterized by cycles of binge eating and purging (through self-induced vomiting or the use of laxatives, purgatives, or diuretics). For university men, the prevalence of bulimia is between 0.2 percent and 1.5 percent (Averett and Korenman, 1996: 305–06).

	Men	Women	Extremely Dissatisfied Women
I always or often:			
Compare myself with models in magazines	12	27	43
Carefully study the shape of models	19	28	47
Very thin or muscular models make me:			
Feel insecure about my weight	15	29	67
Want to lose weight	18	30	67

TABLE 11.1

The Influence of Fashion
Models on Feelings about
Appearance, North America
(in percent; *n* = 4000)

Source: From "The 1997 Body Image
Results" by David M. Garner,
Psychology Today, Vol. 30, No. 1,
pp. 30–44. Reprinted with
permission from *Psychology Today
Magazine*, copyright © (1997)
Sussex Publishers, Inc.

Male–Female Interaction

The gender roles children learn in their families, at school, and through the mass media form the basis of their social interaction as adults. For instance, by playing team sports, boys tend to learn that social interaction is most often about competition, conflict, self-sufficiency, and hierarchical relationships (leaders versus the led). They understand the importance of taking centre stage and boasting about their talents (Messner, 1995). Because many of the most popular video games for boys exclude female characters (*Game Boy* wasn't named *Game Boy* for nothing!), use women as sex objects, or involve violence against women, they reinforce some of the most unsavoury lessons of traditional gender socialization (Dietz, 1998). However, by playing with dolls and baking sets, girls tend to learn that social interaction is most often about maintaining cordial relationships, avoiding conflict, and resolving differences of opinion through negotiation (Subrahmanyam and Greenfield, 1998). They are informed of the importance of giving advice and not promoting themselves or being bossy.[4]

Because of these early socialization patterns, misunderstandings between men and women are common. A stereotypical example: Harold is driving around lost. However, he refuses to ask for directions because doing so would amount to an admission of inadequacy and therefore a loss of status. Meanwhile, it seems perfectly "natural" to Sybil to want to share information, so she urges Harold to ask for directions. The result: conflict between Harold and Sybil (Tannen, 1990: 62).

Gender-specific interaction styles also have serious implications for who is heard and who gets credit at work. Here are some examples uncovered by Deborah Tannen's research (1994a: 132–59):

- A female office manager doesn't want to seem bossy or arrogant. She is eager to preserve consensus among her co-workers. So she spends a good deal of time soliciting their opinions before making an important decision. She asks questions, listens attentively, and offers suggestions. She then decides. But her boss perceives her approach as indecisive and incompetent. He wants to recruit leaders for upper-management positions, so he overlooks the woman and selects an assertive man for a senior job that just opened up.
- Male managers are inclined to say "I" in many situations where female managers are inclined to say "we"—as in "I'm hiring a new manager and I'm going to put him in charge of my marketing division" or "This is what I've come up with on the Lakehill deal." This sort of phrasing draws attention to personal accomplishments. In contrast, Tannen heard a female manager talking about what "we" had done, when in fact she had done all the work alone. This sort of phrasing camouflages women's accomplishments.

The contrasting interaction styles illustrated above can result in female managers not getting credit for competent performance. That may be part of the reason why women sometimes complain about a **glass ceiling**, a social barrier that makes it difficult for them to rise to the top level of management. As we will soon see, factors other than interaction styles, such as outright discrimination and women's generally greater commitment to family responsibilities, also support the glass ceiling. Yet gender differences in interaction styles seem to play an independent role in constraining women's career progress.

HOMOSEXUALITY

The preceding discussion outlines some powerful social forces that push us to define ourselves as conventionally masculine or feminine in behaviour and appearance. For most people, gender socialization by the family, the school, and the mass media is compelling and is sustained by daily interactions. A minority of people, however, resists conventional gender roles.

Transgendered people defy society's gender norms and blur widely accepted gender roles (Cole, Denny, Eyler, and Samons, 2000: 151). About 1 in every 5000 to 10 000 people in North America is transgendered. Some transgendered people are **transsexuals**. Transsexuals are individuals who want to alter their gender by changing their appearance

The glass ceiling is a social barrier that makes it difficult for women to rise to the top level of management.

Transgendered people break society's gender norms by defying the rigid distinction between male and female.

Transsexuals believe they were born with the "wrong" body. They identify with, and want to live fully as, members of the "opposite" sex.

NEL

or resorting to medical intervention. Transsexuals believe they were born with the "wrong" body. They identify with, and want to live fully as, members of the "opposite" sex. They often take the lengthy and painful path to a sex change operation. About 1 in every 30 000 people in North America is a transsexual (Nolen, 1999). **Homosexuals** are people who prefer sexual partners of the same sex, and **bisexuals** are people who enjoy sexual partners of either sex. People usually call homosexual men *gay* and homosexual women *lesbians*. In 2000, about 6 percent of Torontonians identified themselves as homosexual or bisexual ("Homosexuality and Bisexuality," 2000). In 2003, 1.8 percent of Canadian men and 1.5 percent of Canadian women described themselves as homosexual or bisexual in response to surveys (Statistics Canada, 2004c). The most comprehensive survey of sexuality conducted in North America reports that an approximately comparable 2.8 percent of American men and 1.4 percent of American women pick homosexual or bisexual as self-descriptions. However, the American investigation also discovered that 10.1 percent of men and 8.6 percent of women think of themselves as homosexual or bisexual *or* have had some same-sex experience or desire (see Table 11.2; Laumann, Gagnon, Michael, and Michaels, 1994: 299). It seems likely that because of widespread animosity toward homosexuals, some people who have desired or engaged in same-sex acts do not identify themselves as gay, lesbian, or bisexual (Flowers and Buston, 2001; Herdt, 2001).

Homosexuality has existed in every society. Some societies, such as ancient Greece, have encouraged it. More frequently, however, homosexual acts have been forbidden (see Box 11.1 on page 320). In both the past and present, most laws prohibiting homosexual behaviour have targeted male rather than female homosexuality (Brown, 2000). Worldwide as of 2008, 7 countries mandated the death penalty for male and female homosexuality, while 76 countries and 6 other jurisdictions mandated imprisonment. Some 49 countries and 33 other jurisdictions had antidiscrimination laws on the books. Only 19 countries and 14 other jurisdictions legally recognized same-sex unions. A mere 5 countries (Belgium, Canada, the Netherlands, South Africa, and Spain) allowed same-sex marriage (International Lesbian and Gay Association, 2008).

Homosexuals were not identified as a distinct category of people until the 1860s, when the term *homosexuality* was coined. The term *lesbian* is of even more recent vintage.

We do not yet understand well why some individuals develop homosexual orientations. Some scientists believe that the cause of homosexuality is mainly genetic (Hamer, Copeland, Hu, Magnuson, Hu, and Pattatucci, 1993; Pillard and Bailey, 1998), others think it is chiefly hormonal, while still others point to life experiences during early childhood as the most important factor (Brannock and Chapman, 1990; Doell, 1995). The scientific consensus is that homosexuality "emerges for most people in early adolescence without any prior sexual experience . . . [it] is not changeable" (American Psychological Association, 1998). A study of homosexual men in the United States found that 90 percent believed they were born with their homosexual orientation and only 4 percent felt that environmental factors were the sole cause (Lever, 1994). Gallup poll findings also suggest that the general public increasingly believes that homosexuality is not so much a "preference" as an innate orientation (13 percent in 1977 compared with 34 percent in 1999; Gallup Organization, 2000). Beliefs about the causes of homosexuality are also related to people's attitudes

Homosexuals are people who prefer sexual partners of the same sex. People usually call homosexual men *gay* and homosexual women *lesbians*.

Bisexuals are people who enjoy sexual partners of both sexes.

	Men	Women
Identified themselves as homosexual or bisexual	2.8	1.4
Had sex with person of same sex in past 12 months	3.4	0.6
Had sex with person of same sex at least once since puberty	5.3	3.5
Felt desire for sex with person of same sex	7.7	7.5
Had some same-sex desire or experience or identified themselves as homosexual or bisexual	10.1	8.6

TABLE 11.2

Homosexuality in the United States (in percent; *n* = 3432)

Source: Michael, Gagnon, Laumann, and Kolata, 1994: 40.

BOX 11.1
Sociology at the Movies

NO. | TAKE | ROLL

Brokeback Mountain (2005)

It would not be an exaggeration to say that Westerns—often called "Cowboy and Indian" movies—shaped a generation of North Americans' expectations about gender and sexuality. John Wayne, Gary Cooper, Jimmy Stewart, and many others became role models for North American men and their idea of masculinity: silent but strong, gentle toward the weak (women and children) but ferocious toward the evil (often Aboriginals), community-minded but ultimately lone, rugged individualists. Even today, it's hard not to be stirred and engrossed by such classic Westerns as *The Man Who Shot Liberty Valance* and *High Noon.*

Jack (Jake Gyllenhaal; left) and Ennis (Heath Ledger) in *Brokeback Mountain*

Westerns, however, have not been a popular genre since the 1970s. The Civil Rights movement questioned the racial ideology of many Westerns, which presumed the superiority of the white race against the native populations. The movement against the War in Vietnam challenged the vision of the world as a place that ought to be pacified and ruled by whites. The feminist movement criticized the patriarchal masculine viewpoint of Westerns. The few Westerns since the 1970s have therefore deviated from classical Westerns, often parodying them.

Brokeback Mountain (2005), nominated for the 2005 best picture Oscar, traces the romantic love between two cowboys. They fall in love in the early 1960s, when both are 19 years old, long before they had heard of gay culture or

even the notion of homosexual identity. They lead seemingly conventional married lives. Yet they continue to love each other and carry on their affair for two decades, periodically telling their wives that they are going on fishing trips together but raising suspicions when they fail to bring any fish home. More than the passion, however, what the movie depicts is the high emotional cost of keeping one's sexual orientation and one's love a secret. Eventually, their marriages crumble, their social relationships suffer, and happiness and fulfillment prove elusive.

One of the reasons that Ennis (the late Heath Ledger, nominated for the 2005 best actor Oscar) cannot imagine the possibility of settling down with Jack (Jake Gyllenhaal,

nominated for the 2005 best supporting actor Oscar) is a childhood experience. His father took him to see two men who were beaten to death, two "tough old birds" who happened to be "shacked up together." Fear of expressing his homosexuality was thus instilled early on. (In fact, both men deny their homosexuality. After their first night together, Ennis says to Jack, "You know I ain't queer." To which Jack replies, "Me neither.") Jack and Ennis's affair ends when Jack is beaten to death by homophobic men. Three grisly murders of gay men, then, provide the tragic backdrop to *Brokeback Mountain.* How much have things changed since the 1960s, '70s, and '80s? Could *Brokeback Mountain* be set in 2009?

toward homosexuals. For example, one national poll reported that "those who believe homosexuals choose their sexual orientation are far less tolerant of gays and lesbians and more likely to conclude homosexuality should be illegal than those who think sexual orientation is not a matter of personal choice" (Rosin and Morin, 1999: 8).

In general, sociologists are less interested in the origins of homosexuality than in the way it is socially constructed, that is, in the wide variety of ways it is expressed and repressed (Plummer, 1995). It is important to note in this connection that homosexuality

Especially since the middle of the twentieth century, gays and lesbians have gone public with their lifestyles. They have organized demonstrations, parades, and political pressure groups to express their self-confidence and demand equal rights with the heterosexual majority. This has done much to legitimize homosexuality and sexual diversity in general.

has become less of a stigma over the past century. Two factors are chiefly responsible for this, one scientific, the other political. In the twentieth century, sexologists—psychologists and physicians who study sexual practices scientifically—first recognized and stressed the wide diversity of existing sexual practices. Alfred Kinsey was among the pioneers in this field. He and his colleagues interviewed thousands of men and women. In the 1940s, they concluded that homosexual practices were so widespread that homosexuality could hardly be considered an illness affecting a tiny minority (Kinsey, Pomeroy, and Martin, 1948; Kinsey et al., 1953; see also Box 2.2 in Chapter 2, How Sociologists Do Research).

Sexologists, then, provided a scientific rationale for belief in the normality of sexual diversity. However, it was sexual minorities themselves who provided the social and political energy needed to legitimize sexual diversity among an increasingly large section of the public. Especially since the middle of the twentieth century, gays and lesbians have built large communities and subcultures, particularly in major urban areas, such as Vancouver, Winnipeg, Toronto, and Montreal (Greenhill, 2001; Ingram, 2001). They have gone public with their lifestyles (Owen, 2001). They have organized demonstrations, parades, and political pressure groups to express their self-confidence and demand equal rights with the heterosexual majority (Goldie, 2001). This has done much to legitimize homosexuality and sexual diversity in general.

Yet opposition to people who don't conform to conventional gender roles remains strong at all stages of the life cycle. When you were a child, did you ever poke fun at a sturdily built girl who was good at sports by referring to her as a "dyke"? As an adolescent or a young adult, have you ever insulted a man by calling him a "fag"? If so, your behaviour was not unusual. Many children and adults believe that heterosexuality is superior to homosexuality and they are not embarrassed to say so. "That's so gay!" is commonly used as an expression of disapproval among teenagers.

Among adults, such opposition is just as strong. What is your attitude today toward transgendered people, transsexuals, and homosexuals? Do you, for example, think relations between adults of the same sex are always, or almost always, wrong? If so, you are again not that unusual. A national survey of Canadians conducted in 2000 found that almost one in three Canadians believed same-sex relations were "always wrong." Although discouraging to some people, this figure represents an increase in Canada's acceptance of homosexuality over the past three decades. In 1975, 63 percent of Canadians viewed homosexuality

WHERE DO
YOU FIT IN?

in this disapproving way (*Maclean's*, 2002: 12). Another indication of changing sentiments is that in 2005 Parliament authorized marriage for same-sex couples, making Canada the world's fourth country to adopt such legislation (the Netherlands was first in 2001). Nonetheless, a 2005 survey showed that only 48 percent of Canadians favoured same-sex marriage (CBC News, 2005). Tolerance is advancing and is most widespread among young Canadians, but substantial hostility remains.

Antipathy to homosexuals is so strong among some people that they are prepared to back up their beliefs with force. A study of about 500 young adults in the San Francisco Bay area (one of the most sexually tolerant areas in North America) found that 1 in 10 admitted physically attacking or threatening people he or she believed were homosexuals. Twenty-four percent reported engaging in anti-gay name-calling. Among male respondents, 18 percent reported acting in a violent or threatening way and 32 percent reported name-calling. In addition, a third of those who had *not* engaged in anti-gay aggression said they would do so if a homosexual flirted with, or propositioned, them (Franklin, 1998; see also Bush and Sainz, 2001; Faulkner and Cranston, 1998).

The consequences of such attitudes can be devastating. For example, 14-year-old Christian Hernandez of Niagara Falls, Ontario, told his best friend that he was gay. "He told me he couldn't accept it," recalls Hernandez. "And he began to spread it around." For two years, Hernandez was teased and harassed almost daily. After school one day, a group of boys waited for him. Their leader told Hernandez that "he didn't accept faggots, that we brought AIDS into the world" and stabbed him in the neck with a knife. Hernandez required a week's hospitalization. When he told his parents what had happened, his father replied that he'd "rather have a dead son than a queer son" (Fisher, 1999).

Research suggests that some anti-gay crimes may result from repressed homosexual urges on the part of the aggressor (Adams, Wright, and Lohr, 1998). From this point of view, aggressors are **homophobic** or afraid of homosexuals because they cannot cope with their own, possibly subconscious, homosexual impulses. Their aggression is a way of acting out a denial of these impulses. Although this psychological explanation may account for some anti-gay violence, it seems inadequate when set alongside the finding that fully half of all young male adults admitted to some form of anti-gay aggression in the San Francisco study cited above. An analysis of the motivations of these San Franciscans showed that some of them did commit assaults to prove their toughness and heterosexuality. Others committed assaults just to alleviate boredom and have fun. Still others believed they were defending themselves from aggressive sexual propositions. A fourth group acted violently because they wanted to punish homosexuals for what they perceived as moral transgressions (Franklin, 1998). It seems clear, then, that anti-gay violence is not just a question of abnormal psychology but a broad cultural problem with several sources.

Anecdotal evidence suggests that opposition to anti-gay violence is also growing (see Box 11.2). The 1999 movie *Boys Don't Cry* also raised awareness of the problem of violence directed against sexual minorities. The movie, for which Hilary Swank won the Best Actress Oscar, tells the true story of Teena Brandon, a young woman with a sexual identity crisis. She wants a sex-change operation but can't afford one. So she decides to change her name to Brandon Teena and pass as a man. She soon develops an intimate relationship with a woman by the name of Lana Tisdel. When Lana's ex-boyfriend and his friend discover the truth about Teena, they beat, rape, and ultimately murder her. Teena's only transgression was that she wanted to be a man.

In sum, strong social and cultural forces lead us to distinguish men from women and heterosexuals from homosexuals. We learn these distinctions throughout the socialization process, and we continuously construct them anew in our daily interactions. Most people use positive and negative sanctions to ensure that others conform to conventional heterosexual gender roles. Some people resort to violence to enforce conformity and punish deviance.

Our discussion also suggests that the social construction of conventional gender roles helps create and maintain social inequality between women and men. In the remainder of this chapter, we examine the historical origins and some of the present-day consequences of gender inequality.

Homophobic people are afraid of homosexuals.

BOX 11.2
It's Your Choice

Hate Crime Law and Homophobia

On November 17, 2001, Aaron Webster, a 42-year-old gay man, was beaten to death in Vancouver. Tim Chisholm, Aaron's friend for 15 years, discovered Aaron's bloodied body, naked except for his hiking boots, in a parking lot in Stanley Park. Aaron had been bludgeoned with either a baseball bat or a pool cue by a group of three to four men. After phoning 911, Chisholm attempted CPR on his unconscious friend. It was no use. Aaron died in Chisholm's arms before help could arrive.

This brutal murder is believed to have been British Columbia's first fatal "gay bashing." At a memorial service for Webster that drew more than 1500 people, Vancouver Police Inspector Dave Jones identified Webster as the victim of "a hate crime, pure and simple" and pledged that the city's police department would "do everything in our power" to find the perpetrators and "bring them to justice" (Associated Press, 2001; Nagle, 2001).

One issue raised by Webster's death concerns the definition of hate crime (Wetzel, 2001). Hate crimes are criminal acts motivated by a victim's race, religion, or ethnicity. Under section 319 of the Canadian Criminal Code, the willful promotion of hatred against any identifiable group (that is, "any section of the public distinguished by colour, race, religion, or ethnic group") and the advocating of genocide are crimes punishable by up to two years' imprisonment. In 1999, following the gay bashing of a student in Fredericton, New Brunswick, then Justice Minister Anne McLellan announced that she would introduce amendments to protect lesbians and gays from hate crimes. She did not do so. Following Webster's murder, MP Svend Robinson introduced a Private Member's Bill that sought to include sexual orientation among the grounds protected by hate crimes legislation.

If hate motivates a crime, Canadian law requires that the perpetrator be punished more severely than otherwise. Under section 718.2 of the Criminal Code of Canada, "evidence that the offence was motivated by bias, prejudice or hate based on race, national or ethnic origin, language, colour, religion, sex, age, mental or physical disability, sexual orientation or any other similar factor" is to be considered an aggravating circumstance only in sentencing convicted offenders. For example, assaulting a person during an argument generally carries a lighter punishment than assaulting a person because he or she is gay or Jewish or black. However, despite this provision in law, "gay-bashers are often able to rely on the discredited 'homosexual panic' defence, claiming they were justified in committing murder because the victim 'came on' to them" (EGALE, 2001).

Do you think crimes motivated by the victim's sexual orientation are the same as crimes motivated by the victim's race, religion, or ethnicity? If so, why? If not, why not? Do you think crimes motivated by the perceived sexual orientation of the victim should be included in the legal definition of a hate crime? Why or why not?

GENDER INEQUALITY

The Origins of Gender Inequality

Contrary to what essentialists say, men have not always enjoyed much more power and authority than women have. Substantial inequality between women and men has existed for only about 6000 years. It was socially constructed. Three major socio-historical processes account for the growth of gender inequality.

Long-Distance Warfare and Conquest

The anthropological record suggests that women and men were about equal in status in nomadic hunting-and-gathering societies, the dominant form of society for 90 percent of human history. Rough gender equality was based on the fact that women produced a substantial amount of the band's food, up to 80 percent in some cases (see Chapter 15, Families). The archaeological record from "Old Europe" tells a similar story. Old Europe is a region stretching roughly from Poland in the north to the Mediterranean island of Crete in the south, and from Switzerland in the west to Bulgaria in the east (see Figure 11.3 on page 324). Between 7000 and 3500 BCE, men and women enjoyed approximately equal

FIGURE 11.3
Old Europe

Source: Gimbutas, 1982: 16.

status throughout the region. In fact, the religions of the region gave primacy to fertility and creator goddesses. Kinship was traced through the mother's side of the family. Then, sometime between 4300 and 4200 BCE, all this began to change. Old Europe was invaded by successive waves of warring peoples from the Asiatic and European northeast (the Kurgans) and the deserts to the south (the Semites). Both the Kurgan and Semitic civilizations were based on a steeply hierarchical social structure in which men were dominant. Their religions gave primacy to male warrior gods. They acquired property and slaves by conquering other peoples and imposed their religions on the vanquished. They eliminated, or at least downgraded, goddesses as divine powers. God became a male who willed that men should rule women. Laws reinforced women's sexual, economic, and political subjugation to men. Traditional Judaism, Christianity, and Islam all embody ideas of male dominance, and they all derive from the tribes that conquered Old Europe in the fifth millennium BCE (Eisler, 1987; see also Lerner, 1986).

Plow Agriculture

Long-distance warfare and conquest catered to men's strengths and so greatly enhanced male power and authority. Large-scale farming using plows harnessed to animals had a similar effect. Plow agriculture originated in the Middle East around 5000 years ago. It required that strong adults remain in the fields all day for much of the year. It also reinforced the principle of private ownership of land. Since men were on average stronger than women were, and since women were restricted in their activities by pregnancy, childbirth, and nursing, plow agriculture made men more powerful socially. Thus, men owned land and ownership was passed from the father to the eldest son (Coontz and Henderson, 1986).

The Separation of Public and Private Spheres

In the agricultural era, economic production was organized around the household. Men may have worked apart from women in the fields but the fields were still part of the *family* farm. In contrast, during the early phase of industrialization, men's work moved out of the

NEL

household and into the factory and the office. Most men became wage or salary workers. Some men assumed decision-making roles in economic and political institutions. Yet while men went public, women who could afford to do so remained in the domestic or private sphere. The idea soon developed that this was a natural division of labour. This idea persisted until the second half of the twentieth century, when a variety of social circumstances, ranging from the introduction of the birth control pill to women's demands for entry into higher education, finally allowed women to enter the public sphere in large numbers.

So we see that, according to social constructionists, gender inequality derives not from any inherent biological features of men and women but from three main socio-historical circumstances: the arrival of long-distance warfare and conquest, the development of plow agriculture, and the assignment of women to the domestic sphere and men to the public sphere during the early industrial era.

The Earnings Gap Today

After reading this brief historical overview, you might be inclined to dismiss gender inequality as a thing of the past. If so, your decision would be hasty. Gender inequality is evident if we focus on the earnings gap between men and women, one of the most important expressions of gender inequality today.

Canadian data on the earnings of women and men were first reported in 1967. At that time, the ratio of female to male earnings stood at around 58 percent. In 1992, it passed 70 percent and has fluctuated near that level since then (Figure 11.4).

Figure 11.5 on page 326 shows that women earn less than men do at every level of education. However, the wage gap between men and women varies among different categories. For example, Table 11.3 on page 327 illustrates the gender wage gap in the average earnings of people in the 10 highest-paying and 10 lowest-paying occupations in Canada. If the wage gap were due to universal gender differences, it would not vary across occupations. But it does vary considerably, suggesting that social conditions specific to given occupations account in part for the magnitude of the gender wage gap.

Four main factors contribute to the gender gap in earnings (Bianchi and Spain, 1996; England, 1992):

1. *Gender discrimination.* In February 1985, when Microsoft already employed about 1000 people, it hired its first two female executives. According to a well-placed source involved in the hiring, both women got their jobs because Microsoft was trying to win a U.S. Air Force contract. Under the government's guidelines, it didn't have enough women in top management positions to qualify. The source quotes then 29-year-old Bill

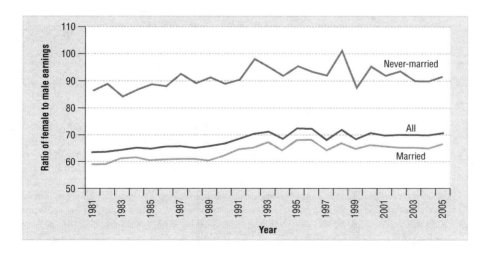

FIGURE 11.4
Ratio of Female to Male Earnings, Canada, 1980–2005

Source: Statistics Canada, 2008, CANSIM Table 2020104. Retrieved May 2, 2008 (http://dc1.chass. utoronto.ca.myaccess.library.utoronto. ca/cgi-bin/cansimdim/c2_ search Cansim.pl).

FIGURE 11.5

Hourly Wages by Educational Attainment for Men and Women, Canada, 2003

Source: Adapted from Statistics Canada, 2003, "The Canadian Labour Market at a Glance," Catalogue 71-222. Retrieved November 17, 2004 (http://www.statcan.ca/english/freepub/71-222-XIE/71-222-XIE2004000.htm).

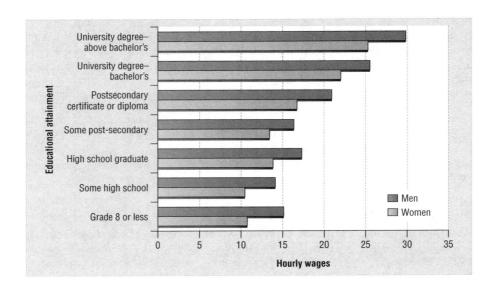

Gender discrimination involves rewarding men and women differently for the same work.

Gates, president of Microsoft, as saying: "Well, let's hire two women because we can pay them half as much as we will have to pay a man, and we can give them all this other 'crap' work to do because they are women" (quoted in Wallace and Erickson, 1992: 291). This incident is a clear illustration of **gender discrimination**, rewarding women and men differently for the same work. Discrimination on the basis of sex is against the law in Canada. Yet progress is slow; as noted earlier, the female–male earnings ratio has not improved since 1992. If the rate of improvement between 1980 and 2005 were to persist, women would not earn as much as men until 2118.

2. *Women tend to be concentrated in low-wage occupations and industries.* The second factor leading to lower earnings for women is that the programs they select in high school and afterwards tend to limit them to jobs in low-wage occupations and industries. The concentration of women in certain occupations and men in others is referred to as *occupational sex segregation.* Although women have made big strides since the 1970s, especially in managerial employment, they are still concentrated in lower-paying clerical and service occupations and underrepresented in higher-paying manual occupations (Table 11.4 on page 328). This is particularly true for women of colour, Aboriginal women, and women with disabilities (Chard, 2000: 229). In contrast to men in visible minority groups, who are concentrated in professional occupations and service jobs in higher proportions than Canadians are overall, women in visible minority groups are more likely than Canadian women as a whole to do manual labour. Similarly, working-age women with disabilities are less likely than working-age men with disabilities to be employed (Shain, 1995).

3. *Heavy domestic responsibilities reduce women's earnings.* In 2005, Canadian women who had never been married earned 91.7 cents for every dollar earned by men. The comparable figure for married women was 66.7 cents (see Figure 11.4). A substantial part of this 25-cent gap represents the economic cost to women of getting married and assuming disproportionately heavy domestic responsibilities. Of course, raising children can be one of the most emotionally satisfying experiences. That should not, however, blind us to the fact it is also work that decreases the time available for education, training, and paid work. Because women are disproportionately involved in child rearing, they suffer the brunt of this economic reality. They devote fewer hours to paid work than men do, experience more labour-force interruptions, and are more likely than men to take part-time jobs, which pay less per hour and offer fewer benefits than full-time work does (Waldfogel, 1997). Women also do considerably more housework

TABLE 11.3

Earnings of Men and of Women and Gender Composition in the Ten Best Paid Occupations, Canada, 2000

Note: Only full-time, full-year workers are included.

Source: Adapted from Statistics Canada, Publication Profile of the Canadian Population by Age and Sex: Canada Ages, 2001 Census, Catalogue No. 96F0030XIE2001002.

Occupation	Number Employed	Average Earnings in $	Average Male Earnings in $	Average Female Earnings in $	Female Percentage in Occupation	F/M Earnings Percentage
Judges	1 825	142 518	146 008	131 663	24.4	90.2
Specialist physicians	12 480	141 597	160 833	98 383	30.8	61.2
Senior managers: Financial, communications carriers, and other business services	40 910	130 802	141 829	90 622	21.5	63.9
General practitioners and family physicians	22 040	122 463	133 789	96 958	30.8	72.5
Dentists	8 710	118 350	129 104	82 254	22.9	63.7
Senior managers: Goods production, utilities, transportation, and construction	44 630	115 623	120 914	75 267	11.6	62.2
Lawyers and Quebec notaries	47 290	103 287	114 894	77 451	31.0	67.4
Senior managers: Trade, broadcasting and other services, N.E.C.	37 690	101 176	108 527	67 161	17.8	61.8
Securities agents, investment dealers, and traders	17 765	98 919	124 290	55 299	36.8	44.5
Petroleum engineers	4 370	96 703	100 633	61 057	10.0	60.7
Babysitters, nannies, and parents' helpers	26 670	15 846	15 310	15 862	97.1	104.3
Food counter attendants, kitchen helpers, and related occupations	54 290	19 338	20 241	19 053	71.8	94.1
Food and beverage servers	54 660	18 319	22 671	17 030	77.1	75.1
Service station attendants	8 315	18 470	19 475	15 750	9.2	80.9
Bartenders	16 175	19 877	22 008	18 347	58.2	83.4
Cashiers	58 775	19 922	22 925	19 391	85	84.5
Harvesting labourers	2 215	20 158	21 971	18 246	48.8	83.0
Tailors, dressmakers, furriers, and milliners	13 425	20 499	27 690	18 882	81.6	68.2
Sewing machine operators	31 040	20 575	26 782	19 997	91.5	74.7
Ironing, pressing, and finishing occupations	3 860	20 663	23 041	19 319	63.9	83.8

NEL

277

TABLE 11.4

Percentage Female in Broad
Occupational Categories
in Canada, 1987, 1997,
and 2007

Source: Adapted from the Statistics
Canada, 2008, CANSIM Table 282-
0010. Retrieved May 2, 2008
(http://dc1.chass.utoronto.ca.
myaccess.library.utoronto.ca/cgi-bin/
cansimdim/c2_getArrayDim.pl).
Computations by Robert Brym.

Occupational Category	1987	1997	2007
	Percentage Females in Occupation		
Senior management	21.2	27.1	26.5
Other management	31.3	37.5	37.8
Professions in business and finance	38.6	47.8	50.6
Financial, secretarial, and administrative	83.2	85.1	82.9
Clerical	68.0	69.2	71.1
Scientists	20.0	20.0	22.1
Health professions (including nursing)	79.3	79.1	80.9
Social science, government, and religion	57.4	64.8	68.4
Teachers and professors	52.8	60.3	64.1
Artistic/literary/recreational	48.5	52.6	54.7
Sales and service	55.5	56.3	56.9
Trade and transport	5.2	6.1	6.9
Primary industry	19.6	20.7	20.0
Processing, manufacturing, utilities	33.2	31.9	31.2
All occupations	43.2	45.4	47.1

and elder care than men do (Sauve, 2002). Globally, women do between two-thirds and three-quarters of all unpaid child care, housework, and care for aging parents (Boyd, 1997: 55). Even when they work full-time in the paid labour force, women continue to shoulder a disproportionate share of domestic responsibilities (Chapter 15, Families).

4. *Finally, work done by women is commonly considered less valuable than work done by men because it is viewed as involving fewer skills.* Women tend to earn less than men do because the skills involved in their work are often undervalued (Figart and Lapidus, 1996; Sorenson, 1994). For example, kindergarten teachers (nearly all of whom are women) earn less than office machine repair technicians (nearly all of whom are men). It is, however, questionable whether it takes less training and skill to teach a young child the basics of counting and cooperation than it takes to get a photocopier to collate paper properly. As this example suggests, we apply somewhat arbitrary standards to reward different occupational roles. In our society, these standards systematically undervalue the kind of skills needed for jobs where women are concentrated.

We thus see that the gender gap in earnings is based on several *social* circumstances rather than on any inherent difference between women and men. This fact means that people can reduce the gender gap if they want to. Below, we discuss social policies that could create more equality between women and men. But first, to stress the urgency of such policies, we explain how the persistence of gender inequality encourages sexual harassment and rape.

Male Aggression against Women

Serious acts of aggression between men and women are common. The great majority are committed by men against women. For example, 6 percent of Canadian women under the age of 25 reported being sexually assaulted and 9 percent reported being stalked in 2004 alone (Johnson, 2006: 36).

Rape is one of the most violent forms of sexual assault. Although rapists have typically been regarded as deranged individuals, research on acquaintance rape—sexual assaults committed by someone the victim knows—demonstrates that normal men are capable of acts of coercive sex (Meyer, 1984; Senn, Desmarais, Veryberg, and Wood, 2000). One study found that more than 20 percent of female Canadian postsecondary students said they gave in to unwanted sexual intercourse because they were overwhelmed by a man's continued arguments and pressure, nearly 7 percent reported they had unwanted sexual intercourse because a man threatened or used some degree of physical force, and nearly 14 percent claimed that, while they were either intoxicated or under the influence of drugs, a man had attempted unwanted sexual intercourse (DeKeseredy and Kelly, 1993).

Another study found that half of first- and second-year university women reported unwanted attempts at intercourse by males of their acquaintance. In 83 percent of cases, they knew the man at least moderately well. One-third of these attempts were accompanied by "strong" physical force and another third by "mild" physical force. The women seemed constrained by traditional roles in their responses, which were largely passive and accepting; 37 percent did nothing. Only a minority gave a strong verbal response (26 percent) or a physical response (14 percent). Half the attacks succeeded; the stronger the victim's response, the less likely it was that the attempted rape was completed. None of the women reported the attack to the authorities and half talked to no one about it. The remainder told friends. Only 11 percent ended the relationship, whereas almost three-quarters either accepted or ignored the attack. Half continued to be friends (25 percent) or dating or sex partners (25 percent). Most blamed themselves at least partially (Murnen, Perot, and Byrne, 1989; Figure 11.6).

Why do men commit more frequent (and more harmful) acts of aggression against women than women commit against men? It is not because men on average are physically more powerful than women are. Greater physical power is more likely to be used to commit acts of aggression when norms justify male domination and men have much more *social* power than women do. When women and men are more equal socially, and norms justify gender equality, the rate of male aggression against women is lower. This is evident if we consider various types of aggressive interaction, including sexual assault and sexual harassment (see also the discussion of wife abuse in Chapter 15, Families).

Sexual Assault

Some people think rapists are men who suffer a psychological disorder that compels them to achieve immediate sexual gratification even if violence is required. Others think rape

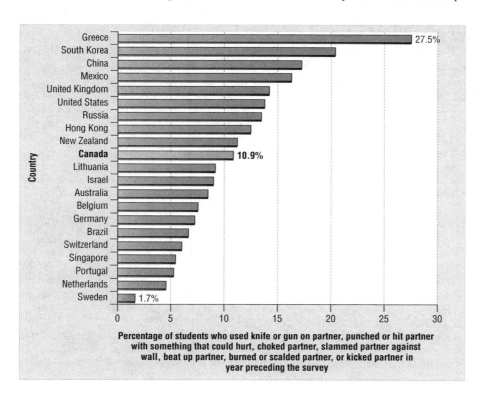

FIGURE 11.6

Percentage of University Students Who Severely Assaulted a Dating Partner in the Past Year, by Country, 2001–2005 (n = 6700)

Note: Some of the American data were collected in 1998.

Source: From International Dating Violence Study, tabulation courtesy of Murray A. Straus based on Emily M. Douglas and Murray A. Straus, (2006) "Assault and injury of dating partners by university students in 19 nations and its relation to corporal punishment experienced as a child," *European Journal of Criminology* 3: 293–318. Reprinted with permission.

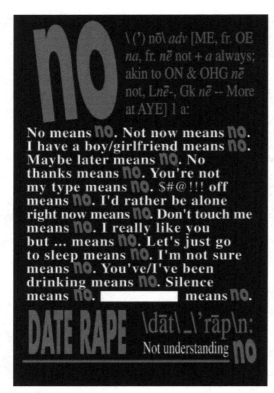

no \(') nō\ adv [ME, fr. OE na, fr. nē not + a always; akin to ON & OHG nē not, Lnē-, Gk nē -- More at AYE] 1 a:

No means no. Not now means no. I have a boy/girlfriend means no. Maybe later means no. No thanks means no. You're not my type means no. $#@!!! off means no. I'd rather be alone right now means no. Don't touch me means no. I really like you but ... means no. Let's just go to sleep means no. I'm not sure means no. You've/I've been drinking means no. Silence means no. _____ means no.

DATE RAPE \dāt_\'rāp\n: Not understanding no

This poster suggests that men still need to be reminded that no means no.

occurs because of flawed communication. They believe some victims give mixed signals to their assailants by, for example, drinking too much and flirting with them.

Such explanations are not completely invalid. Interviews with victims and perpetrators show that some offenders do suffer from psychological disorders. Others misinterpret signals in what they regard as sexually ambiguous situations (Hannon, Hall, Kuntz, Laar, and Williams, 1995). But such cases account for only a small proportion of the total. Men who commit sexual assault are rarely mentally disturbed, and it is abundantly clear to most assailants that they are doing something their victims strongly oppose.

What then accounts for sexual assault being as common as it is? A sociological answer is suggested by the fact that sexual assault is sometimes not about sexual gratification at all. Some offenders cannot ejaculate or even achieve an erection. Significantly, however, all forms of sexual assault involve domination and humiliation as principal motives. It is not surprising, therefore, that some offenders were physically or sexually abused in their youth. They develop a deep need to feel powerful as psychological compensation for their early powerlessness. Others are men who, as children, saw their mothers as potentially hostile figures who needed to be controlled or as mere objects available for male gratification. They saw their fathers as emotionally cold and distant. Raised in such an atmosphere, rapists learn not to empathize with women. Instead, they learn to want to dominate them (Lisak, 1992).

Other social situations also increase the rate of sexual aggression. One such situation is war. In war, conquering male soldiers often feel justified in wanting to humiliate the vanquished, who are powerless to stop them. Rape is often used for this purpose, as was especially well documented in the ethnic wars that accompanied the breakup of Yugoslavia in the 1990s (Human Rights Watch, 1995).

The relationship between male dominance and sexual aggression is also evident in research on American fraternities. Many fraternities tend to emphasize male dominance and aggression as a central part of their culture. Sociologists who have interviewed fraternity members have shown that most fraternities try to recruit members who can reinforce a macho image and avoid any suggestion of effeminacy and homosexuality. Research also shows that fraternity houses that are especially prone to sexual assault tend to sponsor parties that treat women in a particularly degrading way. By emphasizing a very narrow and aggressive form of masculinity, some fraternities tend to facilitate sexual assault on campuses (Boswell and Spade, 1996).

Another social circumstance that increases the likelihood of sexual assault is participation in athletics. Of course, the overwhelming majority of athletes are not rapists. However, there are proportionately more rapists among men who participate in athletics than among non-athletes (Welch, 1997). That is because many sports embody a particular vision of masculinity in North American culture: competitive, aggressive, and domineering. By recruiting men who display these characteristics and by encouraging the development of these characteristics in athletes, sports can contribute to off-field aggression, including sexual aggression. Furthermore, among male athletes, there is a distinct hierarchy of sexual aggression. Male athletes who engage in contact sports are more prone to be rapists than are other athletes. There are proportionately even more rapists among athletes involved in collision and combative sports, notably football (Welch, 1997).

Sexual assault, we conclude, involves using sex to establish dominance. Its incidence is highest in situations where early socialization experiences predispose men to want to control women, where norms justify the domination of women, and where a big power imbalance between men and women exists.

NEL

Sexual Harassment

There are two types of sexual harassment. **Quid pro quo sexual harassment** takes place when sexual threats or bribery are made a condition of employment decisions. (The Latin phrase *quid pro quo* means "something for something.") **Hostile environment sexual harassment** involves sexual jokes, comments, and touching that interferes with work or creates a hostile work environment. Research suggests that relatively powerless women are the most likely to be sexually harassed. Specifically, women who are young, unmarried, and employed in non-professional jobs are most likely to become objects of sexual harassment, particularly if they are temporary workers, if the ratio of women to men in the workplace is low, and if the organizational culture of the workplace tolerates sexual harassment (Rogers and Henson, 1997; Welsh, 1999). However, female doctors (Schneider and Phillips, 1997) and lawyers (Rosenberg, Perlstadt, and Phillips, 1997) also report high rates of sexual harassment, in the first case by male patients and in the second by male colleagues.

Ultimately, male aggression against women, including sexual harassment and sexual assault, is encouraged by a lesson most of us still learn at home, in school, at work, through much of organized religion, and in the mass media—that it is natural and right for men to dominate women. Despite change, it is still more common for men to hold positions of power and authority, than for women to hold such positions. Along with this comes widespread willingness to tolerate or even encourage dominance in males and to discourage it in females. Daily patterns of gender domination, viewed as legitimate by most people, are built into our courtship, sexual, family, and work norms. As a result, aggressive behaviour by males against females typically encounters less notice, resistance, or sanctions than would similar behaviour by females toward males.

This does not mean that all men endorse the principle of male dominance, much less that all men are inclined to engage in sexual assault or other acts of aggression against women. Many men favour gender equality, and most men never abuse a woman (Messerschmidt, 1993). Yet the fact remains that many aspects of our culture legitimize male dominance, making it seem valid or proper. For example, pornography, jokes about "dumb blondes," and leering might seem harmless. At a subtler, sociological level, however, they are assertions of the appropriateness of women's submission to men. Such frequent and routine reinforcements of male superiority increase the likelihood that some men will consider it their right to assault women physically or sexually if the opportunity to do so exists or can be created. "Just kidding" has a cost. For instance, researchers have found that university men who enjoy sexist jokes are more likely than other university men to report engaging in acts of sexual aggression against women (Ryan and Kanjorski, 1998).

We conclude that male aggression against women and gender inequality are not separate issues. Gender inequality is the foundation of aggression against women. In concluding this chapter, we consider how gender inequality can be decreased in the coming decades. As we proceed, you should bear in mind that gender equality is not just a matter of justice. It is also a question of safety.

TOWARD 2118

The twentieth century witnessed growing equality between women and men in many countries. In Canada, the decline of the family farm made children less economically useful and more costly to raise. As a result, women started having fewer children. The industrialization of Canada, and then the growth of the economy's service sector, increased demand for women in the paid labour force (Figure 11.7 on page 332). This change gave them substantially more economic power and also encouraged them to have fewer children. The legalization and availability of contraception made it possible for women to exercise unprecedented control over their own bodies. The women's movement

Quid pro quo sexual harassment **takes place when sexual threats or bribery are made a condition of employment decisions.**

Hostile environment sexual harassment **involves sexual jokes, comments, and touching that interferes with work or creates an unfriendly work environment.**

FIGURE 11.7

Percentage of Men and Women in Paid Labour Force, Canada, 1946–2007

Source: Adapted from Statistics Canada, 1983, "Historical Statistics of Canada," Catalogue 11-516, July 29, 1999, Series D160-174. Retrieved May 2, 2008 (http://www.statcan.ca/english/freepub/11-516-XIE/sectiond/sectiond.htm), and from the Statistics Canada CANSIM database, Table 282-0002, using E-STAT (distributor). Retrieved May 2, 2008 (http://estat.statcan.ca/cgiwin/CNSMCGI.EXE?CANSIMFILE-Estat\English\CII_1_E.htm); Statistics Canada, 2008, "Labour Force Indicators by Age Groups for Males, Participation Rate (2006), for Canada, Provinces and Territories—20% Sample Data." Retrieved May 2, 2008 (http://www12.statcan.ca/english/census06/data/highlights/Labour/Table601.cfm?SR=1).

GLOBAL PERSPECTIVE

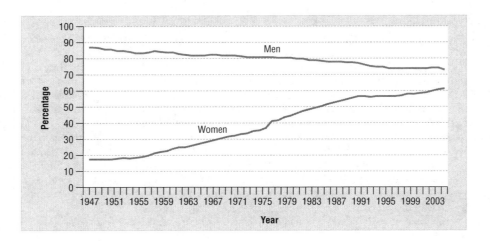

FIGURE 11.8

Gender Empowerment Measure, Top 10 and Bottom 10 Countries, 2007

Note: Data are available for 93 countries.

Source: United Nations, 2007–2008, *Human Development Report 2007–2008*. Retrieved May 2, 2008 (http://hdrstats.undp.org/indicators/280.html). The United Nations is the author of the original material.

fought for, and won, increased rights for women on a number of economic, political, and legal fronts. All these forces brought about a massive cultural shift, a fundamental reorientation of thinking on the part of many Canadians about what women could and should do in society.

One indicator of the progress of women is the Gender Empowerment Measure (GEM). The GEM is computed by the United Nations. It takes into account women's share of seats in Parliament; women's share of administrative, managerial, professional, and technical jobs; and women's earning power. A score of 1.0 indicates equality with men on these three dimensions.

As Figure 11.8 shows, Norway, Sweden, Finland, and Denmark were the most gender-egalitarian countries in the world in 2007. They had GEM scores ranging from 0.910 to 0.875. On average, women in these countries are about 87 percent of the way to equality with men on these three dimensions. Canada ranked tenth in the world, with a GEM score of 0.820.

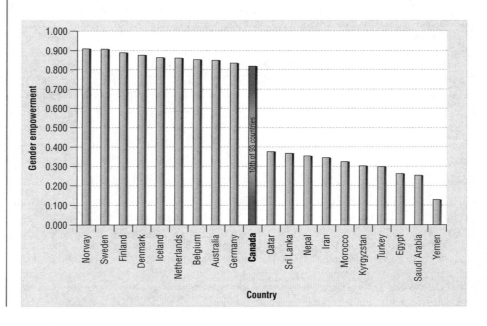

In general, there is more gender equality in rich than in poor countries. Thus, the top 11 countries shown in Figure 11.8 are all rich. This suggests that gender equality is a function of economic development. However, our analysis of the GEM data suggests that there are some exceptions to the general pattern. Gender equality is also a function of government policy. Thus, in some of the former communist countries of Eastern Europe—such as Slovakia (ranked at 26), Latvia (29), and the Czech Republic (30)—gender equality is *higher* than we would expect given their level of economic development. Meanwhile, in some of the Islamic countries, gender inequality is *lower* than we would expect given their level of economic development (e.g., Bahrain and Saudi Arabia). These anomalies exist because the former communist countries made gender equality a matter of public policy while many Islamic countries do just the opposite (Brym et al., 2005). To cite just one extreme case, in 1996 authorities in the Islamic country of Afghanistan made it illegal for girls to attend school and women to work in the paid labour force. (The situation has improved in some areas since the overthrow of the Taliban regime in 2001.)

The GEM figures suggest that Canadian women still have a considerable way to go before they achieve equality with men. We have seen, for example, that the gender gap in earnings is shrinking but will disappear only in 2118—and then only if it continues to diminish at the same rate as it did between 1980 and 2005. That is a big "if," because progress is never automatic.

Socializing children at home and in school to understand that women and men are equally adept at all jobs is important in motivating women to excel in non-traditional fields. Hiring more women to compensate for past discrimination in hiring, firing, promotion, and training is also important. However, without in any way minimizing the need for such initiatives, we should recognize that their impact will be muted if women continue to undertake disproportionate domestic responsibilities and if occupations containing a high concentration of women continue to be undervalued in monetary terms.

Two main policy initiatives will probably be required in the coming decades to bridge the gender gap in earnings. One is the development of a better child-care system. The other is the development of a policy of "equal pay for work of equal value." Let us consider both of these issues.

Child Care

High-quality, government-subsidized, affordable child care is widely available in most Western European countries but not yet in Canada (Chapter 15, Families). Sixty percent of children in the United Kingdom are in regulated child care as are 69 percent of children in France and 78 percent in Denmark. But a team from the Organisation for Economic Co-operation and Development (OECD) strongly faulted Canada's efforts as a patchwork that has been chronically underfunded. Only 20 percent of Canadian children under the age of seven are in regulated child care (OECD, 2004a: 7). As a result, many Canadian women with small children are either unable to work outside the home or able to work outside the home only on a part-time basis.

A universal system of daycare was proposed in Canada as early as 1970 but little was done at the federal level or in most provinces and territories. Quebec is an exception. In 1997 that province introduced a comprehensive family policy that attempts to integrate family benefits, paid parental leave, child care, and kindergarten. Its child-care component heralded universally available, affordable child care. A rapid expansion in the number of spaces occurred, although waiting lists grew as well. By 2004, 40 percent of the regulated daycare spaces available in Canada were in Quebec. Unfortunately, that was in part because no new spaces had been added outside Quebec in the preceding decade.

There is no lack of need. In 2001, 52 percent of Canadian preschoolers received some kind of care outside of the home, up from 42 percent just seven years earlier. But only 25 percent of these children were enrolled in daycare programs; a growing number were cared for by relatives: 14 percent, up from 8 percent in 1994 (Statistics Canada, 2005b).

In 2004, affordable, high-quality, regulated daycare was a central electoral promise of the victorious Liberal Party. By mid-2005, the beginnings of a national system began to take shape when the federal government reached child-care agreements with Saskatchewan, Manitoba, Ontario, and Newfoundland and Labrador. The system, had it taken root across the country, would potentially have paid for itself. One study estimated that a high-quality, affordable, universal system of child care and early child-care education would cost $7.9 billion, while the increased employment of mothers would be worth $6.2 billion and the improvement in child development would be worth $4.3 billion (Cleveland and Krashinsky, 1998). However, after his election in 2006, Prime Minister Stephen Harper scrapped the agreements in favour of taxable benefits of $1200 paid to parents for each child under age six. The amount and the targeting were widely criticized as failing to address what women who work for pay needed to support their families.

Equal Pay for Work of Equal Value

On paper, Canadian women have had the right to equal pay for the same jobs done by men since the 1950s. But although early laws proclaimed lofty goals, they failed to result in fair wages. Because of occupational sex segregation, few men and women were doing the same jobs, and "women's" jobs paid less than "men's" jobs.

In the 1980s, researchers found women earned less than men did partly because jobs in which women are concentrated are valued less than jobs in which men are concentrated. They therefore tried to establish gender-neutral standards by which they could judge the dollar value of work. These standards include such factors as the education and experience required to do a particular job and the level of responsibility, amount of stress, and working conditions associated with it. Researchers felt that, by using these criteria to compare jobs in which women and men are concentrated, they could identify pay inequities. The underpaid could then be compensated accordingly. In other words, women and men would receive **equal pay for work of equal value**, even if they did different jobs.

In the mid-1980s, some governments amended the law to state that women should be paid equally for work of equal value. Employers were now required to compare the rates of pay for women and men in dissimilar jobs that nevertheless involved the same skill, effort, responsibility, and working conditions. In 1985, Manitoba became the first Canadian province to demand that its public sector implement equal pay for work of equal value—or "pay equity," as it came to be called. Pay equity is now official policy in 10 of 13 Canadian jurisdictions (Alberta, Saskatchewan, and the Northwest Territories are the exceptions). However, provisions for pay equity vary widely. In some provinces they apply only to the public sector and even where they apply more broadly, such as in Ontario and Quebec, small businesses are exempt. In many cases it has been argued that there are no "male" jobs that can be reasonably compared to jobs in which women are segregated. In one case (Newfoundland and Labrador), the provincial government has argued it simply cannot afford a pay equity settlement. Enforcement mechanisms are meagre and employers have found various ways to argue that unequal wages do not signify discrimination based on sex. As a result, only about a fifth of female-dominated jobs have received pay equity adjustments (Moorcroft, 2005; Smeenk, 1993). Thus, while pay equity is undoubtedly a significant step toward achieving gender equality, inequity remains, as evidenced by the persistence of the wage gap between working men and working women.

The Women's Movement

Improvements in the social standing of women do not depend just on the sympathy of government and business leaders. Progress on this front has always depended in part on the strength of the organized women's movement. That is likely to be true in the future, too. In

Equal pay for work of equal value refers to the equal dollar value of different jobs. It is established in gender-neutral terms by comparing jobs in terms of the education and experience needed to do them and the stress, responsibility, and working conditions associated with them.

concluding this chapter, it is therefore fitting to consider the state of the women's movement and its prospects.

The first wave of the women's movement emerged during the late nineteenth century and lasted into the early 1920s. Its most important public achievements in Canada were the right to vote and the right (granted in 1929) to be considered *persons,* and not chattels (personal property), under Canadian law. In 1916, women in Alberta, Manitoba, and Saskatchewan were granted the right to vote in provincial elections. All the other provinces followed suit by 1925 except Quebec, which granted women the right to vote only in 1940. These rights were first granted to white women. Women from certain ethnic and racial groups did not receive the franchise until later (Nelson and Robinson, 2002).

In the mid-1960s, the second wave of the women's movement emerged. Second-wave feminists were inspired in part by the successes of the civil rights movement in the United States. They felt that women's concerns were largely ignored despite persistent and pervasive gender inequality. Like their counterparts more than a century earlier, they held demonstrations, lobbied politicians, and formed women's organizations to further their cause. They demanded equal rights with men in education and employment, the elimination of sexual violence, and control over their own reproduction. However, the second wave of the women's movement did not always or consistently recognize, include, or champion the needs of all Canadian women equally. It is only recently that the second wave of the women's movement has begun to respond positively to the claim that white, middle-class feminists have "denied, dismissed, and denigrated" the experiences of women of different races, abilities, and classes (Cassidy, Lord, and Mandell, 1998: 26).

There is considerable diversity in the modern feminist movement concerning ultimate goals. Three main streams can be distinguished (Tong, 1989):

1. *Liberal feminism* is the most popular current in the women's movement today. Its advocates believe that the main sources of women's subordination are learned gender roles and the denial of opportunities to women. Liberal feminists advocate nonsexist methods of socialization and education, more sharing of domestic tasks between women and men, and the extension to women of all the educational, employment, and political rights and privileges men enjoy.
2. *Socialist feminists* regard women's relationship to the economy as the main source of women's disadvantages. They believe that the traditional nuclear family emerged along with inequalities of wealth and that the economic and sexual oppression of women has its roots in capitalism. Socialist feminists also assert that the reforms proposed by liberal feminists are inadequate, because they can do little to help working-class women, who are too poor to take advantage of equal educational and work opportunities. Socialist feminists conclude that only the elimination of private property and the creation of economic equality can bring about an end to the oppression of all women.
3. *Radical feminists,* in turn, find the reforms proposed by liberals and the revolution proposed by socialists inadequate. Patriarchy—male domination and norms justifying that domination—is more deeply rooted than capitalism, say the radical feminists. After all, patriarchy predates capitalism. Moreover, it is just as evident in self-proclaimed communist societies as it is in capitalist societies. Radical feminists conclude that the very idea of gender must be changed to bring an end to male domination. Some radical feminists argue that new reproductive technologies, such as in vitro fertilization, are bound to be helpful in this regard because they can break the link between women's bodies and child bearing (see Chapter 15, Families). However, the revolution envisaged by radical feminists goes beyond the realm of reproduction to include all aspects of male sexual dominance. From their

The second wave of the women's movement started to grow in the mid-1960s. Members of the movement advocated equal rights with men in education and employment, the elimination of sexual violence, and control over their own reproduction.

NEL

point of view, pornography, sexual harassment, restrictive contraception, sexual assault, incest, sterilization, and physical assault must be eliminated for women to reconstruct their sexuality on their own terms.

This thumbnail sketch by no means exhausts the variety of streams of contemporary feminist thought. For example, since the mid-1980s, *anti-racist* and *post-modernist* feminists have criticized liberal, socialist, and radical feminists for generalizing from the experience of white women and failing to understand how women's lives are rooted in particular historical and racial experiences (hooks, 1984). These new currents have done much to extend the relevance of feminism to previously marginalized groups.

Partly because of the political and intellectual vigour of the women's movement, some feminist ideas have gained widespread acceptance in Canadian society over the past three decades. Most Canadians, men and women, agree or strongly agree that being able to have a paying job is either important or very important for women's personal happiness. About 7 of 10 Canadian men and women agree or strongly agree that both spouses should contribute to household income. However, these values appear to conflict with other attitudes and beliefs. For example, more than half of Canadians agree or strongly agree that preschool-age children are likely to suffer if both parents are employed. And around 45 percent of Canadians agree or strongly agree that a "job is alright, but what most women really want is a home and children" (Ghalam, 1997: 16). It appears that the tapestry of our social lives features interwoven threads of the new and the old.

NOTES

1. Freud called this set of emotions the *Oedipus complex* after the ancient Greek legend of Oedipus. Oedipus was abandoned as a child. When he became an adult he accidentally killed his father and unwittingly married his mother. Discovering his true relationship to his mother, he blinded himself and died in exile.

2. Freud called this set of emotions the *Electra complex* after the ancient Greek legend of Electra. Electra persuaded her brother to kill their mother and their mother's lover to avenge their father's murder. Incidentally, some sexologists call into question the existence of vaginal orgasm and stress the importance of clitoral stimulation (Masters, Johnson, and Kolodny, 1992, 1994). This viewpoint emerged around the same time as the modern feminist movement and as more and more people came to view sexuality not just as a means of reproduction but also as a means of enjoyment.

3. This message is borne out by research in the United States, Germany, and Britain that finds that upwardly mobile women "are much thinner than their counterparts who marry men of the same social class or lower" (Etcoff, 1999: 200–201).

4. Displaying direct aggression is more strongly associated with peer rejection for girls than for boys (Bukowski, Gauze, Hoza, and Newcomb, 1993). Also, compared with boys, girls demonstrate higher levels of indirect or relational aggression— acts designed to damage another's peer relationships or reputation (e.g., gossiping, spreading malicious rumours, exclusionary acts)—than boys do (Crick, 1997).

SUMMARY

1. Are sex and gender rooted in nature?
   Sex refers to certain anatomical and hormonal features of a person, while gender refers to the culturally appropriate expression of masculinity and femininity. Sex is largely rooted in nature, although people can change their sex by undergoing a sex-change operation and hormone therapy. In contrast, social as well as biological forces strongly influence gender. Sociologists study the way social conditions affect the expression of masculinity and femininity.

2. What are some of the major social forces that channel people into performing culturally appropriate gender roles?
   Various agents of socialization channel people into performing culturally approved gender roles. The family, the school, and the mass media are among the most important of these agents of socialization. Once the sex of children is known (or assumed), parents and teachers tend to treat boys and girls differently in terms of the kind of play, dress, and learning they encourage. The mass media reinforce the learning of masculine and feminine roles by making different characteristics seem desirable in boys and girls, men and women.

3. What is homosexuality and why does it exist?
   Homosexuals are people who prefer sexual partners of the same sex. We do not yet well understand the causes of homosexuality—whether it is genetic, hormonal, psychological, or some combination of the three. We do know that homosexuality does not appear to be a choice and that it emerges for most people without prior sexual experience in early adolescence. Sociologists are, in any case, more interested in the way homosexuality is expressed and repressed. For example, they have studied how, in the twentieth century, scientific research and political movements made the open expression of homosexuality more acceptable. Sociologists have also studied the ways in which various aspects of society reinforce heterosexuality and treat homosexuality as a form of deviance subject to tight social control.

4. Aside from agents of socialization, are there other social forces that influence the expression of masculinity and femininity?
   Yes. One of the most important non-socialization forces that influences the expression of masculinity and femininity is the level of social inequality between men and women. High levels of gender inequality encourage more traditional or conventional gender roles. There are fewer differences in gender roles where low levels of gender inequality prevail. Historically, high levels of gender inequality have been encouraged by far-ranging warfare and conquest, plow agriculture, and the separation of public and private spheres. Each of these changes enhanced male power and added a layer of what we now consider tradition to gender roles.

5. How does the existence of sharply defined gender roles influence men's and women's income?
   The gender gap in earnings derives from outright discrimination against women, women's disproportionate domestic responsibilities, women's concentration in low-wage occupations and industries, and the undervaluation of work typically done by women.

6. What helps explain male aggression against women?
   Male aggression against women is rooted in gender inequality. Thus, where women and men are more equal socially, and norms justify gender equality, the rate of male aggression against women is lower.

7. How might the gender gap in earnings be reduced or eliminated?
   Among the major reforms that could help eliminate the gender gap in earnings and reduce the level and expression of gender inequality are (a) the development of an affordable, accessible system of high-quality daycare and (b) the remuneration of men and women on the basis of their work's actual worth.

KEY TERMS

bisexuals (p. 319)

equal pay for work
  of equal value (p. 334)

essentialism (p. 308)

gender (p. 307)

gender discrimination (p. 326)

gender identity (p. 307)

gender ideology (p. 314)

gender role (p. 307)

glass ceiling (p. 318)

heterosexuality (p. 307)

homophobic (p. 322)

homosexuals (p. 319)

hostile environment sexual
  harassment (p. 331)

intersexed (p. 306)

quid pro quo sexual harassment (p. 331)

sex (p. 307)

transgendered (p. 318)

transsexuals (p. 318)

QUESTIONS TO CONSIDER

1. By interviewing your family members and using your own memory, compare the gender division of labour in (a) the households in which your parents grew up and (b) the household(s) in which you grew up. Then, imagine the gender division of labour you would like to see in the household you hope to live in about 10 years from now. What accounts for change over time in the gender division of labour in these households? Do you think your hopes are realistic? Why or why not?

2. Systematically note the roles played by women and men on TV programs and ads one evening. Is there a gender division of labour on TV? If so, describe it.

3. Are you a feminist? If so, which of the types of feminism discussed in this chapter do you find most appealing? Why? If not, what do you find objectionable about feminism? In either case, what is the ideal form of gender relations in your opinion? Why do you think this form is ideal?

WEB RESOURCES

Companion Website for This Book

http://www.compass3e.nelson.com

Begin by clicking on the Student Resources section of the website. Next, select the chapter you are studying from the pull-down menu. From the Student Resources page you have easy access to InfoTrac® College Edition, additional Weblinks, and other resources. The website also has many useful tips to aid you in your study of sociology, including practice tests for each chapter.

InfoTrac® Search Terms

These search terms are provided to assist you in beginning to conduct research on this topic by visiting http://www.infotrac-college.com:

gender
glass ceiling
gender discrimination
sexual harassment
gender role

NEL

Recommended Websites

For a useful discussion of women and work worldwide see the article "Women, Gender and Work: Part II" by Janneke Plantenga and Johan Hansen, available on the World Wide Web at www.ilo.org/public/english/revue/download/pdf/intro994.pdf.

To learn about the history of women and gender in Canada, go to the World History Archives page at http://www.hartford-hwp.com/archives/44/index-eb.html.

For information on gender roles and stereotyping in children's literature, see http://www.indiana.edu/~reading/ieo/bibs/childgen.html.

A variety of useful links about gender can be found at Gender.org.uk: http://www.gender.org.uk.

Visit the website of Status of Women Canada at http://www.swc-cfc.gc.ca.

For more on the United Nations Gender Empowerment Measure (GEM) discussed in the text, see http://hdr.undp.org/en/statistics/indices/gdi_gem.

CengageNOW™

http://hed.nelson.com

This online diagnostic tool identifies each student's unique needs with a Pretest that generates a personalized Study Plan for each chapter, helping students focus on concepts they're having the most difficulty mastering. Students then take a Posttest after reading the chapter to measure their understanding of the material. An Instructor Gradebook is available to track and monitor student progress.

NEL

Chapter 8: Political Studies

INTRODUCTION
The Study of Political Science

Political science is the systematic study of *government* and *politics,* terms that are defined at greater length in Chapter 1. But before getting into the subject matter, students may find it useful to learn something about the discipline itself.

HISTORY OF POLITICAL SCIENCE

The origins of political science lie in the classical period of Greek philosophy, whose greatest writers were Plato and Aristotle. The Greek philosophers did not approach political science as a specialized discipline in the modern sense, but they thought and wrote systematically about government. They were concerned above all with how politics can contribute to a life of excellence and virtue. The long quotation from Aristotle printed in Historical Perspectives I.1 gives some idea of how this great philosopher saw political science as a moral endeavour committed to the betterment of the human condition. Greek philosophy, and with it the habit of systematic reflection upon government, became part of the cultural tradition of the Western world. Political science continued to exist as a branch of moral philosophy, and important contributions were made by authors who also wrote in other areas of philosophy, such as Thomas Aquinas, Thomas Hobbes, and John Locke. Such writings, extending over more than two millennia, constitute a rich body of wisdom that is still the foundation of political science.

In the eighteenth century, political science started to differentiate itself from moral philosophy—not yet as an independent study, but as part of the new science of political economy. Writers such as Adam Smith, who held the chair of moral philosophy at the University of Glasgow, began to study and write about the workings of the market. They did not do this in a vacuum; in the society of the time, market processes were being freed from mercantilist policies predicated on governmental control of the economy. The study of government was a junior partner in the new science of *political economy,* which emphasized market forces. Government was seen as a limited auxiliary that could carry out a few functions not performed well in the marketplace. In the late eighteenth and early nineteenth centuries, universities established chairs of political economy. During this period, much work that today we would call political science was also done in faculties of history and law, especially under the guise of comparative and constitutional law.

Aristotle on Political Science

"Now it would be agreed that [the Supreme Good, the purpose of human existence] must be the object of the most authoritative of the sciences—some science which is pre-eminently a master-craft. But such is manifestly the science of Politics; for it is this that ordains which of the sciences are to exist in states, and what branches of knowledge the different classes of the citizens are to learn, and up to what point; and we observe that even the most highly esteemed of the faculties, such as strategy, domestic economy, oratory, are subordinate to the political science. Inasmuch then as the rest of the sciences are employed by this one, and as it moreover lays down laws as to what people shall do and what things they shall refrain from doing, the end of this science must include the ends of all the others. Therefore, the Good of man must be the end of the science of Politics. For even though it be the case that the Good is the same for the individual and for the state, nevertheless, the good of the state is manifestly a greater and more perfect good, both to attain and to preserve. To secure the good of one person only is better than nothing; but to secure the good of a nation or a state is a nobler and more divine achievement."

Source: Aristotle, *The Nicomachean Ethics,* I, ii, 4–8, tr. H. Rackham (London: William Heinemann, 1934, rev. ed.; Loeb Classical Library, vol. 19), pp. 5–7.

Economics and political science began to diverge in the second half of the nineteenth century as scholars began to specialize. The discovery of the principle of marginal utility in the 1870s made it possible for economics to become mathematical, and hence more specialized and remote from the everyday concerns of government and politics. Universities in the United States took the lead in establishing autonomous departments of political science, which united the work of professors who might previously have gravitated to political economy, history, and law. Political science in its modern academic form thus stems from developments in the United States in the late nineteenth century. The first American department of political science was founded at Columbia University in 1880; by the outbreak of World War I in 1914, there were 40 such departments in U.S. universities.[1]

Why in the United States? Partly because this rapidly expanding country was opening scores of new universities not bound by old traditions about academic specialties. But the more important reason is that the United States—a nation founded on a political act of revolution—has always been fascinated with government. Political science at the university level was a logical extension of the civics education that was so important in the public schools. Also, these early political scientists tended to be moralistic crusaders for governmental reform—a good example being Woodrow Wilson, the only political science professor ever to become an American president.

In the first half of the twentieth century, political science as an academic discipline remained largely an American phenomenon, with only a few chairs established in universities in other countries. Of course, the substance of political science was pursued elsewhere, but it was usually conducted within departments of law, political economy, economics, and history. However, after World War II, political science was adopted as an independent discipline around the world. This was partly in imitation of the American cultural behemoth. A deeper reason, perhaps, was the tremendous expansion of the scope of government in the second half of the twentieth century. The small state of the *laissezfaire* era could be understood fairly easily within the study of political economy; the large, interventionist state of the present era seems to demand its own specialized discipline.

Political science in Canada must be seen in this historical context. In 1950 there were only about 30 political scientists in Canada, most of them employed in university departments of political economy.[2] Their main periodical was the *Canadian Journal of Economics and Political Science (CJEPS)*. In the 1960s, as enrollments increased and more staff were hired to cope with an unprecedented expansion of universities, these departments began to split into separate departments of economics and political science. In 1967 the *CJEPS* was split into the *Canadian Journal of Economics (CJE)* and the *Canadian Journal of Political Science (CJPS)*, while two separate professional associations also emerged: the Canadian Economics Association (CEA) and the Canadian Political Science Association (CPSA). Some years later, as part of the general movement of Quebec nationalism, political scientists in that province formed their own association, the Société québécoise de science politique, with its own journal, *Politique et Sociétés*. The two associations maintain cooperative relations with one another, and there is a good deal of cross-membership; but in political science, as in so many other areas, the reality of Canada is that Quebec is a "distinct society."

The term political economy no longer embraces the entire territory of economics and politics as it once did. It now has several special uses. In some circles, it refers to the study of certain narrower subjects—such as economic intervention by government—that require information and insights from both disciplines in order to be understood. In other circles, it denotes a historical–materialist approach to the study of politics that draws heavily, though not exclusively, on the thought of Karl Marx and other writers in the Marxist tradition. Within the Canadian political-science community, the practitioners of political economy in this latter sense are a recognized subgroup whose members tend to work together with like-minded historians, economists, and sociologists. Together, they maintain their own academic network and help to support an interdisciplinary journal, *Studies in Political Economy*, which is based at Carleton University in Ottawa.

APPROACHES TO POLITICAL SCIENCE

When political science achieved academic autonomy, its practitioners brought to it the methods of their forebears in philosophy, political economy, law, and history. These methods were chiefly the narrative, chronological, and descriptive study of political institutions, complemented by philosophical reflection about matters of good and evil in the sphere of government. Great changes have taken place since that beginning.

In the 1940s, sociology and social psychology began to exert enormous influence, and political scientists became familiar with methods of research common in those disciplines, such as attitude scales, sample surveys, and statistical analysis. The rapidly increasing use of these methods was closely tied to a shift in emphasis away from formal constitutional structures and toward political parties, pressure groups, elections, and collective behaviour. This transition—often referred to as the *behavioural revolution*—brought political science closer to the other social sciences.

A second phase of the behavioural revolution began in the 1950s and is still far from ending. It is characterized by the influence of rational-choice models of analysis that were first developed in economics and mathematics. Increasingly, some political scientists are using deductive models derived from branches of mathematics such as game theory and information theory to explain the data gathered in their empirical investigations. This phase is more abstract and theoretical in nature than the first and is drawing political science closer to natural sciences such as biology and cybernetics, which often utilize similar mathematical models.

There were acrimonious divisions within the discipline in the 1950s and 1960s between supporters and opponents of the new methods, with many extreme claims being made on both sides. That furor, however, has now largely subsided. Political scientists who use quantitative methods now coexist peacefully with colleagues who rely on the old techniques of description and reflection. It seems to be accepted that political science is inherently pluralistic and is united not by adherence to a single method, but by concern with a common subject. Because different questions of politics and government lend themselves to different approaches, political scientists may resemble philosophers, sociologists, historians, lawyers, economists, or anthropologists in their research methods; yet all feel that they are united in a joint enterprise to understand the many facets of government and politics.

The methodological battles have subsided but have been followed by equally noisy ideological strife. In the late 1960s, political economists and others rooted in the Marxist tradition enunciated a vigorous challenge to what they saw as the capitalist bias of most political science. Their criticism was soon augmented by distinctive new points of view such as environmentalism, feminism, and multiculturalism, each arguing in its own way that fragile and ill-defended assumptions amounting to bias exist in conventional political science. There is no immediate prospect for consensus on such issues, and political science remains what it has always been—an inherently pluralistic discipline in which different points of view clash and final victory is never achieved.

In this respect, political science is very different from the natural sciences. At any given time, probably 99 percent of physicists, chemists, or biologists agree on about 99 percent of the contents of their respective disciplines. They may disagree heatedly about research on the frontiers, but overall the areas of such disagreement are small.

Those who challenge the fundamentals of such disciplines are often regarded as cranks and banished to the periphery. In contrast, political science is an ongoing debate in which honest differences of opinion over fundamental issues are the norm.

Nonetheless, in spite of such deep-seated divisions, there are large areas of agreement. Although feminist and conservative political scientists may disagree profoundly on the larger implications, they should be able to agree on how many women sit in the House of Commons, on what the statistical trend has been over time, and on at least some of the reasons why the percentage (1) used to be extremely low, (2) rose rapidly from the 1960s to the mid-1990s, and (3) has levelled off since the election of 1997 at about 21 percent, still far below the level for men in Canada and also below the level for women in the legislatures of some European countries. Such agreement is important in itself, even if it is immersed in vigorous polemics about whether the trends are good or bad, and whether additional measures ought to be enacted to accelerate the changes.

To introduce some technical terminology, political scientists can hope for agreement on *empirical* (i.e., factual) questions, such as what is the shape of the political world, and how does that world function? Although disagreement on such questions always exists, it can in principle be overcome by more research and better evidence. But disagreement on *normative* (i.e., evaluative) questions is harder, perhaps impossible, to resolve, because it may stem from different value commitments. To go back to the preceding example, even after feminist and conservative political scientists reach agreement on a host of empirical issues relating to the representation of women in the House of Commons, they might continue to disagree on the normative question of whether one *ought* to take steps to increase that level of representation.

Pulling these strands of historical background together, one can identify four leading contemporary approaches within the discipline of political science. These are not the only ones, to be sure, but they are so widespread that everyone studying political science must be aware of them. Few political scientists would maintain that any of these approaches is the only correct one, but in practice most political scientists depend on one of them most of the time in the research that they do. Consequently, the discipline as a whole consists of the aggregate of these different and sometimes conflicting approaches to the study of politics.

Institutionalism

Institutionalism focuses on the detailed, systematic analysis of the working of political organizations, such as legislatures, cabinets, political parties, interest groups, and courts. Obviously, any political scientist has to be an institutionalist to some extent because the political world consists of institutions and you cannot understand politics without knowing what these institutions are and how they work. You could, for example, hardly presume to speak about American politics without understanding that the Congress is divided into two branches called the Senate and the House of

Representatives, that legislation must be approved by both branches, that the president has the right to veto legislation, and that the Congress can override a presidential veto under certain circumstances. Institutionalism, however, is sometimes criticized for being nothing more than formalistic description, devoid of deeper insight into political processes. Dissatisfaction with institutionalism, which was the dominant approach to political science up to the 1950s, led to the development of behaviouralism.

Behaviouralism

Behaviouralism focuses on the behaviour of individuals rather than on the structure of institutions. Behaviouralists typically study topics such as political culture and socialization, public opinion, and voting, where people think and make decisions as individuals, not as cogs in the wheel of an organization. They often use methods such as sample surveys, which allow them to ask people questions and record their responses as individual-level data, after which they use statistical methods to find correlations among variables. This type of research can tell you, for example, which categories of people tend to vote for the candidates of the various political parties—information that is not only interesting in itself but also of great practical importance to the strategists who craft the appeals that parties make to voters during elections.

Behaviouralism has undoubtedly made great contributions to the development of political science, but it has some obvious limitations. Public opinion and elections are interesting and important, but in themselves they do not decide anything except who will fill elected political offices. Those elected officeholders are the ones who actually make decisions, and they do so not as unconstrained individuals but as role-players in institutions. A balanced view, therefore, would see institutionalism and behaviouralism as complementary rather than contradictory approaches to the study of politics, both being necessary for a complete explanation of political outcomes.

Public Choice

Public choice is sometimes called "the economics of politics." It represents the application of assumptions about human behaviour that are standard in economics—rationality and the maximization of individual utility—to the explanation of political phenomena. In its purest form, public-choice analysis begins with abstract reasoning to devise a model of how rational, self-interested, utility maximizers would act in stipulated political circumstances, and of how their behaviour would respond to changes in those circumstances. Would such people vote for Party A or Party B? Would they join a political party? Would they bother to vote at all? The predictions of the model are then tested against data collected from the real world of politics.

One of the great advantages of public choice is its applicability to both individual behaviour and institutional structure. Practitioners of public choice analyze institutions as the aggregation of individual choices. To the extent that this approach works, it has the potential to overcome the split between behaviouralism and institutionalism. Another advantage of public choice is that it operates with a single, explicit theory of human nature, which helps to give it consistency across different applications. However, the critics of public choice believe that interpreting human behaviour as self-interested utility maximization is too narrow and too dependent upon the capitalist theory of economics from which public choice was imported into political science. Many critics denounce public choice as simply an ideological rationalization for a conservative, market-oriented brand of politics.

Even though we admit the significance of some of the criticisms of public choice, the authors of this book have been influenced by it, and one of us has even written a book attempting to interpret Canadian politics in public-choice terms.[3] Public-choice interpretations, therefore, crop up here and there throughout this text. But we do not believe that public choice is the only valid way of doing political science, and the text draws as much, if not more, on the findings of researchers committed to institutionalism and behaviouralism.

Political Economy

Political economy, like public choice, is also an application of economic theory to the explanation of political life, but it mobilizes a different version of economics. Political economy, at least as the term is generally understood today in Canada, derives from the Marxist view that politics is conditioned by and expresses the class struggle, and that the ruling class uses organized government as a tool to maintain its position of dominance. Starting from this premise, practitioners of political economy refuse to analyze politics and government as such; they believe that satisfying explanations can be found only by linking political phenomena to the underlying realities of class conflict.

As part of its Marxist heritage, political economy also rejects the notion of value neutrality that tends to dominate in other contemporary approaches to political science. Political economists do not see themselves merely as value-free analysts of political life; on the contrary, they hope that by exposing the realities of class conflict, they will hasten the approach of a less exploitive, more egalitarian form of economy and society.

The strengths and weaknesses of political economy are in some ways like those of public choice. Political economy transcends the divide between behaviouralism and institutionalism; and its explicit theory of human nature as a product of social circumstances, particularly of the class struggle, gives it rigour and consistency. But as with public choice, those who question the underlying economic premises will have further doubts about the validity of applying them to the interpretation of politics.

ORGANIZATION OF THE DISCIPLINE

Political science, like all academic disciplines, has become so large that internal specialization is necessary. Political scientists typically think of themselves as working in one or two particular fields, and university and college departments of political

NEL

299

science organize their course offerings accordingly. The following, most common, way of carving up the discipline is based more on convenience than on any profound intellectual rationale:

- Political philosophy
- Canadian politics
- Comparative politics
- International relations

Political philosophy, which goes back to Plato and Aristotle, is treated as a separate field because it has its own long tradition and because its methods are mainly reflective and conceptual rather than empirical. Yet political philosophy often generates empirical hypotheses that can be tested against evidence in all of the other fields.

Canadian politics is treated as a field simply because we live in Canada and the requirements of citizenship make it important to understand the politics of the country where we live. Each country treats its own national politics as a distinct field. Thus, American and British universities have separate fields of American and British politics and teach Canadian politics (if they do) as part of comparative politics.

It is important to note that Canadian politics does not operate only at the national level. Provincial and municipal governments are important political arenas that for many students are closer to their own experience than the more remote field of national government. Recent developments in aboriginal self-government have further enriched the field of local government. At one time aboriginal communities were simply administered by the Department of Indian Affairs and thus were not of much interest to political scientists; but the more than 600 Indian bands, today usually called First Nations, now have governments that are just as worthy of study as other local governments in Canada.

Comparative politics is the study of politics in different countries. Canadian universities teach American and British politics as part of comparative politics, even though these would be considered separate fields in the United States and Great Britain. This is mainly a matter of convenience. Politics has many similarities and differences all around the world, and everyone understands their own national politics better through comparison with those of other countries. This book, while written for Canadian students, tries to bring in comparative material from many other countries, particularly the United States and Great Britain, to give Canadians a better understanding of their own system.

Comparative politics can also be conceptualized as a method of analysis. Studying multiple cases and looking for both similar and divergent features helps to build a body of knowledge applicable to the entire world, not just to the country in which you happen to live.

International relations studies the way in which independent states relate to one another. As explained at greater length in Chapter 8, international politics is characterized by the absence of overall sovereignty, which makes it a unique field of study. In fact, it is so different that some universities have separate programs or even departments of international relations.

Beyond this traditional fourfold division of political science, still found in almost every university catalogue, there are a variety of fields and subfields that crop up more or less widely. The department of political science in which you are studying may group courses under headings such as public administration, public law, public policy, political behaviour, and research methods. These groupings usually cut across the traditional divisions among the four fields described above. For example, public policy—e.g., the study of government's role in health care—will be both Canadian and comparative. Researchers study the origin and implementation of such policies and also attempt to evaluate their effectiveness in attaining their stated objectives. Policy studies thus have both philosophical and empirical dimensions to the extent that values are involved and evaluations of effectiveness are made. The field of public policy is of particular practical importance because many positions in government are filled by graduates of public-policy programs. A well-known Canadian example of this kind of work is *How Ottawa Spends,* an annual series of volumes produced by the School of Public Administration at Carleton University in Ottawa.

When we debated these matters in our department at the University of Calgary, someone proposed the metaphor of "fields and streams," based on the title of a well-known hunting and fishing magazine. The four traditional areas can be thought of as expansive territorial divisions—the fields—while the special concerns, such as public policy, can be seen as streams meandering through all the fields. Don't take it too seriously; it's just a metaphor. But we have found it helpful in organizing our research and teaching in political science.

HOW SCIENTIFIC IS POLITICAL SCIENCE?

The answer to this question depends upon what you mean by *science.* If you take highly mathematical, theoretical disciplines such as physics and chemistry as the model, political science does not measure up very well. Those sciences operate according to the hypothetical-deductive method, in which hypotheses are logically derived from abstract theories and then tested against real-world data. A famous example is the verification of Einstein's theory of relativity—in itself merely a complex mathematical model—by testing its prediction that the path of light passing close to the sun should be bent by the enormous force of its gravitational field.

Among contemporary approaches to political science, public choice makes the loudest claims to apply the hypothetical–deductive method. Yet many public-choice predictions, including some of the best-known ones, have not been supported very well by empirical evidence.[4] Because of discrepant data, public choice has had to refine its predictions so often that many of them begin to look less like broad generalizations than like specific descriptions of particular cases—in other words, not scientific in the sense of physics or chemistry.

Political science stacks up better against disciplines such as biology and geology, in which systematic observation and careful description still play a larger role than abstract model-building. If biologists can demonstrate how differences in precipitation or soil nutrients affect the growth of plant species, political scientists can show how changes in the electoral system affect the competition of political parties in democracies. If geologists can offer a plausible explanation of many features of the earth's surface in terms of plate tectonics, political scientists can explain elections in terms of the formation and breakup of political coalitions. Geology cannot predict the timing of an earthquake in advance, and political science cannot predict when a realignment of coalitions will take place; but both disciplines can offer enlightening after-the-fact explanations. Political scientists often disagree among themselves about many topics; but meteorologists, geologists, and biologists also sometimes disagree strenuously, for example, about whether global warming is a reality, what its causes might be (if indeed it exists), and how it might be combated (if indeed it ought to be combated).

Political scientists have much to be modest about. The history of the discipline is filled with failed predictions, unsubstantiated claims to scientific rigour, and unproductive ideological controversy. Nonetheless, it is not an unrealistic aspiration for political scientists to build a body of knowledge composed of careful description together with well-tested generalizations about political phenomena.

WHY STUDY POLITICAL SCIENCE?

There are at least four answers to this question.

1. There is no professional category of political scientist, as there is of economist, chemist, or geologist. Nonetheless, the knowledge imparted by political science is highly useful in several professions, and many students major in political science as a sort of pre-professional degree. One can take political science as a preparation for studying law, entering the civil service, or working in party politics. Political science is an obvious springboard for anyone interested in these professions, although other disciplines such as history and economics can also serve the same purpose.

2. Political science is a form of education for citizenship. Everyone in the modern world lives under the jurisdiction of a government and is a potential participant in politics. Even those who are not particularly interested in politics—and not everyone is or needs to be—are required to pay taxes and encouraged to vote. Studying political science can help you become a more effective citizen by enhancing your understanding of the environment in which you operate.

3. The study of political science can be part of a broad liberal-arts education. Political philosophy is particularly useful in this respect. Systematic reflection on government has natural linkages to other liberal disciplines such as philosophy, history, and literature.

NEL

302

4. For a few who have the time, inclination, and ability to go on to postgraduate studies, political science can lead to a career in research and teaching in universities, colleges, and research institutes. Someone who takes this path becomes part of the same type of scientific community that exists for all disciplines. It is a life dedicated to the advancement of knowledge in your chosen field.

All of the above are valid reasons for studying political science. Whatever your own reasons—you probably have more than one—we hope this book provides an entry into the discipline. It's just a first step, not the last word. Take what you learn and build on it. We, as the authors, will be more than compensated if you remember the aphorism of the philosopher Friedrich Nietzsche: "You badly repay your teacher if you always remain a student."

Questions for Discussion

1. Do you agree with Aristotle that politics is not a proper study for young people?

2. Give an example of a normative statement. Do you think that such statements merely reflect personal preferences, or do they have some stronger foundation?

3. Would you personally want to major in political science? Why or why not?

Internet Links

1. Nelson Education Political Science Resource Centre: **www.polisci.nelson.com.** A comprehensive reference site maintained by Nelson Education, the publisher of this book. Includes many links to various topics.

2. Website of the Canadian Political Science Association: **www.cpsa-acsp.ca.**

3. Website of the American Political Science Association: **www.apsanet.org.**

4. The Ultimate Political Science Links Page: **www.rvc.cc.il.us/faclink/pruckman/ PSLinks.htm.** Many links to various topics.

5. Bourque Newswatch: **www.bourque.org.** Gateway to top stories in current events in Canada and around the world.

Further Reading

Archer, Keith, et al. *Parameters of Power: Canada's Political Institutions.* 3rd ed. Toronto: Nelson Canada, 2002.

Baxter-Moore, Nicolas, Terrance Carroll, and Roderick Church. *Studying Politics: An Introduction to Argument and Analysis.* Toronto: Copp Clark Longman, 1994.

Clement, Wallace. *The Challenge of Class Analysis.* Ottawa: Carleton University Press, 1988.

———, ed. *Understanding Canada: Building on the New Canadian Political Economy.* Montreal: McGill–Queen's University Press, 1997.

Dahl, Robert Alan, and Bruce Stinebrickner. *Modern Political Analysis.* 6th ed. Englewood Cliffs, NJ: Prentice-Hall, 2003.

Dyck, Rand. *Canadian Politics: Critical Approaches.* 4th ed. Toronto: Thomson Nelson, 2003.

Goodin, Robert E., and Hans-Dieter Klingemann, eds. *A New Handbook of Political Science.* Oxford: Oxford University Press, 1996.

Guy, James John. *People, Politics & Government: Political Science: A Canadian Perspective.* 5th ed. Scarborough, ON: Prentice-Hall, 1995.

Howlett, Michael, Alex Netherton, and M. Ramesh. *The Political Economy of Canada: An Introduction.* Don Mills, ON: Oxford University Press, 1999.

Johnson, David B. *Public Choice: An Introduction to the New Political Economy.* Mountain View, CA: Mayfield Publishing, 1991.

Jones, Laurence F., and Edward C. Olson. *Political Science Research: A Handbook of Scopes and Methods.* New York: Longman, 1996.

Marsh, David, and Gerry Stoker, eds. *Theory and Methods in Political Science.* London: Macmillan, 1995.

Richter, Melvin. *The History of Political and Social Concepts: A Critical Introduction.* New York: Oxford University Press, 1995.

Shively, W. Phillips. *The Craft of Political Research.* Upper Saddle River, NJ: Prentice Hall, 2002.

Stoker, Gerry, *Why Politics Matters: Making Democracy Work.* New York: Palgrave MacMillan, 2006.

White, Louise G. *Political Analysis: Technique and Practice.* 3rd ed. Belmont, CA: Wadsworth, 1994.

CHAPTER 1

Society, Government, and Politics

In the Introduction, we used terms such as *politics, government,* and *authority* without attempting to define them or to analyze them carefully. We could do that because everyone knows from ordinary life experience, as well as from attending school, more or less what they mean. But knowing "more or less" what key terms mean is not good enough for students of political science. It is time to take a more systematic and detailed look. Government and politics are features of all human societies; we would not be human without them. Hence, in undertaking a careful exploration of the meaning of key terms, we are not just playing around with words—we are coming to grips with human nature itself.

SOCIETY: LIVING TOGETHER

We are all social beings who need the support of others not merely to live well but to survive. There is no record of a time when human beings lived as isolated individuals, coming together only to mate. As far as we know, people have always lived in groups at least as large as the family or band. The usual term for such groups, large or small, is *society.*

Sociologists usually define **society** as a human group whose members live by common rules of conduct and which has a plausible claim to self-sufficiency. Both of these points need clarification. By rules of conduct we mean not just enforceable commands but also regular and predictable behaviour. All human activities, such as marriage, work, and recreation, are carried on within a framework of such rules. Society exists when people share so many rules of conduct that they are able to understand and predict one another's behaviour.

For example, adults in North America and northern Europe have a clear conception about how close to each other two people should stand or sit. In impersonal business situations, they generally maintain a distance of between one and two metres. But the people of Middle Eastern countries do not use this intermediate spacing; they transact business either closer together or farther apart—the distance depends on factors that would not be immediately apparent to us.[1] Such behavioural differences may cause considerable discomfort and misunderstanding in cross-cultural contact. The physical distance between people is not important in itself, but it is vital that it be understood in the same way by everyone concerned. Understanding and living by the rules that govern interpersonal relations is the essence of social order.

Human beings are not the only social animals. There are social insects (bees, termites, ants) and mammals (hyenas, wolves, chimpanzees, baboons). In recent decades the study of animal societies has grown to become one of the most dynamic scientific fields and has yielded many insights that, with appropriate caution, can sometimes be transferred to the study of human society.[2] The common denominator in both animal and human societies is rules of conduct—predictable, regular patterns of behaviour that integrate the individual with the social whole. The major difference between animal and human societies is this: the vastly greater intelligence of human beings allows them not only to understand social rules of conduct but also to change them by conscious decision.

It is impossible to draw clear lines between societies in the modern world. The international movement of people, commodities, and ideas is so vast that self-sufficiency has almost vanished. Rules of conduct have also become widely diffused. The ascendancy of Western society since the fifteenth century has spread many Western cultural practices around the earth: formal education and literacy, modes of dress, table manners, forms of economic activity, and much more. To a great extent, the world has become one society, with regional differences increasingly blurred. A person can travel to and even work in any major city on any continent without feeling that any profound lines of social demarcation have been crossed. Nonetheless, we often speak of societies as if their boundaries were the same as the legal and territorial boundaries established by governments. Thus, it is common to refer to Canadian society or American society, and even to "Alberta" or "Toronto" society, but for analytical purposes it is essential to remember that societies are not sharply distinguished from one another, certainly not by boundaries of governmental jurisdiction.

GOVERNMENT: MAKING PUBLIC DECISIONS

Society is a field of voluntary interaction. People make their own decisions about whom to marry, how to make a living, who their friends will be, and where to shop. **Government,** in contrast, has to do with compulsion, not voluntary decision making. Government is a specialized activity of those individuals and institutions that make and enforce public decisions that are binding upon the whole community. All effective governments carry out at least the following functions: they protect society from external attack, enforce rules of conduct within society, and settle disputes between members of society. The common denominator of these functions is *order,* both internal and external. Governments selectively use force to maintain a stable and durable social order. Beyond this minimum function, government also provide services for members of society. This is particularly true of modern governments, which deliver mail, pave highways, operate health insurance schemes, and provide old-age pensions. But the essence of government is to maintain peace within the social order by enforcing rules of conduct.

But why do rules of conduct need enforcement? Why do human beings not always obey them spontaneously? The problem of obedience is vastly more complicated in our species than in any other because of our greater intelligence. Humans are able not only to follow rules but also to understand and formulate them, reflect upon them, and manipulate them for their own ends. Because of this, there may be differences of opinion about what rules of conduct apply to particular situations.

Even if we could always agree in the abstract about which rule of conduct to follow, there would still be the problem of enforcement. In many situations, cooperation offers benefits, yet the existence of those benefits creates an incentive for self-interested individuals to cheat. For example, almost all of us benefit from paying taxes if the money is used to pave the roads; yet any one person will benefit still more by evading the taxes while continuing to drive on the roads which others pay to maintain. However, the benefit disappears if enough people default on their taxes, in which case there will not be enough revenue to pay for paving the roads. It is an outcome that no one really wants but that no one can avoid if all are motivated only by narrow self-interest.

THE PRISONER'S DILEMMA

The problem of achieving social cooperation is illustrated by the so-called "Prisoner's Dilemma," which is one of the most widely applied models of game theory. Assume that two men, Mark and Tom, are arrested by the police for possession of illegal drugs and suspected of trafficking. The police interrogate them separately and do not allow them to communicate with each other. The police, furthermore, say the same thing to each prisoner: "We know you are guilty, but we need proof. If you inform on your partner while he remains silent, you can go free, and he will get ten years in jail. But if the situation is reversed—if he informs on you while you remain silent—he will go free and you will get ten years. If you both talk, you will both get eight years. But if neither of you talks, you will each get one year on the lesser charge of possession, which is all that our evidence will sustain without further testimony from one of you."

Mark and Tom will achieve the most favourable outcome if they both keep silent; if they do that, each will escape with a light sentence. But that is not likely to happen in the situation as described; instead, each will probably end up informing on the other and thus both will receive the heavier sentence of eight years. To understand why, consider the following payoff matrix:

Prisoner's Dilemma		Mark	
		Silent	Talk
Tom	Silent	−1,−1	−10,0
	Talk	0,−10	−8,−8

Each cell in the matrix contains a pair of numbers separated by a comma. The first number represents the payoff in a given situation to the row player (Tom), the second number represents the payoff in the same situation to the column player (Mark). The upper right-hand cell, for example, shows that if Mark talks while Tom remains silent, Mark will go free (0) while Tom will get ten years in jail (–10).

Now consider how each player will reason if he has complete information about the game and if he is rational in the sense of caring first about his own self-interest. Tom will say to himself, "I face two possibilities. Mark can either remain silent or talk. If he remains silent, I can either remain silent or talk. If I remain silent, I get one year in jail (–1); if I talk, I go free (0)—so I had better talk (0 > –1). But Mark may talk, in which case I again have two choices. If he talks and I remain silent, I get ten years in jail (–10). If he talks and I also talk, I only get eight (–8)—so in this case also, it is better for me to talk (–8 > –10). No matter what Mark does, I will be better off if I talk." Mark will reason the same way, for his column payoffs are a mirror image of Tom's row payoffs.

This result is both interesting and paradoxical. By a rigorous analysis of his self-interest, each prisoner is led to talk, which ensures that they both achieve the less desirable outcome of eight years in jail (–8). If each could trust the other to remain silent, both could achieve the more desirable outcome of only one year in prison (–1). But in the game as described, if we assume self-interested players, neither has reason to have faith in the other's reliability.

The players might hope to obtain a better joint outcome if the rules of the game were relaxed so they could communicate with each other. They could then agree in advance not to inform on each other. But communication in itself is not sufficient to resolve the prisoner's dilemma, for each player still has an incentive to break the agreement if he believes he can count on the other to keep his side of the bargain. That is, if Tom and Mark agree to keep silent, thus ensuring their best possible joint outcome, Tom (or Mark) can do even better by breaking the agreement and playing the other for a sucker. Thus we may still expect each to betray the other.

The game of Prisoner's Dilemma is a model of the general problem of obtaining social cooperation. In the terminology of the social sciences, a model is a simplified abstraction, often mathematical in character, used to represent a more complex process. No one pretends that a model can capture all the aspects of a situation. Prisoner's Dilemma is an obvious simplification: people are not just individuals but also members of families and communities, and they are not purely self-interested but also care about others and feel obligated to follow general rules of conduct. Nonetheless, a model can illuminate important aspects of a given situation—in this case, the tendency to abandon cooperation in the pursuit of self-interest. Of course, in this particular instance, what is good for the two players is bad for the larger society. But it still shows that voluntary cooperation requires a degree of confidence that the behaviour will be reciprocated.

There are two ways to resolve the Prisoner's Dilemma. One is iteration. If the game is played repeatedly, Mark and Tom can learn from experience how to achieve the best outcome for both. A brilliant study based on computer simulations of iterated

Prisoner's Dilemma has shown that the most effective strategy is tit for tat. Do not be the first to defect; trust the other player as long as he cooperates, but punish him if he defects. At the same time, do not hold a grudge: return to cooperation as soon as he does.[3] Perhaps not surprisingly, this conforms to the working morality of most normal social behaviour: approach others in a cooperative way; cooperate as long as they do, but don't let yourself be played for a sucker. The other way to resolve the Prisoner's Dilemma is to enforce agreements. If Tom and Mark can find some way to ensure—or at least to increase the probability—that both will keep their promises, each will be able to rely on the other and be willing to cooperate to their mutual benefit.

The enforcement of agreements by an external authority is one of the most important things that government does. By promising to serve as an enforcement agency, government promotes social cooperation by overcoming the self-interested logic of the Prisoner's Dilemma game. Remember the example of taxation mentioned earlier in this chapter. The public services paid for by taxation benefit everyone, yet everyone has an incentive to evade taxation and let others carry the burden. It is a multi-sided cooperation problem (*n*-person Prisoner's Dilemma, in the jargon of game theory). By enforcing the payment of taxes, government resolves the dilemma and ensures that resources are made available to provide the public services that people actually want but might not get if all were left to pursue their narrow self-interest.

POLITICS: GATHERING SUPPORT

A concept always associated with government is **politics.** The word comes from the Greek *polis,* usually translated as "city-state." The ***polis*** was the typical Greek form of political community at the time of Socrates, Plato, and Aristotle, the founders of political science. The *polis* consisted of a city, such as Athens or Sparta, plus some surrounding hinterland, including smaller towns and villages. It has given us a number of related words having to do with the idea of the common good, such as *politics* and *police.*

Curiously, politics is one of the most disputed terms in the vocabulary of political science. Almost everyone uses it as an occasional synonym for government, but beyond that it has taken on a wide variety of meanings, some of which are discussed in this chapter. The various definitions tend to emphasize different aspects of politics. We believe that each contains an element of truth and that a satisfactory understanding of politics must be comprehensive and multifaceted. It may seem odd to the student reader to have to slog through a whole range of definitions of a term that is so basic to the discipline, but the reality is that different writers define politics in different ways, so you must be ready for the variety that you will encounter.

One definition comes from a French writer, Bertrand de Jouvenel. According to Jouvenel, "We should regard as 'political' every systematic effort, performed at any place in the social field, to move other men in pursuit of some design cherished by the mover."[4] For him, politics is the activity of gathering and maintaining support for human projects.

Jouvenel's conception of politics emphasizes support. Another common approach is to equate politics with conflict. J. D. B. Miller writes that politics "is about disagreement or conflict."[5] Alan Ball carries this even further; for him, politics "involves disagreements and the reconciliation of those disagreements, and therefore can occur at any level. Two children in a nursery with one toy which they both want at the same time present a political situation."[6]

Ball's definition is not too far from Jouvenel's, for in real life mobilizing supporters for a project almost always involves overcoming conflicts of opinion or desire. Certainly conflicts arise that do not seem political in any usual sense: there is conflict if a mugger tries to take my wallet, but it is a simple crime, not a political action, because no collective project is envisioned. To be political, a crime must be linked to some vision of reordering society. It is thus a political act—as well as a crime—for a revolutionary group to kidnap a politician in the hope of exciting the people to rise against the government.

Yet another conception of politics is expressed in the title of Harold Lasswell's famous book, *Politics: Who Gets What, When, How.*[7] In Lasswell's view, politics is the distribution of the good things of earthly life, such as wealth, comfort, safety, prestige, and recognition. David Easton means the same thing when he says that politics is the "authoritative allocation of values"—values meaning not moral ideals but those things in life that people desire.[8] There is certainly much merit in this approach, in that it draws attention to the fact that the winners in a conflict—that is, those who succeed in mobilizing support for their projects—usually allocate to themselves and their followers a generous share of material and social benefits. At the same time, however, the distributive approach tends to risk merging politics with other activities. Wealth, for example, can be distributed through the impersonal economic transactions of buying and selling, which are not in themselves political acts because they do not involve mobilizing support for a common project. I do not have to be a supporter of Tim Hortons to buy a doughnut and a double-double; I just have to be hungry and have a little money to spend in order to engage in an act of exchange.

Funky Winkerbean © Batom, Inc. North American Syndicate

Having looked at many definitions, we would promote the following, which is a slight variation on Jouvenel's: Politics is a process of conflict resolution in which support is mobilized and maintained for collective projects. Government—which involves making and enforcing rules—is thus laden with politics at every stage. A government cannot carry out its various functions unless it has some popular support. It will probably lose that support if it is unable to maintain internal and external peace and to provide services desired by the population. Government in a democracy must have an especially high level of popular support, and elections are an important way of acquiring it. This is why the term *politics* has come to be associated with elections and related phenomena, such as political parties. The phrase "going into politics" usually implies running for elective office. This popular usage is valid as far as it goes but is only one aspect of politics in the broader sense.

Politics has been called the art of the possible and the art of compromise because it must resolve disagreements among people with different opinions and desires. Compromise is usually necessary if violence and coercion are to be avoided. Political problems rarely have a satisfying solution; usually the best that can be obtained is a settlement—that is, an arrangement that makes no one perfectly happy but with which everyone can live.[9] When this is achieved, politics approximates the definition put forward by the English political scientist Bernard Crick: "The activity by which different interests within a given unit of rule are conciliated by giving them a share in power in proportion to their importance to the welfare and the survival of the whole community."[10] Citing Aristotle, Crick argues that politics is not unity but harmony—that is, the peaceful and cooperative coexistence of different groups, not their reduction to a single imposed pattern. This is a good description of politics as it can be and sometimes is practised; but in reality harmony often breaks down and people resort to coercive measures.

COALITIONS: POLITICS IN ACTION

The fundamental unit of political activity is the **coalition,** defined as "the joining of forces by two or more parties during a conflict of interest with other parties."[11] Coalitions involve both conflict and cooperation. They draw a boundary within which cooperation takes place to defeat or gain advantage over an external opponent. Political coalitions are formed precisely to exclude others and thereby exercise power over them.

There are at least three kinds of coalitions. The first kind has parallels among the primates and the social carnivores, whose coalitional behaviour can be observed both in zoos and in natural settings; the other two are distinctively human because they depend on language and the manipulation of symbols.

1. In small-scale settings, coalitions are based on personal relationships among individuals. For example, in any parliamentary system the prime minister must keep

the support of the party caucus—the party's elected members of parliament—in order to remain in office. Jean Chrétien showed himself to be adept at this while he was prime minister during the 1990s. His caucus contained a so-called "right wing" interested in balancing the budget, reducing taxes, and creating a favourable climate for business, as well as a "left wing" interested in causes such as preserving public health care, expanding publicly funded child care, and promoting gay rights. The prime minister expelled one member from caucus during this period—the Toronto MP John Nunziata—but generally succeeded in keeping these two internal factions cooperative with each other and with the party leadership.

2. Coalitions can also be formal alliances. The North Atlantic Treaty Organization (NATO) is a coalition of 26 European and North American countries that have agreed to defend each other in case of attack. In domestic politics, cabinets are sometimes formed by coalitions when no single party has a majority of seats in the elected legislature. The party caucuses, acting through their leaders, make an explicit agreement to support each other and to divide up the seats in the cabinet. The cabinets of many European democracies—for example, Germany, Italy, Denmark, and the Netherlands—are routinely put together in this way. The most recent Canadian example is the Liberal–NDP coalition cabinet formed in Saskatchewan after the 1999 provincial election left the NDP with exactly half the seats, one seat short of a controlling majority. That coalition lasted until the election of 2003, at which time the NDP won a narrow majority (30–28) over the opposing Saskatchewan Party and the Liberals failed to win any seats at all.

3. Less formally, the building of coalitions is a characteristic of the mass politics of modern democracies. Party leaders form electoral coalitions by proposing policies to attract certain groups of voters. Each party tends to be backed by a distinctive array or coalition of groups defined by geography or demography. For example, major elements in the Republican coalition in American national politics are white Southerners, suburban and rural voters (especially in the Great Plains and Rocky Mountain states), private-sector businesspeople, and (increasingly) Roman Catholics. The Democratic coalition, in contrast, emphasizes blacks, Latinos (except Cubans, who tend to vote Republican), Jews, organized labour (especially teachers and other government employees), and urban voters (especially in the Northeast and on the Pacific coast). Of course, these divisions are not absolute: the Democrats get 90 percent of the black vote in presidential races, while the Republicans get only about 10 percent; but even 10 percent of this large ethnic group is still a lot of people.

The individuals or groups that make up any type of coalition are not necessarily permanent partners. Southern whites and Roman Catholics used to support Democrats in American politics but have changed allegiance over time, as have blacks, who used to vote Republican. In Canada, a dominant coalition virtually monopolized federal politics between 1946 and 1984; as a result, Liberal governments were elected for 32 of those 38 years. Significant groups in this coalition included Quebeckers, both francophone and anglophone; immigrants and ethnic minorities in many parts of the country; Roman Catholics; and many individuals in the media and in the academic community. One factor holding these disparate groups together was a belief in the state's ability to guide change, progress, and economic development in Canadian society. When those years produced expensive bureaucracies and programs that did not always work as intended, the stage was set for the breakup of the dominant coalition, and the Conservatives in 1984 seized the opportunity to create a new one, which in turn fell apart in the early 1990s.

To recapitulate: government and politics are universal aspects of human existence. *Government is the process that makes and enforces rules and decisions for society; politics is the activity of reconciling conflicts and gathering support that makes government possible.* Government and politics both arise from the need for people to live in societies; for a society to succeed, people must settle conflicts and abide by common rules in such a way that the community is not endangered. Government and politics involve coercion, but not for its own sake. One reason why rulers resort to force is to lessen the use of force by private individuals against each other.

Government and politics become more and more indispensable as civilization advances. The more complicated our way of life becomes, the less we can afford to have our plans upset by random intrusions of others on our person, property, or expectations. Government can be the great guarantor of the stability of expectations and the force that makes it possible for other human endeavours, such as religion, art, science, and business, to flourish. When a government is working well, the political process continually and unobtrusively resolves those conflicts that might otherwise tear society apart. In fact, politics may work so well that the ordinary person may take it for granted and have very little need to be concerned with it.

Even though government is essential, we are not always reconciled to it. There is a persistent belief that we may someday attain a perfectly harmonious, conflict-free society in which government will be unnecessary. One form of this belief is the Judeo-Christian tradition of the Kingdom of the Saints or the Kingdom of God on earth.[12] According to this idea, human conflict will cease with the advent (Judaism) or return (Christianity) of the Messiah, and there will be no ruler except this divinely authorized figure. Related ideas in Islam involve the appearance of the Mahdi or the return of the Twelfth Imam—enlightened teachers who presage the coming of the Last Days.

Secular versions of this scenario also exist.[13] The early French socialist Henri de Saint-Simon (1760–1825) wrote that eventually "the government of men" would be replaced by the "administration of things"—a formula later echoed by Lenin.[14] They both hoped that in a future world, where everyone was comfortable and gross inequalities had vanished, people would become so peaceable that governmental coercion would be unnecessary. The same expectation is embodied in the Marxist doctrine of "the withering away of the state," which teaches that government will eventually become obsolete after a communist revolution.[15] But none of these visions has ever come to pass, and still we must rely on politics and government to mediate the conflicts that arise among self-interested individuals.

Canadian Focus 1.1

Conservative Coalition-Building

When Jean Chrétien was prime minister of Canada (1993–2003), the conservative side of the spectrum in federal politics was represented by two political parties, the Reform Party of Canada (later renamed the Canadian Alliance) and the Progressive Conservative Party of Canada. Neither party could get enough votes to wrest control of the government from the Liberals until, in 2003, Alliance leader Stephen Harper invited PC leader Peter MacKay to form a coalition. However the two leaders agreed to go even farther and merge, and large majorities in each of the two parties voted in favour of the merger. The new Conservative Party of Canada went on to bring the Liberals down to a minority in the 2004 election and then win a minority government for themselves in the 2006 and 2008 elections.

These events illustrate coalition-building at all three levels described in the text. First, Stephen Harper and Peter MacKay had to build a personal coalition between themselves before anything else could happen. Then, the members of the two parties had to approve a merger of organizations. Finally, voters who were used to supporting the old merger partners had to play follow-the-leader and support the new Conservative Party in federal elections, thus building a mass electoral coalition.

Questions for Discussion

1. Can you think of examples of political conflicts that you have encountered outside of government, for example, in school, clubs, or athletic teams?

2. Can you think of real-world examples of Prisoner's Dilemma games—that is, situations where everyone involved would like something to happen but no one seems to be willing to contribute to getting it done?

3. Compare the various definitions of politics quoted in this chapter. How different are they, really?

Internet Links

1. Government of Canada home page: **www.gc.ca.** Links to all departments of the government of Canada.

2. Encyclopedia Wikipedia: **http://en.wikipedia.org.** A vast storehouse of information. Search for articles on key terms such as government, politics, primitive government, and so on.

3. Prisoner's Dilemma: **www.princeton.edu/~mdaniels/PD/PD.html.** An interactive site where you can play Prisoner's Dilemma games.

Further Reading

Ball, Alan R., and B. Guy Peters. *Modern Politics and Government.* 7th ed. London: Palgrave Macmillan, 2005.

Bateman, Thomas M. J., Manuel Mertin, and David M. Thomas, eds. *Braving the New World: Readings in Contemporary Politics.* Scarborough, ON: Nelson Canada, 1995.

Blakeley, Georgina, and Valerie Bryson. *Contemporary Political Concepts.* Sterling, VA: Pluto Press, 2002.

Brams, Steven J. *Game Theory and Politics.* New York: Courier Dover Publications, 2004.

Brodie, M. Janine, ed. *Critical Concepts: An Introduction to Politics.* Toronto: Prentice Hall, 2002.

Crick, Bernard. *In Defence of Politics.* Rev. ed. London: Pelican Books, 1964.

Evans, Peter, ed. *State–Society Synergy: Government and Social Capital in Development.* Berkeley, CA: University of California at Berkeley, International and Area Studies, 1997.

Flanagan, Thomas. *Game Theory and Canadian Politics.* Toronto: University of Toronto Press, 1998.

Franks, C. E. S., et al. *Canada's Century: Governance in a Maturing Society: Essays in Honour of John Meisel.* Montreal: McGill–Queen's University Press, 1995.

Hawkesworth, Mary, and Maurice Kogan. *Encyclopedia of Government and Politics.* 2nd ed. London: Routledge, 2004.

Klosko, George. *The Principle of Fairness and Political Obligation.* 2nd ed. Savage, MD: Rowman & Littlefield, 2003.

Lasswell, Harold D. *Politics: Who Gets What, When, How.* New York: Meridian Books, 1958.

Leftwich, Adrian, ed. *What Is Politics? The Activity and Its Study.* Oxford: Blackwell Publishing Ltd., 2004.

McMenemy, John. *The Language of Canadian Politics: A Guide to Important Terms and Concepts.* 3rd ed. Waterloo, ON: Wilfrid Laurier University Press, 2001.

MacLean, George A., and Brenda O'Neill, eds. *Ideas, Interests and Issues: Readings in Introductory Politics.* Toronto: Pearson Prentice Hall, 2006.

Miller, J. D. B. *The Nature of Politics.* Rev. ed. Harmondsworth, UK: Penguin Books, 1965.

Pierson, Paul. *Politics in Time: History, Institutions, and Social Analysis.* Princeton, NJ: Princeton University Press, 2004.

Poundstone, William. *Prisoner's Dilemma: John von Neumann, Game Theory, and the Puzzle of the Bomb.* New York: Doubleday, 1992.

Roninger, Luis, and Ayse Gunes-Ayata, eds. *Democracy, Clientelism, and Civil Society.* Boulder, CO: Lynne Rienner, 1994.

Tansey, Stephen D. *Politics: The Basics.* 2nd ed. London: Routledge, 2000.

Tremblay, Reeta Chowdhary. *Mapping the Political Landscape: An Introduction to Political Science.* Toronto: Nelson, 2004.

Walsh, David F. *Governing through Turbulence: Leadership and Change in the Late Twentieth Century.* Westport, CT: Praeger, 1995.

CHAPTER 2
Power, Legitimacy, and Authority

Power in the broadest sense is the capacity to achieve what you want. The word is related to the French verb *pouvoir,* "to be able." Power can be the physical ability to perform a task such as lifting or running, the intellectual capacity to solve a problem, or the social ability to induce others to do what you want.

In political science, power has this latter meaning. Political science is centred around the study of political power, seeking answers to questions such as the following: Who has power and who does not? Are those who exercise power held accountable in some way to those who do not? Can those who wield power be replaced peacefully or only with violence? What beliefs justify the distribution and exercise of power in political systems?

Power is to politics what money is to economics: the medium of exchange, the universal common denominator. Political power, however, is not a homogeneous quantity like money, and it does not have a simple unit of measurement, such as dollars. There are, in fact, three main forms of power—influence, coercion, and authority—which have to be discussed separately.

INFLUENCE

Influence is the ability to persuade others to do your will, to convince them to want to do what you want them to do. The important point is that the targets of persuasion act voluntarily; they are not conscious of restraints on their will because they have freely chosen to agree. Of course, they may agree either because they have come to think that the action is right and justified in itself or because they think they will reap personal benefit from it. Influence takes many forms, which in the hard light of reality often overlap:

- Appeals to the intellect (i.e., convincing people that a given action is intrinsically best)

- Appeals to the passions (i.e., persuading people to act by playing directly on the emotions)

- Appeals to self-interest (i.e., persuading someone to support a cause because of "what is in it for me")

- Appeals to group solidarity (i.e., persuading people to work on behalf of a community to which they belong)

Because there are so many ways to influence others, there are also many resources that can be deployed in the task. The following list, while by no means exhaustive, enumerates some possibilities:

- Intelligence, knowledge, and research can be used to construct convincing arguments.

- People with money and expertise can produce effective advertising.

- People who control wealth can offer financial inducements (bribes).

- People with organizational connections can offer career prospects (jobs, contracts, patronage in all its forms).

- Officials who control the apparatus of government can offer what political scientists call "policy outputs" (i.e., promises to legislate in ways that will benefit their supporters).

Influence is always at work in government. Candidates for office in a democratic system win elections by persuading their fellow citizens to vote for them. Once in office, they are in turn besieged by individuals and groups who want government to do something on their behalf—for example, to build a road along one route rather than another, or to lower their taxes. For its part, government seeks to influence the behaviour of the electorate. For example, the government of Canada has run extensive advertising campaigns exhorting Canadians to exercise more, stop smoking, drink less alcohol, conserve energy, and support Canadian unity.

Democratic politics is a giant web of influence and persuasion. Consider the position of the Conservative government of Canada elected October 14, 2008. They got to that position by persuading 38 percent of eligible voters to vote for them. In order to accomplish that feat, they had to persuade members to join the party, activists to work during the campaign, and donors to contribute money. Having gotten elected through this exercise of influence, the Conservative government became subject to all sorts of influence from those wanting action of various kinds. Business, labour, and agricultural groups lobby for legislation to benefit their members. Advocacy groups, such as Greenpeace, carry out campaigns to steer public opinion in one way or another, with the ultimate aim of influencing government to do something those groups desire. Moreover, because this was a minority government (i.e., the Conservatives won only 143 of 308 seats in the House of Commons), they had to persuade members of one or more opposition parties to support, or at least not oppose, their legislation if they hoped to get anything passed. At the same time, opposition parties were attempting to persuade the Conservatives to make changes in legislative proposals as the price of such support. And, while all of this was going on, all parties were hoping to influence voters to support them in the next election, whenever that would come.

COERCION

Coercion is the deliberate subjection of one will to another through fear of harm or threats of harm. When coercion is applied, compliance is not voluntary but results from fear of unpleasant consequences.

Coercion can take many forms. **Violence** involves physical harm, such as beatings, torture, and murder. Imprisonment, while not directly violent, is enforced by violence if the prisoner tries to leave custody. Other forms of coercion include monetary penalties (e.g., fines imposed by government) and strikes, in which workers combine to threaten employers with losses in the marketplace. The number of ways of harming or threatening people is infinite, but most methods ultimately rely on violence. We must pay a fine for a traffic violation to avoid imprisonment. Employers must submit to the economic setback of a legal strike. If they repudiated their agreements to bargain collectively with the unions, discharged their workers, and tried to hire a new workforce, they would be breaking the law and could be fined or even imprisoned.

A case that straddles the border between coercion and persuasion involves the manipulation of individuals by means of false or misleading information. Motivating someone to act on false information is tantamount to coercion even though it has the appearance of persuasion. The actions of the one who is persuaded would not have been voluntary had the truth been available, so the result is similar to coercion in that it secures involuntary compliance.

Manipulation is a ubiquitous reality in politics. Political leaders rehearse their statements with professional advisers to test them for effect. Words are chosen, and themes are omitted or included, to achieve a desired result. Statements about future consequences of policies generally emphasize the positive and suppress the negative. Political advertising is even more manipulative than politicians' statements because it is often designed to appeal directly to the emotions.

Modern governments try to control most forms of outright coercion, especially violence. Ordinary people are prohibited from violently assaulting each other or seizing property. They are supposed to refrain from violence except in self-defence and limits are enforced even in such situations. Government uses its near-monopoly on violence to protect society from external attack, and to enforce rules of conduct and punish those who violate them. To these ends, every government has developed a complex apparatus of armed forces, police forces, prisons, and courts.

One partial exception to the governmental control of coercion involves industrial relations. During the twentieth century, governments accepted that collective bargaining is an arena in which employees and employers may resort to economic coercion to achieve their objectives. Yet the exception is perhaps not as great as it seems: collective bargaining was introduced to civilize labour relations, which were for a long time marked by a great deal of overt violence. Governments now try, more or less successfully, to legalize a degree of economic coercion and thus keep both sides from resorting to violence.

Government forbids all individuals or groups to use violence against it. Whatever their other differences, all governments are identical in their resistance to acts of political violence, because such acts undermine the very existence of the state. The use of force and the threat to use force against government are defined as political crimes. A government that cannot resist such threats will not survive long. Liberal democracies define political crimes narrowly as the use of force, or the advocacy of such use, against the state. Totalitarian and authoritarian regimes extend the definition to include peaceful opposition to or criticism of the state. The definition of a political crime is an almost infallible test for the genuineness of liberal democracy.

Coercion is a powerful tool, yet no government can depend on it entirely. Society has so many members engaging in so many different activities that everything cannot be coercively directed. Even if it were possible, it would be too expensive because coercion is so labour-intensive. In any case, it is logically impossible for everything to depend on coercion because there must be a coalition of the coercers to get the job done. What holds them together? More coercion? If so, who provides it? At some point, societies must go beyond coercion to a principle that holds its followers together for joint action and that makes it possible for them to coerce others—in a word, *authority*.

The Chinese communist leader Mao Zedong (1893–1976) expressed this truth when he wrote, "Political power grows out of the barrel of a gun. Our principle is that the Party commands the gun; the gun shall never be allowed to command the Party."[1] (The first sentence of this statement is often quoted out of context, as if coercion were the ultimate reality of politics.) To be sure, the gun is significant, as was demonstrated at Tiananmen Square in 1989, when the Chinese government put down the democracy movement with tanks. But it is noteworthy that the army did nothing until the Communist Party had sorted out its internal disagreements and resolved upon a repressive course of action. Until there was clear direction from the party, the army was unwilling to use its firepower against unarmed civilians. The point is that coercion is not the ultimate form of power but a highly useful adjunct to authority.

AUTHORITY

Authority is a form of power in which people obey commands not because they have been rationally or emotionally persuaded or because they fear the consequences of disobedience, but simply because they respect the source of the command. The one who issues the command is accepted as having a right to do so, and those who receive the command accept that they have an obligation to obey. The relationship between parents and young children is a model of authority. Sometimes the parents will persuade the child to do something, and occasionally they may have to resort to coercion, but most of the time they can command with the expectation of being obeyed.

All governments possess at least some authority and strive to have as much as possible, for obvious reasons. Something more than influence is necessary to guarantee predictable results. Coercion produces compliance, but it is also very expensive and furthermore is possible only if a substantial number of agents of coercion are held together by authority. Clearly, authority is an inescapable necessity of government.

It is safe to say that most people most of the time are acting in deference to authority when they do what their government wishes. They stop at red lights and file tax returns because they realize that such actions have been commanded. (Of course, they may have other motives as well.) Perhaps their consciences bother them if they disobey authority. How else can we explain such obedience even in circumstances where punishment is highly unlikely? Most drivers obey traffic lights even at 3 a.m. on a deserted street, and not solely because they fear a hidden police cruiser—almost certainly, they feel a little uncomfortable about violating an authoritative rule. Nevertheless, not everyone is always deferential to authority; this is why coercion is extremely useful—it motivates by fear those who are not susceptible to feelings of obligation. Coercion is present as a background threat, as with a soldier who may be prompted to obey out of fear of a court-martial. But this coercion, though important, is only a tool of authority. Coercion by itself could not produce the united action necessary to hold a court-martial. On the other hand, authority without powers of coercion to back it up is likely to become ineffectual. We have seen this situation in "failed states" such as Somalia, where the government, though still recognized internationally, has lost effective control. In such cases, authority becomes purely nominal and is no longer a form of real-world power.

We must also distinguish between **natural** and **public authority.** The former exists whenever one person spontaneously defers to the judgment of another. Little children tagging after big children, and students seeking out teachers in the early days of the medieval university, are instances of natural authority. Every individual is always surrounded by numerous natural authorities—friends, relatives, colleagues—and acts as an authority to others on occasion. Natural authority is simply another term for the human tendencies to follow and imitate, as well as to lead and initiate. These are some of the bonds that hold society together.

Public authority, in contrast, is deliberately created by human agreement. The English language recognizes the difference between natural and public authority in an interesting way. We say that an expert on baseball statistics is "an authority" in his chosen field, but not that he is "in authority" in that field. But when we describe, for example, a police officer, we do not say she is "an authority" by virtue of any personal quality, but rather that she is "in authority" by virtue of the power entrusted to her by government. Her uniform is a visible sign of the public or artificial authority that she wields. To be a natural authority, you must have special personal qualities; to hold public authority, you have only to be in a position or office that carries with it rights of command.

What is the relationship between public authority and social order? Power is required to order any society, but it must be more than coercive power if a given society is to be open and free. An advantage of authoritative power over coercive power is that most individuals voluntarily submit to it. But why would people submit to any power that restricts their freedom of action? The answer is not easy to find, and political philosophers have grappled with the question for centuries, searching for the roots of consent to authority. One writer has put the issue this way:

> . . . the authority of government does not create the order over which it presides and does not sustain that order solely by its own fiat or its accredited power. There is authority beyond the authority of government. There is a greater consensus without which the fundamental order of the community would fall apart.[2]

LEGITIMACY

Although we often speak of *having* or *possessing* authority, that usage is misleading because it makes authority sound like a quality some people have, like red hair or a deep voice. In fact, authority is a social relationship; an individual has it only if others respect and obey it. Authority is one pole of a relationship in which the other pole is **legitimacy.** When we emphasize the right to command, we speak of authority; when we emphasize the acceptance of command, we speak of legitimacy. Authority is focused in the one who commands; legitimacy is the feeling of respect for authority that exists in those who obey—it is what makes authority possible. It is the same type of relationship as exists between leadership and "followership." Neither makes sense without the other.

Both authority and legitimacy are moral or ethical concepts; that is, they involve perceptions of right and wrong. We feel that someone in authority has a right to command. Similarly, we feel that it is right to obey, that we have a duty or obligation to do so. Governmental power without legitimacy is only coercion or force; with legitimacy, power becomes authority.

Legitimacy creates a sense of obligation, as illustrated in the following diagram:

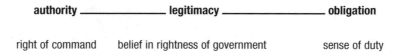

authority ———————— legitimacy ———————— obligation

right of command   belief in rightness of government   sense of duty

We feel obligated to respond to commands when we are convinced that those who exercise authority are justified in doing so.

Public authority survives only as long as it has some degree of legitimacy in society. It is not necessary that literally everyone, or even a numerical majority, accept the legitimacy of a particular government; but there must be at least a loyal minority, strong and united, to withstand potential opposition. If such a minority exists and is willing to use coercion, it can sustain itself in power for a surprising length of time in the face of widespread popular opposition.

It was obvious for decades that the numerical majorities in the Republic of South Africa and in the communist countries of Eastern Europe would have chosen other rulers if they had been effectively consulted. Yet those governments were in little danger of falling as long as they maintained their weapons monopoly and the political support of a determined minority. All these regimes finally changed when reform movements were established within the governments themselves. In each case, substantial elements of the ruling elite, led by the head of government, decided to break with the past. In each case the system had long ago lost its legitimacy, but this in itself was not sufficient to topple the structure of authority.

Legitimacy rests upon beliefs and values that are not static; these things change over time, and legitimacy is challenged when government actions no longer correspond with them. According to Carl Friedrich:

> The process of aging leadership in consensual power situations is usually associated with the disintegration of authority. The actions of the "old one" are no longer understood, because they make no sense in terms of the altered values and beliefs; his capacity for reasoned elaboration is declining and finally is gone. This often carries with it a decline of power, though just as often the power continues, but it gradually becomes more coercive, less consensual.[3]

Power, authority, and legitimacy are integral components of government and politics. Power without legitimacy represents coercion—naked force. Power combined with legitimacy represents authoritative force—the force required to order a diverse society.

One of the great advantages of democracy is that regular, nonviolent changes of government are possible at periodic intervals. If a government ignores ongoing changes in beliefs and values, it can be voted out of office. Democracy provides a safety valve that enables voters to change governments without having to change the nature of the political system. Legitimacy is maintained for the system as a whole even as authority is transferred within it.

Because authority and legitimacy are so central to political life, they are an important focus of study in political science. One of the most important contributions to understanding them was made by the German sociologist Max Weber (1864–1920), who identified three kinds of authority/legitimacy: *traditional, legal,* and *charismatic.*[4] These "ideal types," as Weber called them, are always found mixed together in political systems. They are intellectual models that never exist in pure form in the real world yet help observers to understand what they see.

TRADITIONAL AUTHORITY

Traditional authority is domination based on inherited position. Hereditary monarchs are a good example of traditional authority. They hold the right of command not because of extraordinary personal qualities or because they have been chosen by others, but because they have inherited a position from a parent or other relative. The arrangement is regarded as legitimate because it has the sanction and prestige of tradition: things have been done that way from time immemorial. The principle of inherited authority also draws support from its similarity to the workings of the family, the most fundamental social institution.

The feudal system of medieval Europe was based mainly on traditional authority. At the apex of authority were the hereditary monarchs. They appointed judges, administrators, and military commanders who owed them personal allegiance; their authority was only an extension of the monarch's. Many governmental functions were performed by members of the nobility, whose social positions also stemmed from right of birth. The system depended on the work of the common people, who were born into a social position out of which it was extremely difficult to rise. Throughout the system, command and obedience were associated with inherited social rank and sanctified by tradition. Similar arrangements characterized much of the rest of the world until very recently; traditional authority still prevails in Saudi Arabia and other Gulf sheikhdoms, where authority is vested in the royal family and a number of related clans.

LEGAL AUTHORITY

The central concept of **legal authority** is that of general rules binding on all participants in the system. Authority is exercised only when it is called for by these rules. It is not associated with individuals who inherit their status, but with legally created offices that can be filled by many different incumbents. It is, to quote an ancient phrase, the "rule of law, not of men." (See Chapter 7 for a further discussion of this phrase.)

In Canada and Great Britain, authority is primarily legal, although the external symbolism is still traditional. A hereditary monarch reigns but does not rule, and actual power is wielded by politicians who are elected to office under a strictly defined system of laws. A prime minister is in authority while in office but has no personal status once dismissed. Those who work for government are no longer the personal servants of the monarch; their allegiance to the Crown means loyalty to the government as a whole, not to a particular person within it. There is no longer a hereditary class of nobles carrying out governmental functions. The House of Lords still survives in Great Britain, but it is mainly a symbolic reminder of the vanished age of traditional authority. The system derives its legitimacy not from the acceptance of status or from loyalty to personal authority, but from loyalty to the constitution, which is a legal system stronger than any individual.

However, some traditional elements still survive within contemporary legal authority. Law itself is hallowed by tradition. As rule-following animals, we quickly build up habits of compliance to those in power. Over time, it begins to seem right to obey, simply because that is the way things have been done in the past. It is undoubtedly true that habit is a powerful source of governmental legitimacy. We obey because we are accustomed to, because we have always done so. Reflective thought is not necessarily involved.

Such habits of obedience are necessary, for if we continually had to reconsider the legitimacy of government we would have time for little else. Those habits break down in times of revolutionary transition, when one form of authority is replaced by another. Yet they quickly re-establish themselves as part of the new government's legitimacy.

The great trend of development in modern political history is for traditional authority to be replaced by legal authority. This long, slow, and painful process began in Great Britain and its American colonies in the seventeenth century, continued in Europe in the eighteenth and nineteenth centuries, and engulfed the entire world in the twentieth century. It is the political aspect of the wider social process known as **modernization.** Social changes gradually and cumulatively modified people's notions of political legitimacy; this process was punctuated at certain times with the dramatic collapse of a traditional regime and its replacement by a new system of legal authority. The great popular revolutions of modern history must be seen in this context:

1688	Glorious Revolution	Stuarts overthrown by English Parliament
1776	American Revolution	American colonies declare independence from British Crown
1789	French Revolution	Bourbon dynasty replaced by a republic
1911	Chinese Revolution	Manchu dynasty replaced by a republic
1917	Russian Revolution	Romanov dynasty overthrown; Russian Empire becomes Soviet Union

These are only a few of the many revolutions that in three centuries have transformed the political face of the globe. Together they make up what is often called the world revolution. The French writer Alexis de Tocqueville, who made an extended tour in 1831–32 of the United States and Canada and noted the great social inequality of the traditional order of Europe, memorably stated the essence of the transition from traditional to legal authority:

> On the one side were wealth, strength, and leisure, accompanied by the refinements of luxury, the elegance of taste, the pleasures of wit, and the cultivation of the arts; on the other were labor, clownishness, and ignorance. But in the midst of this coarse and ignorant multitude it was not uncommon to meet with energetic passions, generous sentiments, profound religious convictions, and wild virtues. The social state thus organized might boast of its stability, its power, and, above all, its glory. But the scene is now changed. Gradually the distinctions of rank are done away; the barriers which once severed mankind are falling down; property is divided, power is shared by many, the light of intelligence spreads and the capacities of all classes are equally cultivated.[5]

This social equalization described by de Tocqueville is inseparable from legal authority, in which individuals are governed by universal rules applicable to all. It cannot coexist for long with the hereditary classes and ranks of traditional authority.

The worldwide transition from traditional to legal authority is the single most important political event of our times, and furnishes the context in which everything else takes place.

The collapse of communism in the Soviet Union and Eastern Europe was a further development in this direction. Communism as an ideology promised the benefits of legal authority and social equalization, but the communist regimes never came close to attaining these goals. In practice, they resembled a kind of bureaucratic feudalism, with great emphasis on the personal authority of the party leaders and disregard for impersonal legal norms. The party leaders constituted an elite as privileged and oppressive as any traditional aristocracy.

CHARISMATIC AUTHORITY

Charismatic authority is based on the projection and perception of extraordinary personal qualities. Weber defined charisma as "a certain quality of an individual personality by virtue of which he is set apart from ordinary men and treated as endowed with supernatural, superhuman, or at least specifically exceptional powers or qualities."[6]

Charisma was originally a theological term, derived from the Greek word for "grace" or "spiritual favour." Generally speaking, charismatic leaders are prophets, saints, shamans, or similar figures. Their legitimacy does not depend on tradition or law but on their followers' belief that they speak to them directly from God. Their transcendental claim to authority often places them in conflict with traditional or legal authorities. Some of our most striking and well-known historical figures were charismatic in this sense: the biblical prophets of the Hebrews, as well as Joan of Arc, whose heavenly visions inspired her to help drive the English from France. (For a Canadian example of charisma, see Historical Perspectives 2.1 on Louis Riel.)

The term *charisma* is also applied to political leaders who base their claim to rule on an alleged historical mission. Adolf Hitler, for example, believed that he had a special mission to restore Germany's greatness. He came to this conviction as he lay in hospital in 1918, having been blinded by a British gas attack on the Western front. His blindness coincided in time with Germany's surrender, and when he recovered his sight he became convinced that he might also be the means of Germany's restoration to greatness. The title he always preferred was *Führer*, the German word for leader; it emphasized that his authority radiated from his personality, not from any office that he happened to occupy.

Charisma is sometimes collectively shared, as in the political thought of the Ayatollah Khomeini (1900–89), the symbol and leader of the revolution that swept the Shah of Iran from power in 1979. Khomeini was a jurist who specialized in the study of the *Shari'a,* the Islamic law. "The jurists," according to Khomeini, "have been appointed by God to rule."[7] The state, he said, must also have secular legislative and executive authorities, but the jurists as a group have an overriding and divinely

Historical Perspectives 2.1

Louis Riel

Louis Riel is Canada's best-known example of a charismatic leader. On December 8, 1875, he experienced a mystical illumination that convinced him he was the "Prophet of the New World." He saw himself as endowed by God with a personal mission to create a new religion in North America in which his own people, the Métis, would be a chosen people like the Hebrews. Riel wanted the Métis to adopt certain Old Testament practices, such as polygamy and the Saturday sabbath; these would eventually be merged with a revised version of Roman Catholicism. Riel preached this novel doctrine to the Métis at Batoche during the North-West Rebellion of 1885. The rebels formed a sort of provisional government, but Riel did not hold office in it—he preferred to be recognized as a prophet. Each morning he assembled the Métis forces to tell them of the divine revelations he had received during the night. He promised his followers that God would work a miracle to defeat the expeditionary force sent by Canada. The miracle did not happen and the uprising was crushed. Riel was later convicted of high treason. He went to the scaffold believing that he, like Christ, would rise from the dead on the third day after his execution. His execution served as a form of martyrdom that ensured his reputation would persist and grow across subsequent generations of history.

In eastern Canada, Riel seemed like a madman, and in fact his friends and relatives in Montreal had him committed to a lunatic asylum in the years 1876–78. But the Métis saw him as charismatic. His inspiration played off the desperation of the buffalo-hunting Métis, as they were increasingly marginalized by the opening of the Canadian West to agricultural immigration and economic development.

given power and responsibility to ensure that all government is carried on within the principles of the *Shari'a*. Khomeini saw himself less as a special individual than as the most prominent representative of a charismatic class. This class of jurists still exercises considerable power in the contemporary Islamic Republic of Iran, though it is also paralleled by a more conventional structure of legal authority based on a written constitution and elections.

The term charisma is also often applied to politicians who have never made claims like those of Louis Riel or Joan of Arc. Two good examples from twentieth-century history in North America were the American president John Kennedy and the Canadian prime minister Pierre Trudeau. Both were young, handsome, athletic, intelligent, and highly educated men who stirred up unusual excitement among the public. Both ran for office under the aegis of idealistic slogans—Kennedy's "New Frontier" and Trudeau's "Just Society." In Canada in 1968, observers referred to Trudeau's first national election campaign as "Trudeaumania." Yet, although both Kennedy and Trudeau enjoyed a type of adulation usually reserved for movie stars, rock musicians, and professional athletes, neither claimed to be anything more than an officeholder in a structure of legal authority. Certainly, neither man claimed a right to rule on the basis of divine inspiration or a world-historical mission. If political leaders such as Kennedy and Trudeau are to be called charismatic, it should be remembered that this is a looser use of the term than when it is applied to genuinely charismatic authorities such as Louis Riel.

Charisma, like authority in general, is not a thing that a leader has; it is a social relationship based on the followers' perception of the legitimacy of the leader's claims. The most important question is not how Joan of Arc, Louis Riel, or Adolf Hitler could utter such extraordinary claims about themselves, but how they could find such a receptive audience. The short answer is that charismatic leaders are accorded legitimacy in times of crisis or grave unrest when other forms of authority appear to have failed. Joan of Arc came to the rescue of France during the Hundred Years' War at a time when England had the upper hand and France was in danger of being conquered. The traditional authority of the French monarch seemed incapable of meeting the challenge. Riel preached his radical gospel to the Métis at a time when the disappearance of the buffalo and the replacement of ox-trains by railways and steamboats threatened to destroy the Metis' way of life. It was a challenge that the traditional Métis authorities, the patriarchs of the clans, were helpless to meet. Hitler came to power during a turbulent phase of German history. The traditional authority of the Kaiser had been destroyed by Germany's defeat in World War I; and the legal authority of the Weimar Republic, never deeply rooted, was gravely shaken by the runaway inflation of the early 1920s and the international depression of the early 1930s. Driven to desperation, the German people, particularly the middle class, listened to Hitler's promises of salvation.

If charisma is a response to crisis, it is difficult to see how it can be very long-lasting. As stability is restored, we would expect a return to traditional or legal authority. Weber was well aware of this tendency, which he called the "routinization of charisma."[8] The more success prophets or leaders have in creating a following, the more either they or their followers find it necessary to create an enduring structure of authority that can exist over generations. If Riel had been successful in the North-West Rebellion, he would eventually have had to take on some role other than prophet. Once the Shah was overthrown, Khomeini approved a new Iranian constitution that institutionalized and regularized the authority of the Islamic jurists, who have carried on since his death. Political history seems to alternate short, intense upheavals of charismatic authority with longer periods of normalcy.

Questions for Discussion

1. Some people talk about hunger, poverty, and disease as forms of violence directed against the poor. Would you agree or disagree with extending the concept of violence to cover these things? Why or why not?

2. The traditional model of authority presents government as a sort of extended family. Based on your experience, what similarities and differences do you perceive between government and the family?

3. Politicians and rock stars can both be charismatic. What do they have in common?

Internet Links

1. Nelson Education Ltd. Political Science Resource Centre: **www.polisci.nelson. com.** Links to studies of political violence.

2. Use "charismatic authority" as a search term. The Internet will give you dozens of discussions of the subject, in both general and specific contexts.

3. Much of this chapter is based on the work of Max Weber. For an informative site on Weber, go to **www.faculty.rsu.edu/~felwell/Theorists/Weber/Whome.htm.** If the link is balky, use "Max Weber" as a search term.

Further Reading

Baldwin, David Allen. *Paradoxes of Power*. Oxford: Blackwell, 1989.

Connolly, William, ed. *Legitimacy and the State*. Oxford: Basil Blackwell, 1984.

Frank, Thomas. *The Power of Legitimacy among Nations*. New York: Oxford University Press, 1990.

Friedrich, Carl J., ed. *Authority*. Cambridge, MA: Harvard University Press, 1958.

Jaffe, Erwin. *Healing the Body Politic: Rediscovering Political Power*. Westport, CT: Praeger, 1993.

Kittrie, Nicholas N. *The War against Authority: From the Crisis of Legitimacy to a New Social Contract*. Baltimore: Johns Hopkins University Press, 1995.

Lukes, Steven. *Power: A Radical View*. 2nd ed. London: Palgrave Macmillan, 2005.

Madsen, Douglas, and Peter G. Snow. *The Charismatic Bond: Political Behavior in Time of Crisis*. Cambridge, MA: Harvard University Press, 1991.

Mumford, Michael D. *Pathways to Outstanding Leadership: A Comparative Analysis of Charismatic, Ideological, and Pragmatic Leaders*. Philadelphia: Lawrence Erlbaum Associates, 2006.

Nelson, Daniel N. *After Authoritarianism: Democracy or Disorder?* Westport, CT: Greenwood Press, 1995.

Raz, Joseph. *Authority*. Oxford: Blackwell, 1990.

Russell, Bertrand. *Authority and the Individual*. Boston: Beacon Press, 1960.

———. *Power: A New Social Analysis.* New York: Routledge, 2004.

Sennet, Richard. *Authority.* New York: Knopf, 1980.

Shaar, John H. *Legitimacy and the Modern State.* New Brunswick, NJ: Transaction Publishers, 1989.

Vidrich, Arthur J., and Ronald M. Glassman, eds. *Conflict and Control: Challenge to Legitimacy of Modern Government.* Beverly Hills, CA: Sage, 1979.

Wrong, Dennis H. *Power: Its Forms, Bases and Uses.* Oxford: Basil Blackwell, 1979.

Zartman, I. William, ed. *Collapsed States: The Disintegration and Restoration of Legitimate Authority.* Boulder, CO: Lynne Rienner, 1995.

CHAPTER 3
Sovereignty, State, and Citizenship

SOVEREIGNTY

The term **sovereign,** derived from the Latin *super,* meaning "above," literally denotes one who is superior. Human beings naturally associate superiority with the physical quality of elevation. We put kings and queens on high thrones to make them taller; and we picture God, the highest of all authorities, as living in the heavens above the earth. Conversely, we lower ourselves to recognize authority. We bow or curtsy when we address royalty, and we kneel or even prostrate ourselves when we pray.

Sovereignty was first used in its modern sense by the French author Jean Bodin toward the end of the sixteenth century. Writing at a time of fierce wars between Catholics and Protestants, Bodin sought to obtain civil peace by establishing the king as the supreme authority whose will could decide such disputes. Bodin's idea was that in any community there ought to be a single highest authority who is not subject to other human authority. He wrote in *Six Livres de la République* (1576) that "sovereignty is the absolute and perpetual power of a commonwealth. The sovereign Prince is only accountable to God . . . Sovereignty is not limited with respect to power, scope, or duration . . . The Prince is the image of God."[1]

Bodin, who was a student of Roman law, was trying to revive the idea of centralized power in an age in which it did not exist or existed only in an imperfect way. To understand why this was so, we must recall some facts about the feudal society of medieval Europe. Everyone was subject to a feudal overlord, but there was no effective pyramid of authority with the monarch at its peak. For all practical purposes, the nobles were often autonomous, as were many city-states in Italy and along the Rhine. The pope exercised a claim to rule in religious matters through his bishops. The Church maintained its own system of ecclesiastical courts; it even had the power to gather taxes, by which means money flowed to Rome. Nowhere was there a single sovereign—a highest authority—and, indeed, except for the authority of God, the concept did not exist. This helps to explain why the religious wars of the Protestant Reformation were so protracted. Various nobles gave their support to one side or the other, and there was no effective central power to keep them all in check. Bodin's idea of the sovereign took hold at a time of revulsion against this warfare and became well established in the seventeenth and eighteenth centuries. This was the age of *absolute monarchs*—so called not because they could do whatever they pleased, but because there was no human authority superior to theirs.

However, it is less the person than the power that is of interest here. **Sovereignty** is the authority to override all other authorities. Family, employer, church—all social authorities—must yield to the sovereign's power when it is turned in their direction. More concretely, sovereignty is a bundle of powers associated with the highest authority of government. One is the power to enforce rules of conduct—by establishing tribunals, compensating victims, punishing offenders, and so on—and includes the power of life and death. Another is the power to make law; that is, to create new law, amend existing law, and repeal old law. Sovereignty also includes the control of all the normal executive functions of government such as raising revenue, maintaining armed forces, minting currency, and providing other services to society. In the British tradition sovereignty also implies an underlying ownership of all land. Private ownership of land "in fee simple" is a form of legal delegation from the sovereign, who can reclaim any parcel of land through expropriation. Compensation to the private owner is customary but not required. Finally, sovereignty always means the power to deal with the sovereigns of other communities as well as the right to exercise domestic rule free from interference by other sovereigns.

Sovereignty was exercised by individual sovereigns in the Age of Absolutism, in the seventeenth and eighteenth centuries, but it can also be placed in the hands of a small group or an entire people. In England, the Stuarts' claims to absolute monarchy were decisively defeated by Parliament in the Glorious Revolution of 1688. This victory ultimately led to the theory of **parliamentary sovereignty,** articulated by William Blackstone in his *Commentaries on the Laws of England* (1765–69). Blackstone held that the supreme authority in England was Parliament, defined as the Commons, Lords, and Crown acting together under certain procedures.

Parliamentary sovereignty is still the main principle of the British constitution. It means that Parliament may make or repeal whatever laws it chooses; one Parliament cannot bind its successors in any way. Parliament is still the highest court in the land and cannot be overruled by the judiciary. The executive authority of government symbolized by the Crown can be exercised only by ministers who are responsible to Parliament.

One hundred years ago, A. V. Dicey, one of the greatest British constitutional experts, claimed facetiously that "Parliament can do anything except make a man into a woman." The invention of sex-change surgery has now removed even that limitation! However, in other ways Parliament has conceded some of its sovereignty in recent years. By entering into the European Union, Britain has voluntarily subjected itself to decisions of the EU bureaucracy and the European Court of Justice. Britain could leave the EU, but as long as it remains a member the sovereignty of Parliament is functionally limited.

While Blackstone was developing the theory of parliamentary sovereignty, the French philosopher Jean-Jacques Rousseau's book *The Social Contract* (1762) set forth the great alternative of **popular sovereignty.** Rousseau taught that supreme authority resided in the people themselves and could not be delegated. Laws should be made by the people meeting in direct-democratic fashion, not by electing representatives to legislate for them (indirect democracy). "The people of England," wrote Rousseau, "deceive themselves when they fancy they are free; they are so, in fact, only during the election of members of Parliament: for, as soon as a new one is elected, they are again in chains, and are nothing."[2]

Because Rousseau's ideal of direct democracy is extremely difficult to attain in a commonwealth of any great size, subsequent writers have kept alive the notion of popular sovereignty by softening the definition. For example, the American Declaration of Independence (1776) states that governments derive "their just powers from the consent of the governed." This moderate formulation of popular sovereignty, which stresses consent rather than direct rule, underlies modern representative democracy.

The three alternatives of personal, parliamentary, and popular sovereignty are not mutually exclusive. All three have to be examined to explain the present reality of, for example, British government. Queen Elizabeth II is still sovereign in the symbolic sense that she represents the power of the state; she "reigns but does not rule," as the saying goes. Parliament is legally sovereign in its control over legislation and all aspects of government, but Parliament does not exist in a political vacuum. The most important part of Parliament is the House of Commons, whose members are elected by the people at large. Interpreters of the British system argue that popular sovereignty exists in the political sense that Parliament depends on public support. If Parliament uses its legal sovereignty in a way that runs counter to public opinion, the people will elect new members to the House of Commons when the opportunity arises. In the long run, popular sovereignty is as much a fact of British politics as is parliamentary sovereignty.

The British situation is complex, the Canadian one even more so. Canada has a heritage of representative democracy based on the British model, and Canadians share the same balance of personal, parliamentary, and popular sovereignty. The Queen is the sovereign of Canada, as she is of Great Britain and of some other members of the Commonwealth, and Canada has a legally sovereign Parliament whose political composition is determined by a voting population. But Canada's political system also divides power among levels of government. The national Parliament and the provincial legislatures each have a share of sovereign lawmaking power. The provinces, for example, have control of education but cannot issue money or raise an army. The government of Canada controls trade and commerce but not property and civil rights, which are provincial matters.

The inevitable disputes between levels of government regarding the precise distribution of powers are settled in the courts, which have a power not needed or possessed by the British courts: judicial review. **Judicial review** is the power of the courts to declare that actions taken by other branches of government violate the Constitution. Canadian courts have the power to nullify legislation passed by one level of government that invades the jurisdiction of the other. The Canadian system is thus a variant of British parliamentary sovereignty, in the sense that sovereignty is shared by a number of parliaments or legislatures and tempered by the courts' power to declare legislation unconstitutional. In other words, Canadian sovereignty is divided, not concentrated.

This arrangement is vastly different from Bodin's original conception of sovereignty as a single, undivided centre of power.

The same is true in the United States, where sovereign power is also divided among levels of government. A further complexity of the American constitution is that the president, the chief executive officer, must cooperate with Congress in order to make law, wage war, and perform other governmental acts.

Sovereignty may also be delegated to administrative agencies or even private bodies. Marketing boards enforcing production quotas, professional associations licensing practitioners, corporations exploiting mineral rights obtained from the Crown, and trade unions requiring all employees to abide by a collective agreement are all exercising a small, delegated share of sovereignty. Much of modern politics consists of a competitive struggle among organized groups to get the government to delegate a share of sovereign power to them, so that they may use it to benefit their members.

Clearly, Bodin's original desire to locate sovereignty entirely in one place has not been fully realized. The bundle of sovereign powers that exists conceptually may be divided among different hands. Some fragmentation of power helps to ensure that sovereignty is exercised within the rules established by the constitution. It is perhaps better for a free society that power be divided in this way, for concentrated, unopposed power is a standing temptation to abuse by those who wield it.

It might even be best to abandon the concept of sovereignty altogether for purposes of domestic politics and to admit that no person or group is sovereign in the original sense of the term. Metaphorically, we might say that the constitution is sovereign; that is, that all political power is constrained by constitutional rules that establish and limit the exercise of public authority. Different authorities exercise sovereign power at different moments in the political process: the people in voting for candidates to office, parliamentarians in voting on legislation, the head of state in giving assent to legislation, the courts in exercising judicial review. Each exercise of power takes place within constitutional limits, so that no one group or person is sovereign in the original sense.

However, even if sovereignty is internally constrained, divided, and delegated within the state, it still makes sense to inquire whether a government is able to control a certain population or a given territory, free from interference by other governments. This is actually the most frequent use of the term today—that is, to denote autonomy from outside control in international affairs. Sovereignty in this sense is claimed by all governments and recognized by international law.

THE STATE

The preceding discussion of sovereignty makes it possible to develop the concept of **state,** which has been mentioned previously but not fully explained. A state is defined by the joint presence of three factors: population, territory, and sovereignty. A state exists when a sovereign power effectively rules over a population residing within the boundaries of a fixed territory. As the sociologist Max Weber put it, "a state is a human community that (successfully) claims the *monopoly of the legitimate use of physical force* within a given territory" [Weber's emphasis].[3]

Canada is a state, as are Great Britain and France. Quebec, on the other hand, is not a full-fledged state in this sense; it has people and territory but not a sovereign government (except to the limited extent in which a province in the Canadian system has a share of sovereignty). It is the program of the Bloc Québécois and the Parti Québécois to turn Quebec into a state by attaining full sovereignty, but that is a project for the future, not a current reality.

The state is the universal form of political organization in the modern world. The earth's entire land mass, with the exception of Antarctica, is divided into territories under the control of sovereign states. At the time of writing, 192 states are members of the United Nations. It is difficult to say precisely how many states there are in total, because of certain anomalous cases. Some mini-states, such as Monaco, Andorra, and San Marino, do not carry on a full range of relationships with other states; their foreign policy is conducted by larger neighbours. Other difficult cases include *governments-in-exile,* states that lack universal recognition—for example, Taiwan—and puppet or buffer states. Various states claim portions of Antarctica, but the claims conflict and have never been resolved. Despite all this, we tend to take the state for granted as the only conceivable form of political organization, even though the combination of people, territory, and sovereignty that we call the state is, historically speaking, a fairly recent invention. The word itself was not widely used before Machiavelli wrote *The Prince* (1513).

Governmental processes in tribal societies are carried on without the state form of organization. Like hunting societies, the earliest agricultural societies were also stateless. Farming took place in autonomous villages that could handle their collective affairs without a specialized machinery of government. How then did the state arise? The answer almost certainly lies in warfare. Armed clashes between hunting tribes do not lead to the formation of a state as long as the losers can migrate to new hunting grounds; roughly the same is true of primitive agriculturalists, as long as arable land is available. But where new land is not readily accessible, warfare produces a social hierarchy of victors and vanquished that is enforced by coercion. A specialized state machinery of armies, courts, tax gatherers, and other officials evolves as the conquerors enrich themselves at the expense of the conquered.[4] When a strong monarch consolidates conquered territory, the state form of organization emerges.

Research in anthropology and human biology has stressed that reproductive competition was interwoven with competition for land and other resources in the rise of the early states.[5] Tribes victorious in warfare commonly killed or enslaved the men seized among their conquered opponents while making wives or concubines of the captured women. Chiefs and headmen used their power to take and support a larger number of wives. Early states were almost all characterized by polygamy in the upper classes, with kings and powerful noblemen maintaining harems of remarkable size. The Hebrew king Solomon reputedly had 700 wives and 300 concubines.[6]

Once created, the state was a powerful and expansive force. It easily prevailed over neighbouring agricultural communities if these had not formed their own states. It found tougher opposition in warlike nomads, who at times overran even territorial states, as happened often in the history of Europe and Asia. Over thousands of years, tribe after tribe of invaders from the steppes of Eurasia descended upon the empires of China, India, the Middle East, and Europe. Often the conquerors did not destroy the state; rather, they took it over and installed themselves as rulers, and were sometimes able to extend the state's territories. At other times, the conquest was such a shock that the state machinery deteriorated and required a long period to be rebuilt.

The modern European states arose from such an interregnum after invasions by Germans and other peoples destroyed the highly developed Roman Empire. The invaders installed themselves as rulers in medieval Europe but did not initially create a full-fledged state system. There were rudimentary specialized structures of government, but territorial boundaries between authorities were not clear. The Norman conquest of England in 1066 led to a situation that seems bizarre by today's standards. For hundreds of years England's Norman kings were nominally feudal vassals of the French kings, because they still had important territorial holdings in France. The Roman Catholic Church in all parts of Europe carried on activities, such as raising revenue and conducting court trials, that today would be considered governmental. The political history of modern times is the history of the emergence of separate, sovereign states out of the overlapping, interlocking jurisdictions of medieval Europe. For more on the development of European states, see Historical Perspectives 3.1.

Historical Perspectives 3.1

The Development of European States

The development of the state runs like a thread through the familiar epochs into which Western history is customarily divided. Although the subject is far too big for a complete discussion here, we can at least mention some of the main stages.

During the Renaissance (in the fifteenth and sixteenth centuries) there was a great revival of interest in classical antiquity. Knowledge of Latin and Greek became more widespread, and many forgotten works of art, literature, and science were recovered. This revival culminated in *humanism,* one of the great contributions of the Renaissance. One consequence of this was a heightened knowledge of Roman law, whose concept of *imperium* helped clear the way for sovereignty. Legal advisers trained in Roman law guided monarchs toward assertion of centralized control over their territories.

The Reformation (in the sixteenth and seventeenth centuries) broke the political power of the Roman Catholic Church. In England and parts of Germany, new Protestant churches

Historical Perspectives 3.1

were created that were firmly subordinated to the state. (The Queen is still head of the Church of England, for example.) In countries such as France and Spain, which remained Roman Catholic, church administration was shorn of independent political power and the pope lost the ability to intervene in internal political disputes. Another aspect of the Reformation, the increased use of vernacular languages rather than Latin, strengthened the developing states of Europe by fostering the notion of a different official language for each state. The dialect of Paris became the language of France, the "King's English" became the standard speech of Britain, and so on.

The Enlightenment (in the eighteenth century) saw a relaxation of religious tensions. Exhausted by more than a century of religious warfare, people turned their energies to secular matters. Science and philosophy flourished under the patronage of kings, who founded institutions such as the Royal Society of London to promote the advancement of learning. Scepticism, science, and individual freedom contributed to the development of the name by which the Enlightenment is best known: the Age of Reason. Hope and optimism became the qualities of a civilization that perceived itself as peaceful and reasonable.

Interestingly, the Enlightenment in its political aspect is often known as the Age of Absolutism. The European continent was now more or less clearly divided into territorial states ruled by strong monarchs, who established standing armies,

court systems, and police forces and in other ways developed a virtual monopoly of law enforcement and armed coercion. Further, they founded a professional bureaucracy that was capable of raising money through taxes and of offering public services to the population, such as the construction of harbours and highways and the promotion of agriculture. It was in the eighteenth century that the state first took on a shape we would recognize if we could return to that era.

There was an important contradiction between the political thought of the Enlightenment, which was generally individualistic, and the political practices of that age, which were absolutist and monarchical. "*L'état c'est moi*" ("I am the State"), said Louis XIV, emphasizing his personal sovereignty. In England this contradiction had been partly resolved through the establishment of parliamentary sovereignty in 1688. On the continent of Europe the revolution was delayed for a century and was correspondingly more violent when it came. The year 1789 saw a popular uprising against the French monarchy that proved to be the beginning of the end of personal sovereignty and traditional authority. Since then, all the great royal dynasties have been overthrown or made merely symbolic, as in Britain. Yet the age of popular revolutions did not abolish the states created by the absolute monarchs; on the contrary, it extended and perfected those states. Modern governments control armies, police, and bureaucracies that Louis XIV could never have imagined.

CITIZENSHIP

Remember that the state is defined as a sovereign authority exercising a legitimate monopoly of physical force as it rules over a population inhabiting a fixed territory. Just as the legal boundaries of the state mark the limits of its territory, so the concept of citizenship marks its demographic boundaries. The modern state is not just an organized structure of governmental power, it is also an association of members. **Citizenship** is membership in the state.

When the concept of citizenship first arose in the world of the classical *polis,* its meaning was somewhat different than it is today. Citizenship in the *polis* meant the right to participate in public affairs, to vote and hold public office; it was restricted to a minority of those residing in the city. Only free adult males—not slaves, women, or children—could be citizens. Also, ancient cities typically contained large numbers of resident aliens who lived and worked in the city but did not possess citizenship unless granted as a special favour.

Modern citizenship, in contrast, is universal. Citizens are not a special category within the state; they are the state. The essential feature of modern universal citizenship is the right to live within the territorial boundaries of the state. In Canada this is now protected by Section 6 of the Canadian Charter of Rights and Freedoms: "Every citizen of Canada has the right to enter, remain in and leave Canada." Non-citizens require special permission to become permanent residents; and as long as they do not become citizens, they can be deported for reasons such as having entered the country under false pretences or being convicted of a serious criminal offence.

Beyond this minimal right of residence, modern citizenship has also come to include and universalize the classical notion of the right to participate in politics. This happened in degrees throughout the nineteenth and twentieth centuries as the rights to vote and run for office were gradually extended to women as well as to men who were not property-owners. Today, except in a very few countries where democratic institutions do not exist, political rights are seen as an attribute of citizenship. The relationship is protected in Section 3 of the Canadian Charter of Rights and Freedoms: "Every citizen of Canada has the right to vote in an election of members of the House of Commons or of a legislative assembly and to be qualified for membership therein." Many other imputed attributes of citizenship, both rights and obligations, also appear in public discussion. People often speak of the payment of taxes, military service, reception of economic benefits, and freedom from discrimination as if these things were part of citizenship; but there is in fact considerable variation in these matters among political communities. They are not nearly as universal as the right of residence and the right to participate in politics.

There is also a great deal of variation in the rules that different communities use to determine who is qualified for citizenship, either by birth or by **naturalization,** the procedure by which an adult is granted citizenship. Amidst all the variation, however, one can discern two basic principles known by their Latin names: *jus soli* (right of soil) and ***jus sanguinis*** (right of blood). According to *jus soli*, which is the basic principle of citizenship law in the United Kingdom, France, Canada, the United States, and most other states in the New World, anyone born within the boundaries of the state automatically becomes a citizen. Thus women from Mexico occasionally go to great lengths to have their baby born during a visit to the United States, so that the child will be able to claim citizenship, including the right of residence, at the age of eighteen. In much of Europe, in contrast, the basic principle is *jus sanguinis* (right of blood), which means that only the children of citizens acquire citizenship by birth.[7] In Germany, which is quite strict in applying the *jus sanguinis,* millions of Turkish and other foreign workers do not have German citizenship even though they were born in Germany. Most states have elements of both *jus soli* and *jus sanguinis* in their citizenship law, but the balance may be tilted quite far toward one side or the other.

The category of Canadian citizenship did not exist until January 1, 1947, when the first Citizenship Act came into effect. Prior to that time, the key status was that of "British subject," which supposedly carried with it not only the right to vote but also the right to live anywhere within the British Commonwealth (in practice, immigration to Canada from non-white countries such as India and Hong Kong was restricted to almost nothing). Before 1947, residents of Britain, Australia, and New Zealand could without limitation immigrate to Canada whenever they chose and could vote or run for office immediately upon taking up residence; Canadians had the same right to move to those countries and exercise political rights. The establishment of a separate Canadian citizenship was an important step in the emergence of a Canadian state distinct from the rest of the British Commonwealth. Canadian Focus 3.1 provides a summary of the types of Canadian citizenship.

As a summary, let us link together the four key concepts that have been discussed thus far: society, state, politics, and government. *Society* is the voluntary, spontaneously emerging order of relationships in which we coexist with and serve the needs of one another. It is what makes possible human comfort and even survival. The *state* is the community organized and armed with coercive power to protect the social order from internal disruption and external attack, and to provide certain public services to the community. *Government* is the decision-making structure and process of the state, while *politics* is the never-ending struggle for support in the public realm. Social factions put pressure on public authorities hoping to influence their decisions in certain ways, and provide support if the desired decisions are made.

Although the concepts of state and government overlap to a considerable extent, there is a subtle distinction of emphasis between them. Government is the process of decision-making and the structure of offices that sustains the process. The state is the entire territorial community, organized for collective action through its government. The state is a more abstract and permanent entity. Governments come and go as politicians and civil servants change in office, but the state remains, unless it is destroyed through civil war, conquest, or annexation by another state.

Canadian Focus 3.1

Canadian Citizenship

According to the Citizenship Act, the following categories of people are deemed Canadian citizens:

- A person born in Canada (*jus soli*).

- A person born outside of Canada if at least one parent is a Canadian citizen (*jus sanguinis*). Such people lose their Canadian citizenship unless they apply for it and live in Canada for a year before they become 28.

- An immigrant who, after living in Canada for three of the last four years, applies for citizenship, demonstrates knowledge of French or English, and passes a simple test of knowledge about Canada (*naturalization*). Dependent children receive citizenship along with their parents.

Questions for Discussion

1. Economists often speak of "consumer sovereignty," by which they mean that, in a competitive market, producers will be able to sell only those goods and services that consumers are willing to pay for. Compare this to the meaning of sovereignty as used in the study of government and politics. Do you see any important differences?

2. Politicians in Quebec routinely refer to their provincial government as "*l'état du Québec*" ("the Quebec state"). How does this way of speaking differ from the definition of state offered in this chapter?

3. Under current law, Canadians can hold dual citizenship. Do you personally favour this? Regardless of your personal view, what advantages and disadvantages do you see in allowing dual citizenship?

Internet Links

1. Bloc Québécois home page: **www.blocquebecois.org.** Parti Québécois home page: **www.pq.org.** These two sites will give you access to documents explaining Quebec separatists' understanding of sovereignty.

2. United Nations home page: **www.un.org.** By following the links, you can get an up-to-date list of member states (192 at time of writing).

3. Citizenship and Immigration Canada home page: **www.cic.gc.ca.** Gateway to information about Canadian citizenship.

4. Dual Citizenship FAQ: **www.richw.org/dualcit.** Highly informative, non-technical source of information about dual citizenship in United States law. This could be of practical significance to you if you are one of the many Canadians who would like to work in the United States or who have an American family background.

Further Reading

Albo, Gregory, David Langille, and Leo Panitch. *A Different Kind of State? Popular Power and Democratic Administration.* Toronto: Oxford University Press, 1993.

Boyer, Pierre, Linda Cardinal, and David Headon, eds. *From Subjects to Citizens: A Hundred Years of Citizenship in Australia and Canada.* Toronto: University of Toronto Press, 2004.

Camilleri, Joseph. *The End of Sovereignty? The Politics of a Shrinking and Fragmenting World.* Aldershot, UK: Elgar, 1992.

Courchene, Thomas J., and Donald J. Savoie. *Art of the State: Governance in a World without Frontiers.* Montreal: Institute for Research on Public Policy, 2003.

Elkins, David J. *Beyond Sovereignty: Territory and Political Economy in the Twenty-first Century.* Toronto: University of Toronto Press, 1995.

Esberey, Joy E., and L. W. Johnston. *Democracy and the State: An Introduction to Politics.* Peterborough, ON: Broadview Press, 1994.

Foisneau, Luc. *Leviathan after 350 Years.* New York: Oxford University Press, 2004.

Gidengil, Elisabeth, André Blais, Neil Nevitte, and Richard Nadeau. *Citizens.* Vancouver: University of British Columbia Press, 2004.

Gill, Graeme. *The Nature and Development of the Modern State.* London: Palgrave Macmillan, 2003.

Godfrey, Sima, and Frank Unger, eds. *The Shifting Foundations of Modern Nation-States: Realignments of Belonging.* Toronto: University of Toronto Press, 2004.

Guehenno, Jean-Marie. *The End of the Nation-State.* Trans. by Victoria Elliott. Minneapolis: University of Minnesota Press, 1995.

Harding, Alan. "The Origins of the Concept of the State," *History of Political Thought 15,* Spring 1994.

Harmes, Adam. *The Return of the State: Protestors, Power-Brokers and the New Global Compromise.* Vancouver/Toronto: Douglas & McIntyre, 2004.

Jouvenel, Bertrand de. *Sovereignty.* Chicago: University of Chicago Press, 1963.

Magocsi, Paul Robert. *The End of the Nation-State? The Revolution of 1989 and the Future of Europe.* Kingston, ON: Kashtan Press, 1994.

McLennan, Gregor. *The Idea of the Modern State/The State and Society*. Milton Keynes, UK: Open University Press, 1984.

Pierson, Christopher. *The Modern State*. New York: Routledge, 2004.

Poggi, Gianfranco. *The State: Its Nature, Development, and Prospects*. Stanford, CA: Stanford University Press, 1990.

Tivey, Leonard, ed. *The Nation State: The Formation of Modern Politics*. Oxford: Martin Robertson, 1981.

Vincent, Andrew. *Theories of the State*. Oxford: Blackwell, 1987.

Chapter 1

Introduction

If you are reading this book, you are probably already open to the excitement and importance of the subject of politics and government in Canada. How a whole society makes collective, public decisions is a fascinating question. Political personalities can be as interesting as movie stars, and the conflicts between them and their respective teams are as hard-fought as any hockey game. Politics often brings out the worst in human nature—ambition, selfishness, greed, and the will to control—but it is sometimes characterized by the best—an altruistic desire to serve the public interest and to improve the lives of the less fortunate. Politics and government are the only way to solve many societal problems, and may well be the best way to solve some of your own!

Chapter Objectives

After you have completed this chapter, you should be able to:

Identify the many ways in which government action affects your life

Draw a model of the Canadian political system

Explain the main function of each of the major institutions of Canadian government, including the prime minister and Cabinet, House of Commons, Senate, bureaucracy, and judiciary

Appreciate the concentration of power in the executive branch of the government

Outline the basic differences between the Canadian and American systems of government regarding the separation or fusion of powers, party discipline, and the framework of federalism

The Political System

Perhaps it is best to begin with the 34 million residents of Canada. All these individuals have an array of needs that they attempt to satisfy, ranging from water, food, and shelter through security and friendship to self-esteem and self-fulfillment. Some of these needs are felt personally and individually, while others are concerns shared with people of similar position, in small or large groups. Most of us spend much of our time trying to satisfy such needs.

In the first instance, we do so by our own efforts, in pairs, in families, in organizations of all kinds, at work, and at play. By not automatically calling for government help, we are essentially operating in the **private** or **voluntary sectors**. At some point, however, we may begin to feel that the satisfaction of our needs is beyond personal, interpersonal, family, or group capacity, and we come to the conclusion that the government should step in to help us. When we express the opinion that the government should take some action, we are converting a "need" into a "demand" and crossing the threshold between the private or voluntary sectors and the **public sector**. We can say that a demand is the expression of opinion that government take some action (or desist from an action that it is already taking).

The first fundamental question that arises in politics and government is therefore whether people should solve their own problems or whether they should ask the government or the state to intervene. Almost everyone agrees that the government should provide certain security measures, such as police services and armed forces. Most people also support public highways and a public education system. The population may be more divided, however, on the extent to which the government should provide such programs as social assistance, social housing, public pensions, and universal health care. One of the main reasons for such divisions of opinion is that government intervention normally costs money and usually relies on taxes of one kind or another. People also disagree on which areas of life the state should regulate and on how much regulation is appropriate. There is currently much controversy in Canada over the role of government in the protection of the environment. What combination of taxation, regulation, and incentives would be most effective?

The largest group of people reading this book will be young students. If you think about the role of government in your life, many interesting questions come to mind. To what extent should you be expected to pay for your postsecondary education, and to what extent should it be financed by the state? Why do tuition fees keep increasing, and what form and level of student assistance is most appropriate?

The Canadian Federation of Students demonstrates against rising tuition fees. (*CP Photo/Toronto Star/Steve Russell*)

Should the state (provincial or municipal) provide a transit system and/or subsidize bus or subway fares for students travelling to school or work? Should the state (federal or provincial) intervene to regulate the price of gasoline? For the housing needs of students living away from home, should the province regulate the private rental market, or should the municipality, university, or college provide public housing? For those who work, should there be a minimum wage, and if so, what is an appropriate rate? Should all colleges and universities be public institutions, or is private postsecondary education a good idea?

Many of these and other questions go beyond one's status as a student. For example, should affluent people be able to get quicker medical attention because they can pay for such health care, or should Canada maintain a universal system in which no one can jump the queue? Should the public health care system be extended to pharmaceutical drugs and dental care, or should physiotherapy and chiropractic treatment be removed?

Should the state put more restrictions on carbon production, gasoline exhaust, and other environmental hazards, or should companies be minimally constrained in their pollution emissions in the interest of providing jobs? How far should the state go in prohibiting discrimination in the workplace? Should it engage in employment equity programs to enhance the employment prospects of those who were discriminated against in the past? Should the federal government enact a national daycare program, or should it give cash to families and let them find their own childcare solutions? Should people be able to enjoy pornographic materials, or should these be censored by the state? Such a list barely scratches the surface of issues involving potential government action, but it serves to demonstrate the relevance of government to our daily lives.

Many demands arise from deep, persistent divisions within society that political science calls "cleavages." The cleavages in Canadian society that generally have the greatest political significance are those between the geographic regions; between English, French, Aboriginal, and other ethnocultural and linguistic groups; and between various socioeconomic classes. Other common cleavages are related to gender, religion, and age. The relative importance and nature of these cleavages changes over time, and they are the subject of Chapters 2, 3, and 4.

Another way to look at these characteristics of Canadian society is in terms of identities. Each of us has many identities—male or female, Newfoundlander or Albertan, Roman Catholic or Muslim, francophone or Aboriginal, young or old. Indeed, issues relating to ethnicity, gender, and sexual orientation are commonly referred to today as the "politics of identity." But only if people are conscious of a particular characteristic—if it is part of their identity—are they likely to act on it politically. In any case, many of the demands with which the authorities have to contend originate from such cleavages and identities.

Linking People to Government

Both those who seek state intervention and those who prefer that the authorities leave them alone must transmit their demands to the government. In either case, such action requires knowledge and other resources that may well exclude a large proportion of people on the margins of society. On the other hand, those in authority may seek out such demands, asking what different groups in the electorate really want.

Figure 1.1 shows that individuals can communicate their needs directly to the government. This can be done on a personal basis, such as by means of a letter, fax, telephone call, e-mail, or face-to-face encounter. Sometimes such directly transmitted demands achieve their desired result, but very often they do not. When they fail, it may be time to consider some kind of group action.

Canadian society contains many groups, and quite likely a group already exists to articulate the demand that any individual decides to transmit to the government. If such a group is not already in existence, it may be worthwhile to create

Figure 1.1 A Model of the Political System

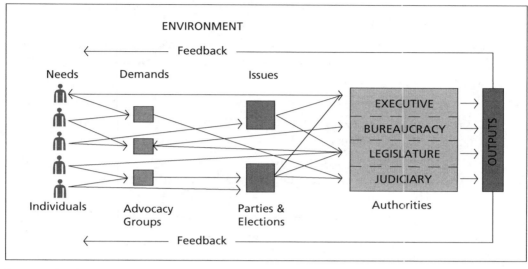

Source: Rand Dyck

one, since, as a general rule, the authorities are more likely to respond to a demand coming from a group than from a single individual. Such groups are usually called **advocacy groups**, **interest groups**, **pressure groups**, or social movements, and they constitute an important part of Canadian political activity. The Canadian Chamber of Commerce, the Canadian Labour Congress, and the Canadian Federation of Students are prominent examples. Corporations and other institutions also make demands, either individually or in groups.

A special kind of group that is even more overtly political is the **political party**, and it can also be used to transmit demands to the government. People join a political party or support it financially and try to get it to recognize their concerns in its platform or policies. If the party comes to power, it can incorporate the demand into government policy; if the party is in opposition, it may be able to press the government to address it or use the mass media to bring the problem to national attention. Parties are particularly responsive to people's demands during an election campaign, as they appeal for the support of large numbers of individuals and groups by promising to take the action they seek. Those dissatisfied with how existing parties are responding to their demands can create new parties, such as occurred with the appearance of the Green Party, the Reform Party, and the Bloc Québécois.

Another means of transmitting the demand to the government is, as suggested earlier, via the **mass media**—principally television, newspapers, and radio. The media are usually eager to publicize controversial issues and often delight in pointing out problems that the government has failed to resolve. They pay attention to individual and advocacy group concerns on a regular basis, cover political party activities, and are especially active in election campaigns, all of which help to bring demands to the attention of the government. More than that, the media also provide the electorate with most of its information about politics, and in so doing serve to shape the whole nature of political discourse in Canada. All of these aspects of linking people to government are discussed in Chapters 6 to 10.

Despite the various avenues that can be used to transmit demands to the government, relatively few demands have any impact. The authorities are likely to ignore demands that do not concern very many people or that are contrary to their own values. Since the number of demands under serious consideration at any given time constitutes such a small proportion of the total number being made, it is sometimes useful to distinguish between demands and "issues," the latter including only those demands that the government has taken under serious consideration. It should be added that those in authority usually have their own concerns, which sometimes carry more weight than demands arising from the wider society.

Government authorities are thus bombarded by demands from all directions, but even more striking than the vast quantity of demands is the usually intense conflict among them. The essence of politics and government, therefore, is choosing among competing demands, trying to resolve conflict, or making social choices in the midst of social conflict. **Politics** can be defined as that activity in which conflicting interests struggle for advantage or dominance in the making and execution of public policies. Politics is closely linked to the concept of **power**, which is often defined as the ability of one actor to impose its will on another, to get its own way, or to do or get what it wants.

Government

Having repeatedly mentioned **government**, we may now define it as the set of institutions that make and enforce collective, public decisions for a society. In Canada, those institutions primarily consist of the prime minister and Cabinet, the House of Commons and Senate, the bureaucracy or public service, and the courts. Backed up by armed forces, police, and punishments, if necessary, government possesses a particular kind of power called **coercion**. That is, it has the ability to impose its will upon us by means of sanctions or penalties. Indeed, as a general rule, only the government, as an agent of the state, is allowed to use force or coercive power in society. But if we (or our ancestors) had a hand in the creation of such a government apparatus, as well as in the selection of the current governors, then we have in a sense agreed to be bound by its decisions. In other words, we have cloaked the government's power with legitimacy, a term defined as "being accepted as morally binding." Such legitimate power is often called "authority," and a synonym for government is "the authorities." To some extent, we obey the government because of the threat or expectation of penalties if we do not, but we also obey because we accept government decisions as binding upon us and necessary for the general good. Think of stopping at a red light or paying income taxes.

Individuals and groups raise conflicting demands, but because there is a widespread consensus on the legitimacy of the government, people generally abide by its authoritative decisions, even when they disagree with them. It is sometimes said, therefore, that politics and government are characterized by both conflict and consensus. The daily conflict normally operates within an underlying consensus about the decision-making apparatus and about remaining together as part of a united political community. Moreover, the authorities usually seek to develop some kind of consensus out of the conflicting demands.

A couple prepare for another federal election. (Graham Harrop/Artizans.com)

Who are these government authorities? As can be seen in the diagram in Figure 1.1, political scientists usually divide them into four branches: the **legislature**, the **executive**, the **bureaucracy**, and the **judiciary**. The authoritative decision that a demand seeks can sometimes be made by a single branch of government. The legislature or Parliament passes laws, so if the demand requires the passage of a law, action by the legislative branch will be necessary. The executive, consisting of the prime minister and Cabinet, has a wide variety of powers. These include deciding where the government will spend money and appointing people to public positions. Thus, if the demand can be satisfied by an appointment or large monetary grant, it should be addressed to the executive. The bureaucracy is made up of public servants who work for the government, providing services, advising the politicians, and issuing regulations. If the demand is for the provision of routine government services or for changes in regulations, bureaucratic action will probably suffice. Finally, the judiciary comprises the courts, which interpret the laws and make other decisions in case of dispute, and if the demand can be settled only by a judicial ruling, it should be transmitted in that direction.

In many instances, however, the demand will require the combined actions of any two of the executive, legislative, and bureaucratic branches, or even all three working together, such as in the formulation, passage, and implementation of a new law. The courts normally stand somewhat apart, and judicial decisions usually follow authoritative actions in other branches of government. For example, the Supreme Court invalidated the abortion provisions of the Criminal Code as being a violation of the Charter of Rights and Freedoms. But judicial decisions may also lead to subsequent legislative action. For example, after the Supreme Court ruled that a total ban on tobacco advertising was unconstitutional, the government introduced a revised law with fewer restrictions.

Government decisions take many forms—laws, regulations, appointments, grants, contracts, services, and judgments—that are sometimes called "outputs." Authoritative decisions are also made in the provinces and territories and in an assortment of regional and local councils and boards, and they often require the agreement of two or more levels of government.

Completing the Picture

Whatever the type of authoritative decision, it usually sparks a reaction in the rest of the system. This leads us to the concept of "feedback"—that is, a communication of the outputs back into the system. If a decision satisfies a particular demand, that demand will no longer have to be articulated. For example, many

French-speaking Canadians demanded that their language be designated as equal to English in federal government operations. The Pearson and Trudeau governments, which grasped at the opportunity to counter nationalism in Quebec, enacted the Official Languages Act as a result. But that was not the end of it: there was feedback or reaction to this decision. On the one hand, some francophones then demanded French-language services at the provincial as well as the federal level. On the other, many anglophones protested that the Act (as well as Quebec language legislation favouring French) went too far. Thus, the reaction to one demand created a new pattern of demands, and the language issue is still very much alive. The political system is thus characterized as a dynamic, circular process in which the authorities react to demands, convert some of them into decisions, and then respond in turn to whatever changes in the pattern of demands have resulted from the feedback from such decisions.

The modern world is composed of some 200 states such as Canada, and each has a government that makes its public decisions. Each state claims its own **sovereignty**, that is, its right to be self-governing; it has the final say over its own territory and people. But today's world is characterized by a tremendous amount of interplay among such states, as well as cross-border interaction and movement in terms of individuals, corporations, other organizations, and information. States often join international organizations and sign international agreements, and transnational corporations operate around the world. These developments constitute the phenomenon of **globalization**. Beyond the internal demands discussed above, such external actions increasingly serve as the source of demands on national political systems, such as the 1997 Kyoto Protocol which Canada ratified but failed to implement. Other external influences such as the North American Free Trade Agreement act as constraints upon domestic policymaking. As noted in Chapter 5, external pressures of these kinds often lead a government into actions that it otherwise would not take, and no state is as sovereign as it would like to be. Especially since the terrorist attacks on the United States in September 2001, governments have had to give additional attention to the adequacy of their security measures.

What Do You Think?

Is it fair to owners of apartment buildings, hotels, bars, and restaurants to prohibit smoking by means of provincial laws or municipal bylaws? Is it fair to smokers? Whose interests should prevail: those of smokers, non-smokers, owners, employers, customers, tenants, or employees?

Foundations of Canadian Government Institutions

The state called Canada was created in 1867, but remained a British colony until the Statute of Westminster provided for complete autonomy in 1931. At its origins, Canada was a federation composed of four provinces, but it eventually grew to encompass ten provinces and three territories.

The Parliamentary System

Before going any farther, let us outline more specifically the basic institutions of government in Canada, which are dealt with in detail in Chapters 11 to 16. Within the central or national government in Ottawa (often called the "federal government"), the British parliamentary system provides the foundations of these governmental institutions. This system is based on the popular election of the members of the House of Commons. Parliament also has a second or "upper" chamber, the Senate, whose members are appointed by the prime minister. Such a two-chamber legislature is labelled "bicameral." The third part of Parliament is the monarch or the Crown. Because it was a British colony at the time the Constitution was adopted in 1867, Canada automatically shared the British monarch. The current monarch, Queen Elizabeth II, still resides in Britain, so on a practical basis, her representative, the governor general, exercises the functions of the Crown.

The British system is sometimes called the **Westminster model** or **parliamentary government**, but the latter label is somewhat misleading. The core of the parliamentary system, even in 1867, was the executive branch—the prime minister and the Cabinet ministers. Although they must be members of Parliament (MPs), they are such an important part of Parliament that they often relegate both the monarch and other members of the House of Commons and Senate to a position of insignificance. Like the executive of any organization, the prime minister and Cabinet are given the powers to lead and make the most important decisions. But the principle of **responsible government** holds that they retain their position and powers only as long as they are supported by a majority in the House of Commons. If the House of Commons declares a lack of confidence in the prime minister and Cabinet, they must either resign and make way for another group to take their place or call an election. Because the prime minister and Cabinet ministers have seats in the legislative branch, mostly the House of Commons, the system is often described as involving a "fusion of powers"—that is, a combination of legislative and executive powers.

The executive dominance of the parliamentary system can be seen in the power of the prime minister and Cabinet ministers to control most of the agenda of the legislature and to introduce most legislation. They have the exclusive power to introduce legislation of a financial nature—laws either to raise or to spend money. They have other wide powers as well: to make appointments, to draft subordinate legislation under the authority of laws, and to make decisions relating to international affairs—essentially all powers necessary to provide effective political leadership for the country. Other members of Parliament may criticize, delay, and propose amendments, but the prime minister and Cabinet almost always get their way. This is because a majority of the members of Parliament normally belong to the same political party as the prime minister and Cabinet; together they constitute a **majority government**. In this situation prime ministers usually impose rigid party discipline on their MPs to support their every move. On the other hand, Canada is increasingly characterized by **minority governments**, in which the opposition members outnumber those on the government side. In such a situation, the PM may be somewhat less dominant.

The significance of the Senate has declined since Confederation because being appointed rather than elected diminishes its members' legitimacy in a democratic age. The powers of the Senate have remained virtually equal to those of the House of Commons, but senators have rarely felt it proper to exercise them. Moreover, independent behaviour has been discouraged by the fact that the same party has usually held a majority both in the Senate and in the Commons. If for any reason the Senate should ultimately defeat a government bill, such an action does not affect the constitutional standing of the prime minister and Cabinet. The model outlined here is also operational in each of the provinces, except that they all possess one-chamber ("unicameral") legislatures.

Government was small and simple at the time of Confederation, but it has gradually developed another important branch, the bureaucracy or public service. The bureaucracy essentially advises the prime minister and Cabinet ministers on their decisions and then carries out whatever government programs have been authorized. The current Canadian bureaucracy consists of about 400 000 public servants who make a vast array of government decisions.

....

Figure 1.2   An Outline of Canadian Political Institutions

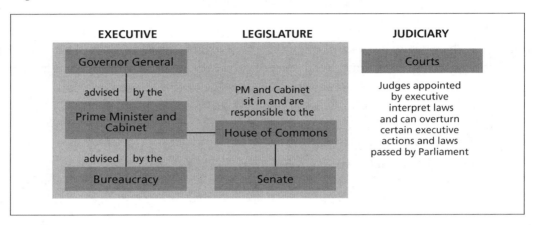

Source: Rand Dyck

The British parliamentary system also incorporates the principle of judicial independence. Although courts are established by acts of Parliament, and judges are appointed by the prime minister and Cabinet, the whole judicial system is expected to operate independently of the executive and legislative branches of government, as can be seen in Figure 1.2. In the case of Britain itself, judges have considerable discretion in interpreting laws but lack the power of judicial review, that is, the power to declare them invalid. The Canadian judiciary soon appropriated to itself the power to invalidate laws that violated the federal–provincial division of powers but was otherwise quite restrained.

Since the Canadian institutional structure was established in 1867, the only major change has been the adoption of the Charter of Rights and Freedoms in 1982. That addition had the effect of expanding the scope of judicial review to include the new task of protecting individual rights and freedoms. Henceforth, the courts could disallow federal or provincial legislation or other government actions that violated the Constitution in terms of either the division of powers or the Charter of Rights and Freedoms.

The British parliamentary system is distinct in many ways from the presidential–congressional system of the United States. There, the president and the two houses of the legislature (Congress) are independently elected, and no one is permitted to sit in more than one branch of government. The "separation of powers" means that executive, legislative, and judicial powers are distributed to three separate branches of government: president, Congress, and the courts respectively. Moreover, as indicated in Figure 1.3, the U.S. system is also

Figure 1.3   U.S. System of Separation of Powers and Checks and Balances

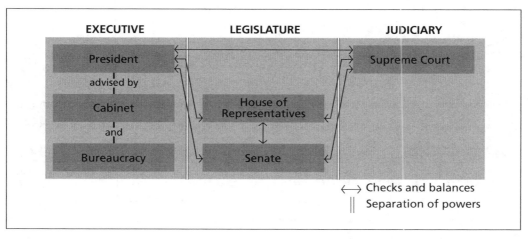

Source: Rand Dyck

characterized by a maze of "checks and balances" designed to ensure that the actions of any one branch of government are subject to veto by another. Members of the House of Representatives and the Senate have much more legislative power than their counterparts in the parliamentary system, in terms of both initiating bills themselves and amending or vetoing those bills emanating from the executive. Party discipline is also much looser. Even if a majority of the members of Congress belong to the same party as the president, there is no guarantee that the legislature will pass the president's initiatives. The Supreme Court also has the power of judicial review and can overturn any legislation that it feels is in violation of the Constitution. Thus, even though it often appears that the U.S. president has enormous power, largely because of the manner in which that country often tries to enforce its will across the globe, the fact is that, at least in domestic policy areas, the president actually has less control than the prime minister does in Canada.

Federalism

The Fathers of Confederation were dealing with a large piece of territory and were contending with colonies that had separate identities and a previous semi-autonomous existence. In this respect, the new country had to be a **federation** of some kind. **Federalism** is characterized by two levels of government—central and provincial—and a division of powers between them.

NEL

Confederation was, to a large extent, the work of Sir John A. Macdonald, who went on to become the first Canadian prime minister. Macdonald preferred a unitary state or legislative union, in which the new central government would have almost all the powers, and the provinces would be little more than munici- palities. But Quebec and the Maritimes were not prepared to join such a system. Quebec demanded an autonomous provincial government so that its cultural con- cerns, such as education and civil law, would be placed in the hands of a French- speaking majority. Hence, the logical compromise was a system that contained a central government to deal with purposes common to the whole country and provincial governments to look after local concerns.

Macdonald accepted a federal form of government, allowing the former colo- nies to retain some of their political and economic independence, but he intended the new country to be highly centralized. He felt that its economic and defensive objectives required a strong central government. This conviction was reinforced by the predominant view that the American Civil War (which was ending just as they began their deliberations) had been the result of leaving too much power at the state level. Thus, at their creation, the Canadian and American federations were quite different. The United States deliberately established a weak central government and strong states, while Canada preferred a strong central govern- ment and weak provinces.

Besides dividing powers between the two levels of government, constitutional architects in both the United States and Canada had to decide how the provinces or states would be represented at the national level. In both cases, the lower house of the legislature would be based on the principle of representation by population, so that the most populous provinces or states would have the largest number of members in that chamber. To protect the interests of the smaller states, however, the U.S. decided that each state, regardless of population, would have two sena- tors at the national level. Some Fathers of Confederation also preferred this idea, but others wanted representation by population in both houses of Parliament. The Canadian compromise was to base the Senate on the principle of equal *regional* representation rather than equal provincial representation.

Fusing the Parliamentary System with Federalism

The basic governmental institutions established in 1867 thus combined the par- liamentary system from Britain with a more centralized form of federalism than that found in the United States. But the whole ethos underlying the Canadian and U.S. systems was different. In the parliamentary system, everything is designed to *facilitate* government action by concentrating power in the hands of the executive, in terms of its relationship both with other institutions of government, such as Parliament and the courts, and with territorial units, such as provincial and local governments. In the American system, everything is designed to *inhibit* government action by preventing the concentration of power in the hands of any government. In the United States, the individual institutions of the national government are able to veto each other and are collectively kept in line by a division of powers that was intended to give most authority to the states. It is largely because the British system is designed to facilitate government action, whereas the American system is designed to inhibit it, that the fusion of the two systems in Canadian Confederation was such a distinctive creation. Macdonald saw the contradiction and therefore tried to establish a federal system that was much more centralized than that next door. He would turn over in his grave if he saw how powerful Canadian provinces have become and how much of a constraint they impose on the actions of the national government!

As well, all provinces in Canada have found it convenient to delegate certain powers to local municipal governments. These are often headed by a mayor and council, usually include an autonomous school board, and sometimes incorporate other local elected or appointed authorities. Their responsibilities vary from province to province, and sometimes within a province, but municipal authorities are a significant part of the government structure in Canada. Unlike the federal and provincial governments, which are not subordinate to each other and whose specific powers are laid out in the Constitution, municipal governments are subordinate to provincial governments, and their responsibilities and taxing powers can be expanded or contracted at the province's whim. Municipalities typically have more responsibilities than their taxation powers can support, leading them to plead for increased provincial (or federal) funding.

This book concentrates on the federal or national system of government in Canada but does not deny the significance of the provinces and municipalities. Indeed, Chapter 12 deals with the relationship between the provinces and the national government. It also notes that municipalities have succeeded in recent years in getting the federal government to pay them more attention.

SUMMARY

This chapter illustrates the many ways in which government action affects our everyday lives. It provides a model of the Canadian political system, showing how demands are transmitted from individuals and groups to, or solicited by, the main institutions of government and are sometimes transformed into public decisions. It outlines the main function of each organ of the Canadian government, emphasizing the concentration of power in the executive branch. The chapter contrasts this concentration with the separation of powers in the U.S. system of government, and it also shows the differences between Canada and the United States as federations.

DISCUSSION QUESTIONS

1. Which actions of the federal government or your own provincial or municipal governments do you disagree with? Should a different approach be used, or should these actions not be taken at all? Which additional actions should one or more of these governments undertake?
2. What are the relative advantages and disadvantages of the structures of the Canadian and U.S. systems of government?
3. Do you feel that you are part of the political process? What would prompt you to be more involved?

KEY TERMS

Advocacy group/interest group/pressure group Any group seeking to influence government policy without contesting elections; an organization whose members promote their common interest by acting together to influence public policy.

Bureaucracy The permanent officials employed by the government, also known as the public service.

Charter of Rights and Freedoms Part of the Constitution Act, 1982, that guaranteed fundamental freedoms and legal, democratic, linguistic, mobility, and equality rights.

Coercion Power based on authorized physical force, including police, armed forces, and jails, on which government has a near-monopoly.

Executive That branch of government which provides leadership and makes the major decisions.

Federalism (federation) A system of government characterized by two levels of authority (federal and provincial) and a division of powers between them such that neither is subordinate to the other.

Globalization The pattern of deepening supraterritorial interaction around the world, characterized by comprehensive free trade agreements, massive diffusion of technological change, and worldwide corporate competition or mega-mergers that challenge the sovereignty of the state.

Government The set of institutions that make and enforce collective, public decisions for a society.

Judicial independence The constitutional principle that the courts should function independently of the rest of the government apparatus, especially of the politicians.

Judicial review The power of the courts to overturn legislation or actions of the executive branch of government.

Judiciary The court system.

Legislature That branch of government whose function is to represent the people and make laws.

Majority government A situation in which the party in power has over 50 percent of the seats in the House of Commons.

Mass media Sources of information for the mass public—principally radio, television, and newspapers.

Minority government A situation in which the government party has fewer than 50 percent of the seats in the House of Commons.

Parliamentary government A form of government, distinct from the U.S. congressional system, characterized by the dominance of the political executive whose members also sit in parliament.

Political party An organized group that makes nominations and contests elections in the hope of influencing the policy and personnel of government.

Politics The activity in which conflicting interests struggle for advantage or dominance in the making and execution of public policies.

Power The ability of one actor to impose its will on another, to get its own way, or to do or get what it wants, usually considered to be the essence of politics and government.

Private sector That part of the economy operated by individuals and corporations, based on the profit motive.

Public sector That part of the economy operated or financed by government.

Responsible government A form of government in which the political executive must retain the confidence of the elected legislature and resign or call an election if and when it is defeated on a vote of non-confidence.

Sovereignty Ultimate control or independence, such as Canadian national sovereignty vis-à-vis that of other countries.

Voluntary Sector That part of the economy operated on a not-for-profit basis by non-governmental groups.

Westminster model The model of government developed in Britain in which the political executive is given extensive power to provide effective leadership.

Chapter 12

The Provinces and the
Federal System

The adoption of a federal system was one of the crucial decisions taken in the creation of Canada, and the shape of the federal–provincial relationship remains at the heart of contemporary Canadian politics. After introducing the role of the provinces, this chapter outlines the federal system in Canada at its creation and then traces the evolution of that system, especially through changes in the division of powers and federal–provincial financial relationships. The chapter concludes with a discussion of Canadian federalism today and an enumeration of recent developments.

Chapter Objectives

After you have completed this chapter, you should be able to:

Define federalism and distinguish it from other forms of intergovernmental relations

Enumerate the ingredients of the Confederation Settlement

Distinguish the intended division of powers between federal and provincial governments from the actual judicial interpretation of these sections

Discuss the evolution of federal–provincial finance, including taxation agreements, different kinds of grants, and equalization payments

Explain how the centralized federation of 1867 became the decentralized Canada of today

Discuss the concepts of executive and bureaucratic federalism, and outline the major features of Canadian contemporary federalism

The Provincial Political Systems

Canada is composed of ten provinces and three territories (see Figure 12.1). The provinces are autonomous within the powers given them by the Constitution, but the territories are constitutionally subordinate to the federal government. Although the territories increasingly function as provinces, exercising similar powers, these powers could theoretically be revoked; moreover, the territories are heavily dependent on Ottawa for their finances.

Each of the provinces can be considered a separate political system. Each has a full complement of governmental institutions and a somewhat distinctive political culture, party system, and array of advocacy groups. The distinctiveness of each province is the principal reason for establishing Canada as a federation, yet their governmental operations bear a striking resemblance to those at the federal level.

Figure 12.1   Canada's Provinces, Territories, and Capitals

ARCTIC OCEAN

ALASKA

YUKON TERRITORY
Whitehorse

NORTHWEST TERRITORIES
Yellowknife

NUNAVUT

Iqaluit

ATLANTIC OCEAN

PACIFIC OCEAN

NEWFOUNDLAND AND LABRADOR

HUDSON BAY

St. John's

BRITISH COLUMBIA

ALBERTA
Edmonton

MANITOBA

QUEBEC

Charlottetown
P.E.I.

SASKATCHEWAN

ONTARIO

N.B.

NOVA SCOTIA

Victoria

Regina

Winnipeg

Quebec City
Fredericton

Halifax

U.S.A.

Ottawa ☆
Toronto

U.S.A.

Each province is formally headed by the lieutenant governor, the equivalent of the governor general, who represents the Queen and primarily performs ceremonial and social functions. The effective head of the provincial government is the premier, analogous to the prime minister, along with the Cabinet, who are officially called the executive council. As in Ottawa, the provincial cabinet sets priorities, especially financial; determines policies; gives direction for the preparation of legislation; oversees departmental administration; and makes order in council appointments.

The provincial legislatures consist of the elected representatives of the people, usually called MLAs (Members of the Legislative Assembly). Each provincial legislature has only one chamber, which is divided between government and opposition members, and functions quite similarly to the House of Commons. A number of provinces have opted for fixed election dates at four-year intervals.

Given the expansion of provincial government operations, at least until 1990 or so, provincial politicians are increasingly dependent on the bureaucracy or public service to advise them on their decisions and the implementation of their programs. The most important provincial responsibilities are health and education, and those two departments consume the largest share of each province's finances. Provinces have their own sources of revenue, but as noted later in this chapter, they also depend heavily on transfers from the federal government. In fact, despite the division of powers between the two levels of government, there is a great deal of interaction between them, especially at the ministerial and bureaucratic levels.

Each province also establishes its own hierarchy of courts and its own system of municipal government. Since the province determines the structures, responsibilities, and financial powers of its local governments, the latter are constitutionally subordinate. In theory, there is no connection between municipal authorities and the federal government—those two levels of government communicate via the provinces. In practice, however, actions of the federal government often have serious consequences for municipalities. More and more observers are recommending that large cities in particular be somehow brought into the ambit of Canadian federalism.

Federalism and the Confederation Settlement

In a formal sense, **federalism** can be defined as a system of government characterized by two levels of authority—federal and provincial—and a division of powers between them, such that neither is subordinate to the other. This definition distinguishes the relationship between provincial and national governments from that between municipal and provincial governments, for in the latter case the municipalities are clearly subordinate entities. This federal–provincial equality of status is provided for in the constitutional division of powers between the two levels of government that is found primarily in sections 91 and 92 of the Constitution Act, 1867. Other aspects of federalism are also important, however, such as federal–provincial financial relations and joint policymaking mechanisms. The recent tendency of federal and provincial governments to download their responsibilities illustrates the increasingly significant role of municipalities.

The fundamentals of Canadian federalism, often called the **Confederation Settlement**,[1] were incorporated into the **Constitution Act, 1867**. As noted in Chapter 1, the principal architect of Confederation was Sir John A. Macdonald, who intended the new country to be a highly centralized federation, with Ottawa retaining most of the power. In fact, the Confederation Settlement was not consistent with the modern definition of federalism because in certain respects the provinces were made subordinate to the central government.

The Confederation Settlement consisted of five principal components:

- the division of powers between federal and provincial governments,
- the division of financial resources,
- the federal controls over the provinces,
- the provincial representation in central institutions, and
- cultural guarantees.

The Fathers of Confederation gave the provinces 16 specific **enumerated powers** in section 92 (e.g., hospitals and municipal institutions) and then left everything else—the **residual powers**—to Ottawa in section 91. For greater certainty, however, they also listed 29 federal powers such as trade and commerce and national defence (see Table 12.1). Two **concurrent powers**—agriculture and immigration—were listed in section 95, and the treaty power in section 132 gave the federal government the power to implement Empire treaties, regardless of their subject matter.

In the division of financial resources, federal dominance was even more apparent. The 1867 settlement gave Ottawa the power to levy any mode or system of taxation, including both direct and indirect taxes. Since the only tax widely used at the time was the customs duty, an indirect tax, the provincial power over direct taxation was not considered to be significant. Instead, the provinces were expected to raise their revenues from the sale of shop, saloon, tavern, and auctioneer licences, as well as to rely on federal subsidies. The federal government was to

TABLE 12.1   THE CORE OF THE FEDERAL–PROVINCIAL DIVISION OF POWERS

Federal Powers	Provincial Powers
Trade and commerce	Direct taxation within the province
Any form of taxation	Public lands
National defence	Hospitals and health care
Banking	Municipal institutions
Indians	Education
Criminal law	Property and civil rights
Interprovincial transportation and communication	Administration of justice

pay each province an annual per capita grant of 80 cents plus a small subsidy to support its government and legislature. The act also stated that the federal government would assist the provinces by assuming their pre-Confederation debts. It should be added that the provinces were authorized to raise revenues from their natural resources, but this source was not taken seriously at the time because few such resources had yet been discovered.

In addition, in a clear departure from what is now regarded as the federal principle, Ottawa was given several means of controlling the provinces. As an alternative to granting royal assent, the lieutenant governor, a federal appointee, was permitted to "reserve" provincial legislation for the consideration of the federal Cabinet, which could then approve or reject it. Even if the lieutenant governor gave assent to a piece of provincial legislation, however, the federal Cabinet could subsequently "disallow" it. As well, the federal government could declare any local work or undertaking to be for the general advantage of Canada and unilaterally place it within federal jurisdiction. These three controls are respectively referred to as reservation, disallowance, and the declaratory power.

Given the highly centralized nature of the division of powers, the limited financial resources of the provinces, and the federal controls, it is clear that the Confederation Settlement of 1867 placed the provinces in a subordinate position, somewhat akin to municipalities, rather than giving them the equal or coordinate status provided for in the modern definition of federalism.

In the light of the federal government's dominant position, it is not surprising that the smaller provinces were concerned with their representation in Ottawa.

The fourth aspect of the 1867 Settlement, therefore, dealt with provincial representation in the House of Commons and the Senate, a question of much more concern at the time than the division of powers. The great compromise that allowed Confederation to go forward was the agreement that the provinces would be represented according to population in the Commons but that regional equality would prevail in the Senate. Thus, each of the three original regions—the Maritimes, Quebec, and Ontario—received 24 senators, appeasing smaller provinces that could be easily outvoted in the lower chamber.[2]

Confederation was more than just a union of provinces; it was also seen as a union of two cultural groups, English and French. Thus, the fifth aspect of the Confederation Settlement might be called cultural guarantees. Considering the anxiety of French Canadians about the preservation of their language and culture, these guarantees were surprisingly minor. Section 133 of the 1867 act made French and English official languages in the federal Parliament and federal courts as well as in the Quebec legislature and Quebec courts—but nowhere else. At the time, religion was probably of greater concern than language, so existing separate school systems in the provinces (especially Ontario and Quebec) were guaranteed by allowing the federal government to step in to restore them, if necessary. French Canada was also protected by giving power over property and civil rights to the provinces, so that Quebec could maintain certain cultural particularisms, including its civil law system.

Of the five components of the Confederation Settlement, only three relate directly to the relationship between federal and provincial governments. This chapter will therefore proceed to track the evolution of the division of powers, financial resources, and federal controls. In discussing this evolution, it is critical to understand how the very centralized federation created in 1867 became the highly decentralized Canada of today. This trend is apparent in all three areas.

John A. Macdonald, the architect of a centralized federal system. (William James Topley/Library and Archives Canada PA-027013)

Division of Powers

If changes to the **division of powers** between federal and provincial governments have resulted in the provinces being more important today, there are two ways in which this could have happened. First, formal constitutional amendments could have altered the division of powers in the provinces' favour; second, judicial decisions interpreting sections 91 and 92 of the Constitution Act, 1867, could also have had this effect.

Since 1867, only four formal constitutional amendments have been adopted that directly affected the division of powers. In 1940, unemployment insurance was added to the list of federal powers in section 91 after the courts had earlier declared that it belonged to the provinces. In 1951, old age pensions were made a concurrent power, allowing the federal government into this area as well. In 1964, Ottawa's jurisdiction was enlarged to include widows' and survivors' benefits and disability pensions. In 1982, the new section 92A increased provincial jurisdiction over natural resources, while at the same time the Charter of Rights and Freedoms generally reduced the powers of both levels of government. Thus, in the first three cases, the net result was a slight increase in federal powers, but this increase was accomplished with the unanimous consent of the provinces. The 1982 amendment was the only formal constitutional amendment that in any way increased provincial powers at the expense of the federal government. Formal constitutional amendments, therefore, do little to explain the more powerful provinces of today.

Judicial interpretation of the federal and provincial powers in the 1867 act is a much more complicated and significant subject. Before 1949, the **Judicial Committee of the Privy Council (JCPC)** in London was Canada's final court of appeal, and its decisions had a major impact in transforming Canadian federalism from a centralized to a decentralized system. The most important JCPC decisions related to the federal "peace, order, and good government" clause as opposed to the provincial power over "property and civil rights."

The **peace, order, and good government (POGG) clause**, one of two parts of section 91 in the 1867 act, says that all powers not given to the provinces in section 92 are left with the federal government. This clause is also known as the residual clause. The second part of section 91 provides, "for greater certainty," a list of 29 examples of federal powers. In the course of its judgments, the Judicial Committee drove a wedge between these two parts of section 91, deciding that the 29 specific items listed were the *real* federal powers rather than just examples, and ignoring the peace, order, and good government clause except in cases of national emergency. But in times of national emergency, as determined by the JCPC, federal powers were almost unlimited. This became known as the **emergency doctrine**, and how the courts managed to transform the residual clause into an emergency power is a very long story. In normal times, on the other hand, the JCPC gave an extremely broad interpretation to section 92-13, property and civil rights in the province, finding that almost any matter that was the subject of a federal–provincial constitutional dispute could be incorporated within this provincial power.[3] That is why so little was left over for the federal residual clause.

The effect of the judicial interpretation of the peace, order, and good government clause, along with other clauses such as the trade and commerce and treaty powers, was to reduce significantly the intended dominance of the federal government. The complementary broad interpretation of property and civil rights increased substantially the scope of provincial powers. This influence has been very controversial in political, judicial, and academic circles, because it was clearly contrary to John A. Macdonald's conception of Canadian federalism in not permitting Ottawa to take initiatives that centralist advocates often desired.[4]

Other observers contend, however, that the Judicial Committee's line of interpretation was consistent with the increasing size and distances that characterized the country as time went on, as well as with societal forces and public orientations, at least outside Ontario. They argue that the provincial bias pervading so many of the JCPC's decisions was "in fundamental harmony with the regional pluralism" of the federal, decentralized, diversified nature of Canadian society. However desirable centralization may have seemed at the outset, it was inappropriate in the long run "for the regional diversities of a land of vast extent and a large, geographically concentrated, minority culture."[5]

What Do You Think?

Are you a centralist or a decentralist? Would you give more power to the federal or provincial level of government? What are the advantages and disadvantages of each approach to Canadian federalism?

Federal–Provincial Finance

In the Confederation Settlement, the federal government was given the power to levy any kind of tax, while the provinces were restricted to direct taxation.[6] The federal government was also committed to pay the provinces small annual grants.

While the intention was thus to create a highly centralized federation, the financial factor also ultimately contributed to the increased power of the provinces. This situation came about because the provinces levied direct taxes that they were not expected to use, such as income taxes; because the provinces successfully lobbied for larger federal grants; and because some provincial revenues, such as those from natural resources, turned out to be more significant than anticipated.

Provincial revenues proved to be inadequate from the beginning, and it did not take long for the provinces to begin levying their own direct personal and corporate income taxes and to demand larger sums from Ottawa. With both levels of government taxing the same personal and corporate incomes, but in a totally uncoordinated fashion, and with provinces always lining up for more federal funds, the federal–provincial financial situation became very complicated. This muddied state of affairs worsened with the advent of the Depression, when even fewer funds were available to go around. As a result, Prime Minister Mackenzie King appointed the Rowell-Sirois Commission, officially the Royal Commission on Dominion–Provincial Relations, in 1937. One of its recommendations was immediately implemented: the costly responsibility for unemployment insurance was transferred to the federal government.

Before 1940, therefore, the two levels of government were relatively independent on both the taxation and expenditure sides of public finance. Since the Second World War, on the other hand, they have become intimately intertwined, and Ottawa has taken the lead (sometimes with provincial encouragement) in coordinating the various ingredients of the financial relationship. The complicated federal–provincial financial situation since 1940 might be simplified somewhat by considering three aspects separately: taxation agreements, conditional and block grants, and equalization payments.

Taxation Agreements

Between 1942 and 2001, the taxation side was characterized by a series of five-year federal–provincial taxation agreements. The name and terms of the agreements changed over the years, but the basic objective was the same: to effect a degree of coordination in the field of federal–provincial taxation. The main taxes in question were personal and corporate income taxes. While the federal personal income tax was standard across the country (except for Quebec), each province was able to determine its own rate as a percentage of the federal tax, so that the provincial portion varied widely. Except for Quebec, all personal income taxes were collected

Provinces' view of Fiscal Imbalance teeter-totter.
(Michael de Adder/Artizans.com)

by Ottawa in the first instance, after which the provincial portion was transferred back, an arrangement that was found to be satisfactory to all concerned. Quebec has always collected its own personal income tax, so that its residents complete two separate income tax forms. By 2001, however, all provinces had separated their provincial income tax from the federal income tax system, meaning that the provincial tax is no longer necessarily calculated as a percentage of the federal tax, although Ottawa still collects both portions.

Conditional and Block Grants

The second aspect of the federal–provincial financial picture was **shared-cost programs**. These expanded considerably after 1940 in the joint development of a **welfare state**. The most important shared-cost social programs were postsecondary education (1952), hospital insurance (1957), the Canada Assistance Plan (1966), and medical insurance (1968). Hospital and medical programs were later combined as health insurance or "medicare." These programs are termed the "major" federal transfers to the provinces, but a large number of smaller transfer programs also exist.

Federal grants for postsecondary education have always been of a **block grant** variety, that is, a sum of money given to each province for the operating costs of universities and colleges but without any conditions or strings attached. Such a grant significantly helped to fund universities and colleges and allowed provinces to keep tuition fees relatively low. The other major shared-cost programs originally fell into the **conditional grant** category. The usual pattern here was for the federal government to pay approximately 50 percent of the cost of each program provided that the provinces met Ottawa's conditions. For example, Ottawa would fund half of any provincial health care program that was comprehensive (covering all necessary health services provided by hospitals and medical practitioners), universal (covering the whole population), portable (covering the costs of provincial residents while temporarily absent from the province), accessible (not impeding or precluding reasonable access to services by extra charges), and publicly administered. Under the Canada Assistance Plan, Ottawa similarly provided half the funding for almost any provincial or municipal program that provided social assistance and welfare services to persons in need. In this case, the main condition was that anyone in need had to be included, and no one could be forced to work for welfare. Without federal contributions to health and social assistance programs, many provinces would not have been able to finance them.

Most of these programs fell constitutionally within provincial jurisdiction, but Ottawa maintained that its **spending power** allowed it to make payments to individuals, institutions, and other governments in fields over which Parliament did not necessarily have the power to regulate. The federal government even claimed that it could attach conditions to such spending and often did so. In the exercise of its spending power, Ottawa was able to establish national standards in a number of social programs.

While a combination of provincial pressure and federal political and bureaucratic expansionism inspired most of these programs, the provinces often criticized the federal conditions attached to them as being out of place in areas of provincial jurisdiction. Quebec in particular took this point of view in the early 1960s. In response, the Pearson government allowed the provinces to opt out of certain conditional grant programs and continue to receive federal funding as long as they maintained an equivalent program.

Then, in the 1970s, Ottawa became upset at the rapidly escalating costs of many of these programs and its commitment to finance 50 percent of whatever the provinces spent on them. In 1977, therefore, the federal government removed the detailed conditions attached to the health insurance programs, as many provinces wished. But in return, it no longer felt obliged to pay 50 percent of the provincial program costs. The federal grants took the form of tax transfers (giving the provinces more room to levy their own taxes) as well as cash, and henceforth Ottawa would increase its funding of such programs only by a certain annual percentage. Removing the conditions from health insurance grants, however, led to problems such as hospitals introducing user fees, doctors practising double- or extra-billing, and provinces using health care funds for other purposes.

Unhappy with these developments, the federal government consequently passed the **Canada Health Act** in 1984. The act resurrected the five earlier conditions connected to health care and provided for penalizing those provinces that permitted extra charges. At the same time, the federal share of such programs fell below 50 percent, and the 1990s saw a progression of freezes and cuts in funding.

Finance Minister Paul Martin's 1994 federal budget announced a freeze on all major federal transfers except equalization payments, and his 1995 budget inaugurated a significant transformation of federal–provincial transfers. Beginning in 1996–97, postsecondary education, health insurance, and the Canada Assistance Plan (social assistance and welfare services) were combined into a block grant called the **Canada Health and Social Transfer (CHST)**.

The CHST was a combination of cash payments and tax points (federal withdrawal from joint tax fields), but it represented a significant reduction from previous amounts. It was at this time that postsecondary education fees began to skyrocket, as provinces in turn reduced university and college funding. As a block grant, the CHST did not contain the conditions of CAP, nor were Ottawa's expenditures driven by provincial costs. The only condition on welfare transfers was that provinces not impose a minimum residency requirement. As a result, many provinces reduced social assistance programs and/or brought in workfare. Despite the protests of almost all social reformers, who did not trust provincial governments to provide adequate social assistance programs, Ottawa felt that it could not retain such conditions when it was reducing its contributions. On the other hand, the federal Liberal government continued to defend the principles of the Canada Health Act and fought with provinces that appeared to be in violation of the act.

Equalization Payments

The third aspect of federal–provincial finance consists of **equalization payments**. In 1957, the federal government began to pay these unconditional grants to have-not provinces based on provincial need so that all provinces could offer a relatively equal standard of services. The essence of equalization payments was to bring the have-not provinces up to the national average tax yield per capita. Typically, Ontario, British Columbia, and Alberta were above the national average and did not receive equalization payments, while the other seven provinces received an annual payment based on the per capita shortfall of tax revenues multiplied by the province's population. In the first decade of this century, however, provincial rankings changed: in particular, Saskatchewan and Newfoundland and Labrador rose above the national average, while Ontario fell below it. In 2004, the Canada Health and Social Transfer was divided into two separate parts—Canada Health Transfer and Canada Social Transfer. Table 12.2 shows the major federal transfers to the provinces in 2010–11.

TABLE 12.2 MAJOR FEDERAL TRANSFERS TO PROVINCES/TERRITORIES, 2010–11 ($ MILLIONS)

	Health Transfer	Social Transfer	Equalization	Other	Total
Newfoundland/ Labrador	439	167	—	397	1 003
Prince Edward Island	110	47	330	3	490
Nova Scotia	725	308	1 110	477	2 620
New Brunswick	580	246	1 581	80	2 488
Quebec	6 093	2 587	8 552	—	17 232
Ontario	9 965	4 321	972	214	15 472
Manitoba	953	405	1 826	175	3 359
Saskatchewan	829	350	—	7	1 186
Alberta	2 071	1 238	—	—	3 309
British Columbia	3 582	1 482	—	—	5 064
Yukon	26	11	—	653*	691
Northwest Territories	25	14	—	920*	959
Nunavut	28	11	—	1 091*	1 130
Total	25 426	11 186	14 372	4 018	55 002

*Territorial Formula Financing

Source: Department of Finance Canada, Major Transfers to Provinces and Territories—2010–11, available at http://www. fin.gc.ca/fedprov/mtpt-ptfp10-eng.asp, retrieved April 20, 2010.

Provincial Finances

In addition to their grants from Ottawa, the provinces have levied over 30 forms of direct taxation that were unanticipated in 1867. The enormous natural resource revenues that some provinces (especially Alberta) receive on top of direct taxation and federal contributions are also significant. A comparison of federal transfers and the provinces' own revenues (taxes plus natural resource and other revenues) is shown in Figure 12.2.

Thus, the combination of unanticipated federal grants, direct taxes, and natural resource revenues has contributed significantly to the enhanced status of the provinces in the Canadian federal system. It should also be reiterated that the two

Figure 12.2   Provincial and Territorial Own-Source Revenue as Percentage of Total Revenue, 2008

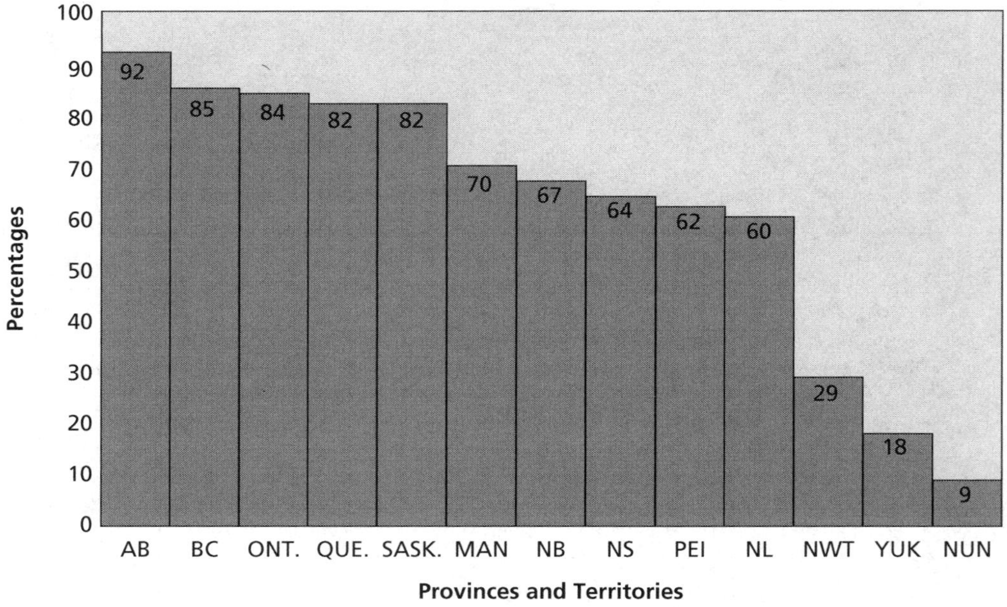

levels of government began by operating more or less independently of each other, taxing and spending in different areas, with federal grants being unconditional in nature. Then, from about 1940 onward, the federal and provincial governments became closely intertwined by taxation agreements on the revenue side and by conditional and block grant programs in terms of expenditures. At the beginning of the 21st century, however, the degree of integration declined somewhat, especially with the disengagement of federal and provincial personal income tax systems. The richest and most autonomy-minded provinces continue to argue for greater decentralization of powers and more tax room, but the have-not provinces are not capable of increasing their own tax revenues, so they have a stake in keeping a strong central government that can act as a redistributive agency.

Federal Controls

As mentioned, the 1867 Constitution Act contained three specific federal controls over the provinces: reservation, disallowance, and the declaratory power. In the first 30 years after Confederation, all three controls were actively used, and this had the effect of keeping the provinces subordinate to Ottawa. Their use gradually declined and then ceased completely: the reservation and declaratory powers were last used in 1961, and disallowance, in 1943. As these were the federal powers that originally precluded Canada from being classified as a true federation, their disuse has meant that the provinces have shrugged off their subordinate status. Canada is now a genuine federation, and a highly decentralized one at that.

Modern Canadian Federalism

Federal–provincial relations in Canada have gone through many different phases since 1867, depending on shifting attitudes of federal and provincial governments, states of war and peace, and variations in judicial interpretation. In fact, Canadian federalism has experienced pendulum-like swings between centralization and decentralization, and the evolution from a centralized to a decentralized federal system has not been a unilinear process.

Executive Federalism

The phase of Canadian federalism that began after the Second World War might be called **cooperative federalism**. The essence of this concept is that while neither level was subordinate to the other, the federal government and the provinces were closely intertwined rather than operating independently. Here the crucial variable was financial relations. As noted earlier, the post-1945 period has been marked by federal–provincial taxation agreements on the revenue side and a host of shared-cost programs in terms of expenditures.

Cooperative federalism resulted from several developments.[7] First, federal and provincial objectives often had to be harmonized if public policy was to be effective. Second, public pressure forced the federal government to establish minimum national standards throughout the country in certain public services even within provincial jurisdiction such as health care. Third, the two levels of government competed for tax revenues and needed to coordinate these efforts to some extent, at least for the convenience of taxpayers. Fourth, given a generally vague division of powers, federal and provincial ministers and bureaucrats usually sought to maximize their jurisdiction and the programs of the two levels of government eventually overlapped.

Cooperative federalism was made operational by hundreds of federal–provincial conferences at all levels—first ministers, departmental ministers, deputy ministers, and even lesser officials—who engaged in almost continuous consultation, coordination, and cooperation. Cooperative federalism can be conducted on a multilateral basis, involving the federal government and several or all provinces, or on a bilateral basis, in which Ottawa interacts with individual provinces. Since the ministers and bureaucrats involved are all part of the executive branch of government, cooperative federalism is sometimes called **executive federalism**. Two main implications of executive federalism are that legislatures, political parties, and the public at large are not given much role to play in decisions that emerge from the secrecy of such meetings and that federal–provincial conflicts are worked out in conferences or meetings rather than being referred to the courts.

Executive federalism can therefore be defined as "relations between elected and appointed officials of the two levels of government."[8] It is often practised at the level of first ministers, even though the **first ministers' conference**—that is, a conference of premiers and the prime minister—is not provided for anywhere in the written Constitution and rests upon a conventional base. This institution made many significant policy decisions with respect to constitutional issues, shared-cost programs, and taxation and fiscal arrangements. Some of these had to be ratified later by federal and provincial legislatures, but except on constitutional matters, legislative ratification was usually a formality. Such agreements could rarely be altered in any legislature because they would then have to be changed in all 11 legislatures. First ministers' conferences became more elaborate and institutionalized over time. They could be televised, in whole or in part, but it was generally agreed that any serious negotiation had to take place behind closed doors. The prime minister functioned as chair, in addition to representing the federal government, and individual ministers from either level of government were usually allowed to speak as well. Every delegation brought along a host of advisers. After the collapse of the Charlottetown Accord, however, such first ministers' conferences fell into disrepute and were replaced by occasional first ministers' dinners at the prime minister's residence.

Executive federalism conducted at the level of departmental ministers and leading bureaucrats is sometimes labelled "functional" or "bureaucratic" federalism. This form of executive federalism is usually more successful than first ministers' meetings, partly because the officials involved often share certain professional norms and, once they reach a consensus, these experts may be able to "sell" it to their departmental and first ministers.

Canadian federalism between 1945 and 1960 may have been "cooperative" in the sense that the two levels of government were closely intertwined, but it

Prime Minister Paul Martin and his provincial and territorial counterparts participate in session at the First Ministers' Conference on Health in September 2004. (The Canadian Press/Fred Chartrand)

continued to be highly centralized in the immediate postwar period. The ministers and bureaucrats in Ottawa who had almost single-handedly run the country during the Second World War were reluctant to shed their enormous power. Moreover, they had discovered **Keynesian economics**, which prescribed a leading role for the central government in guiding the economy. The Diefenbaker government after 1957 was more sensitive to provincial demands, and the whole picture was increasingly complicated from 1960 onward by the Quiet Revolution in Quebec. This period still manifested an intertwined, non-subordinate relationship between the two levels of government, but with Quebec regularly rejecting federal initiatives, cooperation was sometimes harder to come by. The concept of "opting out" was a hallmark of this phase of federalism, which saw a significant degree of decentralization take place.

Between about 1970 and 1984, federal–provincial relations were racked with conflict. Quebec and the other provinces were more aggressive than ever, but the Trudeau government was not prepared for any further decentralization. Thus, taxation agreements were accompanied by more provincial unhappiness, and block funding replaced conditional grants in important areas, leaving the two levels less intertwined than before. Moreover, especially at the level of first ministers, federal–provincial conferences frequently failed to come to any agreement, and Ottawa often chose to act unilaterally. In this phase, federal–provincial conflicts were more frequently referred to the courts, resulting in a renewed emphasis on the judicial interpretation of the division of powers.

The Trudeau era was characterized by years of federal–provincial discord over resource and energy policies, especially the National Energy Program, conflict with Newfoundland over offshore oil, and conflict with Saskatchewan over the regulation and taxation of that province's oil and potash industries. When these disputes coincided with Trudeau's attempt to unilaterally amend the Constitution and entrench official bilingualism as a national policy, many Western Canadians began to re-examine their place in the federation. Some of the heat was reduced when Trudeau conceded the new section 92A of the Constitution Act, 1982, which enhanced provincial jurisdiction over natural resources. He made this concession in order to secure federal NDP support for his constitutional package and as a peace offering to the West.

Canadian Federalism, 1984–2000

When Brian Mulroney came to power in 1984, he was determined to improve federal–provincial relations and embark on another period of decentralized, genuinely cooperative federalism. In this objective he was somewhat successful, for much of the federal–provincial animosity of the Trudeau years seemed to dissipate. Concerns about energy resources were resolved to a large extent in the 1985 Western and Atlantic Accords. During its second term, however, the Mulroney government increasingly aroused provincial anger, especially as it became obsessed with deficit reduction and cut back on grants to the provinces. The Mulroney government even enforced the Liberals' Canada Health Act, imposing penalties on provinces that allowed doctors to extra-bill or permitted hospitals to charge user fees. The major federal–provincial dispute of the Mulroney years concerned the Goods and Services Tax (GST). To some extent it was just "good politics" for provincial premiers to jump on the anti-GST bandwagon because of widespread popular opposition. Most provinces refused to integrate their sales taxes with the new federal tax, even though many mutual advantages would have accrued from doing so.

The Chrétien Liberals were initially popular with provincial governments in offering funds under the national infrastructure program, and they were somewhat successful in negotiating a reduction in provincial barriers to the free movement of

What Do You Think?

The most persistent federal–provincial issue in recent times concerns health care. If the federal government makes substantial annual contributions to provincial health care programs, is Ottawa entitled to insist that they not be spent to finance health care services that are privately provided or that a two-tier health care system develop? Some provinces contend that as long as people do not have to pay extra for privately provided services, that is, as long as these services are covered by the provincial medicare plan, this is acceptable. Other health care advocates argue that public funds should not leak out into the pockets of profit-making ventures. Should those who can afford to pay for their own health care be allowed to do so and get faster service?

people, goods, services, and capital across the country in the Agreement on Internal Trade. They had only partial success in implementing their promise to replace the GST (in reality, harmonizing it with the provincial retail sales tax in a handful of provinces), and then they angered the provinces with reductions in their transfers, especially after 1995. The provinces' principal complaints included severe reductions in health, postsecondary education, and welfare transfers, although provinces also joined in to protest the cuts to almost every other aspect of federal government operations, such as a wide range of transportation subsidies. On the other hand, Ottawa did not cut equalization payments.

More harmoniously, the Chrétien government transferred responsibility for labour market training to the provinces by means of bilateral deals rather than constitutional amendment and replaced the Child Tax Benefit with a new integrated National Child Benefit system developed through federal–provincial cooperation. It was also during this era that the federal and provincial governments (minus Quebec) signed the 1999 **Social Union Framework Agreement (SUFA)**, a framework on which to construct or modify federal, provincial, or joint social programs.

Canadian Federalism in the 21st Century

Canadian federalism in the 21st century demonstrates aspects of both continuity and change. Despite the fact that the formal Constitution lists only three concurrent powers, the federal and provincial governments continue to be intertwined in programs in almost every area. In other words, Canada is characterized by a large amount of *de facto* concurrent jurisdiction.[9] Moreover, an enormous degree of federal–provincial interaction will be required in the future to come up with solutions to many public problems.[10] While most of the interaction takes place at the ministerial and bureaucratic levels, Paul Martin began his regime by being much more open than his predecessor to talking individually and collectively to provincial premiers themselves.

Meanwhile, at the initiative of Quebec Premier Jean Charest, the annual premiers' conference has been transformed into the Council of the Federation. Its objective is to speak with a strong, united voice for the provinces and territories in their relations with the federal government, at least on issues on which they all agree. Indeed, the whole structure of Canadian federalism has been somewhat transformed by new players and new relationships: Aboriginal self-government, direct contact between the federal government and cities, and relations between provincial governments and foreign states.

Health care continues to be the hottest issue in federal–provincial relations. The Accord on Health Care Renewal in 2003 promised the provinces an increase of $35 billion over five years. About the same time, most provinces agreed to join the Health Council of Canada, an independent body to advise Canadians on the performance of their health care systems. At the September 2004 first ministers' meeting, Ottawa promised the provinces an additional $18 billion over six years to be used to reduce waiting times, and the provinces committed to establish and publish benchmarks and targets to monitor progress in meeting this goal. The ten-year plan allowed Quebec to implement its own plan, a recognition of the principle of asymmetrical federalism. These funds exemplify a new type of transfer, somewhat similar to block grants, sometimes called "targeted funding," which does not require the provinces to meet specific conditions, but which is intended for certain purposes.[11]

Another contentious issue is the formula used to determine equalization payments. Besides a demand from have-not provinces for a general increase in the amount of the payments, Newfoundland and Labrador and Nova Scotia had a specific complaint with respect to their offshore petroleum revenues. They claimed to be losing 70 cents in equalization payments for every new dollar of petroleum revenue they took in. Paul Martin eventually allowed them to retain offshore petroleum revenues with no reduction in equalization payments, which only angered other provinces. Not having Alberta's abundant revenues nor receiving equalization payments, Ontario then complained that the federal government extracted over $20 billion more from the province annually than it returned, and Martin agreed to give it some $6 billion over five years for various purposes.

Martin also promised a "new deal for cities," and established a Ministry of State for Infrastructure and Communities. He exempted municipalities from paying the GST on their purchases and then shared the revenues from the federal gasoline excise tax with the provinces with the aim of having these funds transferred to municipalities to help finance environmentally friendly infrastructure projects.

Aboriginal issues were another priority of the Martin government. Martin convened a meeting of first ministers and Aboriginal leaders in Kelowna in 2005 and announced that the federal government would commit $5 billion over five years to close the gap in the quality of life between Aboriginal peoples and other Canadians. The premiers were enthusiastic participants and pledged to make significant contributions of their own.

Stephen Harper came to power with expectations of being even more generous to the provinces. The 2007 budget was designed to redress the "fiscal imbalance" between Ottawa and the provinces, especially as articulated by Quebec, although some observers argued that it was a myth disguising Quebec's *spending* more per capita than other provinces. The Harper government also brought in a new, more generous equalization formula, but managed to alienate Newfoundland and Labrador, Nova Scotia, and Saskatchewan in its treatment of natural resource revenues.

The Harper government did not honour the full Kelowna commitment with respect to Aboriginal peoples, and it cancelled the early childhood and child care agreements that the Martin government had just signed with all ten provinces. The health care wait-times guarantee Harper signed with the provinces was generally considered very weak. On the other hand, Harper introduced a parliamentary resolution to recognize the Québécois as a nation within a united Canada and allowed Quebec to have a seat in the Canadian delegation to UNESCO. In general, Harper seemed prepared to engage in further decentralization to the provinces, mainly to consolidate his party's support in Quebec, which he labelled "open federalism."

Addressing environmental issues is an increasingly urgent problem and one that is complicated in Canada by the division between federal and provincial jurisdictions. Some observers have anticipated a major constitutional confrontation between the federal and Alberta governments over capping emissions from the oil sands, but the Harper government rejected the Kyoto Protocol in favour of a less stringent approach. No such conflict is expected on his watch unless the U.S. forces Canada to take the environment more seriously.

After the 2008 economic meltdown, infrastructure stimulus spending became a high priority of both federal and provincial governments. By means of the Building Canada Fund, Ottawa not only helped provincial and municipal governments, but also ensured that their infrastructure spending was aligned with federal thinking.

SUMMARY

This chapter examined the relationship between the provinces and the federal government. It began by defining federalism as a system in which neither level of government is subordinate to the other and by setting out the five main provisions of the Confederation Settlement. The heart of the chapter demonstrated how the provinces have become more powerful than originally intended, partly through judicial (mis)interpretation of the division of powers, partly through the enormous increase in provincial financial resources, and partly because the federal government no longer uses its means of controlling the provinces. The evolution of federal–provincial finance is particularly important, replete with taxation agreements, shared-cost programs, and various kinds of grants. The chapter showed that despite the division of powers, the two levels of government are closely intertwined, and that almost all powers, in practice, are concurrent. The chapter concluded with descriptions of developments in Canadian federalism in recent years and of future challenges.

DISCUSSION QUESTIONS

1. Should the federal government increase its financial transfers to the provinces, or should it give them increased taxation room instead?
2. Should the federal government be able to spend money for any purpose, even within provincial jurisdiction?
3. Should Ottawa be able to deal directly with large cities, and should provinces be able to deal directly with neighbouring U.S. states?

KEY TERMS

Block grant A federal grant to the provinces that is given for a specific purpose, such as postsecondary education, but does not contain rigid conditions or standards.

Canada Health Act The 1984 act that re-imposed conditions on federal grants to the provinces for health programs, especially to prevent extra-billing, privatization, or other moves toward a two-tier health system.

Canada Health and Social Transfer (CHST) The annual federal block grant to the provinces between 1996 and 2004 intended to be used for health, postsecondary education, and welfare, now replaced by the Canada Health Transfer and the Canada Social Transfer.

Concurrent powers Powers officially shared by the federal and provincial governments, namely agriculture, immigration, and old age pensions.

Conditional grant A federal grant to the provinces, usually in support of a shared-cost program within provincial jurisdiction, to which Ottawa attaches conditions or standards before the province receives the money.

Confederation Settlement The deal made among the Fathers of Confederation that entailed setting up a new federal system of government with a division of powers, including financial powers, federal controls over the provinces, provincial representation in federal institutions, and certain cultural guarantees.

Constitution Act, 1867 The new name for the British North America Act, 1867, which united the four original provinces.

Cooperative federalism A variant of Canadian federalism since the Second World War in which neither level of government is subordinate to the other and in which there is an extensive degree of interaction between them.

Division of powers The distribution of legislative powers between the federal and provincial governments, largely contained in sections 91 and 92 of the Constitution Act, 1867.

Emergency doctrine A constitutional doctrine invented by the Judicial Committee of the Privy Council that in times of national emergency, the peace, order, and good government clause became an emergency clause, increasing the powers of the federal government.

Enumerated powers The powers of the provincial governments that are explicitly listed in section 92 of the Constitution Act, 1867.

Equalization payments Large annual cash payments made by the federal government to have-not provinces to help them provide a satisfactory level of public services.

Executive federalism A variant of cooperative federalism characterized by extensive federal–provincial interaction at the level of first ministers, departmental ministers, and deputy ministers.

Federalism A system of government characterized by two levels of authority (federal and provincial) and a division of powers between them such that neither is subordinate to the other.

First ministers' conference A federal–provincial conference consisting of the prime minister and provincial premiers (and, increasingly, territorial leaders).

Judicial Committee of the Privy Council A committee of the British parliament
that functioned as Canada's final court of appeal until 1949.

Keynesian economics An economic theory that to promote general economic
stability, the government should counterbalance the private sector, spending
(running deficit budgets) in periods of unemployment when the private sector
doesn't spend, and taxing (withdrawing money from the system) in periods of
inflation when the private sector is spending too much.

Peace, order, and good government (POGG) clause The words in the opening
sentence of section 91 of the Constitution Act, 1867, which state that the
residual powers rest with the federal government but which has been often
misinterpreted by the courts as providing only an emergency power.

Residual powers Those powers not given to the provinces in the Constitution
Act, 1867, that were assigned to the federal government under the POGG
clause in section 91.

Shared-cost programs Government programs whose cost is shared by the federal
and provincial governments.

Social Union Framework Agreement An overall framework of federal–provincial relations agreed to in 1999 by all governments except Quebec that sought
to end long-standing irritants on both sides.

Spending power The unofficial power of the federal government to spend money
in any field, including those within provincial jurisdiction.

Welfare state The characterization of most Western democracies from about
1950 to 1985 in which governments functioned as provider and protector of
individual security and well-being through the implementation of a wide array
of social programs and income transfers to individuals.

FURTHER READING

Bakvis, Herman, Gerald Baier, and Douglas Brown. *Contested Federalism: Certainty
and Ambiguity in the Canadian Federation*. Toronto: Oxford University Press,
2009.

Bakvis, Herman, and Grace Skogstad, eds. *Canadian Federalism: Performance,
Effectiveness, and Legitimacy*, 2nd ed. Toronto: Oxford University Press, 2008.

Canadian Tax Foundation. *Finances of the Nation*. Toronto: CTF, biennial.

Harrison, Kathryn, ed. *Racing to the Bottom? Provincial Interdependence in the
Canadian Federation*. Vancouver: UBC Press, 2005.

Institute of Intergovernmental Relations. *Canada: The State of the Federation*.
Kingston: Queen's University, annual.

Rocher, François, and Miriam Smith, eds. *New Trends in Canadian Federalism*, 2nd ed. Peterborough: Broadview Press, 2003.

Russell, Peter. *Constitutional Odyssey*, 3rd ed. Toronto: University of Toronto Press, 2004.

Smith, Jennifer. *Federalism*. Vancouver: UBC Press, 2004.

Stevenson, Garth. "Federalism and Intergovernmental Relations." In Michael Whittington and Glen Williams, eds. *Canadian Politics in the 21st Century*, 7th ed. Toronto: Thomson Nelson, 2008.

———. *Unfulfilled Union: Canadian Federalism and National Unity*, 5th ed. Montreal: McGill-Queen's University Press, 2009.

Chapter 9: Democracy in Canada

Chapter Ten

DEMOCRACY IN ACTION: Elections, Political Participation, and Citizens' Power

Brenda O'Neill

After you have completed this chapter, you should be able to:

- describe the difference between direct democracy and representative democracy

- describe the functions of elections

- compare the plurality, majoritarian, and proportional representation electoral systems

- understand why voters vote the way they do

- describe the many forms of political participation and explain what influences the decision to participate in politics

- explain the use of tools of direct democracy for increasing citizens' political power

Popular Perceptions of Democracy

In the fall of 2007 two events made dramatic headlines: the protests in Myanmar (also known as Burma) and the imposition of emergency rule and suspension of the constitution in Pakistan. Both underscore the importance assigned to democracy and democratic practices around the world. In Myanmar, thousands of monks in red vestments engaged in a silent and peaceful pro-democracy protest against the long-standing military dictatorship, only to be met with curfews, attempted crackdowns on news links to the outside world, riot police, arrests, and deaths. In Pakistan, the imposition of emergency rule was loudly condemned as it allowed for the suspension of political and civil rights and restrictions on the press. So, too, was the arrest and removal of the chief justice of the supreme court following the court's ruling on the illegality of President Musharraf's decision to run for office without stepping down from his military position.

Elections are often seen as the key mechanism for granting citizens a measure of power in democracies, but democracies require far more than elections to be considered legitimate. What additional criteria make for democracies that are acceptable to the international community? Why is judicial independence so important for the democratic legitimacy? What is it about democracy that would lead Buddhist monks to defy government restrictions on protest? Why is democracy valued so highly?

This chapter hopes to help answer these questions and more. Many of us employ the word *democracy* in everyday conversation, but the term is often ill defined or misunderstood. Few citizens in Western states are fully aware of the underlying assumptions, goals, and mechanisms required for the successful adoption and implementation of democracy.

Although there exist many academic definitions of the term, most agree that democracy is something close to "the rule of the people." The main principle is that political power should originate with the people rather than with those who rule. Modern democracy argues that the government's authority rests on the free and fair participation of all who are subject to its rule. Respect for the rule of law also ensures that political leaders do not govern arbitrarily, but rather follow the rules as laid out in the laws and the constitution. An independent judiciary ensures that governments respect the rule of law.

Western states and their citizens rarely challenge the normative superiority of democracies. Democracy is without question the *best* form of government. Unlike authoritarian systems, democracies provide opportunities for citizens to make decisions about the state, its citizens, and its relationship with other states, because ultimately those very citizens will have to live with the consequences of those decisions. In other words, citizens are politically powerful. Citizen participation is assumed to lead to *better* decisions than any alternative system.

The study of politics requires us to challenge popular perceptions in an effort to better understand the use and distribution of political power. Important questions include: What are the requirements of a democratic political system? Do democracies actually provide citizens with such opportunities? Are modern democracies successful? Answering such questions requires a basic

Buddhist monks march on a street in protest against the military government in Myanmar (Burma), September 2007.

AP Photo

understanding of the structures, procedures, and requirements adopted by modern democratic states in an attempt to meet the "democratic ideal." It is not an ideal easily met by regimes—sometimes called *fledgling democracies*—that have only recently adopted the democratic system. But established democracies, while undoubtedly more successful at the democratic challenge, are not without their own weaknesses. Few offer many opportunities for direct rule. Citizens get to vote in regular elections to select representatives in a number of legislative and executive bodies. Citizens might have an opportunity to vote in referendums on whether they support specific pieces of legislation or constitutional changes. They may also be given the opportunity to initiate their own pieces of legislation. But most democratic opportunities provide little by way of direct control over the day-to-day workings of the state. Instead of citizen rule, we have something closer to citizen choice over who will rule. For some, this is an unacceptable alternative; for others, the opportunities afforded by democracies for citizen decision-making are quite sufficient. One goal in this chapter is to explore the basis for such contradictory conclusions.

Citizen Power

In a majority of the world's states, citizens are granted a measure of power to make public decisions. The ideal of democratic governance is to ensure that citizens "enjoy an equal ability to participate meaningfully in the decisions that closely affect their common lives as individuals in communities."[1] In other words, democracy advocates that the ultimate source of political power is the people, and that the best method for deciding upon questions that affect the community is to allow its members to debate alternatives freely and openly and to select the option that receives support from more than half of those affected.

The ideal of democratic governance, however, is rarely met. Modern democracies provide citizens with only an indirect ability to influence public decisions, and not all citizens enjoy equal ability to participate effectively in politics. The lack of formal restrictions on participation is very different from the existence of equal means and skills for participation purposes. What sets democracies apart is the belief that vesting political power in citizens is a laudable goal.

In the 5th century BCE in the city-state of Athens in ancient Greece, citizens were more intimately involved in the day-to-day decision-making required for the community.[2] Given a marked commitment to civic virtue, politics played a part in everyday life. In this version of democracy, called **direct democracy**, citizen power came from participation in popular assemblies—the equivalent of modern-day legislatures. Citizens, not politicians, were responsible for making key political decisions. Consensus was preferred, but the support of a majority of those assembled could also decide on the alternatives. A key difference from today's legislatures is that *all* citizens were meant to participate in these assemblies, not only a smaller number of elected representatives. Democracy, rule of the people, was direct: the people sitting in the assemblies debated and ruled on community questions. And the debate that took place in these assemblies was crucial: if citizens were made aware of alternatives, were allowed to voice their own concerns, and could hear the concerns of others, the outcome of the deliberation was believed to be *better* than that offered by some smaller, select group of individuals. Moreover, in the Athenian system, appointment to offices and executives occurred by lot, in an effort to avoid the problems that accompanied direct election.

Before concluding that this is a system on which to pattern modern democracy, take note of the fact that the ability to meet in assembly requires a limited number of citizens. Gathering thousands of people together anywhere to debate and render decisions is unlikely to be easy or successful; indeed, think about how hard it is to get even a small group of friends to agree on which restaurant to choose for a dinner out. Direct democracy in ancient Greece worked because the city-state was small (an average of 2,000 to 3,000 of the approximately 50,000 citizens would attend an assembly) and citizenship was not extended to slaves, women, and children. These exclusions meant that the men sitting in these assemblies constituted a minority of the population. This minority imposed its will on the majority, an outcome that would be unacceptable in modern democracy. It also worked because slavery provided Athenian citizens with plenty of free time. While this application of direct democracy is likely to leave us uncomfortable, the ideal of all citizens having an equal and direct say in public decisions remains an important standard by which to judge modern democracies.

Few modern democracies are able to employ the model of direct democracy of ancient Greece. Indeed, even among ancient political systems, the Athenian model was atypical. Democracy has evolved in response to the requirements of modern living, and representative assemblies have replaced Athenian popular assemblies. Instead of making public decisions directly on a regular basis, citizens vote for individuals who will act as their representatives in these assemblies. In some modern systems, elements of direct democracy are nonetheless incorporated into the system in an effort to increase citizen participation in decision-making, as we will see later.

Representative democracies retain the important deliberative element of earlier assemblies— decision-makers must be able to gather and debate options before coming to any conclusions—but not the popular basis for filling these assemblies. The considerable time requirement imposed by politics on Athenian citizens is made today only of citizens who choose to stand for public office. The compromise works, however, only if representatives are conscious of the needs, desires, and concerns of the people they are elected to represent; that is, citizens are powerful only if their representatives act in ways that correspond with the desires of the represented. Most modern democracies attempt to ensure this consciousness by requiring periodic elections. Elections mean that representatives must present themselves regularly before those who selected them to defend their actions and to receive the privilege of continuing on in their role. What is often overlooked in this process is each citizen's personal responsibility. To keep modern democracies from degenerating into **elite** rule, citizens must stay informed, active, and committed to the public project to ensure the accountability of elected representatives. Thus elections assume a crucial role in the maintenance of modern democracies. According to Joseph Schumpeter, democracy is the "competitive struggle for the people's vote."[3] Because elections have degenerated to some extent into negative ad campaigns, leader image contests, and fundraising competitions, many challenge the degree to which the democratic ideal is currently being met in modern democracies.

Technology and Democracy

Technological innovation provides the potential for allowing modern democracies to incorporate the popular participation found in direct democracy and perhaps to counter the excesses of elections. E-democracy and **digital democracy** have been championed by many who consider communications technology the perfect vehicle for allowing citizens to regain some of the direct political power lost under representative systems. One estimate suggests that, as of 2007, over 1.2 billion users around the world were connected to the Internet: approximately 19 percent of the world's population.[4] Given the ease of access to and the wealth of information available on the Internet, this medium provides the potential for citizens to become proactive democratic participants. Citizens can be tremendously empowered by communicating directly and instantly with each other, with elected representatives, and with the government. Local government in Bristol, England, for example, launched a website designed specifically to allow young people to upload text, MP3 files, and images in an effort to encourage them to participate more in local politics. The site includes a number of e-petitions launched by youth on such issues as the funding of school kitchens and public swimming pools.[5] Another option rests in the possibility for completing political transactions online, for example by e-voting. Experiments with tele-voting have been conducted in a number of party leadership races in Canada.[6] Information communication technologies (ICTs) offer a whole range of options for increased citizen political participation: text messaging, blogs, websites (including YouTube and Facebook), and e-mail provide opportunities and tools for participation that were unknown even 20 years ago. In July 2007, for example, Democratic presidential candidates squared off in a debate with a twist: questions were submitted online via YouTube.[7] Technological innovation provides the potential for getting many more citizens to discuss, get information about, and participate in politics.

The potential that exists in digital democracy is mitigated, however, by a number of difficulties. Tele-voting experiments have had their share of technological problems: lost PINs (personal identification numbers), computer incompatibilities, site crashes, software glitches, and security breaches. Such concerns are at least as troubling as the problems encountered with the traditional technology of the "butterfly ballot" employed in the 2000 American elections. The ballot used in Palm Beach, Florida, had two vertical columns listing candidates and parties (resembling the wings of the butterfly), and voters punched a hole in the centre to indicate their preference. Unfortunately, the holes were not well aligned with the party and candidate names, and the resulting confusion probably cost the Democrats enough votes to lose the presidency.

Yet there are bigger issues than simply getting the systems to work properly and securely. There is a "digital divide"—that is, a vast gulf separating the rich and the poor with respect to accessing this technology. Remember for a moment that the democratic ideal is to allow citizens *equal ability* to participate meaningfully in public decision-making. There is little doubt that if democracy embraces technology, a number of citizens will be left behind. Democracies such as Denmark, the United States, Sweden, and Canada boast that over 65 percent of their populations have Internet access.[8] Read differently, that means that about 35 percent do not. And those without access are disproportionately made up of the poor, the uneducated and illiterate, and ethnic minorities. Estimates suggest that less than 20 percent of the population in the Middle East and less than 5 percent in Africa have access to the Internet.[9] Unequal access translates into unequal ability. Greater access, however, is not enough to breach the divide. Broadband access in every city may help, but it cannot guarantee ability—citizens must possess the requisite skills to employ this technology successfully. If this fact is overlooked, our democracies might eventually consist of two groups: the powerful and the increasingly powerless.[10] As some point out, however, this would not be very different from the current state of affairs.

One difficulty with which modern democracies grapple is the conflicting desire to increase citizen power while at the same time ensuring that those very citizens respect the rights and obligations of others.[11] Historically, majorities have sometimes voted to remove the freedoms of minorities. While citizens in modern democracies are quick to assert the rights owed them by virtue of their citizenship, fewer acknowledge the obligations involved for greater responsibility for public decision-making. Increasing citizens' political power might result in greater rates of participation, but only if the citizens have both the capacity and the desire to participate. Creating civic capacity by increasing skills and means is partly the responsibility of government, and governments might increase the desire to participate if political systems, structures, and processes were modified to create more effective citizen power. Technology may well provide one potential mechanism for increasing this power.

A further challenge for modern democracy is **globalization**,[12] which has served to erode state sovereignty in such a way that modern democratic institutions may no longer be effective. If important political decisions are being made by nongovernmental organizations (NGOs) or by international political organizations, rather than by democratically elected governments, then increasing citizen political power might ultimately be in vain. Democracy is meant to provide a mechanism by which a community can render decisions on how it will be governed. If institutions and groups outside the community are making such decisions, existing democratic structures are inadequate, as discussed in Chapter 16.

Elections

One of the key democratic instruments is the **election**. Elections are the primary mechanism through which citizens in democratic states participate in the political system. And in terms of citizen power, citizen political decision-making takes place mainly through elections. Elections can provide much information about the condition of democracy in a country. When Canadians went to the polls in the 2006 general election, only 64.7 percent of registered voters bothered to take advantage of their civic right (see Figure 10.1).[13] The turnout rate has been declining in Canada, although it did rebound slightly in 2006, and many take this to indicate that Canadians are dissatisfied with—rather than merely apathetic about—their governments, politics, and democracy.

Elections provide the prime mechanism in representative democracies for holding governments accountable. Governments are made up of representatives belonging to various political parties who are often selected on the basis of territory. Voters are provided an opportunity for retrospective evaluation—they can render a decision on whether they believe the government has done a good job while in office and whether it should be returned to power. At the same time, voters have an opportunity to assess the alternative parties and their promises to see whether another party might deserve a shot at governing on the basis of the platform it puts forward. Elections should occur on a regular basis to ensure that representatives and governments are aware of the need to "face the voters." Competitive or effective elections, then, determine—either directly or indirectly—the composition of the government and attempt to ensure government accountability to citizens.[14] Competitive elections have a number of requirements.[15] Elections should not unnecessarily restrict citizens' right to vote—called the **franchise**—and most modern democracies have relatively

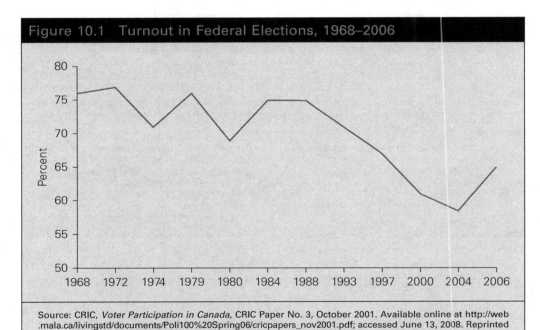

Figure 10.1   Turnout in Federal Elections, 1968–2006

Source: CRIC, *Voter Participation in Canada*, CRIC Paper No. 3, October 2001. Available online at http://web .mala.ca/livingstd/documents/Poli100%20Spring06/cricpapers_nov2001.pdf; accessed June 13, 2008. Reprinted by permission of the Centre for Research and Information on Canada (CRIC); 2004 and 2006 election turnout data obtained from http://www.electionscanada.ca

few limitations on this right. The removal of property qualifications, the extension of the right to vote to women and Aboriginal people, and the lowering of the voting age greatly increased the number of voters in Canada. Free and fair elections require at the very least that political parties be relatively free to assemble and put forward candidates, as noted in Table 10.1. Citizens must be presented with alternatives at elections; if they are not, the process is devoid of meaning. Not all groups, however, are given the freedom to associate and contest elections. In the Federal Republic of Germany, for example, "parties which, by reason of their aims or the behaviour of their adherents, seek to impair or destroy the free democratic basic order or to endanger the existence of the Federal Republic of Germany" are deemed unconstitutional, with the Federal Constitutional Court having the ultimate authority to decide on the question of unconstitutionality.[16] German history helps us to understand why such restrictions are in place.

Intimidation, violence, threats, and bribes should occur neither during election campaigns nor at the polls. The use of the secret ballot was adopted in part to curtail such practices. Finally, the administration of elections should be fair; the counting and reporting of votes cast, for example, should occur in an honest and consistent manner. The recent election ballot reform adopted in Florida came in response to the difficulties encountered in the 2000 presidential election. Optical scan ballots have replaced the butterfly ballot punch card system in the hope of preventing a repeat of that fiasco; counting votes fairly should not require that individual vote counters attempt to "guess" voter intent according to the depth of a dimpled chad on a punch card. More recently, 13 centres served as pilot projects in e-voting during local elections in Britain in May 2007, but the results suggested that security concerns and vote-counting problems continue to plague this modern twist on an ancient act.[17]

Table 10.1   Criteria of Free and Fair Elections

	Free	Fair
Campaign Period	• freedom of expression • freedom of assembly • freedom of association • universal suffrage • right to stand for office	• transparent election process • equality of political parties and groups • equal access to public media by parties and candidates • impartial, independent electoral commission • no impediments to voter registration • equal access to party information by voters
Election Day	• opportunity to vote • secret ballot • absence of intimidation of voters • accessible polling stations	• access to polling stations for party representatives, media, and election observers • impartial ballots • tamper-resistant ballot boxes • effective and transparent ballot counting procedures • effective and transparent procedures for determining invalid ballots • security measures for the transportation of ballot boxes • protection of polling stations
After Election Day	• ability to legally contest election results	• impartial and prompt treatment of election complaints • official and timely announcement of election results • unbiased media reporting of results • acceptance of results by all involved • installation in office of winners of the election

Source: Adapted from Richard Rose, ed., *The International Encyclopaedia of Elections* (Washington, DC: CQ Press, 2000), p. 133. © 2000 Congressional Quarterly Inc.

Function of Elections

What are the effects of competitive elections, and what exactly do elections do?[18] There are two contradictory views on the main function of elections in competitive democracies. The first, called the bottom-up view, suggests that elections are mechanisms for allowing citizens to select their governments, to influence public policies, and to be represented. The alternative, top-down view emphasizes the controlling elements of elections. Competitive elections provide mechanisms for governments to control the democratic process—by focusing dissent, by limiting political participation primarily to elections, and by legitimizing a system in which citizens have little effective power. Most people accept a middle ground between these two positions: elections provide opportunities for exchange between governments and citizens. This conclusion sets the stage for assessing how well elections perform their purported functions.

Choosing a Government

A key function of elections is to decide who will govern. In many liberal democracies, however, this is true only to a degree. Elections normally allow citizens to choose members of the legislature, but legislatures rarely govern, the American

A demonstrator dressed as Uncle Sam holds up a sign rejecting Governor George W. Bush as president during a rally in support of Vice-President Al Gore in Tallahassee, Florida, in December 2000.

CP Photo/Dave Martin

Congress being an exception (see Chapters 7 and 8). Moreover, the formation of a government in parliamentary systems often results from bargaining among the parties represented in the legislature (known as coalition governments) or from some long-standing convention, rather than from direct election. When one party wins a majority of seats in the legislature, it is normally asked to form government (known as a *majority government*). If, on the other hand, a party with the greatest number of seats in the legislature holds only a plurality but is deemed capable of governing, it can nonetheless be asked to form government (known as a *minority government*). It is also the case that parliamentary governments can change between elections. A majority of presidential systems, on the other hand, allow for direct election of the president.[19] Yet the American president, contrary to popular belief, is not directly elected. When American voters cast a vote for president, they are actually voting for a slate of electors called the Electoral College; these electors pledge to vote for the winning candidate in their state when they formally elect the president roughly a month later. Electoral College votes are distributed on a state-by-state basis, equal to the number of members sent from the state to the two houses of Congress, making them roughly proportional to each state's population. Because most states' college electors vote as a block, it is possible for the college to elect a candidate who lost the nationwide popular vote, as was the case in the 2000 American presidential election: Al Gore won 48.4 percent of the popular vote but only 267 of the 537 Electoral College votes. George W. Bush, on the other hand, won only 47.9 percent of the popular vote but captured 271 Electoral College votes to win the presidency.[20] Finally, the public service, courts, and military play an important role in helping the executive to govern, although executive appointment rather than election is normally the rule employed to fill the vast majority of these positions. Accordingly, "competitive elections play an important part in government formation but the relationship is less tight, less strict, than many people imagine."[21]

Mechanism of Accountability

Elections are also mechanisms designed to ensure government accountability. This claim may seem suspect, given the fact that elections do not always directly determine the government. They can, however, force a change in government, particularly if the people are especially unhappy with decisions made during the government's tenure and if a clear alternative party exists. Democratic governments understand that at some point they must face the electorate, a knowledge that can constrain their behaviour to some degree. It cannot guarantee, however, that all government decisions will be popular: the Mulroney government, for example, imposed the Goods and Services Tax (GST) on Canada despite widespread public hostility.

Selection of Representatives

Elections allow citizens to choose their political representatives; they necessarily determine who serves as the representative or representatives of individual territorial districts. But the concept of representation is a difficult one to pin down, as mentioned in Chapter 8. What does it mean to represent others politically? One common interpretation proposes three styles of electoral representation: trustee, party, and constituency.[22] The trustee model emphasizes that although representatives take the interests and concerns of their electors into account, decisions are ultimately made according to the representatives' own judgment. Citizens should, the argument goes, trust their judgment. Such an argument might seem immediately unacceptable, but democracy does value the importance of debate and the articulation of alternative viewpoints for political decision-making—and this is exactly what is supposed to take place in the legislature. Only a minority of ordinary citizens have the information, expertise, and awareness of consequences that would allow them to render equally valid judgments on many current political questions.

The party model, on the other hand, emphasizes that legislators are chosen on the basis of their party membership—very few independents ever get elected—and as a result their responsibility is to support the party position in the legislature. This argument focuses on the fact that many people vote according to party rather than individual candidate; once elected, legislators should be bound to support that party's platform. Such an argument is often heard in Canada to criticize MPs who "cross the floor" to join another political party, a recent example being that of Belinda Stronach, who left the Conservative Party to become a Liberal Party cabinet minister in May 2005.

Finally, the constituency model emphasizes the role that representatives play in supporting the interests of their constituents by helping them to deal with the large government bureaucracy, promoting government spending in the constituency and, in some cases, generating employment opportunities. For many Canadian backbench MPs, this casework can take up a significant portion of their time.

Political representation is particularly important in democracies given that legislators are elected to "represent" the interests of citizens. Political scientists have engaged in a continuing debate on the nature of the concept, making a distinction between substantive and descriptive representation. Is it more important to have political representatives, regardless of who they are, who will make decisions that are in the best interests of a particular constituency (substantive), or to have political representatives whose physical characteristics, such as gender, ethnicity, and age, mirror those of their constituency (descriptive)? In the latter argument, it is often assumed that if a group of legislators physically resemble those they are meant to represent then their decisions are likely to mirror the decisions that would have been made by the very people they represent. Although the descriptive versus substantive representation dichotomy is to some extent a false one, it has nevertheless generated significant discussion in some areas, such as **feminist** political theory where the question of who can "best" represent the interests of women has been raised (see Box 10.1).[23]

How the Canadian Electoral System Discourages Women's Participation   BOX 10.1

The Royal Commission on Electoral Reform and Party Financing reported in 1991 its findings concerning the principles and processes governing elections to the House of Commons. In setting out the objectives of Canadian electoral democracy, the study suggested the importance of ensuring equitable access to candidacy. And while few formal restrictions exist, the commission noted that women have been greatly underrepresented among those running as candidates for and those elected to the House. For example, in 1988 women made up only 19 percent of candidates and only 13 percent of those elected. This virtual exclusion of women, it argued, was no longer acceptable. According to the report, "It is not merely a matter of political symbolism; elected representatives will not and cannot effectively represent the full range of Canada's interests if they do not reasonably reflect its society. To this extent, the electoral system fails to secure the best persons to sit in the House of Commons" (p. 8).

Two of the key barriers for women's entry into the House of Commons are the nomination process and the inattention of political parties. The nomination process presents a particular financial barrier to women, whose earnings continue to be less than those of men. First, women are more likely to find themselves in expensive contested nominations rather than in acclamations to run as the party's candidate. And second, they receive fewer and smaller donations than men, in part due to their different social and professional contacts.

To deal with these problems, the report recommended the imposition of spending limits on nomination contest campaigns and the issuing of tax receipts to those who donate money toward nomination contests. The report also highlighted the role played by political parties in increasing the representation of women in the House. Although it noted that the major parties at the federal level had measures designed to assist prospective women candidates (especially the New Democratic Party), progress had been slow. Women continued to be underrepresented in "safe" ridings, which decreased their chances of getting elected. They also continued to work in "pink-collar" positions within party hierarchies (e.g., as constituency association secretaries), rarely stepping stones to political office. The report recommended that "the by-laws and constitutions of registered political parties require the establishment of formal search committees and commit the parties to processes that demonstrably promote the identification and nomination of broadly representative candidates" (p. 121).

Have we made any progress in the years since the report came out? In the 2006 federal election, women made up 23 percent of all candidates and 21 percent of those elected to the House of Commons. Should there have been greater progress than this since 1988? Does it matter whether more women get elected? What do you think?

SOURCE: Royal Commission on Electoral Reform and Party Financing, *Final Report, Vol. 1*, pp. 8 and 121, 1991. Reproduced with the permission of the Minister of Public Works and Government Services, 2008, and courtesy of the Privy Council Office.

Conferral of Legitimacy

Elections are also the mechanism through which governments are granted a measure of **legitimacy**. As a key element of democratic systems, fair and free elections provide a chance for citizens to participate in politics and to decide who will hold political power. With this opportunity, however, comes the expectation that the people will comply with government decisions. The opportunity to choose the rulers in a fair and legitimate manner obliges citizens to obey the decisions of that popularly elected government. The legitimacy of the electoral process provides the government with political authority, but an obligation to obey does not remove the right of political dissent and the opportunity to change such policies.

Establishing a Policy Mandate

Elections are also meant to supply governments with a specific policy mandate for their tenure in office. Understanding the nature of elections provides insight into why this function is rarely fulfilled. Political parties offer specific campaign platforms, filled with a number of policy prescriptions. One might, then, conclude that the winning party has been given a vote of support for its specific policy proposals. In order for this to occur, however, voters must be voting for the party *because* of its policy positions and for no other reason, which is not often the case. A majority of the electorate must also support the party and its platform, which is not always true either. Although Brian Mulroney claimed that the election of the Progressive Conservative Party in 1988 indicated that Canadians wished to go forward with the Canada–U.S. Free Trade Agreement, he failed to mention that the party had won only 43 percent of the popular vote. One cannot make the claim that elections determine public policy if more people vote against than for the positions ultimately adopted. In addition, once parties have formed the government, they can drop key elements of their electoral platforms without major repercussions. This seriously weakens the argument that elections shape public policy. In 2003, for example, Ontario Premier Dalton McGuinty broke an election promise not to raise taxes while in government. The need for the increased taxes notwithstanding, such reversals make it difficult to claim that elections constrain policy choices in government.

Mechanism for Political Education, Mobilization, and Socialization

Finally, elections provide opportunities for political education, mobilization, and socialization. Elections allow for the political education of both voters and members of political parties. Voters can learn about political campaigns, candidates, and party leaders, and the major issues facing the government. Parties and candidates have an opportunity to find out what the people are thinking and also to shape their opinions. Such education can provide an incentive for people to get out and vote and possibly become politically involved in additional ways. Elections can also socialize citizens regarding the requirements of democracy and the importance assigned to politics within a particular country. If such learning is to occur, however, citizens must already be interested enough in politics to pay attention to the media coverage of campaigns. The most recent Canadian election study reveals that on a scale of 0 (not at all interested) to 10 (extremely interested), Canadians possess an average interest of 5.3 for politics in general. This average jumps to 5.9, however, when people are asked more specifically about their interest in the federal election.[24]

Elections and the Media

Any discussion of elections in modern democracies must address the role played by the **mass media**. Television, radio, and newspapers provide an important source of information for voters, a point not lost on politicians and campaign managers. More often than not, the media present the electoral contest as a "horse race." The focus is on which party and leader are ahead on any particular day, rather than on more substantive policy issues or the parties' platforms. This sensational treatment makes for entertaining viewing, listening, or reading; it does little, however, to advance the political education of voters or the message that politics and elections are more than games. Party leaders and candidates have also had to learn to speak in sound bites, since the media like answers in the form of 10-second clips. Not all political questions, however, can be reasonably answered in so short a time.

Style over Substance?

This focus on style, often over substance, leads politicians to hire professional image consultants and speech specialists. The transformation of Preston Manning during his tenure as leader of the Reform Party in Canada suggests the importance assigned to image: a change from glasses to contact lenses, a change in hairstyle (and colour?), a serious overhaul of his wardrobe, and voice lessons. Selecting the proper media image is not always easy. Prime Minister Stephen Harper has suffered his own image problems. He appeared in 2005 at the Calgary Stampede in a too-small leather vest and odd-looking cowboy hat; in 2006 he was criticized on an official visit to Mexico for wearing what appeared to be a fishing vest compared to the starched crisp white shirts worn by Presidents Fox and Bush; and the news media have often remarked on the size of his

Conservative leader Stephen Harper attending the Calgary Stampede in a cowboy outfit.

Stephen Harper photo taken by Mikael Kjellstrom, July 7, 2007. Reprinted with permission of the *Calgary Herald*.

stomach. And although none of this ought to matter for the quality of governance in democracies, the prominence of media coverage has increased the degree to which it does. Citizens need to feel that their leaders are competent, honest, able, and trustworthy. The image that they portray through the media directly determines these attitudes.

Tighter regulation might be the solution to ensuring more realistic, informative, and substance-driven media coverage of politics, but the media's portrayal of politics and politicians would be extremely difficult to control. Although public broadcasters exist (CBC Radio and Television in Canada, for example), much of the industry is dominated by commercial (private) broadcasters and publishers, whose bottom line is either circulation numbers or size of the audience. Maximizing paper sales and viewing audience would prove difficult if the media were forced to provide in-depth and substantial coverage of politics and elections (especially given the low level of interest that Canadians have in politics and elections as noted above). And while regulation might prove successful in altering coverage, the cost to political freedom, namely freedom of expression, would certainly prove too high.

Media Concentration

A further concern is the growing concentration of mass media ownership and its increased commercialization. In the United States, giants such as AOL/Time Warner and Viacom increasingly dominate all forms of mass communication, driven by a set of values not always in line with journalistic ones.[25] The rise in commercialization has meant a simultaneous decrease in the importance of public broadcasting based on a greater sense of public purpose and responsibility. Public broadcasters offer more current affairs and political news programs than commercial broadcasters, and help to produce a politically informed and aware citizenry. Increased concentration also raises concerns about the responsiveness of media empires to local political issues, as exemplified by CanWest Global's decisions to adopt common editorials for various newspapers across the country and to refocus journalists' stories that were at odds with the views of the owners (see Chapter 4). A challenge to media ownership concentration comes from citizen journalism, made possible by the expansion of the Internet. Blogs, wikis, and websites provide almost unlimited alternative sources of information.

Electoral Rules

In each country, the conduct of elections is governed by a set of rules and regulations, which detail the offices that will be filled by the election; financial, nomination, and reporting requirements for candidates and parties that wish to run in the contest; voting eligibility requirements; regulations concerning the drawing of electoral boundaries; and even the requirements for the ballot, such as the order of candidates' names.

Campaign Finance

Key among these rules are those concerning matters of party and election finance: for example, the amount and sources of party funds, party and candidate spending, and *third-party advertising*—a term encompassing spending by organizations other than political parties during elections.[26] The need for financial regulation stems from a concern for equity and fairness among those contesting elections; the control of how money is raised and spent can help "level the playing field" and limit the degree to which money influences electoral outcomes and ultimately government decisions. Restricting how parties can spend during campaigns diminishes their need for raising funds, makes elections more equitable, and reduces candidates' and parties' obligations to those donating the funds.

In 2000, the government of Manitoba adopted legislation designed to address concerns regarding the perception that money unduly influences politics and elections. This legislation bans contributions from corporations and unions to political parties, limits individual contributions to $3,000 per year, limits third-party spending during election periods to $5,000, and reinstates limits on political party advertising during elections. Similar legislation has existed in Quebec since 1977. The National Citizens' Coalition, a right-wing nonprofit organization in Canada, has fought hard against restrictions on third-party election advertising, which it calls "gag laws." On three separate occasions, Alberta courts agreed with the organization's argument that the rules represent an unreasonable violation of the right of freedom of expression. The Supreme Court, however, ruled in favour of the restrictions imposed on third-party spending in the Canada Elections Act in *Harper v. Canada* in 2004. The challenge is to balance the desire for a level playing field with the desire for ensuring free and open debate during elections.

Similar campaign finance legislation was adopted for Canadian general elections by the Chrétien Liberal government in 2003. Designed to enhance the fairness and transparency of the electoral system, Bill C-24 brought the *Canada Elections Act* in line with elections regulation in Manitoba and Quebec by restricting contributions, imposing spending limits on parties and candidates, enhancing financial reporting requirements, and increasing the regulation of political broadcasting. In an effort to level the political playing field and to reduce the perception of undue influence in politics, the system of public financing of election expenses was also further enhanced.[27] Although the 2004 election took place under the new regulatory framework, its overall impact on parties, elections, and participation remains unclear.[28] The Harper government's *Federal Accountability Act* attempted to plug the last loopholes in this field.

Similar legislation was adopted in 2002 at the federal level in the United States. The key element of the *Bipartisan Campaign Reform Act* was the regulation of "soft money" and "issue advocacy," the former involving donations to parties not specifically directed toward the support or opposition of a candidate and the latter involving campaign communications that do not expressly advocate for the election or defeat of candidates. Spending in both has skyrocketed given dramatic increases in the costs of campaigns (mass media and technology costs) and the need to overcome the limits on "hard money" and "express advocacy."[29] Unlike in Canada, however, the U.S. Supreme Court has been less willing to accept that campaign finance regulation be employed to "level the playing field" across political parties (see Chapter 12).

Electoral Districting and Apportionment

Another key set of electoral rules governs electoral districting and apportionment, particularly in electoral systems based on territorial representation, such as those of Canada and the United States. *Districting* (or *redistribution*, as it is called in Canada) refers to the drawing of electoral boundaries in order to establish territorial districts or constituencies from which one or more representatives will be sent to the legislature. The manipulation of district boundary lines to advantage a particular group (or to disadvantage another) is referred to as *gerrymandering*. In an effort to reduce the likelihood of such manipulation, the responsibility for the drawing of electoral boundaries has been placed in the hands of independent bodies, rather than those of the sitting government.

The principle of **representation by population** ("rep by pop") advocates that electoral districts should be roughly equal in population in order to ensure that individuals receive a proportionate share of representation in government, so that each vote is of equal weight. *Apportionment*—the determination of representative seats according to population—should occur regularly, normally after a census, to account for shifting population bases. The rep by pop principle, however, recognizes that other considerations can come into play in drawing boundaries, including a desire to keep the geographic expanse of a district to a manageable size and to ensure minority groups are not scattered across several districts, which would minimize their electoral influence. In federal states, such as Canada and the United States, rep by pop is adopted for the lower house at the national level but not for the upper house. In the United States, representation in the senate occurs on a state basis (two representatives per state). In Canada's senate, representation occurs on a more complicated regional basis. In both instances, however, population size is not a consideration in apportioning seats to the upper house.

Electoral Systems

The rules employed to translate votes into seats have been the subject of great debate in many countries.[30] New Zealand, Japan, and Italy have recently changed their electoral systems in an attempt to address various concerns. Such changes reflect the importance of electoral systems— systems that set the rules for determining how individual votes are translated into legislative seats. To better understand the importance of rules for outcomes, let us employ an academic analogy. Imagine your response if a professor decided to change the format of an exam from multiple-choice to essay questions one day before you were scheduled to write it. Rules (in this example, the format of the exam—multiple choice or essay questions) determine how you will study for the exam and possibly the grade you will receive. Electoral systems are no different—they shape electoral strategies, electoral outcomes, and voter behaviour. Because of this, students of politics require a basic understanding of the various electoral systems in use in today's democracies.

One common method for distinguishing electoral systems focuses on the electoral formula employed—that is, the rule for determining how many votes are required to earn a seat. Two main types of electoral systems are proportional and nonproportional systems (see Table 10.2). Nonproportional systems (such as in Canada, the United States, and Britain) are defended for their tendency to produce majority governments, for encouraging the development of two-party systems, and for encouraging strong territorially defined links between representatives and their constituents. Proportional systems, on the other hand, are defended for the greater fairness in awarding seats that are roughly proportional to the share of votes obtained by each party.

Table 10.2 Electoral Systems

Nonproportional Systems

(a) Plurality (first-past-the-post)

Candidate who wins more votes than any other (i.e., wins the plurality of votes) is awarded the seat. This method is used most often in combination with single-member districts. *Examples:* Canada (House of Commons); United States (House of Representatives).

(b) Majority

Candidate must win a majority of votes (50% + 1) in order to win the seat. Majority is achieved by employing one of three methods:

- *Runoff:* The second ballot lists only the top two candidates from the first ballot round. This method is used most often in combination with single-member districts. *Example:* French presidential elections.
- *Plurality:* A second ballot is also employed, but the winner needs to obtain only a plurality of votes. There is no significant reduction in the number of candidates on the second ballot, although a threshold may be imposed. *Example:* French legislative elections.
- *Alternative:* A single election occurs, but voters rank the candidates in order of preference. Winner must obtain a majority of first preferences. If no candidate earns a majority of first preferences, the second preferences of the last-place candidate are transferred to the remaining candidates until one candidate achieves a majority. *Example:* Australia (House of Representatives).

Proportional Systems
(all in multimember districts)

(a) List System

Seats are awarded to parties that meet or exceed an electoral quota. In a closed-list system, voters cast a single ballot for a party, and candidates from that party's list are elected in the order in which they appear on the list. In the more common open-list system, in addition to choosing to award their votes to a single party, voters can instead choose to award their votes individually to specific candidates on the party lists. *Examples:* Israel; Switzerland.

(b) Single Transferable Vote (STV)

Voters rank their candidate choices across parties. Candidates meeting a quota are awarded a seat. Initial counting looks at first preferences only; any candidate meeting the quota is elected. Second preferences of any surplus votes (in excess of the quota) are then transferred to any remaining candidates. Again, the candidates who meet the quota after the second preferences have been transferred are elected. If seats are still vacant, the weakest candidate is eliminated and the second preferences from those ballots are allocated to the remaining candidates until the quota is met and all seats are allocated. *Examples:* Ireland; Australia (Senate).

MIXED SYSTEMS

Such systems combine elements of nonproportional and proportional electoral systems. The mixed member proportional (MPP) system is an example. Voters have two votes: one for the constituency representative and a second for a party. A share of seats is allocated through single-member districts, while the remaining seats are allocated in order to bring each party's seat share in line with the party's popular vote share. Examples: Germany (Bundestag); New Zealand.

Source: Adapted from André Blais and Louis Massicotte, *"Electoral Systems,"* in Lawrence LeDuc, Richard G. Niemi, and Pippa Norris, eds., *Comparing Democracies: Elections and Voting in Global Perspective* (Thousand Oaks, CA: Sage, 1996). Reprinted by permission of Sage Publications, Inc.

Electoral systems are not merely of academic concern; by the end of 2007, three Canadian provinces (British Columbia, Ontario, and Prince Edward Island) had held referendums on the question of reforming the electoral system.

Nonproportional Systems

Nonproportional type electoral systems are constituency-based (the country is divided into geographically defined constituencies represented by one elected representative) and voters select a candidate on the ballot rather than a party. This group of electoral systems includes the one most familiar to North Americans: the plurality system. The requirement for winning in a plurality system is *to earn more votes than any other candidate but not necessarily a majority*—hence its more common name, **first-past-the-post (FPTP)**. In elections to the Canadian House of Commons, for example, the country is divided into single-member districts: one representative is selected from each territorially defined district. Since a number of political parties nominate a single candidate to run in each district, the winner rarely earns a majority of the votes cast. The cumulative effect of this "wasting of votes" can lead to serious distortions in the vote-share-to-seat-share ratio at the national level (see Table 10.3 for the distortion in Canada's 2006 federal election).[31] Such distortions have fuelled efforts to change Canada's electoral system at both the federal and provincial levels. Since the governing parties often achieve power as a direct result of this distortion, however, one can understand why they might be hesitant to change the system.

An additional but less common nonproportional electoral system is the **majoritarian system**. The distinction between such systems and FPTP is that the winning candidate is required to earn a majority of votes in order to be declared the winner (a majority being 50% + 1). This requirement means that one election will often not produce a winner, since elections normally involve more than two candidates. As a result, majoritarian systems employ one of three mechanisms for producing a winner. Two of these systems require a second election in the event that no candidate earns a majority of votes in the first. The majority runoff systems include only the top two finishers from the first race in the second election. Limiting the subsequent election to only two candidates virtually ensures that a majority winner will be produced. In majority plurality systems, on the other hand, a second election is held without any reduction in the number of candidates (although some countries adopt a threshold to eliminate candidates who earned a small share of the vote). The winner in the second election is the candidate who obtains a plurality of votes—that is, more votes than any other candidate.

The third mechanism, the alternative vote, requires only one election, which many see as its advantage: voters are asked to rank the candidates listed on the ballot in order of preference (e.g., putting a "1" next to the candidate who is their first choice, a "2" next to their second choice, and so on). The winner is the candidate earning a majority of first preferences, or "1"s. If no such

Table 10.3 Distorting Effects of the Canadian Electoral System, 2006

Party	Seats	Seat Share (percent)	Vote Share (percent)	Seat-to-Vote (ratio)
Conservative Party	124	40.3	36.3	1.11
Liberal Party	103	33.4	30.2	1.11
Bloc Québécois	51	16.6	10.5	1.58
New Democratic Party	29	9.4	17.5	0.54
Total seats	**308***			

Note: If the seat-to-vote ratio is greater than one, the party has been awarded more seats than it deserved on the basis of its vote share. If the ratio is less than one, the party has been underrewarded. *One seat was won by a candidate running as an independent.

Source: Elections Canada, "Percentage of Valid Votes, by Political Affiliation" and "Distribution of Seats, by Political Affiliation and Sex"; available at http://www.elections.ca/scripts/OVR2006/25/table7.html and http://www.elections.ca/scripts/OVR2006/25/table9.html; accessed June 13, 2008.

majority is achieved, the second preferences of the candidate with the fewest number of first preferences are then transferred to the remaining candidates. If a majority is still not achieved, the process continues until transferred preferences provide a majority of votes to a candidate.

Proportional Systems

In **proportional representation (PR)** systems, the priority lies in awarding seats to parties in rough proportion to the share of votes earned rather than in awarding the seat to a single candidate from each district. One key to understanding PR systems is that they use multimember districts rather than single-member districts; the allocation of seats according to the proportion of votes earned is only possible if there is more than one seat available. The higher the number of members to be elected per district, the more proportional the system is likely to be. In Israel, the entire country serves as a single constituency, allowing for a large degree of proportionality in seat allocation. The other key to understanding PR systems is that seats are generally allocated to parties rather than to candidates; although there is significant variation across PR systems, political parties are considered to be more powerful in PR than non-PR systems, in part because they often have a greater say than voters in determining which party members get elected to the legislature.

Two specific PR systems are the list system and the single transferable vote. Most PR systems use the **list system**, which requires voters to choose from among lists of candidates prepared by the parties. In a *closed-list system*, voters are presented with a ballot that lists each of the parties contesting the election and the rank-ordering of the candidates each party has selected as their representatives if they win seats in the legislature. Voters cannot indicate preferences for individual candidates on a party's list, but instead select one party's list as their choice. The share of votes the party receives in the constituency determines the number of candidates who will sit in the legislature. Parties derive tremendous power in this system through their ability to set candidate lists. An *open-list system*, on the other hand, allows voters to choose and rank as many specific candidates from among the different party lists as there are seats to be allocated, thereby weakening the power of party officials to determine who gets elected to the legislature. While the power of parties is stronger in closed-list than open-list systems, the former more easily allow for the adoption of measures by parties for targeting certain demographics for increased representation. For instance, "zippering" party lists— making every second candidate on the closed list a woman—has been shown to be a particularly effective mechanism for increasing their numbers in legislatures.

The procedure employed for allocating seats in proportional systems varies, but it normally involves dividing the number of votes cast for the party or candidate by a quota or divisor. Seats are allocated to the parties according to the resulting figure. As an example, the "droop quota" is calculated in the following manner:

$$\frac{\text{total number of votes}}{\text{number seats to be filled} + 1} + 1$$

Each party's total votes earned are then divided by the quota to determine the number of seats they are awarded; any unallocated seats are awarded to the parties with the highest remainders (i.e., the number of votes "left over" after dividing by the quota). The end result is that the "cost" for each seat (in terms of votes) is roughly equal. Some PR systems also adopt thresholds that deny seats to parties that receive very small shares of the vote, normally around 5 to 6 percent. The argument for adopting thresholds is that it keeps extremist parties from gaining a measure of legitimacy, at least that afforded by a legislative seat. Such thresholds necessarily introduce distortion in the seat-to-vote ratio, however, a criticism often aimed at nonproportional systems.

Israel's electoral system provides a simple example of the application of a PR electoral system. As previously mentioned, Israel consists of a single electoral district with a district magnitude of 120 (the number of seats to be filled in the Knesset, Israel's legislature). A closed-list system is in place; more than a month before election day, political parties are required to submit their ordered candidate lists to the Central Elections Committee and voters are provided with a ballot that allows them to allocate a single vote to one of the party lists (rather than to individual candidates). After all the votes have been counted, parties that do not meet the existing threshold (currently 2 percent of all votes cast) are not awarded a seat in the legislature. The *d'Hondt formula* is then employed to allocate seats among the remaining parties. That is, the total votes earned by each party is divided by a set of numbers (1, 2, 3, 4, 5, etc.) and the result (the quotient or average votes per seat earned) determines the allocation of seats; then the first seat is awarded to the party with the highest quotient or average, the second seat to the party with the next highest average, and so on until all seats are awarded.

An alternative to the list system, the **single transferable vote (STV)**, used in both Australia and Ireland, allows voters to rank their candidate preferences on the ballot. As in the alternative vote system, voters can rank as many candidates as there are seats to be allocated in the constituency. This ballot structure provides voters rather than parties with a greater measure of power than many other PR systems. The increased choice offered to voters, and the associated decrease in the power of parties to choose the representatives to send to the legislature, was one of the rationales offered by B.C.'s Citizens' Assembly in 2004 for their selection of STV as the recommended alternative to FPTP.[32] The procedure for determining which candidates are elected involves the use of the droop quota (explained above). Each candidate's first preference votes are counted, and those whose total number of first preference votes received meets the required quota are each awarded a seat. Any surplus or remaining votes over the quota for these elected candidates are then transferred to the second-preference candidates on the winning candidates' ballots. If a candidate earned 40 percent of the winning candidate's overall second preferences, then that candidate receives 40 percent of the winning candidate's surplus votes. Candidates who meet the quota with the addition of these transferred votes are then awarded a seat. If seats remain unallocated at this point, the candidate with the fewest first preferences is eliminated, and the second preferences listed on those ballots are transferred proportionately to the remaining candidates. The process (which at times can be very lengthy given its complexity) continues until all seats are allocated.

Mixed Systems

Several countries have adopted an electoral system that combines elements of the proportional and nonproportional electoral systems into mixed systems. Japan, for example, elects 300 members of its house of representatives using a first-past-the-post system with single-member constituencies. An additional 200 members are independently elected from 11 regional multimember constituencies through a PR system. New Zealand's system also creates two sets of elected members: those elected under the traditional FPTP system in 65 single-member districts and another 55 elected under a PR closed-list system. The difference, however, is that the 55 PR members are awarded to the parties in order to "top up" the seat shares awarded by the single-member districts to ensure proportionality of all seats with party vote shares cast under the list system. Since FPTP over-rewards larger parties, the PR seat allocation corrects this distortion. Most mixed electoral systems hope to maintain the territorial link between the representative and his or her constituents while injecting greater proportionality between each party's vote and seat shares in the legislature.

Electoral reform has recently become a key issue on the political agenda in Canada in light of growing concerns over citizen disengagement and increased political cynicism. The most common criticism directed at FPTP relates to the system's distorting effects when vote shares are translated into seat shares. Because it is a "winner take all" system, votes for parties with anything less than a plurality are essentially wasted. This distortion leads to overrepresentation for parties that win a plurality of the vote (creating "artificial majorities" in the legislature) and underrepresentation for most other parties, as seen in Table 10.3. This distortion can at times be extreme. In 2001, the Liberals came to power in British Columbia with 97 percent of the seats in the legislature, having earned only 57.6 percent of the popular vote. The New Democratic Party, on the other hand, won only 2 of 79 seats despite having earned 21.6 percent of the provincial vote share.

An additional criticism of FPTP relates to the fact that parties whose support is concentrated in a particular region are likely to be overrepresented in the legislature, while parties with weak but more broadly dispersed support are likely to be underrepresented. In Canada, the Bloc Québécois receives an inflated share of seats in the House of Commons because it receives a plurality of votes in a limited number of regionally concentrated ridings. The NDP, on the other hand, is significantly underrepresented despite receiving a fairly consistent level of support across the country, because it fails to achieve a plurality in many ridings, leading to many votes being effectively wasted. Proponents of electoral reform have argued that this regionalizing effect has exacerbated regional tensions in Canada. The underrepresentation of women and Aboriginal peoples has also been identified as a weakness of FPTP. Alternatively, supporters of FPTP point to its tendency to produce majority governments capable of implementing electoral mandates, its encouragement of a territorial link between elected representative and constituents, and its overall simplicity.[33]

Although several Canadian provinces have examined the question of electoral reform, and in some cases held referendums on the question, FPTP remains in place at both the provincial and federal level in Canada. As noted above, the B.C. Citizens' Assembly on Electoral Reform recommended STV as an alternative to FPTP in 2004; a similar assembly in Ontario recommended MMP as the preferred alternative in 2007. Both recommendations were subsequently defeated in provincial referendums. We can nevertheless identify a number of potential consequences resulting from the move to a more proportional electoral system. First, the incentives for voting (fewer wasted votes) and for voting for smaller parties (because they would be more likely to gain seats in proportion to the votes they earn) would likely increase. Accordingly, turnout would likely improve and the party system might become more fractionalized (see Chapter 11). Second, electoral results would likely become proportional; political parties would likely earn seat shares that more closely reflect the share of votes earned. At the federal level, this might help parties such as the NDP and the Green Party, who have been underrewarded historically in seat shares. Third, the representation of minorities and women in legislatures could improve; a move to an electoral system that allowed political parties to more directly determine which of their candidates earned legislative seats might result in more representative chambers. Fourth, some PR systems would allow voters, rather than parties, more say in determining which candidates get elected. Fifth, greater proportionality would likely translate into fewer majority governments and more coalition governments. Without the representational "boost" afforded to winning parties in FPTP, governments are more likely to be formed from the merger of two or more parties than from only one.

Voting

Elections are the primary mechanism for engaging the people in democracies. The study of voting behaviour and the way voters decide have preoccupied political scientists for quite some time, especially since the advent of public opinion polling in the 1940s. Why do people vote as they do? Three theories can be identified that together provide a fairly complete answer to this rather complex question.[34]

Sociological Model

The first theory, the sociological model, explains voting by identifying the social forces that determine individual values and beliefs. People make their decisions on the basis of such things as

- place of residence
- religious group to which they belong (if any)
- ethnic background
- social class
- age
- gender

These important factors work their influence indirectly. For example, gender might affect how one votes by increasing the value one places on publicly funded child care, which in turn would increase the likelihood of voting for parties that endorse such policies. An explanation like this takes us only so far, however, as people belong to many groups, often with conflicting interests; and although group memberships are fairly stable, voters often switch parties from one election to another.

Sociopsychological Model

The second model, the sociopsychological model, casts a wider net in search of an explanation of vote decisions. The focus in this model is on the psychological process of voting—how people come to make their individual choices. The result is a much more complex model of the various factors. One group of influences mirrors the social group influences identified in the sociological model. Friends and family, ethnic groups, and social cleavages are likely to shape the interests and values that voters bring to their vote decisions. But more important are the personal and political factors that often occur closer in time to the decision itself. Key among these is **party identification**—the long-standing psychological attachment or loyalty to a party that can directly influence where one is likely to put one's X on the ballot. Party identification acts as a filter through which individuals interpret election issues, candidates, parties, and leaders; it can serve as a shortcut in what can be the daunting process of gathering the information necessary to make a rational voting choice. But if the explanation for why a person voted for the Liberal Party, for example, is "because I always vote that way," the result is that we really have not explained very much. Moreover, evidence suggests that the importance of party identification is decreasing; younger and more educated voters are less likely to defer to partisan loyalties at the ballot box.

Like Canadians, the British keep electing people they don't like.

Bruce MacKinnon/Halifax Herald/Artizans

Rational Voting Model

The third model of voting stresses the actual calculus that voters employ. According to this model, voting is a rational decision rather than one based on social ties or partisan identification. The **rational voting** model assumes that, in deciding how to cast their ballot, voters employ a process of evaluation, involving the important issues in the campaign, their assessment of the candidates and the parties' platforms, and their evaluations of the party leaders. This process might compare the alternatives in the search for the "right" choice or it might simply involve an evaluation of the sitting government in an attempt to determine whether a change is needed. This retrospective approach to voting is assumed in campaign slogans that emphasize "a time for change" and helps to explain why voters often punish governments in periods of economic downturn that are at least partly beyond their control. Research suggests, however, that campaigns and campaign strategies set the stage for or frame the evaluations that individuals undertake in elections.[35] A party's ability to remain in government is not, then, completely outside its control. An opposition party's ability to become the government is similarly dependent on its ability to shape the electoral agenda. The rational model also helps explain the current preoccupation with party image and the attention directed to leaders.

The important part played by **public opinion polling** in modern elections should also not be overlooked.[36] Modern polling techniques allow parties to quickly and accurately gauge public opinion and potential reaction. Such information has implications for the timing of elections, the selection of leaders, and campaign strategies, tactics, and slogans. Published polls can also influence voter behaviour, in deterring them from voting for "lost causes" or in providing them with the information necessary for casting a strategic vote. The importance of polls in elections is underscored by the adoption of restrictions on their publication at certain times during election campaigns. The degree to which such restrictions unnecessarily restrict freedom of expression continues to be debated.

Political Participation

A young mother joins a parent–teacher organization to try to change school policy. A university student jumps on a bus to attend a rally in another city to protest against increasing corporate power. A senior citizen attends a political party's constituency meeting to help select the party's candidate in the next election. Each of these is an example of **political participation**, and each provides a measure of political power to the citizens who employ it. If democracy is supposed to afford political power to the people, one could make the claim that healthy democracies are those with high rates of political participation among their citizens.

The avenues available to citizens in liberal democracies for influencing political decisions are many, ranging from the simple act of voting to more involved acts such as running for political office or organizing a petition-signing campaign. Participation can occur on several different levels: individual (voting or attending a rally), organizational (volunteering time to an interest or community group or donating money to a political candidate's campaign), and professional (working as a paid lobbyist or a political appointee). More often than not, such action is undertaken to bring about some kind of political change (including a return to the status quo), directly by influencing decision-makers, or indirectly by gaining sympathetic media coverage or public support for the cause. Participation can also occur for purely expressive rather than instrumental reasons; that is, one may participate to feel a sense of belonging with the community as much as to influence political decisions.[37]

Most liberal democracies make participation voluntary, except for the few that legally require citizens to vote, such as Australia. Note that while a failure to vote in Australia may be illegal, the penalty is minor: only $20.[38] The objective of such laws is to instil a belief in the importance of political participation, which can result in higher rates of participation than one finds in countries such as Canada and the United States. Some have suggested that a similar law should be adopted in Canada in order to increase the rate of participation in elections—a rate that has been steadily dropping. While the adoption of such a law would no doubt increase the number of Canadians who vote, it would do little to change the underlying causes of low voter turnout.

The vast majority of political acts in liberal democracies are legal, but some actors choose other means to affect political decisions. Civil disobedience—that is, breaking laws in a nonviolent fashion to increase public awareness of their injustice—can often be successful. Recent examples in Canada include blockades of logging roads by environmentalists and of public highways by Native groups. The emphasis on nonviolent protest and on accepting punishment willingly helps to generate support for the cause. **Terrorism**, on the other hand, is a more violent but less effective technique sometimes employed by marginal groups in an effort to dramatically focus attention on their cause. The Front de Libération du Québec (FLQ) kidnapped British trade commissioner James Cross in Montreal in 1970 to pressure the federal government to release 23 members of the group imprisoned for terrorist acts. The group, committed to Quebec independence, resorted to murdering Quebec cabinet minister Pierre Laporte in response to the invoking of the *War Measures Act* by Prime Minister Pierre Trudeau. While dramatic, the events did little to increase public support for the group's cause. The terrorist acts committed on September 11, 2001 in the United States are a vivid reminder that the use of illegal acts for political purposes continues.

Early studies of political participation constructed a hierarchy of political activity in the shape of a triangle, with simple activities such as voting at the base and more demanding activities such as running for office at its peak. The width of the base of the hierarchy meant that a good portion of the population were engaged in the simple activities; the narrowness of the top of the hierarchy meant that relatively few were involved in the more demanding ones. Early researchers also assumed that citizens in democracies naturally progressed from simple activities to more demanding ones—from voting to canvassing for a political party to running for office, for example.[39] Reflecting the traditional domination of male thinking in the study of politics, the most active participants were labelled "gladiators," the less active "spectators," and the uninvolved "apathetics." The general conclusion was that many democracies did not meet the level of participation one would expect.

Early research also suggested that those who could afford to participate and those who had the time to participate made up the largest share of the politically active.[40] This included men and those from historically dominant groups, such as the British and to a lesser extent the French in Canada.[41] More recent studies point to the importance of the definition of politics one employs in determining whether certain groups can be considered to be politically active. Immigrant women, for example, have organized immigrant and ethnocultural associations in response to the lack of attention from the women's movement and minority organizations.[42] Such associations have not traditionally been defined as political, however, and as such, immigrant women's level of political participation has been underestimated. More recent studies have also abandoned the conclusion that citizens progress from simple to more demanding political activities. Data suggests that people's political activity tends to cluster into types, the three most common being voting, campaign activity, and communal activity.[43] People choose political activity partly on the basis of the amount of effort required, the degree of cooperation needed among a number of people, the degree of potential conflict involved, and the nature of the issue addressed.

One of the most striking findings regarding political participation is how few people actually participate in traditional activities. A comparison of average turnout rates between 1961 and 1999 in free elections in 40 democracies suggests that where you live determines in large measure the likelihood that you vote; while only 50 percent of eligible voters cast their ballots in Lithuania, 95 percent do in Australia.[44] The rates of participation are much lower for activities that require greater time commitments and resources. Evidence from Great Britain gives a sense of how dramatically the rates drop as the demands of the activity increase; while voting turnout in the 1990s was 72 percent, only 4 percent of the population belonged to a political party, and only 2 percent had canvassed for a candidate.[45]

The rate of participation in various political activities varies by country depending on whether the culture encourages participation and whether the institutional structure makes it easy. Electoral turnout in the United States is relatively low, partly due to the fact that electoral registration depends on individual effort. Some estimates suggest that the rate could increase by several percentage points if a centralized and less demanding system of registration was adopted.[46]

Participation also varies according to the characteristics of individuals, regardless of geography. If those who participate are not drawn equally from all groups in society, government decision-making may not accurately reflect the desires of the population. If age is an important predictor of political activity (see Box 10.2), so too are gender, class, and attitudes. Women are significantly underrepresented in elite political activity, constituting only 17.4 percent of members of national parliaments around the world.[47] The poor and those of lower social classes are less likely to engage in political activity than those with greater access to resources. Political dissatisfaction, political apathy, and political cynicism are likely to turn people away from the political system.

Another striking finding is the degree of change taking place in the kind of political activity that citizens are willing to engage in. Evidence suggests that there has been a rise in the numbers willing to engage in protest behaviour in democracies, both lawful (signing petitions and joining a boycott)

Why Don't Young Canadians Participate More in Politics?   BOX 10.2

How closely do you follow politics? Have you voted every time the opportunity was available to you? You have much in common with your peers if your answers are "not very closely" and "not always." Research tells us that young Canadians are less likely to vote than older Canadians. It also reveals that they are less interested in politics but are also happier with democracy and government (see Table 10.4).

Life cycle explanations for this pattern suggest that young people are not participating at high rates because their interests are such that politics is not a priority. Once they start paying taxes, acquire a mortgage, and think about public school for their children, however, they will naturally become more involved. Evidence from a Canadian poll taken in the

spring of 2000 by the Institute for Research on Public Policy suggests that the life cycle explanation can help us understand this pattern in opinion and behaviour. Today's young Canadians will be participating at higher rates in 10 years' time. The study also reveals, however, that if we compare the participation rates of today's young Canadians to those of Canadians of the same group in 1990, youth are now participating at lower levels than they were only 15 years ago. Although they will become more politically active as they age, they are unlikely to catch up to the rates exhibited by the previous generation. Can you think of an explanation for why today's young people are less politically active than in previous generations?

SOURCE: IRPP, *Policy Matters* 2(5) (October 2001). Reprinted by permission of IRPP.

Table 10.4 Generational Patterns in Canadian Political Opinion and Behaviour, 2000

	18–27 (percent)	28–37 (percent)	38–47 (percent)	48–57 (percent)	Over 57 (percent)
Attention to Politics					
Not very closely or not at all	59	41	42	36	32
Voted in the 1997 election	66	69	85	92	91
Very or fairly satisfied with democracy	82	75	74	70	65
Total number of respondents	**271**	**268**	**281**	**224**	**211**

Source: Brenda O'Neill, "Generational Patterns in Political Opinions and Behaviour of Canadians," Policy Matters 2(5) (October 2001), pp. 11–12, 16.

and unlawful (attending unlawful demonstrations and occupying buildings), especially in Canada and among younger citizens.[48] Protest activity can be explained by deprivation—political alienation and frustration with the system can lead individuals to pursue unconventional modes of political activity. Alternatively, the resource model stresses that protest behaviour is merely an alternative mechanism for drawing attention to a cause; those with the political skills and resources are more likely to undertake such activity.

Explanations for the changing nature of political participation in modern democracies point to the changing nature of **civil society** or of overall patterns of social interaction (sometimes called *social capital*) and the increasing dissatisfaction with politics and governments. Robert Putnam suggests that citizens in the United States are less engaged at the civic level than they were previously and that this has important implications for the health of that democracy.[49] Community activities, ranging from bowling leagues to parent–teacher associations, provide opportunities for community members to build the social trust and social capital necessary for democratic government. There is debate, however, over whether social capital has indeed declined, or whether it may simply be manifesting itself in different ways, such as recycling (a community-minded event), and in different forums, such as the Internet (through discussion lists and "zines"—noncommercial publications of small circulation).

Neil Nevitte suggests that participation rates have changed due to increased education, the expansion of mass communications, and the rise of a knowledge-based economy. Today people are smarter and can access information much more easily than previous generations. Combine this with a loss of confidence in traditional political institutions, and the result is a shift from traditional to non-traditional forms of participation, including protest (see Figure 10.2).[50]

Is there such a thing as too much democratic participation?[51] Some argue that effective political decision-making requires that leaders enjoy a degree of freedom from democratic demands. Decision-makers are better informed than ordinary citizens and are more likely to be able to make decisions in the general public interest. Individual citizens are more likely to think about the costs and benefits to their own neighbourhoods and groups, for example, and are less likely to have as much information or expertise as political elites. Besides, the argument goes, people are generally politically apathetic. The participation of apathetic citizens leads to uninformed decision-making. To this way of thinking, too much democracy is definitely a bad thing.

For others, however, full participation by an informed and rational citizenry is a necessary and crucial condition for democracy. Such an argument rests on the assumption that the pursuit of individual truths—a goal of liberalism—can and will lead to conflicting interests. The mechanism for controlling such disputes is to establish laws on the basis of popular consent. Popular consent, the argument continues, can be established only through full political participation, and without it the legitimacy of political authority is in doubt. Participation also helps citizens learn greater tolerance, achieve greater rationality, and develop an appreciation for civic activism.

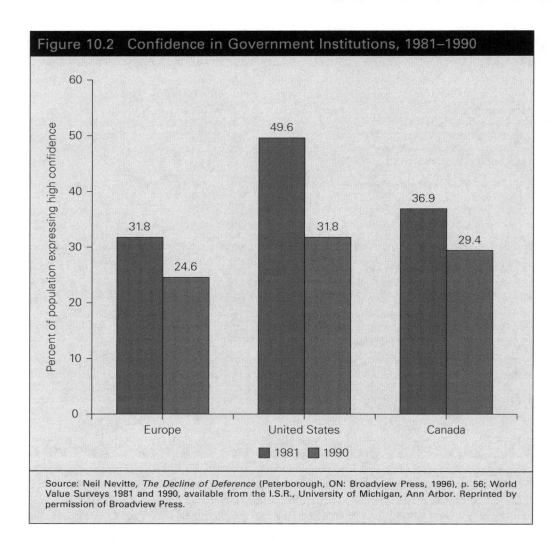

Figure 10.2   Confidence in Government Institutions, 1981–1990

Source: Neil Nevitte, *The Decline of Deference* (Peterborough, ON: Broadview Press, 1996), p. 56; World Value Surveys 1981 and 1990, available from the I.S.R., University of Michigan, Ann Arbor. Reprinted by permission of Broadview Press.

Tools of Direct Democracy

A number of devices have the potential for increasing direct citizen political power in representative democracies. Populist movements and parties in the western United States and Canada have successfully pushed for the adoption of these mechanisms to return a measure of power to citizens to balance that enjoyed by governments. The three most common are the referendum, the initiative, and the recall. Despite their potential, they are not immune from manipulation by governments and powerful groups of citizens alike. The result is that few governments have adopted such mechanisms wholeheartedly; most employ them on occasion, sometimes in an attempt to manipulate the political outcome.

Referendums provide opportunities for citizens to vote directly on pieces of legislation or on constitutional questions. The *binding* referendum requires that the government act on the result of the referendum, and thus provides the greatest potential for citizen power. Such referendums are employed in Australia for constitutional change. *Nonbinding* referendums (sometimes referred to as *plebiscites*) do not tie a government's hands as binding referendums do. In democracies with politically interested, informed, and active populations, however, the reality is that the results of nonbinding referendums would be hard for any government to ignore. In 1992, Canada employed a referendum to determine whether citizens accepted the constitutional changes that the prime minister and premiers had set out in the Charlottetown Accord. The results of that vote were surprising, in that a majority of citizens voted to defeat a constitutional package that had been the result of intense and protracted negotiations between the federal and provincial governments and leaders of Aboriginal communities in Canada. While this was only the third referendum used at the national level, thousands have been used at the municipal level and over 60 at the provincial level, most notably within Quebec regarding secession[52] and in British Columbia, Prince Edward Island, and Ontario on electoral reform.[53] Referendums have both advantages and disadvantages. One advantage is that public decisions are arrived at in a public manner—through free and open public debate.[54] Such debate leads to political education: people are more likely to inform themselves about issues if they have a direct say in the outcome. A second advantage lies in allowing the people to voice their own interests, rather than having those interests filtered through political representatives and political parties. This empowering mechanism provides a potential counter to the increased apathy and growing cynicism occurring in many democratic states; the knowledge that one has an ability to take part in deciding fundamental public questions is likely to increase satisfaction with democracy and the political system. Perhaps most importantly, the use of referendums, especially on divisive issues, can provide a measure of legitimacy to the outcome, since it can be said that "the people have spoken." But such a result is likely only if the public believes that the process was conducted fairly.

The use of referendums can also be problematic. Opponents highlight the fact that referendums can be employed strategically by the political elite for purposes other than to solicit the people's views on the issue. Such concerns were raised in the referendums on sovereignty held in Quebec, for the way the question is phrased can encourage, although rarely guarantee, a particular outcome. Second, referendums do not provide the public with a mechanism for shaping the policy agenda; instead, the people are provided with an opportunity merely to veto a government's proposal.[55] Some observers have also questioned the capacity of the general public to deal with complex issues. Finally, referendums can be highly divisive when the issue is a salient one and if it engenders strong opposing positions in various groups in society.

The **initiative**, on the other hand, is a device that allows registered voters to use petitions to propose the introduction of new laws or change existing ones. Initiatives were meant to complement representative democracy by providing citizens with a populist mechanism for introducing laws the government might be avoiding for whatever reason. One possibility is that a successful petition can force a referendum on the proposed bill, and, if sufficient support is achieved, the bill automatically becomes law. Alternatively, a successful petition can result in the bill being introduced into the legislature, where it follows the normal legislative process.

A successful initiative process should set the requirements fairly high to ensure that minority interests do not hijack the democratic process. In 23 of the 50 U.S. states, on the other hand, initiatives appear on the election ballot if a previously circulated petition receives only a small proportion of the population's signatures; voters then have the opportunity to agree or disagree with the initiative. The process can also be taken over by wealthy interest groups and industries that hire professional signature gatherers to collect the signatures at $1.50 each.[56] Once on the ballot, many of these initiatives pass, even though a majority of the state's population opposes the measure. If only a small proportion of the population actually votes, a minority of dedicated voters can wield tremendous but unrepresentative influence. In some cases, the proposed legislation is even inconsistent with existing laws or constitutional requirements. In others, it dangerously ties the legislature's hands. Proposition 13, for example, which passed in California in 1978, prohibited the state's government from ever increasing property taxes (one imagines it was not too difficult to gather support!). The result, however unintended, is one of the worst public school systems in the nation. Minority interests do not always correspond with those of the greater public good.

The third mechanism of direct democracy employed in representative democracies is the **recall**, which allows registered voters to petition to remove a member of the representative assembly between elections. The mechanism is intended to increase representative accountability by providing a direct means for unhappy electors to "de-elect" their representative without having to wait for the next general election. The same concerns about the initiative exist with the use of the recall. The number of signatures required on the petition to trigger the recall of an elected member should not be so low that the process can be hijacked by a small group of disgruntled voters, for elections are costly affairs in terms of both time and money; but neither should the number be so high as to render the recall process meaningless.

Recall provides an important mechanism for ensuring that representatives keep the interests of their constituents in mind. At the same time, however, the parliamentary system makes it particularly difficult for representatives to always act according to the wishes of constituencies (assuming for the moment that such wishes are easily determined). Party discipline, for instance, requires that the interests of the party determine the actions of each representative, given the constraints of responsible government. In addition, representatives may be provided with information that makes it clear that constituents' interests may be best served in a manner that contradicts their own wishes.

CONCLUSION

Democracy is based on putting a certain measure of political power in the hands of the people. Modern representative democracies provide only a few mechanisms by which citizens are able to influence government policy. Encouraging the use of the referendum, the initiative, and the recall for increasing citizen power rests on the presumption that the citizenry desires to participate more fully in democratic decision-making. Declining voter turnout in Western nations and increased political cynicism suggest that attention should be focused on problems other than simply the lack of opportunity for political participation. Successful democracy requires above all else that citizen participation is effective—citizens must believe that legitimate political action will result in clear and understandable initiatives that respond to that action. The most fundamental of democratic institutions, the election, provides the clearest mechanism for instilling that belief. In too many instances, however, electoral results are ambiguous, do not directly reflect the choices made by the voters, and appear to shut out a number of groups and interests whose chances are directly dependent on achieving electoral success. The democratic ideal will remain an elusive goal until citizens believe they are powerful, regardless of whether they choose to act on that power.

DISCUSSION QUESTIONS

1. What factors do you consciously consider when deciding how to cast a vote in a general election? Can you think of any factors that might affect your decision unconsciously?

2. When should referendums be used? For what issues? Can you think of any occasions or reasons when the use of a referendum might be ill advised?

3. Explain why students' participation in university politics is so low. Does your answer help explain participation in politics more broadly?

4.   Should a more proportional electoral system be adopted at the federal and/or provincial level in Canada? Why or why not?

5.   What do you consider the greatest challenge facing modern democracies? Why?

KEY TERMS

DIGITAL DEMOCRACY: A broad term meant to encompass the application of technological innovations to politics and political participation; also called *e-democracy* or *e-politics*. (285)

DIRECT DEMOCRACY: A political system in which citizens hold power directly rather than through elected or appointed representatives. (284)

ELECTION: A mechanism by which the expressed preferences of citizens in democratic states are aggregated into a decision regarding who will govern. (287)

FIRST-PAST-THE-POST (FPTP): An electoral system that requires the winning candidate to receive more votes than any other in order to win the seat—that is, to receive a plurality of votes. The majority of first-past-the-post systems employ single-member electoral districts. (297)

FRANCHISE: The right to vote in public elections. (287)

INITIATIVE: A mechanism that allows citizens to petition the government to introduce or adopt specific pieces of legislation or force a referendum on an issue. (307)

LIST SYSTEM: The most commonly adopted form of proportional representation, employing relatively large multimember electoral districts and a ballot that requires voters to choose from among party lists or candidates on party lists. (298)

MAJORITARIAN SYSTEM: An electoral system that requires the winning candidate to receive a majority of votes to win the seat. The majority is normally achieved through a second ballot or by an alternative voting system. (297)

MASS MEDIA: The methods of mass communication, such as television, radio, and newspapers, designed to reach large numbers of people. (292)

POLITICAL PARTICIPATION: Actions taken by individuals and groups in an attempt to influence political decisions and political decision-makers. (302)

PROPORTIONAL REPRESENTATION (PR): An electoral system that attempts to award seats to parties in proportion to the share of votes earned. Such systems must be combined with multimember constituencies. (298)

PUBLIC OPINION POLLING: The use of survey interviews, often conducted over the telephone, with a representative, randomly selected sample of people, providing an accurate description of the attitudes, beliefs, and behaviour of the population from which the sample was drawn. (302)

RATIONAL VOTING: A model that seeks to explain voting decisions by emphasizing the rational evaluation of alternatives (parties and candidates) and the retrospective assessment of the governing party. (301)

RECALL: A mechanism that allows citizens to petition to remove their political representative before the next election period. (308)

REFERENDUM: A mechanism that provides citizens with the ability to vote directly on pieces of legislation or constitutional changes. (306)

REPRESENTATION BY POPULATION: The principle suggesting that the allocation of seats in assemblies should occur in a manner that encourages an equal division of the population across electoral districts, so that each vote is of equal weight. (295)

REPRESENTATIVE DEMOCRACY: A political system in which citizens hold power indirectly by selecting representatives who render public decisions on their behalf in popular assemblies. (285)

SINGLE TRANSFERABLE VOTE (STV): A proportional electoral system that elects candidates in multimember ridings and provides voters with significant freedom by allowing them to rank-order their choices within and across party lists. (299)

WEB LINKS

Elections Canada:
http://www.elections.ca

The U.S. Federal Election Commission:
http://www.fec.gov

Stanford University's Comparative Democratization Project:
http://democracy.stanford.edu

IFES Election Guide:
http://www.electionguide.org

International Institute for Democracy and Electoral Assistance:
http://www.idea.int

Fair Vote Canada:
http://www.fairvotecanada.org

Canadian Election Study:
http://ces-eec.mcgill.ca

FURTHER READING

Butler, David, and Austin Ranney, eds. *Referendums Around the World: The Growing Use of Direct Democracy*. Washington, DC: American Enterprise Institute, 1994.

Courtney, John C. *Elections*. Vancouver: UBC Press, 2004.

Dalton, Russell J. *Citizen Politics: Public Opinion and Political Parties in Advanced Industrial Democracies*. 4th ed. Washington, DC: CQ Press, 2006.

Everitt, Joanna, and Brenda O'Neill, eds. *Citizen Politics: Research and Theory in Canadian Political Behaviour*. Don Mills, ON: Oxford University Press, 2002.

Gidengil, Elisabeth, André Blais, Neil Nevitte, and Richard Nadeau. *Citizens*. Vancouver: UBC Press, 2004.

Harrop, Martin, and William L. Miller. *Elections and Voters: A Comparative Introduction*. Basingstoke, UK: Macmillan, 1987.

LeDuc, Lawrence, Richard G. Niemi, and Pippa Norris, eds. *Comparing Democracies 2: New Challenges in the Study of Elections and Voting*. Thousand Oaks, CA: Sage, 2002.

O'Neill, Brenda. "Indifferent or Just Different? The Political and Civic Engagement of Young People in Canada," prepared for Canadian Policy Research Networks (CPRN) research series *Charting the Course for Youth Democratic and Civic Participation*, September 2007, 48 pp. Available at http://www.cprn.org/doc.cfm?doc=1751&l=en (Document Number 48504); accessed June 13, 2008.

ENDNOTES

1. Darin Barney, *Prometheus Wired: The Hope for Democracy in the Age of Network Technology* (Chicago: University of Chicago Press, 2000), p. 22.

2. This section relies heavily on David Held, *Models of Democracy*, 2nd ed. (Stanford: Stanford University Press, 1996), ch. 1.

3. Joseph Schumpeter, *Capitalism, Socialism and Democracy* (New York: Harper, 1942), p. 265.

4. The percentages vary dramatically around the world, from a high of 70 percent in North America to a low of 4.7 percent in Africa. See Internet World Stats, "Internet Usage Statistics: The Internet Big Picture"; available at http://www.internetworldstats.com/stats.htm; accessed June 13, 2008.

5. See the Ask Bristol website at http://www.viewfinder.public-i.tv/askbristol.php; accessed June 13, 2008.

6. See David Stewart and Keith Archer, *Quasi-Democracy? Parties and Leaders in Alberta* (Vancouver: UBC Press, 2000).

7. Associated Press, "Democratic Presidential Hopefuls Face Off in YouTube Debate," July 24, 2007; available at http://www.foxnews.com/story/0,2933,290514,00.html; accessed June 13, 2008.

8. See Internet World Stats, "Internet Usage Statistics."

9. *Ibid.*

10. For an excellent review of the interplay between democracy and information and communications technology, see Darin Barney, *Communication Technology* (Vancouver: UBC Press, 2005).

11. Held, *Models of Democracy*, p. 317.

12. *Ibid.*, pp. 353–60.

13. See the Elections Canada website at http://www.elections.ca for information on the 2006 and previous general elections.

14. In most parliamentary systems, voters choose the members of the legislature, and the share of seats held by parties within that body determines the government. Hence, voters only indirectly determine which party forms the government.

15. These requirements follow those set out by David Butler, Howard Penniman, and Austin Ranney, eds., *Democracy at the Polls: A Comparative Study of Competitive National Elections* (Washington, DC: American Enterprise Institute, 1981), p. 4.

16. See "The Basic Law for the Federal Republic of Germany," September 23, 1990; available at http://www.psr.keele.ac.uk/docs/german.htm; accessed June 13, 2008.

17. "Halt E-voting Says Election Body," BBC News International online, August 2, 2007; available at http://news.bbc.co.uk/2/hi/uk_news/politics/6926625.stm; accessed June 13, 2008.

18. See Martin Harrop and William L. Miller, *Elections and Voters: A Comparative Introduction* (Basingstoke, UK: Macmillan, 1987), ch. 9.

19. André Blais, Louis Massicotte, and Agnieszka Dobrzynska, "Direct Presidential Elections: A World Summary," *Electoral Studies* 16 (1997): 441–55.

20. See "2000 Presidential Electoral and Popular Vote," U.S. Federal Election Commission; available at http://www.fec.gov/pubrec/fe2000/elecpop.htm; accessed June 13, 2008.

21. Harrop and Miller, *Elections and Voters*, p. 251.

22. Hanna Pitkin, *The Concept of Representation* (Los Angeles: University of California Press, 1967).

23. See, for example, Anne Phillips, "Democracy and Representation: Or, Why Should It Matter Who Our Representatives Are?," in Anne Phillips, ed., *Feminism and Politics* (New York: Oxford, 1998), pp. 161–92.

24. The *2006 Canadian Election Study* is available at http://ces-eec.mcgill.ca/index.html; accessed June 13, 2008. André Blais, Elisabeth Gidengil, Neil Nevitte, Patrick Fournier, and Joanna Everitt were the study's co-investigators. The survey was conducted by the Institute for Social Research at York University and funded by Elections Canada.

25. Peter Dahlgren, "The Transformation of Democracy?," in Barrie Axford and Richard Huggins, eds., *New Media and Politics* (Thousand Oaks, CA: Sage Publications, 2001), pp. 69–70.

26. See Donald Blake, "Electoral Democracy in the Provinces," *Choices: Strengthening Canadian Democracy* 7(2) (2001).

27. James Robertson, "Bill C-24: An Act to Amend the Canada Elections Act and the Income Tax Act," February 5, 2004, Parliamentary Research Branch, Library of Parliament. Available at http://www.parl.gc.ca/37/2/parlbus/chambus/house/bills/summaries/c24-e.pdf; accessed June 13, 2008.

28. See Anthony Sayers and Lisa Young, "Election Campaign and Party Financing in Canada," paper prepared for the Democratic Audit of Australia, September 2004, available at http://www.partyfinance.ca/publications/AustraliaDemAudit.pdf; accessed June 13, 2008.

29. Richard Briffault, "Soft Money, Issue Advocacy and the US Campaign Finance Law," *Electoral Insight* 4(1) (May 2002): 9–14.

30. This section closely follows André Blais and Louis Massicotte, "Electoral Systems," in Lawrence LeDuc, Richard G. Niemi, and Pippa Norris, eds., *Comparing Democracies 2: New Challenges in the Study of Elections and Voting* (Thousand Oaks, CA: Sage, 2002), pp. 40–69.

31. The equivalent distortions in the 2004 election were as follows: Liberal, 1.19; Conservative, 1.08; Bloc Québécois, 1.41; and NDP, 0.39.

32. See http://www.citizensassembly.bc.ca/public, accessed June 13, 2008, for an overview of the mandate of the Assembly, and for its procedures and reports.

33. A number of the arguments for and against the FPTP can be found in Law Commission of Canada, *Voting Counts: Electoral Reform for Canada* (Ottawa: Public Works and Government Services, 2004) and in Louis Massicotte, "Changing the Canadian Electoral System," in Paul Howe, Richard Johnston and André Blais, eds., *Strengthening Canadian Democracy* (Montreal: IRPP, 2005), pp. 65–98.

34. See Mebs Kanji and Keith Archer, "The Theories of Voting and Their Applicability in Canada," in Joanna Everitt and Brenda O'Neill, eds., *Citizen Politics: Research and Theory in Canadian Political Behaviour* (Don Mills, ON: Oxford University Press, 2002), pp. 160–83.

35. Richard Johnston, André Blais, Henry Brady, and Jean Crête, *Letting the People Decide: Dynamics of a Canadian Election* (Montreal and Kingston, ON: McGill-Queen's University Press, 1992).

36. See David Butler, "Polls and Elections," in LeDuc, Niemi, and Norris, *Comparing Democracies 2*, pp. 236–53.

37. Sandra Burt, "The Concept of Political Participation," in Everitt and O'Neill, *Citizen Politics*, pp. 232–46.

38. Australian Electoral Commission; available at http://www.aec.gov.au/Elections/ australian_electoral_system/electoral_procedures/Electoral_Offences.htm; accessed June 13, 2008.

39. Lester Milbraith, *Political Participation: How and Why Do People Get Involved in Politics?* (Chicago: Rand McNally, 1965).

40. Sidney Verba and Norman H. Nie, *Participation in America: Democracy and Social Equality* (New York: Harper & Row, 1972).

41. John Porter, *The Vertical Mosaic: An Analysis of Class and Power in Canada* (Toronto: University of Toronto Press, 1965).

42. Yasmeen Abu-Laban, "Challenging the Gendered Vertical Mosaic: Immigrants, Ethnic Minorities, Gender and Political Participation," in Everitt and O'Neill, *Citizen Politics*, pp. 268–83.

43. Russell J. Dalton, *Citizen Politics: Public Opinion and Political Parties in Advanced Industrial Democracies*, 4th ed. (Washington, DC: CQ Press, 2006), p. 38.

44. Mark Franklin, "Electoral Participation," in LeDuc, Niemi, and Norris, *Comparing Democracies 2*, 148–68.

45. Dalton, *Citizen Politics*, ch. 3.

46. *Ibid.*, p. 41.

47. Inter-Parliamentary Union, "Women in National Parliaments"; available at http://www .ipu.org/wmn-e/world.htm; accessed June 13, 2008.

48. Neil Nevitte, *The Decline of Deference* (Peterborough, ON: Broadview Press, 1996).

49. Robert Putnam, "Bowling Alone: America's Declining Social Capital," *Journal of Democracy* 6 (1995): 65–78.

50. Nevitte, *The Decline of Deference*.

51. See the discussion in William Mishler, *Participation in Canada* (Toronto: Macmillan, 1979).

52. Patrick Boyer, *Direct Democracy in Canada: The History and Future of Referendums* (Toronto: Dundurn Press, 1992).

53. See Elections BC at http://www.elections.bc.ca/elections/ge2005/referendum.htm; accessed June 13, 2008.

54. This section relies heavily on David Butler and Austin Ranney, eds., *Referendums: A Comparative Study of Practice and Theory* (Washington, DC: American Enterprise Institute for Public Policy Research, 1978) and Patrick Boyer, *The People's Mandate: Referendums and a More Democratic Canada* (Toronto: Dundurn Press, 1992).

55. Mendelsohn and Parkin, "Introducing Direct Democracy in Canada," *Choices: Strengthening Canadian Democracy* 7(5) 2001: 7.

56. Doug Sanders, "Practical Pitfalls of the Plebiscite," *The Globe and Mail*, October 24, 2000, p. A3.

Chapter 10:
Political Inequality

CHAPTER 17

Liberal Democracy

In today's world, virtually every government claims to be democratic; and when we criticize a government, it is often for not being democratic enough. But democracy was not always so popular. Its universal acceptance stems only from the years of World War I, which was fought, in the famous words of the American president Woodrow Wilson, "to make the world safe for democracy." Despite its popularity, democracy is often misunderstood and, in recent years, has suffered from what many now refer to as "democratic malaise."

Democracy in itself is a technique, a way of making certain decisions by privileging the will of the majority. Democracy is characterized as a system that involves those affected by the decisions in the process of making them. In our view, it becomes a legitimate form of government only when it is united with the traditional Western ideals of constitutionalism, rule of law, liberty under law, and the limited state. And, conversely, it is not the only legitimate form of government. Although only a relatively small number of people could vote, aristocratic rule was not always considered oppressive. Our current democratic government carries on British constitutionalism while bringing the common people into the political realm.

The most basic conceptual problem today is that the two dimensions of the "how" and the "who" of government have become blurred in the single term *democracy*. Its current usage suggests not only majority rule, but also a condition of freedom in which a limited state respects people's rights. Freedoms of speech, religion, and so on are commonly identified as democratic liberties, though they aren't necessarily found in a democracy. To cloud the issue even further, democracy outside the Western world often means government allegedly for the many, but conducted by a ruling elite, such as a vanguard party or a military *junta* (Spanish for a group of individuals forming a government, especially after a revolution), rather than the majority and that faces few constitutional limitations.

All of this raises so many problems that we will restrict ourselves for the moment to a discussion of Western democracy, which in itself is extremely complex. As one writer has stated:

> In the nineteenth century, democratic government was seen mainly in terms of equality of political and legal rights, of the right to vote, to express differing political opinions and to organize political opinion through political parties, of the right of elected

representatives to supervise or control the activities of the government of the day. Today, much more stress is laid upon the need for the State to guarantee to everybody certain economic and social rights, involving the elimination of educational and social inequalities.[1]

During the twentieth century, the concept of democracy expanded. As Giovanni Sartori has written:

> Up until the 1940s people knew what democracy was and either liked or rejected it; since then we all claim to like democracy but no longer know (understand, agree) what it is. We characteristically live, then, in an age of confused democracy. That "democracy" obtains several meanings is something we can live with. But if "democracy" can mean just anything, that is too much.[2]

Democracy has now come to imply freedom—encompassing political, economic, and social rights—as well as the rule of the many.

Brief reflection is enough to show that these two dimensions are quite different and that no inevitable connection exists between them. Freedom is made possible by the rule of law, which minimizes arbitrary coercion and maximizes universal submission to equal laws. Yet the rule of the many, as Aristotle saw, may or may not be lawful. Specifically, a majority might take away the property, language, or religious rights of a minority unless the majority itself is restrained by the constitution. Democracy requires freedom only in the limited and partial sense that a certain amount of political freedom is necessary if the people are to choose officials: they must have a chance to nominate candidates, discuss issues, cast ballots, and so on. But beyond this necessary minimum, democracy in other realms of life could be quite oppressive.

For example, in the southern United States white employers sometimes refused to hire blacks. And in Canada, employers have sometimes refused to hire Aboriginal people. Such job discrimination can limit freedom in that the denial of a job possibility may be the denial of an opportunity to improve one's lot in life. In most democracies today, the definition of democracy includes the assumption that all individuals have an equal legal right to be considered for employment.

From now on, we will use the term *constitutional* or *liberal democracy* to denote a system in which the majority chooses rulers, who must then govern within the rule of law. This is what Plato and Aristotle meant by polity. The term *liberal democracy* refers to liberalism in the broadest sense, without distinguishing between classical and reform liberalism. Whatever their disagreements about *laissez faire,* redistribution, and government intervention, classical and reform liberals are united in their support of constitutional procedures, the limited state, and a private sphere of personal freedom. Liberal democracy, based on this common ground, is broad enough to encompass different experiments in economic policy. The moderate form of socialism that we have called social democracy is also compatible with liberal democracy as a system of government. The limited amounts of nationalization, central planning, and egalitarianism advocated by social democrats are subordinated to majority rule and respect for constitutional procedure.

Communism, however, was never compatible with liberal democracy. In the people's democracies of Eastern Europe, the Leninist theory of democratic centralism, as converted into the operating philosophy of the communist state, did not allow for political freedom and the right of constitutional opposition. The uncontested elections that were the hallmark of communism in power were sharply different from the practice of liberal democracy. When democratization began in Eastern Europe in 1989, those countries repudiated communism and democratic centralism as quickly as they could. From the West they imported the entire apparatus of liberal democracy, including competitive elections, multiple political parties, an executive answerable to an elected legislature, and an independent judiciary. Based on the historical record thus far, we can say that liberal democracies are not easily transplanted, especially in countries with low economic development, or where ethnic and religious interests are strongly entrenched.

Liberal democracy can be briefly defined as a system of government in which the people rule themselves, either directly or indirectly (through chosen officials) but in either case subject to constitutional restraints on the power of the majority. This definition can be expanded through an examination of four operating principles of liberal democracy: equality of political rights, majority rule, political participation, and political freedom. Let us look at these one by one.

EQUALITY OF POLITICAL RIGHTS

Equality of political rights means that every individual has the same right to vote, run for office, serve on a jury, speak on public issues, and carry out other public functions. Obviously, political rights are a matter of degree, and it was only in the twentieth century, when women and ethnic minorities obtained these rights, that full equality was approached in most Western systems. There is no hard-and-fast rule for determining how much political equality is enough for democracy to exist; that being said, universal adult male suffrage was an important threshold because it broke through the barrier of socioeconomic class. Prior to its introduction, suffrage was limited to a small portion of the population, largely made up of affluent men. Another was the extension of the franchise to women, which doubled the electorate.

By these criteria, the United States was the first democracy of modern times. Equality of political rights, however, was not attained all at once because the constitution of 1787 let the individual states determine the franchise. In the first decades of the nineteenth century, the states one by one adopted universal male suffrage, except in the South, where slaves were excluded. The emancipated slaves were theoretically enfranchised after the Civil War, but most were prevented from voting by various tactics until the 1960s. Women received the right to vote in federal elections at a single stroke, through the Nineteenth Amendment (1920).

Figure 17.1 Number of Persons Having Right to Vote per 100 Adults, Britain, 1800–1928

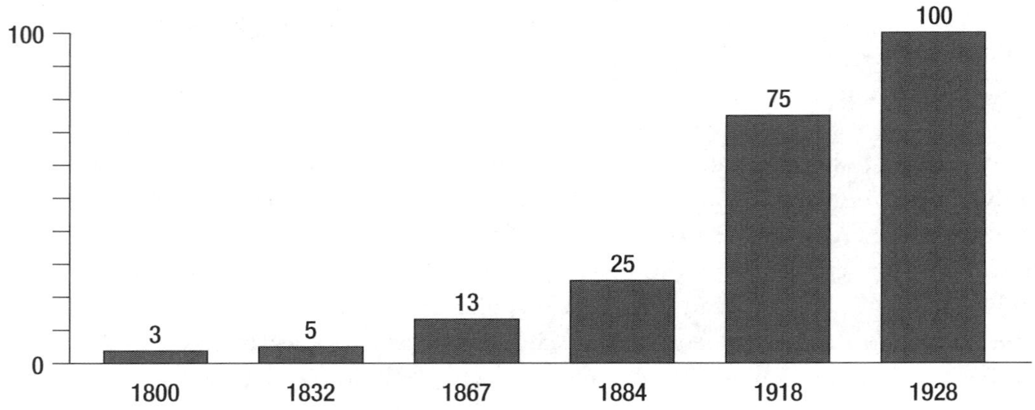

Source: J. Harvey and L. Bather, *The British Constitution,* 2nd ed. (London: Macmillan, 1968), p. 51.

Great Britain was somewhat behind the United States in providing equality of political rights. At the beginning of the nineteenth century, there was still a restrictive franchise that allowed only about 200,000 male property owners to vote in elections for the House of Commons. The parliamentary Reform Acts of 1832, 1867, and 1884 gradually extended the franchise to include the middle class and the more prosperous elements of the working class. The remaining men, as well as women aged 30 and older, received the vote in 1918; women were granted suffrage on equal terms with men in 1928. The growth curve of the British electorate is illustrated in Figure 17.1.

The expansion of the franchise in Canada is more difficult to describe because it was intricately involved in federal–provincial relations. Before 1885, qualifications to vote in parliamentary elections had been determined by the provinces. In that year, Sir John A. Macdonald pushed a uniform Electoral Franchise Act through Parliament, in part because he did not like the tendency of provinces to abolish the property franchise.[3] The Act of 1885 established a moderate property qualification that remained until 1898, when the government of Sir Wilfrid Laurier returned the franchise to the domain of the provinces. Most property qualifications disappeared around that time.

From 1898 to 1917, the provinces controlled the federal franchise, but they could not disenfranchise particular groups of people: if people could vote in provincial elections, they could also vote in federal elections. In other words, provinces could not, through legislation, isolate certain groups demographically and deny them the right to vote in federal elections. In the Military Voters Act and the Wartime Elections Act (1917), the federal government was selective in extending and restricting the suffrage. Under the former, all men and women on active service were permitted to vote. Under the latter, conscientious objectors and those of enemy alien birth were denied the franchise, while wives, widows, and female relatives of men overseas were enfranchised.[4] In 1920, with the passage of the Dominion Elections Act, the federal government resumed control of qualifications for voting in federal elections, while qualifications for voting in provincial elections remained the responsibility of provincial governments. In 1918 women aged 21 and older gained the right to vote in federal elections. Provincially, women were first enfranchised in Manitoba, in 1916; not until 1940, however, were they allowed to vote in Quebec.[5] Registered Indians received the federal franchise in 1960, although they had been allowed to vote in some earlier provincial elections.

Although each country's history is unique, the general pattern in the Western world has been a step-by-step extension of the franchise, with universal adult male suffrage being reached at the end of the nineteenth or beginning of the twentieth century. In most countries, women were given the vote during or shortly after World War I. Switzerland was one exception; women received the right to vote in that country's federal elections only in 1971, and even later in some cantonal (provincial) elections. Indeed, the men of one laggard canton did not agree to grant the franchise to women until 1989.

Today, the franchise can hardly be extended further in most liberal–democratic countries except by giving it to non-citizens, children, prisoners, those with no fixed address, and the mentally disabled. The latter received the right to vote at the federal level in Canada beginning with the election of 1988. The right of prisoners to vote was re-affirmed in 2002 by the Supreme Court of Canada, when it held that the legislation depriving prisoners of the franchise unjustifiably conflicted with Section 3 of the Canadian Charter of Rights and Freedoms, which states that "every citizen has the right to vote in an election of members of the House of Commons or of a legislative assembly."[6] We have virtually reached the end of a process that has transformed the vote from a trust exercised by property owners or heads of families into a universal right of adult citizens.

MAJORITY RULE

Majority rule is the normal working principle of decision-making in democracies. It can be derived logically from the prior principle of political equality. If each vote is to be counted equally, the decision of the majority must be accepted because any other procedure would inevitably weigh some votes more heavily than others.

Yet in some circumstances democracies depart from majority rule. Election to public office in Canada, Britain, and the United States is normally by **plurality** rather than **majority.** In these systems, the winning candidate need only obtain more votes than any other candidate, even if the number fails to reach the "50 percent plus one" requirement for a majority. The plurality criterion is both simple and efficient. If candidates for office were always required to receive a majority, there would have to be an expensive series of runoffs to reduce the candidates to two; only then could it be guaranteed that a plurality would also be a majority of votes cast. In fact, some countries—France, for example—do employ runoff elections. The French president must receive an absolute majority of votes cast, which in practice means a two-stage election.

The majority requirement is also sometimes raised (for example, to three-fifths, or two-thirds, or three-fourths) in what is known as a **qualified majority.** This is done to protect the rights of minorities. Because a qualified majority is obviously harder to obtain than a simple majority, it becomes more difficult for larger groups to act against the rights of smaller ones.

The qualified majority, while a constraint upon democracy, is within the spirit of the rule of law. It is incorporated in most modern democracies as part of the process of constitutional amendment, on the assumption that the fundamental laws of the state are so important that they should not be easily altered by a simple majority. A constitutional amendment in the United States, after being passed by two-thirds of the Senate and House of Representatives, must be ratified by three-fourths of the states. In Canada, amending most parts of the Constitution requires ratification by the Senate, the House of Commons, and the legislative assemblies of "at least two-thirds of the provinces that have, in the aggregate, according to the latest general census, at least fifty per cent of the population of all the provinces." On certain matters of fundamental importance, such as recognition of the monarchy, the consent of all provinces is required.[7]

A variation of the qualified majority is the **concurrent majority,** which was sometimes used in the legislature of the old united province of Canada (1840–67). In that specific case, laws had to receive a majority of votes from representatives of both Canada East (Quebec) and Canada West (Ontario). This was supposed to prevent the two regions, one English and one French, from oppressing each other. A special form of the concurrent majority is **bicameralism,** the practice of dividing the legislature into two chambers. The requirement that a bill be passed in two different houses of the assembly is meant to be a safeguard against precipitous action. John A. Macdonald called the Canadian Senate "the sober second thought in legislation." He also supported the requirement, entrenched in Section 23(4) of the Constitution Act, 1867, that a senator's "Real and Personal Property shall be together worth Four thousand Dollars over and above his Debts and Liabilities," a substantial amount at that time. According to Macdonald, "a large property qualification should be necessary for membership in the Upper House, in order to represent the principle of property. The rights of the minority must be protected, and the rich are always fewer in number than the poor."[8]

While the Senate no longer plays the role Macdonald envisioned for it, its continued existence illustrates the principle that liberal democracy sometimes accepts restraints on the will of popular majorities in order to protect the legal rights of minorities. A requirement for **unanimity** would be the ultimate in protection for minorities, because then no one could be required to do anything against their will. But the practical task of getting unanimous agreement is so formidable that political systems have had to settle for a qualified or concurrent majority as a restraint on popular powers. Balancing majority and minority rights remains one of the major challenges in a democratic system of government.

NEL

POLITICAL PARTICIPATION

Democratic institutions are founded on mass participation. The two great varieties of democracy, which differ in the nature of this participation, are **direct democracy,** the only kind known to the ancient world, and **representative democracy** (or *indirect democracy,* as it is sometimes called), the predominant form in modern times.

The city-states of Greece practised direct democracy. The highest authority was the assembly of all male citizens (slaves were not citizens and could not vote). Executive officers were either elected by this body or chosen by lot—a random procedure that was considered superbly democratic because it gave everyone an equal chance of being selected to serve. In either case, terms of office were very short—usually a year or less. Citizens were paid to hold office and even to attend assembly meetings, so that poverty would not prevent participation.

Assembly-style direct democracy faces two obvious problems. One involves the practical difficulty of assembling more than a few thousand individuals to discuss public issues. If direct democracy was just barely possible in the Greek city-state, how could it exist in the modern nation-state, which is so much larger? The other problem concerns the quality of decisions made at large meetings, where emotional rhetoric and appeals to prejudices, emotions, and fears can easily sway votes. The democracy of Athens destroyed itself by enthusiastically voting for a disastrous military campaign against Syracuse. The best minds of antiquity, including Plato and Aristotle, were so unimpressed with direct democracy in action that they turned decisively against it.[9]

Representative democracy tries to address both problems. It overcomes the obstacles of population and distance while providing the means for choosing rulers whose talents are presumably superior to those of the people at large. These rulers are kept in check, and directed by the majority, through the machinery of elections. A ruler elected for life would be effectively insulated from the popular will. This is why democracy requires regular elections that those in power cannot indefinitely postpone: to ensure the accountability of government to its citizens.

The rationale behind representative government was clearly stated in 1825 by James Mill, the first important political philosopher to argue in favour of what we would today call democracy. "The people as a body," he wrote, "cannot perform the business of government for themselves."[10] What was required, he continued, was the creation of a system of "checks" that would induce rulers to act for the general benefit. These checks would be provided by representatives elected by the community for a limited period of time. Limiting the duration of rule was, according to Mill, "an old and approved method of identifying as nearly as possible the interests of those who rule with the interests of those who are ruled."[11]

It cannot be emphasized too strongly that democratic elections do not and cannot decide questions of policy. Citizens vote for representatives but do not make policy decisions; elected representatives make those decisions for the society. Citizens probably agree with some opinions of their favourite candidates and disagree with others.

Also, neither voters nor candidates can be sure of what the future will bring. Politicians are notorious for breaking campaign promises not because they are especially dishonest, but because things may look different a year or two after the election, particularly when seen from the perspective of public responsibility. Elections are much more a judgment on recent policies than a decision about the future. If voters are dissatisfied with the past record of the incumbent government, elections provide an opportunity for installing another party into power.

Many contemporary critics of representative democracy focus on the idea that elected officials have their own political agendas and disregard the wishes of the public. Such critics advocate a move toward some form of direct democracy, or at least more public involvement in the policy-making process. One way to do this would be to institutionalize direct-democratic practices such as the referendum, the initiative, and the recall.

In a **referendum,** electors are asked to vote directly on a constitutional amendment, piece of legislation, or other policy proposal. Some authors use the term **plebiscite** for a nonbinding, advisory referendum,[12] but we will not follow this usage because it is not universal. Both binding and nonbinding referendums are common around the world.

Referendums are used frequently in Switzerland at all levels of government, and in the United States at the state and local levels. They are required in Australia for the approval of all constitutional amendments. All Canadian provinces provide for advisory referendums in some circumstances at the local and provincial level, and there have been three federal referendums: one in 1898 on the prohibition of alcohol, one in 1942 to release Prime Minister William Lyon Mackenzie King from his promise not to send conscripted soldiers overseas, and one in 1992 on the Charlottetown Accord. More recently, three provinces (B.C., Ontario, and PEI) have held referendums on electoral reform; all were defeated (see Chapter 24). Because legislation in Canada is technically made by the Crown with the advice of Parliament or of a provincial legislature, Canadian referendums can be only advisory in a legal sense unless the Constitution is amended; under present conditions, a legally binding referendum would be an unconstitutional restriction on the authority of the Crown.

In Switzerland, however, the vote in a referendum legally determines the legislative outcome of an issue. In France, the president can call a binding national referendum. President Charles de Gaulle (in office 1959–69) used this power on six occasions as a way of circumventing a legislature that would not cooperate on his policy proposals. Not all French presidents have been successful in their use of the referendum. Jacques Chirac called a referendum in 2005 on the proposed Constitution of the European Union expecting victory; instead, the proposal was defeated, which was seen as a devastating blow to his presidency.

The British government has used consultative referendums to clear the air on divisive issues. In 1975 the government called a national referendum on membership in the European Economic Community. It was the first ever held in Britain.

The Conservatives had decided on membership three years earlier, but many Labour Party members remained opposed to the decision. So the newly elected Labour government of Prime Minister Harold Wilson called a referendum in hopes of laying the matter to rest. British voters endorsed membership by slightly more than a two-thirds majority. In 1979, referendums were held in Scotland and Wales as a way of deciding the issue of devolution. Voters in Wales rejected the proposal for a regional parliament. The proposition also failed in Scotland, even though it received the support of 52 percent of voters, because turnout (33 percent) failed to meet the minimum required (40 percent). In 1997, however, voters in both Scotland and Wales accepted regional parliaments in referendums held after Tony Blair's Labour Party came to power.

A second form of direct democracy is the **initiative.** The mechanism is a simple one: if a minimum number of voters sign a petition dealing with a particular issue (the number would be spelled out in legislation), then the government is required to act on it. The required action may be either that the legislative body enact the proposal outlined in the petition or that it submit the proposal to voters in a referendum. A referendum originates in the legislative body and is "referred" to the electorate; in contrast, an initiative moves from the people to the legislature.

In Switzerland, 50,000 voters are enough to force the government to hold a referendum. Initiatives are also popular in California. The famous Proposition 13 was committed to a state-wide referendum in 1978 as a result of an initiative signed by 1.5 million voters. The voters of California proceeded to endorse a forced limit on local property taxes—a move that naturally was unpopular with politicians but very popular with the electorate.[13]

Several standard arguments are made against referendums and initiatives—that legislation is too complex, that voters become fatigued when asked to decide too many issues, and that these instruments can be used to restrict the rights of minorities. There is undoubtedly some truth in these contentions, and, therefore, important reasons for limiting the use of the referendum and initiative. However, voters do not seem to rule out direct democracy as an occasional supplement to representative democracy. Of the arguments in favour of direct democracy, the most interesting comes from former Progressive Conservative MP Patrick Boyer, Canada's leading authority on and advocate for referendums. Boyer argues that referendums are particularly useful in a parliamentary system of disciplined parties where the legislative agenda is controlled by politicians who believe that electoral victory has given them a mandate to legislate as they please.[14] Mechanisms of direct democracy provide a means for testing policy options against the judgment of the public. To date, referendums and initiatives have been used sparingly in Western democracies, but the development of electronic communications may soon make these consultative processes more cost-effective and lead to their increased use.

A third and less common element of direct democracy is the **recall,** which enables voters to remove an elected representative from office.[15] This practice was introduced in the United States at the turn of the century. Its purpose was to rid constituencies of representatives controlled by "political machines" (i.e., party organizations dominated by a few backroom leaders). Provisions for recall usually require a petition signed by a substantial number of voters, and a successful recall vote requires at least a simple majority of those voting. These provisions are designed to protect representatives from a minority of voters who may not like a particular stand. Recall is used in some cities and states in the United States, though less frequently today than in the 1920s. In 2003 California voters recalled Governor Gray Davis and replaced him with Arnold Schwarzenegger; Davis was only the second governor ever to be successfully recalled in the United States.

Venezuela is the only country where the head of the national government is subject to recall. The procedure was tested in 2004 with a recall campaign against President Hugo Chavez, who is considered by his opponents to be too left-wing and too close to Cuban leader Fidel Castro. Forty-two percent voted to recall President Chavez but 58 percent voted to affirm him in office, so he remained president.

In Canada, there is less support for a recall mechanism than for other forms of direct democracy. At the present time only the province of British Columbia has recall legislation, which came into effect in 1995. Since then, 20 recall petitions have been issued but none have been successful. This is due partly to the high bar set for success: the applicant has 60 days to obtain the signatures of 40 percent of registered voters in the previous election in the member's electoral district. The recall may be a fine idea in the United States, where elected officials serve fixed terms and are judged as individuals because party discipline is weak or nonexistent. But in a parliamentary system such as Canada's, elected officials are members of a team that functions collectively—the Cabinet and caucus in the case of the government, the caucus in the case of the opposition. In 1992, Joe Clark spent all his time as a cabinet minister on the constitutional negotiations that led to the Charlottetown Accord, and then on trying to get the Accord passed in the referendum. Now it is clear that the voters in his Alberta riding (Yellowhead) did not like the Accord: almost 70 percent voted no when the referendum was held. But should they have had the right to recall their hardworking MP because he was working on a project whose outcome they eventually disapproved? The answer may be yes if we think of MPs primarily as representatives of their constituencies, but it is probably no if we think of them as members of a team pursuing national policies.

Today, public-opinion polls also play an important advisory role in all democratic countries. An enthusiast for direct democracy will periodically remind us that it is now technically possible to wire all citizens into one computer system and let them decide questions of public policy. But even if such a nonstop referendum were possible, it is doubtful that it would be a good idea. Complex questions of public policy need the attention and deliberation of informed minds, and both legislators and the public need time to digest various views. Representative democracy is not just a second-best substitute for direct democracy, made necessary by the size of modern states; rather, it is a mechanism for seeking the consensus that is essential to good government. However, direct-democratic devices could be a useful supplement when such wisdom does not emerge from representative institutions.

Democratic participation involves far more than the election of representatives. It also involves influencing government policy either through public debate or by making submissions to elected representatives. Governments today often consult extensively with the public before passing major legislation. A general policy statement may be published, followed by a draft of the statute. Often there are public hearings at which interested parties express their views. In fact, participation has expanded so much in recent years, particularly at the level of local government, that it is sometimes seen as unduly slowing decision making and offering too much influence to vocal and well-organized minorities.

Even when they possess a strong parliamentary majority, governments will occasionally withdraw or modify policy proposals in the face of public criticism. Public participation and consultation is now an ongoing process in democratic government. Elections punctuate the process; when governments are not responsive, voters change the participants.

Access to the decision makers is a major problem in contemporary democracies; this issue will be discussed in more detail in Part Four. Critics of democracy say that powerful interests dominate the political process and that groups more marginal to the system have difficulty in influencing decisions. For example, women's and environmental groups claim they have been shut out of the process in the past. However, the existence of elections as open contests at least offers a possibility, if not the certainty, that marginalized groups will be able to exert more influence on decision makers.

POLITICAL FREEDOM

Meaningful participation is possible only if political freedom prevails. Limited participation or directed mobilization of the masses is characteristic not of genuine democracy but of totalitarian pseudo-democracy. An infallible test for political freedom is the legitimacy of opposition: freedom is meaningful only if it extends to those whose opinions differ from the opinions of those in authority. Freedom only to agree is no freedom at all. If freedom does not exist, public support or opposition can only be speculative, and this uncertainty can be very convenient for manipulative rulers. At the same time, the opposition in a liberal democracy must operate within the rule of law. When it resorts to unlawful means—for example, terrorist acts or plotting an insurrection—its actions are not compatible with political freedom in a liberal democracy.

Political freedom has numerous aspects: the right to speak freely, even to criticize the government; the right to form associations, including political parties that may oppose the government; the right to run for office; and the right to vote without intimidation and to choose from a slate of at least two candidates. Without these rights, democracy might be "for the people," but it is certainly not "by the people."

Extensive and important as it is, political freedom is only a part of the whole range of personal freedoms. For instance, it does not include the right to own property or to use one's chosen language. It is quite possible for very wide political freedom to coexist with, and even be the cause of, reduced freedom in other areas. An example can be taken from Quebec: all citizens have full political freedom in that province, but businesses have been restricted by legislation from posting signs in languages other than French. In 1989 the provincial government used its override power, as provided by Section 33 of the Canadian Charter of Rights and Freedoms, to reinstate its language legislation after the Supreme Court of Canada had ruled that the law violated the freedom of expression guaranteed by the Charter.[16] Both the legislation and the use of the notwithstanding clause (as Section 33 is often called) were and remain popular with the francophone majority in Quebec. In this instance, a majority used its political freedom to reduce the linguistic freedom of minorities.

This example highlights what is sometimes seen as a general problem of liberal democracy. Can law restrain the power of the majority so that it does not use its political freedom to take away other freedoms from minorities? The tension between democracy and the rule of law is illustrated in this passage from Xenophon, a pupil of Socrates. It had just been proposed to the Athenian Assembly—the democratic gathering of all male citizens—that certain alleged enemies of the regime be arrested:

> Great numbers cried out that it was monstrous if the people were to be prevented from doing whatever they wished . . . Then the Prytanes [the executive committee of the Assembly], stricken with fear, agreed to put the question [to a vote]—all of them except Socrates . . . he said that in no case would he act except in accordance with the law.[17]

Socrates was ultimately put to death by a democracy that ignored the rule of law and heeded only its own will.

A fear first voiced by Aristotle, and echoed since by countless other writers, is that in a democracy, the many would use their political power to expropriate and distribute the wealth of the few. In the words of John Adams, the second American president, "Debts would be abolished first; taxes laid heavy on the rich, and not at all on the others; and at last a downright equal division of everything be demanded and voted."[18] In fact, the record of liberal democracy does not bear out this gloomy prediction of a dramatic clash of rich and poor. In those countries where liberal democracy has been successful, society has not been polarized into extremes of wealth and poverty.

Political freedom helps to ensure that the interests of citizens are voiced, an important step providing governments with an ability to remain accountable to them. But political freedom, and more specifically the political participation that it encourages, can be argued to be valuable in and of itself. As one political scientist has argued, "good citizens are made, not born."[19] One of the values of democracy is that it encourages citizens to participate in the political process and, in so doing, encourages them to develop the skills, knowledge, and tolerance that can enhance their participation and the quality of collective decision making.

PROBLEMS OF LIBERAL DEMOCRACY

To paraphrase Winston Churchill, liberal democracy is not the perfect form of government, it is only the least worst. For discussion purposes, we will consider three basic problems that have been present since the creation of liberal democracies: elite rule, majority versus minority rights, and public versus private interests.

Elite Rule

One common, and serious, criticism of liberal democracy is that it is elitist—that democracies are, in effect, ruled by elites and therefore undemocratic. It is true that representative democracy is a form of elite rule, if by an **elite** we mean "a minority of the population which takes the major decisions in the society."[20] But to see the place of political elites in modern politics, one must compare them with the elites that were found in traditional societies of earlier centuries. In the latter, a tiny and interlocking group of families dominated the social, economic, and political life of society. In most instances, these families owned large estates, which their children inherited along with all the wealth and responsibilities that went with their status. Traditional societies were highly stratified; that is, there was a large gap between the elite and the masses. This simple, dichotomized society was perpetuated as the children of the elite inherited their positions, while opportunities for the masses were restricted. There was little if any social mobility between the elite and the masses.

In most Western countries this situation has gradually been transformed. The Industrial Revolution broke the hold of the landed aristocracy and created new sources of wealth and employment; mass education created opportunities for many in the lower classes; guilds and unions helped artisans and workers to get better working conditions and wages; urban centres served as the base for dynamic marketing systems; and new attitudes about equality and freedom led to more participatory politics. Modern society is characterized by a large middle class, not by polarization between wealth and poverty. Opportunities for education and jobs are extensive, and this promotes social mobility between classes. Politics is charged with new sources of authority and legitimacy. In short, the old dualism of the traditional society has given way to a complex and dynamic modern social order.

Correspondingly, the old idea of a traditional elite was replaced by the concept of pluralism. New elites began to spring up and challenge the agrarian aristocracy. An industrial elite, a commercial elite, a financial elite, a military elite, and even a political elite emerged; and each had a degree of wealth and power that posed a threat to the old guard with its roots in the land. In modern societies, elites have not disappeared; rather, they have become more numerous and more diverse. Many Marxists tend to deny that this change has really affected societies much. They still see a simple dichotomy—the rulers and the ruled. The two-class situation dominates their frame of reference; except in socialist societies, rulers are thought to exploit the masses. But other observers recognize that modern societies have become pluralistic, and that so have their politics. As the French author Raymond Aron wrote:

> Democratic societies, which I would rather call pluralistic societies, are full of the noise of public strife between the owners of the means of production, trade union leaders and politicians. As all are entitled to form associations, professional and political organizations abound, each one defending its members' interests with passionate ardour. Government becomes a business of compromises.[21]

In democracies, those who aspire to rule must build a power base. They must first of all be chosen by the electorate; then, if they are to remain in office, their policies must be responsive to the needs of some coalition of groups. Contemporary theorists of democracy emphasize the competition of diverse elites. They suggest that the representative system is an instrument for ensuring that no single elite can attain power unless it reflects the desires of some fraction of the ordinary people. While it is true powerful groups may monopolize contemporary politics, if elections are working as they were intended there should be no contradiction between liberal democracy and elite rule.

Majority versus Minority Rights

Liberal democracies operate on the majoritarian principle. Political party nominations, elections to office, and legislative decisions are decided on the basis of a majoritarian vote. But how do minorities fare under majoritarian government? Is it true, as the proponents of liberal democracy claim, that minority rights can be reconciled with majority rule? For example, in a multicultural society, when one or two ethnic groups (or nationalities) occupy a dominant position, can it be guaranteed that the rights of minority cultures will be protected? Can the rights of Native peoples in Canada be protected when they make up less than 4 percent of the total population? How can the rights of cultural minorities such as the Chinese or West Indians, or the political rights of gays and lesbians, be guaranteed when the vast majority of Canadians are European, English- or French-speaking, and heterosexual?

One argument is that all majority and minority rights are protected on the floor of the House of Commons and the Senate. This argument revolves around the assumption that most elected representatives want to be re-elected and so must appeal to a broad coalition of groups in their constituencies. They try not to alienate any voters—and certainly as few as possible, if they have to legislate in a way that will alienate any. But the fact remains that winning coalitions need not be, and probably will not be, all-inclusive. Some minorities, particularly small ones, are

NEL

438

likely to be left out, which opens up the possibility that an elected assembly could become a "tyranny of the majority" that consistently votes to override minority rights.

A second way of protecting minority rights is through a constitution and the judicial process. Since the passage of the Canadian Charter of Rights and Freedoms in 1982, individual rights for all Canadians have been spelled out in the Constitution. If the rights of a minority may have been violated by a legislative assembly, representatives of that minority are entitled to challenge the constitutionality of the legislation in the courts. If members of a legislative assembly choose to ignore the rights of a certain segment of society, the citizens affected have recourse through the courts. While there is no guarantee that court rulings will satisfy either the majority or the minority, the judicial system is another possible venue for reconciling majority rule with minority rights.

Public versus Private Interests

Another difficult problem to resolve in liberal democracies relates to the conflict between public and private interests. Ideally, the public interest involves the well-being of all individuals or all groups in society. It is difficult, however, to find an interest that is equally shared by everyone. In practice, therefore, the term *public interest* refers to interests that are relatively broadly shared, such as national defence, enforcement of the law, protection of life and property, stable prices, low taxation, public education, accessible health care, and a social safety net. *Private interests* include the interests of specific groups such as business people, unionized workers, farmers, and students and professors. Most such groups attempt to achieve certain ends through the political process. They may seek concessions of some kind from governments, and these concessions may or may not be in the public interest. For example, postsecondary students may want to have free college or university tuition. Most colleges and universities are public institutions in Canada, so taxes would have to be increased accordingly. Since college and university graduates usually get better-paying jobs than non-graduates, it seems reasonable that these students should pay at least some tuition. However, society (public interest) benefits from the presence of educated young people (private interest), so it pays most of the costs of higher education.

Few conflicts between public and private interest are as easy to reconcile. Often such conflicts centre on definitions of the public interest and the presence or absence of a level playing field. Disputes between developers and environmentalists are notoriously difficult to resolve. Private interests will push for what they see as a healthy economic-development project. It might be a water-storage project for irrigation, or a timber-cutting licence for a pulp mill. In either case, it will be argued that private industrial activity will, through capital investment and job creation, also serve the broader public interest by enhancing the local or regional economy. Developers often make the case, particularly in times of recession, that a softening of environmental regulations would reduce the cost of the project. The argument is usually that increased costs will make the project uncompetitive and that investment and jobs will for that reason be lost.

At the same time, governments are also pressured by those who want to preserve the quality of the air and water in the region. These people argue that poor air and water quality affects the health not only of local residents but also of the environment itself. They argue, as well, that a healthy environment will attract environmentally "clean" industries. In effect, there is a political clash not only between private interests but also between differing conceptions of the public interest. Whichever side the government comes down on, it will claim that its decision is in the public interest.

When legislators write lax environmental regulations, or loosen existing regulations to lure industry, environmentalists claim that private interests have prevailed at the expense of the public interest—that the playing field has been tipped to favour developers. When legislators support strict environmental regulations, industrialists claim that narrow but powerful environmental interests have thwarted the public interest, which is for more jobs and increased investment—that the field was tipped to favour environmentalists. Here again, the challenge facing public decision makers is to balance the demands of conflicting private interests with their different conceptions of the public interest.

These classic problems are not the only ones facing liberal democracies today. Powerful interests, political party responsiveness, influence of the media, voter apathy, representation of the electorate, and the role of the courts are challenges in most current liberal democracies. There is insufficient room in this chapter to discuss these problems individually, so each of these issues will be addressed in chapters on the political process in Part Four.

DIFFERENT PATTERNS OF POLITICS IN LIBERAL DEMOCRACIES

Liberal democracies operate in different ways. For example, within one liberal–democratic system, interest groups such as business organizations, labour unions, or farmers' associations may have a great deal of political **autonomy**—that is, they have a great deal of freedom to pursue political objectives with little interference from the state. In other liberal–democratic systems, political organizations may be highly restricted in their political activity by a powerful regulatory state. Mexico, prior to political reforms instituted after 1994, is a case in point. These different patterns of politics in liberal democracies can be classified as pluralist, corporatist, or consociational (see Concept Box 17.1).

Concept Box 17.1

Liberal Democracies

Pluralist

Liberal democracies in which highly autonomous groups compete freely and openly in the political process are labelled **pluralist.** Robert Dahl's term for this pluralist form of liberal democracy is **polyarchy,** which means many different sources of power. For Dahl, "the characteristics of polyarchy greatly extend the number, size, and diversity of the minorities whose preferences will influence the outcome of governmental decision."[22] In a polyarchy, control of the governmental process may change hands frequently as different groups compete for political power.

Features of pluralist liberal democracies include:

a. a high degree of autonomy for political interests in society to pursue their political ends;

b. equality of all groups in the political process—ideally, there is a level playing field on which political interests compete; and

c. an absence of monopoly control of government or state power by any one group. The power of groups ebbs and flows with societal conditions, as coalitions are accepted or rejected by the voters.

Corporatist

Liberal democracies in which there is a significant lack of autonomy for groups are labelled *corporatist.* In the corporatist pattern, the state is the dominant force in society and the activities of all interests in society are subordinate to that force. One of the principal writers on **corporatism,** Philippe C. Schmitter, has defined corporatism as follows:

> Corporatism can be defined as a system of interests representation in which the constituent units are organized into a limited number of singular, compulsory, non-competitive, hierarchically ordered and functionally differentiated categories, recognized or licensed (if not created) by the state and granted a deliberate representational monopoly within their respective categories in exchange for observing certain controls on their selection of leaders and articulation of demands and supports.[23]

Features of corporatist liberal democracies include:

a. the components of the political process are arranged in a hierarchy and are not equal;

b. the components have limited autonomy, with the state restricting their actions;

c. competition is limited, in the sense that the various components are not free to compete with each other for political ends;

d. the components in the process are dependent on the state; and

(continued)

e. the relative power of different components may vary, depending on their relationship to the state.

Consociational

Liberal democracies in which elites and organized interests play a special and distinctive role are labelled *consociational*. This form is found in several countries, including the Netherlands, Switzerland, and (to a lesser degree) Canada. Arend Lijphart suggests that the basis for **consociationalism** is a society so sharply divided along linguistic, ethnic, or religious lines that the segments have their own social institutions and live largely apart from one another.[24] The Netherlands is a classic case: although everyone speaks Dutch, the society is divided into Roman Catholic, neo-Calvinist, liberal, and socialist "spiritual families," each of which has its own schools and universities; newspapers and radio and television programs; and labour unions and recreational associations. Switzerland is similarly divided, by language as well as by religion and ideology.

Features of consociational liberal democracies include:

a. each social segment has a high degree of autonomy over its internal affairs, particularly language, culture, religion, and education;

b. a rule of proportionality is followed in allocating government jobs, expenditures, and benefits among the segments;

c. all important segments have the power to veto major changes affecting their vital interests; and

d. government is carried on through a "grand coalition" of political representatives of all the main segments.

Different patterns of politics seem to follow particular cultural attributes of societies. For example, politics in the United States, a country with a strong liberal, anti-state tradition, comes close to the pluralist process that Robert Dahl described as polyarchy. In Canada and Great Britain, where elites have played a greater role in the political process, one finds traces of corporatist and consociational thinking and institutions.[25] And, until the late 1990s, in countries such as Mexico and Brazil the corporatist tradition was very strong—to the point that one can rightly ask how democratic these political systems were. The lines of demarcation between political systems can be just as porous as those between political ideologies.

CONTEMPORARY CRITICISMS OF DEMOCRACY

Up to this point, our discussion of liberal democracy has been mainly theoretical, with a review of some of the traditional problems encountered in this particular form of government. However, we should not give the impression that all is well with liberal democracies. Any perceptive person today knows that nothing could be further from the truth. In most Western democracies, criticisms abound. And most of those criticisms are justified. People feel that political leaders are unresponsive, that they have their own agendas. There is a common perception that the relationship among the cabinet, high administrative officials, and powerful lobbyists is too cozy, that governments are ignoring the demands and expectations of large segments of the population. As a result, there is a great deal of cynicism about modern politics: people feel manipulated by the media and politicians, and powerless in a decision-making process in which, theoretically, citizen participation is valued. Never have people had so many opportunities to participate in politics; yet, paradoxically, never have more people been so critical of the political process. Importantly, there is widespread and overwhelming support around the world for the idea of democracy as a system of governance; there is less, however, for its practice.[26]

The polls verify this sense of disillusionment. In the spring of 1966, in the midst of the Vietnam War and race riots, a survey revealed that 66 percent of Americans disagreed with the statement "the people running the country don't really care what happens to you." When the same question was asked in December of 1997, during a time of relative peace and economic prosperity, 57 percent of the American public *agreed* with it.[27] This trend extends beyond the United States: only one in five British citizens is likely to trust politicians to tell the truth.[28] The public in many Western democracies has simply lost faith in the system and in politicians. We can identify at least three major reasons why: the overall performance of the system, the workings of cabinet government, and the changing nature of society itself.

With respect to the first issue, for the past 50 years Canadian governments have followed a highly interventionist course under the assumption that the state can guide the economy; solve social problems such as unemployment, poverty, and prejudice; care for the aged and infirm; and inspire loyalty to and support for the nation-state. A vast amount of legislation has been passed in those 50 years relating to unemployment insurance, welfare payments, old-age pensions, health care, family allowances, civil rights, and government assistance to businesses. Multiculturalism has been strengthened. Even our flag and our anthem date from this time. In effect, the state has been intervening to regulate society and to provide services to create a more just society. Throughout, most people have supported these actions, in part because most have benefited from them in one way or another.

These programs have been both extensive and expensive. Between the 1960s and the 1990s, government was a growth industry. Budgets and bureaucracies grew, but because public-sector expansion was undertaken at a time when the economy was also expanding rapidly, governments could, and did, increase taxes to pay for the increased services and regulations. Canadians were earning enough discretionary income that most middle-income citizens could pay more taxes and still maintain their standard of living. As government expenditures rose, revenues could be increased to sustain the policies and programs. When the economy faltered, however, and revenues levelled off, governments began to borrow in order to maintain their services and programs, under the assumption that the economy would soon return to a growth cycle, at which time taxes could again be increased. The result was high and rising levels of public debt. The Canadian federal budget now includes an item of $33 billion for debt-service charges, amounting to 15 percent of all tax revenues collected. Although the situation is gradually improving, the necessity to pay so much in interest on past loans still squeezes expenditures on social programs.

The heavy burden of taxation, coupled with the debt legacy that the present generation is leaving for the future, led to an outcry against politicians and their recent performance. Citizens now expect better fiscal management.

Since about 1993 most Canadian jurisdictions responded to this concern and, until the economic problems in 2008–09, were operating with balanced budgets (see Figure 17.2).

Interestingly, at the beginning of the twenty-first century, the debate has shifted from deficits and debt to a growing concern about governments adequately supporting programs such as education and especially health care. Again, this debate also is influenced by ideology. There are those who feel that these vital programs are being underfunded, and at a time when we can ill afford a second-class health and educational system. At the same time, there are those who feel that the state should not try to support all costs involved in education and health care, and that some of this

Figure 17.2 Federal and Provincial–Territorial Budgetary Balances (Public Accounts Basis)

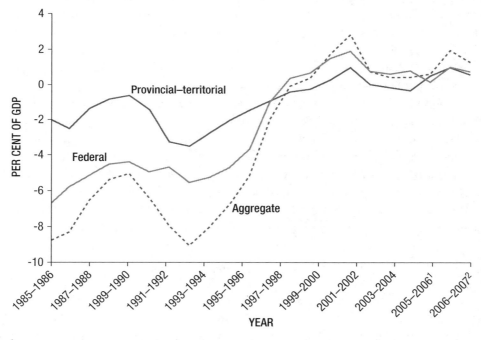

[1]For this and subsequent charts, figures for the combined provincial-territorial sector and the aggregate surplus for 2005–06 are estimates.

[2]Projection.

Source: Department of Finance, Canada "Budget Plan 2007," Chart A1.1, p. 300. http://www.budget.gc.ca/2007/pdf/bkfbsfe.pdf. Reproduced with the permission of the Minister of Public Works and Government Services Canada, 2008.

responsibility should be privatized. This is a contentious debate, and no doubt its outcome has relevance for the question raised by Aristotle about polarization of society along the lines of rich and poor. It will be interesting to see whether resolution of this issue will restore some of the citizens' confidence in government.

A second reason why citizens are criticizing the democratic process relates to the parliamentary process, with its cabinet government and disciplined political parties. This system developed in the nineteenth century, before universal suffrage was introduced and social relationships were democratized. Cabinet ministers still cling to this elitist system; they claim it cannot work without party discipline because changes in government could lead to political instability. Their argument is that a strong executive is vital to the parliamentary system. But this executive-dominated process has now given rise to a populist reaction, as illustrated in the widespread opposition to the Meech Lake and Charlottetown Accords. That opposition did not focus entirely on proposed changes to the Constitution; much of it stemmed from the fact that citizens felt the country's first ministers were imposing these changes on the people. Thus, with the heavy hand of the executive strengthened by political-party discipline, many people question whether their representatives can truly represent them. (More on this in Chapters 23 and 27.)

A third cause of widespread criticism of the present democratic process has to do with changes that have occurred in Canadian society. Many writers and analysts today are talking about a "new politics." What they mean by the phrase is that beliefs and values have changed considerably over the past half century. Among younger generations, there is much less deference toward all social authorities, and especially toward politicians. Many citizens are highly educated; have had a great deal of business, professional, and political experience; and are quite willing to challenge any direction public leaders are embarking on. A symptom of this change is decreased trust in politicians; another is dropping voter turnout levels. Many now view voting as a less than effective use of their time; instead, they prefer to involve themselves in interest groups or community efforts tackling problems and issues directly.

While citizen engagement ought to be applauded, if it comes at the expense of electoral participation then democracy suffers since one of its operating principles is political participation. Democratic legitimacy and the articulation of interests require an informed and engaged voting population.

Can changes be made to restore Canadians' faith in the democratic process? In general, there are two alternatives in this age-old debate: find "better" people to rule, or change the system itself. We believe that systemic change is the better solution to the problem of good government.

As mentioned earlier, mechanisms like referendums and initiatives would involve the public more directly in decision making. While these mechanisms are not without their problems, they do provide a means by which the public, if mobilized, can initiate action. In that sense, they may provide a safety valve when governments become paralyzed and are unable to respond.

Another approach might be to develop more opportunities for the public to influence policymaking earlier in the process and more directly. As mentioned earlier, governments often follow elaborate consultative procedures when formulating policies on particular issues. Cabinets consult with major interests; there are royal commissions; and parliamentary committees sometimes have elaborate cross-country hearings. But these devices, valuable and necessary as they may be, do not appear to be enough. Politicians are now experimenting with new forms of consultation, such as electronic forums, citizen juries, and deliberative dialogues. Such mechanisms require a great deal of time on the part of political leaders, but the dividends in terms of rapport with the people may be great. And given the cynical view people now have about the process, such mechanisms may help to break down the feeling many Canadians have that elected officials are sheltered, unresponsive, and unavailable to the public they are supposed to serve. In short, the public seems to want a more open political process; a process operating from the bottom up rather than the top down. (More on this in Chapter 26.)

Globalization and the reaction to it call into question the actions of the state and protest groups in liberal democracies. Supporters of the idea of globalization argue that free trade among nations will stimulate economic growth, especially in non-industrialized nations. They suggest it is the best way to redistribute wealth. Opponents of globalization in most established democracies argue that it does move manufacturing to non-industrialized nations, but essentially it is a way for multinational corporations to exploit cheap labour in the non-industrialized world, and to be able to do it with few restrictions on working conditions, minimum wages, and environmental protection.

Activities surrounding the concept of globalization have become an issue in a number of Western liberal democracies. Critics of the concept accuse political leaders of negotiating, behind closed doors, world trade deals with multinational corporations. They claim they must protest in the streets in order to open the issue for public debate. Political leaders and supporters of globalization claim discussions of trade arrangements are in a preliminary stage and there will be open debate before agreements are made. Meetings between political and economic leaders and international trade organizations in Seattle; Prague; Davos, Switzerland; Washington, D.C.; and Quebec City did turn violent, with clashes between police and protesters. Thus, the issue of globalization not only raises questions about the idea itself, but also about the conduct of the state and protesters in liberal democracies.

Using the 2001 Quebec City Summit of the Americas trade meetings as an example, note that the Canadian and Quebec governments prepared for the event by constructing a three-metre-high fence around the perimeter of the meeting area to separate protesters and those attending the meetings. The authorities mobilized hundreds of police, claiming the protesters included agitators who intended to provoke violence. Protesters were met with rubber bullets and tear gas.

Whatever one's opinions on globalization, responses by both sides on the issue raise questions of behaviour in liberal democracies. Crises are not new. In the early twentieth century, there were conflicts over legalizing labour unions and over extending the right to vote. As such, one wonders whether they are an inevitable part of life in a free society; if so, liberal democracies ought to do a better job of managing internal conflict. For more on the role of the state in society, see World View 17.1.

World View 17.1

The Third Way

In all democratic systems of government, the role of the state in society is an issue. Whether the state should play a greater or lesser role is at the core of ideological debates. Those on the left of the political spectrum advocate a more interventionist state; those on the right advocate reducing state involvement in society. Anthony Giddens adds to the conceptualization of this debate in *The Third Way:*

> The neoliberals want to shrink the state; the social democrats, historically, have been keen to expand it. The third way argues that what is necessary is to reconstruct it—to go beyond those on the right who say government is the enemy; and those on the left who say government is the answer. (Giddens, 1998, p. 70)

The idea of a "third way" gained credence in academic and political circles with the Clinton administration in the United States (1992 and 1996) and the election of the Labour government of Tony Blair in the United Kingdom (1997). While the Liberal government did not use the term *third way* in Canada,

after their elections in 1993, 1997, and 2000 they did claim their policies were "centralist." They suggested their policies represented a balance between those of the NDP on the left, and the Alliance (known as Reform prior to 2000) and the Progressive Conservative parties on the right.

This pragmatic approach to policy-making has meant many things by those advocating a third way. However, one of their fundamental claims is that government should abandon the old idea of welfare, "the direct provision of economic maintenance" (Giddens, 1998, p. 117), and instead invest in human capital—or *social capital,* as it is frequently called. The claim is that the state's role is to help individuals help themselves; to strengthen policies like education and health care.

For more information on the third way, see Anthony Giddens, *The Third Way: The Renewal of Social Democracy* (Cambridge: Polity Press, 1998) and Anthony Giddens, *The Third Way and Its Critics* (Cambridge: Polity Press, 2000).

CONCLUSION

A liberal–democratic political system, then, is one in which, on the basis of universal adult suffrage, citizens select their governors (representatives); these representatives can be changed by the electorate through periodic elections; individual or group opinions can be discussed freely without fear of retaliation by public officials or private individuals; a legal opposition is free to criticize; and an independent judiciary resolves disputes between citizens, between citizens and government, and between levels of government. If this seems excessively long for a definition, that is because it is not easy to characterize in fewer words a form of government that seeks to reconcile freedom with majority rule.

Liberal democracy is an expression of the political experience of the Western world. It is now practised in every country of Western Europe, although Spain and Portugal did not emerge from authoritarian rule until the 1970s, and Greece underwent a period of military dictatorship in the same decade. Liberal democracy is also strongly entrenched in countries that are essentially transplanted European states; for example, Canada, the United States, Australia, New Zealand, and Israel.

While liberal democracy is a product of Western European traditions and culture, democrats believe that it can be adopted successfully outside that milieu. Two good examples are Japan and India. Both countries have ancient cultural traditions that are quite distinct from those of Western Europe, yet they have successfully operated reasonable approximations of liberal democracy for more than 50 years. There was an initial period of transplantation, to be sure—from the American occupation in Japan, and from the British Raj in India—but since those times, liberal democracy has continued successfully on its own. The economic contrast between Japan and India is also significant. Both countries are heavily populated. Japan is now wealthy, with a standard of living similar to Canada's. India, though now growing more quickly than before, is still poor, with a largely agricultural economy. Nonetheless, in spite of severe religious differences, it has been able to make liberal democracy work. This shows that a high standard of living is not absolutely vital for liberal democracy to work. It is probably true, however, that it is more likely to succeed in countries where the economy is highly developed.

In the beginning of the twenty-first century there is good reason for optimism about liberal democracies. It still remains true that no two liberal democracies have gone to war against each other. The widespread adoption of democracy may be the best available strategy for reducing conflict in the world.

Nevertheless, many analysts still believe that liberal democracies are quite fragile and need to adapt constantly to changing conditions in society. Certainly problems such as human rights, economic inequalities, political alienation, or globalization will provide major challenges for these systems of government. Stand by; politically speaking, the next few decades should be exciting times.

Questions for Discussion

1. How does liberal democracy attempt to reconcile majority and minority rights?

2. What are the responsibilities of citizens in liberal democracies?

3. Which constitutional devices do you see as providing the most effective protection for minority rights?

Internet Links

1. The International IDEA (Institute for Democracy and Electoral Assistance): **www.idea.int.** An intergovernmental organization promoting and supporting democracy around the world.

2. FairVote: The Center for Voting and Democracy: **www.fairvote.org.** American centre; emphasis on elections, voting rights, and electoral systems.

3. Freedom House: **www.freedomhouse.org.** Annual rankings of all nations of the world on indicators of freedom and democracy.

4. World Movement for Democracy: Network of Democracy Research Institutes: **www.wmd.org.** Gateway to centres for the study of democracy all over the world.

5. Rights & Democracy: **www.ichrdd.ca.** Canadian organization promoting democracy around the world.

Further Reading

Ajzenstat, Janet. *The Once and Future Canadian Democracy: An Essay in Political Thought.* Montreal and Kingston: McGill–Queen's University Press, 2003.

Alexander, P. C. *The Perils of Democracy.* Bombay: Somaiya Publications, 1995.

Arthur, John, ed. *Democracy: Theory and Practice.* Belmont, CA: Wadsworth Publishing Co., 1992.

Bachrach, Peter. *The Theory of Democratic Elitism.* Rev. ed. Washington, DC: University Press of America, 1980.

Banting, Keith, Thomas J. Courchene, and F. Leslie Seidle, eds. *Belonging? Diversity, Recognition and Shared Citizenship in Canada.* Montreal: IRPP, 2007.

Barney, Darin. *Communication Technology.* Vancouver: UBC Press, 2005.

Brooks, Stephen. *Canadian Democracy: An Introduction.* 5th ed. Toronto: Oxford University Press, 2007.

Cain, Bruce E., Russell J. Dalton, and Susan E. Scarrow, eds. *Democracy Transformed.* Toronto: Oxford University Press, 2004.

Chapman, John W., and Ian Shapiro. *Democratic Community.* New York: New York University Press, 1993.

Dahl, Robert A. *On Democracy.* New Haven, CT: Yale University Press, 1998.

———. *Polyarchy: Participation and Opposition.* New Haven, CT: Yale University Press, 1971.

Dalton, Russell J. *Democratic Challenges, Democratic Choices.* Toronto: Oxford University Press, 2004.

Di Palma, Giuseppe. *To Craft Democracies: An Essay on Democratic Transitions.* Berkeley: University of California Press, 1990.

Downs, Anthony. *An Economic Theory of Democracy.* New York: Harper and Row, 1957.

Eagles, Munro, Christopher Holoman, and Larry Johnston. *The Institutions of Liberal Democratic States.* Peterborough, ON: Broadview Press, 2003.

Elshtain, Jean Bethke. *Democracy on Trial.* Concord, ON: Anansi, 1993.

Esposito, John L. *Islam and Democracy.* New York: Oxford University Press, 1996.

Evans, Mark, Michael Slovodnik, and Terezia Zoric. *Democracy and Government in Canada: Participating for Change.* Toronto: ITP Nelson, 1996.

Fischer, Mary Ellen. *Establishing Democracies.* Boulder, CO: Westview Press, 1996.

Fishkin, James S. *The Voice of the People: Public Opinion and Democracy.* New Haven, CT: Yale University Press, 1995.

Giddens, Anthony. *The Third Way: The Renewal of Social Democracy.* Cambridge: Polity Press, 1998.

———. *The Third Way and Its Critics.* Cambridge: Polity Press, 2000.

Keane, John. *Democracy and Civil Society.* London: Verso, 1988.

Klosko, George. *Democratic Procedures and Liberal Consensus.* Toronto: Oxford University Press, 2004.

Kymlicka, Will. *Multicultural Citizenship: A Liberal Theory of Minority Rights.* Oxford: Clarendon Press and New York: Oxford University Press, 1995.

Lijphart, Arend. *Democracy in Plural Societies.* New Haven, CT: Yale University Press, 1977.

———. *Patterns of Democracy: Government Forms and Performance in Thirty-Six Countries.* New Haven, CT: Yale University Press, 1999.

Lindsay, A. D. *The Modern Democratic State.* New York: Oxford University Press, 1962.

Mackie, Gerry. *Democracy Defended.* Toronto: Cambridge University Press, 2003.

Manji, Irshad. *Risking Utopia: On the Edge of a New Democracy.* Vancouver: Douglas & McIntyre, 1997.

March, James G., and Johan P. Olsen. *Democratic Governance.* New York: Free Press, 1995.

Mouffe, Chantal. *Democracy and Pluralism: A Critique of the Rationalist Approach.* Toronto: Faculty of Law, University of Toronto, 1995.

Nevitte, Neil. *The Decline of Deference: Canadian Value Change in Cross-National Perspective.* Peterborough: Broadview, 1996.

Parry, Gerraint. *Political Elites.* London: George Allen and Unwin, 1969.

Pateman, Carole. *Participation and Democratic Theory.* Cambridge: Cambridge University Press, 1970.

Sartori, Giovanni. *The Theory of Democracy Revisited: Part I, The Contemporary Debate.* Chatham, NJ: Chatham House, 1987.

———. *The Theory of Democracy Revisited: Part II, The Classical Issues.* Chatham, NJ: Chatham House, 1987.

Saul, John Ralston. *The Unconscious Civilization.* Concord, ON: Anansi, 1995.

Turner, Stephen P. *Liberal Democracy 3.0: Civil Society in an Age of Experts.* Thousand Oaks, CA: Sage, 2003.

Unger, Roberto Magabeira. *Democracy Realized: The Progressive Alternative.* New York: Verso, 1998.

Watson, Patrick, and Benjamin R. Barber. *The Struggle for Democracy.* Toronto: Key Porter, 2000.

CORPORATISM

Cawson, Alan. *Organized Interests and the States: Studies in Meso-Corporatism.* London: Sage, 1992.

———. *Corporatism and Political Theory.* New York: Basil Blackwell, 1986.

Harrison, Reginald James. *Pluralism and Corporatism: The Political Evolution of Modern Democracies.* London: George Allen and Unwin, 1980.

Wiarda, Howard J. *Civil Society: The American Model and Third World Development.* Boulder, CO: Westview Press, 2003.

———, ed. *New Directions in Comparative Politics.* 3rd ed. Boulder, CO: Westview Press, 2002.

Wilensky, Harold, and Lawell Turner. *Democratic Corporatism and Policy Linkages: The Interdependence of Industrial, Labour Market, Incomes and Social Policies in Eight Countries.* Berkeley, CA: University of California Press, 1987.

Williamson, Peter J. *Corporatism in Perspective: An Introductory Guide to Corporatist Theory.* London: Sage, 1992.

Ziegler, L. Harman. *Pluralism, Corporatism and Confucianism: Political Associations and Conflict Resolution in the United States, Europe and Taiwan.* Philadelphia: Temple University Press, 1988.

CONSOCIATIONALISM

Lamy, Steven Lewis. *Consociationalism, Decentralization and Ethnic Group Equalization: The Case of Constitutional Engineering in Belgium.* Ann Arbor, MI: University of Michigan Press, 1980.

Lijphart, Arend. *The Politics of Accommodation: Pluralism and Democracy in the Netherlands,* 2nd ed. Berkeley, CA: University of California Press, 1975.

McRae, Kenneth Douglas, ed. *Consociational Democracy: Political Accommodation in Segmented Societies.* Toronto: McClelland & Stewart, 1974.

CHAPTER 23

Political Parties, Interest Groups, and Social Movements: The Organization of Interests

Political parties, interest groups, and social movements are vital parts of the political process. Each provides a function essential to the conversion stage of the political process (refer to Figure 22.2). Political parties try to capture the reins of power of government; they want to control the institutions of government by winning a majority in elections. Interest groups, on the other hand, attempt to influence governments; they try to persuade public officials to enact legislation in their or the public's interest. Like interest groups, social movements attempt to influence governments but they go beyond this in attempting to bring about some type of wider social change. In this chapter, political parties, interest groups, and social movements will be discussed separately.

POLITICAL PARTIES

Political parties are an essential feature of politics in the modern age of mass participation. In liberal–democratic systems, they help to keep governments accountable to public opinion. Even in autocratic systems of government, they help the government maintain its hold on power. In either case, political parties are an important link between government and the people.

Political parties are a rather recent phenomenon, having evolved with the extension of the franchise. In the eighteenth century, the Tories and Whigs dominated the British Parliament as political clubs of the upper class. They had little in the way of strong connections with the general population. But as the Reform Acts of 1832, 1867, and 1884 extended suffrage to most adult males, these clubs were transformed to accommodate the influx of voters, and the Conservative and Liberal Parties were formed. The tendency toward greater mass participation continued with the development of the Labour Party in the late nineteenth century as a party of the working class. By the

1930s, it had replaced the Liberals as the principal competitor to the Conservatives, leaving the Liberals a third and minor party in the British system. As reforms expanded the electorate in liberal democracies, political parties were viewed as the primary political organization facilitating mass politics. Political parties not only were the vehicle through which individuals could become involved in politics, but also were considered the primary institutions shaping public policy.

A political party performs so many tasks in the political process that it is difficult to establish a simple definition. However, Joseph LaPalombara's working definition can serve as a point of departure:

> A political party is a formal organization whose self-conscious, primary purpose is to place and maintain in public office persons who will control, alone or in coalition, the machinery of government.[1]

These organizations are not usually part of the formal–legal machinery of government. In most Western nations, they do not derive power from a constitution. Any power they have depends on how the electorate responds in elections. However, there is an increasing tendency in many countries for political parties to be drawn into the formal sphere of government. In Canada, for instance, donations to parties are eligible for tax credits, while party finances are regulated by government and subject to disclosure laws. Their very success as informal institutions is pushing them toward formal–legal status.

The Roles of Political Parties

The first and most important goal of the political party in a democratic system is electoral success. An election win entitles the party to dominate the governmental machinery and perhaps enact some of the proposals to which it is committed. Electoral success short of outright victory may enable it to participate in a coalition government and thus achieve at least some of its aims.

A number of other roles complement the primary objective of winning power. A political party is the mechanism by which candidates are chosen to run for public office. A person may choose to run as an independent, but almost all successful candidates for public office are members of an organized party. A related role is to influence voters during campaigns. A great deal of the work of a party organization involves trying to get voters to support its candidates.

At the governmental level, the members elected with the support of the party put forward and pass legislative proposals in the assembly. Obviously, in a parliamentary body of 308 members (Canada) or 646 members (United Kingdom), there must be some organization. The cabinet of the governing party determines which legislative proposals are to be considered, drafted, debated, and (the governing party hopes) passed.

The party also acts as an intermediary between elected members and the public; that is, between people and their government. While the bulk of party activity occurs at election time, this continuous interchange between people and government can be an important function of the party.

Finally, the political party provides a training ground for political leaders. The party ranks are a pool from which political leaders are recruited. Party workers in constituency organizations often choose to run for office; if elected, they may work their way up from the back benches to a ministerial post. In Canada, however, there has been some tendency in recent decades for leaders of the major national parties to be brought in "sideways," as it were. Pierre Trudeau was a university professor and journalist before being invited into the cabinet and was chosen leader after only three years in Parliament. Brian Mulroney had long been a Conservative activist and insider, but had never held an elected office before becoming a Conservative leader. John Turner came back from political retirement to lead the Liberals, a feat that Jean Chrétien repeated in 1990. Paul Martin, however, became prime minister after serving ten years as finance minister in Jean Chrétien's government, so his success came very much from the inside.

Political leadership means building conditions. For example, in the 2000 and 2004 elections, president George W. Bush pulled together a winning coalition of conservative Republicans, large business interests, and fundamentalist Christians in the southern, mid-western, and northern industrial states. In 2008, Barack Obama mobilized moderate Democrats as well as black and Hispanic voters, and was able to make inroads in the south (Florida, North Carolina, and Virginia), the mid-west (Iowa, Colorado, New Mexico, and Nevada), and in Ohio. This aggregation of specific and regional interests enabled Obama to win the presidency over John McCain.

Another important function of the democratic political party is the aggregation of interests. Various groups make a great many demands on government, and it is never possible for a government to meet all of them, mainly because many of the demands are mutually incompatible. For example, organized consumer groups will demand that import quotas on shoes be abolished, while manufacturers will demand that those quotas be made more restrictive. The political party is a forum at which conflicting interests may be at least partially reconciled, where compromises can be reached and then bundled into a program that most party supporters can accept.

In autocratic systems, the party also aggregates demands to some extent, although because of the lack of political freedom this must be done behind the scenes. Specialists in Soviet politics often suggested that the monolithic façade of the Communist Party concealed squabbling factions representing such interests as the military and agriculture. More obvious is the totalitarian party's function of promoting support for the regime. The party is the government's instrument for enhancing popular acceptance of its policies. To this end, the party coordinates publicity in the mass media, organizes meetings and demonstrations, and carries out persuasion through its cells in workplaces.

It must be remembered that we are speaking of political parties in general. Not all parties perform all of the above roles, and the roles may be played in different ways. For example, the role of political parties in the Canadian system has changed over time. They remain the primary vehicle through which politicians are recruited, and they continue to mobilize the electorate at election time. But their function has changed in the area of policy formation. Most policy proposals come from the political executive—the prime minister and other cabinet ministers and their personal advisers—or from the permanent administration. The work of developing policy proposals is not so much the effort of the party faithful as it is of the senior people working for members of cabinet, some of whom may not even belong to the party organization. Thus, while local, regional, provincial, and national party organizations meet and make policy recommendations to the party leadership, the policy proposals that emerge from the government may not reflect opinions at the grassroots level of the party. This is why most analysts now agree that the role of political parties in the legislative process has declined and that the executive and bureaucracy are now more influential. (More on this issue in Chapter 27.)

Because no two parties function in the same way, it is necessary to have a scheme of classification. Without pretending to be definitive, the following typology captures some of the main types: pragmatic, ideological, interest, personal, and movement parties.

The Pragmatic Party

One of the more common party types in Western society is the **pragmatic party.** The dictionary defines *pragmatism* as a "philosophy that evaluates assertions solely by their practical consequences and bearing on human interests."[2] In other words, a pragmatist's actions are less likely to be driven by a set of basic principles and doctrine than by a concern for the consequences of those actions. The pragmatic political party gears its campaign promises not to beliefs founded on doctrine, but to programs that it believes have the greatest appeal to the public. It is thus open to the criticism of having no principles and of moving with the wind, and its programs sometimes appear to reflect nothing more than a cynical desire for power.

The mass parties in the Anglo-American tradition are generally classified as pragmatic: Conservatives and Labour in Great Britain, Conservatives and Liberals in Canada, Republicans and Democrats in the United States. The pragmatism of such parties always generates confusion about where they stand. Brian Mulroney's Conservatives, for example, were attacked by voices on the left for pursuing a "right-wing, neoconservative" agenda; yet organizations on the right, such as the Fraser Institute and the National Citizens Coalition, condemned Mulroney for failing to implement a conservative agenda. Pragmatic parties sometimes appear more ideological—as the British Conservatives did under Margaret Thatcher—but this usually reflects not so much a fundamental change in the party as the temporary ascendancy of one faction within it. With the passage of time, the party usually reverts to a more pragmatic and less ideological stance, as happened when John Major replaced Thatcher as leader.

When pragmatic parties compete head to head, they characteristically make overlapping proposals, even to the extent of borrowing each other's ideas. For example, the proposal for a comprehensive Free Trade Agreement with the United States arose from a royal commission appointed by the Liberal government of Pierre Trudeau and chaired by Donald Macdonald, a former Liberal cabinet minister. Brian Mulroney opposed the idea when he was running for the leadership of the Conservatives, but later adopted it as the most important policy initiative of his first term in office. The Liberals strenuously opposed the Free Trade Agreement while it was being negotiated, but Jean Chrétien's government gave it final approval for implementation.

This mutual borrowing is not confined to particular policies; it also extends to broader party positions. Between the 1950s and the 1970s, the welfare state and government interventionism were dominant ideas, and the pragmatic parties of the right had to accept them or face electoral extinction. "We are all Keynesians now," said Republican Richard Nixon when he was president of the United States. But during the 1980s and 1990s, when the fiscal difficulties of the welfare state led to the revival of conservatism, the pragmatic parties of the left had to come to terms with privatization, deregulation, and balanced budgets. Bill Clinton was elected president in 1992 and re-elected in 1996 in part because he acknowledged the importance of traditional conservative objectives such as reducing the deficit, tightening up welfare programs, and enhancing business competitiveness; indeed, he claimed to be more able than President George H. W. Bush (1988–92) to attain these ends, albeit using different means. Tony Blair's Labour Party regained power in the British election of 1997 in part by promising to leave Margaret Thatcher's reforms undisturbed (see World View 17.1 in Chapter 17).

The Ideological Party

The **ideological party,** in contrast, emphasizes ideological purity more than the immediate attainment of power. Party doctrine takes precedence over electoral success. Such parties are criticized, of course, for their inflexibility. Often they put doctrine before the wishes of the voters, convinced that in time voters will come around to their way of thinking. The Communist Party is a good example of an ideological party, as are socialist parties and even some social democratic parties. On the right, some conservative parties are as doctrinaire as any on the left.

The New Democratic Party is the most ideological of the traditional Canadian parties. As a party of the left, its major policy commitments have focused on social rights (e.g., opposition to the privatization of health care) and economic rights (e.g., review NAFTA to achieve fairer trade). The Reform Party (1987–2000) was understood by most observers to be an ideological party of the right, in that it also presented a simple, doctrinaire program: balance the federal budget, reduce taxes and government spending, abolish official bilingualism, introduce recall legislation, and so on. More careful observers, however, noted that Reform positions were often phrased with a "calculated ambiguity" suggesting a pragmatic party in waiting.[3]

When the Reform Party merged itself into the Canadian Alliance in 2000, it abandoned or watered down a number of its more radical positions, thus taking further steps toward becoming a pragmatic party; and that process was completed in 2003 when Reform merged with the Progressive Conservatives to form the Conservative Party of Canada.

When pragmatic parties adopt policies that are very similar, they run the risk that new parties may appeal to voters who perceive the pragmatic parties as no longer standing for anything. In Canada, Brian Mulroney's success at adopting many positions previously associated with the Liberals (bilingualism, multiculturalism, employment equity) led many ideological conservatives to defect from the Progressive Conservatives in favour of the Reform Party, which offered a more consistent ideological stance. The Reform Party, however, found its potential limited because it was perceived by many voters as excessively ideological, leading to its reunion with the Progressive Conservatives in 2003. The point is not that pragmatic parties are good and ideological parties are bad, or vice versa; it is that each type of party offers something different to voters and may fail or succeed under various sets of circumstances.

The Interest Party

Another type of party is the **interest party.** Here we find people converting their interest group into a full-fledged political party that runs candidates and attempts to obtain power. Such a group feels that it can best achieve its ends by acting as a party rather than trying to influence existing parties, but its narrow basis of support makes it hard for it to win control of the state. In Australia, the National Party (previously known as the Country Party) began as a farmers' party. There have also been peasants' parties in Eastern Europe and Latin America. In Scandinavia, industrialists have formed conservative parties. Around the world, Green parties have developed from environmental movements when they became convinced of the need to have political parties win seats in legislatures to fight for environmental issues from within rather than outside government. In Canada, the Green Party was established in 1983 and in the 2006 and 2008 general elections, that party earned 4.5 percent and 6.8 percent respectively of the national vote. While not an insignificant share, it was not high enough to win a seat in the House of Commons.

There is vigorous debate about the merits of pragmatic, ideological, and interest parties. Some believe that pragmatic parties contribute to the stability of the political system—that they cover the waterfront, so to speak, in their response to demands made by groups in society. These parties endeavour to include something for everyone in their platforms. They appeal to diverse groups—employers and labour unions, farmers and consumers, conservationists and developers. Many people see pragmatic parties as mechanisms for aggregating interests and mending the fault lines in a pluralistic society.

Those who advocate the virtues of interest and ideological parties make their arguments from the standpoint of representation. They are quite critical of pragmatic parties, suggesting that by making broad appeals to all groups such parties dilute their platforms so that in the end they represent no one. This is the position taken by Maurice Duverger, a noted authority on political parties, whose comparative work is still basic in the field.[4] An interest or ideological party, according to this view, can cater its platform to a specific interest or to a group with a defined ideology. Political parties of this type are able to offer voters a clear choice, and elected members have a responsibility to a specific clientele. But what is made up in representation could be lost in stability. The advocates of pragmatic parties suggest that interest and ideological parties tend to intensify cleavages in society rather than reconcile them. Moreover, when these parties are unwilling to compromise at the legislative level little is accomplished, and governmental instability and inaction may well result.

In fact, both pragmatic parties and interest or ideological parties have shown themselves capable of aggregating interests and reconciling conflicts. In the Anglo-American model of pragmatic parties, the resolution of conflicts takes place within the party. Labour, business, and agricultural organizations come to some sort of compromise with the government of the day, which is almost always formed by a single party. In contrast, in democracies where coalition governments of ideological or interest parties are the norm, interest reconciliation takes place among parties. Parties do not have to surrender their principles internally, but they have to make compromises to keep a coalition cabinet in power. This illustrates the general principle that the necessary functions of the political process may be accomplished in quite different ways in different systems. Any successful political system must resolve conflicts of interest among different social groups; but this task can be carried out within parties, among parties, or by other institutions in the governmental process. The method may not matter very much as long as the job gets done. The advantage of approaching politics as a process is that one becomes sensitive to relationships of this type and learns to look at institutions not in isolation but rather as they relate to other institutions.

The Personal Party

Another type of party is the **personal party,** which is founded around a single, influential political leader. After World War II, supporters of Charles de Gaulle formed the Gaullist Party, which became the strongest political force in France after de Gaulle established the Fifth Republic in 1958. With the support of this party, called the Union for the Defence of the Republic (UDR), de Gaulle was elected president in 1958 and 1965. The Gaullists, under a variety of party names, survived the General's retirement in 1969 and today represent a coalition of moderate conservatives. Juan Perón of Argentina also developed a political party from his personal following. His supporters elected him president in 1946 and 1951. Perón, however, was removed from office after a *coup d'état* in 1955. The Peronistas were the main force behind the election of President Carlos Menem in 1989 and 1995, reinforcing the fact that personal parties need not die with their founders.

NEL

459

Personal parties have been common in the Third World, particularly in Africa. Jomo Kenyatta of Kenya was one of the chief architects of KANU—the Kenya African National Union. KANU provided a base of support for Kenyatta, who attempted to use the party to integrate Kenya's many tribal groups. Kenyatta died in 1978, but his party has remained a dominant force in Kenya. For years Robert Mugabe of Zimbabwe dreamed of establishing his Zimbabwe African National Union–Patriotic Front (ZANU–PF) as the single party under which racial and ethnic groups would be united. This was accomplished in December 1987 and he was re-elected president in 1990, 1996, and 2002. In the 2008 election, however, Morgan Tsvangirai, leader of the Movement for Democratic Change (MDC), earned a sufficient number of votes to force a runoff election for the presidency. Mugabe won the runoff when Tsvangirai withdrew, accusing the government of mounting a campaign of violence against his supporters.

All these examples show that the personal party, like the other types of parties, is not an entirely clear-cut category. All parties have leaders who are usually quite prominent even in a thoroughly democratic party; and even the most dominating leader has to have an organization to be effective. Thus parties that may be considered personal vehicles at the outset often evolve into long-lasting pragmatic, ideological, or interest parties.

The Movement Party

A **movement party** is a political movement that evolves into a party apparatus. A movement is a union of people that aims at a profound social change, such as national independence, but does not itself aspire to govern. A movement sometimes is converted into a party when the prestige it gains by achieving its goals makes it a logical choice to become the government. The Congress Party in India is a good example. The Indian National Congress, organized in 1885, became the instrument by which Indians sought independence from Great Britain. The party became the focus of nationalist feeling throughout India and mobilized popular pressure against the British. After achieving independence in 1947, it became the dominant political force in the federal Parliament, a position that it long maintained, although it slipped a good deal during the 1990s. In Canada, the Bloc Québécois could be considered a movement party. Its only real program is the sovereignty of Quebec. If it ever achieves this goal, it will probably break up into ideological factions. In the meantime, it uses the House of Commons as a forum for promoting the independence of Quebec. For a list of other movement parties throughout Canadian history, see Canadian Focus 23.1.

Political Party Systems

Political party systems also influence the manner in which parties carry out their roles. There are basically three types of party systems: one-party, two-party, and multiparty.

Canadian Focus 23.1

New Political Parties in Canada

For a very long period of time, the two regions of Canada most dissatisfied with the status quo in Canada have been Quebec and the West. It is not surprising, then, that these two regions, so different in other ways, have both given rise to a long series of political parties challenging the constitutional order in fundamental ways. Below are lists of the main parties created in these two regions. The symbol P means provincial party, F means a federal party, and F+P indicates that the party operated at both levels.

New Political Parties Founded in Western Canada

Provincial Rights Party (P)	1905
Non-Partisan League (P)	1916
Progressives (including United Farmers' parties) (F+P)	1919
Co-operative Commonwealth Federation (F+P)	1932
Social Credit (F+P)	1935
Social Credit Party of British Columbia (P)	1952
Western Canada Concept (F+P)	1980
Western Canada Federation (F+P)	1980
Confederation of Regions (F+P)	1983
Reform Party of Canada (F)	1987
Reform Party of British Columbia (P)	1989
National Party (F)	1992
Progressive Democratic Alliance of British Columbia (P)	1993
Saskatchewan Party (P)	1997
British Columbia Unity Party (P)	2001
Alberta Alliance (P)	2002
Wildrose Alliance Party (P)	2008

New Political Parties Founded in Quebec

Parti National (P)	1885
Nationalist League (as political party) (F)	1911
Action Libérale Nationale (P)	1934
Union Nationale (P)	1935
Union des Electeurs (F+P)	1939
Bloc Populaire Canadien (F+P)	1942
Ralliement des Créditistes (F)	1957
Parti Québécois (P)	1968
Ralliement Créditiste du Québec (P)	1970
Equality Party (P)	1989
Bloc Québécois (F)	1990
Action Démocratique du Québec (P)	1994
Québéc Solidaire (P)	2006

The One-Party System

This type includes true **single-party systems** and **one-party-dominant systems.** In the former, there is only one party in the political system, and no political alternative is legally tolerated. The former Communist Party of the Soviet Union, whose leading role was guaranteed in the Constitution, was the classic example. Where political leaders are building a utopian order according to an ideological blueprint, political opposition becomes heresy. Under such conditions any political alternative is prohibited.

In a one-party-dominant state, a single political party dominates the political process without the official support of the state. While a number of minor parties offer political alternatives, the electorate usually votes overwhelmingly for the dominant party. The Institutionalized Revolutionary Party (PRI) of Mexico was an example until the 2000 elections. After the Mexican Revolution began in 1910, a fierce struggle occurred during which many leaders, such as Pancho Villa and Emiliano Zapata, fought to gain control of the national government. Plutarco Calles consolidated power in the late 1920s and developed a party organization that in time emerged as the PRI. Even today the party claims to stand as a symbol of the ongoing revolution. Its critics suggest that the party is more institutionalized than revolutionary. The PRI maintained power by clever use of the state apparatus, especially through patronage and corruption. Electoral reforms initiated under President Ernesto Zedillo (1994–2000) played a role in the victory of the National Action Party under the leadership of Vicente Fox in 2000.

Finally, there are times when one party dominates without in any way using the state machinery to support its position. For whatever reason, voters seem content with a single party for long periods of time. The Democrats dominated the American South for a century after the Civil War. In Canada, the province of Alberta has had the curious habit of endorsing one party for long periods, then suddenly turning to another. Since 1905, no party in Alberta having once formed a government and then lost an election has ever returned to power. The result has been a sequence of one-party-dominant situations rather than sustained competition between two or more credible contenders. This assertion was reinforced in 2008 when the Progressive Conservatives won their eleventh straight election since 1971.

Canadian federal politics also entered a one-party-dominant phase with the 1993 election, which persisted through the elections of 1997 and 2000. The Liberals were the only party able to elect MPs in all regions of the country, while each of the other parties had a much narrower geographic and demographic base. The Bloc Québécois appealed only to francophones in Quebec. The Reform Party and its successor, the Canadian Alliance, were strong in the West but unable to win appreciable numbers of seats elsewhere. The NDP had pockets of support in inner-city ridings, in strongholds of organized labour, and since 1997 in Atlantic Canada. However, the merger of the Progressive Conservatives and the Canadian Alliance in 2003 moved the system back to the two-party-plus system that dominated Canadian federal politics throughout most of the twentieth century.

The Two-Party System

A **two-party system** exists when two parties are credible contenders for power and either is capable of winning any election. The United Kingdom and the United States are commonly cited as illustrations, but neither is literally a two-party system. In Britain, the Conservatives and Labour have been challenged by the Liberal Democrats, plus several regional parties operating in Scotland, Wales, and Northern Ireland. In the American election of 1992, Ross Perot, an independent candidate for president, received 19 percent of the popular vote, although he did not get any electoral votes. Perot then transformed his movement into a more conventional political party, borrowing the name Reform Party from Canada. When he ran for president again in 1996, however, he received only 9 percent of the popular vote and again failed to win any votes in the Electoral College. In 2000, Ralph Nader ran for the Green Party and received only about 3 percent of the popular vote and no Electoral College votes. However, it has been argued that Nader's candidacy was significant. The approximately 100,000 voters he took in Florida might have tipped the balance in favour of Al Gore. This is an example of how even a minor third party may influence a close political race. (For further discussion of this disputed election, see Chapter 25.)

In Britain and the United States there have been many third parties, but they have rarely gained enough popular support to threaten the two major parties. Thus, when we speak of a two-party system, we mean that victory at the polls is likely to go to the Conservatives or Labour (or to the Democrats or Republicans), even though other parties may also contest the election. In systems where third parties receive a significant but minor share of the vote, it might be more accurate to call these systems **two-party-plus systems,** as some observers do.

Germany furnishes an example of two-party-plus politics. The Christian Democrats and Social Democrats there are so evenly matched at the polls that the small Free Democratic Party, the Left, and/or Greens can determine who will govern by throwing their parliamentary weight to one side or the other. The current government, however, is a "grand coalition" between the Christian Democrats and the Social Democrats, the two major parties.

Canada was close to a strict two-party system in the first 50 years of Confederation. From 1867 to 1917, only the Conservatives and Liberals mattered in federal politics. But from 1921 onward, there have always been more than two parties represented in the House of Commons. The Progressives were the first successful third party, followed by Social Credit and the CCF, which both entered the House of Commons in 1935. The CCF continues in the form of the NDP, while more recently we saw the rise of the Bloc Québécois and the Reform Party/Canadian Alliance.

The election of 2004 saw a return to the classic two-party-plus configuration of Canadian federal politics. A close race to the end, the Liberals won only a minority government, with 37 percent of the popular vote and 135 seats; the Conservatives became the Official Opposition with 30 percent of the vote and 99 seats. The 2006 election confirmed the return to the two-party-plus system, only with the Conservatives forming a minority government (with 36 percent of the vote and 124 seats) and the Liberals the official opposition (with 30 percent of the vote and 103 seats). The NDP and Bloc Québécois were never a threat to win, but each secured an important niche in Parliament (29 seats for the NDP, 51 for the BQ). After the 2008 election, the number of seats won by the political parties were: Conservatives 143; Liberals 76; NDP 37; Bloc 50; and Independents 2.

The two-party system is widely praised as a source of political stability, especially in parliamentary systems, in which the cabinet must maintain the confidence of an elected assembly. A two-party system is likely to yield majority governments that can hold office for a respectable length of time. Less convincing is the common argument that a two-party system serves the interests of voters by offering them a clear choice between two responsible aspirants to power. Parties in two-party systems are often highly pragmatic, so that for long periods of time their platforms may greatly resemble each other, giving voters little real choice. American and Canadian politics are like this at most elections. This is not to say that the two-party system is necessarily any worse than the multiparty alternative—only that it is not as obviously superior as newspaper editorials in the Anglo-American democracies often maintain.

The Multiparty System

In a **multiparty system,** three or more political parties have a realistic chance of partici-pating in government. In most cases, the parties are either interest parties or ideological parties, which consider the interests of their supporters their first priority. Sweden is a multiparty system. From left to right on the political spectrum, one could find seven political parties represented in the Riksdag (parliament) after the 2006 election: Left, Greens, Social Democrats, Centre, Christian Democrats, Liberals, and Moderates. The Left Party is the residue of the old Communist Party and is supported by workers; the Greens, as their name implies, are an expression of the environmentalist movement; the Social Democrats are a pragmatic socialist party; the Centre is an agrarian party with some urban support; Christian Democrats advocate Christian values; the Liberals represent professionals and intellectuals; the Moderates represent free-enterprise finan-cial and business interests.

Cabinet instability sometimes occurs in parliamentary systems in which there are many parties. When representatives are drawn from a number of parties, majority govern-ments are difficult to come by, and coalition governments may become the norm. Where the parties in a coalition government hold to principle and refuse to compromise, govern-ments tend to change frequently. This was the case in the Fourth Republic of France in the 1950s, which saw 13 governments in one period of 18 months. The same is true of Italy, which has averaged about one government a year since the end of World War II.

However, in political science generalizations seldom apply without exceptions. Instability does not occur in all multiparty systems. The multiparty systems of Denmark, Norway, and Sweden, for example, have usually produced durable coalitions that cannot be characterized as unstable. The difference has an interesting and logical explanation. Italy and France at various times had large extremist parties of both the left and the right. Because some of these parties were fundamentally opposed to the constitution, they were not acceptable coalition partners, which restricted the number of possible coalitions. Under such conditions, when a working partnership among parties breaks down there may be no alternative to re-establishing it, except perhaps by replacing the cabinet. The result is a game of political musical chairs in which cabinets succeed each other with monotonous regularity. In contrast, the Scandinavian countries do not have large extremist parties. All important parties are acceptable coalition partners, so there is more room to manoeuvre and create durable coalitions.

Assessing Political Parties

Political parties developed in concert with the extension of the franchise and they have helped to legitimize mass democracy. But this does not mean that all political parties are mass organizations with every voter holding a membership; on the contrary, in most Western societies the actual number of party members is very small. In Canada, fewer than 5 percent of voters belong to any federal or provincial party. Moreover, most of those who do are in the middle and upper-middle income brackets, are relatively well educated, and generally feel they have something at stake in the political process. For this reason, political parties have been criticized as representing not the masses but the social and economic elite in society. Indeed, when one examines a sociological profile of party activists, the criticism may seem valid. Oligarchies of a kind do run political parties.

This point was made early in the century by Roberto Michels in his classic work *Political Parties*. Michels argued that even the parties that talked the most about democracy, such as the social democratic parties of his day, inevitably fell under the control of small, self-perpetuating elites. He went so far as to state that an "iron law of oligarchy" represented the real truth about democracy.[5]

However, the charge of elitism conveys the idea of a group closed off from the rest of society by restricted membership; this is not really the case with political parties in most Western democracies. While there may be only a few militants, and they may represent the upper echelons of society, the doors of party organizations are not closed. On the contrary, anyone who pays the nominal membership fee is welcomed with open arms, and anyone who volunteers for party work is quickly inundated with tasks. The ranks of political parties may be filled by a few middle-class activists because they are the ones who choose to become involved. Many people simply may not have an interest in the mundane tasks that accompany political party membership. In most cases, the individual reward or payoff for party work is relatively small when measured against the effort involved.

In another sense, parties are elitist. Modern political competition depends heavily on public relations, advertising, polling, and fundraising—the so-called "black arts" of politics. These tasks require special skills and connections possessed by only a few insiders. While there may be many ordinary people serving as foot soldiers in the trenches of political warfare, the commanders and strategists are well-paid, well-connected people possessing unusual skills. This makes it difficult for the rank and file to feel they have any impact on policy directions of the party.

Be that as it may, we are seeing a remarkable proliferation of new political parties in Western Europe and North America. On the left, the main entrants are the "Green" parties, which represent environmentalism as a rising political issue. There are also a number of "new" socialist parties, which are actually recycled versions of older communist parties. On the right, the picture is even more complex. New "populist" conservative parties emerged recently in several countries; for example, the New Democracy in Sweden and the Reform Party/Canadian Alliance in Canada had temporary but important life spans. These parties tended to be market-oriented, to advocate direct democracy, to be opposed to large-scale immigration, and to be rather antagonistic to corporations, trade unions, government bureaucracies, and other large organizations. Further to the right are nationalistic, even racist, parties like the National Front of Jean Le Pen in France, the Republicans in Germany, and the Freedom Party in Austria.

At one level, these new parties are responding to emerging issues. Green parties are responding to environmental concerns; populist conservative parties are driven by the fiscal problems of the welfare state; and nationalist–racist parties represent a backlash against the flood of refugees and other immigrants into Western Europe. But at another level, this does not explain why the established parties have not responded adequately to these new issues, as they have to other emerging issues in previous decades.

Without pretending to give a complete explanation of why so many new parties have arisen in so many countries in recent decades, we would draw attention to one factor that is surely involved, namely the rise of post-materialism as discussed in Chapter 5. Voters influenced by the post-materialist political culture are more concerned about self-expression and less willing to defer to the compromises engineered by political brokers. This may point toward the emergence of new political parties catering to the demands of a more diverse, opinionated, and fractious electorate. However, with the success of the Liberals and, more recently, the new Conservative Party here in Canada (since 1993), the Labour Party in the United Kingdom (since 1997), and in the United States Republicans (2000–2008) and Democrats (2008–), that is assuming both Republican and Democratic Parties are pragmatic, it appears that pragmatic, centre parties remain the key to electoral success, at least in the Anglo-American world.

INTEREST GROUPS

In addition to political parties, the articulation of interests is also undertaken by particular social groups, usually called interest groups. An **interest group** is defined as "any organization that seeks to influence government policy, but not to govern."[6] It represents people who band together to accomplish specific objectives. Because interest groups exert political pressure to achieve their ends, they may also be called pressure

In 2003, the Progressive Conservative Party of Canada merged with the Canadian Alliance. The cartoon, showing PC leader Peter MacKay and Alliance leader Stephen Harper, poses the question—widely asked at the time—whether the two parties could be successfully merged.
© Graeme MacKay/Artizans.com

groups. Obviously, not all groups are political; people may organize for any number of reasons. There are social groups such as bridge and dance clubs, sports clubs, community associations, and professional organizations. Most of these voluntary organizations will never become involved in politics; however, if they do, they become interest groups in the political process. As such, they facilitate popular participation in politics. By coordinating political activities, they offer individuals an opportunity to become involved in the complex process of politics. Politics is an endless cycle because there are always new demands, generated by a variety of interests, with which government must deal.

Unlike political parties, interest groups do not seek to control the entire machinery of government; they seek merely to influence the political process with the goal of achieving certain legislative or policy ends. Interest groups may work with political parties and may even become affiliated with them—as in the relationship between the New Democratic Party (NDP) and some, but not all, member unions of the Canadian Labour Congress (CLC). Generally, however, parties and interest groups are conceptually distinct, even if their activities sometimes overlap.

Interest groups can be categorized according to the degree to which the benefits that they seek largely benefit their own members (i.e., selective benefits) or the wider community more generally (i.e., diffuse benefits). While the distinction is not watertight and is sometimes subjectively determined, it is important nonetheless to understand that not all interest groups are motivated by self-interest.[7]

The function of an interest group in politics is to articulate the interest of its members with the goal of changing laws and influencing policies. Interest groups seek to achieve their ends by persuading public officials. Land developers may try to influence a city council's decisions on planning and zoning; labour unions may try to persuade the provincial cabinet to amend collective-bargaining legislation; conservation organizations may seek to influence public policies relating to national or provincial parks. Interest groups also address themselves to public opinion; in the Canadian election of 1988, business, labour, and other groups all spoke out vigorously about free trade, although the business community, led by the Canadian Council of Chief Executives (formally the Business Council on National Issues) and the Canadian Manufacturers' Association, had much more money to spend on advertising. In all such cases, citizens with a common goal band together in an effort to shape legislation that they believe affects their lives.

In the second half of the twentieth century, one of the great developments in the political process in Western democracies was the proliferation of organized interest groups. Before World War II, organized interest groups were relatively few in number and consisted chiefly of economic producer groups with a specific focus: business and industrial associations, labour unions, farmers' associations, and the organized professions, such as doctors, lawyers, and teachers. Because groups had to operate with whatever resources they could collect from their members, those representing a well-to-do clientele tended to be the most effective.

The present-day picture is radically different. First, there are now many more politically active groups. Second, there are politically effective groups representing not only traditional producers but also diverse consumer interests (consumer associations, environmental protection groups), as well as a host of moral, cultural, and symbolic causes. Social movements arise (discussed at greater length further on) and organizations are created in rapid succession; witness the way in which the original ethno-linguistic liberation movements of the 1960s (black civil rights in the United States, bilingualism in Canada) have been followed by feminist, gay liberation, and animal-rights movements. Each of these movements has stimulated the growth of a number of organized interest groups to formulate and express distinct political views in the contemporary political process.

Many reasons are suggested as causes for interest-group proliferation. Here we can mention only a few factors. One is the expansion of formal education. More people now have the skills required to run an organization—public speaking, keeping minutes and financial records, doing research on political issues, writing and submitting briefs to public officials. Another is the ongoing revolution in transportation and communication, which has dramatically lowered the costs of building and maintaining a national organization. Modern communication technology, especially fax machines, cell-phones, and e-mail, makes possible the creation of organizations that could not have existed 50 years ago. The same technology has also revolutionized fundraising methods. Even relatively small groups can raise significant amounts of money through telephone solicitation, direct mail driven by computerized lists of target recipients, and credit-card donations on the Internet. Finally, with the declining role of political parties as formulators of public policy, individuals may be more inclined to associate and work for interest groups supporting causes with which they identify because they are perceived to be more effective. This trend is especially true of recent generations (see Figure 23.1).

Ottawa is not the only Canadian city to witness the proliferation of interest groups. In provincial capitals and even at the municipal level, interest groups have become a key part of the political process. Many community or neighbourhood associations are politically active when city councils consider by-laws or otherwise make decisions that have an impact on their section of the city. With governments becoming more involved in all facets of social life, more groups are trying to influence legislation. And many citizens are participating in these groups. According to a recent study undertaken in the United States, almost half of the respondents (48 percent) reported being affiliated with an interest group that took a stand on a political issue.[8] A number of

Figure 23.1 Attitudes on the Most Effective Way to Work for Change by Age Group, Canada, 2000 Strengthening Canadian Democracy Survey

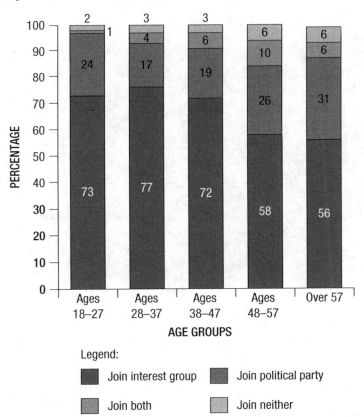

Source: Adapted from Brenda O'Neill, "Generational Patterns in the Political Opinions and Behaviours of Canadians," Policy Matters 2001, 2(5), p. 14. Used with permission of the Institute for Research on Public Policy, www.irpp.com

political scientists have argued that interest groups provide an important opportunity for political participation; participating in an interest group not only provides members with an opportunity for acquiring civic skills and knowledge, but also can provide the "glue" that makes for stronger communities (in political science terminology, this glue is referred to as *social capital*).[9]

A standard typology for classifying interest groups is the fourfold division of **anomic, associational, institutional,** and **nonassociational groups.**[10] For more detail, see Concept Box 23.1 on interest group typology.

A number of issues arise when considering just how interest groups work as part of the political process. For example, an important theoretical analysis by Mancur Olson

---

Concept Box 23.1

Interest Group Typology

Anomic Groups. Spontaneous groups formed by citizens concerned about a specific issue. They usually disband after resolution of the single issue.

Example: Friends of the Calgary General Hospital Society (FCGHS)

After 1994, the Government of Alberta closed three hospitals in Calgary, all of which were in the downtown core. The last closure, the Calgary General Hospital, caused considerable controversy. A group formed to protest the closure, arguing that the downtown needed a full-service hospital. The group continued for a while after demolition of the hospital, taking the government to court on the grounds that the land was set aside for purposes of a hospital and therefore should not be used for anything else; but it faded away after its judicial challenge was unsuccessful.

Associational Groups. Formal organizations set up to articulate the interests of their members over a long period of time.

Examples: Canadian Labour Congress, Canadian Manufacturers and Exporters, Canadian Medical Association

Associational groups are established to further the interests of their members or the public interest. They usually charge their membership a fee and use the proceeds to support a permanent staff to conduct the business of the organization. Most of the large associational groups have representatives in provincial capitals and Ottawa to lobby for their organization.

Institutional Groups. Organizations closely associated with government that act internally to influence public decisions.

Examples: Canadian Union of Public Employees, National Council of Veterans' Associations of Canada.

While people in these groups are part of government and in theory politically neutral, they have interests to articulate and seek specific goals. Like associational groups, they have the advantage of large memberships, permanent organizations, and continuity.

Concept Box 23.1

There are certain associational groups that, according to this classification, might almost be labelled "institutional" because of their close association with governments. Such ties are usually financial. Aboriginal associations are examples, as are francophone and anglophone minority-language associations and multicultural ethnic societies. All such groups receive substantial financial support from the federal government, from departments such as Indian and Northern Affairs, and Canadian Heritage. This funding is often crucial to their existence.

Non-Associational Groups. Unorganized groups made up of individuals who perceive a common identity on the basis of culture, religion, or some other distinctive quality.

Examples: Youth, Catholics, Westerners, Maritimers

Non-associational groups lack formal organizations designed for political activity even though often they are considered as if they were organized. The term *latent groups* captures the significance of these people—at any time, given the right issue, they could mobilize and possibly become a political force. For that reason, politicians take the interests of such groups into account.

suggests that the costs in time and money of organizing for political action often outweigh the benefits that an individual can expect to gain by lobbying, especially when the potential benefits are diffuse.[11] This is another aspect of the free-rider problem discussed in Chapter 10. Why should I spend my time working, for example, in an environmental association when the benefits of cleaner air and water will be enjoyed by all who live in the community, whether or not they contribute to the movement? It might be rational for me to contribute my time and money if I could be sure that others would do likewise, but how can I obtain that guarantee?

One answer is that when a group is already organized for other reasons, its incremental costs of entry into the political system may be much lower. A group may also provide nonpolitical benefits, such as the recreational activities sponsored by the Sierra Club.[12] In both these ways, pre-existing associations have an advantage in undertaking pressure-group activity. The prediction that pre-existing associations such as labour unions and professional associations should be formidable lobbyists seems to be borne out empirically.

Government support of interest groups first became important in Canada as part of Pierre Trudeau's "Just Society." The rationale for it was that Aboriginal peoples, women, and ethnic and linguistic minorities were disadvantaged or even oppressed groups that could not hope to compete on equal terms in the political marketplace. It was thought that giving them financial assistance to form interest groups would enable them to exert political pressure for economic and social reforms and thereby improve their position over the long run. Public support of interest groups was thus a logical corollary of reform liberalism. The public funding of interest groups has declined significantly, however, beginning with the Mulroney government in the 1980s.[13]

It is perhaps surprising that such federally funded interest groups often became the severest critics of federal policy, sometimes in unexpected ways. For example, the National Action Committee on the Status of Women actively opposed most of the initiatives of the Mulroney government, including the FTA and NAFTA, the Charlottetown Accord, and many changes in social policy. But if one considers that such groups received funding because of their relative disadvantage and oppression, then their criticisms are perhaps easier to understand.

Public funding of interest groups raises a number of questions. While the funding provides some groups with the only possibility for participating effectively in the political system, it can also compromise their ability to protect the interests of their members. Government funding also means that certain interests are provided the means with which to organize while others are not; government, in effect, can directly determine which marginalized interests are voiced and heard through its funding decisions. If, however, one accepts that not all interests are equally capable of mobilizing, then public funding remains an important mechanism for ensuring the articulation of a diversity of interests.

Political Consultants and Lobbying

The expansion of interest-group activity has given rise to a new profession, that of the **political consultant.**[14] Consultants often are former politicians, public servants, or military officers who see the opportunity to put their expertise to work in the private sector. For a fee, they keep clients informed of new developments within government and advise them on how to pursue their goals effectively. After consultants have been retired from the public service long enough to avoid charges of conflict of interest, they may also engage in lobbying.

The term **lobbying** is derived from the old practice of individuals and groups buttonholing MPs in the lobby of the British House of Commons. The practice now involves many different methods for influencing decisions: arranging an interview with a cabinet member, submitting a brief to a royal commission or parliamentary committee hearing, writing letters to elected representatives, advertising in the media to generate public pressure over an issue, and offering gifts of various kinds to public officials. In every case, the objective is the same: to influence governors and the public so that they will be favourably disposed to the interest group's position on an issue.

Lobbying has become an accepted part of today's political process. In 2006–07, 9,656 lobbyists were registered under Canada's federal Lobbying Act.[15] While the term carries certain derogatory connotations, many public officials admit that they depend on lobbyists as a source of information. Typically, elected officials depend on members of the administration or bureaucracy to supply the facts they require to make a political decision. But the administration has its own views and biases, or may not have all the information pertinent to a decision; as a result, resorting to lobbyists for a range of views has become a recognized part of politics. In this sense, interest-group lobbying can be seen as a positive part of politics, in that it counters the entrenched views of bureaucrats or cabinet members.

The focus of lobbying depends on the institutional arrangements of government. In the United States, where Congress is a more autonomous body and is not controlled by party discipline, lobbyists concentrate on swaying the minds of individual representatives and senators. Such a strategy would have little payoff in Canada, or in other parliamentary systems in which elected representatives must vote according to party discipline. In the parliamentary milieu, the ultimate goal is to influence members of cabinet and the senior advisers of the prime minister. In practice, however, these people are extremely difficult to reach, so Canadian lobbyists do much of their work with the civil servants who offer advice to politicians over the long term. And in countries like the United States and Canada, where judicial review is an important factor in the political process, interest groups may also devote resources to sponsoring litigation.

Determinants of Influence

An important question is why some groups are more influential in their lobbying than others. What makes an interest group powerful? A number of factors have been suggested: the size and cohesion of the group; its wealth, organizational abilities, and leadership; and the nature of the issue at hand. For a further discussion, see Concept Box 23.2 on determinants of interest-group influence.

Interest groups tend to be particularly influential when several of these factors coincide. Provincial medical associations are an example. While their members are few in relation to the larger society, they are cohesive because their members share a common education and body of professional practices. They have great financial resources as well as excellent leaders and organizational capabilities. All this has made them effective lobbyists on the political scene.

Interest Groups and the Political System

Let us make some general observations about the place of interest groups in contemporary liberal democracies. First, there is a correlation between interest-group activity and the guarantee of political freedom in a society. Without constitutional guarantees of free speech, a free press, and the right to assemble, the political activities of interest groups would be seriously jeopardized. Governments seldom cherish criticism, and a good portion of an interest group's activities involves criticizing proposed or existing laws and policies. Without immunity from reprisal, there would be considerably less enthusiasm

Concept Box 23.2

Determinants of Interest-Group Influence

Numbers. The size of the group cannot help but count in democratic politics. Legislators listen when a group represents a large membership. Numbers, however, do not tell the whole story.

Cohesion. To be effective, members of a group must act cohesively. Organized labour, for example, is one of the largest groups in Canada, and if its members voted as a bloc they could carry many ridings. While labour organizations often endorse political party candidates, the members usually vote across the party spectrum.

Organizational Skills. Effective groups maximize the use of human resources and have the ability to translate emotion into action. No matter how strongly individuals feel about an issue, ad hoc and sporadic complaints may be ineffective. Coordinating individual responses under an effective organization is more likely to have an impact on public policy.

Financial Support. It costs money to set up an organization, monitor government decisions, and engage in lobbying. The main sources of support are large contributions by corporations or unions, small contributions by grassroots members, grants from foundations, and subsidies from government. Interest groups vary greatly in how they combine these sources of revenue, but none can function without money.

Leadership. Good leadership can mobilize concerned individuals and make a difference by inspiring coordinated action on the part of the group.

Nature of Issue. The issue must have significant appeal to legislators and to the public, or there is little chance of obtaining results in politics. Over time, however, appeal for an issue can develop. For example, when the antismoking movement began in the 1970s, it seemed to have little chance of success. More than half of North American adults smoked; and not only was smoking in public taken for granted, it was on the increase. There was already substantial medical evidence about the harmful effects of smoking, but it had made little impact on the public consciousness. Then, as part of wider trends involving diet, fitness, health, and the environment, the medical evidence began to register, public opinion began to turn against smoking, and antismoking groups became highly successful lobbyists, achieving higher taxes on tobacco products, limitations on tobacco advertising, and restrictions on smoking in public places.

for this type of public participation. Even in our own relatively free society, governments are sometimes accused of withholding vital information and even using intimidation.

Second, interest-group activity may be good "therapy" in the participatory society. While all groups cannot achieve all their ends in the political process, most of them are successful at least occasionally. The theory of group politics suggests in part that successful participation in the political process through interest-group activity reinforces confidence in the system. Group politics thus has the potential to enhance the legitimacy of the system in the minds of citizens. To deny groups an opportunity to participate in politics would be to undermine this perceived legitimacy.

The increase in the activity of interest groups is a fact, but it is also a fact that only a small number of people become activists in interest-group politics. Are non-participants—those not affiliated with an interest group—excluded from the benefits of public decisions? Certainly to some extent, but perhaps not entirely, because the unorganized still have the potential to organize and therefore constitute latent interests.[16] In other words, when public officials distribute benefits through the political process, they cannot afford to bypass unorganized interests totally, because the unorganized are voters and have the potential to become organized into effective groups.

Political freedom has nurtured a great deal of interest-group activity, with the benefits described above; yet there are ways in which interest groups may damage the community. For one thing, interest-group activity is closely interwoven with a distributive approach to politics in which political activity represents an exchange: voters render their support (votes) to politicians, and politicians in turn enact programs and policies for the benefit of those groups that support them. Although this may reflect much that occurs in the politics of liberal democracy, it is hard to view it without concern. Liberal democracy as a form of government rests ultimately on the notion that these are universal laws that apply equally to all citizens. It is this general equality before the law that justifies equal political rights for all citizens. But aggressive interest-group activity may easily become a pursuit of special privileges, which is inimical to equality before the law. Manufacturers of certain products lobby for protective tariffs to prevent consumers from buying cheaper foreign products. Organized labour uses collective-bargaining legislation to win benefits denied to the rest of the workforce. Organized farmers use their political power to get government to set up marketing boards to raise prices in their favour. As one special-interest group succeeds in its objectives, other interests may be stimulated to organize themselves for entry into the lobbying contest. If this process continues over many decades, a society of equality before the law can transform itself into a society of entrenched privilege, with each interest group jealously defending its special prerogatives.

A related phenomenon is the tendency to politicize issues. Once groups learn that they can use government to their particular advantage, they tend to begin looking for political rather than economic or social solutions to problems. For example, owners of declining industries, faced with severe competition from foreign producers, may seek protective tariffs and quotas rather than new outlets for their capital. Similarly, the workers in such industries may pressure government to protect their jobs by propping up or even nationalizing faltering companies. What were once economic matters decided in the marketplace can become political issues decided by a preponderance of power. Politicization can jeopardize the fundamental liberal concept of the limited state by injecting government into more and more realms of social activity. If each group single-mindedly pursues its own interests, all groups together may bring about a general situation that none of them would ever have chosen in the first place.

The Dilemma of Interest-Group Politics

Interest-group politics can be seen positively as part of the tendency toward democratization in modern society. The increase in the number of effective interest groups has likely produced a more level playing field in politics. As more people participate in politics, the number of interest groups grows accordingly. Environmental and anti-globalization groups are current examples of different segments of the population organizing around new political issues.

But interest-group politics also has a negative aspect. The playing field in the competition of interest groups is not perfectly level. Some have greater financial resources or better access to the levers of power and therefore get more than their fair share of benefits. Others, like business groups, occupy a privileged position relative to other groups in pluralist societies, and governments are generally more responsive to their interests than to other groups.[17] This reflects the overall importance of the economy on the political agenda rather than anything more sinister but highlights the fact that structural factors can limit the effectiveness of certain groups.

Yet imagining modern participatory politics without interest groups is difficult. So, to curb the possibilities of unfairness in the operations of interest groups, there has been a growing tendency toward public regulation of interest-group activity, including public identification as well as tighter definitions of conflict of interest on the part of politicians and civil servants.

Such problems cause some analysts to see interest-group politics as a long-term threat to liberal democracy. Legislators at all levels of government have voiced the concern that powerful lobbying by special interests can dominate the process for distributing public goods and services. Mancur Olson suggests that small but cohesive organizations with a single purpose have a great capacity for influencing public officials. Because the goals of these groups are usually self-centred, they may create economic inefficiency for the larger society.

Political thinkers at the dawn of the democratic era were acutely aware of these problems. Rousseau went as far as wishing to outlaw organized groups.[18] His view was that individuals could exercise their political responsibilities in the spirit of what he called the "general will"—that is, the good of the whole community—but that the formation of groups fostered a selfish spirit of particular advantage.

Rousseau's diagnosis was undoubtedly shrewd, but his remedy of banning private associations was extreme and perhaps totalitarian in its implications. James Madison suggested a more moderate approach in *The Federalist,* where he discussed interest groups (then called **factions**).[19] Madison realized that factions could not be banned without destroying liberty itself. His remedy (which Rousseau had also accepted as a second-best solution) was to promote the existence of a great number and variety of factions, so as to maintain an approximate balance or equilibrium among them. This fundamentally defensive strategy is based on the hope that a drive for special privilege by one group will generate contrary political pressure from other groups that stand to be adversely affected.

SOCIAL MOVEMENTS

While interest groups continue to play an important role in political systems, social movements have become increasingly important political actors. Interest groups are often elements of social movements but movements encompass more than these traditional political organizations. Social movements are identified by their form (relatively unorganized and fluid); goals (sweeping political, social, and cultural change); structure (non-hierarchical and participatory); and techniques (often non-traditional, including protests—both legal and illegal—and boycotts).[20] An interest group is a hierarchical organization working to influence public policy on issues of concern to its members; **social movements** are loose organizations of groups and individuals working to bring about wholesale change by influencing multiple actors, including governments, business, and individuals. For social movements, the objective is to change more than public policy and legislation, but also political priorities, social values, and individual values and behaviour. And the focus often extends beyond national borders towards transnational actors.

Social movements are not a recent phenomenon, but contemporary movements can be distinguished from earlier ones. "Old" social movements include agrarian, labour, and religious reform movements, spurred in part by the processes of industrialization and urbanization. Examples of "new" social movements, on the other hand, include those focusing on the environment, women's equality, peace, and, most recently, anti-globalization. In line with post-materialism, new social movements focus on issues of identity and non-material goals rather than on questions of redistribution and class. The 1960s are normally identified as the years during which new social movements appeared. Societal changes taking place at that time furnish part of the explanation for their rise, including increased secularization, access to higher education, and the availability of the birth control pill. In 1970, for example, in one of the first examples of national feminist protests, Canadian women organized an abortion caravan, which travelled from Vancouver to Ottawa and ended with demonstrators chaining themselves to the gallery in the House of Commons, to protest amendments made a year earlier to Section 251 of the Criminal Code dealing with abortion.

Political parties frequently emerged from old social movements—the CCF, the British Labour Party, and Christian Democratic parties in a number of Latin American countries. The same is true of new social movements; for example, Green parties have grown out of environmental movements in many countries, including Canada. And as support for the cause grows, existing political parties attempt to adopt the programs of new social movements as part of their party policy.

Social movements often develop from grassroots efforts directed at a particular issue. Interest groups can develop from the efforts, or existing organizations can join in the effort. Mentioned earlier, the Sierra Club lobbies the American government on a number of environmental issues, including the building of dams and carbon emissions. These organizations can also be involved in activities besides lobbying and advocacy such as direct action (e.g., Earth First! employs tree sits and illegal tree spiking in its conservation efforts), conducting research to better understand issues (e.g., Earthwatch supports scientific research around the world to assist sustainability), and changing public attitudes (e.g., the Friends of Nature encourages green tourism to develop an increased love and understanding of nature). Importantly, movements also include unorganized individuals whose behaviour and attitudes reflect the goals of the movement (e.g., the many individuals who use blue boxes to collect recyclables).

The fluid and relatively unorganized nature of social movements means that while there is general agreement on goals (the transformation of community and society), there is often much less agreement on how best to pursue them. Some of the organizations and individuals within a movement may seek change by working with governments to influence policies and legislation (sometimes referred to as "mainstreaming" or "large-P" politics). Others will argue that working with governments can lead to co-optation by requiring that the organizational goals be compromised to some degree to win concessions, an option they flatly reject; instead, their position is one of disengagement or a focus on "small-p" politics. Some will argue that actions should always and everywhere be legal, in part to ensure that public support for the movement remains strong; others argue that the slow pace of change and the consequences of non-action demand the use of illegal means to raise awareness and increase the speed of change. And yet others will adopt a mix of positions, their pragmatic positions responding to changing circumstances.[21]

Anti-globalization protestors provide a current example of a new social movement. They have organized demonstrations, sometimes violent ones, in cities around the world to oppose what they see as the anti-democratic practices of economic globalization. Maude Barlow's Council of Canadians is an important interest group in Canada taking this position. Proponents of globalization argue that reduced trade restrictions will stimulate the economies of all countries, especially the industrializing, transitional democracies, and that this economic growth will in turn enhance democratization. The forces of anti-globalization counter with three points: the process of globalization is undemocratic because discussions on its particulars are closed to the public; the economic growth experienced in industrializing, transitional democracies is uneven, creating great disparities of wealth; and the lack of a regulatory process leads to environmental degradation and poor working conditions.[22]

The anti-globalization movement presents an important example of contemporary interest mobilization: it is transnational; fights for increased citizen access to decision-making processes; focuses on the media, corporations, and international trade organizations in addition to states; and combines the use of "old" techniques (e.g., demonstrations and protests) with new mechanisms for mobilization (e.g., cellphones, text messaging, and the Internet).[23] Many major political issues of the past and present, such as feminism, gay and lesbian rights, and environmentalism, started with the noisy protests of relatively small numbers of people and went on from there to enter the political mainstream.

Questions for Discussion

1. Which political party comes closest to your political positions on issues? Which political issues do you consider to be priorities?

2. When (if ever) is illegal political protest defensible?

3. Are interest groups and social movements a response to increasing political complexity or do they unnecessarily complicate politics?

Internet Links

1. Liberal Party of Canada: **www.liberal.ca**

2. Conservative Party of Canada: **www.conservative.ca**

3. New Democratic Party: **www.ndp.ca**

4. United States Democratic National Committee (DNC): **www.democrats.org**

5. United States Republican National Committee (RNC): **www.rnc.org**

6. Canadian Labour Congress (CLC): **http://canadianlabour.ca**

7. Canadian Council of Chief Executives: **www.ceocouncil.ca**

8. The Global Greens Charter, a statement of the values and principles of Green parties and movements: **www.global.greens.org.au/charter.htm**

9. Greenpeace: **www.greenpeace.org/international**

10. National Organization for Women: **www.now.org**

11. Assembly of First Nations: **www.afn.ca**

Further Reading

INTEREST GROUPS AND SOCIAL MOVEMENTS

Baumgartner, Frank R., and Beth L. Leech, *Basic Interests: The Importance of Groups in Politics and Political Science*, Princeton, NJ: Princeton University Press, 1998.

Berry, Jeffrey M. *The Interest Group Society*. 3rd ed. New York: HarperCollins, 1997.

Chong, Dennis. *Collective Action and the Civil Rights Movement*. Chicago: University of Chicago Press, 1991.

Coleman, William, and Grace Skogstad. *Policy Communities and Public Policy in Canada: A Structural Approach*. Mississauga, ON: Copp Clark Pitman, 1990.

Dalton, Russell J., and Manfred Kuechler, eds. *Challenging the Political Order: New Social and Political Movements in Western Democracies*. New York: Oxford University Press, 1990.

Duverger, Maurice. *Party Politics and Pressure Groups: A Comparative Introduction*. New York: Thomas Y. Crowell, 1972.

Finkle, Peter, et al. *Federal Government Relations with Interest Groups: A Reconsideration*. Ottawa: Supply and Services Canada, 1994.

Hein, Gregory. *Interest Group Litigation and Canadian Democracy*. Montreal: Institute for Research in Public Policy, 2000.

Kingdon, John W. *Agendas, Alternatives and Public Policies*. 2nd ed. New York: HarperCollins, 1995.

Kwavnick, David. *Organized Labour and Pressure Politics: The Canadian Labour Congress 1956–1968*. Montreal and Kingston: McGill–Queen's University Press, 1972.

McAdam, Doug, John D. McCarthy, and Mayer N. Zald, eds. *Comparative Perspectives on Social Movements: Political Opportunities, Mobilizing Structures, and Cultural Framings*. New York: Cambridge University Press, 1996.

Montpetit, Eric. *Misplaced Distrust: Policy Networks and the Environment in France, The United States and Canada*. Vancouver: University of British Columbia Press, 2003.

Olson, Mancur. *The Logic of Collective Action*. Rev. ed. Cambridge, MA: Harvard University Press, 1971.

Petracca, Mark P., ed. *The Politics of Interests: Interest Groups Transformed*. Boulder, CO: Westview Press, 1992.

Pross, Paul A. *Governing Under Pressure*. Toronto: Institute of Public Administration of Canada, 1982.

———. *Group Politics and Public Policy*. 2nd ed. Toronto: Oxford University Press, 1992.

———, ed. *Pressure Group Behavior in Canadian Politics*. Toronto: McGraw-Hill Ryerson, 1975.

Sawatsky, John. *The Insiders: Government, Business, and the Lobbyists*. Toronto: McClelland & Stewart, 1987.

Seidle, F. Leslie, ed. *Interest Groups and Elections in Canada*. Royal Commission on Electoral Reform and Party Financing, vol. 2. Toronto: Dundurn Press, 1991.

Smith, Miriam, ed. *Group Politics and Social Movements in Canada*. Peterborough, ON: Broadview, 2008.

———. *A Civil Society? Collective Actors in Canadian Political Life*. Peterborough, ON: Broadview, 2005.

Tarrow, Sidney. *Power in Movement: Social Movements, Collective Action, and Politics.* New York: Cambridge University Press, 1994.

Truman, David B. *The Governmental Process.* New York: Knopf, 1958.

Verba, Sidney, Kay Lehman Schlozman, and Henry E. Brady. *Voice and Equality: Civic Voluntarism in American Politics.* Cambridge: Harvard University Press, 1995.

Walker, Jack L., Jr. *Mobilizing Interest Groups in America: Patrons, Professions, and Social Movements.* Ann Arbor: University of Michigan Press, 1991.

Wright, John R. *Interest Groups and Congress: Lobbying, Contributions, and Influence.* Boston: Allyn and Bacon, 1996.

Young, Lisa, and Joanna Everitt. *Advocacy Groups.* Vancouver: University of British Columbia Press, 2004.

POLITICAL PARTIES

Ajzenstat, Janet, and Peter J. Smith, eds. *Canada's Origins: Liberal, Tory, or Republican?* Ottawa: Carleton University Press, 1995.

Archer, Keith, and Alan Whitehorn. *Canadian Trade Unions and the New Democratic Party.* Kingston: Industrial Relations Centre, 1993.

Bashevkin, Sylvia B. *Toeing the Lines: Women and Party Politics in English Canada.* 2nd ed. Toronto: Oxford University Press, 1993.

Bickerton, James, Alain-G. Gagnon, and Patrick J. Smith. *Ties That Bind: Parties and Voters in Canada.* Toronto: Oxford University Press, 1999.

Brodie, M. Janine, and Jane Jenson. *Crisis, Challenge and Change: Party and Class in Canada, Revisited.* Rev. ed. Ottawa: Carleton University Press, 1988.

Campbell, Colin, and William Christian. *Parties, Leaders, and Ideologies in Canada.* McGraw-Hill Ryerson, 1996.

Carty, R. Kenneth, et al., eds. *Leaders and Parties in Canadian Politics: Experiences of the Provinces.* Toronto: Harcourt Brace Jovanovich, 1991.

Carty, R. Kenneth, William Cross, and Lisa Young. *Rebuilding Canadian Party Politics.* Vancouver: University of British Columbia Press, 2000.

Christian, William, and Colin Campbell. *Political Parties and Ideologies in Canada.* 3rd ed. Toronto: McGraw-Hill Ryerson, 1990.

Courtney, Johon. *Do Conventions Matter? Choosing National Party Leaders in Canada.* Toronto: Macmillan, 1995.

Cross, William. *Political Parties.* Vancouver: University of British Columbia Press, 2004.

Dalton, Russell J., and Martin P. Wattenberg. *Parties without Partisans: Political Change in Advanced Industrial Democracies.* Oxford: Oxford University Press, 2000.

Duverger, Maurice. *Political Parties*. 3rd ed. New York: Wiley, 1978.

Flanagan, Tom. *Waiting for the Wave: The Reform Party and Preston Manning*. Toronto: Stoddart, 1995.

Gagnon, Alain-G., and A. Brian Tanguay, eds. *Canadian Parties in Transition*. 3rd ed. Peterborough, ON: Broadview, 2007.

Ingle, Stephen. *The British Party System: An Introduction*. London: Routledge, 2008.

Katz, Richard S. *A Theory of Parties and Electoral Systems*. Baltimore: Johns Hopkins University Press, 1980.

Klingemann, Hans-Dieter, Richard I. Hofferbert, and Ian Budge. *Parties, Policies, and Democracies*. Boulder, CO: Westview Press, 1994.

Laver, Michael, and Norman Schofield. *Multiparty Government: The Politics of Coalition in Europe*. New York: Oxford University Press, 1990.

Mair, Peter. "Comparing Party Systems," in Lawrence LeDuc, Richard G. Niemi, and Pippa Norris, eds. *Comparing Democracies 2: New Challenges in the Study of Elections and Voting*. London: Sage Publications, 2003.

Michels, Robert. *Political Parties*. New York: Free Press, 1962. First published in 1911.

Paterson, William E., and Alastair H. Thomas, eds. *Social Democratic Parties in Western Europe*. London: Croom Helm, 1977.

Piven, Frances Fox, ed. *Labor Parties in Postindustrial Societies*. Cambridge: Polity Press, 1991.

Rose, Richard. *Do Parties Make a Difference?* 2nd ed. London: Macmillan, 1984.

Rose, Richard, and Neil Munro. *Elections and Parties in New European Democracies*. 2nd ed. Washington, DC: CQ Press, 2009.

Sáez, Manuel Alca ntara. *Politicians and Politics in Latin America*. Boulder, CO: Lynne Reiner, 2008.

Sartori, Giovanni. *Parties and Party Systems: A Framework for Analysis*. Colchester: ECPR, 2005.

Sayers, Anthony M. *Parties, Candidates, and Constituency Campaigns in Canadian Elections*. Vancouver: University of British Columbia Press, 1999.

Seidle, Leslie F., ed. *Comparative Issues in Party and Election Finance in Canada*. Royal Commission on Electoral Reform and Party Financing, vol. 4. Toronto: Dundurn Press, 1991.

———. *Issues in Party and Election Finance in Canada*. Royal Commission on Electoral Reform and Party Financing, vol. 5. Toronto: Dundurn Press, 1991.

———. *Provincial Party and Election Finance in Canada*. Royal Commission on Electoral Reform and Party Financing, vol. 3. Toronto: Dundurn Press, 1991.

Thorburn, Hugh G., and Alan Whitehorn, ed. *Party Politics in Canada*. 8th ed. Scarborough, ON: Prentice Hall Canada, 2000.

Ware, Alan. *Political Parties and Party Systems*. Oxford and New York: Oxford University Press, 1996.

Wearing, Joseph. *Strained Relations: Canadian Parties and Voters*. Toronto: McClelland & Stewart, 1988.

Webb, Paul, David Farrell, and Ian Holliday, eds. *Political Parties in Advanced Industrial Democracies*. Oxford: Oxford, 2002.

Young, Walter D. *Democracy and Discontent: Progressivism, Socialism and Social Credit in the Canadian West*. 2nd ed. Toronto: McGraw-Hill Ryerson, 1978.